Discovering Christ

In

The Gospel Of John

Volume 1

Discovering Christ
In
The Gospel Of John

Donald S. Fortner

Volume 1

Go *publications*

Go Publications
Gibb Hill Farm, Ponsonby, Seascale, Cumbria, CA20 1BX, United Kingdom

© Go Publications 2017
First Published 2017

British Library Cataloguing in Publication Data available

ISBN 978-1-908475-07-7

*Printed and bound in Great Britain
By Lightning Source UK Ltd.*

Dedication

To Pastor Gary Vance

"our dear fellowservant ...
a faithful minister of Christ"

Contents

Foreword

The Gospel of John is in some respects the most unique book in holy scripture. The first sentence, "In the beginning was the Word and the Word was with God and the Word was God", sets forth the majesty and glory of the person of Christ. In mostly one-syllable words the Holy Spirit through John sets forth the infinite truth of Christ. Who can plumb the depths of, "I am the way, the truth, and the life"? In this book Pastor Don Fortner faithfully sets forth the glories of the person of Christ and the completeness of the salvation that is in Him. Every believer responds to this with Paul, "Oh that I may win Christ, and be found in Him."

Todd Nibert , Pastor
Todds Road Grace Church
Lexington, Kentucky

Chapter 1

Christ The Son Of God

The apostle John tells us exactly what his purpose was in writing his gospel narrative. He says, 'Many other signs truly did Jesus in the presence of his disciples, which are not written in this book: But these are written, that ye might believe that Jesus is the Christ, the Son of God; and that believing ye might have life through his name' (20:30, 31). John wrote his Gospel to show us that Jesus of Nazareth is the Christ, the Son of God; and he begins his message by stating that fact clearly, emphatically, and beautifully, 'In the beginning was the Word, and the Word was with God, and the Word was God. The same was in the beginning with God' (1:1, 2).

There is one word used repeatedly throughout these 21 chapters. That one word is the key to all things spiritual, the key to spiritual life, spiritual knowledge, and spiritual understanding. The word is 'believe'. John uses it 98 times in this gospel. His intention is that 'we might believe that Jesus is the Christ, the Son of God; and that believing, we might have life through his name'. May the God of all grace give us grace to go on believing 'that Jesus is the Christ, the Son of God'.

Distinctive Features

Matthew, Mark, and Luke are called 'The Synoptic Gospels' because they each give us an orderly, well-arranged narrative of our Saviour's earthly life and ministry, describing (for the most part) the same events in different ways and for different purposes. John's Gospel is different. It was written much later than the other three. In the Gospel of John we are given the inspired reflections of an old man who had faithfully served the Son of God for many, many years. With one foot in heaven he tells us of his all-glorious Saviour, the Son of God, that we might believe him. John's Gospel is neither a historical biography nor a theological textbook. Rather, what we have here is the loving adoration of a saved sinner for his Saviour, describing the greatness, grace, and glory of the Son of God as John had experienced it.

There are several things that stand out as distinctive features of John's Gospel. Unlike Matthew, Mark, and Luke, John does not mention any of our Lord's parables. Yet, he was inspired to describe miracles not recorded by the other writers. John alone tells us about the Lord Jesus turning water into wine at the marriage feast in Cana (2:1-11), the healing of the nobleman's son (4:46-54), the healing of the lame man at the Pool of Bethesda (5:1-9), the feeding of the five thousand (6:1-14), the Lord Jesus coming to his disciples walking across the stormy sea (6:15-21), the healing of the man born blind (9:1-7), and the resurrection of Lazarus (11:38-44).

The miracles described by John seem to have been specifically intended to lay the foundation for something our Lord was about to teach. When the Master was about to teach some great truth, he performed a miracle to illustrate what he was about to say. He had a way of getting people's attention.

Just before he drove the money changers out of the temple and told how that he was about to build a greater, more glorious temple by his death and resurrection, our Saviour turned water into wine. 'This beginning of miracles did Jesus in Cana of Galilee, and manifested forth his glory; and his disciples believed on him' (2:11). Just before declaring himself to be the Son of God, into whose hands the Father has committed all things in chapter 5, our Lord healed the nobleman's son and the impotent man. Just before telling us that he is the Bread of Life in chapter 6, our Saviour fed five thousand men with five loaves of bread and two small fish. The Lord Jesus came walking across the stormy sea, showing his dominion over all things, teaching us to trust him, just before his disciples saw the multitudes abandon him because of the gospel he preached (chapter 6). In John 8:12 our Saviour declared, 'I am the light of the world: he that followeth me shall not walk in darkness, but shall have the light of life'. Then, in chapter 9, he healed the man who was born blind and said, 'I am the light of the world'. After declaring to Martha, 'I am the resurrection and the life' (11:25), the Master went out to the tomb and raised Lazarus from the dead.

'I Am'

Another distinctive feature of John's Gospel is the fact that he alone gives us the seven 'I AM' sayings of Christ. Seven times the Lord says, 'I AM'. These sayings are very precious and give us a delightful, instructive picture of our

Redeemer. 'I AM' is the name by which the Lord God revealed himself to Moses in Exodus 3:13, 14. By taking this title and name as his own the Lord Jesus declared himself to be God, and did so at least seven times. He said, 'I am the bread of life' (6:35). If we would live, we must eat this Bread. He said, 'I am the light of the world' (8:12). If we would see, we must have this Light. He said, 'I am the door of the sheep' (10:7). If we would enter into life, we must enter by this Door. He said, 'I am the good shepherd' (10:11). If we are saved, we must be saved by this Shepherd. He said, 'I am the resurrection and the life' (11:25). If we would be partakers of resurrection glory and eternal life, he who is the Resurrection and the Life must be ours. We must trust him. He said, 'I am the way, and the truth, and the life' (14:6). If we would have eternal life, we must be in the Way, know the Truth, and be given the Life. Then he said, 'I am the true vine' (15:1). If we would bring forth fruit unto God, we must be grafted into this Vine.

The significance of our Lord using the words 'I AM' of himself must not be overlooked. This enraged the Jews because they understood exactly what he meant by it. He was saying, 'I am the eternal God, Jehovah, the Redeemer and Deliverer. I am everything, for I am God.' Using these two words, 'I AM', of himself, he identified himself as the covenant God of Israel. Liberals and religious infidels today may not recognise that fact; but the Jews who heard the Master understood him perfectly (John 8:58, 59; 10:31-33).

John also gives a distinct emphasis to the fact that the Lord Jesus spoke of a specific time and hour for which he came into the world (2:4; 7:6, 8, 30; 8:20; 12:23, 27, 28; 13:1; 17:1).

Divisions
In chapters 1-12, John tells us who Christ is, giving highlights of his life and ministry during the three years of public, earthly ministry. In chapters 13-21 the apostle gives an account (an account none could give except a tender-hearted old man, full of love for Christ) of our Lord's last night upon the earth, his death as our Substitute, and his resurrection.

Christ Our God
That Man Luke described, the Servant Mark portrayed, and the King Matthew declared, Jesus of Nazareth, is himself the Christ, the Son of God, our eternal God and Saviour. That is what John asserts with utter dogmatism in chapter 1. John declares that this man is the Word who is God (v. 1), the second person of the holy trinity, altogether equal with the Father (v. 2), the Creator of all things (v. 3), and the incarnate God our Saviour (vv. 10-18, 29). This Man who is God is the Lamb of God, spoken of and typified throughout the Old Testament, by whose sacrifice our sins are taken away.

Best Things Last
In chapter 2, when our Lord turned the water into wine and began to show forth his glory, the governor of the feast said to the bridegroom, 'Every man at the beginning doth set forth good wine; and when men have well drunk, then that which is worse: but thou hast kept the good wine until now' (v. 10). That is exactly what our Saviour does in his wondrous works of grace. He saves the best wine until the last (1 Corinthians 2:9). As good as the experience of God's grace in Christ is here, it is but a foretaste of that which awaits us in heaven's glory.

The New Birth
In the first chapter we are told that sinners are made to be the sons of God and are born again by the will of God alone (vv. 11-13). In chapter 3 we have our Lord's discourse on the new birth with Nicodemus. Here he shows us both the nature and necessity of the new birth. Until a person is born again he can neither see, nor enter into, the kingdom of God (vv. 3, 5). And this new birth is altogether the work of God the Holy Spirit who sovereignly gives life and faith to whom he will (v. 8). Then, the Master told Nicodemus that the only way any sinner can live before God, the only way we can be saved, is by trusting him as our sin-atoning Substitute (vv. 14-18).

All grace, all salvation, all life, all hope is in Christ. Do you believe on the Son of God? Do you trust Christ alone as your Saviour? That is the one thing that must be settled. To believe Christ is to have life. To abide in unbelief is to abide in death, under the wrath of God. That was John the Baptist's message and that is the message of God's preachers in every age and place. 'The Father loveth the Son, and hath given all things into his hand. He that believeth on the Son hath everlasting life: and he that believeth not the Son shall not see life; but the wrath of God abideth on him' (vv. 35, 36). 'He that hath the Son hath life; and he that hath not the Son of God hath not life' (1 John 5:12).

The Samaritan Woman
In chapter 4 John gives us a tremendous picture of God's grace. Our Lord Jesus 'must needs go through Samaria' because there was an elect sinner there for whom the time of love had come. Grace chose her. Grace marked the place at which grace would be given. Grace brought the Samaritan woman to the appointed place at the time of love. Grace brought Christ to the sinner. And grace brought the sinner to Christ and gave her faith.

The Impotent Man
In chapter 5 our Saviour came to the Pool of Bethesda. There were many around the pool who were impotent, blind, halt, and withered. But the

sovereign Saviour came there to show mercy to one certain man, a certain chosen sinner who had been impotent for 38 years. 'And immediately the man was made whole' (v. 9).

That is another picture of God's saving grace. It is sovereign, distinguishing, effectual grace. Spiritually, God's elect are totally impotent. We could never be saved if any part of salvation depended on us. But that is not the case. The Lord Jesus saves poor, impotent sinners by his own almighty arm of omnipotent mercy (Ephesians 2:1-5).

Witnesses To Christ
In the second half of chapter 5 our Lord Jesus shows himself to be the Christ by numerous witnesses. As we read these verses and others like them (10:16-18), we must not imagine that our Lord is declaring anything that might suggest him being inferior to the Father. Rather, our Lord is declaring his voluntary subjection to the will of his Father (Isaiah 50:5-7) as our Mediator and Surety.

'Then answered Jesus and said unto them, Verily, verily, I say unto you, The Son can do nothing of himself, but what he seeth the Father do: for what things soever he doeth, these also doeth the Son likewise. For the Father loveth the Son, and showeth him all things that himself doeth: and he will show him greater works than these, that ye may marvel. For as the Father raiseth up the dead, and quickeneth them; even so the Son quickeneth whom he will. For the Father judgeth no man, but hath committed all judgment unto the Son: That all men should honour the Son, even as they honour the Father. He that honoureth not the Son honoureth not the Father which hath sent him. Verily, verily, I say unto you, he that heareth my word, and believeth on him that sent me, hath everlasting life, and shall not come into condemnation; but is passed from death unto life. Verily, verily, I say unto you, The hour is coming, and now is, when the dead shall hear the voice of the Son of God: and they that hear shall live. For as the Father hath life in himself; so hath he given to the Son to have life in himself; And hath given him authority to execute judgment also, because he is the Son of man. Marvel not at this: for the hour is coming, in the which all that are in the graves shall hear his voice, And shall come forth; they that have done good, unto the resurrection of life; and they that have done evil, unto the resurrection of damnation. I can of mine own self do nothing: as I hear, I judge: and my judgment is just; because I seek not mine own will, but the will of the Father which hath sent me. If I bear witness of myself, my witness is not true' (John 5:19-31).

John the Baptist bore witness to him as the Christ, the Lamb of God, the eternal Saviour (vv. 33-35). His own works, his miracles, bear witness that he is the Christ, the Son of God, our Saviour (v. 36). The Father bore witness to Christ (v. 37) at his baptism and at his transfiguration, trusting him as our

Surety (Ephesians 1:12), putting all things in his hands as the Son of man (v. 27), and giving him all pre-eminence (Colossians 1:18; Philippians 2:8-11). And the book of God bears witness to him, that he is indeed the Christ (vv. 37-39). Moses (vv. 46, 47), in all the books of the law, bore witness to him, typically and prophetically, as does the veil being rent when he had fulfilled the whole law, satisfying the wrath and justice of God as our Representative.

The Offence Of The Gospel

Multitudes followed our Saviour, not because they were converted by his grace, but because they had eaten the loaves and fish. They were religious because they found religion profitable. They followed Christ outwardly because of what they gained by doing so. But, then, our Lord preached a message that offended the crowd. We read in John 6:66, 'From that time many of his disciples went back, and walked no more with him'. What did he preach? What was it that so greatly offended the multitudes? It was the message of God's free, sovereign, saving grace, the same message that offends lost religious crowds throughout the world today. It was the declaration that salvation is by the will of God alone (vv. 37-40). He asserted that fallen man's natural, total depravity makes salvation by the will of man impossible (v. 44). Our Master declared that salvation is altogether the work of God's free, sovereign, irresistible grace (v. 45) and this salvation can be possessed only by faith in Christ, eating his flesh and drinking his blood, trusting his righteousness and his atonement as our only ground of acceptance with God (vv. 47-58). This salvation was obtained by Christ laying down his life for chosen sinners scattered throughout the world (v. 51).

'These things said he in the synagogue, as he taught in Capernaum. Many therefore of his disciples, when they had heard this, said, This is an hard saying; who can hear it? When Jesus knew in himself that his disciples murmured at it, he said unto them, Doth this offend you? What and if ye shall see the Son of man ascend up where he was before? It is the spirit that quickeneth; the flesh profiteth nothing: the words that I speak unto you, they are spirit, and they are life. But there are some of you that believe not. For Jesus knew from the beginning who they were that believed not, and who should betray him. And he said, Therefore said I unto you, that no man can come unto me, except it were given unto him of my Father. From that time many of his disciples went back, and walked no more with him' (John 6:59-66).

These were the same people who sought just a short while earlier, to take him by force and make him a king (6:15).

'If Any Man Thirst'
In the seventh chapter 'the Jews' feast of tabernacles was at hand. His brethren tried to get the Lord to go up to the feast, to show himself to the world, but he refused. Later, he went up to the feast privately. Then, on the last day of the feast, as our Master beheld the multitudes going home from their empty, meaningless religious ritual, he proclaimed a great, gracious, magnanimous invitation to needy souls that is echoed around the world to this day, wherever the gospel is preached. 'In the last day, that great day of the feast, Jesus stood and cried, saying, If any man thirst, let him come unto me, and drink. He that believeth on me, as the scripture hath said, out of his belly shall flow rivers of living water' (vv. 37, 38).

The Adulterous Woman
The eighth chapter opens (vv. 1-11) with a tremendous picture of redemption and grace in Christ. A woman taken in adultery, scorned by men and condemned by God's holy law, is freely and fully forgiven of all sin by the Son of God who stooped to the earth and rose again.

Disciples Indeed
Beginning in verse 31 of chapter 8 our Lord gives us four unmistakable marks by which true disciples, true children of Abraham, are identified in this world: (1) They do the works of Abraham (v. 39). That is to say, they believe God. (2) True disciples love Christ (v. 42; 1 John 4:19). (3) They receive, bow to, and believe God's word (v. 47). (4) They keep Christ's doctrine (v. 51). They continue in his word (v. 31) and hold fast the gospel.

The Good Shepherd
In chapter 9 our Lord healed a man who was born blind. Because of the goodness of God, which he experienced, the Jews unchurched him. They kicked him out of their church because the Son of God gave him sight. When they did, the Lord Jesus took him into his arms and into the sheepfold of his grace. Then, in chapter 10, John gives us our Saviour's great discourse on the Good Shepherd. Christ is the Good Shepherd. He has some sheep. He voluntarily laid down his life for his sheep. He calls his sheep by name. He must and shall save his sheep. He gives his sheep eternal life. His sheep shall never perish!

Lazarus
Chapter 11 tells us about Mary, Martha, and Lazarus, our Lord's beloved friends, and the sickness and death of Lazarus by the will of God and for the glory of God. We see the Son of God raise Lazarus from the dead by the word

17

of his power. What a picture this is of God's saving operations of grace! Like Lazarus, I was dead. Like Lazarus, the Lord Jesus loved me. He came to where I was. He called me by name. I came forth to him. And he set me free.

Chapter 12 opens with our Lord again in the home of his friends Martha, Mary, and Lazarus. Mary anoints him for his burial. As he sets his face toward Calvary, our Lord declares that which he would there accomplish by the sacrifice of himself, 'Now is the judgment of this world: now shall the prince of this world be cast out. And I, if I be lifted up from the earth, will draw all men unto me. This he said, signifying what death he should die' (vv. 31-33).

Foot Washing

Chapter 13 begins the second section of John's Gospel. Everything, from here through the end of chapter 19 took place in the last hours of our Saviour's earthly life. In chapter 13 he gives us an example of how we ought to love one another by washing his disciples' feet. He did not do this to establish foot washing as a church ordinance, but to show us how to love one another. Love involves action, not sentimental words. Love bows low and gladly performs the most menial task for the sheer comfort of its object. 'By this shall all men know that ye are my disciples, if ye have love one to another' (v. 35).

Then our Lord told Peter how that he would deny him three times before the morning sun arose. 'Simon Peter said unto him, Lord, whither goest thou? Jesus answered him, Whither I go, thou canst not follow me now; but thou shalt follow me afterwards. Peter said unto him, Lord, why cannot I follow thee now? I will lay down my life for thy sake. Jesus answered him, Wilt thou lay down thy life for my sake? Verily, verily, I say unto thee, The cock shall not crow, till thou hast denied me thrice' (vv. 36-38).

Immediately after that, we read those sweet, sweet words of comfort and assurance in John 14:1-3. 'Let not your heart be troubled: ye believe in God, believe also in me. In my Father's house are many mansions: if it were not so, I would have told you. I go to prepare a place for you. And if I go and prepare a place for you, I will come again, and receive you unto myself; that where I am, there ye may be also.' How Peter must have cherished those words after his fall and restoration!

Comfort

Chapters 14, 15, and 16 are filled with words of tender comfort and instruction for God's people in this world in which we must endure constant sorrow and tribulation. 'These things I have spoken unto you, that in me ye might have peace. In the world ye shall have tribulation: but be of good cheer; I have overcome the world' (16:33).

The Lord's Prayer

Then, in chapter 17 John gives us the Lord's great, high priestly prayer for us, in which he prays not for the world but for his elect, asking his Father to keep us throughout our days on earth, through all our tribulations, and then to bring us safe to glory. Only in eternity shall we know the full scope of our Lord's words recorded here.

'And the glory which thou gavest me I have given them; that they may be one, even as we are one: I in them, and thou in me, that they may be made perfect in one; and that the world may know that thou hast sent me, and hast loved them, as thou hast loved me. Father, I will that they also, whom thou hast given me, be with me where I am; that they may behold my glory, which thou hast given me: for thou lovedst me before the foundation of the world. O righteous Father, the world hath not known thee: but I have known thee, and these have known that thou hast sent me. And I have declared unto them thy name, and will declare it: that the love wherewith thou hast loved me may be in them, and I in them' (17:22-26)

When I compare John 17:5 with John 17:22, I am utterly overwhelmed. Can it be true? Has the Lord Jesus Christ, the Son of God, our all-glorious Redeemer given to every one of his elect all the glory the Father gave to him as our covenant Surety and Mediator, all the glory that he now possesses as the God-man in heaven? Are we really and truly so perfectly one with him and so perfectly accepted in him that we shall all fully possess all the glory the Father gave him as the reward of his obedience unto death? Yes, O my soul, yes, it is true! He who is God and cannot lie declares it to be so!

Gethsemane

Chapter 18 brings us with our all-glorious Christ into Gethsemane. But John leaves out most of the things described by Matthew and Luke. Instead, he tells us of our Saviour's care for his disciples when the soldiers came to arrest him, emphasising the fact that he is God in total control, even over those who arrested him. Here again, we have a picture of redemption and grace. As if to demonstrate that he is God over all, not a helpless victim, the Saviour takes the initiative. He asked the soldiers, 'Whom seek ye?' When they told him they had come for that man called Jesus, he declared, 'I AM', and they fell down as dead men. Those men, representing the law by which he was to be executed, were slain before him. Then, the Master said, 'I AM' ('He' is in italics), 'If therefore ye seek me, let these go their way'. That is exactly what our Saviour says to the law of God. You cannot have me and my sheep. If you take me, you must let my people go free.

19

'It Is Finished'
In chapter 19 our Saviour is crucified. In verse 30 we read these great, triumphant words of our victorious Redeemer, 'It is finished'! 'When Jesus therefore had received the vinegar, he said, It is finished: and he bowed his head, and gave up the ghost.' What was finished? The law was finished, being satisfied (Romans 10:4). The prophets were finished, being fulfilled. All the work he came to do (Matthew 1:21) was finished. Atonement was finished. Righteousness was finished. Judgment was finished. Sin was finished.

Restoration
Chapters 20 and 21 tell us about our Lord's resurrection and his appearances to his disciples after the resurrection. By his death and resurrection as our Substitute, our Lord Jesus reconciled us to our God, restored all that we had lost by the sin and fall of our father Adam, and restored us entirely to our God. Is it not most fitting that John shows us the restoration of his fallen disciple in this context? The Lord Jesus came to Peter in grace, assuring him of his love and forgiveness, and assuring Peter of his love for his Saviour.

Conclusion
We read in John 21:25, 'And there are also many other things which Jesus did, the which, if they should be written every one, I suppose that even the world itself could not contain the books that should be written. Amen.' When John says, 'I suppose', he is still writing by inspiration. It is as though the Lord God is telling us, 'You cannot imagine how big my Son is, how great he is, and what wonders he has accomplished. If you go into every detail of who he is and what he has done, the world itself would not hold the books it would take to declare it all.' There could not be a more fitting conclusion of the Gospel of the Son of God.

Chapter 2

'In the beginning ... '

'In the beginning was the Word, and the Word was with God, and the Word was God' (John 1:1).

One of the old writers suggested, 'These words should be written upon tablets of gold and hung in every church building in the world.' In the 2nd century Clement of Alexandria wrote that one of the atheistic Platonic philosophers said of John 1:1, 'This barbarian hath comprised more stupendous stuff in three lines, than we have done in all our voluminous discourses.' May God the Holy Spirit teach us that which he inspired an unlearned and ignorant man like John, the fisherman, the son of Zebedee, to write in these three lines. 'In the beginning was the Word, and the Word was with God, and the Word was God.'

'The Beginning'
The other Gospel writers begin with Bethlehem. John begins with 'the bosom of the Father'. Luke dates his narrative by Roman emperors and Jewish high-priests. John dates his 'in the beginning'. With those words, he carries us into the depths of eternity, before time or creatures were. Both the Book of Genesis and the Gospel of John start from 'the beginning'. Genesis starts with 'the beginning' and works downward, telling us what followed. John starts with 'the beginning' and works upward, telling us what preceded 'the beginning'. Before the beginning, Christ the Word, our God and Saviour, already was.

John's Gospel opens with three simple words that are full of instruction, 'In the beginning'. In the first Epistle of John this same Apostle used similar language to describe our Saviour and speaks of him as, 'That which was from

21

the beginning' (1 John 1:1). But what is he talking about? Certainly, he is not talking about the beginning of eternity, for eternity has no beginning. John is talking about the beginning of the manifestation of Jehovah's purpose of grace, the beginning of his great work of saving his elect by our blessed Lord Jesus Christ, our Saviour, whose 'goings forth have been from of old, from everlasting' (Micah 5:2). It seems to me that he is telling us that there was a beginning before the beginning of time. Our blessed Saviour went forth from the beginning as our covenant Surety to save us from our sins (Proverbs 8:22, 23; Isaiah 46:9, 10; Acts 15:18; Colossians 1:18; 2 Thessalonians 2:13; Hebrews 1:10; 1 John 2:14).

John here teaches us to look upon the Son of God, both as the Essential Word and as the Revealed Word, standing forth in the everlasting councils of the triune God as our Surety and set up as the Wisdom of God from everlasting (Proverbs 8:22-31). In the beginning, before ever the earth was made, Christ stood forth as the Word in and by whom the Lord God would make himself known in the salvation of chosen sinners. He was not only the Word from the beginning, but 'in the beginning'. 'In the beginning' he stood forth as our covenant Surety. 'In the beginning' he was accepted as 'the Lamb slain from the foundation of the world'. 'In the beginning' we were chosen, accepted, blessed, and redeemed in him (Ephesians 1:3-7).

'The Word'
'In the beginning was the Word'. John calls our Lord Jesus Christ 'the Word'. This is a term used in the New Testament almost exclusively by John, identifying Christ as one who is God, and yet a distinct Person from the Father. I can think of only two places in which other inspired writers used this term in the New Testament with reference to our Saviour. In Hebrews 4:12, 13 we read 'For the word of God is quick, and powerful, and sharper than any twoedged sword, piercing even to the dividing asunder of soul and spirit, and of the joints and marrow, and is a discerner of the thoughts and intents of the heart. Neither is there any creature that is not manifest in his sight: but all things are naked and opened unto the eyes of him with whom we have to do.' In 2 Peter 3:5 we read, 'that by the word of God the heavens were of old'.

A word is an expression, a means of manifestation, communication, and revelation. Christ manifests the invisible God, communicates the love, mercy, and grace of God, and reveals the attributes and perfections of God. The word of God, then, is deity expressing itself. Therefore Christ is called the Word of God (Hebrews 1:1-3).

In Revelation 1:8 our Saviour declares himself to be God's alphabet. 'I am Alpha and Omega, the beginning and the ending, saith the Lord, which is, and which was, and which is to come, the Almighty.' Christ is the Word in and by whom the triune God makes himself known to men, the personal enunciation of Jehovah (John 1:18).

Christ, the Word, is one of the Holy Three-in-One that bear record in heaven. 'There are three that bear record in heaven' (1 John 5:7). Bear record of what? That Jesus is the Son of God? No. Heaven needs no evidence of that! These three bear record in heaven that God has given us eternal life, in strict accordance with his just and righteous law, by the merits of Christ's obedience and death as our Substitute. The three Persons of the holy trinity bear record in heaven that Christ has accomplished redemption for God's elect by his blood atonement. 'There are three that bear record in heaven, the Father, the Word, and the Holy Ghost: and these three are one.'

God the Father bears record that redemption is accomplished by his acceptance of Christ as our Representative and Surety (Hebrews 1:1-9; 6:19, 20; 10:11-14). When the Father raised Christ from the dead and received him back into heaven as our Mediator, he accepted all his elect in Christ and bare record that redemption's work was done (Ephesians 1:6; John 17:1-5).

God the Son, the living, eternal Word, the second person of the blessed trinity, bears record of his people's right to eternal life, by his perpetual advocacy and intercession at the Father's right hand (Romans 8:34; 1 John 2:1, 2; Hebrews 6:20; 7:24, 25). The record he bears, which secures the eternal salvation of God's elect, by which we merit heaven and eternal life, is twofold: his righteousness as our Representative and his satisfaction as our Substitute.

God the Holy Spirit, the third person of the holy trinity, bears record of the accomplishment of redemption, by effectually applying the blood of Christ to the hearts of God's elect in effectual calling (John 16:14; Hebrews 9:13, 14). The Spirit of God takes the merit of Christ's blood and righteousness and reveals our acceptance with God to us by the gospel. In effectual calling chosen, redeemed sinners hear the gospel. But they hear more than the bare word of the gospel. They hear the Spirit of God speak in their hearts! Each one hears God speak pardon to his own soul by the gospel of his salvation (Ephesians 1:13; 2 Corinthians 5:16). This is the record of heaven. The Father, the Word, and the Holy Spirit point to the blood and righteousness of Christ and say, 'It is finished! Redemption is accomplished'!

'And these three are one.' The three divine persons are one God. But more, the record of the Father, the record of the Word, and the record of the Spirit are one. What is that record? Redemption is accomplished by Christ alone! Every chosen sinner has the right to enter into heaven by the blood gate, by the merits of Christ. 'God hath given us eternal life, and this life is in his Son.'

Look at this name and title John gives to the Lord Jesus again. 'The Word'. 'In the beginning was the Word'. That is a statement so full of meaning that it cannot be adequately declared. Christ is called the Word because he is the

Wisdom of God. He is called the Word because he is the person spoken of in all the Old Testament prophecies and the sum of all the promises. Our Redeemer is called the Word because he is the Speaker, the Revealer, and the Interpreter of the Father's will. And he is called the Word because he is the image of the invisible God, the Offspring of the Father's mind, the express image of his person, just as our words (if honestly spoken) are the express image of our minds.

'Was'

John says, 'In the beginning was the Word'. He does not say, In the beginning came the Word, or began the Word, but was the Word. The word translated 'was' literally means 'was existing'. John is telling us that whenever the beginning was, the Word already was. He is declaring that he who is God our Saviour is the eternal One. He is that One who 'was, and is, and is to come' (Revelation 4:8).

'In the beginning was the Word'. No created mind can plunge the depths of this vast ocean or traverse its shoreless breadth. When time and creatures came into being, the Word was. 'In the beginning was the Word'. No words could have been chosen by God the Holy Spirit that could more perfectly or more emphatically declare that our Lord Jesus Christ is the absolute, uncreated, eternal God.

'With God'

'And the Word was with God'. With those words, John declares that Christ the Word is one with and co-eternal with God. John is declaring the eternal existence of the Word with the Father, his relation and nearness to him, his equality with him, and particularly the distinction of the Word from the Father. He was always with him, and is with him, and ever will be with him. From all eternity, there was an intimate and ineffable union between the first and second persons in the blessed trinity, between Christ the Word and God the Father. Though John here speaks of the Father and the Son, as we saw in 1 John 5:7, the same is true of God the Holy Spirit.

John seems to be emphasising, not just the eternality of the Word and the eternal union of the Father and the Son, but the eternal communion of the Divine Persons. The preposition 'with' is a preposition of direction and means 'toward', or 'face to face with', suggesting both equality and agreement. The phrase might be translated, 'and the Word was toward God'. It expresses the idea of motion.

We are reminded of Micah's description of our Saviour as him whose 'goings forth have been from of old, from everlasting'. In perfect union, communion, and being with one another, the Father and the Son, the Word and

God went forth toward us in everlasting mercy and love in the beginning, from eternity! Christ, the Word, was with the Father in the covenant of grace. He was with the Father in the creation of the universe, and is with him in the providential government of the world. He was with him as the Word and Son of God in heaven, while he as man, was here on earth. And he is now with him as our Advocate on High (1 John 1:1, 2).

There is now, always has been, and always will be a reciprocal, conscious communion, and the active going out of love between the three persons of the triune God; the Father and the Son and the Holy Spirit, regarding the Salvation of our souls. Imagine that! As the three persons of the eternal Godhead are equal in divinity, but distinct in personality, so all three of the divine persons are equal in grace, but distinct in the operations of grace; and all three are and were and forever will be moving toward us in grace!

God the Father is set before us as the Fountain of all grace (Ephesians 1:3-6). It was God the Father who in the covenant of grace proposed redemption, devised the plan, and chose the people whom he would save by his almighty grace. He found a way whereby his banished ones could be brought back to him and never expelled from his presence. Then, 'in the fulness of time', he sent his Son to be the Medium or Mediator of grace to his chosen (Galatians 4:4-6).

God the Son, the Lord Jesus Christ, is the channel of all grace (Ephesians 1:7-12). All grace comes to sinners through Christ the Mediator. In the first chapter of Ephesians Paul tells us fourteen times that everything God requires of sinners, does for sinners, and gives to sinners is in Christ. Apart from Christ there is no grace. God will not deal with man, but by Christ. Man cannot deal with God, but by Christ. Christ is the Revelation of God, the incarnation of God, and the only way to God. Are we chosen of God? We are chosen in Christ. Are we blessed of God? We are blessed in Christ. Are we predestinated by God? We are predestinated to be conformed to the image of Christ. Are we adopted as the children of God? We are adopted in Christ. Are we accepted of God? We are accepted in Christ. Are we redeemed by God? We are redeemed in Christ. Are we forgiven by God? We are forgiven in Christ. Are we justified before God? We are justified in Christ. Are we sanctified by God? We are sanctified in Christ. Do we know God? We know him in Christ. Do we have an inheritance from God? We have it in Christ. Are we called of God? We are called in Christ.

Do you see this? All grace comes to chosen sinners through Christ, the Word, who is from everlasting 'with God'. There is no other way the grace of God can reach a sinner. It is the work of Christ upon the cross which has brought grace and justice together in the salvation of sinners. It is through his blood, only through the blood of the cross, that 'mercy and truth are met together; righteousness and peace have kissed each other' (Psalms 85:10). Blissfully lost in the contemplation of God's matchless grace in Christ, John Bunyan penned the following rapturous words,

> O Thou Son of the Blessed! Grace stripped Thee of thy glory. Grace brought Thee down from heaven. Grace made Thee bear such burdens of sin, such burdens of curse as are unspeakable. Grace was in Thy heart. Grace came bubbling up from Thy bleeding side. Grace was in Thy tears. Grace was in Thy prayers. Grace streamed from Thy thorn-crowned brow! Grace came forth with the nails that pierced Thee, with the thorns that pricked Thee! Oh, here are unsearchable riches of grace! Grace to make sinners happy! Grace to make angels wonder! Grace to make devils astonished!

The Fountain of all grace is God the Father. The medium of all grace is God the Son. And God the Holy Spirit is the Administrator of all grace (Ephesians 1:13, 14). It is God the Holy Spirit who effectually applies the blood of Christ to chosen, redeemed sinners. He regenerates the dead by omnipotent power (John 6:63). He calls the redeemed with irresistible grace (Psalms 65:4; 110:3; John 16:8-11). He gives faith to the chosen by almighty operations of grace (Ephesians 2:1-9; Colossians 2:12). He seals God's elect unto everlasting glory.

Redemption was effectually accomplished for God's elect by Christ at Calvary. It is effectually applied to all the redeemed by God the Holy Spirit in effectual calling (Hebrews 9:12-14). Without the sovereign, gracious operations of God the Holy Spirit in conversion, no sinner would ever become the beneficiary of grace. He takes the things of Christ and shows them to his people. He quickens those the Father chose. He reclaims those the Son redeemed. He leads to the Good Shepherd every one of those lost sheep for whom the Good Shepherd laid down his life (John 10:11). C. D. Cole wrote,

> He conquers the stoutest hearts and cleanses the foulest spiritual leper. He opens the sin-blinded eyes and unstops the sin-closed ears. The blessed Holy Spirit reveals the grace of the Father and applies the grace of the Son.

All three persons in the Godhead are equally gracious; and all three must be equally praised. In fact, whenever the three persons of the holy trinity are presented together in the scriptures, it is always in connection with redemption, grace, and salvation. I have not found an exception. Thomas Ken wrote,

Praise God from whom all blessings flow!
Praise Him all creatures here below!
Praise Him above, ye heavenly hosts!
Praise Father, Son, and Holy Ghost!

Sometimes God the Father is presented alone, as when he stood upon Mount Sinai, clothed with thunder and lightning, delivering the law to Moses. So terrible was his presence that the very mountain shook in the prospect of God's awesome judgment (Exodus 20:18).

Sometimes God the Son appears alone, as when he appears in his glorious second advent. Then men and women who have despised and rejected him will cry for the mountains to fall upon them and pray in terror that they might be saved from 'the wrath of the Lamb' (Revelation 6:14).

When God the Holy Spirit is represented alone, the consequences are the same. Those who blaspheme him, committing that sin which can never be forgiven, are reserved as reprobates unto everlasting judgment (Matthew 12:31, 32). Whenever one person in the trinity is presented alone, the result is judgment.

However, when all three of the divine persons are set before us together, as in John 1:1, the consequence is always mercy, grace, redemption, and salvation (Ephesians 1:3-14; Revelation 1:4-6). In other words, the whole Being of God, in all his attributes, in all his glory, in the trinity of his persons is set for the everlasting salvation of his elect (Jeremiah 32:41; Romans 8:28-32).

'Was God'
'And the Word was God.' It is impossible for anyone to read those words with honesty and misunderstand them. John here asserts that the Lord Jesus Christ, the eternal Word, was, is, and ever shall be in nature, essence, and substance very God of very God, and that as the Father is God, so also the Son is God. Our Saviour's divinity could not be more positively stated. There is no inferiority in the Word to God the Father. The eternal and unchangeable Godhead of the Father, of the Son, and of the Holy Ghost is all one.

'And the Word was God.' He was not made God, as he was made flesh. He was not constituted or appointed God, or declared God by office and title. 'The Word was God', truly and properly God, in the highest sense of the word. Jesus Christ, our Saviour, the Word, is Jehovah, our God, God with us, the mighty God, God over all, the great God, the living God, the true God and eternal life. All the perfections of divinity are his. All the fulness of the Godhead dwells in him. The works of his hands are the works of him who is God. Creation and

27

providence, redemption and forgiveness, life and death, judgment and mercy are all works of God attributed to our Lord Jesus Christ.

Heresy Abolished
'In the beginning was the Word, and the Word was with God, and the Word was God.' With this one sentence, John sweeps away and abolishes every heresy, by which Satan has harassed the Church of God from its beginning.

Arianism, which asserts that Christ is a being inferior to God; Sabellianism, which denies the distinction of persons in the trinity, and says that God sometimes manifested himself as the Father, sometimes as the Son, and sometimes as the Spirit; Socinianism, Unitarianism, which declares that Jesus Christ was not God at all, but mere man, a good and great man, but only a man; and Arminianism, which declares God to be changeable, as one whose love, will, purpose, and grace are all subject to the will of man; all are swept away by this one blessed declaration of God in his holy word, 'In the beginning was the Word, and the Word was with God, and the Word was God.'

Without question, there are deep mysteries here, which no man can comprehend, and no language can explain. How can there be a plurality in unity and a unity in plurality, three persons in the trinity and one God in essence? How can Christ be at the same time in the Father and with the Father? These are matters far beyond our feeble understanding. Blessed are they who are content simply to believe the Revelation of God. As one old writer put it, 'It is rashness to search too far into it. It is piety to believe it. It is life eternal to know it. And we can never have a full comprehension of it, till we come to enjoy it.'

The Blessedness Of It
Let me show you something of the blessedness of that which is here asserted. 'In the beginning was the Word, and the Word was with God, and the Word was God.' Christ the Word, who is our God, is eternal life (1 John 1:1-3). Christ, the Word of Life, Christ who is life essential, swallowed up death in victory, and 'brought life and immortality to light by the gospel' (2 Timothy 1:10). 'Truly our fellowship is with the Father and with his Son'. Union being the ground of communion, all that is theirs is ours. This made Moses cry out, 'Happy art thou, O Israel' (Deuteronomy 33:29).

'The life was manifested, and we have seen it, and bear witness, and show unto you that eternal life, which was with the Father, and was manifested unto us' (1 John 1:2). Christ is Eternal Life! Look at 1 John 1:5. 'God is light, and in him is no darkness at all.' With those words, John tells us what the message is that we are sent to proclaim. He is talking about the revelation of God, whom no man has seen or can see, apart from Christ, the Word, who is both God himself and the Light of life, in and by whom God is revealed. God the Holy Spirit has given us 'the light of the knowledge of the glory of God in the face of Jesus Christ' by the gospel (2 Corinthians 4:6). Oh, may 'the Spirit of the living God' write these things, 'not in tables of stone, but in fleshy tables of our heart', for Christ's sake, that we may know him who is Eternal Life, and that we may forever walk together in sweet fellowship with one another, and truly in fellowship 'with the Father, and with his Son Jesus Christ', that our joy may be full!

Nothing revealed in holy scripture more forcibly inspires unity among true believers than the revelation of the trinity. This is not some abstract point of theological speculation, or some profitless point of doctrinal refinement. This is a subject so far above our comprehension, that it should inspire our deepest reverence and humility, as well as the most circumspect consecration and unity.

In our baptism you and I have publicly avowed our consecration to our God (Romans 6:4-6). Being baptised in the name of the Father, and of the Son, and of the Holy Spirit, we publicly declared our consecration and commitment to obey the will of the Father, live for the glory of the Son, and submit to the leadership of the Holy Spirit. Let every thought about the holy trinity stimulate in us a desire that we may be one, even as God the Father, God the Son, and God the Holy Spirit are one (John 17:20-22). Said J. M. Pendleton,

> Who can think of the Father, the Son, and the Holy Spirit as one, one in nature, one in love, one in purpose, and not hope for the day when the intercessory prayer of Christ will be answered in the union of all his followers?

All true believers should earnestly devote themselves, as the sons and daughters of the triune God, to unity. Oh, that God's saints on earth might truly be one in purpose, seeking the glory of God; one in labour, serving the cause of Christ; and one in the love of Christ (Philippians 2:2-5). As the children of God in this world, for Christ's sake (Ephesians 4:32-5:1), for his glory, let us learn by the grace of God to be patient with one another, to highly esteem one another, to forgive one another, to be forbearing with one another, and to give deference to one another. Soon, we shall be one in glory (John 17:22; Ephesians 4:1-6).

Chapter 3

The Eternal Christ

'In the beginning was the Word, and the Word was with God, and the Word was God. The same was in the beginning with God. All things were made by him; and without him was not any thing made that was made. In him was life; and the life was the light of men. And the light shineth in darkness; and the darkness comprehended it not' (John 1:1-5).

These five verses set before us the matchless sublimity of our Lord Jesus Christ in his eternal being and character. In these five verses, inspired by God the Holy Spirit, John sets before us heights no mortal mind can hope to scale and depths that none can fathom. Yet, he sets these things before us in such simple, clear, language that they cannot be misunderstood, except by those who are willingly ignorant.

John's Gospel is the gospel of the eternal Christ. We do not have to guess what John's purpose was in writing. He tells us plainly in the last verse of chapter 20, 'These are written, that ye might believe that Jesus is the Christ, the Son of God; and that believing ye might have life through his name.' His great aim in these 21 chapters is not merely to inform us of historical facts relating to the life of Christ on this earth. John's purpose is to show us the deity and eternal Godhead of that man who is known the world over as 'Jesus of Nazareth', that we might trust him as God our Saviour, and obtain eternal life in him.

What man could have been better suited to show us our Saviour's glorious Godhead? John was distinctly prepared of God for the work. He had been with the Lord from the beginning of his earthly ministry as a chosen Apostle. John was there when the Lord Jesus performed his mighty miracles. John was with

31

him when the Master instituted the Supper. John heard the Saviour's many sermons, his parables, and his explanation of the parables. John laid his head upon the Lord's chest, as only a loving brother or friend might do. He was with the Lord Jesus in Gethsemane. He was by his side as the Saviour poured out his life's blood upon the cursed tree. John took the Saviour's mother into his own household and provided and cared for her until her death. He was present when the risen Christ ascended back into heaven. He saw the destruction of the Jewish nation, the temple, and the City of Jerusalem. And it was to this man, John, that our Lord appeared on the Isle of Patmos, showing him all that he would accomplish before time is no more.

In these opening verses of his Gospel John shows us the eternal Christ in his relationship to time, to the Godhead, to creation, and to men.

Relationship To Time

First, John declares our Saviour's relationship to time. Our Saviour is not a mere creature of time. He is before all time and the Creator of time. Christ is eternal. John tells us 'in the beginning was the Word'. He did not begin to exist when the heavens and the earth were made. He was with the Father 'before the world was' (John 17:5), possessing from the beginning all the glory that he now possesses as our successful Surety. He was already existing when matter was first created and before time began. He is 'before all things' (Colossians 1:17). He is eternal.

'In the beginning was the Word, and the Word was with God, and the Word was God. The same was in the beginning with God' (vv. 1, 2). Christ, the Word, was continually in being with God, in perfect union, communion, and being with God the Father and God the Spirit. In time he came to be with man; but in the beginning he was with God. The Lord Jesus Christ is God the eternal Son. He is our eternal Surety, 'the Surety of a better covenant', our eternal Sacrifice, 'the Lamb slain from the foundation of the world', our eternal Shepherd, and our eternal Saviour (2 Timothy 1:9, 10; Ephesians 1:3-6).

I want you to get the sweet honey found in the honeycomb of our Saviour's glorious eternality. For as long as he has had being, we have had being in him. As soon as he stood forth in the beginning with God, as our Head and Representative, we stood forth in him, as one with him. We were in him as his seed (Psalms 22:30, 31). And we were in him as his body (Psalms 139:14-18).

God's elect are the members of Christ's mystical body, the church. All the members of his body were written in his book, the book of life, when as yet, as regarding their actual existence, there was none of them. We were given to him in eternity, when he was constituted our covenant Head in the everlasting covenant, ordered in all things and sure. Thus, we became, in prospect of our Saviour's incarnation, 'members of his body, of his flesh, and of his bones'.

How tenderly our blessed Redeemer reminded his Father of these covenant transactions, when he said in his great intercessory prayer, 'I pray for them: I pray not for the world, but for them which thou hast given me; for they are thine. And all mine are thine, and thine are mine; and I am glorified in them' (John 17:9, 10).

Being thus given to Christ, and constituted members of his mystical body, we can no more perish than Christ himself. He is our Head, and as he is possessed of all power, full of all love, filled with all wisdom, and replete with all mercy, grace, and truth, how can he, how will he, allow any of his members to fall out of his body and be lost and separated from him forever? Will any man willingly allow his eye, or his hand, or his foot, or even the tip of his little finger to be cut off? If any member of our body perishes, if we lose an arm or a leg, it is because we have no power to prevent it. But all power in heaven and in earth belongs to Christ. Therefore, not one member of his mystical body, 'the fulness of him that filleth all in all', can perish for lack of power in him to save it.

We do not become members of his body when we believe. We were members of his body when he was 'in the beginning with God'. When we are quickened and made alive unto God savingly and experimentally, by the regenerating work of the Spirit, we are brought into the realisation of this blessed eternal union with Christ; but the union was from everlasting.

Relationship To God
Second, John shows us our blessed Saviour's eternal relationship to the triune Godhead. He was from the beginning with God, because he is God, one with the Father and the Spirit. We rejoice to know that Christ our Saviour is God. But, I want you to see the significance of the fact that John here declares that he is the Word, the eternal Logos of the triune God.

Christ 'was in the beginning with God', as the unuttered speech and thought of the triune God. It is only in Christ that God is fully told out. He so fully and so perfectly reveals God that he declares, 'He that hath seen me hath seen the Father' (John 14:9). To know him is to know God (John 17:3). The 'light of the knowledge of the glory of God' is seen only 'in the face of Jesus Christ' (2 Corinthians 4:6).

It is Christ the Word, our crucified Substitute, the Lamb of God, who opens the sealed book of God's eternal purpose, reveals it to us, and fulfils it in the accomplishment of redemption (Revelation 5:1-10). It is Christ the Word, crucified as our Substitute and risen as our Saviour, who interprets and fulfils all the Old Testament scriptures (Luke 24:25-27, 45-47). It is Christ the Word whom we preach to men, by whom the veil of spiritual darkness is taken away and the glory of God is revealed (2 Corinthians 3:14-18).

Relationship To Creation

Third, John shows us, with sublime simplicity, the relationship of our Lord Jesus Christ to creation. 'All things were made by him; and without him was not any thing made that was made' (v. 3). In the book of God creation is almost always associated with redemption, because he who is our Creator is our Redeemer, and because creation is meaningless apart from redemption.

Liberals, Mormons, and Russellites (Jehovah Witnesses), and countless other heretics tell us that Christ is but a creature of God, but holy scripture declares that he is God our Creator! Our Lord Jesus Christ is the Word by whom the worlds and all that they contain were made (Psalms 148:5; Ephesians 3:8, 9; Colossians 1:15-19). 'By (Christ) the word of God the heavens were of old' (2 Peter 3:5).

'All things were made by him; and without him was not anything made that was made.' He who is before all things is eternal, he who made all things is omnipotent, and he who is eternal and omnipotent is God. This great God, our Creator, who made all things, is he who has made peace for us by the blood of his cross (Colossians 1:20). In the new creation of grace, as in the creation of the world itself, Christ is the Creator. It is Christ who declares, 'Behold, I make all things new' (Revelation 21:5). 'If any man be in Christ, he is a new creature'! And of the new creation, the book of God everywhere declares, 'Without him was not anything made that was made'! Without him there can be no new covenant, no new name, no new and living way, no new heart, no new spirit, no new garment, no new song, no new heaven, and no new earth. 'Thou art worthy, O Lord, to receive glory and honour and power: for thou hast created all things, and for thy pleasure they are and were created' (Revelation 4:11). If all things were created for his pleasure, it cannot be doubted that 'he shall see of the travail of his soul and shall be satisfied'!

Relationship To Men

Fourth, John shows us Christ's relationship to men. 'In him was life; and the life was the light of men. And the light shineth in darkness; and the darkness comprehended it not' (vv. 4, 5).

Christ is Life. 'In him was life'. All natural life, all spiritual life, the resurrection life, and eternal life are all from him who is Life. He who created all things must be the Fountain of life and Giver of life. The word 'life' is used here in its widest sense. All creature life comes from him, for 'in him we live and move and have our being'. All spiritual life or eternal life comes from and is found in him. He has given us eternal life (1 John 5:11; John 11:25, 26).

And Christ is Light. 'And the life was the light of men.' The natural light of reason and conscience, as well as spiritual light and heaven's eternal light, come from him who is the Light of men. Christ is the only moral, spiritual Light there is. He is that 'true light, which lighteth every man that cometh into the world' (v. 9). Every rational man is morally enlightened (Romans 2:15; Romans 1:18-21). That means all are responsible and accountable. Though all men are by nature dead in trespasses and sins, all are responsible before God and shall give an account (Hebrews 9:27; Revelation 20:12) for the 'Light' they have despised and refused.

Look at verse 5 again. John tells us that Christ, the Light, blazes forth in the darkness of man's depraved heart and sin-darkened soul. That is clearly the meaning of the first part of verse 5. 'The light shineth in darkness'! Then we read, 'and the darkness comprehended it not', meaning the darkness perceived no light, though the Light shines ever so brightly.

The word translated 'comprehended' is sometimes translated 'overtake' (1 Thessalonians 5:4). Blessed be his name forever, when Christ comes to shine in the hearts of his own, he does not just give light, he causes his own to see the Light. He shines with such irresistible Light in the hearts of his redeemed that we simply cannot overtake the Light. Rather, the Light completely overtakes us! As it was in the old creation, so it is in the new. God says, 'Let there be light', and there is light (Genesis 1:1-3).

'In the beginning was the Word, and the Word was with God, and the Word was God. The same was in the beginning with God. All things were made by him; and without him was not any thing made that was made. In him was life; and the life was the light of men. And the light shineth in darkness; and the darkness comprehended it not.' With those words the Apostle John was inspired to begin his Gospel, showing us the eternal Christ, 'Who only hath immortality, dwelling in the light which no man can approach unto; whom no man hath seen, nor can see: to whom be honour and power everlasting. Amen.'

Chapter 4

'a man sent from God'

'There was a man sent from God, whose name was John. The same came for a witness, to bear witness of the Light, that all men through him might believe. He was not that Light, but was sent to bear witness of that Light. That was the true Light, which lighteth every man that cometh into the world. He was in the world, and the world was made by him, and the world knew him not. He came unto his own, and his own received him not. But as many as received him, to them gave he power to become the sons of God, even to them that believe on his name: Which were born, not of blood, nor of the will of the flesh, nor of the will of man, but of God. And the Word was made flesh, and dwelt among us, (and we beheld his glory, the glory as of the only begotten of the Father,) full of grace and truth' (John 1:6-14).

Find a man sent from God, and you have found a man you would be wise to hear. Find a man sent from God, and you have found a man just like any other man; sinful, weak, and in constant need of grace, and yet a man unlike any man. Find a man sent from God, and you will have found a prophet, a messenger of God to your soul.

A Man Sent
The first thing set before us in this portion of holy scripture is 'a man sent from God'. John begins his Gospel narrative by declaring that Jesus Christ is God our Creator, asserting without explanation that the Man Christ Jesus is the eternal God (vv. 1-5). Having declared our Saviour's eternality and eternal Godhead, John shows him to be the Creator of all things, the source of all life,

37

and the Light of the world. Then, John proceeds to introduce us to John the Baptist and his ministry. This prophet, John the Baptist, is held before us as an exemplary gospel preacher. Like John the Baptist, every true gospel preacher is 'a man sent from God'.

Here is a divinely inspired description of every man sent from God. He is sent 'for a witness, to bear witness of the Light, that all men through him might believe'. Preachers are not priests. They are not mediators between God and men. Christ alone is our Priest and Mediator. Gospel preachers are not social workers, psycho-therapists, counsellors, educators, or religious cheerleaders. And they certainly are not trained religious parrots, who simply repeat what they have heard others say! Those men who are sent of God are witnesses. They are sent to bear testimony to God's truth, as first-hand witnesses, telling what they know by personal experience.

A man I know very well, after preaching the gospel for nearly thirty years, began to alter his doctrine. He sent out what he called 'a clarification'. This is what he said about the message he once preached. 'What I might have said or written in the past was because others said it.' That man who is sent of God does not parrot what others have said. He bears witness to that which he has seen for himself and knows for himself, by personal experience. That is precisely what John the Apostle said about John the Baptist here; and that is also what he says about himself in the first verses of 1 John (1 John 1:1-3).

Specifically, that man who is sent of God bears witness to this blessed revelation of grace: The Lord Jesus Christ is the only Saviour of men, the only Light through whom lost sinners believe. Peter did this on the day of Pentecost. 'With many other words did he testify and exhort, saying, Save yourselves from this untoward generation' (Acts 2:40). Paul tells us about his own preaching. He preached, 'Testifying both to the Jews, and also to the Greeks, repentance toward God, and faith toward our Lord Jesus Christ' (Acts 20:21).

Gospel preachers testify what they know by the word of God, the teaching of the Holy Spirit, and their own experience of grace, bearing faithful witness to Christ. Any preacher who does not bear faithful witness to Christ in all the fulness of his person and work is not sent of God. So long as the preacher bears faithful witness of the Light, so long as he faithfully preaches Jesus Christ and him crucified, he performs his work faithfully. His preaching is honouring to God and is honoured by God, whether those who hear him believe or do not believe (2 Corinthians 2:14-17).

The preacher's object in preaching is 'that all men through Christ might believe'. The words 'all men' must be understood in a limited sense. They do not refer to every person in the world. Obviously, the Spirit of God does not intend for us to understand that there is the possibility that every person in the world might believe. Some were already in hell when John came preaching.

38

They could not believe. Those who never hear the gospel cannot believe. And those to whom the Spirit of God is not given cannot believe.

The words 'all men' simply refer to all classes of men. We preach the gospel to all men for the salvation of God's elect scattered among all men. The gospel of Christ is the means by which God the Holy Spirit gives chosen, redeemed sinners life and faith in Christ (Romans 10:17; 1 Peter 1:23-25).

Yet, no man can preach the gospel effectually, in the power of the Spirit, except he be sent of God. 'How shall they preach, except they be sent?' (Romans 10:13-17). I ask you to pray for me and for our brethren around the world that, having been sent of God, we may be sent every time we stand to preach, that we may, like those of old, 'be filled with the Holy Ghost and speak as the Spirit gives us utterance'. As you send your pastor out to do the work of an evangelist, pray for him, 'that utterance may be given unto (him), that (he) may open (his) mouth boldly, to make known the mystery of the gospel' (Ephesians 6:19), 'that God would open unto us a door of utterance, to speak the mystery of Christ' (Colossians 4:3).

Verse 8 might seem to be a redundant statement. 'He was not that Light, but was sent to bear witness of that Light.' But the sad fact is, many treat preachers as though they were Christ himself. There was an ancient, heretical sect which held that John the Baptist was the Messiah. Some in his own day presumed that the Baptist prophet was the Christ. Therefore, he said in verse 20, 'I am not the Christ'! You may think, 'No one today would be that foolish'. But multitudes are! Papists treat the pope and their priests as if they were themselves Christs. Multitudes of Protestants treat preachers and religious leaders as though they were Christs.

What is a preacher? Ask any true prophet, and he will tell you plainly. 'I am the voice of one crying in the wilderness, Make straight the way of the Lord' (v. 23; Isaiah 40:3). Does anyone ask, 'What is a preacher?' I like the answer I heard pastor Scott Richardson give to that question many, many years ago. 'A preacher is a nobody sent to tell everybody about somebody who can save anybody.'

Christ The Light

In verse nine the Holy Spirit tells us, secondly, as he did in verse 4, that Christ is the Light. 'That was the true light, which lighteth every man that cometh into the world.'

Christ is to the souls of men what the sun is to the world: The Light. Twice our Saviour declared, 'I am the light of the world' (John 8:12; 9:5). Christ is that Light of whom all gospel preachers bear witness. He is the Light and the fountain of all light to all creatures. He is the true Light, in distinction from typical lights of the Mosaic, Levitical ceremonies in the Old Testament. Christ the Light gave light to the dark earth in the beginning, and spoke light out of darkness. Christ the Light is the Light of all men, 'which lighteth every man that cometh into the world'.

Both the light of reason and the light of conscience come from Christ. All natural light and understanding comes from him. But the light of nature, of reason, and of conscience, while sufficient to render all without excuse before God (Romans 1:18-20), is not and never can be spiritual, saving light. The Lord Jesus warns us plainly and solemnly that the light that is in men by nature, as it relates to spiritual things, is utter darkness (Matthew 6:23; Luke 11:35; John 3:18-21).

When John says that Christ 'lighteth every man that cometh into the world', it is obvious that he is talking about natural, not spiritual light. I say that is obvious, because all men do not have spiritual light. But if you do, if you have light in your soul, if you possess the light of the knowledge of the glory of God, if you have the light of life, and grace, and salvation, it is because Christ has given it to you by the gospel. And whatever light you have regarding the things of God is the gift of Christ, the Light.

God 'hath saved us, and called us with an holy calling, not according to our works, but according to his own purpose and grace, which was given us in Christ Jesus before the world began, But is now made manifest by the appearing of our Saviour Jesus Christ, who hath abolished death, and hath brought life and immortality to light through the gospel' (2 Timothy 1:9, 10).

Unknown By The World
Thirdly, in verses 10 and 11 John tells us that Christ, who is the Light of the world, is completely unknown by the world. 'He was in the world, and the world was made by him, and the world knew him not. He came unto his own, and his own received him not.'

Read those five statements just as they stand in this chapter. John is not here describing our Lord's earthly life and ministry. These five rich and instructive statements illustrate and explain the glorious things John has been declaring in the first nine verses of this chapter about our Saviour.

'He was in the world'. When was he in the world? This does not refer to our Lord's incarnation. John speaks of that in verse 14. This statement, 'He was in the world', speaks of a past existence in the world. It is written, as A. T. Robertson points out, in the 'imperfect tense of continuous existence in the universe before the incarnation as in verses 1 and 2'. 'The word "was" denotes past existence in the world, even all the time past from the creation of the world' says John Gill. When was he in the world? He was in the world from all eternity. He was not in the world in his human nature, for the world had not yet been created by him and he had not become flesh. And it cannot be understood that John refers to him being in the world merely in his divine nature, because that would have been a needless observation. But he was in the world when in his covenant character he was set up from everlasting, and when Jehovah possessed him (as he himself states it), 'from the beginning or ever the earth was' as our Surety and Mediator, when he stood up in the council chambers of eternity as our Wisdom, 'Rejoicing in the habitable part of his earth' and delighting himself in his chosen (Proverbs 8:22-31). Then read ...

'And the world was made by him'. This is exactly what John told us in verse 3. 'Through faith we understand that the worlds were framed by the word of God, so that things which are seen were not made of things which do appear' (Hebrews 11:3).

'And the world knew him not.' By the sin and fall of our father Adam, the whole human race was plunged into darkness and 'knew him not' (Psalms 14:1, 2; 10:4). The world knew him not as their Creator. The world refused to acknowledge the mercies they received from him. The world refused to worship, serve, obey, love, and fear him as God. Then read,

'He came unto his own'. The words might be read, 'He came unto his own people', referring not to his elect and redeemed people, who shall be made willing in the day of his power and shall receive him (Psalms 110:3; John 6:37), but I am more inclined to think the Holy Spirit is referring to his own physical people, the Jews, to whom he gave the law, the prophets, the service of God, and the promises. Throughout the Old Testament 'he came unto his own', to the Jewish people, before his incarnation. He came in the types and pictures given to the nation of Israel. He came in promises and prophecies, and in the word and ordinances of the Old Testament. He came to them personally, in person, as he did to Moses in the burning bush. He came in person to deliver the children of Israel out of Egypt on the night of the Passover. The Lord Jesus himself came and redeemed them with a mighty hand and an outstretched arm; and in his love and pity he led them through the Red Sea as on dry ground and through the wilderness in a pillar of cloud by day and a pillar of fire by night. He came to them in person at Mount Sinai, and gave them the oracles of God. He came in person to Abraham, Isaac, and Jacob, to Gideon, Manoah, and his wife, to Daniel in the lion's den, and Shadrach, Meshach, and Abednego in the furnace. Throughout the days of the Old Testament, 'he came unto his own'.

'And his own received him not.' They did not believe in him and refused to obey his voice. They rebelled against him and tempted him often. They provoked him to anger and vexed and grieved his Holy Spirit. They despised his prophets, generation after generation. Then, after he came into the world, the Jews despised him and his gospel, fulfilling their own scriptures by their rejection of him (Hosea 9:17; Acts 13:27).

41

Oh, how wicked, how desperately wicked the heart of man is! Christ was in the world invisibly, long before the Word was made flesh. He was in the world from the very beginning; ruling, ordering, and governing the whole creation, 'upholding all things by the word of his power'. He gave to all life and breath, rain from heaven, and fruitful seasons. By him kings reigned and nations were increased or diminished. Yet, 'the world knew him not', and honoured him not. They 'worshiped and served the creature more than the Creator' (Romans 1:25).

Then, when the Son of God came visibly into the world, when he was born at Bethlehem, he fared no better. He came to the very people he had brought out of Egypt, to the Jews, whom he had separated from other nations, and to whom he had revealed himself by the prophets. He came to those Jews who read of him every sabbath day in their synagogues, and professed to be waiting for his coming. But, when he came, they received him not, but crucified him!

But there is far greater proof of the wickedness and depravity of the human heart than all of that. How often the Lord Jesus Christ has come to you by the gospel, being 'evidently set forth, crucified among you' (Galatians 3:1). Yet, you obstinately refuse to obey the truth, and receive him not! To such rebels he says, in Lamentations 1:12, 'Is it nothing to you, all ye that pass by? behold, and see if there be any sorrow like unto my sorrow, which is done unto me, wherewith the LORD hath afflicted me in the day of his fierce anger.'

Another People
Fourth, John tells us about another people. The Jewish nation refused him; but the purpose of God is not thwarted (Romans 3:3, 4). Blessed be his name, there is another people, a spiritual seed, who are his people by election and redemption, a people who will be willing and will receive him in the day of his power. 'But as many as received him, to them gave he power to become the sons of God, even to them that believe on his name' (v. 12).

Saving faith is here spoken of as receiving Christ. To believe on the Lord Jesus Christ is to receive him, to reach out and take him for your own. That is what the word 'receive' means here, to take. We receive him as the Word of God. We receive him as God our Saviour. We receive him as our Lord and Redeemer. We receive grace. We receive pardon, forgiveness, righteousness, and an inheritance among the sons of God by his blood. We receive life by his death. Receiving him, we receive all by him and with him and in him!

Who are these many who receive him? The scriptures tell us plainly. They are the many, out of every nation, kindred, tribe, and tongue, who were ordained unto eternal life (Acts 13:48), the many who were redeemed by his precious blood (Isaiah 53:10-12), the many whom the Lord our God shall call by his Spirit (Psalms 65:4; Acts 2:39).

Blessedness Of Faith
Look at verse 12 again. Here is a brief description of the blessedness of faith in Christ. 'But as many as received him, to them gave he power to become the sons of God, even to them that believe on his name.'

Several years ago, one of the men in our congregation asked me about this statement: 'To them gave he power to become the sons of God'. He asked, 'Does that word 'power' mean ability or authority?' I answered, 'Yes.' It means ability and authority. This is not the word translated power in Romans 1:16. This is a different word altogether. In Romans 1:16 the word translated 'power' means 'mighty ability, violent strength, or abundant might'. It is the word from which we get our word 'dynamite'. The gospel of Christ is the mighty, explosive, violent power of God unto salvation.

The word translated power here means both authority and ability. It is similar to our word 'exercise'. It has the idea of putting something to use, or of putting something into operation, by right and with skill and ability (John 5:27; 17:2). As the Lord Jesus Christ has been given power (the right and authority) to execute judgment with skill and ability, and to govern the universe, so the Lord Jesus gives to every believing sinner the power (the right to execute with skill and ability) his adoption. We were adopted in eternity and named the children of God in election before the worlds were made; but now, believing on the Lord Jesus Christ, we are the sons of God, and have every right (the authority and ability) to call God our Father (1 John 3:1, 2; Galatians 4:6, 7; Colossians 1:12-14).

We who believe are 'the children of God by faith in Christ Jesus' (Galatians 3:26). All who trust Christ are, as J. C. Ryle wrote, 'born again by a new and heavenly birth, and adopted into the family of the King of kings. Few in number, and despised by the world as they are, they are cared for with infinite love by a Father in heaven, who, for his Son's sake, is well pleased with them. In time he provides them with everything that is for their good. In eternity he will give them a crown of glory that fades not away.' These are great things, privileges beyond expression! But faith in Christ gives sinners like us the right to possess them.

New Birth
This faith we have in Christ is the result of the new birth, the result of being born again by God the Holy Spirit. Here in verse 13 we are told in no uncertain terms that the new birth, by which God gives us faith in Christ, is altogether the gift of God. 'Which were born, not of blood, nor of the will of the flesh, nor of the will of man, but of God.'

The new birth has nothing to do with who our parents may or may not be. It is 'not of blood'. It does not come by family descent. Having Abraham for your father does not give you a step up toward God. Nothing derived by human generation from our depraved fathers, nothing arising out of the corrupt stock of a fallen race can contribute anything to spiritual life. The new birth, and that faith in Christ which comes with it is not something we obtain by 'the will of the flesh', by the exercise of our imaginary free will (Romans 9:16). And this new birth is not something one man can will, or bequeath, to another. It is not by 'the will of man'. Abraham desired it for Ishmael, and prayed for God to let Ishmael live before him; but he could not will Ishmael into life and salvation. David desired it for Absalom, but Absalom still perished. No father or mother can will a son or daughter into life! No man can will, or talk, or persuade, or scare a dead sinner into life and faith in Christ.

All who are born again are born again by the sovereign, eternal, irresistible will 'of God'. All who receive Christ, all who trust him believe by 'the working of his mighty power, which he wrought in Christ when he raised him from the dead' (Ephesians 1:19, 20). Oh, how great, how precious, how wonderful is God's saving grace and distinguishing mercy to poor sinners!

> Sons we are, through God's election,
> Who in Jesus Christ believe;
> By eternal destination,
> Saving grace we now receive.
> Our Redeemer, our Redeemer
> Does both grace and glory give!

Would you be numbered among the sons of God? Receive Christ. 'Believe on the Lord Jesus Christ, and thou shalt be saved'! Oh, may God give you faith in his dear Son, faith to behold the glory of God in the face of Jesus Christ (John 1:14; 2 Corinthians 4:6, 7).

'And the Word was made flesh, and dwelt among us, (and we beheld his glory, the glory as of the only begotten of the Father,) full of grace and truth.' In order to save such things as we are, the Son of God took on himself our humanity, dwelt among us, and laid down his life as the sinners' Substitute, that we might be made the righteousness of God in him! Now, believing on him, we behold 'his glory, the glory as of the only begotten of the Father, full of grace and truth'. This faith in Christ is the blessed gift of grace, begotten in us by the preached gospel (1 Peter 1:23-25), by a man sent from God (Isaiah 52:7-10; 1 Thessalonians 5:12, 13).

Chapter 5

Have You Seen His Glory?

'And the Word was made flesh, and dwelt among us, (and we beheld his glory, the glory as of the only begotten of the Father,) full of grace and truth' (John 1:14).

Have you seen the glory of Christ? When Philip went down to Samaria 'he preached Christ unto them, and there was great joy in that city'. Why do you suppose the Apostle Paul wrote to the Corinthians, 'I determined not to know anything among you, save Jesus Christ and him crucified'? Without question, he made that determination because Jesus Christ crucified is the message of holy scripture. Paul was determined to preach Jesus Christ crucified to all men everywhere, because the only thing in the world that can give peace to the souls of men is 'Jesus Christ and him crucified'.

Poor, lost sinners vainly imagine that they must find something good in themselves before they can trust the Saviour. What a sad, foolish thing! They seek rest where no rest can ever be found: their good works, their feelings, their experience, their religious duties, their remorse over sin, even their faith! They make a refuge of lies that must be swept away. They lay on a bed that is too short to stretch themselves upon. They wrap themselves in coverings too narrow to cover. And they wonder why they cannot find rest for their souls!

There is no place of rest for our souls but Jesus Christ crucified. There is nothing in this world that can give us rest except a sight of the crucified Lamb of God. If you would have rest, you must get a sight of the glory of Christ, 'the glory as of the only begotten of the Father, full of grace and truth'. John 1:14 is a text so deep and full that I approach it with fear and trembling, lest I

45

misstate that which is here revealed. Yet, I am certain that if the Lord God will, by the grace and power of the Holy Spirit, enable you to behold the glory of Christ you will be blessed with rest in your soul. 'The Word was made flesh, and dwelt among us, (and we beheld his glory, the glory as of the only begotten of the Father,) full of grace and truth.'

The Tabernacle

John here compares Christ to that which was the greatest glory of the Jewish Church. Let me read it giving another translation, the NKJV states, 'And the Word became flesh, and did tabernacle among us, and we beheld his glory, glory as of an only begotten of a father, full of grace and truth.' The word 'dwelt' in our translation comes from the Greek word for 'tabernacle'. When the Son of God became flesh, he tabernacled among us.

In the Jewish Church of the Old Testament its greatest glory was the fact that God tabernacled in its midst. God did not dwell (tabernacle) in the tent of Moses, or in the tents of the princes of Israel, but in the tabernacle in the wilderness. There God dwelt, and that tabernacle was Israel's glory. They had God himself in their midst. The tabernacle was a tent to which men went when they would commune with God. It was the place to which God came manifestly when he would commune with man. There God and his chosen people met each other through the slaughter of bullocks and lambs. It was there in the tabernacle that the two (God and man) were reconciled.

All of this pointed to and was typical of our Lord Jesus Christ. Christ's human body is God's tabernacle; and it is in Christ that God meets with man, and in Christ that man has dealings with God. As the ancient Jews went to God's tent in the centre of the camp to worship, so we come to Christ to worship the triune God. If the Jew would be released from any ceremonial uncleanness by which he was polluted and ceremonially separated from his God, he went up to the sanctuary of God, the tabernacle. There he found cleansing by the sacrifice God required, and peace was restored between God and his soul. So, too, you and I, being washed in the precious blood of Christ, have access with boldness unto God, even the Father, through Jesus Christ our Lord, who is our Tabernacle and the Tabernacle of God among men.

The Shekinah

Follow the parallel a little further. The greatest glory of the tabernacle was the most holy place. There stood in the most holy place the Ark of the Covenant, with its golden lid called the mercy-seat. Over the mercy-seat stood the cherubim, whose wings met each other, as they looked downward toward the mercy-seat. Rising above the mercy-seat, there was a bright light called 'the Shekinah'. That light represented the continual, abiding presence of God in the tabernacle. Immediately above that light stood a pillar of fire by night, and by day a spiral column of cloud. The cloud expanded over all the camp of Israel and shielded God's chosen people from the broiling sun. The Shekinah was glory.

Here in John 1:14, God the Holy Spirit declares that the incarnate Christ is God's Tabernacle and John says, 'we beheld his glory, the glory as of the only begotten of the Father'. I am not simply telling you what Christ was. I am declaring what he is. Our Lord Jesus Christ is himself God and he is God's Tabernacle, 'the true Tabernacle, which the Lord pitched, and not man' (Hebrews 8:2), 'for in him dwelleth all the fulness of the Godhead bodily'. In this Tabernacle, the Lord Jesus Christ, we have and we behold the Shekinah, the glory of God.

Grace And Truth
Here is the great, surpassing excellence of Christ the true Tabernacle, by which he wondrously excels the typical tabernacle of the Old Testament. He is 'full of grace and truth'. The Jewish tabernacle was full of law. Its rites and ceremonies foreshadowed and typified grace; but those typical sacrifices, repeated continually, did nothing to remove sin and guilt. As with all the law, all they could do was remind the people of their sin and guilt. That is what the Holy Spirit tells us in the opening verses of Hebrews 10.

> Not all the blood of beasts,
> On Jewish altars slain,
> Could give the guilty conscience peace,
> Or wash away the stain.
>
> But Christ, the heavenly Lamb,
> Takes all our sins away;
> A Sacrifice of nobler name,
> And richer blood than they.
>
> My faith would lay her hand,
> On that dear head of Thine,
> While, like a penitent, I stand,
> And there confess my sin.
>
> My soul looks back to see,
> The burdens Thou didst bear,
> When hanging on the cursed tree,
> And hopes her guilt was there.

Believing, we rejoice,
To see the curse remove;
We bless the Lamb with cheerful voice,
And sing redeeming love!

The old tabernacle had a barrier, a wall, a thick veil that separated God and man. That veil represented the law of God we have broken. The worshippers of old, as they came to the tabernacle, were reminded of their sin and guilt, and could never enter into the presence of God in the most holy place behind the veil. But in Christ, the true Tabernacle, there is no separating veil. He destroyed the barrier separating his people from God by fulfilling and satisfying God's law. Now, as I said before, we draw near to God by faith in his blood, with full assurance, because Christ is 'full of grace' (Hebrews 10:19-22).

How I love those words 'full of grace'! There is not a little grace in him, or much grace in him; but such a rich abundance of grace is treasured up in the Lord Jesus that he is 'full of grace'! In him all fulness dwells!

The old tabernacle was full of imagery, and shadows, and symbols, and pictures, and types; but Christ, the true Tabernacle, is 'full of truth'. Christ is the substance, not the picture, the reality, not the shadow. Here is our great joy. Coming to Christ, we come to the true Tabernacle of God. We come not to the Shekinah that represented the glory of God, but to him who is the glory of God. We come not to the representation of grace, but to him who is Grace. We come not to the shadow of truth, but to him who is the Truth, by which our souls are accepted of God.

Have you come to Christ? Have you beheld his glory? Are you numbered among those who can say with John, 'We beheld his glory, the glory of the only-begotten of the Father, full of grace and truth.'

The Incarnate Word

First, the Apostle speaks of the incarnate Word. If there is any verse in the Bible marked with the special emphasis by God the Holy Spirit, surely this is one. Every word is of immense importance. Here is the glorious person so highly spoken of in the preceding 13 verses of this chapter. The Word is declared to be 'made flesh'. The Son of God was 'made flesh'.

The word translated 'flesh' is very strong. It is the same word used in Romans 3:20, where we are told no flesh can be justified by the deeds of the law. In Romans 8:3 Christ is said to have been made 'in the likeness of sinful flesh'. The word here translated 'flesh' has the same significance as the Hebrew words used in Genesis 6:12 to speak of 'corrupt' flesh. John could not have used a stronger, more emphatic word to speak of our Saviour's great condescension and humiliation in assuming of our nature. Had John merely said, 'the Word was made man', the meaning would not have been so emphatic a declaration of degradation. (Philippians 2:5-8).

'The Word was made flesh'! The Son of God was made what we are, made to be our full nature, body and soul, a complete man. He who is God became man. He did not cease to be God; but he took our human nature into union with his nature, so that the Lord Jesus Christ is God and man, the God-man, our Mediator. 'The Word was made flesh', as Augustine put it in the 4th century, 'Not by changing what he was, but by taking what he was not.' This union of God and man in one person is indissoluble and forever. Jesus Christ our Saviour, our God-man Mediator is 'the same yesterday, and today, and forever' (Hebrews 13:8).

I have no idea what the length, breadth, height or depth of what I am about to say is; but I cannot help linking these words to those of the Apostle Paul in Ephesians 5:30. 'The Word was made flesh;' and 'we are members of his body, of his flesh, and of his bones'! So is it now, so it has been in all ages of the Church, and so shall be forever.

The Favoured People
Second, John describes a favoured people. 'And we beheld his glory'. Who are these favoured people? They are an elect people, a chosen company. The Lord Jesus said, 'I know whom I have chosen'. He said, 'Ye have not chosen me, but I have chosen you'. He came unto his own, and his own received him not; but they who did receive him are described as people who were 'born not of blood, nor of the will of the flesh, nor of the will of man, but of God'. The elect in Christ's day, though they were but a small remnant, nevertheless did exist. There were but few who followed him; but there were a few who followed the Lamb whithersoever he went. The 'we', then who beheld Christ's glory were a chosen company. So it was then, and so it is now. Thank God for his electing love! Those who behold his glory are those who were chosen from eternity to behold his glory (Acts 13:48). And those who behold his glory here will behold his glory forever in the world to come (John 17:24).

Those who behold Christ's glory are a graciously called people. We behold his glory because we have been specifically called by him to behold his glory. 'He calleth unto him whom he would' (Mark 3:13). 'He calleth his own sheep by name' (John 10:3). It is written of those he delivers from going down to the pit, 'his life shall see the light' (Job 33:28). 'Many shall see it, and fear, and shall trust in the LORD' (Psalms 40:3). 'They shall see the glory of the LORD, and the excellency of our God' (Isaiah 35:2).

49

The Son of God calls his own sheep by name and leads them out. If you and I behold Christ's glory, it is because he has called us to himself; and that call is the result of his election of us unto salvation.

These who behold his glory are also a divinely illuminated people. If others do not see what we see, and we are as blind as they by nature, our seeing his glory must be because of something he has done for us, and not because of anything in us or done by us (2 Corinthians 4:6). C. H. Spurgeon said,

> None of the princes of this world knew him. The priests who had studied the law could not discover him; the members of the Sanhedrim, who were under some expectation of his advent, could not perceive him. In vain the star in the east; in vain the miraculous appearance of angels to the shepherds; the blind generation would not perceive him. In vain the opening of blind eyes and the preaching of the gospel to the poor; in vain the raising of the dead; in vain all those innumerable signs and wonders; they could not perceive his glory; but of those who did perceive it may be said, as of Simon Barjonas, 'Blessed art thou, for flesh and blood hath not revealed this unto thee'.

'Blessed are your eyes, for they see'! None believe in Christ but those who are his sheep. No man comes unto him except the Father who sent him draws them; and none ever perceive him but those whose eyes are opened by his own healing fingers. Do you behold his glory? If so, beloved, it is because he chose you, he called you, and he illuminated you by his grace.

The Thing Revealed

Third, John speaks about the thing revealed. 'We beheld his glory'. 'We beheld'. The text does not say, we heard about his glory, we read about his glory, but 'we beheld his glory'. What a privilege that is!

This is much more than a physical, carnal vision of the Lord Jesus. Many saw him with the eyes in their heads who never saw him with the eye of faith, who never beheld his glory. And many today behold him with the eye of carnal reason, who never behold his glory, because they do not know him and do not behold him by faith, not having him revealed in them by the Spirit of God.

When John says, 'We beheld his glory', he is saying the very same thing Peter said when he wrote, 'We have not followed cunningly devised fables, when we made known unto you the power and coming of our Lord Jesus Christ, but were eyewitnesses of his majesty' (2 Peter 1:16). He is talking about that which he, with Peter and James, beheld on the Mount of Transfiguration. Christ was transfigured before them. They saw him as he now appears in heaven, glorified with the glory he had with the Father before the world was. They saw the Lord Jesus Christ as the sinner's Substitute who accomplished redemption by his death upon the cursed tree (Luke 9:28-31).

'And it came to pass about an eight days after these sayings, he took Peter and John and James, and went up into a mountain to pray. And as he prayed, the fashion of his countenance was altered, and his raiment was white and glistering. And, behold, there talked with him two men, which were Moses and Elias: Who appeared in glory, and spake of his decease which he should accomplish at Jerusalem' (Luke 9:28-31).

The word 'decease' in Luke 9:31 is literally the word 'exodus'. These disciples beheld his glory upon the mount, the very same glory that is revealed to us by the saving operations of his Spirit. By the death he accomplished, he fulfilled the law and the prophets, he pleased the Father (Matthew 17:5), he obtained eternal redemption, he earned the right to be Lord as our Mediator, he revealed the glory of God as 'a just God and a Saviour' (Isaiah 45:20-22). In Christ crucified God sent forth 'his mercy and his truth' from heaven and saved us (Psalms 57:3; 85:10; 115:1; Proverbs 3:3; 16:6; Micah 7:20).

I ask you again, have you seen his glory? Have you beheld the glory of Christ by the Spirit's gift of faith? If you would behold his glory, he says, 'Look unto me'! Look and you will see. He does not say, work for me, but 'look unto me'. He does not say, figure me out, but 'look unto me'. He does not say, serve me, but 'look unto me'. He does not say, feel after me, but 'look unto me'. He does not even say, pray to me, but 'look unto me'. Look away to Christ and, looking, you will behold his glory.

Trusting Christ, we see his glory, just as Isaiah did, 'the glory as of the only-begotten of the Father, full of grace and truth' (Isaiah 6:1-7). It is by faith, only by faith, that we behold his glory (John 11:40). Trusting the Lord Jesus Christ, we behold his glory in redemption, in the saving operations of his grace, and in his providence!

The Blessed Vision
Fourth, John describes the blessed vision before us, as we behold the glory of our Saviour. It is just this: 'The glory as of the only begotten of the Father, full of grace and truth'. What glory we have before us, as we behold the glory of Christ by faith! It is:

The Glory of his wonderful person, God and Man.
The Glory of his perfect righteousness as our Representative.
The Glory of his sin-atoning sacrifice (2 Corinthians 5:21).
The Glory of his sovereign dominion.
The Glory of tender, sympathizing humanity.

The Glory of his heavenly intercession (1 John 2:1, 2).
The Glory of his persevering love (John 13:1).
The Glory of his final triumph (Revelation 19:1-6).

The Witness Given
Fifth, one reason why the Lord God has so graciously given us grace to behold his glory is that we might bear testimony to others of his glory as 'eye witnesses of his majesty' (1 John 1:1-3). As soon as Isaiah beheld his glory, the Lord God said to that sinner whose lips still burned with the purging fire of his altar, 'Go tell this people'! That is what we must do. Proclaim the Glory! Jesus Christ is the only Saviour of poor sinners. He is the only begotten of the Father. He is full of grace! Charles Wesley wrote,

> Plenteous grace with Him is found,
> Grace to cover all my sin:
> Let the healing streams abound,
> Make and keep me pure within.

The Lord Jesus Christ is full of truth! He is Truth! He is the Truth of all the Prophets, all the Law, and all the Promises of God!

> All hail Immanuel, all divine,
> In Thee Thy Father's glories shine;
> Thou brightest, sweetest, Fairest One,
> That eyes have seen or angels known.
>
> O may I live to reach the place,
> Where He unveils His lovely face.
> Where all His beauties saints behold,
> And sing His name to harps of gold!

Have you beheld his glory? May God give you grace to behold his glory from this day forth and forever more! 'The Word was made flesh, and dwelt among us, (and we beheld his glory, the glory as of the only begotten of the Father,) full of grace and truth.'

Chapter 6

God's Jubilee Message

'John bare witness of him, and cried, saying, This was he of whom I spake, he that cometh after me is preferred before me: for he was before me. And of his fulness have all we received, and grace for grace. For the law was given by Moses, but grace and truth came by Jesus Christ. No man hath seen God at any time; the only begotten Son, which is in the bosom of the Father, he hath declared him' (John 1:15-18).

We read about the year of Jubilee in Leviticus 25. Every forty-ninth year God required the nation of Israel to begin a yearlong sabbath called, 'The Year Of Jubilee'. Every fiftieth year was a sabbatical year.

In the Old Testament everything revolved around the sabbath. At the end of creation, the Lord God rested on the seventh day, the sabbath. In the giving of the law the Lord commanded Israel to keep the sabbath day holy. But, did you ever notice how many sabbath days the Lord required the children of Israel to keep? He required them to keep a seventh day sabbath, a seventh week or fiftieth day sabbath, a seventh year sabbath, and a fiftieth year sabbath!

This fiftieth year sabbath, 'The Year Of Jubilee', was, like everything else in the law, typical and prophetic of our Lord Jesus Christ, our Sabbath, our salvation in him, and of the gospel of God's free grace. This year of jubilee was a season appointed by God during which the children of Israel were required to adjust their social affairs once every fifty years, setting their brethren free from bondage and free from all debt, and restoring lost possessions, lost property, and lost inheritances to those who had lost them. It portrayed and typified the great work of our Lord Jesus Christ in restoring chosen sinners to God and to one another, and bringing us at last into that great sabbath of eternal rest in 'the glorious liberty of the sons of God'. To many throughout the land the year of jubilee was 'the accepted time' and 'the day of salvation'. The year of jubilee was announced by the blowing of a trumpet throughout all the land. That is, of course, a representation of gospel preaching (Isaiah 27:13; Psalms 89:15). Blessed are those ears that have been made to hear the joyful sound of God's free grace, of God's everlasting salvation in Christ!

Four Trumpets
There were four distinct and special sounds of the trumpet in the camp of Israel. Each one distinctly portrayed the preaching of the gospel. Memorial trumpets were sounded to announce the new moon and call the people together in a joyful assembly of worship (Leviticus 23:24; Psalms 81:3). Battle trumpets, trumpets of war (Judges 3:27) were sounded to gather the people to battle (1 Corinthians 14:8). Trumpets of alarm warned men of impending judgment and called them to repentance (Joel 2:1). And the jubilee trumpet announced the beginning of that joyous year of restoration (Leviticus 25:9).

The jubilee trumpet was different from the others. This trumpet's sound was never heard except once every fifty years. Yet, its sound was so sweet and so distinct that no poor captive in the land of Israel was at a moment's loss to know its music and its gracious meaning.

That is just exactly the way it is when God the Holy Spirit causes a poor, needy, captive sinner to hear the gospel. When the Holy Spirit proclaims pardon to the guilty, pardon by the blood of Christ, he causes the sinner to understand that atonement has been made and accepted. At that very moment, jubilee commences. The soul, long held captive to sin, to Satan, and to the law, is set free and walks and dances in liberty. What a joyful sound! What a joyful day! When the gospel jubilee trumpet sounds in the soul, the acceptable year of the Lord begins (Isaiah 61:1, 2; 63:4).

> Oh for a thousand tongues to sing
> My great Redeemer's praise!
> The glories of my God and King,
> The triumphs of His grace!
>
> He breaks the power of cancelled sin
> And sets the prisoners free!
> His blood can make the foulest clean
> His blood availed for me!
>
> Charles Wesley

The Jubilee Trumpet

The jubilee trumpet, like the gospel of Christ, proclaimed seven things, seven things that sound like heavenly music in the sinner's ear.

1. Atonement: the jubilee trumpet was to be sounded on the day of atonement (Leviticus 25:9). That is where gospel preaching always begins. The gospel has not been preached until atonement has been proclaimed. There can be no joyful sound apart from the sin-atoning blood of Christ. The jubilee trumpet declared the shedding of the atonement blood, the atonement blood accepted, and atonement finished. The Lord Jesus Christ, the Son of God, was delivered unto death under the wrath of God because he was made sin for us and our sins were imputed to him. He was raised again the third day because our justification was accomplished, because our sins were forever put away!

2. Liberty: the year of jubilee began on the day of atonement, and it began with the proclamation of liberty. Liberty according to the very demands of God's holy law (Leviticus 25:10). Our Lord Jesus Christ tells us plainly that he is the Liberator and the One who proclaims liberty (Luke 4:17-21). Be sure you do not miss this. The liberty proclaimed in the year of jubilee, the liberty proclaimed in the gospel is the blessed liberty of grace; but it is liberty demanded by God's holy law. Unlike the other ceremonies of the Levitical law, this law concerning the year of jubilee was given at Sinai, at the very time God gave the law to Moses (Leviticus 25:1). The law of God, being totally satisfied by the blood of our Substitute, demands the liberty of every redeemed sinner. Grace reigns through righteousness unto eternal life, by Jesus Christ our Lord (Romans 5:20, 21).

3. Forgiveness: the year of jubilee was a time of forgiveness (Leviticus 25:35). The poor wretch who had lost everything, who had incurred such a tremendous load of debt that he sold his land, then his house, and at last sold himself into bondage, was released when the jubilee trumpet sounded; released from bondage and released from debt, forgiven completely, freely, and forever. His debt did not bar him from the joy of jubilee. His debt qualified him as the one for whom the trumpet sounded. Hear me, now. I am sent to preach the gospel, to blow the jubilee trumpet, to the poor.

4. Rest: the year of jubilee was a year of rest (Leviticus 25:3-5). The gospel of Christ proclaims rest. It calls weary sinners to rest and promises eternal rest (Matthew 11:28-30; Hebrews 4:1-11; Psalms 116:7; Galatians 5:1-4).

5. Bounty: the year of jubilee was a year of great, unparalleled bounty. 'Ye shall eat your fill, and dwell therein in safety' (Leviticus 25:19). Oh, what a gospel this is! In Christ we are made to dwell in complete safety in a land of infinite bounty. Here we lie down in green pastures and fear no evil. Our treasury is the unsearchable riches of Christ. 'All things are yours, for ye are

Christ's'. We who have been brought by the grace of God into the liberty of the gospel have been brought into his fulness. Let us therefore be careful for nothing, but in all things give thanks.

6. Restoration: in the year of jubilee every man who had lost his inheritance had it returned to him in total, free and clear, with no mortgage of any kind, no lien of any kind against it (Leviticus 25:13). All that we lost in Adam, Christ has restored. All that we lost by our own wilful rebellion and sin, Christ has restored. David understood this. He sang, 'He restoreth my soul'! We who 'were by nature children of wrath, even as others', are now made to be 'heirs of God and joint-heirs with Jesus Christ'.

7. Brotherly love: in the year of jubilee the children of Israel were required by law to love their brethren. 'Ye shall not therefore oppress one another; but thou shalt fear thy God: for I am the LORD your God' (Leviticus 25:17). In the gospel jubilee saved sinners are constrained and taught by grace to love one another. 'By this shall all men know that ye are my disciples, if ye have love one to another.' Have I been loved freely? Let me love freely. Have I been forgiven freely? Let me forgive freely. We read in Matthew 18 of a forgiven servant who took his fellow servant by the throat and demanded payment on the spot. He was obviously bold enough to deal with the man face to face; but he was utterly destitute of the grace, compassion, and forgiveness he had experienced from his master. Have I received freely? Let me give freely.

Do you know who began preaching at the start of the very last jubilee? John the Baptist. He was sent of God to proclaim that the year of the Lord had come, to tell sinners that he who would perform all that was promised, typified, and hoped for in the year of jubilee, the Lamb of God, had come.

The Baptist's Witness

As the year of jubilee began, 'There was a man sent from God, whose name was John.' In verse 15 we have John the Apostle's description of the ministry of John the Baptist. He describes John's whole work as that of a witness. Here is the Baptist's witness. 'John bare witness of him, and cried, saying, This was he of whom I spake, he that cometh after me is preferred before me: for he was before me'.

'John bare witness of him'. That is what a preacher does. He bears witness of the Saviour. He tells what he knows. We bear witness of him, the Lord Jesus, not of a doctrine, but of him, not of a denomination, but of him, not of a theological system, but of him! Like John the Baptist, God's servants are sent 'for a witness, to bear witness of the Light' (v. 7). Faithful men bear faithful witness of him who loved us and gave himself for us.

'John bare witness of him, and cried'. As the voice of one crying in the wilderness (Isaiah 40:3), John the Baptist came crying like the crier sent to blow the jubilee trumpet when atonement was made and the year of jubilee began. John cried. That is what the preacher does. He cries, 'Redemption is done! Justice is satisfied! Sin is put away!' They cry with earnest zeal and fervency, 'Repent, for repentance, the turning of sinners to God by the blood of Christ is accomplished!' They cry, 'This is the Christ!' John said, 'This was he of whom I spake. He that cometh after me is preferred before me: for he was before me.' Christ came into the world six months after John the Baptist; and he came after him to be baptised by him. But he was before him. He is the eternal God. The Christ is preferred before him, preferred before John, preferred before Moses, any of the prophets, any apostle, any preacher, any man, any angel, or anything (Colossians 1:18, 19).

The Redeemer's Fulness
'And of his fulness have all we received, and grace for grace' (v. 16). All fulness is in Christ. That is God's jubilee message. All fulness is in Christ as our Mediator. It is in him for us. Everything we lost in the sin and fall of our father Adam has been recovered for us by Christ and is found in him. It is Christ, and Christ alone who supplies all the needs of our souls. 'Of his fulness have all we received, and grace for grace.'

There is an infinite fulness in our Saviour! 'It pleased the Father that in him should all fulness dwell.' 'In whom are hid all the treasures of wisdom and knowledge.' 'For in him dwelleth all the fulness of the Godhead bodily. And ye are complete in him' (Colossians 1:19, 2:3, 9, 10). There is in the Lord Jesus Christ a boundless, infinite supply of grace for poor, needy sinners, exceeding great riches of grace for time and eternity! His fulness! What a thought! 'His fulness' is all fulness. All the fulness of God's love, mercy, and grace; purpose, providence, and promises; greatness, goodness, and glory; purity, prudence, and power; wisdom, will, and work; righteousness, redemption, and revelation.

'Of his fulness have we all received'. All we who were chosen in him, redeemed by him, called to him, born of him, and given faith in him, all God's elect, every heaven-born soul, every believing sinner has received, is receiving, and shall receive of his fulness by the gift of God's grace, by the operation of God's power, and by the hand of faith.

'Of his fulness have we all received, and grace for grace.' In Christ we have received, from his boundless fulness, grace because of grace. Redeeming grace because of electing grace. Regenerating grace because of redeeming grace. Sanctifying grace because of regenerating grace. Believing grace because of sanctifying grace. Persevering grace because of preserving grace. Grace in time because of grace in eternity. Experimental grace because of covenant grace. Pardoning grace because of promised grace. Imparted grace because of imputed grace. Everlasting grace because of everlasting grace. The fulness of grace because of the freeness of grace. Heaps of grace upon heaps of grace.

'Of his fulness have we all received, and grace for grace.' Blessed be his name forever!

The Saviour's Supremacy

'For the law was given by Moses, but grace and truth came by Jesus Christ.' The opening word of verse 17, 'for', connects this with what we have just seen. We have received grace for grace out of the fulness of Christ our Redeemer and Mediator for this reason. 'The law was given by Moses, but grace and truth came by Jesus Christ.'

Be sure you get this. That which the law commands, grace bestows. God's promise runs side by side with his precept. Indeed, grace turns precepts into promises and promises into performances. This is our Saviour's great supremacy over Moses. It was he who gave the law by Moses, and he who fulfilled the law by grace. The law he gave demanded righteousness. The grace he performed brought in righteousness, complete justification. The law he gave demanded satisfaction. The grace he performed gave satisfaction, perfect redemption. The law he gave demanded our death. The grace he performed accomplished death for us, substitutionary atonement. The law he gave demanded holiness. The grace he performs gives holiness, and perfect sanctification in regeneration. And all this grace, by which the Lord Jesus has magnified the law and made it honourable, in the everlasting salvation of his people, was done in truth, without the least compromise of God's holy law and justice (Romans 3:24-26; 8:1-4).

The Son's Declaration

In verse 18 the Spirit of God speaks about the Son's declaration of the Father. It is in Christ alone and by Christ alone that men and women know God. 'No man hath seen God at any time; the only begotten Son, which is in the bosom of the Father, he hath declared him.'

God is Spirit, without form or shape. He is immense, infinite, and incomprehensible. No man has ever seen him or heard his voice. No man has ever been found who could know the counsel of his will, not Moses, not Elijah, not you, not me. No man was ever found worthy to take the book of his decree and loose its seals, except that man who is himself God in all his fulness, the Lord Jesus Christ, our Saviour, he who is in the bosom of the Father, because he is one with the Father.

He stood forth before the heavenly angels in the beginning as the Lamb that had been slain in the midst of the throne and took the book as our Surety. He showed himself in human form throughout the prophetic age of the Old

Testament. At last, the Word was made flesh, dwelt among us, and was crucified for us. And now, in the crucified Christ the very glory of God shines forth in the redemption and salvation of his people.

That is what John 1:18 is talking about. The words 'he hath declared him' speak of something done at one time, with finality, in the past. At Calvary, in his substitutionary accomplishments on the cross, our blessed Saviour declared the Father, the triune God, in all the fulness of his Being and glory to man! That is God's jubilee message. As we blow the jubilee trumpet, as we preach the gospel, God who alone commands the light to shine out of darkness shines forth in the dark, depraved hearts of lost, condemned sinners, giving the light of the knowledge of the glory of God in the face of Jesus Christ!

What the hand is to the lute,
What the breath is to the flute,
What is fragrance to the smell,
What the spring is to the well,
What the flower is to the bee,
That is Jesus Christ to me.

What is the mother to the child,
What the guide in pathless wild,
What is oil to troubled wave,
What is ransom to the slave,
What is water to the sea?
That is Jesus Christ to me.

C. H. Spurgeon

Chapter 7

Christ's Fulness, Our Inexhaustible Supply

'And of his fulness have all we received, and grace for grace' (John 1:16).

John 1:16 should be understood as a continuation of John's description of our Lord Jesus Christ. Verse 15 is a parenthetical insertion in which John the Apostle tells us, as he did in verses 6 and 7, that John the Baptist preached the same message he preached. Read verses 14 and 16 together.

'And the Word was made flesh, and dwelt among us, (and we beheld his glory, the glory as of the only begotten of the Father,) full of grace and truth ... And of his fulness have all we received, and grace for grace.'

Our Lord Jesus Christ is the revelation of the triune God. In him we behold the glory of the triune God. By this I mean that in his crucifixion, his resurrection, his ascension, his session at the right hand of God and his second advent, beholding him as our all-sufficient Saviour, we behold his glory, 'the glory as of the only-begotten of the Father, full of grace and truth'. And 'of his fulness' all God's elect in all ages receive an inexhaustible supply of grace. That is the meaning of John's words in these two verses.

Our Glorious Saviour
First, John's words direct our hearts and minds to the person of our glorious Saviour himself, the Word who was made flesh and dwelt among us. John Newton rightly observed,

> I am well satisfied it will not be a burden to me at the hour of death, nor be laid to my charge at the day of judgment, that I have thought too highly of the Lord Jesus Christ or laboured too much

in commending and setting him forth to others, as the Alpha and Omega, the Lord our Righteousness, the sufficient atonement for sin, the only Mediator between God and men, the true God and eternal life. On the contrary, alas! My guilt and grief are that my thoughts of him are so faint, so infrequent, and my commendations of him so lamentably cold and disproportionate to what they ought to be.

Others are mentioned here as receivers, but they are insignificant. 'All we' are mentioned; but we are only receivers 'of his fulness'. All honour is reserved for Christ alone. 'Not unto us, O LORD, not unto us, but unto thy name give glory, for thy mercy, and for thy truth's sake' (Psalms 115:1). 'Of his fulness have all we received'. Christ is, and ever must be, preeminent.

He is 'the Word', the Speech of God, the distinct, intelligible declaration and revelation of the eternal God, the unfolding of the Father's being, character, thoughts, will, and heart. Would you see God? Behold Christ, for he is God's Word, the Revelation of Deity. He declares, 'He that hath seen me hath seen the Father.'

But our blessed Saviour is much more than a mere word, a mere expression of God's thoughts.

He is God the eternal Son, from whose fulness we receive all grace. Look at verses 1-5. 'In the beginning was the Word'. With those words, the Holy Spirit asserts Christ's eternality. 'And the Word was God'. With those words, our Saviour's deity is declared. John also ascribes to our Saviour the acts of God. 'Without him was not anything made that was made'. He declares that Christ is self-existent, which is but another way of saying he is God. 'In him was life'.

In 1 John 1:5 John declares, 'God is light, and in him is no darkness at all' and he tells us in verse 9 of this chapter that the Word is 'the true light, which lighteth every man that cometh into the world'.

John could not have been more explicit in his declarations of the fact that he from whom we receive grace and salvation is himself God over all and blessed forever. And the Apostle is quick to assert that he who is God our Saviour is bone of our bones and flesh of our flesh, a real man. 'The Word was made flesh'. He did not merely assume our nature, but was 'made flesh'. John does not even say the Word was made a man. He says, 'The Word was made flesh, and dwelt among us'. He pitched his tent with the sons of men. He dwelt among sinners and sufferers, among mourners and mortals, completing his pilgrimage among us by becoming obedient to death, even the death of the cross.

The triune God has treasured up the fulness of his infinite grace in a person so august that heaven and earth tremble at the majesty of his presence, and yet in a person so humble that he is not ashamed to call us 'brethren'. With Joseph Hart, God's saints delight to sing,

> A Man there is, a real Man,
> With wounds still gaping wide,
> From which rich streams of blood once ran,
> In hands, and feet, and side.
>
> 'Tis no wild fancy of our brains,
> No metaphor we speak;
> The same dear Man in heaven now reigns,
> That suffered for our sake.
>
> This wondrous Man of whom we tell,
> Is true Almighty God;
> He bought our souls from death and hell;
> The price, His own heart's blood.
>
> That human heart He still retains,
> Though throned in highest bliss;
> And feels each tempted member's pains;
> For our affliction's His.
>
> Come, then, repenting sinner, come;
> Approach with humble faith;
> Owe what thou wilt, the total sum
> Is cancelled by His death!
>
> His blood can cleanse the blackest soul,
> And wash our guilt away;
> He will present us sound and whole
> In that tremendous day.

Throughout this chapter, John purposefully takes our thoughts away from any other, and points us to Christ alone, as if to say, 'Christ alone is important'. Others are mentioned, but each one as he is introduced, is immediately followed with a disclaimer. He mentions John the Baptist, the greatest of all the prophets, several times, but each time with a disclaimer. John came 'to bear witness of the Light' (v. 7); but 'he was not that Light' (v. 8). John was the forerunner of Christ; but he declared, 'I am not the Christ' (v. 20). Moses is mentioned (v. 17); but he bows before the Lamb of God because, though 'the law was given by Moses, grace and truth came by Jesus Christ.' Andrew, Simon, Philip, Nathanael, even the angels of God are named in the chapter; but everything ascends and descends upon the Son of man, our all-glorious Lord Jesus Christ.

That is as it should be and must be, because God has ordained that in all things he must have the pre-eminence. Prophets, Apostles, all men, and all angels must decrease and be decreased before him, and he must increase and be increased by us (John 3:30). Nothing and no one shines in the light of the Sun of Righteousness except the Son himself. Christ stands alone as the Word of God, as Life, as the Light of men, and as the infinite Fountain of all grace. Oh, that we might so see the Lord Jesus Christ in his glorious majesty and greatness as our Saviour, that, as the disciples on the Mount of Transfiguration, we may see 'no man, save Jesus only'! Make much of Christ and little of everything else.

His Fulness

God the Holy Spirit teaches two things in verse 16 that are indescribably precious to those who, by the grace of God, have experienced them. First, he tells us that all fulness is treasured up in this glorious person, our Lord Jesus Christ. Second, he tells us that all the fulness treasured up in Christ is an inexhaustible supply of grace from which all God's elect receive all grace.

First, think about the fulness that is treasured up in the Lord Jesus. 'His fulness'. Here is a fulness which cannot be measured. John is talking about 'the fulness of him that filleth all in all'! It is an infinite fulness (Colossians 1:18, 19; 2:9, 10). The fulness from which we receive all grace is in Christ, in him alone, in him and nowhere else! There is no fulness to be found in any man, in any church, in any religious ritual, ceremony, or ordinance, or in any experience!

Paul tells us 'it pleased the Father that in him should all fulness dwell'. 'His fulness' is 'all fulness'. All fulness is in him, infinite, incomprehensible, divine, saving fulness, all of it is in Immanuel. God has placed all fulness in his Son. Where else could he put it? All fulness is in Christ radically. It cannot be had anywhere else. It is not in his doctrine, but in him. It is not in his word, but in him. It is not in his blood, but in him. It is not in his righteousness, but in him. It is the Person of Christ that gives worth, weight, merit, and efficacy to his word, his offices, and his work, not the other way around. Would you get grace? Would you get salvation? You must get Christ. You must receive it from 'his fulness'. Christ alone is great enough to contain all fulness, immutable to retain all fulness, and suitable to distribute all fulness.

I repeat, 'his fulness' is 'all fulness'! What a superlative wealth of meaning there is in that statement! What a word of comfort this is for us poor, bankrupt sinners! By nature, we are all emptiness and vanity; but 'all fulness' is in Christ. In us there is an utter lack of merit before God, a total absence of power to gain merit with God, and a complete absence of will to obey God, even if we had the ability to do so. But in Christ there is 'all fulness'!

O my heart, Rejoice in this! O my soul, dance before the Ark of God! Everywhere else in this vast universe there is nothing but barrenness and emptiness. 'Vanity of vanity all is vanity'! But, blessed be our God forever, he has provided all fulness in Christ. In us there is all emptiness and utter vanity. 'In me, that is, in my flesh, there dwelleth no good thing' (Romans 7:18). But in Christ there is 'all fulness'.

As I said before, in us there is a lack of all merit, an absence of all power to procure any, and even an absence of will to procure it if we could. Our nature is a desert, empty and void and waste, inhabited only by sin, darkness, and death. We are all emptiness; but in Christ dwells all fulness. Are you dead? Christ is Life! Are you sin? Christ is Righteousness. Are you naked? Christ is Clothing. Are you hungry? Christ is Bread. Are you thirsty? Christ is Water. Are you dirty? Christ is Cleansing. Are you blind? Christ is Light. Are you weary? Christ is Rest. Are you a debtor? Christ is Ransom. Are you helpless? Christ is Strength. Are you guilty? Christ is Pardon. Are you a prisoner? Christ is Liberty. Are you condemned? Christ is Deliverance. Are you emptiness? Christ is Fulness.

Christ is substance, not the shadow of fulness. Fulness, not the foretaste of fulness. The reality, not the picture of fulness. Let me show you what I mean. The Old Testament types are instructive, but not saving. The ordinances and ceremonies of the law pointed us to One who would put away sin; but they could never do so. Those sacrifices were beautiful, costly, and impressive; but they could never satisfy the justice of God, never silence a guilty conscience, or put away a single sin.

Christ is all the fulness of all the Old Testament types and pictures (Hebrews 10:1-14).

Now, if those rituals and sacrifices ordained by God could never put away sin, then what you do certainly cannot! Christ is all fulness!

Christ is all the fulness of the law (Romans 10:1-13). Christ is all the fulness of all God's eternal purposes (Romans 8:28-31). And there is in the Lord Jesus Christ all the fulness of the triune Godhead (Colossians 2:9, 10). Jesus Christ the Man is the eternal God, possessing all the attributes of divinity. Obviously, his manhood is neither eternal, omnipotent, nor omnipresent. Yet, his manhood is so united with his Godhead that that Man who sits in glory is himself God. He is 'the mighty God'!

Still there is more. All the fulness of the infinite, triune God; Father, Son, and Holy Spirit, resides in the body of that Man who died at Calvary and now reigns over all things. Jesus Christ is God. Jesus Christ is all of God we now know, and all of God we shall ever know. Jesus Christ is all there is of God! We are Trinitarians (1 John 5:7). However, all fulness of the triune God resides in and is known by Jesus Christ alone, in whom all fulness dwells.

Yet, there is more still. All the fulness of grace is in Christ. This 'all fulness' is in Christ mediatorially. It is in Christ for us. His fulness is the fulness of the one Mediator between God and men. As the result of our Lord's mediatorial work as our Surety, Substitute, and Representative before God, as the result of all that he has done in bringing in everlasting righteousness, in putting away sin by the sacrifice of himself, and in the redemption he accomplished at Calvary, all fulness dwells in him. All fulness for us toward God. And all fulness for us from God!

All fulness for us toward God dwells in Christ. That is to say, all that God Almighty requires of us dwells in Christ, perfectly and perpetually (1 Corinthians 1:30, 31). And all fulness for us from God dwells in Christ. 'Of his fulness have we received, and grace for grace'! Everything we need, everything our souls require is in Christ, our all-glorious, all-sufficient Saviour. With confident joy we sing with Charles Wesley;

> Thou, O Christ, art all I want,
> More than all in Thee I find!

'He that spared not his own Son, but delivered him up for us all, how shall he not with him also freely give us all things?' (Romans 8:32).

Blessed be the God and Father of our Lord Jesus Christ, who hath blessed us with all spiritual blessings in heavenly places in Christ: According as he hath chosen us in him before the foundation of the world, that we should be holy and without blame before him in love: Having predestinated us unto the adoption of children by Jesus Christ to himself, according to the good pleasure of his will, To the praise of the glory of his grace, wherein he hath made us accepted in the beloved. In whom we have redemption through his blood, the forgiveness of sins, according to the riches of his grace' (Ephesians 1:3-7).

What do you want? What does your soul need? It is in Christ. All fulness dwells in Christ. Go to Christ for your soul's need. Do you need a new heart? Do you want a broken heart? Do you want faith? Do you want repentance toward God? Do you want life eternal? Do you want certain preservation? Does your soul crave cleansing? Does your heart need consolation? Do you crave the blessed assurance of grace and salvation? Go to Christ for your soul's need. It is in him. All fulness is in our Saviour.

What mortal tongue can express this infinite bounty? All fulness is in Christ. And this Christ is ours. 'The Lord is the portion of mine inheritance and of my cup' (Psalms 16:5). Try to get hold of this. If you are in Christ 'his fulness' is yours! Infinitely yours! Eternally yours! Presently yours! What can you lack? (1 Corinthians 3:21-23).

Fulness Of Grace
His fulness is the fulness of grace. It was a fulness of grace in him that made him enter into the eternal covenant and undertake suretyship engagements for us. It was a fulness of love and grace which sustained him in the discharge of his liabilities as our great Surety. It is the fulness of grace that yet constrains him to persevere in his work, saying, 'For Zion's sake I will not rest, and for Jerusalem's sake I will not hold my peace.'

In Christ there is a fulness of grace to bestow upon needy sinners: a fulness of pardoning grace, so that no sin can ever exceed his power to forgive; a fulness of justifying grace, so that he 'justifieth the ungodly'; a fulness of converting grace, so that he calls to himself whom he will; a fulness of quickening grace, for 'he quickeneth whom he will'; a fulness of purifying grace, for his blood 'cleanseth us from all sin'; a fulness of comforting grace, for he will never leave you comfortless; a fulness of sustaining grace, for 'he that keepeth Israel shall neither slumber nor sleep'; a fulness of satisfying grace, for with Christ as our Shepherd we shall not want; a fulness of restoring grace, for 'he restoreth my soul'; a fulness of sufficient grace, for he has said, 'my grace is sufficient for thee'!

The Lord Jesus Christ is never limited in any gift or grace, but always full. Drink of 'his fulness'. Dive into this vast ocean of 'his fulness', and you will know far more than any man can ever teach you.

Infinite Fulness
His fulness is infinite fulness, an inexhaustible barrel of fulness. 'And of his fulness have all we received, and grace for grace.' Mark those words 'all we'. 'All we', John says, 'have received grace for grace.' Yet, he calls it 'fulness' and, as we see in Colossians 1:19, the Spirit of God calls it 'all fulness'. It was a fulness before the first sinner came to it to receive pardon, before the first sinner drank of that river, the streams whereof make glad the City of God; and now, after myriads of blood-bought sinners have drunk of this life-giving stream, it is just as full as ever. Christ is still an infinite ocean of fulness! This 'barrel of meal shall not waste'!

Fulness Received

God's saints have all 'received' of 'his fulness', 'grace for grace', heaps upon heaps of grace. The word 'received' is the same word as is used in verse 12. It is not a passive verb, but a verb of action. It refers to the act of faith, believing in Christ. All God's elect who have believed on the Lord Jesus have received and are receiving of 'his fulness' heaps upon heaps of grace. If you would have grace, you too, must receive it of 'his fulness'.

But you will never receive of 'his fulness' until he has filled you with emptiness (Psalms 107:9; Proverbs 27:7; Matthew 5:6). May the Lord God graciously empty you, that you may be filled. And if you are empty, it is because Christ has come to fill your hungry soul with the fulness of his grace; and you shall receive 'of his fulness' heaps upon heaps of grace!

If you have received of 'his fulness' heaps upon heaps of grace, you shall yet receive more of the same until grace brings you to glory. 'Of his fulness have all we received, and grace for grace.' This 'barrel of meal shall not waste'!

Chapter 8

Three Questions That Identify A True Prophet

'And this is the record of John, when the Jews sent priests and Levites from Jerusalem to ask him, Who art thou? And he confessed, and denied not; but confessed, I am not the Christ. And they asked him, What then? Art thou Elias? And he saith, I am not. Art thou that prophet? And he answered, No. Then said they unto him, Who art thou? that we may give an answer to them that sent us. What sayest thou of thyself? He said, I am the voice of one crying in the wilderness, Make straight the way of the Lord, as said the prophet Esaias. And they which were sent were of the Pharisees. And they asked him, and said unto him, Why baptisest thou then, if thou be not that Christ, nor Elias, neither that prophet? John answered them, saying, I baptise with water: but there standeth one among you, whom ye know not; he it is, who coming after me is preferred before me, whose shoe's latchet I am not worthy to unloose. These things were done in Bethabara beyond Jordan, where John was baptising. The next day John seeth Jesus coming unto him, and saith, Behold the Lamb of God, which taketh away the sin of the world' (John 1:19-29).

No one can question the fact that John the Baptist was a true prophet. The Son of God, our Lord Jesus Christ, declared that he was the greatest prophet to be born of a woman. That is some commendation! He was the first Baptist to walk upon the earth, the very first Baptist preacher in the world. He was the first immerser of men in the name of Christ. That is what his title, 'the Baptist', means, the Immerser. Both Isaiah and Malachi foretold his coming and described the ministry he would have. He was sent in the spirit and with the power of Elijah, 'to prepare the way of the Lord'. He was filled with the Holy

Spirit while he was still in his mother's womb. And when he was born, God sent an angel to speak of his birth.

Here, God the Holy Spirit holds this great prophet, John the Baptist, before us. He tells us that John was specifically asked three questions. John's answers to those questions identify him as a true prophet and identify every preacher who follows as either true or false.

1. 'Who art thou?' (v. 19)
2. 'What sayest thou of thyself?' (v. 22)
3. 'Why baptisest thou?' (v. 25)

'Who art thou?'

Just as Isaiah had prophesied, John appeared in the wilderness, preaching Christ, calling sinners to repentance, because the Messiah, the Christ had come, and the kingdom of heaven was at hand. Multitudes heard him and were moved to repentance by the Spirit of God, and being converted by the grace of God, John baptised them in the Jordan River. All of this caused no small stir among the people and no small disturbance among the religious elite in Jerusalem. So the priests and Levites were sent out from Jerusalem to ask John who he was.

'And this is the record of John, when the Jews sent priests and Levites from Jerusalem to ask him, Who art thou? And he confessed, and denied not; but confessed, I am not the Christ. And they asked him, What then? Art thou Elias? And he saith, I am not. Art thou that prophet? And he answered, No' (vv. 19-21).

The Messiah's forerunner stood before them, one who was clearly identified as the forerunner of the Christ. That fact was obvious to everyone, everyone except the spiritually ignorant leaders of the people, the priests and Levites!

When these men asked John, 'Who art thou?' before they could utter another word, John cut them off and said, 'I am not the Christ'! Because the people honoured him, their religious leaders were ready to elevate John highly. Self-serving preachers will do anything to promote themselves, even promote one whose message they despise, if in doing so, they can promote and advance themselves.

Remember, these men were the great Sanhedrim, the spiritual rulers of the Jews. They were the most influential, the most revered, and the most highly educated big wheels in the Jewish church. But they did not have a clue what was going on in the kingdom of God.

They professed to be waiting for the appearance of the Messiah. They took great pride in being the descendants of Abraham, and in their knowledge of the scriptures. They lived by the law of Moses, and rested in their imagined obedience to it. They professed to know God's will and believe his promises. They were confident that they understood the prophets. They were confident leaders of the people. Yet, they were totally ignorant of all things spiritual. They stand before us as sad, glaring examples of the fact that unregenerate souls, no matter how well taught, no matter how well learned, no matter how devotedly religious, are utterly without knowledge spiritually. Spiritual knowledge comes only by divine revelation (Proverbs 2:6), only by the teaching of God the Holy Spirit (1 Corinthians 2:14-16).

Here is the proof of Paul's doctrine in 1 Corinthians 2. The Christ of God, the Messiah, was standing in their midst, as John declares in verse 26; yet they did not recognise him. They saw him, but never saw him. They knew much about him, but did not know him. They lived in his company, but knew him not!

And that which was true of these men is true of men today. It may be that some who read these lines are exactly as they were. The Lord Jesus Christ is set forth crucified among you, but you do not see him, hear his voice, or know him. Another person reading the same words does see him, does hear his voice, and does know him; but you do not. Why? You are not yet born of God. May God the Holy Spirit have mercy upon you and reveal the Lord Jesus to you, visiting you with grace, effectual, free, saving grace in Christ (Luke 19:44; Job 10:12; Isaiah 12:1-6; 25:9).

When these men asked John, 'Who art thou?' before they could utter another word, John cut them off and said, 'I am not the Christ'! They were willing to receive him as a reincarnation of Elijah, or Isaiah, or Jeremiah, or one of the prophets, or even as the Messiah (that Prophet of whom Moses spoke in Deuteronomy 18:15-18, if he would simply accept their praise and be identified with them. But John was a true prophet. He refused their honour and refused to take any honour to himself. Instead, he immediately turned attention away from himself to Christ. Nineteen times, he used a double affirmation to turn attention away from himself, to make certain that he was not misunderstood.

Like John the Baptist, God's servants will not align themselves with God's enemies. They cannot be bribed with money, power, or recognition. And they do not seek the praise, or even the approval of men. God's servants desire no honour, but the honour of Christ. They studiously turn the light away from themselves to him.

'What sayest thou of thyself?'
Look at the next question. When they could get no satisfaction, they pressed on. 'Then said they unto him, Who art thou? that we may give an answer to them that sent us. What sayest thou of thyself?' (v. 22) John might have answered, 'I am the son of Zachariah the priest. I am filled with the Spirit from my mother's womb. I am a remarkable man raised up by God and sent to prepare the way before the Christ in the spirit and power of Elijah, as Malachi prophesied'. But instead 'He said, I am the voice of one crying in the wilderness, Make straight the way of the Lord, as said the prophet Esaias' (v. 23).

Those men who are sent of God seek no glory or acclaim for themselves. They look upon themselves, at best, as nothing but unprofitable servants (Luke 17:10). When John referred to himself as 'the voice', he used the very term the Holy Spirit used of him 700 years earlier in Isaiah 40:3. John's mission was to bear witness of Christ, not himself. A voice is heard and not seen. The Lord Jesus endures long after 'the voice' is silent.

'The voice' cried in the wilderness, not in the temple or in the streets of Jerusalem. Why? Because the Lord was no longer in the temple. Judaism was nothing but an empty shell. The Jews were a nation of religious legalists, steeped in self-righteous formalism, ceremonies, and rituals. There was no place for John in the religion of his day; and he did not want a place in it.

He was a true prophet. He had nothing to say for himself, or about himself. He refused to promote himself, or even to defend himself. He had no cause, but Christ. He knew why God had raised him up and sent him, and he would not be turned aside from it (Isaiah 40:1-11).

John knew exactly who he was dealing with. He was dealing with 'they which were sent were of the Pharisees' (v. 24). They were thoroughly orthodox heretics, self-serving religious politicians, pretentious hypocrites, cruel and persecuting self-righteous legalists, blind leaders of blind people!

'Why baptisest thou?'
These proud Pharisees kept pressing. Because God's faithful servant, this true prophet, refused to accept their honour, and refused to take any honour to himself, because he made no pretentious claim of earthly religious authority, they challenged his right to perform any religious ordinance, let alone a new ordinance. He had not been to seminary. He had not been ordained by any earthly religious body. He had not come up through their ranks. John did not fit any mould. He could not be put in any religious box. He was not a Liberal Sadducee, or a Reformed Pharisee, or a Heretical Herodian. So these good preservers of the religious status quo said, 'Why baptisest thou if thou be not that Christ, nor Elias, neither that prophet?' (v. 25).

That's a question every preacher ought to be required to answer. You can determine whether he is God's servant, or the servant of man, by his answer. I have baptised many; but why? The question is 'Why?' not 'How?'. There can be no question about how baptism is performed. Baptism is immersion. Anything else (sprinkling, pouring, etc.) is not baptism. 'Why baptisest thou?' 'John answered them, saying, I baptise with water: but there standeth one among you, whom ye know not' (v. 26).

The word 'with' in our King James version is a very, very poor translation. The Greek word 'en' is a preposition indicating position. John did not say, 'I baptise with water'. He said, 'I baptise in water'. There is a huge difference. Before I show you the answers given in the New Testament to this third question, 'Why baptisest thou?' let us look at verses 26-28. Again, John focuses our attention, not on the ordinance, but upon the Saviour, because the ordinance is meaningless apart from the Saviour. 'Christ is all', not baptism, not the church, not you, and not me. In all things, he must have the preeminence!

'John answered them, saying, I baptise with water: but there standeth one among you, whom ye know not; he it is, who coming after me is preferred before me, whose shoe's latchet I am not worthy to unloose. These things were done in Bethabara beyond Jordan, where John was baptising' (vv. 26-28).

John stood his ground; but he wanted all to know his true mission, which was to point sinners to Christ. These men were raising questions about church authority and baptism, just as multitudes do today, while they were utter strangers to Christ himself. Multitudes debate and argue about side issues and leave that which is vital undecided. 'What think ye of Christ?' That is the matter that is vital (1 Corinthians 1:17).

'There standeth one among you, whom ye know not' (John 1:10, 11). Standing in their midst was the Seed of woman, Abraham's Seed, David's Son, the fulfilment of all promises, prophecies, and pictures of the Messiah given by the prophets in the holy scriptures; yet, they knew him not.

Then the Baptist said, 'He it is, who is coming after me (coming to be revealed after me) is preferred before me, whose shoe's latchet I am not worthy to unloose'! John could not find words strong enough to express his insignificance or his Saviour's majesty, supremacy, and glory. In verse 20 he says, 'Christ is preferred before me because he was before me'! He came to this earth at God's appointed time, but he is the eternal God and the eternal Saviour (John 8:58; Proverbs 8:24-30).

But why did John baptise people? Why do we baptise people? The word of God gives three very specific answers to that question.

By baptism we show, in this symbolic ordinance, how all righteousness was fulfilled for us by the obedience of Christ, our Substitute, unto death (Matthew 3:15). In believer's baptism the child of God shows, by vivid symbolism, how his sins were washed away by the sin-atoning death of Christ, that we might receive the Spirit of life (Acts 2:38; 22:16; Galatians 3:13, 14). By baptism the believer publicly identifies himself with Christ, with his people, and with his gospel, and publicly avows his commitment to his Lord (Romans 6:1-7).

Christ The Lamb
Like the first Baptist, this preacher would have you see and know, worship and adore, trust and rejoice in Christ alone, the Lamb of God. 'The next day John seeth Jesus coming unto him, and saith, Behold the Lamb of God, which taketh away the sin of the world' (v. 29).

May God the Holy Spirit enable you to now behold and never cease to behold the Lamb of God. In this magnificent sentence John tells us four things about the Lord Jesus Christ, the Lamb of God.

He is the only Object of all true faith 'Behold the Lamb'! God our Saviour says, 'Look unto me and be ye saved' (Isaiah 45:22).

Christ was ordained, given, and sent by God. He is 'the Lamb of God'.

Our Lord Jesus Christ is the one Sacrifice for sin. 'The Lamb'! God has provided 'himself a lamb for a burnt offering' (Genesis 22:8).

This blessed Lamb, the Lord Jesus Christ, is the only Remover of sin. 'Behold the Lamb of God, which taketh away the sin of the world'!

Chapter 9

'Behold the Lamb of God'

'The next day John seeth Jesus coming unto him, and saith, Behold the Lamb of God, which taketh away the sin of the world. This is he of whom I said, After me cometh a man which is preferred before me: for he was before me. And I knew him not: but that he should be made manifest to Israel, therefore am I come baptising with water. And John bare record, saying, I saw the Spirit descending from heaven like a dove, and it abode upon him. And I knew him not: but he that sent me to baptise with water, the same said unto me, Upon whom thou shalt see the Spirit descending, and remaining on him, the same is he which baptiseth with the Holy Ghost. And I saw, and bare record that this is the Son of God. Again the next day after John stood, and two of his disciples; And looking upon Jesus as he walked, he saith, Behold the Lamb of God! And the two disciples heard him speak, and they followed Jesus' (John 1:29-37).

The Lord Jesus Christ, the Son of the living God, is the Lamb of God, who 'taketh away the sin of the world.' In this passage John has been preaching the gospel in Bethabara, beyond Jordan, and baptising those who believed. Then, in verse 29 we read. 'The next day John seeth Jesus coming unto him, and saith, Behold the Lamb of God, which taketh away the sin of the world.'

Christ The Lamb
The Lord Jesus Christ is 'the Lamb'. He is the only sin-atoning sacrifice, the only lamb by whose death atonement could be made, the only lamb by whose blood we have access unto the Father, the only lamb whose blood being sprinkled upon the mercy-seat has obtained eternal redemption for us. Christ

is not a lamb, but the Lamb. He is not a way, but the Way. He is not a door, but the Door. He is not a saviour, but the Saviour. 'Neither is there salvation in any other: for there is none other name under heaven given among men, whereby we must be saved' (Acts 4:12).

Christ is 'the Lamb of God'. He is the Lamb who is of God, who came from God, and who is God. He could not be our Saviour if he is not our God. Only one who is God could offer infinite satisfaction for the sins of his people. This Lamb, the Lord Jesus Christ, 'taketh away the sin of the world.' He is the only sacrifice for sin. It is he and he alone who 'taketh away' sin by the sacrifice of himself. It is the blood of this Lamb, God's dear Son, that 'cleanseth us from all sin.' He is an effectual sacrifice for sin. He does not try to take away sin. He does not offer to take away sin. He does not merely make it possible for sin to be taken away. He 'taketh away sin'! The Lamb of God is a sacrifice of perpetual efficacy.

John 1:29 does not say, 'He took away sin', though that is true. By his one sacrifice he put away sin. But, rather, John the Baptist said, 'Behold the Lamb of God, which taketh away the sin of the world.' Oh, how I love those words, 'taketh away'! Quite literally, John was saying, 'Behold the Lamb of God that continually bears away the sin of the world.' Christ is the sin-bearer; and he continually bears away our sin. Notice the word 'sin' is singular, not 'sins', plural. The Lord Jesus Christ continually bears away both our sins and the curse that sin brings.

This is our Saviour's continual work. Though our salvation was finished in all its details from eternity, though our redemption was fully accomplished at Calvary, the Lord God continually performs it in us and continually assures us that he is doing so by using present tense verbs as simple statements of fact, declaring the reality of every believer's experience of grace. What he did in eternity and what he did at Calvary are things utterly insignificant to me until he performs them in me. He 'redeemeth thy life from destruction' (Psalms 103:4). He 'is near that justifieth me' (Isaiah 50:8). He 'justifieth the ungodly' (Romans 4:5). 'It is God that justifieth' (Romans 8:33). It is Christ the Lamb 'who forgiveth all thine iniquities' (Psalms 103:3), who 'cleanseth us from all sin' (1 John 1:7), and 'taketh away the sin of the world'. What sweet terms of grace these are to our souls!

The Lord Jesus Christ, the Lamb of God, is the universally effectual sacrifice for sin. He 'taketh away the sin of the world.' John does not intend for us to understand that Christ bears away the sin of all who are in the world. We know that is not the case, because there are many who bear the curse of God upon themselves forever in hell, multitudes whose sins shall never be taken away. But Christ is the only sin-bearer there is in all the world; and he takes away sin, all manner of sin from all manner of men, throughout the world.

76

'Behold the Lamb of God'

The Message Of The Book

'Behold the Lamb of God which taketh away the sin of the world.' Behold him in the book of God. I want you to see and see clearly that the Lord Jesus Christ as the Lamb of God is the subject of holy scripture. The theme of the Bible is redemption, atonement, access to, and acceptance with God by a sacrificial Lamb; and that Lamb is the Lord Jesus Christ. Christ is referred to as the Lamb of God in the Book of Revelation alone twenty-seven times. This blessed book is all about the Lord Jesus Christ, the Lamb of God (Luke 24:27, 44-47).

He is the great antitype of all the Old Testament types. He is the One of whom they all speak. He is the One who fulfils them all. As we read through and study the Old Testament, we see the Lord Jesus Christ set forth not only in promise and prophecy, but also in the types and shadows of the Mosaic economy. All of those Old Testament types and pictures speak of Christ as our great and glorious Saviour. The Lord God instituted the whole legal system of the Old Testament to show us the gospel of his grace in Christ. But the most outstanding, the most significant of the instituted types of the Old Testament was the paschal lamb sacrificed every year on the day of atonement (Exodus 12; Leviticus 16; 1 Corinthians 5:7).

Nothing more beautifully, more clearly, or more accurately represented the glorious person and work of our Lord Jesus Christ in the Old Testament than the lamb sacrificed, slain, and offered to God on the day of atonement. Everyone even slightly familiar with the Old Testament knew that when Messiah came he would appear as the Lamb of God. Therefore, when John saw him, he cried, 'Behold the Lamb of God'! And every one who heard him knew exactly what he was saying: 'Behold the Messiah, the Christ, the Son of God has come to redeem and save his people from their sins'!

The scriptures universally declare that Jesus Christ, our Redeemer, is the Lamb of God. We have been redeemed from our sins by the gory, but glorious, bloody, but beautiful sacrifice of the Son of God as a Lamb slaughtered in our place (Isaiah 53:7, 8; 1 Peter 1:18-20).

The Son of God was foreordained and slain for us as the Lamb of God before the foundation of the world (Revelation 13:8). And he was manifested and revealed in the fulness of time to put away our sins by the sacrifice of himself (Hebrews 9:26). Throughout the scriptures we see Christ set before us under the figure of the sacrificial Lamb of God.

1. In Genesis chapters 3 and 4 he is the Lamb typified. Abel brought the blood of a lamb to make atonement for his sins and to worship God, because his father Adam told him how the Lord God slew a lamb for him and his wife Eve in the Garden of Eden and clothed them with its skins. This shows us the way of grace and redemption through the blood of Christ (Ephesians 1:7).

2. In Genesis 22 we see our Lord Jesus presented as the Lamb prophesied. Isaac knew that in order to come to God and worship him a lamb had to be slain. So he asked his father, 'Where is the Lamb for a burnt offering? And Abraham said, My son, God will provide himself a lamb for a burnt offering' (vv. 7, 8). And so he did. God provided for himself that day a lamb to be sacrificed in Isaac's place. But he provided himself as the Lamb to be sacrificed in our place in the person of his dear Son (2 Corinthians 5:21).

3. In Isaiah 53 we see Christ set forth as the Lamb personified. Isaiah told us that the Lamb of God was to be a man, a real man like us, the Servant of the Lord, identified with us, assuming our flesh (Hebrews 2:14-17), assuming our sin (Isaiah 53:6), and dying in our place (1 Peter 3:18).

4. In John 1:29 John the Baptist said, 'Behold, the Lamb of God', and the Lamb is identified. John knew all about those sacrificial lambs of the Old Testament. His father was a priest. When Christ came, he was identified by God's messenger. He said, 'There he is boys. That is the One I have been telling you about. That man is the Lamb of God that has come to put away sin'!

5. In John 19 we see the Lord of glory as the Lamb crucified (vv. 17-19, 28-30). Whenever you look upon the crucifixion of Christ, remember that his death was no accident. The Lamb of God died by the hand of God, according to the purpose of God, at the time appointed by God, and effectually redeemed all the people of God, by satisfying the justice of God (Galatians 3:13; 4:4).

6. In the Book of Revelation the Apostle John saw the Lord Jesus Christ sitting upon the throne as the Lamb glorified. In heaven's glory Jesus Christ is worshipped in his sacrificial character as the Lamb of God who has effectually redeemed his people out of every nation, kindred, tribe, and tongue, by his blood. The Lamb's everlasting glory is the result of his accomplishments in his death as our Substitute (Isaiah 53:10-12; Revelation 5:6-14; 7:9-17; 14:1; 15:3; 21:22, 23; 22:1-3).

The Preacher's Message
If the Lamb of God is the singular message of this book, let him be the singular message of every pulpit. Would to God these words were proclaimed incessantly from every pulpit in the world! I say this without reservation. The Lord Jesus Christ as the Lamb of God is the gospel preacher's message.

I did not say that Christ as the Lamb of God ought to be the gospel preacher's message. I said that if a man is God's servant, if he is God's messenger, if he is a man sent of God, if a man is a gospel preacher, Jesus Christ as the Lamb of God is his message. John the Baptist was the first gospel preacher in this dispensation. He is the example to all who follow him. His message was 'Behold the Lamb of God'! The Apostle Peter was the chief spokesman to the early church and to the Jewish world. His message was the same. Even the deacons who preached, preached the Lamb of God. The Apostle Paul was the first gospel preacher to the Gentiles. His message was the same. In fact, as you read the Book of Acts, you find the whole church going about everywhere talking to sinners about the Lamb of God. They went everywhere preaching Jesus Christ and him crucified as the Lamb of God. Though few these days have any understanding of this fact, I want you to understand that God's servants and God's people still go everywhere talking about the Lamb of God. Look at the example of John the Baptist and learn something about what a gospel preacher is.

A gospel preacher is a man with one purpose, one business, one object in life. His only business is to cry, 'Behold the Lamb of God'! John was born and sent out into the world for this purpose. Indeed, every man called and sent of God into the world has been born for that work and is sent forth of God to proclaim Jesus Christ as the sin-atoning Lamb of God. We are sent to bear witness of him. Those who turn aside to other things and do not declare Christ as the Lamb of God to eternity bound sinners make a mockery of the ministry and of the poor souls who hear them. Like John, we must denounce the religions of the age, denounce the sins of men, and call sinners to repentance; but our message is and always must be, 'Behold the Lamb of God'!

That preacher who fails to point sinners to Christ as the Lamb of God is a traitor to the souls of his hearers. He will in the last day have his portion with the damned (Ezekiel 33:8; 1 Corinthians 9:16).

I cannot imagine a doom more terrible than that which awaits the man who claims to be God's servant but does not faithfully preach the gospel to his hearers. Sermons that do not point sinners to Christ, sermons that are not full of Christ, sermons that leave men looking to anyone other than Christ will be hard to answer for in the day of judgment. It is cruel beyond description for a preacher to amuse eternity bound sinners with the trifles of religious speculation, theological niceties, denominational dogma, and prophetic mysteries. Playing with men's souls is murderous work! And if the Lamb of God is not preached, the man who pretends to be preaching is doing nothing but playing with men's souls! Sermons without Christ are damning to those who preach them and damning to those who hear them! If I am God's servant, I will, I must, God helping me, I shall, like John, have nothing to do when I open my mouth to preach except to preach Jesus Christ and him crucified, saying, 'Behold the Lamb of God'!

John also shows us by example that gospel preachers are men whose eyes are fixed on Christ the Lamb of God. Read verses 35 and 36. 'Again the next day after John stood, and two of his disciples; And looking upon Jesus as he walked, he saith, Behold the Lamb of God'! The preacher's eye must be upon Christ if he is going to point sinners to Christ. They preach him best who see him best. And they see him best whose eyes are fixed upon him. John seems to have had no eye for anyone but Christ. He looked upon him adoringly, as one astonished by him, lovingly, as one ravished by him, and constantly, as one who had no interest but him. Therefore, when he spoke of the Lamb, his words had meaning and power.

Notice this too: John looked to the Lord Jesus when he seemed to be passing him by (v. 36) as well as when he was manifestly coming to him (v. 29). And his message was the same in both cases. John's message did not change. When he preached to a crowd of unbelievers and when he was quietly instructing just two of his disciples, he preached the same message (cf. vv. 29 and 36). He kept to one point. Like Paul, he knew nothing among his hearers save Jesus Christ and him crucified.

I know that I am looked upon as a simpleton by some. But I know what God has sent me to do. Most preachers know too much. They need to learn to be know-nothings, knowing nothing but Christ crucified. No subject is more needful to sinners, more sweet to the saints, more hopeful to the guilty, more sanctifying to the righteous, more convicting to the fallen, more refreshing to the ransomed, or more inspiring to both saints and sinners than this: 'Behold the Lamb of God'! I fully agree with C. H. Spurgeon, who said, 'To harp upon the name of Jesus is the blessed monotony of a true ministry, a monotony more full of variety than all other subjects besides. When Jesus is the first, the midst, and the last, yea, all in all, then do we make full proof of our ministry.'

The Gospel's Revelation
The Lord Jesus Christ, as the Lamb of God, is the gospel's revelation. This is what the gospel reveals, proclaims, and teaches. Jesus Christ is the Lamb of God. All those typical lambs were only types. They did nothing. They accomplished nothing. They did not put away sin. They did not appease God's wrath. They did not satisfy his justice, they did not purge the conscience of guilt. They only pointed to Christ the Lamb of God who put away sin by the sacrifice of himself (Hebrews 10:1-10).

Sin could never be put away without satisfaction. God in his infinite wisdom found a way for us to escape his wrath; but that way does not violate his justice. The Lord Jesus as the Lamb of God has borne every stroke of justice that God's elect should have borne. He alone could do it, because Christ alone is the Lamb God appointed (Hebrews 10:5-7). Christ alone is the Lamb God provided (1 John 4:9, 10). Christ alone is the Lamb God himself sacrificed and offered (Isaiah 53:10). Christ alone is the Lamb God accepted (Hebrews 1:1-3; 9:12; 10:11-14; Ephesians 5:1). And Christ alone is the Lamb God has set forth in his covenant, before the world began, in the types, shadows, and prophecies of the law, and in the gospel (Romans 3:24-26).

Chapter 10

'Behold the Lamb of God' Again

'The next day John seeth Jesus coming unto him, and saith, Behold the Lamb of God, which taketh away the sin of the world. This is he of whom I said, After me cometh a man which is preferred before me: for he was before me. And I knew him not: but that he should be made manifest to Israel, therefore am I come baptising with water. And John bare record, saying, I saw the Spirit descending from heaven like a dove, and it abode upon him. And I knew him not: but he that sent me to baptise with water, the same said unto me, Upon whom thou shalt see the Spirit descending, and remaining on him, the same is he which baptiseth with the Holy Ghost. And I saw, and bare record that this is the Son of God. Again the next day after John stood, and two of his disciples; And looking upon Jesus as he walked, he saith, Behold the Lamb of God'! (John 1:29-36)

Is the Bible a sealed book to you? Do you have great difficulty understanding its doctrine, its precepts, and its ordinances? Many people do. To them it is like a treasure chest with a lock on it. They know that it contains many rich gems. But they have no key to open it.

The Key
There is one key which will open the book to you and reveal its golden treasures. That key is Jesus Christ. Jesus Christ is the Foundation, the Centre, and the Mainspring of all divine truth. This is what he said, 'Search the scriptures; for in them ye think ye have eternal life: and they are they which

testify of me.' If we would avoid error in interpreting and applying the scriptures, we must understand that everything in the Bible speaks of and relates to Christ. Divorce any doctrine from Christ and that doctrine becomes heresy. Divorce any precept from Christ and that precept becomes self-righteous legality.

For example: I have heard men preach on the doctrine of the church as though the church were nothing more than a physical religious organization begun by our Lord during his earthly ministry. But the church is much more. It is the body of Christ. It is a spiritual building made up of men and women redeemed by Christ and vitally joined to him by faith. Christ is the Foundation upon which the church is built, the Head by which the church is governed, and the Bread upon which the church lives.

I have heard men talk about the kingdom of Christ as though it were nothing more than a continuance, or re-establishment, of the physical kingdom of David. Again, the Kingdom of Christ is spiritual. Our Lord entered his kingdom by the door of the cross. And he builds his kingdom upon the cross. Christ sits upon the throne today as a direct result of his finished work at Calvary. Whether we are talking about the kingdom in its present or its future manifestations, being a part of this kingdom is nothing more or less than surrendering to the claims of Christ as Lord and King.

I have even heard men preach on election as though it were nothing more than a logical part of a theological system. Election is a precious truth of divine revelation when it is understood properly. Our election is in Christ. God predestinated us to be conformed to the image of Christ. Election is nothing more or less than God loving a people before all worlds, putting them in Christ, and determining to make them like Christ. Election is God choosing to save us rather than damn us, as we justly deserve, for Christ's sake.

As for the precepts of scripture, these, too, are centred in Christ; and obedience to them is motivated by him. Those things that we call 'practical godliness' ought to be preached. But they must be motivated by gospel principles. The Christian life is not an extension of the Mosaic law, or merely a system of morality. It is obedience to Christ. It is following his example. Wives are to be submissive to their husbands, as the church is submissive to Christ. The husband is to love his wife as Christ loved the church and gave himself for it. Servants (employees) are to serve their masters (employers) 'as the servants of Christ, doing the will of God from the heart'. Believing businessmen are to treat their employees with kindness and generosity, knowing that Christ their Master is in heaven, treating them with kindness and generosity. Believers are to forgive offences against them, even as God for Christ's sake forgives us. We are to love one another, as Christ loved us. We are to give with a willing heart, generously, even as Christ willingly gave all for us and to us. This kind of service to Christ is free, spontaneous, unconstrained, motivated by love and arises from the knowledge of the gospel. I know that these are only a few of the doctrines and precepts of the Bible. But they will suffice to illustrate my point. Christ is the key to sacred scripture. Every doctrine of the Bible must be understood and taught in the light of the gospel. Every precept of godliness must be motivated by gospel principles. We truly preach the whole counsel of God only when we preach it in the light of Christ and him crucified.

The key that opens the treasure chest of holy scripture is Christ crucified. To understand the book of God, we must 'Behold the Lamb of God' in it. This is the message of holy scripture, the message for which the first Baptist is famous, 'Behold the Lamb of God'! I want to do what I can to make everyone who hears my voice, reads what I write, or is in any way influenced by me to see that the Lord Jesus Christ as the Lamb of God is the subject of holy scripture. The Bible is a 'him book'. It is all about him. The preacher's only message (1 Corinthians 2:2; 9:16). The gospel's glorious revelation (vv. 31-34; 2 Corinthians 5:16). The sinner's only hope (1 Timothy 1:1). The believer's only rule (John 13:15). The worshipper's only object (Revelation 4 and 5). The embodiment and glory of the triune God (vv. 14, 16; Colossians 2:9).

John's Message
You will notice in the passage before us that this was John's message on two consecutive days. On the first day, John was preaching to a large crowd in the open air in Bethabara beyond Jordan. It was a mixed multitude. Many were believers he had just baptised, young converts at best, many were lost religionists, Pharisees and their disciples, and many more were on their way to hell and were just curious about this strange man who was regarded by all to be a prophet, though he was rough as a cob and anything but a stereotypical preacher. On the next day, John was privately instructing two of his disciples. Yet, on both days his message was the same 'Behold the Lamb of God'!

Behold him as the Lamb slain from eternity (Revelation 13:8), vicariously sacrificed (Romans 5:8-10), enthroned in glory to save his people (John 17:2), interceding in heaven for God's elect (1 John 2:1, 2), and coming again to judge the quick and the dead (2 Timothy 4:1; 1 Peter 4:5; Revelation 6:12-17).

In the previous chapter I laboured the point that this is the universal message of holy scripture and the singular message of true gospel preachers. In this chapter I want us to behold the Lord Jesus as the Lamb of God again; and I want to make some very practical observations about this message. Jesus Christ as the Lamb of God sacrificed, slain, risen from the dead, and exalted in all his saving efficacy and fulness is the message God has given us to proclaim. Let me give you five reasons why I preach this message exclusively.

Perfect Balance

First, Christ as the Lamb of God is the perfectly balanced message of the gospel. Every time a man wants to excuse himself for not preaching the gospel, or wants to justify his criticisms of those who do, this is the line that is used, 'I believe we ought to have a balanced message'. Yet, those who use that line seem to me to always have a lopsided message of works.

Christ as the Lamb of God is the perfectly balanced message of the gospel. When Christ crucified is a preacher's message, when Christ is all in all in preaching, you have everything in that message. Christ crucified is a message of doctrinal instruction, experimental grace, and practical godliness.

All vital doctrinal instruction is contained in this message. 'Behold the Lamb of God'! That preacher who preaches Christ crucified clearly and constantly gives his people the best possible doctrinal instruction, for he proclaims the eternal deity of Christ. 'He was before me'. The incarnation of Christ. 'This is the Son of God'. The strict justice of God. 'The soul that sinneth it shall die'. The gigantic evil of sin. The Lamb of God was the sacrifice required to put it away. The utter inability of man. There is no need for this Lamb if a sinner can save himself! The glorious efficacy of Christ's atonement. He 'taketh away sin'! The superabundance of God's grace (Romans 5:20, 21). The infinite love of God (Romans 5:6-8). The infallible security of God's elect. How can they perish for whom such a sacrifice was made?

If you want a personal, experimental religion, as I do, if you need experimental grace, grace that is felt in the depths of your soul, this is the message that will promote it. 'Behold the Lamb of God'! Are you vexed with sin? 'Behold the Lamb of God'! Are you troubled with affliction? 'Behold the Lamb of God'! Are you in need of comfort? 'Behold the Lamb of God'! Do you need reviving? 'Behold the Lamb of God'! Are you fearful about your soul? 'Behold the Lamb of God'! Are you concerned about the future? 'Behold the Lamb of God'! If you need instruction in what men call 'practical godliness', you need to hear this message. 'Behold the Lamb of God'! What can be more practical, or so capably promote good works? What can be more inspiring to godliness than Christ crucified? Read Titus 2:1-14 and 3:4-8.

Do you want to learn how to give? 'Behold the Lamb of God' (2 Corinthians 8:9). Do you want to know what kind of father and husband you ought to be? 'Behold the Lamb of God'! Do you want to know how to serve God's church and kingdom? 'Behold the Lamb of God'! Do you want to know how to love your brother? 'Behold the Lamb of God'! Do you want to know how to bear affliction? 'Behold the Lamb of God'! Do you want to know how to pray? 'Behold the Lamb of God'! Read Matthew 6:9-13.

Do you want to how to live? 'Behold the Lamb of God'! Do you want to know how to die? 'Behold the Lamb of God'!

'Behold the Lamb of God' Again

Our Constant Need
Second, Christ must be constantly preached, because we need to always have him before our eyes. Christ Jesus as the sin-atoning Lamb of God ought to be the constant and dominant object of every believer's heart. I know that we live in this world and must, of necessity, give thought and consideration to many things. But the one topic which ought to captivate our hearts and minds is the Lord Jesus Christ, our dear Redeemer (Colossians 3:1-3).

Allow me to paraphrase Psalms 1:1-3 to show you my meaning. 'Blessed is the man that walketh not in the counsel of the ungodly, nor standeth in the way of sinners, nor sitteth in the seat of the scornful. But his delight is in Christ the LORD; and in his Saviour doth he meditate day and night. And he shall be like a tree planted by the rivers of water, that bringeth forth his fruit in his season; his leaf also shall not wither; and whatsoever he doeth shall prosper.'

Great, Ennobling Subject
Third, I preach Christ crucified as the Lamb of God incessantly, because Jesus Christ crucified is the greatest, most glorious, and ennobling subject of thought in all the world. I do not claim to be a scholar, or a man of great brilliance. I am neither. But I have done a little reading, and have had a little experience in many things. I have found nothing to compare with Christ crucified. He is the sum of all truth, the essence of all knowledge, the purpose of all creation, the explanation of all providence, the soul of life, the light of light, the heaven of heaven, and the glory of glory! In a word, 'Christ is All' (Colossians 3:10, 11).

No subject in the world is so vast, so sublime, so elevating as this: 'Behold the Lamb of God'! Talk of mysteries? Try God incarnate, slain, and glorified! Talk of romance? Try describing the love of God! Talk of beauty? Try the glory of God in the face of Jesus Christ! Talk of science? Try the science of substitution, satisfaction, and redemption! Talk of philosophy? Try the philosophy forgiveness. Talk of law? Try justice satisfied with mercy granted at the same time!

Compared with these things, a preacher long ago said, 'What are the sciences but human ignorance set forth in order? What are the classics but the choicest of Babel's jargon compared with His teachings? What are the poets but dreamers, and philosophers but fools in His presence?' Jesus Christ alone is wisdom, beauty, eloquence and power. Compared to Christ crucified, everything else is just contemptible (1 Corinthians 1:17-31).

One Thing Needful
Fourth, I preach Christ as the Lamb of God because he is the one thing needful.

'Now it came to pass, as they went, that he entered into a certain village: and a certain woman named Martha received him into her house. And she had

85

a sister called Mary, which also sat at Jesus' feet, and heard his word. But Martha was cumbered about much serving, and came to him, and said, Lord, dost thou not care that my sister hath left me to serve alone? bid her therefore that she help me. And Jesus answered and said unto her, Martha, Martha, thou art careful and troubled about many things: But one thing is needful: and Mary hath chosen that good part, which shall not be taken away from her' (Luke 10:38-42).

We may forget many things without harm. We may even forget some important things without endangering ourselves or anyone else. But we must have Christ. He is the Bread of life. Without him we cannot live. He is the Water of life. Without him we must die. Christ crucified as the Lamb of God is our faith, our doctrine, and our hope. His blood is the life-blood of true religion. Any other faith is a lifeless, false faith.

Glorifies God

Fifth, I preach Jesus Christ crucified as the Lamb of God for sinners, because this message glorifies God. This message, 'Behold the Lamb of God', declares our God to be both a just God and a Saviour, and calls sinners to him (Isaiah 45:20-22). Salvation begins in the experience of it with beholding the Lamb (Isaiah 45:22). Salvation is maintained beholding the Lamb (Hebrews 12:1, 2). And salvation is consummated and completed beholding the Lamb (1 John 3:2).

'Behold the Lamb of God' with reverence. Lift your eyes up to heaven and behold him now. Trust him. Worship him. Love him. 'Behold the Lamb of God' in the blessed ordinances of the gospel every time a saved sinner is immersed in and rises from the waters of baptism (Matthew 3:13-17), and every time you sit at the Lord's Table with God's saints observing together in memory of him who loved us and gave himself for us (1 Corinthians 11:20-26). In our baptism we confess our faith in and union with the Lamb of God in his death, his burial, and his resurrection. In the ordinance of the Lord's supper we remember our Saviour's work of redemption, beholding the Lamb of God in the bread that symbolises his holy body and in the wine that symbolises his sin-atoning blood. 'Behold the Lamb of God'!

Chapter 11

'I knew him not'

'The next day John seeth Jesus coming unto him, and saith, Behold the Lamb of God, which taketh away the sin of the world. This is he of whom I said, After me cometh a man which is preferred before me: for he was before me. And I knew him not: but that he should be made manifest to Israel, therefore am I come baptising with water. And John bare record, saying, I saw the Spirit descending from heaven like a dove, and it abode upon him. And I knew him not: but he that sent me to baptise with water, the same said unto me, Upon whom thou shalt see the Spirit descending, and remaining on him, the same is he which baptiseth with the Holy Ghost. And I saw, and bare record that this is the Son of God' (John 1:29-34).

Most everyone I meet is assured that he knows Christ. They have been led down the Romans Road to salvation. They have been told that Jesus Christ is the Son of God, that he died upon the cross for their sins, and that he rose from the dead the third day. Then, they were told that if they would repeat what someone called 'the sinner's prayer', they would be saved. They did as they were told; and they are sure that they know the Christ of God.

Have I described you? Is that your experience? If so, you must be shocked every time you read the testimony of John the Baptist in this passage. Here is a man who knew the Lord Jesus intimately as a man, but declares twice, 'I knew him not'. Remember, the one speaking here was John the Baptist, our Saviour's first cousin. Yet, he says, 'I knew him not'. What are we to make of that?

We know that John the Baptist knew Christ. I repeat, he was John's first cousin. Yet, twice he said, 'I knew him not'. What do you suppose that means? What is the significance of that statement? That is the question I want to answer in this study. What did John mean when he said, 'I knew him not'?

John's Message
In this passage the apostle John is giving us his inspired account of the ministry of John the Baptist. The Baptist's message was the proclamation of God's Christ. He was sent as Elijah to prepare the way of the Lord. The first thing John the apostle tells us about that great prophet is that he was 'a man sent from God'. 'There was a man sent from God, whose name was John' (v. 6). The only man who can preach the gospel to us is that man who is sent of God with his message (Jeremiah 23:32; Romans 10:15).

What reason we have to bless God for his goodness in sending a man to tell us about our Saviour, the Lord Jesus, proclaiming his great salvation (Isaiah 52:7). John the Baptist was sent 'to bear witness of the Light' (v. 7). Being a prophet of God, he had only one purpose in life, one function, one work to do, and was useful for only that one thing. He came 'to bear witness of the Light', to point sinners to Christ, who alone is the Light of the world. And he would not be turned aside from that one glorious work. It consumed his life. What a witness he bore of the Light! He declared Christ as the shining Light of the world (v. 5). John the Baptist proclaimed that all the fulness of grace is in Christ alone (v. 16). Then he asserted that all grace and truth come to men only in, by, and through the Lord Jesus Christ (v. 17). In verse 18 the apostle tells us that John the Baptist openly asserted that Christ, who is alone the Revelation of the triune God, is the eternal Word with God in heaven, even when he was here upon the earth. And the first Baptist preacher to walk the earth declared Christ's pre-eminence and pre-existence as our eternal Saviour (v. 30).

Now, look at verse 29. Here is John's message. 'The next day John seeth Jesus coming unto him, and saith, Behold the Lamb of God, which taketh away the sin of the world.'

John the Baptist saw the Lord Jesus walking by. When he did, he called for all who heard his voice to behold him, trust him, and follow him who is the Lamb of God. Our Lord Jesus Christ is 'the Lamb slain from the foundation of the world' (Revelation 13:8). Scripture is filled with pictures, prophecies, and descriptions of Christ as the Lamb of God (Exodus 12; Leviticus 9:3; Isaiah 53:7; Revelation 5:6). He is the Lamb who is God and the Lamb of God's own providing (Romans 3:25). God always gives what he requires, requires only what he gives, and always accepts what he gives.

John the Baptist declared that this Lamb, by the virtue of his sacrifice, 'taketh away the sin of the world'. That is to say, he is taking away the sin of the world perpetually, now and forever, by an eternally perpetual and effectual act. As the sun shines and the spring runs without interruption, so Christ takes away the sins of his people scattered through all the world perpetually! Let that be the perpetual picture we have of him. As we multiply sins, he multiplies pardons (Zechariah 13:1; Isaiah 55:7).

All this John the Baptist preached 'that all men through him might believe' (v. 7). Gospel preachers are men sent of God, preaching the grace and glory of God in Christ the Redeemer, as instruments by whom others believe. 'Faith cometh by hearing, and hearing by the word of God.' In verse 30 John again declares the supremacy and glory of Christ. All this was done and all these things were spoken, after he had baptised the Lord Jesus.

'knew him not'

Then, in verse 31 he throws us this curve ball. 'And I knew him not'. He repeats the same words in verse 33. 'And I knew him not'.

'And I knew him not: but that he should be made manifest to Israel, therefore am I come baptising with water. And John bare record, saying, I saw the Spirit descending from heaven like a dove, and it abode upon him. And I knew him not: but he that sent me to baptise with water, the same said unto me, Upon whom thou shalt see the Spirit descending, and remaining on him, the same is he which baptiseth with the Holy Ghost.'

This is John the Baptist's recollection of meeting Christ in the flesh. When he said, 'I knew him not', he was not saying I had not yet met him in person. John the Baptist was not only God's prophet, he was the Saviour's cousin. He had been brought up with him. His mother, Elizabeth, who called the Lord Jesus her Lord when she welcomed Mary into her home, had (we may be sure) often told John about him. Surely, she would have described the Saviour's wondrous birth many times, as she spoke to her son, whom she knew was to be his forerunner. Elizabeth must have often reminded John of how he leaped in her womb for joy when Mary came to her with her Lord and his Lord in her womb (Luke 1:39-45).

Though we have no record of it, it is likely that John and the Lord Jesus were often together as they grew up. There is no question that John knew who the Saviour was, and that he was convinced that he was the Christ of God. When the Lord Jesus came to be baptised by him, 'John forbad him, saying, I have need to be baptised of thee, and comest thou to me?' (Matthew 3:14).

After The Flesh

What, then, is the meaning of John's twice repeated statement to the Pharisees 'I knew him not'? If you will look back at verses 26 and 27, you will get a hint.

'John answered them, saying, I baptise with water: but there standeth one among you, whom ye know not; he it is, who coming after me is preferred before me, whose shoe's latchet I am not worthy to unloose.'

John said to the Pharisees, 'I was once in the same boat you are in. Though I knew much about the Son of God by the instructions of my parents, though I was, like you, looking for the Messiah, the Christ of God, of whom the prophets spoke, though I knew I knew him after the flesh, I did not know him.' He was saying, 'Until he was revealed to me by God the Holy Spirit, I had not beheld him, but now I do. I knew him not; but now I know him. He walks among you. He is the One with whom you have to do; but you know him not. You do not need to be concerned about who I am. You need to be concerned about who he is! I am nobody, just a voice, a noise in the wilderness; but he who walks among you is the Lamb of God who takes away the sin of the world. Do not concern yourself with me and my baptism; concern yourself with him and his baptism.'

These things are 'written for our learning, that we through patience and comfort of the scriptures might have hope' (Romans 15:4). May God the Holy Spirit, who caused them to be written, use them for that end.

There is no doubt that prior to his birth implanted in his mind and heart was the message of the Messiah. I would not attempt to explain this; but John the Baptist was a prophet from his mother's womb; and he knew Christ by special revelation, even when he was in her womb, leaping for joy because of his incarnation (Luke 1:41, 44; Jeremiah 1:5).

John's knowledge of Christ was a miracle of grace, which is basically the meaning of his name, John, 'God has graced, or Jehovah is gracious'. Yet, when John says, 'I knew him not', he was in fact saying that it had not yet been revealed to him that this man, his cousin, was the Christ; but now he had been revealed to him as the Lamb of God and the Son of God.

Christ Revealed

How was the Lord Jesus revealed and made known to John the Baptist as the Christ, the Lamb of God and the Son of God? The fact that he emphatically declares, and declares twice, 'I knew him not', is of paramount importance, because John uses it as the background for the explanation he gives in verses 33 and 34 of how he came to recognise that this man from Nazareth is the Son of God, the Messiah, the One for whom he was sent to bear witness, and to prepare the way.

'And I knew him not: but that he should be made manifest to Israel, therefore am I come baptising with water. And John bare record, saying, I saw the Spirit descending from heaven like a dove, and it abode upon him. And I knew him not: but he that sent me to baptise with water, the same said unto me, Upon whom thou shalt see the Spirit descending, and remaining on him, the same is he which baptiseth with the Holy Ghost. And I saw, and bare record that this is the Son of God.'

John is saying, 'Though I knew him not, I now know him by the word of God, by the Spirit of God, and by the faith God has given me.' He recognised Christ for who he was based on the word of God (vv. 31-34). He once knew Christ after the flesh, but no more. Now, he knew him after the Spirit (2 Corinthians 5:16).

By The Word Of God

First, John knew Christ by the word of God. God himself had described the Lord Jesus with such clarity that there could be no mistake as to who he was once he was revealed. He said, either by an articulate voice, or by a divine impulse on his mind, or by the revelation of the Spirit, 'Upon whom thou shalt see the Spirit descending and remaining on him, the same is he which baptiseth with the Holy Ghost.' This is a plainly revealed fact: faith in Christ is conveyed to chosen, redeemed sinners by God the Holy Spirit through the word of God (Romans 10:17; James 1:18; 1 Peter 1:23-25).

The word of God, the gospel of Christ, is the power of God unto salvation, the catalyst God uses to give sinners life and faith in Christ. It is the power of God unto salvation in all who believe (Romans 1:16).

The book of God repeatedly asserts that regeneration and faith in Christ, gifts of God the Holy Spirit and operations of his irresistible grace, are communicated to chosen, redeemed sinners through the instrumentality of gospel preaching. The Lord God plainly declares that it is his purpose and pleasure to save his elect through the preaching of the gospel (Romans 1:15-17; 10:13-17; 1 Corinthians 1:21; Ephesians 1:13; 1 Timothy 4:12-16; Hebrews 4:12; James 1:18; 1 Peter 1:23-25).

Perhaps you think, 'What if one of God's elect is in a remote barbarian tribe in the jungles of New Guinea where no gospel preacher has ever been?' I can see how that would create a problem, except for one thing: There are no problems with God! He knows exactly how to get his prophet to the people to whom he has purposed to show his mercy. Just ask Jonah!

We preach the gospel with a sense of urgency, knowing that sinners cannot believe on Christ until Christ is preached to them. Yet, we preach with confidence of success, knowing that our labour is not in vain in the Lord (1 Corinthians 15:58). God's word will not return to him void. It will accomplish his will and prosper in the thing it is sent to do (Isaiah 55:11). Every chosen, redeemed sinner must be regenerated and called by the Holy Spirit. And that work will be accomplished through the preaching of the gospel.

The Spirit Of God

But, if we would know Christ, there must be more than the word of God. We must have the word made effectual to us by the power and grace of God the Holy Spirit. Look at the text at the head of this chapter again. Not only did John the Baptist have the testimony of God's word, he had God's word confirmed to him personally by the Holy Spirit. He saw, as God said he would, 'the Spirit descending and remaining on' the Lord Jesus. Is this not the work of God the Holy Spirit? Is this not exactly what he has done for us in the blessed operations of his saving grace upon us and in us? (See John 14:22, 23; 15:26; 16:8-11, 13-15).

Faith In Christ

Then, as soon as Christ was revealed, he saw, he beheld Christ, he knew him by the gift of faith. This is what he tells us in verse 34. 'And I saw, and bare record (confessed) that this is the Son of God'. Read Zechariah 12:10. In the new birth, in the conversion of sinners, this is always the divinely ordained equation: the word of God, the Spirit of God, and faith in Christ. All are the gifts of God's grace. All are necessary. And all are made effectual to the saving of our souls by the grace of God.

The words of John the apostle, explaining the experience of John the Baptist, were prophetic of every believer's experience of grace. When John baptised the Lord Jesus and saw him owned by God the Father with a voice from heaven and the Spirit descending on him as a dove, he understood that 'the Word was made flesh and dwelt among us and we beheld his glory, the glory as the only begotten of the Father, full of grace and truth' (v. 14). He recognised this man from Galilee for who he was, based on the word of God and by the revelation of God. And he saw in the baptism of our Lord the symbolic picture of righteousness fulfilled by the death, burial, and resurrection of Christ as the sinner's Substitute (Matthew 3:13-17).

As if to reiterate this truth, John tells us that those first men who were found of Christ, who found him by the faith he gave them when he made himself known to them, experienced the same thing (vv. 35-37, 40, 41, 43-45, 49).

Sovereign Election

There is yet another distinction concerning the revelation of Christ by the Spirit, through the word. In verse 26 John the Baptist said to the Pharisees, 'I know him whom ye know not'. Looking at this entire chapter, and others like it, we see that Christ is revealed to sinners he has chosen, redeemed, and called (Acts 2:39; 13:48; Galatians 1:15, 16; 1 Thessalonians 1:4, 5; 2 Thessalonians 2:13; 2 Corinthians 5:16).

Gospel Preaching

All true preaching is, for this reason, limited to the declaration of the gospel. It is by the preaching of the gospel that the word of God is declared to men (1 Peter 1:25). The preaching of the gospel, the preaching of the word of God is the declaration of a person, the declaration of the person and work of the Lord Jesus Christ, the Son of God, the King of Israel, the sinner's Saviour. It is declaring the record that God has given concerning his Son (Romans 1:1-3).

What is the gospel? It is the declaration of a unique person; a man who is like no other; a man who lived like no other, spoke like no other, and died like no other. It is the declaration of a man who is himself God. It is the declaration of the eternal Surety of a chosen people. It is the description of the God-man, who came into the world to seek and save that which was lost, who came into the world to save sinners. It is the description of Jehovah's Servant, the Christ, who finished the work that he came to do. It is the declaration of Jesus the Saviour, who saved all whom he came to save, who loses none who were given to him by the Father, but raises them up in the last day. It is the declaration of the man, that wonderful man who lived among sinners without sin, who was made sin for us and is made the righteousness of God unto us.

It is the description of that man who was and is the Friend of sinners. It is the declaration of him who 'shall not fail', for whom failure is never a possibility. It is the description of him who died, and was buried, and rose again that he might be Lord of both the living and the dead. It is the description of him who is, at this moment, seated on the right hand of the majesty on high, ruling with absolute sway over everything that wriggles and writhes in the whole universe, ruling in calm repose (Numbers 23:9). It is the description of him whose very words are spirit and life. It is the description of him about whom every line, every word, every jot, and every tittle of the Bible is written. It is the description of him who, by the sacrifice of himself, has put away our sins and has 'made us meet to be partakers of the inheritance of the saints in light'. It is the description of him who satisfied the law and justice of God for his people so fully, so infinitely, that the Judge of the all the earth declares them never to have sinned, and accepts them fully as sons and daughters! It is the declaration, the description of him who is made of God unto us wisdom, righteousness, sanctification and redemption. It is the description of him for whom heaven opens and the voice of God declares 'this is my beloved son, hear ye him'.

We preach him, and preach him, and preach him so that when he comes to his chosen, his redeemed, his called, they will immediately recognise him for who he is, and cry with old Thomas, 'my Lord and my God.' We preach that those who hear can say, 'I knew him not, but I now know him, because the word of God has described him so fully that none other will fit the description, because the Spirit of God has revealed him in me, and has given me faith to know and trust him!'

When he comes to his own, their testimony is that God has hung flesh on his Word and we behold his glory, as the only begotten of the Father, full of grace and truth. We keep on preaching him so that every nook and cranny of the believer's existence will be immersed in him (Romans 11:36). We preach him so that every turn of providence, every happenstance, circumstance, and every occurrence will be seen as his hand of love and tender care (Romans 8:28; Colossians 1:16, 17).

I often hear people extolling preachers for being so 'practical', for teaching 'practical truths' on how to live the Christian life. They tell how the preacher comforts them and makes their struggles easier. They talk about how their pastor preaches in an understandable manner, showing them what to do and what not do in order to be 'real Christians'. But in all the preacher praise and promotion I hear, seldom do I hear a man praised because he preaches Christ fully and clearly in all his redeeming, saving glory.

The Bible may be used to show men and women what to do and what not to do. It is full of moral principles. Peoples' lives will be radically changed, if they abide by the principles that are taught in the blessed book. They will probably never be sent to the penitentiary. Moral teachings, however, focus on you. They fix the mind and the eye on self and looking at self. But they will never cause anyone to know Christ in grace or in providence. We preach Christ and him crucified so that sinners might see him and know him, 'that all men through him might believe' and worship him whom we preach (1 Corinthians 2:2-5; 2 Corinthians 4:5, 6).

Can you say, with John the Baptist, 'I knew him not', but now I know him (2 Corinthians 5:16, 17; John 17:3), because the Spirit of God has opened and applied to me the word of God, giving me faith in him who is the Christ of God'? May God the Holy Spirit grant you grace to know my Saviour!

Chapter 12

Peter's Four Calls

'Again the next day after John stood, and two of his disciples; And looking upon Jesus as he walked, he saith, Behold the Lamb of God! And the two disciples heard him speak, and they followed Jesus. Then Jesus turned, and saw them following, and saith unto them, What seek ye? They said unto him, Rabbi, (which is to say, being interpreted, Master,) where dwellest thou? He saith unto them, Come and see. They came and saw where he dwelt, and abode with him that day: for it was about the tenth hour. One of the two which heard John speak, and followed him, was Andrew, Simon Peter's brother. He first findeth his own brother Simon, and saith unto him, We have found the Messias, which is, being interpreted, the Christ. And he brought him to Jesus. And when Jesus beheld him, he said, Thou art Simon the son of Jona: thou shalt be called Cephas, which is by interpretation, A stone' (John 1:35-42).

In these few short verses we have the beginning of the New Testament church, the calling of the Saviour's first disciples. These first three disciples are Andrew and his brother Simon. The third disciple, that unnamed man who with Andrew left John the Baptist and 'followed Jesus', was probably the Apostle John, who always preferred to conceal his identity, never referring to himself by name. As we look at this passage of scripture together, I will call your attention to five things set before us by the Spirit of God.

Faithful Preaching
First, the Spirit of God here shows us an example of faithful preaching (vv. 35-37). The first time that John the Baptist cried, 'Behold the Lamb of John God',

it appears that no one heard his message. No one began following Christ. None obeyed the preacher. None believed on the Son of God. What did John do? Did he quit preaching? No. Did he decide that preaching was now out of date, that educated people required something more than preaching? No. John just kept on doing what he had been doing, what he was sent to do. The next day, he saw the Saviour passing by. Again, he pointed to him and cried, 'Behold the lamb of God'!

The Lord Jesus Christ is the Lamb of God, that Lamb portrayed in all the scriptures, who has, by the sacrifice of himself, put away sin. He is the Lamb set forth in the paschal lamb and typified by that lamb of the morning and evening sacrifices offered every day in the temple at Jerusalem. He is that Lamb without blemish and without spot, who was foreordained as our sin-atoning Sacrifice and Substitute (1 Peter 1:19). In his humiliation, he is the Lamb of sacrifice. In his resurrection, he is the prevailing Lion of the tribe of Judah (Revelation 5:5). As the King of Zion, he is the Ruler of heaven and earth to whom every man must send a lamb (Isaiah 16:1).

God's servants never adjust or alter their message for any reason. Whether men hear or refuse to hear, we will not change our message to suit them. John cried, 'Behold the Lamb of God that taketh away the sin of the world.' It appears that no one responded in any way to his message. So the next day, he went out and preached the very same message. That day, two men heard him and believed. Those two men left John and 'followed Jesus'.

I have no doubt these things are recorded in holy scripture to show us by example how God's servants serve the souls of men. It is by the preaching of Christ that sinners are converted. It is by gospel preaching that God calls out his elect. It is by the preaching of the cross that eternity bound sinners are snatched from the clutches of Satan as brands from the burning (1 Corinthians 1:18-25; 2:1-5; 9:16; Galatians 6:14; 2 Corinthians 5:17-6:2). The preaching of the gospel is the power of God unto salvation. Nothing else is!

It is by this means, the foolishness of preaching, that God has ordained the salvation of chosen sinners (Romans 10:17). Let the world laugh and mock. We will not lay aside this mighty weapon of warfare against the gates of hell. It is like the ram's horns by which the walls of Jericho fell down. The preaching of the gospel, the blowing of the jubilee trumpet, is mighty to the pulling down of strongholds. The story of the crucified Lamb of God has proved to be the power of God unto salvation in every age. Those who have done most for Christ's cause in every part of the world have been men like John the Baptist. They have not cried, Behold me, or Behold the church, or Behold the ordinances, but 'Behold the Lamb of God'. If souls are to be saved, men must be pointed directly to Christ, the Lamb of God!

Let every preacher of the gospel patiently continue in his labour, preaching Christ. Preach him again and again, as the 'Lamb of God that taketh away the sin of the world.' The story of grace must be told repeatedly, line upon line and precept upon precept. God's word shall not return unto him void (Isaiah 55:11).

True Christianity
Second, we see in the conduct of these two disciples a picture of true Christianity. We are told that these two men 'followed Jesus'. The Saviour graciously received them and made himself known to them as they followed him. This was the most blessed day of their lives. From that day on, these two men were Christ's men. They took up the cross, and followed him.

They continued with him in his temptations. They followed him wherever he went. They became chosen apostles, master builders in the temple of grace. Christianity is following Christ, no more and no less than following Christ. Believers are people who 'follow the Lamb whithersoever he goeth'. We seek in all things to follow the doctrine of Christ and the example of Christ (John 13:1-17; Ephesians 4:32-5:2), by the Spirit of Christ. True Christians are people who follow Christ; and they follow him to the end.

Christ's Abode
Third, we see these two disciples as they are received and taught by the Master (vv. 38, 39). 'Then Jesus turned, and saw them following, and saith unto them, What seek ye? They said unto him, Rabbi, (which is to say, being interpreted, Master,) where dwellest thou? He saith unto them, Come and see. They came and saw where he dwelt, and abode with him that day: for it was about the tenth hour'.

The Master asked them what they were seeking, not because he needed to know, but because they needed to know. Take the Saviour's question personally. 'What seek ye?' What is it that you are seeking? Watch their answer. It may seem a strange response to some. To others it is the very response of their own hearts. They said, this is the thing we must know, 'Master, where dwellest thou?'

Is this the earnest quest of your soul? Do you cry like Job of old, 'Oh that I knew where I might find him! that I might come even to his seat' (Job 23:3)? The Master says, 'Come and see.' Come, follow me, and you shall see! Let me show you where he dwells (Isaiah 57:15; Matthew 18:20; Revelation 3:20).

His Dwelling Place Is His People
Isaiah 57:15 says 'For thus saith the high and lofty One that inhabiteth eternity, whose name is Holy; I dwell in the high and holy place, with him also that is

of a contrite and humble spirit, to revive the spirit of the humble, and to revive the heart of the contrite ones.'

Has God, by his Spirit, caused you to hear the Saviour's voice and open to him? Has he broken you and made you contrite before him? I beg for such grace in my soul! May God the Holy Spirit make me what my Father would have me to be, that the triune God may ever dwell in me! The heaven and the heaven of heavens cannot contain our God, the infinite Spirit! Yet, he promises to dwell with his people on the earth, the broken-hearted, the humble, and the contrite. Oh for grace and a sanctity of heart and mind to possess such mercies and be the dwelling place of God! If we are God's, our bodies are the temple of God who dwells in us!

Still, there is more. The Lord's dwelling place is our meeting place, the church of the living God, the assembly of his saints in holy worship (Matthew 18:20; Revelation 3:20; 1 Corinthians 3:16). There is only one place on earth where God our Saviour has promised to meet with and manifest himself to his people, and that place is the assembly of his saints for public worship. Blessed are they who have the privilege of meeting with the saints of God in the house of God to hear the gospel of God to worship the living God. Wherever such gatherings are found, the Spirit of God is present, Christ our Saviour is present, and our heavenly Father is present!

Christ's Witness
Fourth, as soon as Andrew found Christ he became the faithful witness of Christ. He went out and found his brother Simon and brought him to the Saviour (vv. 40-42). Andrew said to his brother Simon, 'We have found the Messiah, the Christ'! We have found him of whom Moses and the prophets wrote: the Lamb of God; the woman's Seed; Abraham's Seed; the One Manoah saw; the true Nazarite; Jehovah's Servant; the Firstborn; the One Isaiah saw in his glory, the Substitute; David's Son; David's Lord; God's Salvation!

Like one who has unexpectedly heard good news, he ran to tell it to his brother, the one nearest and dearest to him. His heart was full of excitement. He had to tell what he knew. And by his testimony, Peter first received light. Peter was brought to the Saviour by the testimony of his brother. He saw no mighty miracle wrought. He was not convinced by any powerful reasoning. He simply heard his brother tell him that he had found the Saviour. The simple witness of a caring brother was the first link in the chain by which Peter was drawn out of the world and joined to Christ.

May God the Holy Spirit make Andrews of all his saints! Well it would be for immortal souls if all who have been converted themselves would speak to their friends and relatives and tell them they have found the Christ. How much good might be done? How many might be led to the Lord? The work of testifying the gospel of the grace of God ought not to be left to preachers alone. All who have received mercy ought to find a tongue and declare what God has done for their souls. All who have been delivered from the power of the devil ought to 'go home and tell their friends what great things God has done for them' (Mark 5:19). Every believer ought to be a missionary to his family, children, neighbours, and friends.

'We have found the Christ'. Do not be afraid of such a statement. All who have found the Christ have been found of Christ, and know that they have been found of him. All who seek him by faith shall find him (Jeremiah 29:10-14).

Peter's Calls
Fifth, I want you to see that this man Peter experienced four gracious, distinct calls from the Lord. They were given and experienced in a certain order; and both the calls themselves and the order in which they were given are instructive.

Peter was called to become a follower of Christ, a disciple, by the testimony of his brother, Andrew.

That is what we have before us in John 1. This is the beginning of grace in the soul. The Lord Jesus Christ begins by first teaching us who we are, showing us our sin, and causing us to know our need of him, and our own sin. Then he reveals himself to us as the Lamb of God, who has put away sin by the sacrifice of himself.

In the fourth chapter of Matthew's Gospel Peter was called by the Lord Jesus, along with his brother Andrew, to abandon all earthly pursuits and devote himself entirely to the cause of Christ as a preacher of the gospel with him (Matthew 4:17-22).

Both Peter and Andrew were believers, true disciples, before they were called to be preachers. They were industrious, labouring men, serving the Lord as fishermen when he called them to be fishers of men. Those men God puts in the work of the ministry are not lazy dolts, but responsible men who work.

The Lord Jesus called Peter to be an apostle (Mark 3:13-16). Some men God sets apart for very special purposes, for works for which he alone can equip them. Certainly, that was true regarding the prophets and the apostles of old. Such men, being called of God to very great work, stand in the forefront of the Master's army. That means that they are sure to bear the full force of Satan's assaults. Peter was just such a man; and he once failed and fell miserably. The Lord Jesus, you will remember, warned him of what he must endure, assuring him that he had prayed for him. Then he said to Peter, 'And when thou art converted, strengthen thy brethren' (Luke 22:32; John 13:37-14:3).

In John 21 we read of Peter's fourth call, the faithful Saviour's sweet, gracious call of restoration, a call every heaven born soul is sure to need, sooner or later (John 21:1-18).

Blessed Saviour, what reason have we to lift our hearts with gratitude and praise to you, because you will never leave us to ourselves! As you restored Peter from his horrible fall, so you alone are the Restorer of our poor souls in our countless falls!

It is a great mercy of our God, and one we commonly fail to appreciate, a mercy for which none of us are sufficiently thankful, that the Lord God graciously hedges us about with strong restraints of providence and omnipotent grace, keeping his people from those grave, outward sins that give Zion's enemies occasion to blaspheme the name our God and mock his gospel. He plants his fear deep in the heart and causes a well of living water to flow through the soul, and keeps us (for the most part) from great acts of iniquity in our outward lives. How we ought to thank him for this great mercy every day, every hour, every moment!

Yes, it is true, sometimes that man who has found grace in the eyes of the Lord will be found in a drunken stupor, with his shame uncovered, in naked sin before the reprobate; and the reprobate will have a hey-day exposing the shame. Sometimes a man of great faith will choose to pitch his tent toward Sodom and choose to stay in the chosen place of wickedness. Sometimes the mighty Samson will lay his head in Delilah's lap. It has happened that a man after God's own heart has committed adultery and even murder. Sometimes even the wisest man upon the earth will bow to the will of a wicked wife and worship at the altar of an idol. Once in a while a great and truly faithful preacher of the gospel, like Peter, will deny the Lord Jesus. Sometimes the most soundly orthodox and most useful and most used of preachers will shave his head and take a Jewish vow.

Such sad falls do occur. They are plainly recorded in holy scripture for our learning and admonition; but they are not common occurrences. For the most part, God's saints in this world are graciously kept from such outward displays of iniquity and sin by the restraints his grace and his providence.

Yet, though we are usually kept from grave and gross outward wickedness, the righteous do fall and all who are righteous know that they fall seven times in a day. 'A just man falleth seven times' (Proverbs 24:16). 'Seven times'! That is to say, 'In the totality of his being, in all that he is and does, the righteous man, the just one continually falls.' Still, Christ is our Keeper and the Restorer of our souls. 'Rejoice not against me, O mine enemy: when I fall, I shall arise; when I sit in darkness, the LORD shall be a light unto me' (Micah 7:8).

Chapter 13

'no guile!' No Exaggeration!

'The day following Jesus would go forth into Galilee, and findeth Philip, and saith unto him, Follow me. Now Philip was of Bethsaida, the city of Andrew and Peter. Philip findeth Nathanael, and saith unto him, We have found him, of whom Moses in the law, and the prophets, did write, Jesus of Nazareth, the son of Joseph. And Nathanael said unto him, Can there any good thing come out of Nazareth? Philip saith unto him, Come and see. Jesus saw Nathanael coming to him, and saith of him, Behold an Israelite indeed, in whom is no guile! Nathanael saith unto him, Whence knowest thou me? Jesus answered and said unto him, Before that Philip called thee, when thou wast under the fig tree, I saw thee. Nathanael answered and saith unto him, Rabbi, thou art the Son of God; thou art the King of Israel. Jesus answered and said unto him, Because I said unto thee, I saw thee under the fig tree, believest thou? thou shalt see greater things than these. And he saith unto him, Verily, verily, I say unto you, Hereafter ye shall see heaven open, and the angels of God ascending and descending upon the Son of man' (John 1:43-51).

When the Lord Jesus saw Nathanael coming to him, he said something that demands our attention. The Son of God, who sees all and knows all, he from whom nothing can be hid, before whose eyes all things are naked and opened, says of this man Nathanael, 'Behold an Israelite indeed, in whom is no guile!'

Only four times in holy scripture do we read of people being free of guile; here, in Psalms 32:2; 1 Peter 2:22, and in Revelation 14:5. In Psalms 32 we are told that the forgiven sinner is one in whose spirit there is no guile. In 1 Peter 2:22 the Holy Spirit tells us that our Lord Jesus had no guile. And in Revelation 14:5 we are told that those who stand before God in heaven have no guile. We

101

read in Revelation 21:27 that none can enter that blessed place called heaven who have any guile, but only those whose names were written as perfect and without guile in 'the book of life of the Lamb slain from the foundation of the world' (Revelation 21:27).

All who are accepted of God are without guile; and when God declares them without guile, there is no exaggeration in the declaration.

In this portion of holy scripture the Spirit of God tells us about the Lord Jesus calling two of his early disciples, Philip and Nathanael. Everything in these verses is precious, sweet and instructive. May God the Spirit write their lessons upon our hearts.

'Jesus would'

First, we are told that the Lord Jesus came into Galilee because he would. 'The day following Jesus would go forth into Galilee' (v. 43). It was his will, resolution, and determination to return to Galilee. Everything our Lord did was on purpose, and everything he does now is on purpose. It was his will, his determined, unalterable purpose, to come to Galilee, there to begin his ministry and his miracles in fulfilment of the scriptures (Isaiah 9:1, 2). It was his will to come to Galilee because Philip and Nathanael were both in Galilee, and the time had now come when Philip and Nathanael must be called.

Look at verses 43-45. We are told plainly that the Lord Jesus found Philip in verse 43. Then, in verse 45, Philip told Nathanael, 'We have found the Messiah.' Which is true? Did the Saviour find Philip, or did Philip find him? Without question, all who get Christ seek him. Seeking him with all our hearts, we find him (Jeremiah 29:11-14). Then, finding him, we discover that we began seeking him because he had found us by his grace. Knowing where he was, as the Shepherd and Bishop of souls, the Lord Jesus looked Philip up, found him out, and called him by his grace. When he was found of the Saviour, Philip found the Saviour. All who are saved, are saved by the will of God our Saviour; and they gladly acknowledge that to be the case (Romans 9:16; John 15:16).

> I sought the Lord, and afterward I knew
> He moved my soul to seek Him, seeking me;
> It was not I that found, O Saviour true,
> No, I was found of Thee.

> Thou didst reach forth Thy hand and mine enfold;
> I walked and sank not on the storm-vexed sea,
> 'Twas not so much that I on Thee took hold,
> As Thou, dear Lord, on me.

'no guile!' No Exaggeration!

I find, I walk, I love, but, O the whole
Of love is but my answer, Lord, to Thee;
For Thou wert long beforehand with my soul,
Always Thou lovedst me.

Same But Different
Second, we see in the experiences of Philip and Nathanael that, though all God's elect experience the same saving operations of his grace, our experiences are all somewhat different. Every saved sinner's experience of grace is as singular as his finger prints.

We are told here of a man named Philip being added to the Lord's disciples. But unlike Andrew and Peter and John, Philip was called directly by Christ himself. He does not appear to have been one of those influenced by the ministry of John the Baptist. Philip was not brought to the Saviour by the witness of a faithful and zealous brother or friend. Yet, his faith in Christ was just as true as that of Andrew, Peter and John. They embraced the same Saviour, believed the same gospel, served the same Master, and reached the same home at last; but each one experienced God's salvation a little differently.

That fact is very important. It throws light on the history of all God's people in every age, and of every tongue. There are diversities of operations in the saving of souls. All true Christians are led by one Spirit, washed in one blood, serve one Lord, lean on one Saviour, and believe one gospel. All are saved by the same grace, through the same blood, by the same Spirit, and have the same Saviour; but all are not converted in precisely the same way. The experience of grace differs. In conversion the Holy Spirit acts as a sovereign. He calls every one severally as he will. A recognition of this would save us much trouble. We must beware of making the experience of other believers the measure of our own; and we must beware of denying another's grace because his experience is not the same as ours. 'Dost thou believe on the Son of God?' That is the only question of importance.

Christ In The Old Testament
Third, the Holy Spirit here reminds us that the message of the Old Testament is the same as that of the New: Christ crucified. We do not have the old Bible and the new Bible. The Bible, the word of God, is one; and its message is one. It is the gospel of Christ. When Philip described Christ to Nathanael, he said, 'We have found him of whom Moses in the law and the prophets did write, Jesus of Nazareth, the son of Joseph' (v. 45).

103

All the Old Testament speaks of just one 'Him'. Christ is the sum and substance of the Old Testament. To him the earliest promises pointed in the days of Adam, Enoch, and Noah, and Abraham, Isaac, and Jacob. To him every sacrifice pointed in the ceremonial worship appointed at Mount Sinai. Of him every high priest was a type, every part of the tabernacle a shadow, and every judge and deliverer of Israel a picture.

If we read only that which was written by Moses in the books of the law, the Pentateuch, we would see the Christ everywhere in the first five books of the Bible. He is the Seed of the woman that would break the serpent's head, and the Seed of Abraham, in whom all nations would be blessed. He is Shiloh, to whom the gathering of the people would be, and the great Prophet like Moses himself, whom God would raise up among the children of Israel, whom they would obey

Not only is Christ crucified the message of Moses, he is the message of all the prophets. 'We have found him of whom Moses in the law and the prophets did write'. All the law and all the prophets spoke of him. They wrote of his birth through a virgin's womb and the place of his birth, Bethlehem. The prophets spoke of the Saviour's sufferings and the glory that should follow. And they wrote about his resurrection from the dead, his ascension to heaven and exaltation at the right hand of God, and many things relating to his person, offices, and work as Jehovah's righteous servant.

They described him plainly as the King of the house of David, who came to be David's Lord as well as his son. He is the Lamb foretold by Isaiah, the righteous Branch mentioned by Jeremiah, the true Shepherd described by Ezekiel, the Messenger of the Covenant promised by Malachi, and the Messiah who, according to Daniel, was to be cut off, not for himself, but for the people.

If you want to know who those saints of old trusted, just read the Old Testament. When Philip said to Nathanael, 'We have found him of whom Moses in the law and the prophets did write', Nathanael knew immediately that Philip was saying, 'Nathanael, we have found the Christ!' The Person they all saw afar off, on whom they all fixed their eyes, was one and the same Christ we trust and worship. The Spirit which was in them testified of Christ (1 Peter 1:11).

Do we find it difficult to see Christ in the Old Testament? If we do, the fault is all our own. It is our spiritual blindness and ignorance that is to blame, not the imaginary ambiguity of the book. The eyes of our understanding need to be enlightened. The veil needs to be taken away. Let us pray, as we open this book, 'O Spirit of God, open this book to my heart and open my heart to this book. Take the things of Christ written upon these pages and show them to me.' The whole book of God is about our Lord Jesus Christ and his glorious accomplishments as our God-man Mediator (John 5:39).

The Nazarite

Then, having given this general account of him, Philip proceeds to name him particularly and affirms that the Christ, the Messiah, is 'Jesus of Nazareth, the son of Joseph.' His name is Jesus, Saviour, of Nazareth. This is that One who is the Nazarene. In God's wise and good providence, our Saviour was brought to Nazareth as a baby by Joseph that he might in fulfilment of the Old Testament prophecy be called a Nazarene (Numbers 6). Let me show you something here. Turn to Matthew 2:23.

'And he came and dwelt in a city called Nazareth: that it might be fulfilled which was spoken by the prophets, he shall be called a Nazarene' (Matthew 2:23). Where in the Old Testament is there a prophecy that says, 'He shall be called a Nazarene'? Have you ever tried to find such a prophecy? If you have, I am sure you were perplexed, because there is no such statement in the Old Testament. In fact, the statement is not found anywhere in the Bible, except in Matthew 2:23. The town of Nazareth was such a small, insignificant place in Zebulun that it is not even mentioned in the Old Testament. So where did Matthew get the idea that the Old Testament prophesied, 'He shall be called a Nazarene'? Did he take an oral tradition and call it a prophecy of the Old Testament? Was he mistaken? Is this an error found in the Bible? Such questions cannot be considered by one who believes God.

Must we simply say to ourselves, 'The fact that I cannot find where it is written in the Old Testament that "He shall be called a Nazarene" does not mean anything. Matthew wrote it by divine inspiration. God the Holy Spirit who inspired this sentence is the same Holy Spirit who inspired the Old Testament writings; and he knows what he wrote better than I do.' That's a pretty good way to handle the text. In fact, that is exactly the way I have handled it for years.

But the fact that the Spirit of God says it is there means that it is there. This is a prophecy written in bold letters throughout the Old Testament scriptures, 'He shall be called a Nazarene.' Everything regarding the law of the Nazarites, as well as the whole Volume of the Old Testament scriptures, declares that he who is the Christ is that One who is pre-eminently the Nazarite, the Separated One. The Jews, contemptuously, called our Redeemer the Nazarite or Nazarene. Spitting on the ground in disgust, his detractors hissed out the name 'Nazarene', as if it were the climax of contempt. Yet, that blessed Nazarene, triumphant and glorious, 'Jesus of Nazareth', is that One whose glory is great in salvation! His is the greatest name among men.

Blind Bartimaeus understood perfectly well that the Christ, the Messiah, would be called 'The Nazarene'. When he heard that it was 'Jesus of Nazareth' who passed his way in Jericho, his heart was filled with hope of mercy from 'the Son of David' (Mark 10:46-48). Dishonoured by his foes, he is adored among his friends. While others deride him as 'a Nazarene', we adore him as Christ the Nazarene, Jehovah-Jesus, King of kings, and Lord of lords.

This great Saviour is the Nazarene (Numbers 6), our mighty, all-glorious Samson. In his death as our Substitute, he destroyed our enemies. In his resurrection, on the third day after his death, he awoke and carried away the gates of the city – bolt, bar, and posts – unto a high mountain.

The gates Samson carried away, we are told, were very large. Yet, Samson snatched them out of the ground, carried them on his shoulders up a mountain next to Hebron some twenty miles; but, by comparison, that was nothing! Our all-glorious Christ was laid in the sepulchre. It was sealed with a huge stone. Soldiers were appointed to keep watch over the tomb, while all hell trembled. Yet, at the appointed time, he arose from the dead, broke the iron bars of death, hell, and the grave, and ascended up into heaven, and laid claim to glory land as our Representative and Forerunner, declaring himself the victorious, all-glorious Son of God, the Sun of Righteousness arisen with healing under his wings! Under all that weight and burden of our sin, he never even staggered!

Scepticism Answered
Fourth, in verse 46 we see the best reply that one can ever give to scepticism. Nathanael's mind was full of doubts about the Saviour of whom Philip spoke. 'Can there any good thing', he said, 'come out of Nazareth?' To Nathanael's scepticism, Philip replied, 'Come and see.' In verse 39, when Andrew and John asked him where he dwelt, our Lord Jesus said to them, 'Come and see.' But there the words are slightly different. Our Saviour's words in verse 39 are emphatic and sure. He said, 'Come and you shall see.' Philip's words to Nathanael, though the same in English, are different in the Greek text. Philip's words essentially mean, 'The only way to see for yourself is to come to him. Come, and it may be he will give you eyes to see. But if you refuse to come, you will never see.'

Wiser counsel he could not have given. If Philip reasoned with Nathanael, he could not have made him see. But by urging him to come, to prove the matter for himself, he showed his entire confidence in the truth of his own assertion and his willingness to have it tested and proved.

We should never be afraid to deal with people about their souls just as Philip dealt with Nathanael. Indeed, always deal with immortal souls this way. 'Come and see.' We have no secrets. We have nothing to conceal. 'Faith cometh by hearing and hearing by the word of God.' Those who do the most good for immortal souls are simple believers who say to their friends, 'I have found a Saviour; come and see him.'

Greater Things

Fifth, in the last verses of this portion of scripture Nathanael saw a great display of Christ's eternal Godhead in his great omniscience. A display by which Nathanael was convinced that he is indeed the Christ. But our Saviour told him that he would see something greater than that (vv. 47-51). This promise is our Lord's promise to all who believe him. 'Thou shalt see greater things than these ... Verily, verily, I say unto you, Hereafter ye shall see heaven open, and the angels of God ascending and descending upon the Son of man.' With those words, our Lord Jesus promises sweet Bethel-visits, like the ladder of Jacob, to all his redeemed. These sweet visits by which he proves himself over and over to our souls are greater things than the mere revelation of divine omniscience and omnipotence. Even the demons have those revelations. But only saved sinners find all the blessings of grace descending from heaven in Christ and realise that they descend only because all the demands of God's law and justice ascended with Christ.

No Guile

Now, let me draw your attention to our Saviour's words about this man Nathanael in verse 47. 'Jesus saw Nathanael coming to him, and saith of him, Behold an Israelite indeed, in whom is no guile!' Nathanael made no protest, but seemed to recognise immediately that the Lord Jesus truly knew him.

First, the Lord Jesus tells us that Nathanael was an Israelite indeed. He was not simply one who was a physical descendant of Abraham (Romans 9:6), but an Israelite indeed, one of the 'children of promise' (Galatians 4:28), one of 'the Israel of God', of Abraham's spiritual seed, one of God's true Israel, an heir of covenant grace.

The second thing our Lord Jesus says about Nathanael is the matter of great importance. 'Behold an Israelite indeed in whom is no guile!' We are often urged to be without guile. But here our Lord declares of a man, 'Behold no guile!' How are we to take those words? Guile is hypocrisy, deceit, cunning, craftiness, duplicity, dishonesty. Does our Saviour mean for us to understand that Nathanael had no guile?

In Psalms 32:1, 2 we discover that a man in whom there is no guile is a man who is forgiven of all sin by the precious, sin-atoning blood of Christ (Romans 4:8). Nathanael was a true child of God, a true believer in difficult times. He was one of a very little flock. Like Simeon and Anna, he was living by faith and waiting prayerfully for the promised Redeemer when our Lord began his ministry. He had that which grace alone can give, an honest heart, a heart without guile.

Without question, pardoned sinners are upright, righteous, and without guile in the course of their lives. They are not dishonest, hypocritical people.

The Lord God declares of all his children that they are 'children that will not lie' (Isaiah 63:8). But that cannot be our Lord's meaning here. He here declares that Nathanael was a man in whom there was 'no guile!' and asserts that they and only they in whom is no guile are true Israelites. Yet, every heaven-born soul knows the plague of his own heart. All who are taught of God know that they are, by nature, full of guile.

When our Lord declares that Nathanael is without guile and asserts that all who are Israelites indeed have no guile, was he exaggerating, or was he stating the truth? He was stating the truth, pure, absolute truth. All who trust Christ are Israelites indeed (Philippians 3:3). All God's elect are a people in whom there is no guile, no duplicity, no hypocrisy, nothing false. This is no avowal of personal, or personally accomplished holiness. Those who know the plague of their own hearts know better. God's people are a people with no guile representatively because we stand guileless before the holy Lord God because we are in Christ, one with Christ.

And God's people are a people with no guile eternally because we have been accepted in Christ, the Lamb slain from the foundation of the world, from eternity, 'accepted in the Beloved' (Ephesians 1:3-6).

They have no guile in their record. The Lord God declares that there is no sin, no iniquity, no guile recorded against us in the record books of heaven (Jeremiah 50:20).

They have no guile in their spirit. In the new birth God the Holy Spirit creates in the chosen, redeemed sinner a new nature that is truly righteous and holy, a nature that cannot sin (2 Corinthians 5:17; Ephesians 4:24; 1 John 3:6-10). That new nature is 'Christ in you' (Colossians 1:27; 2 Peter 1:4).

Because they are in Christ and Christ is in them, every saved sinner is, like Nathanael, an Israelite indeed in whom is no guile! Are you an Israelite indeed, in whom there is no guile?

Chapter 14

Glory Revealed In The Creation Of Faith

'And the third day there was a marriage in Cana of Galilee; and the mother of Jesus was there: And both Jesus was called, and his disciples, to the marriage. And when they wanted wine, the mother of Jesus saith unto him, They have no wine. Jesus saith unto her, Woman, what have I to do with thee? mine hour is not yet come. His mother saith unto the servants, Whatsoever he saith unto you, do it. And there were set there six waterpots of stone, after the manner of the purifying of the Jews, containing two or three firkins apiece. Jesus saith unto them, Fill the waterpots with water. And they filled them up to the brim. And he saith unto them, Draw out now, and bear unto the governor of the feast. And they bare it. When the ruler of the feast had tasted the water that was made wine, and knew not whence it was: (but the servants which drew the water knew;) the governor of the feast called the bridegroom, And saith unto him, Every man at the beginning doth set forth good wine; and when men have well drunk, then that which is worse: but thou hast kept the good wine until now. This beginning of miracles did Jesus in Cana of Galilee, and manifested forth his glory; and his disciples believed on him' (John 2:1-11).

Here we see the Lord Jesus performing his first miracle, turning water into wine at the marriage feast in Cana of Galilee. In performing this miracle the Holy Spirit specifically tells us in verse 11 that 'Jesus manifested forth his glory; and his disciples believed on him.' I take those words to mean that our faith in Christ is created and sustained by the manifestation of his glory to us.

Practical Lessons

Without question, there are several very practical lessons to be drawn from that which is recorded in John 2:1-11. Like all the miracles that were to follow, 'this beginning of miracles', performed by our Saviour just a few days after he began his public ministry, 'manifested forth his glory' and is preserved upon the pages of Inspiration for our instruction and edification. In this miracle there are five things for us to learn.

First, our Lord Jesus Christ our Saviour turned the water into wine, not by his touch, or even by his word, but by his will. This is the omnipotence of God. No prophet or apostle ever did such a thing. He who can turn ordinary water into extraordinary wine, by a mere act of his will, is the omnipotent God. If he wills my salvation, none can prevent it. If he wills my safety, none can harm me. If he wills my everlasting inheritance in heavenly glory – and he does, John 17:24 – I cannot fail to attain it.

Second, the high honour our Lord places upon marriage. By his presence at the marriage feast, the Son of God said, 'This is an honourable thing' (Genesis 1:28; 2:18-25; Hebrews 13:4). One of the first steps toward moral decadence in any society is a low esteem for this ordinance of God. Where there is no sanctity of marriage, there is no regard for God or his law, no regard for moral decency, and no regard for human life. These things stand and fall together!

Third, the propriety of feasting and laughter. In this passage of scripture the Son of God gives his approval both to the party and to the moderate use of wine. 'A feast is made for laughter, and wine maketh merry' (Ecclesiastes 7:19). Christianity was never meant to make people miserable. On the contrary, true Christianity increases real joy among men and makes people happy in this world, as well as in the world to come.

Fourth, the blessedness of obedience to Christ. 'Whatsoever he saith unto you, do it' (v. 5). The Son of God could have supplied all the wine that was needed without employing these servants. He did not need them! But they would have missed the blessed benefit of being instruments by whom the Son of God brought his miraculous boon of mercy to the wedding guests.

Fifth, the character of Christ's gifts. The Son of God always saves the best wine until the last. Marvellous as his grace is, it is only the earnest of our inheritance, a mere foretaste of the glory that is to be revealed in us! In spiritual matters, the best is always kept for the last. The sorrow of repentance is followed by the sweetness of forgiveness. The bitterness of conviction is followed by the gladness of conversion. After the cross follows the crown. After the valley of the shadow of death comes the glory of life eternal with no sorrow, no sin and no death!

Spiritual Significance

Those are very practical things that should not be overlooked; but we should always look beyond the letter of the word for that which is spiritual. Did you notice that this chapter begins with the word 'And'? That indicates that what we read about here is closely connected with what we saw in the first chapter. One of the things prominent in chapter 1 is the failure of Judaism and the turning away from it to Christ. The Priests and Levites came to John to inquire who he was. He said, 'There standeth one among you whom ye know not' (John 1:19-26). They did not know the forerunner and did not know the Christ (John 1:11).

'He came unto his own, and his own received him not' (John 1:11). The Jews were his own nation and all the ordinances of the law (Judaism) were his own things; but neither his own nation nor his own things would have him.

The Holy Spirit uses those exact, same two words, 'his own', in John 13:1 to speak of his true people, God's elect, those who are truly, everlastingly, eternally 'his own'. 'Having loved his own which were in the world, he loved them unto the end.'

'The law and the prophets were until John' (Luke 16:16). John wound up the Old Testament system. When Christ appeared, Judaism was an empty, meaningless, dead, useless religious form. Nothing else! The wine was gone. It had given out. Wine in scripture is the emblem of joy, 'wine maketh glad the heart of man' (Psalms 104:15). Judaism still existed as a religious system, but the joy was gone. It gave no comfort to the heart. It had degenerated into a cold, mechanical routine, utterly destitute of joy in God.

They set six water pots before the Lord Jesus. Those empty water pots of stone represent religion without Christ. Six is the number of man. It was on the sixth day man was created. Six is the number of the beast, antichrist (Revelation 13:18). There were six water pots, not seven, the number of perfection. All that was left of Judaism was the flesh. The feasts of the Lord had become the feasts of the Jews (John 2:13).

The water pots were water pots of stone, not silver which speaks of redemption, not gold which symbolises the divine glory. And they were empty! These water pots were used by the Jews in their observance of their religious traditions, their various religious washings (v. 6); but they were empty. Religion without Christ is empty of joy or comfort!

Notice, too, the Spirit of God specifically calls our attention to the fact that this marriage feast took place on the third day. 'And the third day there was a marriage in Cana of Galilee' (v. 1). But he does not tell us when that was. We may deduce that this took place on the third day after John the Baptist first declared, 'Behold the Lamb of God that taketh away the sin of the world', but we are not specifically told. Why? Is it because there is something significant

111

about the third day? I think so. The third day is the day of resurrection. It was on the third day in creation that the earth was brought forth from its watery grave (Genesis 1:9-11). Our Lord arose from the dead on the third day.

Judging by 2 Peter 3:8, this is the beginning of the third day of time since this gospel day began. Could it be that the marriage supper of the Lamb shall take place in this third day? Perhaps (Hosea 6:1, 2).

Another Marriage Feast
I have no idea when it will take place, but I do know that there is a day appointed when that marriage shall take place (Isaiah 54:1-8). The book of God says, 'Blessed are they which are called unto the marriage supper of the Lamb. And ... these are the true sayings of God' (Revelation 19:9). Jesus our Saviour will be there. All his disciples will be there. And we will never run out of wine!

'And after these things I heard a great voice of much people in heaven, saying, Alleluia; Salvation, and glory, and honour, and power, unto the Lord our God: For true and righteous are his judgments: for he hath judged the great whore, which did corrupt the earth with her fornication, and hath avenged the blood of his servants at her hand. And again they said, Alleluia. And her smoke rose up for ever and ever. And the four and twenty elders and the four beasts fell down and worshipped God that sat on the throne, saying, Amen; Alleluia. And a voice came out of the throne, saying, Praise our God, all ye his servants, and ye that fear him, both small and great. And I heard as it were the voice of a great multitude, and as the voice of many waters, and as the voice of mighty thunderings, saying, Alleluia: for the Lord God omnipotent reigneth. Let us be glad and rejoice, and give honour to him: for the marriage of the Lamb is come, and his wife hath made herself ready. And to her was granted that she should be arrayed in fine linen, clean and white: for the fine linen is the righteousness of saints. And he saith unto me, Write, Blessed are they which are called unto the marriage supper of the Lamb. And he saith unto me, These are the true sayings of God' (Revelation 19:1-9).

The Wine
The water we are told was made wine (v. 9). The water was not made to look like wine. It was made wine. The water was not made to taste like wine. It was made wine. The water was not treated as though it were wine. It was made wine. Here are three other things made to be what they could never be, had not God done the work. The Word was made flesh (John 1:14). Christ was made sin (2 Corinthians 5:21). We have been made the righteousness of God in him (2 Corinthians 5:21).

112

The good wine of the gospel is Christ himself. When he was made sin for us, it was he and he alone who trod the wine-press of his Father's wrath as our Substitute, when the Lord bruised him and put him to grief. This is the wine that cheers both God and men. When God's justice took the full draught of Christ's blood for the sins of his people, the Lord declared himself well pleased. And when the poor sinner, by sovereign grace, is first made to drink of the blood of the Lamb, he feels constrained to cry,

> Hallelujah! I have found Him
> Whom my soul so long has craved!
> Jesus satisfies my longings,
> Through His blood I now am saved.

Moses' first miracle turned water into blood, because the law is a ministration of death. Christ's first miracle turned water into wine, because once he comes into your life, he makes even the most common mercies (water) boons of grace. Truly, the Lord has kept the good wine until now. Never before has my soul been satisfied.

Mary And The Master
It is not accidental that the scriptures frequently show us incidents of the Lord Jesus gently reproving his mother, even publicly. He knew the papists would arise, seeking to deify Mary. Therefore, the Lord Jesus made it obvious that such heresy is altogether of man's doing. But do not imagine that the Lord Jesus was being disrespectful to his mother. He called her 'woman', because that was the common way to refer to married women respectfully. But Mary seemed to be asserting her parental authority, and the Lord Jesus let her know that that authority over him no longer existed. He teaches men (and women) to cut the apron strings! And Mary accepted the Lord's rebuke, recognised his right to act as he pleased, and left the matter entirely in his hands. What a lesson for us!

His Hour
In verse 4 the Saviour said to Mary, 'Mine hour is not yet come.' Seven references are made in the Gospel of John to that 'hour' (John 2:4, 7:30, 8:20, 12:23, 12:27, 16:32, 17:1). Our Lord had lived in quiet seclusion for thirty years. From this point on he would become a public figure and a marked man. His hour refers to the hour of his suffering and death as our Surety. This is the hour for which the world was made (John 12:27-33; Romans 5:5-11).

The Method Of Grace

We have in this story of our Lord turning the water into wine a good picture of God's method of grace, a picture of the way God saves sinners. It was the Lord Jesus Christ who performed the miracle. Yet, men were called to fetch the pots, fill them with water, draw off the wine, and carry it to the governor of the feast. The means used were human; though the power that performed the miracle was divine. It may have seemed foolish to fill the pots with water, but water is a symbol of the written word (Ephesians 5:26); and the way to bring joy and comfort to the human heart today is to fill it with the preached word. God will make it effectual (Romans 10:17).

The sinner is empty like the water pots. He receives the water of the written word at the command of Christ. The water produced the best wine by the power of Christ; and the change wrought in the new birth is a miracle of grace, as clearly miraculous as the water being turned into wine. This miracle manifested forth his glory (v. 11). The governor proclaimed it to be the best wine. Truly the grace and redemption that is ours in our Lord Jesus Christ is far better than the best the world can give.

Glory Revealed

In verse 11 we are told that our Lord Jesus, by performing this miracle, 'manifested forth his glory', and when he did, 'his disciples believed on him'. The long and short of that is just this: faith in Christ depends upon and is caused by the revelation of Christ, the manifesting forth of his glory: the glory of his person, the glory of his accomplished redemption, the glory of his all-sufficient grace, and the glory of his transforming, saving power. The Son of God takes common, ordinary things and transforms them into something that manifests forth his glory (Isaiah 6:1-7; 2 Corinthians 4:6, 7; 1 Corinthians 1:18-31).

May God the Holy Spirit grant us unceasing grace to believe on our Saviour! He promises to all who believe that they shall see the glory of God (John 11:40). 'Come and see'!

Chapter 15

Fury, Forbearance And Faith

'After this he went down to Capernaum, he, and his mother, and his brethren, and his disciples: and they continued there not many days. And the Jews' passover was at hand, and Jesus went up to Jerusalem, And found in the temple those that sold oxen and sheep and doves, and the changers of money sitting: And when he had made a scourge of small cords, he drove them all out of the temple, and the sheep, and the oxen; and poured out the changers' money, and overthrew the tables; And said unto them that sold doves, Take these things hence; make not my Father's house an house of merchandise. And his disciples remembered that it was written, The zeal of thine house hath eaten me up. Then answered the Jews and said unto him, What sign shewest thou unto us, seeing that thou doest these things? Jesus answered and said unto them, Destroy this temple, and in three days I will raise it up. Then said the Jews, Forty and six years was this temple in building, and wilt thou rear it up in three days? But he spake of the temple of his body. When therefore he was risen from the dead, his disciples remembered that he had said this unto them; and they believed the scripture, and the word which Jesus had said'.

'Now when he was in Jerusalem at the passover, in the feast day, many believed in his name, when they saw the miracles which he did. But Jesus did not commit himself unto them, because he knew all men, And needed not that any should testify of man: for he knew what was in man' (John 2:12-25).

'After this ...' In the opening verses of this chapter we see our blessed Saviour attending a wedding feast in Cana. There he performed his first miracle. Turning water into wine, by the mere exercise of his will, the Lord Jesus supplied all the guests with wine to make their hearts merry.

As we behold our Lord Jesus honouring the bridal feast with his presence and the first miracle he performed as our God-man Mediator, our hearts swell with joy in the consideration of a far more astonishing miracle, the great wonder of his grace when the Son of God first betrothed his Church to himself in righteousness and in judgment, in lovingkindness and in mercies, in faithfulness and forever (Hosea 2:19, 20).

As our Lord provided wine for this wedding party, he is, our Ishi, our Husband, ever supplying the wine of his grace to his Church, his Bride, blessing us with his presence, meeting every need, and turning all our earthly water into wine that gladdens our hearts, causing us to believe on him the more. 'This beginning of miracles did Jesus in Cana of Galilee, and manifested forth his glory; and his disciples believed on him' (v. 11).

Oh, may it please him daily to manifest forth his glory and cause us, by the sweet, effectual influences of his Spirit, to unceasingly believe him!

The Passover

'After this he went down to Capernaum, he, and his mother, and his brethren, and his disciples: and they continued there not many days' (v. 12). Our Lord's stay at Capernaum was very brief, because, as we read in verse 13, 'the Jews' passover was at hand, and Jesus went up to Jerusalem. This was about six months after our Lord's baptism. John is the only Gospel writer who tells us that our Saviour went up to Jerusalem to observe the passover four times after his baptism (2:13; 5:1; 6:4; 18:28). Because John identifies these four passovers observed by our Saviour, we know that his public ministry lasted about 3½ years.

The Lord Jesus observed those legal feasts, because he came to fulfil the law; and he did fulfil it in every detail as a man. But he fulfilled the typical ceremony completely when he died as our Substitute, at the last passover. There, at Jerusalem, upon Mount Calvary, Christ our Passover was sacrificed for us (1 Corinthians 5:7).

Temple Purged

Our Lord's second miracle is described in verses 14-17. Like the miracle in Cana, this second miracle performed by the Lord Jesus demands our attention. These two miracles are eminently significant as prophetic signs of things to come. At his first coming, the Lord of glory attended a marriage feast and purged his house, driving out all who profaned the worship of God. When he comes again, the Lord Jesus will hold a marriage feast and purify his Church.

When the Lord Jesus came into the temple, we read that he 'found in the temple those that sold oxen and sheep and doves'. Try to picture what our Lord saw when he went into the temple. What a ghastly sight was before him! There, in the temple, in the house of God, in the place where men and women gathered with their families to worship the triune God were caged birds, stalled oxen, and sheep. Hundreds of them! Imagine the stench! Men were selling them as a convenience (and for a profit, of course) to those who were too busy to bother preparing for worship, too busy to bring a suitable sacrifice to God! Money changers were scattered throughout the courtyard and at the entrance of the temple, sitting at tables to exchange money (for a fee, of course), with those who rushed to the service without the shekel of the sanctuary, with which God must be worshipped. All this was going on with the consent of greedy, self-serving priests, who turned the worship of God into a profitable business. These people professed to have a great zeal for the law of God and the things of God; but their pretended zeal sickened and enraged the Lord of glory.

As the songs of Zion were sung, while the priest read the word of God, while a man taught the scriptures, people were talking, making deals, running in and out of the place, as if they were at a sporting event! In a word, it was chaos. As it is today in most religious assemblies, so it was then. There was no reverence for God in his house and no reverence for the things of God. The Son of God was enraged by what he saw then; and he is enraged by such irreverence today.

Twice, during the three and a half years of his earthly ministry, the Lord Jesus observed the same profane behaviour of men in his Father's house, here at the beginning of his ministry and again at the end (Matthew 21:12, 13). Twice he showed his contempt for the Jews' irreverence in the strongest terms. 'The thing is doubled', J. C. Ryle observed, 'in order to impress a lesson more strongly on our minds.'

Every time I read about our Lord driving these people out of the temple, I am reminded of the young King Josiah in 2 Kings 22 and 23 repairing the breaches of the Lord's house, and remember the wise counsel Solomon gives us in Ecclesiastes 5:1, 'Keep thy foot when thou goest to the house of God'.

The Miracle

Before I get to the spiritual lesson intended by our Lord's action here, let me call your attention to the miracle before us in this passage. It is one of the greatest miracles wrought by the Son of God during his earthly ministry.

Here is the Lord Jesus going through the temple, driving everything before him, literally whipping men and beasts, driving the herds of cattle, overturning tables, and dumping men's money on the floor; and no one dared to resist him, get in his way, or even ask him what he was doing! Their minds must have been utterly overawed by some supernatural display of his invincible power as God. They saw such majesty shining forth in the face of the God-man that they were completely bowed before him. When the Lord's disciples saw what happened, they immediately realised that the scriptures were being fulfilled before their eyes. 'For the zeal of thine house hath eaten me up' (Psalms 69:9). 'My zeal hath consumed me, because mine enemies have forgotten thy words' (Psalms 119:139).

As he drove these self-serving merchandisers out of the temple, with their cattle and their money, the Saviour said, in what must have been a loud voice expressing anger, 'Make not my Father's house an house of merchandise'! No prophet ever used such language. No one but Christ ever called God his Father. And God never called any prophet his Son. This cleansing of the temple by the Christ seems to be precisely what Malachi spoke of in Malachi 3:1-5.

Spiritual Lessons
What are we to learn from this event? What lessons are being taught here? Why has God the Holy Spirit caused this record of our Lord's zeal in purging the temple to be preserved upon the pages of Inspiration? What are the spiritual lessons we are to glean from it?

As you may well know, the physical temple at Jerusalem was symbolic of three things: (1) our Lord's physical body (v. 21), (2) our bodies (1 Corinthians 6:19), and (3) the assembled Church of Christ (1 Corinthians 3:16, 17). The things we see in John 2 are to be applied to all three.

Let take them in this order, first, the temple represented each believer's body. After the temple at Jerusalem was left desolate by the Jews' rejection of Christ, the Holy Ghost came down at Pentecost and took possession of one hundred and twenty temples, so that they became the dwelling places of the Lord Jesus Christ (Acts 1:8). We are admonished repeatedly to look upon and use our bodies as God's temple, that which is dedicated to his honour. We must not defile God's temple by immoral behaviour or by idolatrous religion (1 Corinthians 6:9-20; 2 Corinthians 6:14-7:1).

Blessed Spirit of God, we give praise, with our thanks, for this record of our Saviour's zeal in purging his temple; and we beg of you our Lord, so cleanse our hearts day by day by your grace! Drive out the vain thoughts that lodge deep within our nature, defiling your dwelling place, defiling your temple. Then, by your indwelling presence, grant us grace to glorify our God in our bodies and in our spirits, which are yours, for you have bought us with your blood!

Second, the temple represented the assembled Church of God, the local Church, gathered for worship (Matthew 18:20; 1 Corinthians 3:16, 17). Let us take great care that we do not defile the house of God with corrupt behaviour, strife, gossip, slander, corrupt religious ceremonies, the wood, hay and stubble of human inventions, or with corrupt doctrine

Christ's Body

But, if we read on in John 2, we see that the temple also represents the physical body of our Lord Jesus Christ. Our Saviour seems to have shone the beam of his deity, as our mighty Samson, laying heaps upon heaps, as he marched through his house.

'Then answered the Jews, and said unto him, What sign shewest thou unto us, seeing that thou doest these things? Jesus answered and said unto them, Destroy this temple, and in three days I will raise it up. Then said the Jews, Forty and six years was this temple in building, and wilt thou rear it up in three days? But he spake of the temple of his body. When therefore he was risen from the dead, his disciples remembered that he had said this unto them: and they believed the scripture, and the word which Jesus had said' (vv. 18-22).

It appears, from these men asking the Lord Jesus to show them his authority for purging the temple, that they were unwittingly convinced that he was indeed the Christ.[1] Had this not been so, these men would have been enraged. They would have tried to seize the Saviour and kill him, as they often did later. Instead, they did not oppose anything. They made no effort to resist anything he said or did. They simply asked for a sign of his mission as the Christ. 'What sign shewest thou unto us, seeing that thou doest these things?' (v. 18).

If in the days of his humiliation such glory occasionally shone forth in the Lord Jesus as God incarnate, to the utter consternation of his enemies (John 18:6) and the comfort and joy of his saints (Matthew 17:1-5), what will it be like when he comes in his glory (2 Thessalonians 1:7-10; Revelation 1:7)?

Robert Hawker rightly observed, 'Oh! the forbearance of our adorable Lord, when driving those buyers and sellers from the temple, that he drove them not into hell'!

Though he refused to give a sign to the Jews, though he refused to answer the demand of his foes, our dear Saviour gave a precious sign to his chosen, for whom he had come to lay down his life. It is for his chosen, for his redeemed, that he does all things. When he spoke of the destruction and raising up again of the temple, God the Holy Spirit tells us plainly that he was talking about his body and his resurrection from the dead three days after his crucifixion as our sin-atoning Substitute. 'He spake of the temple of his body' (v. 21; Romans 4:25).

So when the Lord Jesus arose from the dead three years later, his disciples remembered this conversation with the Jews and, by divine conviction, 'they believed the scripture, and the word which he had spoken'. That is another

---

[1] If I am not mistaken, this was their blasphemy against the Holy Spirit (Matthew 12): Though they were convinced that Jesus of Nazareth is the Christ, they ascribed to him the works of the devil, rather than bow to him.

lesson we must not fail to learn from this passage. The word of God often has its efficacy long after it is first heard.

It is upon this same testimony that the whole Church of God rests. Our Redeemer was and is 'declared to be the Son of God with power, according to the spirit of holiness, by the resurrection from the dead' (Romans 1:4). This is the Foundation upon which we are built. Christ is our Resurrection and our Life. As he lives, his redeemed shall live also. Because he lives, I shall live.

As the pillar of cloud and fire at the Red Sea was a light to Israel, but darkness to the Egyptians, this word of our Lord was blinding to the Jews, a stone of stumbling, and rock of offence; but for God's elect it stands as a blessed testimony to that glorious Rock which Jehovah laid in Zion.

The Jews used these words of our Lord as a charge of blasphemy against him, when he was arraigned before Pilate (Matthew 26:61). But we, being taught of God, see his eternal power and Godhead. 'Destroy this temple', he said, this temple of my body; and 'in three days I will raise it up'. When with wicked hands they took and crucified our Lord, they destroyed his body (Acts 2:23). Three days later, by his own almighty power, he arose from the dead.

Do not miss this: he said, 'I will raise it up'! Having loosed the pains of death, because it was not possible that he should be holden of it, he raised up his body by the power of the redemption he accomplished in the sacrifice of himself (Acts 2:24). He could not be held in the grave. The sin he bore in his body on the tree he put away, the debt we owed he fully paid, the demands of justice he fully satisfied (Romans 4:25-5:5; 1 Timothy 3:16; 1 Peter 3:18).

Hearts Read
In the last three verses of this chapter we are reminded of this solemn fact: the Son of God is he who reads and knows the hearts of all.

'Now when he was at Jerusalem at the passover, in the feast day, many believed in his name, when they saw the miracles which he did. But Jesus did not commit himself unto them, because he knew all men, And needed not that any should testify of man; for he knew what was in man'.

Who less than he who made man can know the thoughts of a man's heart (Hebrews 4:12, 13)? You may not know the difference, but he knows the difference between true faith and false faith. Natural faith, faith arising from sight, is a notion of the head. That faith which is the gift and operation of God the Holy Spirit is the commitment of the heart to Christ.[2]

Christ knows all things. He knows what is in you. He knows what is in me. He knows us. That fact terrifies, rightly terrifies the hypocrite. But this is a fact that gives indescribable comfort to the believer (John 21:15-17).

---

[2] The word translated 'believe' in verse 23 is the same word translated 'commit' in verse 24.

Chapter 16

Born Again? What Does That Mean?

'There was a man of the Pharisees, named Nicodemus, a ruler of the Jews: The same came to Jesus by night, and said unto him, Rabbi, we know that thou art a teacher come from God: for no man can do these miracles that thou doest, except God be with him. Jesus answered and said unto him, Verily, verily, I say unto thee, Except a man be born again, he cannot see the kingdom of God. Nicodemus saith unto him, How can a man be born when he is old? can he enter the second time into his mother's womb, and be born? Jesus answered, Verily, verily, I say unto thee, Except a man be born of water and of the Spirit, he cannot enter into the kingdom of God. That which is born of the flesh is flesh; and that which is born of the Spirit is spirit. Marvel not that I said unto thee, Ye must be born again. The wind bloweth where it listeth, and thou hearest the sound thereof, but canst not tell whence it cometh, and whither it goeth: so is every one that is born of the Spirit' (John 3:1-8).

Much has been said and written about Nicodemus, about him coming to the Lord Jesus by night, and about our Lord's discourse with him on the new birth. Some debate about whether Nicodemus was born again. Much has been said and written about the meaning of the word 'water' in verse 5. I will deliberately pass by all those things without comment, because I want to focus your attention on our Lord's message to Nicodemus. His message to Nicodemus is his message to sinners today. It is plain and clear. We have it stated with utmost clarity and simplicity in verse 7. 'Ye must be born again'!

'Born again'. What does that mean? These days, almost everyone talks about being born again; but virtually no one knows what the word of God teaches about the new birth. Therefore, I want to address the subject in simple, clear, unmistakable terms. I want all who read these pages to understand what the new birth is and how it is accomplished. More importantly, I want you to be born again. May God be pleased to make it so, for Christ's sake.

The religious world today, in its apostate rejection of the truth of God, has made the new birth to be nothing more than making a decision, walking an aisle, and saying a prayer. Their abuse and error regarding the new birth, might tempt us to shy away from using the term 'born again', lest we be identified with those who deny the gospel of Christ. But, no matter how much men may pervert the language and the doctrine of Christ, our Lord's admonition to Nicodemus still stands. It is as necessary and urgent today as it was when he first made it more than two thousand years ago. 'Ye must be born again'!

'Ye must be born again'! You may have been in the church for years and yet be without Christ. You may have made a profession of faith a long time ago and still be without life before God. May God the Holy Spirit cause you to hear the Saviour's word to Nicodemus and grant you his grace. 'Ye must be born again'! Read those five words, and ask God to give you wisdom and grace to understand what they mean. 'Ye must be born again'!

'Ye' is a personal word. This message is for you. I know you are moral. I know you are religious. I know you are well instructed in doctrinal truth. So was Nicodemus. He was a respected religious leader, a Pharisee, and a ruler among the Jews. Nicodemus was a teacher who taught the teachers. He was a preacher, but more. Nicodemus was a preacher who taught preachers. He was a theologian. This was a man of highest rank in the Jewish church. But he was spiritually dead. He was without life before God. He was totally ignorant of all things spiritual. He was a lost man. If you are yet without life toward God, I have this word from God for you, 'You must be born again'.

'Must' is a pressing word. Time is short. 'What shall it profit a man if he gain the whole world and lose his own soul?' This is not a good suggestion. This is not wholesome advice. This is imperative. This is vital. This is a necessity. 'You must be born again'! Otherwise, you will perish in your sins. You will die under the wrath of God! Hell will be your portion forever!

'Be' is a passive word. The new birth is not something you do. Rather, it is done to you, it is something God does for you and in you. A man has no more to do with his spiritual birth than he does with his natural birth. In this matter of regeneration man is passive. He has nothing to do with the work (John 1:12, 13). You cannot save yourself. You cannot give yourself life. You cannot be born again by something you do (Titus 3:4-6): No, not by moral reformation, not by baptism, not by religious fervour and devotion, not even by faith in Christ.

Born Again? What Does That Mean?

Faith in Christ is not the cause of the new birth. It is the result of the new birth. We believe according to the working of God's mighty power, by the operation of his grace (Ephesians 1:19; 2:8; Colossians 2:11, 12). The new birth is something done to you, for you, and in you by God's sovereign, irresistible grace. It is not something you do. 'You must BE born again'!

I fully agree with what Martin Luther had to say in this regard. 'If any man ascribes anything of salvation, even the very least thing, to the free will of man, he knows nothing of grace, and he has not learned Jesus Christ rightly.'

'Born' is a powerful word. I am talking to you about a gift; but it is not just any ordinary gift. I am talking to you about the gift of life, eternal life. When our Lord declares, 'Ye must be born again', he is saying you must be the object and recipient of divine power. Just as God created the world, God must create life in your soul. Just as God breathed into Adam and made him a living soul, so God must breathe into you the breath of life by his Spirit, or you will perish in your sins. This is what I am saying: You are spiritually dead, helplessly lost by nature. Your only hope is that God the Holy Spirit will give life to you. 'You must be born again'!

'Again' is a profound word. The new birth is a mystery of grace. It cannot be explained; neither can it be fully understood. It is a work of God beyond our comprehension. When our Lord says, 'Ye must be born again' his meaning is twofold. The word 'again' has two meanings.

First, it means, 'You must be born from above'. James tells us that 'every good and perfect gift is from above, and cometh down from the Father of lights, with whom is no variableness, neither shadow of turning.' Then, in the next verse, James tells us what he is teaching. 'Of his own will begat he us with the word of truth' (James 1:17, 18).

Second, it means, 'You must be born a second time'. Your first birth was of sinful parents, and you were born in their image. The second birth is of God, and we are born in his image. The first birth was of corruptible seed. The second birth is of incorruptible seed. Our first birth is in sin. Our second birth is in righteousness. By our first birth we were polluted and unclean. By our second birth we become holy. Our first birth was fleshy and carnal. Our second birth is spiritual and makes us spiritual. By the first birth all men are foolish and ignorant. By our second birth we become wise unto salvation. By our first birth we were slaves to sin and the lusts of the flesh. By our second birth we are made free from the dominion of sin. By our first birth we are all children of wrath. By our second birth we are children of promise. Our Lord says, 'Ye must be born again', because we were all born wrong the first time.

Our Lord said, 'Ye must be born again', because none shall ever enter into glory except those who are born again by the power and grace of God the Holy Spirit and made to live in and by the Lord Jesus Christ.

In order for God to save a sinner two things must be done. God must do something for you. And God must do something in you. Redemption is the work of God for sinners. Regeneration is the work of God in sinners. Both are the works of God. Man has nothing more to do with regeneration than he has to do with redemption. 'Salvation is of the Lord'!

> Not all the outward forms on earth,
> Nor rites that God has given,
> Nor will of man, nor blood, nor birth,
> Can raise a soul to heaven.
>
> The sovereign will of God alone
> Creates us heirs of grace;
> Born in the image of His Son,
> A new peculiar race.

Why?

Why must we be born again? There are many answers to that question in the word of God. But we will stay with our text. Our Lord gave Nicodemus three reasons why he must be born again. These three things make it imperative that you must be born again.

First, unless you are born again you cannot understand anything spiritual. 'Jesus answered and said unto him, Verily, verily, I say unto thee, Except a man be born again, he cannot see the kingdom of God' (v. 3). The natural man is totally void of spiritual understanding. You may be a logical, reasonable, rational, and well educated person among men, but with regard to the things of God you are as ignorant, foolish, and unreasonable as a madman, unless you are born again. You have no capacity for spiritual knowledge (Romans 8:5; 1 Corinthians 2:14). The heart of stone is hard, cold, unbending, unaffected.

You cannot see the spiritual nature of God's law (Matthew 5:21-27, 38, 43, 48). You cannot see the spiritual nature of sin (Matthew 15:17-19), nor the glory of God in redemption (Romans 3:24-26), nor the spiritual condition of your own heart (Jeremiah 17:9). You cannot see the spiritual nature of salvation. It is a heart work (Ezekiel 36:25-27). You cannot see the spiritual nature of obedience to God (1 Samuel 16:7; Romans 14:17). (All human religion is carnal. It has to do with carnal things.) You cannot see the spiritual nature of faith and worship (Philippians 3:3), nor the true character of God (Exodus 33:18-34:7), nor the glory of God in Christ (2 Corinthians 4:6). You cannot see the gospel of the grace of God (2 Corinthians 5:18-21).

Born Again? What Does That Mean?

Second, unless you are born again by almighty grace, you can never enter into the kingdom of God. 'Jesus answered, Verily, verily, I say unto thee, Except a man be born of water and of the Spirit, he cannot enter into the kingdom of God' (v. 5). You can reform your life without the new birth. You can be baptised without the new birth. You can join the church, be zealous in religion, teach a Bible class, serve as a deacon or elder, you can even preach with great success without being born again. But unless you are born again, you will never enter the kingdom of God. You will never be a part of the church and family of God. You will never have eternal life. You will never enter into the worship and fellowship of God's saints. You will never be admitted into the presence of God's glory in the bliss of heaven (Revelation 20:6; 21:27).

Third, all flesh is defiled. 'That which is born of the flesh is flesh; and that which is born of the Spirit is spirit' (v. 6). All flesh is corrupt. It is sinful. It is condemned. The flesh is your natural, sinful, self and all flesh must die (Psalms 51:5; 58:3; Romans 5:12; Revelation 20:11-15). Unless you are born of the Spirit, you will die in your sins, and your flesh shall be justly damned.

What is the new birth?
I cannot explain the mystery of the new birth. It is an incomprehensible work of God. But there are several things in the word of God which identify God's regenerating grace.

To be born again is to be raised from the dead (Ephesians 2:1-5). To be born again is to be made a partaker of the divine nature (2 Peter 1:4). In regeneration a new nature is created in our souls, so that men and women upon the earth are born in the image of God (Galatians 5:22). Christ is formed in us (Colossians 1:27). To be born again is to have Christ formed in us (Galatians 4:19). To have eternal life is to have the Lord Jesus Christ living in you (Galatians 2:20). To be born again is to have a good seed implanted in you by grace (1 John 3:9, 10). By nature we are all sprung from bad seed Adam. But in regeneration we are sprung from good Seed, the Lord Jesus Christ.

In summary, to be born again is to be made a new creature in Christ (2 Corinthians 5:17). In the new birth God gives chosen, redeemed sinners a new heart to know and love God, a new will to bow to the rule of Christ, a new mind to understand the things of God, a new, spiritual nature to know, enjoy, and live upon spiritual things, new eyes, eyes of faith, with which to see Christ, new ears with which to hear his voice, new hands, hands of faith, with which to lay hold of Christ and do his will, new feet, with which to flee to Christ and walk with him in the newness of life.

Here is the great difference between the law and the gospel. The law demands everything, but gives nothing. The gospel demands nothing, and gives everything!

125

'Run, run and work', the law demands,
Yet gives me neither feet nor hands;
But sweet, good news the gospel brings.
It bids me fly, and gives me wings!

With these my heavy soul may fly
Away to Christ and reach the sky,
Nor faint, nor falter in the race,
But work with cheer and sing of grace!

John Berridge

How?

How are sinners born again by the Spirit of God? Anyone who understands the
nature of man and the nature of the new birth realises that divine, sovereign
power and grace is required to give dead sinners life. Moral reason cannot give
sinners life. Eloquence and logic cannot do it. Emotional stirrings cannot
regenerate. A mere exercise of the will cannot give the dead life. 'Ye must be
born again'.

Regeneration is the sovereign, irresistible work of God the Holy Spirit.
'The wind bloweth where it listeth, and thou hearest the sound thereof, but
canst not tell whence it cometh, and whither it goeth: so is every one that is
born of the Spirit' (v. 8). At the time appointed by God, the Holy Spirit comes
to the sinner who was chosen by grace in eternal election and redeemed by
Christ at Calvary, and creates life in that sinner by his sovereign, irresistible,
effectual grace (Galatians 4:4-7).

The instrument by which the Holy Spirit causes men and women to be born
again is the gospel of Christ (vv. 12-16).

'If I have told you earthly things, and ye believe not, how shall ye believe,
if I tell you of heavenly things? And no man hath ascended up to heaven, but
he that came down from heaven, even the Son of man which is in heaven. And
as Moses lifted up the serpent in the wilderness, even so must the Son of man
be lifted up: That whosoever believeth in him should not perish, but have
eternal life. For God so loved the world, that he gave his only begotten Son,
that whosoever believeth in him should not perish, but have everlasting life'
(vv. 12-16).

'It pleased God by the foolishness of preaching to save them that believe.'
'Of his own will begat he us with the word of Truth'. Sinners are 'born again,
not of corruptible seed, but of incorruptible, by the word of God which liveth

and abideth forever ... And this is the word which by the gospel is preached unto you'.

In preaching the gospel we call upon dead sinners to arise (Ephesians 5:14), knowing full well that the dead cannot hear and obey the command of the gospel. But if God the Holy Spirit will be pleased to speak through his word, the dead shall hear and live (John 5:25; Revelation 20:6).

Four Pictures
How are lost, dead, helpless sinners born again? If one picture is worth a thousand words, let me point you to four thousand words of explanation given in holy scripture. How are sinners born again? You must be born again in the same way and by the same power displayed when:

God recreated the world that was in chaos (Genesis 1:1-3). The dead, polluted infant was restored in Ezekiel's vision (Ezekiel 16:6-8). The dried bones Ezekiel saw were raised to life (Ezekiel 37:1-15). Lazarus was raised from the dead (John 11:43, 44).

Poor, lost, dead sinners are born again by the will of God, by sovereign operations of God the Holy Spirit, through the preaching of the gospel (1 Peter 1:23-25).

When?
When is a sinner born again? I have no interest in answering the foolish questions of men about the chronological sequence of events in a man's salvation. But I do want to show you when a person may with confidence say, 'I am born again by the grace of God.' When you know Christ, you are born again (John 17:3). When you believe on Christ, you are born again (John 3:15, 36; Isaiah 45:22). 'He that believeth on the Son of God hath everlasting life'. When you have Christ, you are born again (1 John 5:10-13). Get Christ and you get life. Miss Christ and you miss life.

Chapter 17

'How can these things be?'

'Nicodemus answered and said unto him, How can these things be? Jesus answered and said unto him, Art thou a master of Israel, and knowest not these things? Verily, verily, I say unto thee, We speak that we do know, and testify that we have seen; and ye receive not our witness. If I have told you earthly things, and ye believe not, how shall ye believe, if I tell you of heavenly things? And no man hath ascended up to heaven, but he that came down from heaven, even the Son of man which is in heaven. And as Moses lifted up the serpent in the wilderness, even so must the Son of man be lifted up: That whosoever believeth in him should not perish, but have eternal life. For God so loved the world, that he gave his only begotten Son, that whosoever believeth in him should not perish, but have everlasting life. For God sent not his Son into the world to condemn the world; but that the world through him might be saved. He that believeth on him is not condemned: but he that believeth not is condemned already, because he hath not believed in the name of the only begotten Son of God. And this is the condemnation, that light is come into the world, and men loved darkness rather than light, because their deeds were evil. For every one that doeth evil hateth the light, neither cometh to the light, lest his deeds should be reproved. But he that doeth truth cometh to the light, that his deeds may be made manifest, that they are wrought in God' (John 3:9-21).

In this third chapter of John's Gospel God the Holy Spirit has recorded for us a conversation between our Lord Jesus Christ and one of the most learned, well-taught, and highly respected religious leaders of his day, Nicodemus. This is one of the most important passages in all the Bible. Its doctrine is both profound and essential. Nowhere in scripture are we given stronger statements about the new birth and salvation by faith in Christ than are found here.

In the first part of our Lord's conversation with Nicodemus he declared the necessity of the new birth, asserting that we must be born again, because until we are born again we cannot see the kingdom of God and cannot enter into it. Without the new birth, no one has the capacity and ability to understand anything spiritual (John 3:3). And without the new birth, without a new, righteous nature being created in us by God the Holy Spirit, we cannot enter into God's heaven (John 3:5, 7; Hebrews 12:14; Revelation 21:27). 'Marvel not that I said unto thee, Ye must be born again' (v. 7).

Then, in verse 8 our Saviour showed Nicodemus, and shows us that the new birth is a sovereign act and work of God the Holy Spirit. 'The wind bloweth where it listeth, and thou hearest the sound thereof, but canst not tell whence it cometh, and whither it goeth: so is every one that is born of the Spirit'.

The wind is invisible. We cannot see the wind; but we can certainly feel the effects. Even so, we cannot see the Spirit of God; but his power and the results of his work are evident.

The wind is sovereign in its actions. It is beyond man's control. The wind does not consult with us and is not regulated by us. So it is with the Spirit of God. The wind blows when it pleases, where it pleases, and as it pleases. So it is with the Spirit (Exodus 33:19; John 5:21).

The wind is irresistible. When it blows in its power, it sweeps all before it. It is so with the Spirit. When he comes in the fulness of his power, he breaks down man's prejudices, subdues his will, conquers and sweetly forces him into the arms of Christ. 'Thy people shall be willing in the day of thy power' (Psalms 110:3). 'Blessed is the man whom thou choosest and causest to approach unto thee' (Psalms 65:4). 'Salvation is of the Lord' (Jonah 2:9).

Our Lord's conversation with Nicodemus continues in verses 9-21. His doctrine of regeneration is immediately followed by his doctrine of justification. Here he tells us how sinners obtain God's salvation by faith alone. After declaring the necessity and nature of the new birth to Nicodemus, 'Nicodemus answered and said unto him, How can these things be?' (John 3:9) Our Lord Jesus answers the question in verses 10-21.

Spiritual Ignorance

The first thing set before us is a glaring display of spiritual ignorance. Here is a man who was 'a master in Israel', learned in all matters of religious thought, fully acquainted with all the theological trends of the day, a man of letters and degrees, who was utterly ignorant of all things spiritual (vv. 9-12).

'How can these things be?'

When he was told about the new birth, Nicodemus immediately exclaimed, 'How can these things be?' This question reveals the spiritual ignorance of all men by nature, even well-trained, academically superior, highly honoured men. Nicodemus was very well educated, very religious, and of high moral character and reputation. A master in Israel! Yet, he was spiritually ignorant. If we would understand the things of God, we must have something more than education, morality, and sincerity. We must be taught of God.

Even though God became incarnate and spoke in human language, men understood him not (Proverbs 4:19; Ephesians 4:18). Even preachers, teachers, religious leaders, and theologians may be ignorant of divine truth. The fact that a preacher has graduated with honours from some theological centre is no proof that he is a man taught of God (John 6:44, 45).

Nicodemus was one of those pastors in Israel who had ceased to feed the people with knowledge and understanding. The blind were leading the blind, and both were falling into the ditch (Matthew 15:14). The successors of such men are found in every age; and they are abundant today. Let most any preacher or religious leader of our day comment on anything spiritual, and you will have a glaring example of Paul's words in 1 Corinthians 2:14. 'The natural man receiveth not the things of the Spirit of God: for they are foolishness unto him: neither can he know them, because they are spiritually discerned.'

Look at the next verse. After chiding Nicodemus for his ignorance, our Lord shows him the reason for it. It was because he refused to receive the Saviour's witness. 'Verily, verily, I say unto thee, We speak that we do know, and testify that we have seen; and ye receive not our witness' (v. 11). The reason sinners do not know the things of God is twofold: First, they are without the ability to discern anything spiritual. Second, they refuse to believe God's revelation of himself.

None are so blind as those who will not see! As we believe God's word, he gives us understanding of what we believe. As we walk in the light revealed, we are given more light. But, if you receive not the witness of God, you have yourself to blame for your ignorance (John 5:40-44).

Earthly Things And Heavenly

Verse 12 might seem a little confusing. What are those earthly things and those heavenly things our Saviour speaks of here? 'Earthly things' refer to the new birth, which takes place on earth, and to the 'wind', by which he illustrated the Spirit's operations of grace in regeneration. These things Nicodemus ought to have known about from Ezekiel 36:24-27. If he did not believe God's word about these earthly things, it would be useless to tell him of 'heavenly things', of things pertaining to the counsels of God, the mysteries of grace, and the things God has prepared for them that love him (1 Corinthians 2:9, 10).

It would certainly be meaningless for our Lord to tell him of those things he had accomplished as the covenant Surety and Mediator of his people. It would be meaningless, that is, unless the Lord himself was pleased to make the word effectual. Yet, having said that, the Lord proceeds to tell him of heavenly things in verse 13. 'And no man hath ascended up to heaven, but he that came down from heaven, even the Son of man which is in heaven.'

These are heavenly things indeed! Here our Saviour asserts that he, the God-man, and no other man but the God-man had already ascended up to heaven. He then asserts that he had come down from heaven. And third, he says that he was in heaven, even while he walked upon the earth. Obviously, our Saviour is talking here about that which he accomplished before the world began, when he stood forth and was accepted as our covenant Surety, as the Lamb slain from the foundation of the world. In a word, our Lord here declared to Nicodemus that the work he came to do on earth was already accomplished by him in heaven (Romans 8:29, 30; 10:4-9; Hebrews 4:3).

It is true that both Enoch and Elijah had ascended up to heaven; and all those who had died in faith were already in heaven. But all who are there, and all who ever shall be there are there because of the efficacy and merit of Christ, the God-man Mediator, our Substitute.

Read our Lord's words in verse 13 again, and rejoice. 'And no man hath ascended up to heaven, but he that came down from heaven, even the Son of man which is in heaven'. If no man but Christ ascends to heaven, then all others, except Christ, are shut out of heaven. Is that not right? How, then, can we enter heaven? The Church of God's elect, the whole election of grace, is the body of Christ (1 Corinthians 12:12). We and our Saviour, the Church and her Head are one Christ! We are described as 'the fulness of him that filleth all in all' (Ephesians 1:23).

Another Necessity
Our Lord Jesus spoke of the necessity of the new birth. 'Except a man be born of water and of the Spirit, he cannot enter into the kingdom of God.' The new birth is a new creation, the imparting of divine, or eternal life. It is having a new, righteous nature imparted to us and created in us by God the Holy Spirit. But, before any sinner could be granted such grace, before any could be born of God, something else had to be done. So, secondly, our Saviour spoke to Nicodemus about another necessity. Before God could do anything for us, he must do something for himself.

'And as Moses lifted up the serpent in the wilderness, even so must the Son of man be lifted up: That whosoever believeth in him should not perish, but have eternal life' (vv. 14, 15).

If eternal life is to be bestowed on us, it must be done righteously and justly. Eternal life could never be bestowed upon men, except by the satisfaction of divine justice. The Son of God must be lifted up. Eternal life must come out of his substitutionary death. The sacrificial work of Christ is the basis of the Spirit's operations and the ground of God's gift of life (Isaiah 53:4-6).

It is the Son of man who must be crucified, for atonement could be made only by one in the nature of him who sinned. Only as man was Christ capable of taking upon himself our guilt and its penalty. The Jews expected the Messiah to be lifted up or elevated to the throne of David; but before this, he must be lifted up on the cross of shame, enduring the judgment of God upon our sins.

To illustrate the character, meaning, and purpose of his death, our dear Saviour refers to the well-known incident of the brazen-serpent in Numbers 21:6-9. The people were bitten by fiery serpents, dying, and without hope. Moses made a serpent in the likeness of the cause and lifted it up. Those who looked in faith lived. Christ is made in the likeness of sinful flesh and crucified. The only animal upon whom the Lord God specifically pronounced his curse was the serpent. So our Lord Jesus who was made sin and made a curse for us was rightly represented by the cursed thing. All who look to him in faith shall live (Isaiah 45:22).

By being 'lifted up', our Lord meant nothing less than his own death upon the cursed tree. That death, he would have us know, was appointed by God for 'the life of the world' (John 6:51). It was ordained from all eternity to be the great propitiation and satisfaction for the sins of his people throughout the whole world. It was the payment of our debt, by an Almighty Substitute and Representative of infinite worth and merit. This is God's scheme of grace and redemption. In infinite wisdom and goodness he purposed to save sinners by the sin-atoning death of his dear Son, the Lord Jesus Christ, on the cross.

When Christ died upon the cross, our many sins were laid upon him. He was made 'sin' for us. He was made 'a curse' for us (2 Corinthians 5:21; Galatians 3:13). By his death he purchased complete pardon for our souls and obtained eternal redemption for us.

The truth set before us here is substitution, the foundation-stone of our faith. Christ's death is our life. His cross is our title to heaven. Christ 'lifted up' and put to shame on Calvary is the ladder by which we 'enter into the holiest' and ascend at last to heavenly glory. We are sinners, but Christ has suffered for us. We deserve death, but Christ has died for us. We are guilty debtors, but Christ has paid our debt with his own blood. This is the good news we preach. This is the gospel we believe. On this let us lean while we live. To this let us cling when we die. Christ has been 'lifted up' on the cross, and has thrown open the gates of heaven to poor sinners!

133

The Cause

Then, our blessed Saviour shows us that the cause of all this is the love of God. 'For God so loved the world, that he gave his only begotten Son, that whosoever believeth in him should not perish, but have everlasting life. For God sent not his Son into the world to condemn the world; but that the world through him might be saved' (vv. 16, 17).

The Lord Jesus declared that his death on the cross was an imperative, a necessity. He did not say, 'The Son of man shall be lifted up', but, 'The Son of man must be lifted up'. There is no alternative if the claims of God are to be met, if the demands of justice are to be satisfied, if sin is to be put away, and if the elect are to be saved, Christ must die (Romans 3:25, 26; 2 Corinthians 5:21). The law and justice of God demand it.

John 3:14 declares the remedy for sin. Christ must be lifted up. Verse 15 is the result. 'Whosoever believeth in him should not perish, but have eternal life'. Verse 16 is the reason. 'For God so loved the world, that he gave his only begotten Son, that whosoever believeth in him should not perish, but have everlasting life'!

The cross is a display of righteousness, justice, truth, and holiness; but there is more in the cross of Christ than an exhibition of the holiness of God. The cross is the great display and manifestation of the love of God. John 3:16 takes us back to the very foundation of everything. God's great salvation was provided by love. Christ came and died because God loved us and was determined to have a people like Christ, not in order to make the Father love us, but because he loved us. The atonement was not the cause but the effect of God's love (1 John 4:9, 10).

'Twas not to make Jehovah's love
Toward His people flame,
That Jesus from the throne above,
A suffering man became.

'Twas not the death which He endured,
Nor all the pangs He bore,
That God's eternal love procured,
For God was love before.

He loved the world of His elect,
With love surpassing thought;
Nor will His mercy e'er neglect
The souls so dearly bought!

The warm affections of His breast
Towards His chosen burn;
And in His love He'll ever rest,
Nor from His oath return.

John Kent

In this sixteenth verse our Lord tells us seven things about the love of God.

1. The tense of his love. 'God so loved'. He always has loved us. It is an everlasting love (Romans 5:8; Jeremiah 33:3).
2. The magnitude of his love. 'God so loved'. It is an infinite love (John 15:13).
3. The scope of his love. 'God so loved the world'. His love is not limited to the Jews only, but to all nations (Revelation 5:9).
4. The nature of his love. 'God so loved ... that he gave'. Real love ever seeks the highest interest and well-being of its object. Love is unselfish; it gives. God gave the greatest gift.
5. The sacrificial character of his love. He not only gave his Son to live on earth among men, but to die the death of the cross (Philippians 2:6-8).
6. The design of his love. 'That whosoever believeth on him should not perish'. God has a people who shall not perish. No condemnation or judgment shall come to them (Romans 8:33, 34).
7. The beneficence of his love. 'But have everlasting life'. This is what our Lord imparts to his own: eternal life and glory (1 John 3:1-3).

The coming of Christ was not to condemn the world; the world was already condemned (Romans 5:18). The Son of God came into the world in human flesh that men and women of all nations might be saved. The word 'might' does not express any uncertainty about the fact of their being saved. It expresses our Lord's purpose and design in coming. He came in order that the world might be saved. His person and work for sinners enabled God to be both just and Justifier of those who believe (1 Peter 3:18; Isaiah 45:20-25).

By Faith Alone
Now, our Lord teaches us that sinners obtain all the blessedness of eternal life in Christ by faith alone.

'He that believeth on him is not condemned: but he that believeth not is condemned already, because he hath not believed in the name of the only begotten Son of God. And this is the condemnation, that light is come into the world, and men loved darkness rather than light, because their deeds were evil. For every one that doeth evil hateth the light, neither cometh to the light, lest his deeds should be reproved. But he that doeth truth cometh to the light, that his deeds may be made manifest, that they are wrought in God' (vv.18-21).

Obviously, faith in Christ does not give sinners life. Faith is the result of life given by God the Holy Spirit. And faith does not accomplish justification. Faith is the result of that justification Christ accomplished at Calvary. Yet, no one is saved without faith; and all who are saved are saved by faith alone, because salvation is by grace (Romans 4:16). Three times our Lord repeats this glorious truth to Nicodemus. Twice he proclaims that 'whosoever believeth shall not perish'. Once he says, 'He that believeth on the Son of God is not condemned'.

Faith in the Lord Jesus Christ is salvation. He that has faith has life, and he that has it not has not life. Nothing is necessary to our complete salvation but faith. Nothing will give us an interest in Christ except faith in him. You may fast and mourn for sin, and do many things that are right, and use religious ordinances, and give all your goods to feed the poor, and yet remain unpardoned, and lose your soul. But if you come to Christ as a guilty sinner, believing on him, eternal life is yours and neither it, nor you, can be lost. Without faith in Christ, there is no salvation; but through faith in the Son of God, the vilest sinner is saved forever.

In this matter of salvation, faith stands alone, without works. If you would know whether you are justified by Christ, there is but one question to be asked. 'Dost thou believe on the Son of God?' 'He that believeth on him is not condemned: but he that believeth not is condemned already, because he hath not believed in the name of the only begotten Son of God' (v.18).

For the believer there is no condemnation (Romans 8:1) because Christ was condemned in our stead (Isaiah 53:4-6). Those who believe not are condemned already. We all came into this world with the curse of sin upon us and were by nature children of wrath (Ephesians 2:3). Guilt and condemnation is increased by persistent unbelief. If any go to hell, it will be because they loved darkness rather than light. It will be because they refused to come to Christ, because they refused to believe on the Son of God (Proverbs 1:23-33; Matthew 11:21-30).

May God the Holy Spirit give you faith in Christ! May he be gracious to you and give you the gift of life, for Christ's sake.

Chapter 18

The Mysteries Of The Brazen Serpent

'And as Moses lifted up the serpent in the wilderness, even so must the Son of man be lifted up: That whosoever believeth in him should not perish, but have eternal life' (John 3:14, 15).

'Say unto them, As I live, saith the Lord GOD, I have no pleasure in the death of the wicked; but that the wicked turn from his way and live: turn ye, turn ye from your evil ways; for why will ye die, O house of Israel?' (Ezekiel 33:11). The Lord God himself declares that he has no pleasure in the death of the wicked, and asks, 'Why will ye die?' It is true, God will punish sin. He must do so. His law, his justice, and his righteousness demand it. But God's law, justice, and righteousness can never find pleasure or satisfaction in the everlasting torments of the damned in hell. Indeed, if all the human race were to suffer the endless fires of hell, God's righteous justice could never find pleasure and satisfaction. Man, who is but a finite creature, can never satisfy the claims of infinite justice. If that were possible, the death of Christ must be needless. If that were possible, the fires of hell must someday burn out. But infinite justice demands an infinite satisfaction. Hell must, therefore, be eternal! God's justice can never be satisfied in the death of the wicked. He has no pleasure in the death of him that dieth.

But God does have pleasure in the death of the sinner's substitute, Jesus Christ. Being the infinite God, our Lord Jesus Christ was able to satisfy, and has fully satisfied all the claims of infinite justice. Being the sinless man, he was able to stand in our room and bear the fulness of God's wrath for us. In his incarnation, his birth, his life, and his death, the Lord God beholds Christ as the Substitute of his people, and says, 'This is my beloved Son, in whom I

137

am well-pleased'. In the death of the God-man, God's law, justice, and righteousness have pleasure and satisfaction. Therefore, there is no possibility of one soul for whom Christ died perishing in hell. The law has no claim against a believing sinner.

It is God's pleasure, for Christ's sake, to be merciful. He gives life to perishing sinners, and forgives all our sins for Christ's sake. So, then, why will ye die? Turn now and seek the Lord, cry out for his mercy, and trust his Son. Only in Christ does God have any pleasure. Lay hold of God's Beloved now. Believe on the Lord Jesus Christ, and you shall never die. Knowing the terror of the Lord, I seek to persuade obstinate, rebel sinners to be reconciled to God, to believe on the Son of God. That is our Lord's intent in John 3:14, 15.

The Old Testament history of the brazen serpent lifted up by Moses was used by our Saviour to show poor, lost sinners the way of life. There is no better type and picture of our blessed Redeemer in all the Old Testament than the brazen serpent. There is no Old Testament type that gives us a clearer, more instructive picture of the way God saves sinners than the one set before us by our Saviour himself in these two verses. 'As Moses lifted up the serpent in the wilderness, even so must the Son of man be lifted up: That whosoever believeth in him should not perish, but have eternal life.' Our Lord Jesus here refers to an event that is recorded in Numbers 21.

'And they journeyed from mount Hor by the way of the Red sea, to compass the land of Edom: and the soul of the people was much discouraged because of the way. And the people spake against God, and against Moses, Wherefore have ye brought us up out of Egypt to die in the wilderness? for there is no bread, neither is there any water; and our soul loatheth this light bread. And the LORD sent fiery serpents among the people, and they bit the people; and much people of Israel died. Therefore the people came to Moses, and said, We have sinned, for we have spoken against the LORD, and against thee; pray unto the LORD, that he take away the serpents from us. And Moses prayed for the people. And the LORD said unto Moses, Make thee a fiery serpent, and set it upon a pole: and it shall come to pass, that every one that is bitten, when he looketh upon it, shall live. And Moses made a serpent of brass, and put it upon a pole, and it came to pass, that if a serpent had bitten any man, when he beheld the serpent of brass, he lived' (Numbers 21:4-9).

A Deadly Poison

The first thing I see in this picture is a humbling fact about our race. We are all infected with the deadly poison of sin and we are all under the judgment of God. This is a fact we prefer not to think about or acknowledge; but it is a fact nonetheless. The sooner we learn it, the better. We are all depraved, diseased at heart, corrupted with sin. This is the natural condition of all mankind. And, until a man is made to know that from the sole of his foot to the crown of his head there is no soundness in him; but wounds, and bruises, and putrefying sores, he will never seek mercy by the merits of Christ. This is clearly represented by the condition of the children of Israel in Numbers 21. We are told, 'The Lord sent fiery serpents among the people, and they bit the people; and much of Israel died' (Numbers 21:6).

Can you imagine the horror and confusion of the camp of Israel? One day they were invaded by an army of fiery, flying snakes! The bite of the snakes was deadly. Their poison caused the body to burn with fever. There was pain throughout the whole body, as though fire was in the veins. Such is the destructive nature of sin. Those who were bitten of the serpents had death in their veins. And such is the deadly nature of sin.

> Sin, like a venomous disease,
> Infects our vital blood;
> The only balm is sovereign grace,
> And the Physician God.
>
> Our beauty and our strength are fled,
> And we draw near to death;
> But Christ, the Lord, recalls the dead,
> With His almighty breath.
>
> Madness, by nature, reigns within;
> The passions burn and rage;
> 'Til God's own Son, with skill Divine,
> The inward fire assuage.

> Isaac Watts

The picture that is set before us is a black one indeed. The Israelites were bitten, they burned with fever, then they died. And so it is with the fallen sons and daughters of Adam. We were all bitten by the old serpent and poisoned with sin in the garden.

Sin is not a social disease which comes by contact with other men. It is an inbred family disease. It comes to us by nature from our father Adam. 'Wherefore, as by one man sin entered into the world ... For by one man's disobedience many were made sinners' (Romans 5:12, 19). David cried, 'Behold, I was shapen in iniquity; and in sin did my mother conceive me'

(Psalms 51:5). 'The wicked are estranged from the womb: they go astray as soon as they are born, speaking lies' (Psalms 58:3).

All men are in bondage to iniquity. All men are taken captive by Satan at his will. All the works of the flesh are evil. 'The works of the flesh are manifest, which are these; Adultery, fornication, uncleanness, lasciviousness, idolatry, witchcraft, hatred, variance, emulations, wrath, strife, seditions, heresies, envyings, murders, drunkenness, revellings, and such like' (Galatians 5:19-21). These are the thoughts of man's heart and the works of his will by nature (Matthew 15:17-20; Mark 7:21, 22).

By nature, man is such an evil creature and so corrupted by evil that everything he does is tainted with sin. Even the sacrifice of the wicked is an abomination to the Lord. Our very righteousnesses are filthy rags in the eyes of God. Mark it down, man by nature is a sinner, utterly obnoxious before the holy Lord God.

Look over the catalogue of sin against God. We have all broken God's holy law in every point from our youth up. We break it continually. Even we who have been washed in the Saviour's blood and regenerated by his grace constantly sin against him.

After the Israelites were bitten by the serpents, they began to burn within. Sin does not instantly produce pain and misery. But give it a little time, and you will find that, like the old serpent himself, no matter how alluring and charming, sin is a painful poison to your soul. It will produce miseries more extreme than the fiery serpents caused Israel. 'At the last it biteth like a serpent and stingeth like an adder' (Proverbs 23:32). The young man casts his restraints to the wind, living riotously, but soon he will find that strong drink is a mocker. The young woman seeks pleasure, popularity, and promiscuity, but soon she will find that the way of the transgressor is hard. Others, because they are restrained by society, by parents, by religion, or by self-esteem, do not indulge in the vices of the day, but within them is a heart that burns with every obscene lust.

But the picture gets darker. Those who were bitten, after much suffering, at last, died. And so it is written, 'Sin when it is finished bringeth forth death'. What a horrible death those people must have died! They cried, they convulsed, they begged, and they died. Soon, you also must die. You have the poison of the serpent in you. Soon, you must die. Soon, unless God intervenes, you will be in hell! Sometimes death comes without warning. Sometimes men are so hardened and calloused that they go to the graves without fear. But often, when they come to die, the wicked have such awakened senses that their souls are terrified. Like Esau, they seek a place of repentance with tears, but find it not. And after death comes hell! All the wicked go down into hell. There the

140

burnings of conscience, the fires of the mind, and the torments of the soul are the everlasting results of sin.

These fiery serpents were the judgment of God upon Israel. Matthew Henry wrote, 'God's wrath against us for sin is as those fiery serpents which God sent among the people, to punish them for their murmurings. The curses of the law are as fiery serpents, so are all the tokens of divine wrath'. Israel had sinned against the Lord; therefore, his judgment came upon them.

The sting of those fiery serpents was a fit representation of God's law when it is applied to the heart of the sinner, by the power of the Holy Spirit (Romans 7:9). The law shows man the exceeding sinfulness of his sin in the light of God's holiness. The law threatens the sinner with divine punishment. Hear what the law says: 'the soul that sinneth, it shall die', 'the wages of sin is death', 'God will by no means clear the guilty'. The law of God shuts us up to Christ alone. 'What things soever the law saith, it saith to them who are under the law: that every mouth may be stopped, and all the world may become guilty before God'. When the law of God is applied to the heart of the sinner, then sin becomes a bitterness in his soul, a fire in his conscience, and a hell in his heart.

This is the work of God the Holy Spirit in conviction. The poor sinner is made to feel death in his members. His pride and self-righteousness wither. His naked sinfulness is laid in open view. Then, and only then will a sinner cry out for mercy. Until a person knows his sin, he will not seek mercy. Until he knows his need of Christ, he will not seek Christ.

It was a serpent that stung the Israelites. And it was that old serpent, the devil that poisoned our nature in the Adam-fall. All his temptations, assaults, and poisons are fiery. And when the dreadful effects of sin are felt in the awakened conscience, how they burn with terrors in the soul!

The Israelites who were bitten of the fiery serpents could do nothing to help themselves. So, too, those who are dead in sin can do nothing of themselves to change their condition. Only when a man knows that his malady is beyond his own power, will he seek the help of Another.

What could the dying Israelite do to heal himself of those venomous bites? Nothing! What medicine could cure his wounds? None! There was no remedy within the power of man. The serpent's poison baffled all science, medicine, skill, and ability. It resisted every attempt of healing. That is sin. No prayers, no tears, no endeavours, no repentance can wash away sin. If the sinner is restored, it must be by the interposition and mercy of God alone.

God's Cure
The second thing set before us in the type of the brazen serpent is God's cure for our curse, God's remedy for our ruin. The only means by which man can

be redeemed from the malady of sin and the burning wrath of God's law is by the sacrifice of the Son of God, the Lord Jesus Christ. This is precisely what our Lord Jesus teaches us in John 3. This is the only way a man can be justified with God: 'As Moses lifted up the serpent in the wilderness, even so must the Son of man be lifted up.' There are several things about the brazen serpent which set forth the substitutionary work of Christ in the place of sinners.

It was God himself who in his sovereign grace and free love provided the remedy. In providing the brazen serpent, God pointed Israel to his own Son, who in the fulness of time would come to make an end of sin. Many must have thought that the brazen serpent was a foolish remedy. After all, it was a serpent that caused the mischief. And many think that it is foolishness to talk of salvation by Christ. But Christ alone is God's appointed Substitute.

The brazen serpent was provided for the Israelites because of God's love and pity. And Jesus Christ was provided for the healing of perishing sinners because of God's love. 'For God so loved the world that he gave his only begotten Son, that whosoever believeth in him should not perish, but have everlasting life.'

The serpent was made of brass. As brass is a base and common metal, it properly represents our Lord's humiliation, who took upon himself the form of a servant. Brass is a bright and shining metal, and so it expresses the glory of Christ, who is the brightness of the Father's glory and the express image of his person. And brass is a durable metal, expressing the strength and power of Christ, who is 'able to save to the uttermost them that come unto God by him'. And it is representative of the immutability of Christ, who is 'the same yesterday, and today, and forever'. But a serpent made of brass, shining brightly in the desert sun, was the most unlikely thing in the world to cure the people. A bright light shining in the eyes of one who has a malady in his head is likely to cause him to be taken with convulsions and seizures.

The brazen serpent had the form of a serpent; but there was no poison in it. Even so, our Lord Jesus Christ was made in the likeness of sinful flesh, and was found in fashion as a man, yet, he is without sin, holy, harmless, undefiled, and separate from sinners.

And there was but one brazen serpent, by which the Israelites could be cured. Even so, there is but one Mediator between God and man, the man Christ Jesus. There is one name given under heaven among men whereby ye must be saved Jesus Christ the Lord.

As the brazen serpent had to be lifted up on a pole, so that all who were bitten could see; even so, the Lord Jesus Christ had to be lifted up on the cross, so that sinners everywhere might look to (believe on) him and live. Specifically, our Lord Jesus is talking about his own crucifixion in the place of chosen sinners, 'the Israel of God', when he says, 'even so must the Son of man be lifted up'. The expression, 'Son of man', was, no doubt, intended to remind us of Daniel's prophecy of the Messiah who must be cut off. The death of Jesus Christ was an absolute necessity.

It was necessary because of God's decrees and purposes. It was necessary because of God's promises and prophecies, because of the types and figures of the Old Testament, because of Christ's eternal agreements as our Surety in the covenant of grace. It was necessary because without it no sinner could ever be accepted of God. God's law had to be fulfilled. God's justice had to be satisfied. The only way a holy God can be merciful and gracious to sinners is if a suitable Substitute suffers and dies in their place. The very love and mercy of God for his people made the sacrifice of his Son necessary!

As the serpent was a cursed creature, the Lord Jesus Christ was made a curse for us when he hung upon the tree. 'Christ hath redeemed us from the curse of the law, being made a curse for us, for it is written, cursed is every one that hangeth on a tree.' 'He hath made him to be sin for us who knew no sin, that we might be made the righteousness of God in him.' 'He, his own self, bare our sins in his own body, on the tree.' The brazen serpent Moses lifted up was a fiery serpent; and our Lord Jesus was made to endure the fiery wrath of God as our Substitute. His very soul was made to burn with the fires of hell for us, when he was made sin for us!

'Even so must the Son of man be lifted up.' Remember, these speak of the Saviour's crucifixion. William Hendriksen wrote, 'The lifting up of the Son of man is a 'must'. It is not 'a' remedy; it is the only possible remedy for sin, for in this way only can the demands of God's holiness and righteousness, and love, be met.'

Yet, there is more in this short passage. The Son of man must also be lifted up in his exaltation. It is only as the exalted Christ that he can be seen by all who are infected with sin. It is only the risen and exalted Saviour who has the power to give lost, ruined, dead sinners eternal life. It is only the exalted Redeemer who is 'able to save unto the uttermost them that come unto God by him'.

The Son of man must be lifted up in the preaching of the gospel. Preachers are like the pole to which the brazen serpent was fastened. We are useful only as long as we lift up and exalt the Son of God before the eyes of perishing men. It is the preacher's one and only business to preach Christ and him crucified. Christ alone can save us. Christ alone can justify, pardon, reconcile, and sanctify us.

Christ alone is our message. We can never heal the sinner's disease; but we can tell sinners who can and does heal all manner of disease. We cannot bring men to Christ; but we can point men to Christ.

Look To Christ

Here is the third thing I want you to see. Every perishing sinner who believes on Christ shall be saved. In the gospel Christ is lifted up before all; but all are not saved. Yet, this I know, (I have the Saviour's own word for it), 'Whosoever believeth on him shall not perish, but have eternal life'. What were the Israelites told to do? They were not told to produce some healing medicine. They were not told to help one another. They were not told to fight the serpents. They were not told to make an offering to the serpent. They were not told to pray to the serpent. They were not told to obey Moses. They were not told to look at their wounds. They were told to look. All who looked up to the serpent, no matter how grievous their wounds, no matter how weak their eyes, if they did but look, they were healed.

If you would be saved, you must look to Christ. Looking to Christ is an expression of faith in him. You desperately need to look to Christ. God himself commands you to look (1 John 3:23); and the Lord Jesus bids you look. 'Look unto me and be ye saved all the ends of the earth, for I am God, and beside me there is none else.' May God the Holy Spirit now enable us ever to look to Christ. Look to his glorious Person. Look to his redeeming blood. Look to his unfailing love. Look to his saving power. Look to his fulness. Holy Spirit, ever cause me to look to him who alone saves poor sinners by his blood!

What is the result of this look? – Eternal life! Not only does the look bring healing to your soul, but you are given eternal life! Look to Christ.

Chapter 19

The Baptist, The Bride, And The Bridegroom

'After these things came Jesus and his disciples into the land of Judaea; and there he tarried with them, and baptised. And John also was baptising in Aenon near to Salim, because there was much water there: and they came, and were baptised. For John was not yet cast into prison. Then there arose a question between some of John's disciples and the Jews about purifying. And they came unto John, and said unto him, Rabbi, he that was with thee beyond Jordan, to whom thou barest witness, behold, the same baptiseth, and all men come to him. John answered and said, A man can receive nothing, except it be given him from heaven. Ye yourselves bear me witness, that I said, I am not the Christ, but that I am sent before him. He that hath the bride is the bridegroom: but the friend of the bridegroom, which standeth and heareth him, rejoiceth greatly because of the bridegroom's voice: this my joy therefore is fulfilled. He must increase, but I must decrease. He that cometh from above is above all: he that is of the earth is earthly, and speaketh of the earth: he that cometh from heaven is above all. And what he hath seen and heard, that he testifieth; and no man receiveth his testimony. He that hath received his testimony hath set to his seal that God is true. For he whom God hath sent speaketh the words of God: for God giveth not the Spirit by measure unto him. The Father loveth the Son, and hath given all things into his hand. He that believeth on the Son hath everlasting life: and he that believeth not the Son shall not see life; but the wrath of God abideth on him' (John 3:22-36).

This is the last testimony of John the Baptist concerning our Lord Jesus Christ. That faithful man of God, John the Baptist, was the same at the end of his ministry as he was at the beginning: the same in his views of himself, the same in his views of Christ, and the same in his views of God's salvation. Blessed is that church whose pastor is as steady, as bold, and as constant in proclaiming the saving majesty and glory of the Lord Jesus Christ as John the Baptist!

145

Much Water

The first thing that is obvious in this passage is the fact that it takes 'much water' to perform the gospel ordinance of believer's baptism. The Holy Spirit tells us plainly that 'John was baptising in Aenon, near to Salim, because there was much water there' (vv. 22-24). You cannot baptise anyone with a few sprinkles, or even a cup of water. It takes 'much water' to perform the gospel ordinance of believer's baptism.

John had not yet been arrested and murdered by Herod. He had not yet reached the end of his time on earth. So his work was not yet over. Here he is baptising all who came to him, wishing to publicly confess their faith in the Lord Jesus Christ as the Lamb of God. Look at these three verses line by line, and learn what they teach.

If we compare what the Holy Spirit says in verse 22 with what he says in John 4:2, we see that that which is done by Christ's servants, in his name and by his authority, is done by Christ himself. God's servants are to be heard, received, and treated as the Lord Jesus himself (2 Corinthians 5:18-6:2; Luke 10:16; Hebrews 13:7, 17).

Verse 23 is one of the most definitive statements in holy scripture with regard to what men call 'the mode of baptism'. 'And John also was baptising in Aenon near to Salim, because there was much water there: and they came, and were baptised'. If baptism could be performed by sprinkling or pouring, 'much water' would not be needed. Baptism is by immersion. The word 'baptised' (both in the Greek and the English) means to dip, to immerse, or to plunge. The example of our Lord himself ought to settle all controversy in this regard. No unprejudiced mind can read the New Testament without seeing that baptism is immersion. The Lord Jesus was immersed (Matthew 3:16). Baptism is a burial (Romans 6:3, 4; Colossians 2:12). It symbolises the fulfilment of all righteousness by Christ's death, burial, and resurrection as our Substitute (Matthew 3:15). And it shows forth our hope of the resurrection (Romans 6:4). These things cannot be symbolically portrayed by sloshing a few drops of water on the head and calling the act baptism. They can only be portrayed by the burial of believing sinners in the watery grave, whence we arise to walk in newness of life with our Saviour. Baptism is immersion, a burial. Anything else that is called baptism is a sham.

Satan's Device

The second thing we have in this passage is a warning against one of Satan's favourite devices. The fiend of hell constantly seeks to divide God's people and to divide his servants.

'Then there arose a question between some of John's disciples and the Jews about purifying. And they came unto John, and said unto him, Rabbi, he that was with thee beyond Jordan, to whom thou barest witness, behold, the same baptiseth, and all men come to him' (vv. 25, 26).

Some of John's disciples and the Jewish religionists were involved in a heated debate about rites and ceremonies of purification. The Jews observed countless many purification ceremonies. Some scriptural, being required by God's law as pictures of his work of grace in saving his people, but most of these ceremonies were observed because of religious tradition, and had no basis at all in holy scripture.

These Jews seem to have thought that John was practicing a new purification ceremony. That would have been alright; but he refused to practice their ceremonies. In Matthew 3, when the Pharisees came to John for baptism, trying to tie his baptism to their traditions, he refused.

Read verse 26 carefully. When we read, 'And they came unto John, and said unto him, Rabbi, he that was with thee beyond Jordan, to whom thou barest witness, behold, the same baptiseth, and all men come to him', the 'they' are not John's disciples, but those same Jews who had been arguing with his disciples in verse 25. They are the same ones who were sent by the chief priests and Pharisees to question John in chapter one (John 1:19).

These same Jews came to John and told him that Jesus of Nazareth, the one to whom he bore witness, was baptising and that all men now were coming to him. What do you suppose their motive was? They were trying to make John jealous and envious. They were trying to divide John's disciples and the disciples of Christ, as if they were serving two different causes.

That is one of Satan's favourite devices. He constantly tries to divide the church of God. He constantly strives to divide God's servants, to make one jealous and envious of another. Satan does everything he can to divide the people of God. We see one example of this after another in scripture (Numbers 11:26-29; Philippians 1:14-18; Ephesians 3:8). All hell must bay and howl when the fiend of hell succeeds in dividing brethren! May God the Holy Spirit protect us from this device of the devil and make us peace-makers (Ephesians 4:1-7). Strife and division are horribly evil. They are insidious, contagious, and injurious to the cause of the gospel. Let us do nothing to cause them and nothing to contribute to them!

A Faithful Servant

Third, John the Baptist is held up by the Spirit of God as a pattern and example of a truly faithful servant of God (vv. 27-35). Here is a man 'clothed with humility' (1 Peter 5:5).

'John answered and said, A man can receive nothing, except it be given him from heaven. Ye yourselves bear me witness, that I said, I am not the Christ, but that I am sent before him. He that hath the bride is the bridegroom:

but the friend of the bridegroom, which standeth and heareth him, rejoiceth greatly because of the bridegroom's voice: this my joy therefore is fulfilled. He must increase, but I must decrease' (vv. 27-30).

Here is one of the most important, most greatly used men in the history of the world, John the Baptist, the forerunner of the Messiah. When men sought to honour him, he turned the honour away from himself to another. In verse 27 John asserts that any honour a man has, any usefulness in the kingdom of God, any place of service, is only that which God gives him. Blessed is that servant who knows this and acquiesces in the sovereign will of his God (1 Corinthians 4:7; 12:11, 18; Ephesians 4:7). John turned the attention of these men away from himself to that other man who came into the world as Jehovah's Servant, Jesus of Nazareth.

In verse 28 John declares himself to be nothing, just a voice, a voice sent to proclaim the coming of the Christ. This was not a sham, pretentious show of humility, but genuine humility. Like Paul after him, he says, 'By the grace of God I am what I am' (1 Corinthians 15:10). We see in John the Baptist a very different spirit from that displayed by these Jewish religionists. He genuinely sought no honour or praise, no recognition or applause from men. Rather than receive it, he turned it to another Servant, to promote another Servant of God. That is a faithful servant. True, that other Servant was the Lord Jesus Christ; but the principle is the same.

Beware of any preacher who courts praise and recognition, who seeks light to shine upon himself, who calls attention to himself, and does nothing to promote the ministries of other men. As John Trapp observed, 'Self-love makes men unreasonable, and ever teacheth them to turn the glass to see themselves bigger, and others lesser, than they are.' Ezekiel uplifted the name of Daniel (Ezekiel 14:14). Paul promoted Epaphras (Colossians 1:7). And Peter praised Paul, though he had been publicly reproved by him at Antioch (2 Peter 3:15; Galatians 2:11). Faithful men promote one another, but never themselves.

God's servants, faithful gospel preachers are friends of Christ, the Bridegroom. Like the best man at a wedding, faithful preachers rejoice to see Christ come to take his bride in his arms. They do not desire to be seen, but for him to be seen with his bride (v. 29). They just hold the ring (the everlasting gospel of peace).

The bride is the church, God's elect of every age and nation, the people of God. They belong to the Bridegroom (given to him by the Father, redeemed by his blood, and brought to him by his Spirit). The friend of the Bridegroom is not jealous and envious. He is truly a friend and loves the Bridegroom, he rejoices in the happiness of the Bridegroom, and his joy is fulfilled when the

Bridegroom is glorified. The servant of Christ is occupied with Christ and his glory, nothing else!

Since the first time I read verse 30, with any sense of its meaning, since the day that it was first brought home to my heart, I have been praying that the Lord God might daily make this the ambition of my heart. 'He must increase, but I must decrease'! This is the will and purpose of God. Let it be my will and purpose, too. 'He must increase, but I must decrease'! He must increase in his greatness; I must decrease. We can never think too highly of Christ. We can never extol him too much, love him excessively, or be overly devoted to him.

Then, in verses 31-35, John begins to increase Christ and decrease himself. 'He that cometh from above is above all: he that is of the earth is earthly, and speaketh of the earth: he that cometh from heaven is above all. And what he hath seen and heard, that he testifieth; and no man receiveth his testimony. He that hath received his testimony hath set to his seal that God is true. For he whom God hath sent speaketh the words of God: for God giveth not the Spirit by measure unto him. The Father loveth the Son, and hath given all things into his hand' (vv. 31-35).

Christ came from heaven and is above all. I am of the earth and speak as one of the earth (v. 31). The Lord Jesus is the perfect revelation of God; but men refuse to hear him (v. 32). Yet, all who receive his testimony, all who believe him set to their seal that God is true (v. 33). Believing on the Lord Jesus Christ, we seal the truth to our own hearts. But, this verse might be translated, 'He that received his testimony is already sealed, because God is true'. Chosen, redeemed sinners come to Christ in faith, we believe him, when Christ has sealed us by his Spirit (Revelation 7:1-3). That translation is verified by scripture (2 Corinthians 1:21, 22; Ephesians 1:12-14; 4:30; Jude 1).

Christ is the only man to whom the Spirit is given without measure (v. 34). He is the full Revelation of God. He is the full Truth. All the fulness of the triune God dwells in him without measure (Colossians 2:9). How vast the difference between the servants of God and the Servant of God!

God the Father has given all things to Christ, as our Mediator, because of his love for him (v. 35; John 10:16-18). 'The Father loveth the Son, and hath given all things into his hand.' You might ask, 'What all does that include?' It includes all things pertaining to the universe, all things pertaining to life, all things pertaining to the new heavens and new earth, all things pertaining to the church, and if there is anything else, all things pertaining to that, too! God has laid help for our souls upon One that is mighty (Psalms 89:19).

Your Responsibility
Fourth, in verse 36 John the Baptist gives us the final point of the last sermon he preached before his execution. Having declared the greatness and glory of

Christ, the Lamb of God, the sinner's Substitute, he asserts that your eternal destiny is your own responsibility. 'He that believeth on the Son hath everlasting life: and he that believeth not the Son shall not see life; but the wrath of God abideth on him.'

Here is the nearness and presentness of God's salvation. John the Baptist declares, 'He that believeth on the Son hath everlasting life'! Pardon, peace, eternal life, and a complete title to Heaven are the immediate possession of every sinner who believes on the Son of God. This salvation in all its fulness is the immediate possession of every believer.

What a glorious assertion! There are no works to be done, no conditions to be fulfilled, no price to be paid, no years of probation to be passed before a sinner can be accepted with God. Believe on Christ, and you are at once forgiven. By Christ, all that believe are justified from all things.

If faith in Christ brings with it present and immediate privileges, to remain unbelieving is to be in a state of tremendous peril. If heaven is so near to the believer, hell is just as near to those who believe not! 'He that believeth not the Son shall not see life; but the wrath of God abideth on him.'

How sure is that soul of blessedness who has the Son! How sure the everlasting misery of hell's torments are to those who have not the Son of God! The wrath of God, not taken away by Christ, 'abideth on' them who believe not the Son of God!

Having said all that, read verse 36 again, paying close attention to the verb tenses. 'He that believeth on the Son hath (present tense) everlasting life: and he that believeth not the Son shall not see life (future tense); but the wrath of God abideth on him.' Why, do you suppose, did the Holy Spirit inspire John to use different verb tenses? Would it not have meant the same thing if he had used either the present tense or the future in both places? No, the meaning would have been completely different.

When John declares, 'He that believeth on the Son hath (present tense) everlasting life', he is telling us that wherever faith in Christ is found life is already present. Faith in Christ does not produce eternal life. Eternal life produces faith in Christ. When he asserts, 'he that believeth not the Son shall not see life', while placing all responsibility upon the guilty soul that chooses not to believe, he shuts the poor sinner up to God's sovereign grace, declaring plainly that unless God the Holy Spirit gives life, you will not and cannot believe on the Son of God. At the same time, John assures us that if we find ourselves believing on Christ, we are born of God. Faith in Christ is the evidence that it is so (1 John 5:1, 10-13).

Chapter 20

Five Things Necessary
For Conversion

'When therefore the Lord knew how the Pharisees had heard that Jesus made and baptised more disciples than John, (Though Jesus himself baptised not, but his disciples,) he left Judaea, and departed again into Galilee. And he must needs go through Samaria. Then cometh he to a city of Samaria, which is called Sychar, near to the parcel of ground that Jacob gave to his son Joseph. Now Jacob's well was there. Jesus therefore, being wearied with his journey, sat thus on the well: and it was about the sixth hour. There cometh a woman of Samaria to draw water: Jesus saith unto her, Give me to drink. (For his disciples were gone away unto the city to buy meat.) Then saith the woman of Samaria unto him, How is it that thou, being a Jew, askest drink of me, which am a woman of Samaria? for the Jews have no dealings with the Samaritans. Jesus answered and said unto her, If thou knewest the gift of God, and who it is that saith to thee, Give me to drink; thou wouldest have asked of him, and he would have given thee living water. The woman saith unto him, Sir, thou hast nothing to draw with, and the well is deep: from whence then hast thou that living water? Art thou greater than our father Jacob, which gave us the well, and drank thereof himself, and his children, and his cattle? Jesus answered and said unto her, Whosoever drinketh of this water shall thirst again: But whosoever drinketh of the water that I shall give him shall never thirst; but the water that I shall give him shall be in him a well of water springing up into everlasting life. The woman saith unto him, Sir, give me this water, that I thirst not, neither come hither to draw. Jesus saith unto her, Go, call thy husband, and come hither. The woman answered and said, I have no husband. Jesus said unto her, Thou hast well said, I have no husband: For thou hast had five husbands; and he whom thou now hast is not thy husband: in that saidst thou truly. The woman saith unto him, Sir, I perceive that thou art a prophet. Our fathers worshipped in this mountain; and ye say, that in Jerusalem is the place where men ought to worship. Jesus saith unto her, Woman, believe

151

me, the hour cometh, when ye shall neither in this mountain, nor yet at Jerusalem, worship the Father. Ye worship ye know not what: we know what we worship: for salvation is of the Jews. But the hour cometh, and now is, when the true worshippers shall worship the Father in spirit and in truth: for the Father seeketh such to worship him. God is a Spirit: and they that worship him must worship him in spirit and in truth. The woman saith unto him, I know that Messias cometh, which is called Christ: when he is come, he will tell us all things. Jesus saith unto her, I that speak unto thee am he' (John 4:1-26).

What does it take to save a sinner? How is conversion accomplished? I want to show you how our Lord Jesus brought the Samaritan woman to himself, giving her life and faith in himself by his omnipotent mercy. In this portion of holy scripture God the Holy Spirit shows us that which is taught throughout the book of God: Conversion is the work of God alone. Here are five things that are necessary for the conversion of a sinner.

1. No sinner will ever come to Christ until Christ first comes to the sinner. No sinner will come to Christ until the Lord Jesus Christ himself crosses the sinner's path. 'When therefore the Lord knew how the Pharisees had heard that Jesus made and baptised more disciples than John, (Though Jesus himself baptised not, but his disciples,) he left Judaea, and departed again into Galilee' (vv. 1, 2).

The Son of God left Judea. What a solemn word this is from God! Our Lord was in the midst of the Pharisees. He preached in their streets. He who is God's salvation walked the streets of Judea and preached the gospel. But the Pharisees despised him and his gospel. They would not receive the word of God. They preferred religion to righteousness. Therefore, the Lord Jesus left them. He left them in the darkness of their imaginary light. He left them to go to hell in the delusion of their self-righteousness. He left them to themselves!

Hear God's word and be warned. If you trifle with Christ and the gospel of God's grace in him, you court the wrath and judgment of God! If God leaves you to yourself, you are as sure for hell as if you were already there. I pray that God will not leave you to yourself.

If you go to hell, you will have no one to blame but yourself. It will be your own work, your own doing, your own fault (Proverbs 1:23-31). But do not be so foolish as to imagine that your unbelief will alter, or in any way affect the purpose of God. It will not (Romans 3:3, 4). God's purpose does not depend upon the consent of man's will, or upon the work of any man. You may not trust Christ. You may never come to him. But someone will. There is an elect remnant who must and shall be saved. At the appointed time of love, Christ will come to the sinner chosen by grace and redeemed by his precious blood. At the appointed time of love the Good Shepherd comes seeking his lost sheep.

'And he must needs go through Samaria. Then cometh he to a city of Samaria, which is called Sychar, near to the parcel of ground that Jacob gave to his son Joseph. Now Jacob's well was there. Jesus therefore, being wearied with his journey, sat thus on the well: and it was about the sixth hour' (vv. 4-6). This looks like a chance meeting, a lucky break; but it was nothing of the kind. In God's eternal purpose, that place had been fixed before the world began. That parcel of ground was bought and that well was dug by Jacob because he desired it. But, more importantly, that parcel of ground was bought and that well was dug so that Christ our Saviour might come there to meet and save a lost, ruined sinner. The Son of God came there seeking one of those the Father gave to him before the world began. The woman did not come to the well seeking Christ; but he came to the well seeking her (Isaiah 65:1).

Divine providence arranged for the needy sinner and the mighty Saviour to be at the well at the same time. She came to the well at noon (the sixth hour of the day), in the heat of the day, when it was most likely that no one else would be there, because she was a woman with a name and a reputation that made her the object of great scorn. Yet, she came at this hour, because this was the hour fixed by God to save her.

Notice this, too: the Lord Jesus arranged to be alone with the object of his mercy, love, and grace. He sent his disciples away to buy (to buy, not to beg[3]) food (v. 8). I am reminded of what we read in the book of Hosea concerning God's method of grace. 'Therefore, behold, I will allure her, and bring her into the wilderness, and speak comfortably unto her' (Hosea 2:14).

'There cometh a woman of Samaria to draw water: Jesus saith unto her, Give me to drink. (For his disciples were gone away unto the city to buy meat.) Then saith the woman of Samaria unto him, How is it that thou, being a Jew, askest drink of me, which am a woman of Samaria? for the Jews have no dealings with the Samaritans' (vv. 7-9).

Observe that, as Robert Hawker pointed out, 'The conversation which took place at the well, between Jesus and this woman began with our Lord. Yes! All the overtures of grace come first from the Lord (1 John 4:19)'.

This Samaritan woman would never have come to Christ had he not first crossed her path and come to her. Second, once he crossed her path, the Lord created an interest in her (vv. 10-14). He asked her for a drink of water, because he was thirsty, yes; but the thirst he had come to quench was his thirst for her soul. His request was designed to get her interest and attention.

The woman answered his request with a rude retort. Essentially, she said, 'You're a Jew. You wouldn't have anything to do with me, if you didn't need me. How dare you ask me to draw water for you! I know what you think of

---

[3] 'Our Saviour lived not upon alms.' – John Trapp

me.' But our Lord is longsuffering toward his elect, not willing that any of them should perish. He ignored her insult and pursued her heart. See verse 10.

'Jesus answered and said unto her, If thou knewest the gift of God, and who it is that saith to thee, Give me to drink; thou wouldest have asked of him, and he would have given thee living water' (v. 10).

There is much more in this verse than I can deal with now; but I want you to see the obvious things. First, salvation is the gift of God (Romans 6:23). Who can measure the gifts of God? They are innumerable! Yet, in one great gift, God gives all. Christ is the gift of God, the unspeakable gift of God. Christ is salvation. Christ is eternal life (Luke 2:30; John 17:3).

You will never be saved, you will never come to Christ, until you are made to know the gift of God. Henry Mahan wrote:

> This is the root of man's whole problem. The gift of God is salvation; it is eternal life (1 John 5:11). God is the Giver; all we do is receive. Man does not know the gift, and he does not know Christ, the Giver! Neither does he know his need for mercy. 'If you knew these things, you would ask of me'. Asking proceeds from knowing. Before we ask, God has to deal with us in conviction and revelation. Notice Christ deals with her on the basis of who, not what; it is not doctrine, any more than doing, that saves. It is the person Jesus Christ!

Salvation is to be had for the asking (John 7:37, 38; Luke 11:9-13). 'Thou wouldest have asked of him, and he would have given thee living water'. How close at hand salvation is! 'But what saith it? The word is nigh thee, even in thy mouth, and in thy heart: that is, the word of faith, which we preach; That if thou shalt confess with thy mouth the Lord Jesus, and shalt believe in thine heart that God hath raised him from the dead, thou shalt be saved' (Romans 10:8, 9). Christ is willing to pour out this living water of grace, salvation, and eternal life to sinners in superabundance! 'Ask and ye shall receive'.

2. All men by nature are totally ignorant of all things spiritual, until we are taught of God the Holy Spirit (1 Corinthians 2:9-14). In verses 11 and 12, this poor woman did what all unregenerate people do when they talk, or try to talk about spiritual things. She showed her total ignorance. She had no idea who she was talking to, or what she was talking about. Like Nicodemus in John 3:4, she was just talking.

'The woman saith unto him, Sir, thou hast nothing to draw with, and the well is deep: from whence then hast thou that living water? Art thou greater than our father Jacob, which gave us the well, and drank thereof himself, and his children, and his cattle?' (vv. 11, 12).

In verses 13, 14 the Lord Jesus declares the vanity of all earthly things. 'Jesus answered and said unto her, Whosoever drinketh of this water shall thirst again: But whosoever drinketh of the water that I shall give him shall never thirst; but the water that I shall give him shall be in him a well of water springing up into everlasting life' (vv. 13, 14).

These words are written by the finger of God over all the wells of this world: 'Whosoever drinketh of this water shall thirst again'. The thirst that is in you, the thirst of your soul is too deep to be quenched by the waters of this world. Have you not found it to be so? But that person who is born of God, who receives the water of life, who has the grace of God, the Spirit of God, the Christ of God, and the light and life of God in his soul shall never thirst again (1 Corinthians 1:30; Colossians 2:9, 10). No sinner will ever come to Christ until Christ comes to the chosen, redeemed sinner and creates a thirst in his soul for something more than can be found in this world.

3. No sinner will come to Christ until he exposes to that sinner his own sin. Before a sinner comes to Christ for mercy, he must be made to know and admit his sin before God. As he intended to be gracious to her, the Lord Jesus made this woman know that she was utterly naked before him: 'The woman saith unto him, Sir, give me this water, that I thirst not, neither come hither to draw. Jesus saith unto her, Go, call thy husband, and come hither. The woman answered and said, I have no husband. Jesus said unto her, Thou hast well said, I have no husband: For thou hast had five husbands; and he whom thou now hast is not thy husband: in that saidst thou truly' (vv. 15-18).

He laid bare what she thought she could keep hidden. This always makes sinners uncomfortable. We love darkness rather than light. We will not come to the light, lest our deeds be reproved. And when the light falls on us, we at once take refuge and try to turn the light away from ourselves. 'The woman saith unto him, Sir, I perceive that thou art a prophet. Our fathers worshipped in this mountain; and ye say, that in Jerusalem is the place where men ought to worship' (vv. 19, 20).

The Samaritan woman immediately changed her tone and the subject. She began to speak respectfully, and started talking religion. She wanted to get away from the subject of her immoral, lascivious, perverse behaviour. Her conscience was pricked; and she tried to soothe her conscience by talking about her religion. She tried to break the barb off the Master's arrow with the shield of religious controversy. Men love to talk about religion in general terms, just like this salty old girl. Here she is, a woman with less respectability than a prostitute, a woman who shacked up with one man, then another, without the least compunction, defending her father's religion! But the Lord Jesus would not be led into her trap. He was far more concerned for her soul than he was in proving a point. So he did what only he can do. He destroyed her refuge of lies.

4. No sinner will come to Christ and find refuge in him, until he destroys every false refuge, every refuge of lies, in which the sinner attempts to hide from God. Every rebel sinner has a refuge of lies, a religious refuge he has built, some kind of fortress around his soul, a refuge in which, like Adam in the garden, he is hiding from God. That refuge must be destroyed.

Notice how the Lord Jesus destroyed this woman's refuge. He did not shake his finger in her face and say, 'You Arminian Samaritans are all going to hell.' He simply told her the truth; and the truth, penetrating her heart, destroyed her refuge. 'Jesus saith unto her, Woman, believe me, the hour cometh, when ye shall neither in this mountain, nor yet at Jerusalem, worship the Father. Ye worship ye know not what: we know what we worship: for salvation is of the Jews. But the hour cometh, and now is, when the true worshippers shall worship the Father in spirit and in truth: for the Father seeketh such to worship him. God is a Spirit: and they that worship him must worship him in spirit and in truth' (vv. 21-24).

God the Holy Spirit gives us his commentary on our Saviour's words in Philippians 3:1-3. 'Finally, my brethren, rejoice in the Lord. To write the same things to you, to me indeed is not grievous, but for you it is safe. Beware of dogs, beware of evil workers, beware of the concision. For we are the circumcision, which worship God in the spirit, and rejoice in Christ Jesus, and have no confidence in the flesh'.

God is seeking sinners to worship him in Spirit and in Truth. If we would worship God, we must worship him in Christ, in the Holy Spirit, in the spirit of sincerity, in the spirit of faith, and in the truth of the gospel (Isaiah 28:14-22; Hebrews 4:14-16; 10:16-22).

5. The Lord Jesus Christ must make himself known to the sinner, before the sinner will come to him. 'The woman saith unto him, I know that Messias cometh, which is called Christ: when he is come, he will tell us all things. Jesus saith unto her, I that speak unto thee am he' (vv. 25, 26).

Slowly, but surely, the word of God had done its work (Romans 10:17; James 1:18; 1 Peter 1:23). This woman was driven from her refuge of lies into the arms of the Son of God. As soon as she expressed a desire for the Christ of God, in whom alone sinners can worship God, he said, 'I am'! 'I am he'. That is salvation. That is what it takes to bring sinners to the Saviour, the revelation of Christ (Zechariah 12:10).

Once Christ is revealed to you and in you it is enough. Nothing more is needed. A needy sinner and the sovereign Saviour met face to face, at Jacob's well and all was settled forever (Isaiah 45:20-25; Matthew 11:28-30).

Chapter 21

The Blessed Constraint Of Grace

'When therefore the Lord knew how the Pharisees had heard that Jesus made and baptised more disciples than John, (Though Jesus himself baptised not, but his disciples,) he left Judaea, and departed again into Galilee. And he must needs go through Samaria. Then cometh he to a city of Samaria, which is called Sychar, near to the parcel of ground that Jacob gave to his son Joseph. Now Jacob's well was there. Jesus therefore, being wearied with his journey, sat thus on the well: and it was about the sixth hour. There cometh a woman of Samaria to draw water: Jesus saith unto her, Give me to drink. (For his disciples were gone away unto the city to buy meat.) Then saith the woman of Samaria unto him, How is it that thou, being a Jew, askest drink of me, which am a woman of Samaria? for the Jews have no dealings with the Samaritans' (John 4:1-9).

In these opening verses of John 4 there are several things that demand our attention. Here are seven lessons the Holy Spirit would have us lay to heart.

1. The Man Who Is God
The very first thing we see in this chapter is the fact that our Lord Jesus Christ, the man who lived and died upon this earth to save us from our sins, is himself the omniscient God. The primary purpose of John's gospel is to show us that the man Christ Jesus is God, God manifest in the flesh. Therefore, he misses no opportunity to display our Saviour's Godhood. There is no hint of anyone having informed him of what the Pharisees were saying and doing, but 'the

157

Lord knew'. There was no need for anyone to inform him of anything, because he is the God before whom nothing is hidden, before whom darkness is light.

That One who humbled himself, who took the infinite stoop of taking into union with himself our humanity, who came down here to dwell upon the earth in human flesh as Jehovah's Servant, is here called 'the Lord' because he is the Lord! This man, whom the Pharisees contemptuously regarded as the Nazarene carpenter, was none other than the Christ of God, in whom 'dwelleth all the fulness of the godhead bodily'!

He who brings in everlasting righteousness as a man for men must himself be the everlasting God. He who obtains eternal redemption for sinners by the shedding of his blood as a man must himself be the eternal God.

2. Opposition To Christ

The religious world is now, always has been, and, until time is no more, always will be set in opposition to the God of glory, his Son, and the gospel of his grace. Mainstream religion has always been opposed to the worship of our God. I know that many talk of days gone by when 'most people believed the things we do, when most people believed the gospel of the grace of God'. I defy anyone to show me such a time.

The fact is, from the days of Cain and Abel, through the days of Enoch, Noah, and Job, while Abraham walked in the earth with God, from the days of Moses, throughout the years of Old Testament history, the vast majority of the people in this world despised the worship of God, even those who professed to worship him and claimed to be his people. All men are idolaters by nature. All men are will-worshippers by nature. All men vainly attempt to mix their works with God's grace to find acceptance with God.

There is a way which seems right to all men. All men walk in that way, defend that way, and oppose anything and anyone who speaks against that way; but the ends thereof are the ways of death (Proverbs 14:12; 16:25).

This is exactly what we see in these Pharisees here in John 4. 'The Pharisees heard that Jesus made and baptised more disciples than John.' Even at this early date in our Lord's public ministry, the Pharisees were obviously plotting to get rid of him.

They were jealous of his following. It was bad enough that they had to put up with John; but here was a man, obviously in league with John, who was even more influential than John the Baptist. The Pharisees were threatened by the Master's influence. They feared losing their position, power, and prestige as religious leaders. The Lord Jesus was looked upon by them as a man from a lower social class, he was from Nazareth of Galilee, from which they thought no prophet could come (John 7:52). They just knew that nothing good could come out of Nazareth. But, primarily, they despised his doctrine. Our Lord openly exposed, reproved, and rebuked their hypocrisy, their tradition, their customs, their doctrine, and their empty religious ritualism.

3. Believer's Baptism
Believer's baptism is an ordinance of divine worship, for which we are responsible, but only an ordinance of worship. Baptism has nothing to do with salvation.

'When therefore the Lord knew how the Pharisees had heard that Jesus made and baptised more disciples than John, (Though Jesus himself baptised not, but his disciples)' (vv. 1, 2). Notice the order here. First, disciples were made. Then, they were baptised, not the other way around. You will search the scriptures in vain to find anyone being baptised as an infant, or being baptised to obtain grace, or being baptised before conversion. Baptism is the believer's public confession of faith in Christ, by which we identify ourselves with and make an avowed, public commitment to Christ, his people, and his gospel (Romans 6:3-6).

'Jesus himself baptised not, but his disciples'. Commenting on that statement, C. H. Spurgeon wisely observed, 'Our Saviour did not himself baptise his followers. Now, if baptism depended upon the character or the office of the baptiser, Jesus would certainly have done it; but to show us that the person baptising does not impart any grace to the person baptised, our Lord baptised not, but left that work to his disciples.'

4. Religion Makes Bigots
Here is another lesson, a lesson which is evident to almost every one, except those who make it evident. Religion without Christ makes people even more proud, bigoted, and mean spirited than we are by nature.

'The Jews have no dealings with the Samaritans' (v. 9). The Jews looked upon the Samaritans as a lower class, an inferior race, and despised them. The Jews had the word and oracles of God; but they would not think of sharing the knowledge and worship of God with the Samaritans. The Jews, particularly the Pharisees, were a heartless people, totally indifferent to the glory of God and the souls of men. They were only concerned for themselves, their appearance before men, and their religion. The proudest, meanest, most dishonest people I have ever known have been religious people, not believers, religious people!

5. Christ Leaves
Light despised will be withdrawn and turned into darkness. What sad, sad words are those found in verse three: he left Judea! Our Lord refused to cast his pearls before swine. He left Judea! What a warning those words give: light

despised will be withdrawn and turned into darkness (John 12:35-46, 2 Corinthians 5:20-6:2).

I urge all to believe the gospel. I call upon sinners everywhere, in God's name, as God's ambassador to their souls, to believe on the Lord Jesus Christ. Yet, I assure you that God's will, God's purpose, God's grace, and God's glory do not depend upon what men do, not in the least.

6. God's Purpose Is Sovereign

The purpose of God is not and cannot be altered by man's unbelief. Far from it! If you go to hell, it will be your fault. There is no question about that. God would save you, if you would obey his voice, if you would trust his Son. If you go to hell, you will, as he says, 'eat the fruit of your own way and be filled with your own devices'. But your unbelief, your rebellion, your despising the counsel of God will not alter the purpose of God, but only fulfil it (Romans 3:3, 4).

God cast off Israel because Israel cast off God. Yet, in their rejection of God's gospel, God's kingdom, and God's Son, the Jews, by bringing judgment upon themselves, became the very instruments by which grace was carried to the Gentiles, that the fulness of the Gentiles might be brought in by the grace of God (Romans 11:1, 25, 26, 29, 33-36). Blessed be God, it is yet true, and forever shall be 'The foundation of God standeth sure, having this seal, The Lord knoweth them that are his' (2 Timothy 2:19).

7. Grace Comes Calling

Though the Jews despised him, though the Pharisees sought to destroy him, though he left Judea, it is written in verse 4, 'He must needs go through Samaria', because there are some people in this world who must and shall be saved by the almighty grace and according to the sovereign, unalterable purpose of our great and glorious God.

Read the text as it stands. 'he must'. It does not say he might, he wants to, he hopes to, he will if, or he is going to try. The text says, 'he must'! That means, 'he must needs go through Samaria'!

This was not a thing he might or might not do, but a thing he must do. Why? Because there was a chosen, blood bought sinner there, for whom 'the time of love' had come. In fact, there were a bunch of chosen, blood-bought sinners[4] down in Samaria, for whom 'the time of love' had now come; and they must now be saved by his almighty grace, every one of them!

---

[4] Yes, I do understand that Christ had not yet shed his blood at Calvary. I also understand that he is the Lamb of God who was slain from the foundation of the world (Revelation 13:8; 17:8). These Samaritans were, like all God's elect, redeemed in the purpose of God from eternity, redeemed by the precious blood of Christ, 'who verily was foreordained before the foundation of the world'!

Though obliged to do nothing, yet, as our Surety, the Son of God obliged himself to perform specific deeds of mercy, love and grace for his elect, that he might bring us to glory. He obliged himself to save his own (John 10:16-18). The salvation of chosen sinners is a thing as certain and as much a matter of necessity with God our Saviour, as his own truth and faithfulness.

'And he must needs go through Samaria' to save his chosen, to seek and save his lost sheep. I know, many say, 'He had to go through Samaria, because that was the nearest way to get from Judea to Galilee.' They are exactly right. The closest route from Judea to Galilee was to go through Samaria. But it was God who, in his wise and adorable providence, made it the closest way, because God in his providence put his elect there. As C. H. Spurgeon put it, 'Providence directed man to build Samaria directly in the road, and grace constrained the Saviour to move in that direction.'

When the time of love comes for the objects of his mercy, love, and grace, the Lord Jesus will come to his chosen in almighty, omnipotent, irresistible, saving power. We bless and praise him for the fact that his people shall be willing in the day of his power. When God says 'must', it must be! There is no standing against God's omnipotent 'must'. Let me give you four reasons for these words, 'He must needs go through Samaria'.

A Divine Purpose
'And he must needs go through Samaria', because of a divine purpose. God purposed it before the world began, and so it came to pass. We believe and rejoice in the grand, glorious, God honouring doctrine of divine predestination. It is a doctrine plainly taught in holy scripture, and a doctrine full of comfort for the believer's heart (Romans 8:28-30; Ephesians 1:3-6, 11).

A Divine Promise
'And he must needs go through Samaria', because of a divine promise. Divine predestination moves according to the promise God himself made in eternity to give eternal life to his elect. Yes, the Bible teaches the doctrine of election. We are told plainly that God promised eternal life to chosen sinners before the world began (Titus 1:1-3; 2 Thessalonians 2:13, 14; 2 Timothy 1:9, 10).

> Father, 'twas Thy love that knew us
> Earth's foundations long before:
> That same love to Jesus drew us
> By its sweet, constraining power,
> And will keep us safely now and ever more.

J. G. Deck

161

Divine predestination arranged all things from eternity, in the purpose of God, according to the divine promise of eternal life to chosen sinners in Christ. This promise of eternal life to God's elect was made in ...

A Divine Pact
'And he must needs go through Samaria', because of a divine pact. We delight to trace everything back to that sovereign pact and blessed covenant of grace made on our behalf with Christ, our Surety, before the world began. There is nothing more delightful to my soul than covenant love (2 Samuel 23:5). It was in that covenant that our Saviour put himself in bondage, put himself under obligation to save his people (John 10:16). 'And he must needs go through Samaria', because some of those other sheep were there, whom he must bring into his fold. Once more, 'he must needs go through Samaria', because of ...

A Divine Purchase
The Lord Jesus came here to fetch this woman, and the others in the city whom he had chosen, because he bought them with his blood. How I rejoice to tell sinners everywhere that the cross of Christ shall never be discovered a miscarriage.

The Lord Jesus must go through Samaria, because there were those in Samaria whom the Father had given him from eternity to save, for whom he voluntarily assumed all responsibility, whom he purchased with his own precious blood, whom he must save.

If you are one of God's elect, there is a needs be for Christ to save you; and save you he will. Perhaps you are yet in your sins. You may have been fleeing from him for years; but when he comes, he will overtake you. He will conquer you. He will have you. I am sent of God to tell you, he is already on his way, and he will have you. Blessed be God, there are some people in this world whom he must save, from whom he will not take 'No' for an answer.

When the Son of God comes to save, he will come to you like he did Zacchaeus of old (Luke 19:5, 9, 10). 'And it shall be said in that day, Lo, this is our God; we have waited for him, and he will save us: this is the LORD; we have waited for him, we will be glad and rejoice in his salvation' (Isaiah 25:9).

This is the blessed constraint of God's grace. His people must be saved because he has purposed to save them. Therefore we read in John 4:4 that our Lord Jesus Christ 'must needs go through Samaria'.

Chapter 22

Two Stories Of Grace

'And he must needs go through Samaria. Then cometh he to a city of Samaria, which is called Sychar, near to the parcel of ground that Jacob gave to his son Joseph. Now Jacob's well was there. Jesus therefore, being wearied with his journey, sat thus on the well: and it was about the sixth hour. There cometh a woman of Samaria to draw water: Jesus saith unto her, Give me to drink' (John 4:4-7).

I am constantly aware of my utter insufficiency for the work of the ministry, for the work of proclaiming the gospel of Christ to eternity bound sinners. What great wisdom and grace is needed to minister, to the souls of men, wisdom and grace that only God the Holy Spirit can give!

We all have different needs, different backgrounds, different experiences, and different circumstances. Yet, we all need the same things spiritually. We all need grace, forgiveness, righteousness, and salvation. In John chapters three and four we see two people who could not have been more different, who were saved by the marvellous, free grace of God in Christ. These two great sinners and Christ, our great Saviour, are set before us in these two chapters of Inspiration in a most remarkable way.

'There was a man of the Pharisees, named Nicodemus, a ruler of the Jews: The same came to Jesus by night, and said unto him, Rabbi, we know that thou art a teacher come from God: for no man can do these miracles that thou doest, except God be with him. Jesus answered and said unto him, Verily, verily, I say unto thee, Except a man be born again, he cannot see the kingdom of God'

(John 3:1-3). 'And he must needs go through Samaria. Then cometh he to a city of Samaria, which is called Sychar, near to the parcel of ground that Jacob gave to his son Joseph. Now Jacob's well was there. Jesus therefore, being wearied with his journey, sat thus on the well: and it was about the sixth hour. There cometh a woman of Samaria to draw water: Jesus saith unto her, Give me to drink' (John 4:4-7).

It is always a mistake to interpret any portion of scripture without considering the context in which it is found. In fact, it is impossible to interpret the word of God correctly, if we do not interpret it contextually. Not only did the Holy Spirit inspire the words of holy scripture, he also inspired and fixed the order in which we are given things in the inspired volume. It is no accident that the two stories of Nicodemus and the Samaritan woman are set before us in the same context. Together they show us that none are beyond the reach of God's saving grace in Christ.

Nicodemus shows us that none can rise too high, and the Samaritan woman shows us that none can sink too low to be saved by the grace of God. At the end of these two stories of grace, we have this great declaration in John 4:42 'This is indeed the Christ, the Saviour of the world.'

The Lord Jesus Christ is the only Saviour there is. He is the Saviour of Jews and Gentiles, men and women out of every nation, tongue, and position in the world (Acts 4:12). All who are saved are saved in the same way. We are saved by grace (Ephesians 2:1-10), through the doing and dying of the Lord Jesus Christ, the sinners' Substitute (2 Corinthians 5:17-21), by the revelation of Christ in us (2 Corinthians 4:3-6; Galatians 1:15, 16).

Yet, we all experience grace in a distinct, personal way. No two sinners find grace in exactly the same way. This is set before us in these two people. Let us look at the way our Lord Jesus dealt with Nicodemus and the Samaritan woman, and see what we can learn from their experience of grace.

A Great Separation
First, we see that there is a great separation between Nicodemus and the Samaritan woman. Both were chosen of God and saved by his grace. We see this fact with regard to the Samaritan woman in the immediate context. Once the Lord revealed himself to her, she immediately left her water pots and said to the men of the city, 'Come, see a man, that told me all things that ever I did. Is not this the Christ?' (v. 29). Many believed because of her word.

Nicodemus was one of those disciples who in John 19 came to bury the Lord Jesus. He was not converted immediately upon hearing the gospel. But he was converted. The Master said to him, 'Ye must be born again' and he was, at the appointed hour, born again by God's omnipotent mercy.

Here are two sinners, chosen, redeemed, and called by grace; but it would be impossible to imagine two people more distinct and separate from one another. The contrast between Nicodemus and the Samaritan woman is obvious to the most casual reader.

Nicodemus was a recognised, important, sophisticated ruler of the Jews, a man of name, rank, and reputation. She was an unnamed, insignificant nobody. Nicodemus was a proud Jew. She was a despised Samaritan. Samaritans were a mongrel people, a people who feared the Lord and worshipped their own gods, mixing the worship of God with the worship of idols.

Nicodemus was a wealthy, well-educated scholar. The woman was poor and uneducated. He was a man. The Samaritan was a woman. He was a man known and respected for his great morality. She was an adulteress.

Nicodemus came to the Saviour by night to protect his reputation. This woman came to Jacob's well at noon to avoid other people, because she had no reputation to protect. Nicodemus sought the Lord Jesus. The Lord Jesus came to Samaria seeking this woman.

The Samaritan woman was converted immediately upon hearing the message of Christ. Nicodemus was converted a good while after he first heard the gospel from the Saviour's lips.

It would be impossible to find two people more diverse, more unalike, or more separate from one another socially. Yet, these two people, Nicodemus and the Samaritan woman, are now seated together around the throne of the Lamb in glory. Only the grace of God can do that. Only in Christ are social barriers demolished; and in Christ they are demolished (Colossians 3:10, 11; Ephesians 2:12-22). Grace reconciles sinners to God; and grace reconciles sinners to one another.

A Great Sameness
Second, though much separated and distinguished Nicodemus and the Samaritan woman from each other, still there was a great sameness about them.

As I look into the faces of the immortal souls sitting before me every time I stand to preach the gospel, I see many things which, naturally, distinguish us from one another. Yet, there is a great sameness about us all. Those who are without Christ may look at the person sitting beside them, in front of them, behind them, or across the room from them, and think, 'I am not like him, (or her)', but they really are exactly the same in many ways. What did Nicodemus and this Samaritan woman have in common? I am sure there was much more than this, but here are just four, four things we all have in common.

1. Self-righteousness: they both thought they were right spiritually, right before God. Neither of them had peace in their hearts. Their souls were troubled. Their consciences were uneasy. But they had both made a refuge of

lies, in which they hid themselves in self-righteousness[5]. Both had a religious refuge, that had to be destroyed before they would flee to Christ for refuge. That fact is true concerning all who do not know God (Isaiah 28:14-20).

2. Spiritual blindness: neither Nicodemus nor the Samaritan woman had even the slightest spiritual understanding or discernment. Neither could see the kingdom of heaven (1 Corinthians 2:14).

3. Rebellion: both the proud Pharisee and the Samaritan adulteress were lost rebels. When he was confronted with things he could neither understand nor refute, Nicodemus poked fun at the Master's doctrine. He ridiculed what he could not comprehend (John 3:4). When the Lord Jesus spoke to the Samaritan woman about living water, because she could not understand his words, she did the same thing (John 4:11, 12).

The fact is, this woman and Nicodemus, like all men and women by nature, like all who are yet without Christ, were lost rebels. As it is written, 'All we, like sheep, have gone astray. We have turned, every one, to his own way' (Isaiah 53:6). 'They are all gone out of the way, they are together become unprofitable; there is none that doeth good, no, not one' (Romans 3:12).

If you are lost, it is because you are an obstinate, stubborn, implacable rebel. If you go to hell, it will be because you have broken God's law, despised God's gospel, rejected God's counsel, laughed at God's reproof, refused to bow to God's Son, and hated God in the very core of your being.

4. Emptiness: both Nicodemus and the Samaritan woman tried hard, just like we all did, to cover it up; but they had an emptiness in their souls, which could not be filled with the water pots of their religions, or their accomplishments, or their lusts.

Augustine said, 'Thou hast made us for Thyself; and our hearts are restless until they find their rest in Thee.'

> All my life long I had panted
> For a draught from some clear spring,
> That I hoped would quench the burning
> Of the thirst I felt within.

> Feeding on the husks around me,
> Till my strength was almost gone,
> Longed my soul for something better,
> Only still to hunger on.

---

[5] Self-righteousness flourishes in human flesh, just as fully among adulterers and adulteresses as among Pharisees and Sadducees, just as well in the hearts of criminals as in the hearts of cardinals. Just as Nicodemus argued theology with the Master, defending himself and his religion, so did this adulteress!

Poor was I, and sought for riches,
Something that would satisfy,
But the dust I gathered round me
Only mocked my soul's sad cry!

Well of water, ever springing,
Bread of life, so rich and free,
Untold wealth that never faileth,
My Redeemer is to me.

Clara Tear Williams

A Great Saviour
Oh, what a great Saviour our Lord Jesus Christ is! Let me show you what he did for these two great sinners. The Lord Jesus did not deal with Nicodemus and the Samaritan woman the same way. Yet, in a very real sense he did. This is always what Christ does when he comes to save a sinner.

He destroyed the refuge of lies in which they hid themselves. He exposed their rebellion, unbelief, and sin. He made himself known to them. He crossed them at their point of rebellion. And he conquered them by his grace.

'Blessed is the man whom thou choosest, and causest to approach unto thee, that he may dwell in thy courts: we shall be satisfied with the goodness of thy house, even of thy holy temple' (Psalms 65:4).

'Thy people shall be willing in the day of thy power, in the beauties of holiness from the womb of the morning: thou hast the dew of thy youth' (Psalms 110:3).

Chapter 23

Christ The Well Of Salvation

'Now Jacob's well was there. Jesus therefore, being wearied with his journey, sat thus on the well: and it was about the sixth hour' (John 4:6).

Christ is a River flowing from the throne of God, the River of the Water of Life (Revelation 22:1). 'There is a river, the streams whereof shall make glad the city of God, the holy place of the tabernacles of the most High' (Psalms 46:4). 'Thou visitest the earth, and waterest it: thou greatly enrichest it with the river of God, which is full of water' (Psalms 65:9).

The Lord Jesus is 'The Fountain of Life' and 'The Fountain of Israel' (Psalms 36:9; 68:26). He is the 'Fountain of Living Waters' (Jeremiah 17:13), from whom we receive the Spirit of God, who springs up in our souls as a Well of Living Water unto everlasting life (John 7:37-39).

And he is 'a Fountain opened' to us for sin and uncleanness by God the Holy Spirit (Zechariah 12:10). How often in scripture our blessed Saviour is spoken of as 'Water'. He is a River of Water and a Fountain of Water. And in John 4:6 we see the Lord Jesus meeting a sinner at a well of water. 'Now Jacob's well was there. Jesus therefore, being wearied with his journey, sat thus on the well: and it was about the sixth hour.'

The Message
There has got to be something special about that. Everything written in the book of God is designed to teach us something about the person and work of the Lord Jesus Christ. Christ is the message of this blessed book. All the laws given to Israel, every aspect of worship under the ceremonial law, all the

prophecies, all the events in the history of Israel, everything in the inspired volume, by design of infallible inspiration, points us to the Lord Jesus Christ. It is of immense importance that we never read the scriptures casually, merely for entertainment, or to fulfil our daily disciplines. We should always seek the spiritual message in every passage we read. I do not mean that we should invent a spiritual message and read it into a text; but we should always seek the spiritual message of the text, understanding that the message of every text is Jesus Christ crucified (Luke 24:27, 44-47; John 5:39; Acts 10:43).

If the whole volume of inspiration is written to reveal the person and work of our beloved Redeemer, as it clearly is, that means, as A. W. Pink observed, 'There is a profound significance to everything in scripture, even the seemingly unimportant details.'

With these things in mind, I call your attention to the place where our Lord Jesus met the adulterous Samaritan woman, the place at which grace was bestowed upon her, the place from which she found that living water, which was made to be in her soul 'a well of water springing up into everlasting life'. 'Now Jacob's well was there. Jesus therefore, being wearied with his journey, sat thus on the well: and it was about the sixth hour.'

Significance Of Places
All that transpired between Christ and this poor sinner took place at the well called, Jacob's well. Frequently, it is impossible to understand the spiritual, gospel meaning of those events recorded in the scriptures until we know the place where those events occurred and understand the significance of it. Let me show you some examples of what I mean.

The children of Israel were in Egypt when the Lord delivered them by blood and by power. Egypt symbolises the world of darkness and the bondage we were in, under the tyranny of Satan and the terror of the law, when God saved us by his grace. John the Baptist came preaching in the wilderness of Judea. That wilderness aptly portrays the emptiness, barrenness, and desolation of religion without Christ. When our Saviour began his public ministry, he went up into the mountain, a place of elevation, to give us the Sermon on the Mount. That mountain displayed the elevation of his throne and the heavenly nature and source of his doctrine. When he gave out the parables of his kingdom, he went down to the seaside. In scripture, the sea represents the Gentile world[6]. Thus, he taught that his gospel, his kingdom, and his salvation were for God's elect throughout all the world, both Jew and Gentile. In the parable of the good Samaritan our Saviour portrays the poor sinners he came to seek and save as a certain man, who went down from Jerusalem (the

---

[6] Isaiah 17:12, 13; Ezekiel 26:3; Daniel 7:2; Revelation 17:5

place of blessedness and peace, the city of God) to Jericho (the place of curse). That is a picture of man's fall. He taught us the same thing in the parable of the prodigal son. The prodigal son left his father's house, ran away into a far country, and brought himself to abject poverty and utter ruin.

I could give many more examples; but these will suffice to demonstrate the need for observing and understanding the meaning of the place where things happen in the scriptures. Everything written in the book of God is written by divine inspiration and is written for a purpose; and that purpose is to teach us the gospel.

The Lord Jesus came to Jacob's well, choosing that spot to be the place where he would make himself known to the adulterous Samaritan woman, because he is himself the Well of Salvation. Let us see if that is not the teaching of holy scripture. In Isaiah 12:3 we read, 'Therefore with joy shall ye draw water out of the wells of salvation.'

Christ is the Well of Salvation; and there are many wells of salvation in him from which we draw the Water of Life. It is a great mistake to limit the accomplishment of our salvation to one thing. Christ is our Salvation; and he accomplished and accomplishes salvation for us by many mighty deeds of grace. There are many wells of salvation in him from which we draw the Water of Life. There is the well of his divinity (John 1:1-3); the well of his humanity (John 1:14); the well of his righteousness (Jeremiah 23:6; 33:6); the well of his atonement (Romans 5:1-11); the well of his resurrection (Philippians 3:10); the well of his exaltation (Philippians 2:8-11); the well of his intercession (1 John 2:1, 2); the well of his indwelling (Colossians 1:27); the well of his second coming (1 Thessalonians 4:13-18); the well of his presentation (Jude 24, 25).

In the Old Testament scriptures the wells around which so many important events took place were typical of our Lord Jesus. We will look at seven wells that stand out as highly significant places in scripture. Remember, however, these seven physical, historic wells, as meaningful as they were historically, are insignificant and meaningless to us, until we see how they represent our great Saviour, who is the Well from which we must draw the waters of salvation and eternal life by faith.

The Well Of Meeting

'But Abram said unto Sarai, Behold, thy maid is in thy hand; do to her as it pleaseth thee. And when Sarai dealt hardly with her, she fled from her face. And the angel of the LORD found her by a fountain of water in the wilderness, by the fountain in the way to Shur' (Genesis 16:6, 7). 'And she called the name of the LORD that spake unto her, Thou God seest me: for she said, Have I also here looked after him that seeth me? Wherefore the well was called Beerlahairoi; behold, it is between Kadesh and Bered' (Genesis 16:13, 14).

171

'Beerlahairoi' means 'the well of him that liveth and seeth me'. This is the first mention of a well in the word of God. It is not insignificant. The poor outcast was found at the well. God saw Hagar, met her, and supplied all her need at the well. The only place where God and sinners can ever meet is Christ. The only place at which God can or will look upon sinners in favour is Christ. The only source from which the needs of our souls can be supplied is Christ.

The children of Israel named that place where the Lord spoke to Moses and promised to give them water 'Beer', meaning 'a well of life'. When they were 'discouraged because of the way' (Numbers 21:4), they returned to the well and 'sang unto it' (Numbers 21:14-18).

'Wherefore it is said in the book of the wars of the LORD, What he did in the Red sea, and in the brooks of Arnon, And at the stream of the brooks that goeth down to the dwelling of Ar, and lieth upon the border of Moab. And from thence they went to Beer: that is the well whereof the LORD spake unto Moses, Gather the people together, and I will give them water. Then Israel sang this song, Spring up, O well; sing ye unto it: The princes digged the well, the nobles of the people digged it, by the direction of the lawgiver, with their staves. And from the wilderness they went to Mattanah' (Numbers 21:14-18).

The fact that they sang not by the well, but 'unto' the well makes it obvious that they were taught to look upon the wells God gave them as being representative of Christ and life in him by the Spirit (John 7:37-39).

The Well Of Revelation
Here again we see Hagar. This time, she has been expelled from the patriarch's home with her son, Ishmael.

'And Abraham rose up early in the morning, and took bread, and a bottle of water, and gave it unto Hagar, putting it on her shoulder, and the child, and sent her away: and she departed, and wandered in the wilderness of Beersheba. And the water was spent in the bottle, and she cast the child under one of the shrubs. And she went, and sat her down over against him a good way off, as it were a bowshot: for she said, Let me not see the death of the child. And she sat over against him, and lift up her voice, and wept. And God heard the voice of the lad; and the angel of God called to Hagar out of heaven, and said unto her, What aileth thee, Hagar? fear not; for God hath heard the voice of the lad where he is. Arise, lift up the lad, and hold him in thine hand; for I will make him a great nation. And God opened her eyes, and she saw a well of water; and she went, and filled the bottle with water, and gave the lad drink' (Genesis 21:14-19).

This well was the place of revelation to Hagar. Here is a poor, outcast sinner, perishing in a desolate wilderness. She is helplessly weeping before the Lord, not really praying, just weeping. Broken-hearted, desperate, helpless, she waited to die, watching her only child die. But God intervened. 'And God opened her eyes, and she saw a well of water'. What a great blessing of grace that was (Proverbs 20:12; 1 John 5:20). If we would be saved, we must know God. But God cannot be known by us, except he reveal himself. And the triune God reveals himself to sinners in Christ alone (John 1:18). Look at another well in this same chapter.

The Well Of A Covenant

'And Abraham took sheep and oxen, and gave them unto Abimelech; and both of them made a covenant. And Abraham set seven ewe lambs of the flock by themselves. And Abimelech said unto Abraham, What mean these seven ewe lambs which thou hast set by themselves? And he said, For these seven ewe lambs shalt thou take of my hand, that they may be a witness unto me, that I have digged this well. Wherefore he called that place Beersheba [well of oath or of promise]; because there they sware both of them' (Genesis 21:27-31).

The patriarchs cherished their wells. They often fought wars to defend and keep them, because without the well they could not survive. That is a good picture of the believer's desperate need of Christ. We must have him! Here, in Genesis 21:27-31, we are told about a covenant sealed by an oath at a well. It was a covenant for good. Does that remind you of anything? It should remind us of that better, everlasting covenant of grace, of which Christ is the Surety (Hebrews 7:20-22).

A Well Of Prayer

In Genesis 24 we find Abraham's servant, Eliezer, seeking a bride for Isaac. As he went about his business, he stopped by a well to pray, seeking God's direction, God's will, God's mercy.

'And the servant took ten camels of the camels of his master, and departed; for all the goods of his master were in his hand: and he arose, and went to Mesopotamia, unto the city of Nahor. And he made his camels to kneel down without the city by a well of water at the time of the evening, even the time that women go out to draw water. And he said, O LORD God of my master Abraham, I pray thee, send me good speed this day, and show kindness unto my master Abraham' (Genesis 24:10-12).

Christ, the Well of Salvation, is that One in whom, through whom, and by whom we have access to God. Christ is for us the Well of Prayer, the Place of Prayer (Hebrews 4:15, 16).

The Well Of Rest

'Then Jacob went on his journey, and came into the land of the people of the east. And he looked, and behold a well in the field, and, lo, there were three flocks of sheep lying by it; for out of that well they watered the flocks: and a great stone was upon the well's mouth. And thither were all the flocks gathered: and they rolled the stone from the well's mouth, and watered the sheep, and put the stone again upon the well's mouth in his place' (Genesis 29:1-3).

This well was found, not in the wilderness, but in the field. Here in green pastures the Good Shepherd makes his sheep lie down and rest and gives his sheep water from the well of his grace, assuring us that all is well with our souls. 'Say ye to the righteous, that it shall be well with him: for they shall eat the fruit of their doings' (Isaiah 3:10). Christ is our Well of Rest. He is our Rest. He is our Well of Satisfaction. 'O that one would give me to drink of the water of the well of Bethlehem' (2 Samuel 23:15).

The Well Of Refuge

'Now when Pharaoh heard this thing, he sought to slay Moses. But Moses fled from the face of Pharaoh, and dwelt in the land of Midian: and he sat down by a well. Now the priest of Midian had seven daughters: and they came and drew water, and filled the troughs to water their father's flock. And the shepherds came and drove them away: but Moses stood up and helped them, and watered their flock' (Exodus 2:15-17).

Thank God, there is One to whom sinners can flee for refuge. Our Refuge is that One to whom this well pointed, the Lord Jesus Christ.

'Behold, a king shall reign in righteousness, and princes shall rule in judgment. And a man shall be as an hiding place from the wind, and a covert from the tempest; as rivers of water in a dry place, as the shadow of a great rock in a weary land' (Isaiah 32:1, 2).

To this well alone we must come, like the daughters of Jethro. The hireling shepherds, those preachers who hate the gospel of the free and sovereign grace of God in Christ, drive sinners away from the well of refuge to a refuge of lies. Yet, even in this dark, dark day, God has his servants who, like Moses, stand up to help thirsting souls, watering the Lord's flock.

Jacob's Well

'Now Jacob's well was there. Jesus therefore, being wearied with his journey, sat thus on the well: and it was about the sixth hour' (John 4:6).

The Lord Jesus Christ is Jacob's Saviour. Jacob was a divinely chosen sinner (Romans 9:11-13). He was a blood-bought, redeemed sinner (Psalms 77:15; Isaiah 43:1), a sinner conquered and saved by God's free grace (Genesis 32:24). Jacob was a sinner who drank from Christ, the Well of Salvation, the Water of Life. Do you drink from this Well?

Chapter 24

Wearied With The Journey

'Now Jacob's well was there. Jesus therefore, being wearied with his journey, sat thus on the well: and it was about the sixth hour' (John 4:6).

Are you weary? Weary with the trials and temptations that vex your soul? Weary with the warfare raging in your heart? Weary with sin? Are you weary with labour and toil? Weary with the heavy burden you carry? Weary with this world? Are you weary with the journey, tired, worn out, beat down, exhausted? If you are the words of John 4:6 should be distinctly meaningful to you.

What a picture we have before us! Here is our great Saviour, the Lord of glory, the Son of God, that One who came to seek and save that which was lost, that One who lived to do his Father's will, 'wearied with his journey'. When we are weary and heavy laden, we are hereby encouraged to look to him. The Lord Jesus Christ was, as a man, as our Saviour, wearied with his journey, as he sat upon Jacob's well.

What does this mean? Why is this fact recorded? What does the Spirit of God intend for us to learn from the fact that our Saviour was tired, weary, beat down, exhausted from the toil and burden of his journey? Obviously, this fact is not recorded to reveal some weakness in our Saviour's character. But this event in the life of our Redeemer was and is intended to teach us that our dear Saviour is a real man, a man touched with the feeling of our infirmities.

A Real Man
First, we see here how truly human the Lord Jesus Christ is. The Apostle John, more than any other of the gospel writers, wrote his gospel narrative to show the divinity of our Lord Jesus Christ. It is John, above all others, who shows

175

us that Jesus the man is God the Son, the second person of the holy trinity (John 1:1-3; 1 John 5:7).

Yet, it is John who seems to go out of his way to show us the real humanity of Christ. Many today, who claim to believe in Christ, deny his true and absolute deity. But in John's day many who claimed to believe in Christ denied his real humanity. And multitudes today lose much benefit to their souls, because they fail to grasp the reality of our Saviour's humanity.

He who is our Redeemer must be both God and man in one glorious person. None but a perfect man could suffer the wrath and judgment of God for man's sin as our Substitute. None but God could satisfy the infinite wrath and justice of God to put away man's sin. That God-man, our Substitute, is Jesus Christ, who died, the just for the unjust, that he might bring us to God.

'God was manifest in the flesh.' 'The Word was made flesh and dwelt among us.' We repeat these words of scripture with ease. But I am sure we have not yet begun to grasp the reality and fulness of our Saviour's manhood. We seem to have more difficulty grasping the real humanity of Christ than we do understanding the glorious godhead of our Saviour. I know I do.

When I read in the Bible that the Lord Jesus Christ is the Creator, Sustainer, and Governor of all things, I have no problem at all in saying, 'Amen, my Saviour is my God.' Yet, I must confess to my shame that, when I read that he was tempted of the devil, that he was troubled in his soul, and that he was weary as a man, my first inclination is to try to explain away the reality of his temptations, troubles, and weariness. In doing so, I dishonour him whom most I long to honour in all things. The humanity of Christ is every bit as necessary to our salvation as his deity, and every bit as comforting.

The fact that our Saviour sat upon Jacob's well as a man wearied with his journey is intended to minister comfort to his people, and is intended to encourage sinners to trust him. Our Saviour's divinity did not in any way or to any degree diminish his capacity for suffering as a man.

You might ask, 'Why is it that he who raised the dead, multiplied the loaves and fishes, and turned water into wine for the benefit of multitudes did not perform a miracle for himself?' That is a good question.

When he was hungry after forty days of fasting, and Satan tempted him to turn the stones into bread, he certainly could have done so with the greatest of ease. Without question, the water in Jacob's well would have gushed out of the ground to quench the thirst of the Son of God and relieve his weariness had he simply willed it. But our Lord Jesus Christ came not to be ministered unto, even by creation, but to minister and to give his life a ransom for many.

If he would be our Saviour, if he would stand to his own bond as our Surety, if he would put away sin as our Substitute, it was absolutely necessary that the Lord Jesus Christ endure all the consequences of sin. 'It behoved him in all things to be made like unto his brethren.' From the moment he became flesh, the curse of the fall began to fall upon the Lord of life and glory.

Though he knew no sin, did no sin, and was altogether holy, harmless, undefiled, and separate from sinners, our blessed Saviour experienced all the frailties and infirmities of fallen humanity, which are the result of sin. He experienced all the calamities human life is exposed to in this world. Our Redeemer was pricked with all the thorns and thistles the earth is made to bring forth to man. He was, at last, brought to the dust of death by his Father, just as he said he must be in Psalms 22:15. These were the conditions to which the Redeemer subjected himself in the days of his flesh, when he was made sin for us who knew no sin, that we might be made the righteousness of God in him.

Our Saviour's whole life was a life of weariness, sorrows, and affliction. He was exposed to all the common miseries of humanity. He knew all the needs you can know in this world of woe, all the sorrows and all the pains. The man Christ Jesus felt in himself every groan he heard from suffering men; and, as the prophet spoke of him, he 'himself bare our sicknesses, and carried our sorrows' (Isaiah 53:4; Matthew 8:17). Now we are told by God the Holy Spirit that our Saviour, 'being wearied with his journey, sat thus on the well'.

This weariness was a real weariness. The word 'wearied' tells us that our Saviour was tired; but wearied is a much stronger word than 'tired'. This word, 'wearied', means tired, sick, worn out, exhausted, beat down, burdened. Our Saviour was 'wearied'! He was weary with fatigue, from his journey. He was weary with care for the souls of men. He was weary with the burden of his heart, the burden he carried throughout the days of his flesh, the fact that soon he must be made sin to put away sin. This weariness was real, more real than any of us can imagine.

Yet, this was a voluntary weariness. This was a part of the curse he had come to remove. I repeat, the consequences of Adam's fall, the consequences of sin, seized upon him as a man, from the moment that he came forth from the womb, saying, 'Lo! I come to do thy will, O my God' (Isaiah 53:4; Matthew 8:17; Hebrews 2:10, 17, 18; 4:15, 16; 7:24-26).

Child of God, when weariness seems to overwhelm you, look up to Christ. What an example he has given us. Though wearied more than any man, his weariness did not prevent him from continuing in his journey. Weariness did not prevent him from pushing forward in his work. Weariness did not keep him from doing his Father's will. Weariness did not keep him from serving the needs of a poor, eternity bound sinner.

Was he wearied with his journey through this world as Jehovah's Servant? He truly was. Yet, he turned not back. Let me also be found faithful to the end, though often wearied in the journey. Was he wearied with his journey? He truly was. Let me never grumble about mine. Was he wearied with his journey, having no place to rest his head? He truly was. Let me not repine if I find the world treating me as an outcast. Was he wearied with his journey, though rich, yet for my sake condescending to be poor, though the Lord of life and glory, yet 'a man of sorrows, and acquainted with grief' subjecting himself to hunger, and thirst, weariness and affliction, tempted, buffeted and despised; yea, 'a worm, and no man, a reproach of men, and the outcast of the people'? He truly was. Spirit of God, grant me grace in every trying circumstance of life, as oft as I am weary of the journey appointed me in this world, to behold my blessed Lord 'Jesus being wearied with his journey, (as) he sat thus on the well'!

Wearied With Sin
However, I have no doubt that this text was written by the finger of God to teach us more. It was given to give us something more than a proof of our Saviour's humanity. It was given to give us more than an example to follow. Great as these things are, there is more. Our Lord Jesus Christ is a Saviour wearied by man's sin and unbelief.

We may be indifferent to sin. Unbelief may seem to be a little, insignificant thing to us. But sin and unbelief are not matters of insignificance and indifference to God. Our text shows us a picture of the Son of God 'wearied with his journey', his journey through this world as the Saviour of the world.

The Son of God is wearied with our sin (Isaiah 43:24). He declares, 'Thou hast bought me no sweet cane with money, neither hast thou filled me with the fat of thy sacrifices: but thou hast made me to serve with thy sins, thou hast wearied me with thine iniquities.' He says, 'Behold, I am pressed under you, as a cart is pressed that is full of sheaves' (Amos 2:13).

The Lord of glory is thoroughly wearied with man's religion, too (Isaiah 1:10-15). Religious formality, ceremonialism, and ritualism are as nauseating to the holy Lord God as fornication, adultery, and homosexuality. In fact, those are the very things to which he compares all Christless, faithless, religious activity in the first chapter of Isaiah (Isaiah 1:10-15; 57:11; Psalms 78:36).

Sinners who persist in rebellion and unbelief, who stop their ears against the gospel and shut their eyes against the light, shoving God out of their way as they run madly on to hell, weary him by resisting the Holy Ghost. Yes, I am fully aware that the grace of God is irresistible (Psalms 65:4; 110:3). How I thank God for that fact! Were it not for irresistible grace, none of us would ever be saved. Yet, the word of God holds sinners accountable. God holds men responsible for resisting his Spirit. 'Ye stiffnecked and uncircumcised in heart and ears, ye do always resist the Holy Ghost: as your fathers did, so do ye'! 'And the LORD said, My spirit shall not always strive with man' (Acts 7:51; Genesis 6:3).

Perhaps you are thinking, 'If grace is irresistible, if all God's elect are sure to be saved, if man's will, or decision, or choice has nothing to do with his salvation, how can you say that men resist the Holy Ghost?' Understand the scriptures: man's will, man's choice, man's decision has absolutely nothing to do with salvation; but has everything to do with damnation! Just as Israel provoked the Lord for forty years in the wilderness, those who hear, but refuse to believe the gospel of Christ provoke his wrath. Just as the Israelites perished in the wilderness because of unbelief, because the word preached to them did not profit them, not being mixed with faith in Christ, just as Israel could not enter into the land of promise, because of unbelief, those who believe not, who refuse the counsel of God shall perish under the wrath of God, because of their own, wilful, deliberate, chosen, decided unbelief! It is man's will that will carry him to hell at last, unless God himself intervenes (Proverbs 1:23-31). 'He, that being often reproved hardeneth his neck, shall suddenly be destroyed, and that without remedy' (Proverbs 29:1). The Lord God says ...

'Turn you at my reproof: behold, I will pour out my spirit unto you, I will make known my words unto you. Because I have called, and ye refused; I have stretched out my hand, and no man regarded; But ye have set at nought all my counsel, and would none of my reproof: I also will laugh at your calamity; I will mock when your fear cometh; When your fear cometh as desolation, and your destruction cometh as a whirlwind; when distress and anguish cometh upon you. Then shall they call upon me, but I will not answer; they shall seek me early, but they shall not find me: For that they hated knowledge, and did not choose the fear of the LORD: They would none of my counsel: they despised all my reproof. Therefore shall they eat of the fruit of their own way, and be filled with their own devices' (Proverbs 1:23-31).

A Weary Sinner

This wearied Saviour came to this specific place, at this specific time, to save a weary sinner. It is this same Christ, the wearied Saviour, who calls sinners to come to him in the most gracious, tender words imaginable. He says, 'Come unto me, all ye that labour and are heavy laden, and I will give you rest' (Matthew 11:28).

Yet, no sinner will ever, of his own accord, come to Christ. At the appointed time of love, the Son of God must needs go to the place where he will meet the object of his mercy, love, and grace to fetch his chosen to himself.

Here is the Christ of God waiting to save a weary sinner, who had wearied him with her sin! I do not suggest that this woman was spiritually weary with her sin; but weary she was. No one ever lived such a life as she lived who did not soon become weary with it.

179

Look away, in your mind's eye, to that little spot outside Sychar in Samaria. What do you see in the picture drawn here by the Spirit of God? 'Now Jacob's well was there. Jesus therefore, being wearied with his journey, sat thus on the well: and it was about the sixth hour'.

Let me tell you what I see in this scene. As I behold the Son of God, sitting thus on Jacob's well. I see the Lord of glory waiting to be gracious (Isaiah 30:18). His prophet declares, 'Therefore will the LORD wait, that he may be gracious unto you, and therefore will he be exalted, that he may have mercy upon you' (Isaiah 30:18). Do you not see him? There he is waiting for a sinner, a specific sinner, waiting to save, waiting to bless!

I see here a God willing to save. How can anyone doubt Christ's willingness to save? How can any question the fact that he who is God, the God against whom we have sinned from our youth up, against whom we sin with every breath we draw, is that God of whom the prophet says, 'He delighteth in mercy'? See the Son of God sitting yonder wearied, yet waiting on Jacob's well, because he is a God willing to save! He was watching for her. He had come there to save her. And save her he did. Yes, he was wearied; but as soon as the woman for whom he had come was present, his weariness seemed to vanish. He was enlivened by the very appearance of the object of his everlasting love.

A Satisfied Redeemer

Let me show you one more thing. That which refreshed and revived our wearied Saviour that day in Samaria, and that which now satisfies the travail of his soul is the salvation of sinners. When the disciples came back from town, the Lord Jesus was still sitting at the well. But, he was no longer thirsty. He seems not to have been weary at all. In fact, he appears to have been refreshed, revived and completely satisfied, 'Jesus saith unto her, I that speak unto thee am he. And upon this came his disciples, and marvelled that he talked with the woman: yet no man said, What seekest thou? or, Why talkest thou with her? The woman then left her waterpot, and went her way into the city, and saith to the men, Come, see a man, which told me all things that ever I did: is not this the Christ? Then they went out of the city, and came unto him. In the mean while his disciples prayed him, saying, Master, eat. But he said unto them, I have meat to eat that ye know not of' (John 4:26-32).

The Master had said to her, 'Give me to drink'. And she did. She did not dip her water pot into the well; but she gave him the water he was seeking. As soon as the Lord Jesus made himself known to her, she believed him. She was what he had come to get; and he was satisfied. It is written, 'he shall see of the travail of his soul, and shall be satisfied: by his knowledge shall my righteous Servant justify many; for he shall bear their iniquities' (Isaiah 53:11).

Chapter 25

If You Knew …

'When therefore the Lord knew how the Pharisees had heard that Jesus made and baptised more disciples than John, (Though Jesus himself baptised not, but his disciples,) he left Judaea, and departed again into Galilee. And he must needs go through Samaria. Then cometh he to a city of Samaria, which is called Sychar, near to the parcel of ground that Jacob gave to his son Joseph. Now Jacob's well was there. Jesus therefore, being wearied with his journey, sat thus on the well: and it was about the sixth hour. There cometh a woman of Samaria to draw water: Jesus saith unto her, Give me to drink. (For his disciples were gone away unto the city to buy meat.) Then saith the woman of Samaria unto him, How is it that thou, being a Jew, askest drink of me, which am a woman of Samaria? for the Jews have no dealings with the Samaritans. Jesus answered and said unto her, If thou knewest the gift of God, and who it is that saith to thee, Give me to drink; thou wouldest have asked of him, and he would have given thee living water' (John 4:1-10).

Our Lord Jesus might have said the same thing to this poor, Samaritan adulteress that he did to the rich young ruler, 'One thing thou lackest'. Like the rich young ruler, this Samaritan woman lacked just one thing. Just one thing kept her from being a believer.

She was an object of electing love. God chose her as such from eternity. She was one of those whose names were written in the Lamb's book of life before the world began. She was predestined to eternal life in Christ. Yet, she was lost. She was still a rebel. She was still an unbeliever. The Lord Jesus Christ came into the world to lay down his life for this woman, to put away her sin by the sacrifice of himself as her Substitute. Yet, she did not trust him.

There was one thing missing. She knew her bible history. She knew her religious dogma. She knew what her church believed, and defended her denomination with a vengeance. She knew that Messiah was coming and that salvation could be found only in him. She knew that Christ alone was the Saviour of men.

Yet, she was still lost, lost because of one thing. What was missing? 'Jesus answered and said unto her, If thou knewest the gift of God, and who it is that saith to thee, Give me to drink; thou wouldest have asked of him, and he would have given thee living water' (v. 10). The one thing which kept this poor sinner out of the kingdom of God, the one thing which keeps sinners out of the kingdom of God, was just this, she did not know the Lord Jesus Christ.

If you knew, if only you knew the Lord Jesus Christ, you would trust him. It is ignorance of Christ that holds you in unbelief. Did not our Lord himself say, 'If you knew me, you would know my Father also' (John 8:19; 14:7)? He wept over Jerusalem, saying, 'If thou hadst known' (Luke 19:42). In fact, the Holy Spirit tells us that if the rulers of this world had just known who he was, they would never have crucified the Lord of glory (1 Corinthians 2:8).

It is a man's spiritual ignorance, the blindness of his soul that holds him still in unbelief, just as it did this Samaritan adulteress. But, blessed be God, when the Light of the world shone upon her, when the Sun of Righteousness arose within her, she saw and she believed. So it is my prayer, every time I preach the gospel, that God the Holy Spirit will be pleased, by the almighty power of his invincible grace, to make the light of the knowledge of the glory of God in the face of Jesus Christ shine in the hearts of chosen, redeemed sinners, and give them life and faith in him.

Saving Knowledge

First, the Lord Jesus spoke to this woman about saving knowledge. He said, 'If thou knewest the gift of God, and who it is that saith unto thee, give me to drink ...' Doctrinal knowledge is not salvation. Be sure you understand that. Doctrinal knowledge is not salvation. Grace is not gained by learning. Righteousness is not the reward of study. Salvation is not the successor of research. You can have all the right doctrine and miss Christ altogether.

Calvinism is no more beneficial to a man's soul than Arminianism. I have no more interest in converting men from Arminianism to Calvinism, than I do in converting men from Hinduism to Catholicism. Salvation is not found in a religious system. Salvation is not in a system of works, a system of rituals, or a system of doctrine. Salvation is in a person. Salvation is in Christ. In fact, salvation is a person. Christ is Salvation! It is what the book says. (John 17:3; Luke 2:29, 30; Exodus 15:1, 2; 2 Samuel 22:1-3; Psalms 27:1; Psalms 35:3).

Salvation is not what you know, but who you know. 'And this is life eternal, that they might know thee the only true God, and Jesus Christ, whom thou hast sent' (John 17:3). What you know, or do not know is really irrelevant. But that does not mean that a person can be saved without knowing Christ, without knowing the gospel. Knowledge is essential to faith in Christ as oxygen is to breathing. But understand this, it is not what we know that saves us, but who.

Our Lord told this Samaritan woman that she would be saved, be a believer, if she knew, if she knew the gift of God, if she knew who he was. Is that what you see in the text? 'Jesus answered and said unto her, If thou knewest the gift of God, and who it is that saith to thee, Give me to drink; thou wouldest have asked of him, and he would have given thee living water' (John 4:10).

Gospel knowledge is essential to saving faith. Let men rattle on all they want about people being saved who do not know God, do not know Christ, and do not know the gospel. It just is not so. It makes just as much sense to talk about Mormons and Russellites being saved as it does to talk about Arminians, will-worshippers, and work mongers being saved. Those who deny the gospel do not know God. Those who despise the character of God do not love the Lord. Those who trample the blood of Christ under their feet as useless waste are not born of God. Those who despise the Spirit of grace do not know the God of grace. Gospel knowledge is essential to saving faith. It is impossible to trust an unknown Saviour (Romans 10:13-17). It is utterly impossible for anyone to call upon and worship the Lord if they do not trust him. It is utterly impossible for anyone to trust Christ until they know him. It is impossible for anyone to know Christ without a preacher. It is utterly impossible for anyone to preach Christ, unless he is sent of God. That is precisely what God the Holy Spirit declares in Romans 10:13-17.

Two Essential Things
Faith in Christ is not a leap in the dark. Faith is walking in the light. There is no saving faith without saving knowledge. I could say many things about this saving knowledge. Indeed, much needs to be said. But our text speaks of two things specifically, which this woman had to know, if she would be saved, two things which no one knows by nature, but which we must know if we are to be saved. Without the knowledge of these two things, there is no faith in Christ. Without the knowledge of these, there is no salvation.

First, all who believe on the Lord Jesus Christ, all who are taught of God and born of God know 'the gift of God'. The Saviour says, 'If thou knewest the gift of God'. What is he talking about? God tells us in his word. The gift of God is eternal life in Christ (Romans 6:23), salvation by faith in Christ (Ephesians 2:8, 9), the unspeakable gift of his dear Son (2 Corinthians 9:15).

The gift of God is Christ himself and the salvation that God gives to sinners in him, as a matter of pure, free, undeserved, sovereign grace. Most all religious people, almost all who claim to be worshippers of Christ, like Simon Magus, vainly imagine that the gift of God can be purchased with money, or human effort, or human merit of some kind (Acts 8:20). All believers know and rejoice in the fact that salvation is the gift of God: Not a present, but a gift! Not an offer, but a gift! Not a proposition, but a gift!

Saving faith involves knowledge, knowing the gift of God, and it means knowing him by whom the gift comes. There is no saving faith in Christ without saving knowledge of Christ. No one is saved who does not know who Christ is and what he has done. 'And this is life eternal, that they might know thee the only true God, and Jesus Christ, whom thou hast sent' (John 17:3).

When our Lord Jesus put the question to the man who had been blind, 'Dost thou believe on the Son of God? He answered and said, who is he, Lord, that I might believe on him?' Then, the Saviour made himself known unto him. 'Jesus said unto him, Thou hast seen him, and it is he that talketh with thee'. His eyes were opened to see him, and his ears now heard him, and both being true in a spiritual sense, he immediately expressed his faith in him, saying, 'Lord, I believe', and as a proof and evidence of his faith in Christ, he 'worshipped him' (John 9:35-38).

Before there can be any faith in Christ as our Saviour, there must be some knowledge of him and of our need of him. As John Gill put it, 'a man must be made sensible of the sinfulness of his nature, of the exceeding sinfulness of sin, of the just demerit of it, and of the miserable state and condition it has brought him into, out of which none but Christ the Saviour can deliver him.'

We then call upon Christ, crying for mercy, as the apostles in distress did, saying, 'Lord, save us, we perish' (Matthew 8:25). But no man will ever call upon Christ to save him, until he is acquainted with his own impotence, until he sees that he cannot save himself, that he cannot contribute anything to his salvation, and that no one else can help him but Christ.

No sinner will ever fall out to Christ, until he is made to see that if ever he is saved, it must be by the grace of God alone, through the blood and righteousness of Christ alone, and not by the work of his own hands or the power of his own will.

Second, there can be no faith in Christ apart from the knowledge of the fulness and ability of Christ as the sinners' Substitute, Surety, and Saviour. We cannot trust him until we see him as the Christ of God, full of grace and truth. We will never trust Christ until we are made to know that he is a Saviour suitable to our souls needs. We cannot trust him as our Redeemer until he makes us to know something about the redemption he accomplished for sinners at Calvary. We cannot trust Christ alone for righteousness until we are convinced of the righteousness of God which is in him, which he established. We cannot trust him for the forgiveness of sin, until we are convinced by the Spirit of God that he has put away our sins by the sacrifice of himself. We cannot trust the Son of God as our Saviour until we see him at the right hand of the Majesty on high, with saving power in his hands. No sinner will ever trust Christ alone as his Saviour, until he sees that all salvation is in him (1 Corinthians 1:30). It is absurd to talk about saving faith without saving knowledge. Knowledge and faith are joined together as inseparable companions, and as expressing the same thing. It is written, 'We have known and believed the love that God hath to us'. We are firmly persuaded of it (1 John 4:16). The strongest acts of faith in God's saints are sometimes expressed by words of knowledge. 'I know that my Redeemer liveth ... I know in whom I have believed' (Job 19:25; 2 Timothy 1:12).

Divine Revelation

This knowledge comes to sinners only by divine revelation. Saving knowledge is something more than a notion, an idea, or even a fact. It is a personal, experimental knowledge of the living God, not an academic knowledge, not a second-hand knowledge, not a textbook knowledge, but a personal knowledge of the Lord Jesus Christ. 'I know whom I have believed'! It is knowledge that is conveyed to and born in the hearts of God's elect by the power and grace of God the Holy Spirit in the new birth through the preaching of the gospel (Romans 1:16, 17; Ephesians 1:13, 14; 1 Peter 1:23-25). It is the spiritual knowledge of God-given faith in Christ (2 Corinthians 5:16).

Faith's Request

Next, our Lord Jesus speaks about a request. Look at John 4:10 again. 'Jesus answered and said unto her, If thou knewest the gift of God, and who it is that saith to thee, Give me to drink; thou wouldest have asked of him, and he would have given thee living water.'

That which is sure to follow the knowledge of Christ, the knowledge of God's free grace gift of salvation and eternal life in him is faith, faith expressed in a request. If you only knew the gift of God, if only you knew my Saviour, you would ask of him. You would cry out to him like the publican, 'God, be merciful to me, a sinner'. You would pray like the leper, 'If thou wilt, thou canst make me whole'. You would pray as Bartimaeus, 'That I might receive my sight'. You would plead as the thief on the cross, 'Remember me'.

Christ's Promise

Now, look at our text one more time, and see what it is that the Lord Jesus Christ promises to poor, needy sinners who ask of him. 'Jesus answered and said unto her, If thou knewest the gift of God, and who it is that saith to thee, Give me to drink; thou wouldest have asked of him, and he would have given thee living water.' 'Ask, and ye shall receive'. Believe, and you shall live. Look, and you will be saved. Ask of Christ, and he will give you living water.

Do you wonder why the Lord here refers to his great salvation as living water? Because water is the gift of God. Water is absolutely essential to life. Water meets a universal need. Water comes down from heaven. Water cleanses and refreshes. Water is free. Water is something no one ever gets tired of having. Christ is the Water of Life; and the salvation he gives is 'living water' springing up in our souls.

Two Views Of Christ

'Jesus answered and said unto her, If thou knewest the gift of God, and who it is that saith to thee, Give me to drink; thou wouldest have asked of him, and he would have given thee living water.' Here are two sweet, precious, instructive views of our Lord Jesus Christ, which he held before the Samaritan woman, by which he graciously and effectually endeared himself to her. Let us ever see our Saviour in these two aspects of his character as our God-man Mediator: first, all that he is in himself, second, the fact he is the gift of God.

These two things give poor, needy sinners both a reason to trust our Lord Jesus Christ and a divine warrant for faith in him. Ignorance of these two great things is the cause of much misery in those poor souls tortured with the guilt of sin, and the cause of much discomfort in believing sinners. Ignorance of these two, sweet revelations of grace greatly hinders our enjoyment of our interest in and union with the Lord Jesus Christ. 'Jesus answered and said unto her, If thou knewest the gift of God, and who it is that saith to thee, Give me to drink; thou wouldest have asked of him, and he would have given thee living water'. May God the Holy Spirit give us grace to prove these words of our Saviour to ourselves.

Christ's Person And Work

I ask you to consider who and what the Lord Jesus is in himself. Consider his magnificent Person and his mediatorial work as the God-man, our Saviour. In all that he is, in all that he performed, in all that he accomplished, and in all that he obtained as the God-man, he acted as the Surety of his elect. And by virtue of all the fulness that is treasured up in him, we have all things. None of the virtue, merit, and power of his work or being as the God-man is for himself, but for us. He does not and cannot need it. We do.

'So that', as Robert Hawker wrote, 'a poor sinner is as much suited to Jesus for him to give out of his fulness, as Jesus is suited for a poor sinner to supply his emptiness.'

If we thus know him and come to him, we find that he is as eager and anxious to receive every poor, needy sinner and to give out of his fulness, as that poor, needy sinner is to come and take!

186

The Gift Of God

Our Lord Jesus declares that he is, in all his mediatorial work and being, 'the gift of God'. Here we are given a warrant from God to come to Christ. God himself gives sinners command to believe on his Son (1 John 3:23). That is the warrant of faith. That is the sinner's right and authority to trust Christ.

Do you know who Christ is and what he has done for sinners? If you know that Jesus Christ the Saviour is the Gift of God, make use of him as such. Use him for every need of your poor soul. Christ is the only Sacrament there is. We receive grace only in and by him. He is the only Way sinners can come to God and find acceptance with him.

May God the Holy Spirit enable us ever to keep in view that Christ is the Gift of God and that God is honoured by us when we honour his dear Son, by believing 'the record, that God hath given to us eternal life, and this life is in his Son'.

The thirst of our souls cannot be quenched from any pool that depends upon dry or wet seasons; but only from the Lord Jesus Christ himself, who gives living water and is himself that everlasting living spring of water in our souls, springing up into everlasting life.

If the one thing which prevents sinners from being saved is their ignorance of Christ, let us make it our life's business to make him known. Go, tell your neighbours, your families, your friends, and your enemies, if they will hear you, who Christ is and what he has done for you. Tell it everywhere! Tell it to everybody!

Chapter 26

'Whence then hast thou that living water?'

'Jesus answered and said unto her, If thou knewest the gift of God, and who it is that saith to thee, Give me to drink; thou wouldest have asked of him, and he would have given thee living water. The woman saith unto him, Sir, thou hast nothing to draw with, and the well is deep: from whence then hast thou that living water?' (John 4:10, 11).

What a blessed gift, 'living water'! What a wondrous giver, the Lord Jesus Christ! What delightful terms, 'Ask, and ye shall receive'! The text before us was inspired and written here in the book of God specifically to teach us that the Lord Jesus Christ has all grace, salvation, and eternal life in himself, that he has it for sinners, to give away freely, and that he gives it to every sinner who asks him for it.

This is the doctrine of the gospel, the message of the Bible. If you trust the Lord Jesus Christ, if you ask him to give you this living water, he will fill you with his grace and put his Spirit in you, 'a well of water, springing up into everlasting life'.

I fear that far too much preaching is designed to impress men, not to convert them. May God save us from such! When our Lord Jesus spoke to eternity bound sinners, he had no interest in impressing his hearers with his oratorical skills. His object was to convince immortal souls of sin, of righteousness, and of judgment. Therefore, he spoke to the hearts of those who heard his voice in plain, simple terms.

May God the Holy Spirit be our Teacher as we seek to answer the question this poor sinner put to the Son of God. 'Whence hast thou that living water?'

The Lord Jesus told this woman plainly that if she had known the gift of God and who he is, she would have asked of him and he would have given her living water. I fully realise that she did not know the full implication of what he had said; but she obviously understood that he was talking about something different from the waters that gathered in Jacob's well. He was talking about water bubbling with life from a constantly renewed and renewing source, an artesian well of water. Therefore, she asked a very reasonable question. She said, 'Whence hast thou that living water?'

Living Water And God's Salvation
Our Lord Jesus here uses the words 'living water' to describe his gift of grace, salvation, and eternal life by the Holy Spirit. In fact, this is the way God's salvation is (Isaiah 12:3; Zechariah 13:1; John 7:37, 38; Revelation 21:6; 22:17). Here, our Lord uses the words 'living water' to describe the whole work and gift of God's grace in salvation. This comparison of his salvation to 'living water' is very suggestive. 'Water' is a most appropriate word to describe God's salvation, the gift of God in Christ.

Water is a gift of God. It is something no man can create. If we have water, God must give it. So it is with God's salvation (Romans 6:23; Ephesians 2:8).

Water is vital. This is not an optional, add on luxury. Water is indispensable to life. No one can survive without it. Without it we die. Again, the comparison is obvious. Without God's grace, God's salvation, God's Spirit, we must forever perish under the wrath of God.

Water meets a universal need. Water is not the requirement of some men, but of all men. All the sons and daughters of Adam stand upon equal footing here. It matters not how rich or poor we are, how learned or illiterate, we must have water. It matters not whether we are male or female, black or white, water is something we all must have. It meets the needs of all men alike. So it is with God's salvation. All who are without Christ are lost. All who have Christ are saved. All who are without Christ are without grace and without hope. All who have Christ have life.

Water comes down from heaven. It is not of the earth and earthly, but from heaven and heavenly. Again, this is true of God's grace and salvation in Christ. 'Salvation is of the Lord'!

God's salvation is well described by the word 'water', because water, like salvation, is a gift that has multiple benefits. It cleanses the filthy. It cools the fevered brow. It quenches the thirsty. It refreshes the weary. It satisfies the soul of a man.

Water is something of which we never tire. You may get tired of city water, with all its human corruptions. You may tire of yuppie, plastic-bottled water, with its stale, stagnancy. But I defy anyone to walk by a cool, mountain spring, gushing out of a hillside, on a hot summer day, without stopping for a drink. So, too, those who drink of this water will never tire of it. Chosen sinners never tire of electing love. Redeemed sinners never tire of blood atonement. Forgiven sinners never tire of divine pardon. Saved sinners never tire of saving grace.

Water is sovereignly distributed. In some places it is abundant. In other places it is scarce. In some places it comes seasonally. In other places it seems to fall freely at all seasons. So it is with God's salvation. In some places God sends the dew of heaven occasionally. In some places he opens the windows of heaven and rains grace every day! In some places he sends not so much as a cloud.

Only Christ

This water, this 'living water' comes to sinners only from Christ. If you would have this water, you must get it from him. Let me make just two statements in this regard.

First, grace, salvation, and eternal life are in Christ, only in Christ, and in Christ in infinite abundance (John 1:16, 17; Colossians 1:19; 2:9, 10; 1 Corinthians 1:30, 31). Salvation is not in the church, but in Christ. Grace is not found in religious 'sacraments', but in Christ. God's salvation is not found in religious ritualism, moral reformation, an emotional decision, or the religious sensationalism of this apostate, charismatic age. Salvation is in Christ. Grace is in Christ. Get Christ, and you get everything. Miss Christ, and you miss everything (John 1:16, 17; Colossians 1:19; 2:9, 10; 1 Corinthians 1:30, 31).

A form of godliness will do you no good. You must have Christ! A religious experience, without Christ, is a damning experience. You must have Christ!

Second, salvation is the gift of God! I gladly run the risk of appearing redundant. I repeat myself deliberately. How I want all who read these lines to see this! Salvation is God's free gift to sinners in Christ. It cannot be bought by sacrifice. It cannot be earned by works. It cannot be given by someone else. It cannot be inherited from your relatives. It is the gift of God! 'Thanks be unto God for his unspeakable gift'!

The Question

Now, look at the question this woman asked. How is it that Christ alone has this gift? 'Whence then hast thou that living water?' How is it that Christ alone has grace, salvation, and eternal life in himself to give to needy sinners, and no one else and nothing else does?

It is true, salvation is the work of the triune God. The Father chose us. The Son redeemed us. The Holy Spirit converts us. But God the Father will not and cannot give us this living water without Christ. God the Spirit will not and

191

cannot give us this living water without Christ. How is it that Christ alone has this living water to give to poor, needy, thirsty sinners? 'Whence then hast thou that living water?'

He has it because he is the only fit person to have it. God could never come down to man. Man could never rise to God. If ever the two come together, they must meet in a Mediator, a Daysman who can lay hold of both God and man. That Daysman, that Mediator, is the Lord Jesus Christ. Christ alone is the Mediator between God and men (Acts 4:12; 1 Timothy 2:5).

Did you ever notice how careful the writers of holy scripture were to refer to the Lord Jesus Christ, almost always, in the most reverent, worshipful terms? Seldom did any speak of him only by his earthly name, 'Jesus'. He is often called by his title, 'Christ', and by the term, 'the Lord'. But he is most commonly called, 'the Lord Jesus Christ', because all that he is is essential to our salvation by him (Galatians 6:14; 1 Corinthians 16:22).

He has all salvation in himself because he is 'the Lord'. Who should have it, but 'the Lord'? 'The salvation of the righteous is of the Lord'! Salvation is his to give because he is 'Jesus', who came into this world to save his people from their sins (Matthew 1:21). He has salvation in himself to give to sinners because he is 'Christ', the Christ of God. He is the Anointed One, sent from God to be our Saviour.

On the day of his immersion in the river Jordan to fulfil all righteousness, the Spirit of God descended upon him in the form of a dove, and abode on him. God gave the Spirit to him, without measure. He was anointed with the oil of gladness above his fellows. This is exactly what he announced to the Jews in the temple, when he began his public ministry (Luke 4:16-21).

He has this 'living water' of salvation, grace, and eternal life to give to sinners because he is the Lord Jesus Christ.

He also has this 'living water' by divine purpose. The Lord Jesus Christ is authorized of God to be our Saviour. He came here by divine appointment to bestow upon needy sinners all the blessings of grace given to us in him before the world began (Romans 3:24-26; 1 Peter 1:18-20).

Christ has this 'living water' in himself to give to sinners because he obtained it by his blood. He earned it by his obedience to his Father's will as our Mediator, Representative, Surety, and Substitute. And he bought it with his blood. This is the reward which his Father promised him and gave him, as the result of his accomplishments as our Mediator (John 17:2; 19:30; Hebrews 9:12; Isaiah 53:10-12).

Look up yonder, there upon the throne of God sits that Man who died in the place of sinners more than two thousand years ago. He ascended up on high and received gifts for men, yea, for the rebellious also, that the Lord God might dwell among men!

The Lord Jesus Christ has this 'living water' in himself to give to us poor sinners because of who he is, because his Father purposed it, because of what he did to obtain it; and the Lord Jesus Christ has grace, salvation, eternal life, 'living water' for poor, needy sinners because of his intercession in heaven as the sinners' Advocate and 'great high priest' (Hebrews 7:25-27; 1 John 2:1, 2).

Ask And Receive
This living water is yours for the asking! Ask, and you shall receive. Is that not what our Lord told this Samaritan woman? 'Jesus answered and said unto her, If thou knewest the gift of God, and who it is that saith to thee, Give me to drink; thou wouldest have asked of him, and he would have given thee living water' (v. 10).

He does not have grace, salvation, eternal life, peace, pardon, atonement, forgiveness, and righteousness for himself. He needs none of these things. He has grace, in all its fulness that he may give it away!

Christ has living water, the living water of salvation and grace for thirsty sinners. He has this living water in an inexhaustible fulness. He promises to give it to all who ask him for it. He needs nothing from you, not even your water pot! Come, poor, needy sinner, come. Come, my soul, come. Come my brother, come my sister, come to the Fountain and drink! 'And the Spirit and the bride say, Come. And let him that heareth say, Come. And let him that is athirst come. And whosoever will, let him take the water of life freely' (Revelation 22:17).

Chapter 27

'Go, call thy husband'
Or
Sin Exposed

'The woman saith unto him, Sir, give me this water, that I thirst not, neither come hither to draw. Jesus saith unto her, Go, call thy husband, and come hither. The woman answered and said, I have no husband. Jesus said unto her, Thou hast well said, I have no husband: For thou hast had five husbands; and he whom thou now hast is not thy husband: in that saidst thou truly' (John 4:15-18).

If ever God is pleased to save a sinner he will cause the object of his mercy to see himself as he really is; and he will cause him to see God as he really is. No one has ever been saved without seeing who he is and who God is. These two things always go together. You can never see God in his greatness, glory, and grace in the face of Christ, without seeing yourself in your corruption, confusion, and condemnation.

This is not a conclusion I have reached by reason. It is a fact plainly revealed in holy scripture. Every person in the book of God, who is set before us as seeing God, immediately fell before him, broken and contrite, confessing his sin. Job (Job 42:16), Moses (Exodus 3:11; 19:16; Hebrews 12:21), David (2 Samuel 7:18), Isaiah (Isaiah 6:1-6), Daniel (Daniel 10:8), Peter (Luke 5:8), Saul of Tarsus (Acts 9:1-9).

No one will ever be saved until he sees who God is and sees who and what he really is, until he is compelled by sovereign grace to bow in the dust before the throne of God Almighty, confessing himself to be a justly condemned sinner before the holy Lord God, whose only hope is Christ. James Boyce wrote, 'Christianity begins by bringing men to the truth about their own depraved condition, but it does so to convince them of their need of Jesus

Christ and to prepare them for understanding who he is and what he has accomplished for them by his death and resurrection.'

The only place you will ever see God in his true character is in the face of his crucified Son, the Lord Jesus Christ, 'in the cleft of the Rock' where he revealed himself to Moses (2 Corinthians 4:4-6). If ever a person sees God in Christ, he will confess and acknowledge his sin. This is where Holy Spirit conviction is wrought; in the hearts of eternity bound sinners (John 16:8-11). As soon as a poor sinner confesses his sin, he obtains the forgiveness of sin by the faithfulness and justice of God, through the blood of Christ (1 John 1:9).

In the story of the Samaritan woman recorded in this chapter, we see the Lord Jesus, the great soul winner, graciously bringing a sinner to just this place. The good Shepherd is here seeking one of his lost sheep; and he will not rest until he has fetched the sheep to himself.

'The woman saith unto him, Sir, give me this water, that I thirst not, neither come hither to draw. Jesus saith unto her, Go, call thy husband, and come hither. The woman answered and said, I have no husband. Jesus said unto her, Thou hast well said, I have no husband: For thou hast had five husbands; and he whom thou now hast is not thy husband: in that saidst thou truly.'

Not Always Climactic
First, in verse 15 we learn that conversion is not always climactic. Redemption is climactic. Regeneration is climactic. But conversion is usually a process. Conversion is an experience of grace that is a process. 'The woman saith unto him, Sir, give me this water, that I thirst not, neither come hither to draw' (v. 15).

I can almost picture the scene. The Lord Jesus has been talking to this woman about eternal life, grace, and salvation. But she did not understand anything he said. She was a little cocky, sarcastic, and rude. She was, she thought, just engaged in another banter about religion. She could not care less about what the Master was telling her. As she drops her water pot into the well, holds the rope with one hand, and wipes the sweat off her face with the other, she says, 'Give me that water and you won't see me doing this again'.

Yet, we should not be too harsh in our thinking about her, and the myriads like her. The carnal mind is always occupied with carnal things. The natural man sees everything with the confined vision of his depraved nature. He lives in the cramped, confined quarters of carnality. Therefore, all he can see, sense, and judge is limited to the carnal, the material, the fleshly. Left to himself, there he will live and there he will die.

Look at this poor woman. The Saviour of the world was standing in front of her, but she did not know him. The Light of the world was in front of her, but she could not see him. The Sun of Righteousness was shining in her face; but she was not warmed by him.

She was, like most, full of questions. The Saviour asked her for a drink of water, and she said, 'How?' He told her to ask him for water, and she said, 'From whence?' He spoke to her about living water, and she replied with a sneer, 'Sir, give me this water, that I thirst not, neither come hither to draw.'

All the while, the Lord Jesus was preparing her for grace. He was in the process of making her willing in the day of his power. Our Lord did not deal with this woman and the woman with an issue of blood the same way. And he does not deal with us all the same way, or bring us all down the same path. We must never presume that a person will never be converted because he is not immediately converted. And we must not presume that a person is not saved because he did not go through the same feelings, throes of the devil, or joyful ecstasy we may have experienced.

Suddenly, the Master did something totally unexpected. He stuck his finger right into this sinner's heart. He raised an issue she had no interest in discussing. He had been sort of poking around until now, waiting for and creating the time to say what he had come there to say. Then, at precisely the right moment, he sticks his finger right into her heart and conscience. Look at verse 16. 'Jesus saith unto her, Go, call thy husband, and come hither.'

Immediately, the woman responded, 'I have no husband' (v. 17). She wanted the conversation to end right there. (At least, she thought she did!) But the Master had her on his hook. He was not about to let her go.

Conviction: The Forerunner

'The woman answered and said, I have no husband. Jesus said unto her, Thou hast well said, I have no husband: For thou hast had five husbands; and he whom thou now hast is not thy husband: in that saidst thou truly.' Here our Lord shows us, secondly, that the conviction of sin is the forerunner of conversion.

Many imagine that such talk is unkind, that preachers ought never make people feel terribly uncomfortable. Preaching these days is intentionally evasive. If evil is dealt with, it is dealt with in such general, ambiguous terms that no one feels as if the preacher might be talking to them.

The Lord Jesus here slapped this woman in the face, at once exposing her deepest guilt, making her know that he knew. That slap across the face was the sweetest, kindest, most gracious and loving thing he could have done for her. Now, her pretensions were useless. She still tried to change the subject (vv. 20 and 25); but the hook was set. She did not really know what was going on; but she knew that all her thoughts and actions were known to this man who spoke to her. She knew that this man was able to tell her all things that ever she had done. Can you imagine how shocked, how utterly horrified she must have been?

Why did the Lord Jesus put her through this? Surely, there must be a better, easier, less painful way to deal with and women than this. There is not. The doctor who promises to cure your cancer without surgery or drugs, discomfort or inconvenience may make you feel good; but he is your enemy, not your friend. Those deceivers of men's souls, who would heal the wounds of your souls 'slightly, crying Peace, peace, when there is no peace', are butchers of souls, not the servants of God.

The fact is no one ever sought Christ who did not need him. You will never be saved until you are lost (Mark 2:17). Salvation is deliverance from danger. You will never flee to Christ for refuge from the wrath of God until you know that you are under the wrath of God and deserve to be. You will never trust Christ until you know you are going to hell, and ought to. There is no conversion without conviction. There is no pardon of sin without a confession of sin. There will never be a confession of sin from you until it is wrung out of you by the power and grace of God the Holy Spirit.

This was the turning point in this woman's life. It is the turning point in every chosen sinner's life. Like the prodigal, you must come to yourself, or you will never come to Christ.

The word of God declares that we are all sinners. The totality of man's depravity, the utter corruption of our hearts and our nature is so plainly and frequently stated in the word of God that it simply cannot be denied. Sin is what we all are, what we all do, and what we all love (Genesis 6:5; Psalms 14:1; 143:2; Romans 3:10-23; 1 John 1:8-10). Solomon said, 'There is not a just man upon earth that doeth good and sinneth not'. Some are hedonists, self-centred, make-me-happy, materialists (Romans 1:18-32). Others are moralists, philosophical ethicists (Romans 2:1-16). Others are religionists (Romans 3:10-23). But all are sinners. None do good, or even know what good is.

Every man's conscience condemns him for his sin. No matter what the rule book is by which you pretend to live, which you claim to be your standard, you do not measure up; and you know it. Some love to pretend that they live by the Ten Commandments, but none do. There is not even one of the commandments we do not all break all the time. Others tell us that they live by the Sermon on the Mount, but none come close to the standard there demanded (Matthew 5:48). Moralists who prefer not to be considered too religious claim Ben Franklin's code of ethics, or something like it, as their guide, but none measure up to the code. Many pretend to live by the Golden Rule; but no one really treats all others as they would have others treat them.

Yet, no man can convince another man of his utter sinfulness, his total depravity, his just condemnation. Only God himself can do that. Milford Hall rightly observed, 'It is as difficult to convince men of their lost condition as it is to recover them from it. Only God can do both! You cannot help anyone until he is willing to be helped; but our Lord can make him willing. A man cannot truly bear the gospel of sovereign grace until he cannot bear himself!'

That is what the Lord was doing with this Samaritan woman. The day of his power had come. Therefore he was making her willing. He makes us willing to be saved by getting us lost. He makes us willing to wash in his blood by making us get a smell of ourselves. He makes us willing to be robed in his righteousness by stripping us naked before him.

What a thought that is! We are naked before the all-seeing eye of holy omniscience! God sees behind the masks we wear. 'Neither is there any creature that is not manifest in his sight: but all things are naked and opened unto the eyes of him with whom we have to do' (Hebrews 4:13).

The Samaritans
Let me show you something else. When the original inhabitants of Samaria were exiled from their land by the Assyrian king, people from five different places, each with their own gods, were brought in from Babylon to inhabit the land (2 Kings 17:29-33). If we would be married to Christ, we must be made to see that the gods of this world are false gods, and the religion of this world is wicked, abominable, and adulterous.

This poor sinner could not be married to Christ (spiritually) until she acknowledged that her Samaritan religion was adultery (whoredom), that her former gods were her adulterous lovers (whoremongers), and that her preachers were prostitutes. You may think I am stretching the allusion just a little. I challenge you to search the scriptures and see if that is not exactly what the book of God tells us about all free will, works religion. Does not the Holy Spirit call the preachers of works dogs (male prostitutes)? Does not the Lord command us to abandon the adultery of false religion, to come out of Babylon, lest we be partaker of her sins and of her judgment? (Revelation 18:4; 2 Corinthians 6:14-7:1).

Christ's Purpose
Look again at John 4:16, and learn this: if the Lord Jesus ever exposes your sin to you, if he brings you down in the dusts of humiliation, it is that he might bring you up to himself. He exposes that he may pardon. He abases that he may exalt. He empties that he may fill. He strips that he may cloth. He slays that he may make alive. He destroys our refuge of lies that he might compel us to flee away to him for refuge.

'Jesus saith unto her, Go, call thy husband, and come hither.' The Master did not simply say, 'Go, call thy husband'. He said, 'Go, call thy husband, and come hither.' I know that our first, immediate reaction, once we have seen ourselves corrupt and naked before God, is to run from him. Our first thought is, 'How can God have anything to do with one so vile as me?' He cannot, except by Christ. Only by Christ's blood atonement and perfect righteousness can the holy Lord God embrace such trash as we are. But, blessed be his name, in Christ he can, and he does! First, the Lord Jesus spoke a word of piercing truth to her conscience. 'Go, call thy husband'. Then, he spoke this word of matchless grace to her heart. 'And come hither.'

Commenting on this portion of holy scripture, A. W. Pink wrote, 'The force of what he said was this: If you really want this living water of which I have been telling you, you can obtain it only as a poor, convicted, contrite sinner. But not only did he say 'Go', but he added 'Come'. She was not only to go and call her husband, but she was to come back to Christ in her true character.'

Chapter 28

Five Husbands Or One?

'Jesus saith unto her, Go, call thy husband, and come hither. The woman answered and said, I have no husband. Jesus said unto her, Thou hast well said, I have no husband: For thou hast had five husbands; and he whom thou now hast is not thy husband: in that saidst thou truly. The woman saith unto him, Sir, I perceive that thou art a prophet. Our fathers worshipped in this mountain; and ye say, that in Jerusalem is the place where men ought to worship. Jesus saith unto her, Woman, believe me, the hour cometh, when ye shall neither in this mountain, nor yet at Jerusalem, worship the Father. Ye worship ye know not what: we know what we worship: for salvation is of the Jews' (John 4:16-22).

You can have five husbands for your soul, or you can have one. If you choose the five, you can never have the One; and the five you choose will be no husband to your soul. But if you choose the One, you will forever despise the five. Does that seem a little bewildering? By the time you finish reading this chapter, I hope God the Holy Spirit will make it perfectly clear to you.

Samaritan Origins
Did you ever wonder who the Samaritans were, where they came from, or why the Jews had no dealings with them? When Shalmaneser, the King of Assyria, conquered the ten tribes of Israel and carried them into bondage, he dispersed the Jews throughout his realm and sent his own subjects from Assyria to occupy and cultivate the land of Israel.

The Assyrians were pagans, idol worshipping pagans. They worshipped gods they could carry from one place to another. When they came into the land of Israel, they brought their own gods with them into the land. In time the Lord God sent lions into the land to devour these idolaters. Terrified of the lions, they asked the King of Assyria to send them a priest to teach them 'the manner of the God of the land', which he did.

Once they had learned 'the manner of the God of the land', they adopted Jehovah as their God, hoping to turn away his wrath; but they continued to serve their own gods. In other words, they professed to worship the Lord God of Israel, because they were afraid of him; but they were not converted to him.

In time, these pagan Assyrians intermarried with the Jews. They became known as Samaritans, a mongrel race, with a mongrel religion, with whom the Jews had no dealings. You may recall that in Nehemiah's day, these Samaritans attempted to unite with the Jews in rebuilding the temple at Jerusalem, but Zerubbabel, Joshua, and the rest of the faithful refused their assistance, saying, 'Ye have nothing to do with us' (Ezra 4:3). Israel's faithful rulers at the time would not allow the Samaritans to join them in their work, not because they were a mixed race, but because they were a people with a mixed religion. Their religion was a mongrel religion. Like multitudes today, they were very religious, full of religious activity, but they knew not what to worship. In the last verse of our text, the Lord Jesus says of these people, 'Ye worship ye know not what'! The Samaritans represent sham conversion, false faith, and religious hypocrisy.

Confused Idolater

The Samaritan woman was now thoroughly confused. She perceived that the Lord Jesus was a prophet; but she did not understand what he was saying to her. She knew that the Jews' religion excluded the possibility of her being saved, because she worshipped different gods, in different places, and in different ways, and the Jews worshipped Jehovah, who alone is God. Yet, the Lord Jesus was talking to her about salvation, eternal life, and acceptance with God; and, with the same breath, he told her that her religion was a religion of uselessness, ignorance, and idolatry.

Since he never went to bible college or seminary, and since he was not trained as either a politician or a preacher, our Master never learned the art of compromise or the trick of talking out of both sides of his mouth. These days, when preachers are confronted with such plain, stark contrasts in religions and religious opinions, they appeal to a vague spirit of ecumenism, and attempt to point to areas of agreement between mutually opposing ideas. Our Lord Jesus Christ was not such a man.

In fact, by the standards of modern religion and political correctness, he would be considered a rude, uncouth, bigot. Instead of dodging the issue, instead of attempting to be polite, the Lord Jesus seems to have stopped this Samaritan woman right in the middle of her words to drive the truth of God home to her heart. He shoots a straight arrow at the very core of her hope. He lays the axe to the root of the tree under which she was hiding. He rips down the veneer walls of her refuge of lies, and tears up the very foundation of her religious house.

He says to her, as she was attempting to defend her religion, 'Ye worship ye know not what'! In other words, he said, 'Woman, what I am telling you is this. You don't know God or anything about God, his worship, his people, or his salvation.' Then, he proceeded to tell her that all who truly worship God and obtain his salvation know who he is. True worship is worship based upon, and arising from, revealed knowledge, the revealed knowledge of God himself!

Question
I have a question which I want you to answer, and answer honestly, for your own soul's sake. Do you know who you worship? Is your religion nothing more than that which has been passed along to you by flesh and blood, by human tradition, and religious ceremony, or do you know the living God? Is your religion the result of you being taught of a man, or the result of you being taught of God?

Many False Religions
There are many false religions by which the souls of men are deceived and damned. This woman's religion was the religion of the world. The Samaritans were a mongrel race with a mongrel religion. You see this clearly in 2 Kings 17. It was about 750 years before our Lord's conversation with this woman that the ten northern tribes of the Jewish nation, Israel, were taken captive by the Assyrians.

Five People, Five Gods
When the original inhabitants of Samaria were exiled from their land by Shalmaneser, the Assyrian king sent people from five different places in Babylon, each group with its own god, to inhabit the land of Samaria. The Jews who were left in Samaria intermarried with these people and incorporated the worship of their gods into the worship of Jehovah. While they continued to claim that they feared and worshipped the Lord Jehovah, and convinced themselves that they did, they became base idolaters and forsook the worship of God altogether. Read 2 Kings 17:29-33.

'Howbeit every nation made gods of their own, and put them in the houses of the high places which the Samaritans had made, every nation in their cities wherein they dwelt. And the men of Babylon made Succothbenoth[7], and the men of Cuth made Nergal[8], and the men of Hamath made Ashima[9], And the Avites made Nibhaz and Tartak[10], and the Sepharvites burnt their children in fire to Adrammelech and Anammelech, the gods of Sepharvaim[11]. So they feared the LORD, and made unto themselves of the lowest of them priests of the high places, which sacrificed for them in the houses of the high places. They feared the LORD, and served their own gods, after the manner of the nations whom they carried away from thence.'

These five gods, like the five husbands this Samaritan woman had had, were all false gods of whoredom. As those men were not this woman's husbands, (They took everything from her and gave her nothing!), so the gods of the heathen were not God and were not husbands to her needy soul. But he who was her Husband, the Lord Jesus, who had espoused her to himself from eternity, had come 'to take the names of Balaam out of her mouth' and to teach her to call him alone, 'My Husband' (Hosea 2:16, 17). O may he do that for you!

After a while, the southern tribes of the nation Judah were taken captive and carried away into Babylon for seventy years. But they never lost their distinct identity as Jews, and stoutly refused to worship the gods of Babylon.

Help Refused

When Judah was delivered from Babylon and began to rebuild the temple in Jerusalem (about 450 BC), the mongrel Samaritans offered to help them; but the faithful men of Judah refused their help. The Samaritans in anger built their own temple in Mount Gerizim; and the Jews and the Samaritans had no dealings with one another from that day forward. With the Samaritans, this was a matter of offended pride. The Jews would not accept them as the people of God. (Nothing more enrages a man than to be told plainly that he is lost, that his religion, the religion of his fathers is a false religion, and that his god is an idol.) With the Jews, at least when the rift occurred, this rift with the

---

[7] Succothbenoth was a god worshipped under the image of chickens, or Pleiades (the seven stars). For whom the women of Babylon and Assyria prostituted themselves at least once during their lives to any man who asked them to do so, in the temple of Venus.

[8] Nergal was the image of a great dog, the god of hunting and of war among the Cuthites.

[9] Ashima was the god of Hamath, worshipped under the image of an ape or a goat with no fur.

[10] Nibhaz was a dog, representing a demon. Tartak was a jackass, representing the prince of darkness. Both were probably made of gold.

[11] Adrammelech was the sun god, in the form of a man. Anammelech was the moon god with the representation of a woman. They were images of Molech, to whom men and women offered their own children as sacrifices in fire.

Samaritans was a matter of spiritual integrity. They could not embrace the Samaritans and their gods without becoming idolaters themselves.

The Samaritans, like the people of this world, had many gods, many religious ceremonies, and many different names for their religion. Yet, like the many religions of the world today, all the Samaritans embraced one another as brethren and worshippers of Jehovah, though they refused to worship in the temple of God, at the altar of God, with the people of God. Though they wore many names and had different religious symbols and ceremonies, the religions of the Samaritans, were all essentially the same, just like the many religions of the world today (Proverbs 14:12; 16:25).

Every man worshipped as he chose. The religions of Samaria, like the religions of my town, Danville, KY, and the religions of your town, were religions based upon human merit, not divine mercy. Being of human origin, all the religions of Samaria, like the religions of this world, were man centred, designed to please, entertain, and indulge the lusts of men. Just in case you are missing my point, let me state the matter plainly. All free will, works religion is idolatrous and damning.

The adherents of such religion may claim to fear the Lord, walk in moral integrity, and talk incessantly about Jesus, God, the Holy Spirit, blood redemption, and salvation by grace; but all who make salvation to be dependent upon or in any way determined by the will, works, and worth of man, rather than the will, worth, and work of Christ alone, are idolaters.

All who seek to establish righteousness by something they do are ignorant of God, ignorant of the righteousness of God in Christ. Refusing to be saved by Christ alone, through grace alone, refusing to count their personal righteousness dung and their religion idolatry, they grope about in darkness, superstition, and ignorance on their way to hell, not knowing what they worship. They go to their high places Sunday after Sunday, observe their holy days, burn their incense, and make great sacrifices to their gods. But they are totally ignorant of the true and living God, totally ignorant of who Christ is and what he has done as the sinners' Substitute.

If we would be married to Christ, we must be made to see that the gods of this world are false gods and the religion of this world is wicked, abominable, and adulterous. There is no salvation for any sinner who refuses to repent of his dead works, whose conscience is not purged from the dead works of human religion by the blood of Christ (Hebrews 9:14). No Pharisee can ever be saved until he is made to see, as Paul declares (Philippians 3:1-9), that his righteousnesses are filthy rags, obnoxious to God, and his religion is nothing but dung. That's right, dung! False religion is not just gutter religion. It is outhouse religion!

One God, One Christ, One True Religion
The fact is there is only one true and living God, one Christ, one Saviour, one Holy Spirit, and one true religion, and one true salvation. Our Lord spoke plainly to this Samaritan woman, both about her spiritual ignorance, and about God's salvation. Let me be just as plain as him.

The world in which we live is under the delusion of antichrist. Arminianism, free-willism, works religion, it matters not whether it wears the name Protestant or Papist, Baptist or Buddhist, is damning religion. The Spirit of God calls all religion that has for its centre-piece the will of man, 'will worship' (Colossians 2:23). And will worship is damning religion.

If this Samaritan woman would drink from the Fountain of living water, she must give up her broken cistern and its polluted waters. If she would have Christ to be her Husband and his salvation her Husband's provision, she must abandon her former husbands. If she found acceptance with God, she must disown the gods, the temple, and people of Samaria. And you and I must do the same.

If we would be saved, the Lord himself must come to us and make himself known to us. We must worship God alone in his true character as he has revealed himself in holy scripture, in the person and work of the Lord Jesus Christ. We must worship God in Christ, the only true Christ! We must worship God by his Priest, Christ Jesus. We must worship at his Mercy-seat, Christ. We must worship God on his Altar, Christ. We must worship the Lord God by his Sacrifice, the Lamb of God. We must worship him in his Temple, Christ, at his throne in his way, by faith alone in Christ alone (1 Corinthians 1:30, 31; Ephesians 2:8, 9; 2 Timothy 1:9; Romans 4:16).

If you would be saved, like this Samaritan woman, you are going to have to identify yourself with Christ, his gospel, his worship, and his people. This identification is made initially in believer's baptism; but it is a constant, lifelong thing. Believer's baptism, like good works, has nothing to do with salvation. And our identifying ourselves with Christ does not contribute one iota to our salvation. Yet, those who refuse to make such an identification with Christ are not saved (Matthew 10:32, 33).

As in the Old Testament men and women found acceptance with God and had a scriptural basis for claiming refuge and salvation in him only when they became Jews, so today, no sinner has a biblical basis for assurance, a biblical basis for claiming grace and salvation in Christ, except those who come into God's kingdom, circumcised in heart, and are numbered among God's Israel.

Ruth the Moabite became Ruth the Jew (Ruth 1:16). Naaman the Syrian idolater became Naaman the worshipper of Jehovah, once the Lord poured out his grace upon him (2 Kings 5:17). Elisha sent him to wash in Jordan. The act meant he had to heed God's word by his prophet and disown the far more physically attractive rivers of his own land, as well as the fake healers who had tried – in the names of their gods – to heal him. The great Naaman had to stoop to be healed God's way, in God's land, among God's people, or perish in his leprosy. The same is true of you!

Once the healing was done, when Naaman went back to Syria, he carried in his great caravan as much of the dirt of Israel as two mules could carry back to Syria, because he had become a Jewish convert, a worshipper of God. He worshipped God on God's altar of earth (Exodus 20:24, 25). Though he lived and died in Syria, Naaman knelt to pray in Syria on Jewish soil, bowing toward the altar of God and the mercy-seat in the temple of God at Jerusalem, as a Jew, a sinner saved by grace alone, through the merits of that Saviour of whom the altar, mercy-seat, temple, and the sacrifices were types!

In the days of Esther, after Haman was hanged on the gallows he had built for Mordecai, many of the Persians became Jews, because the fear of God fell upon them (Esther 8:17).

Do you know who you worship? I do. I worship him who is the Salvation of the Jews, the Seed of Abraham, the Covenant of the people, the Christ of God, the Saviour of the world. I have no righteousness but Christ. I have no atonement but Christ. I have no access to God but Christ. I have no hope but Christ. Christ is my soul's Husband. Christ is enough!

How many husbands do you have? Five or one? If Christ is our Husband, if we are married to him, oh, how devoted we ought to be to him!

Chapter 29

Worship

'But the hour cometh, and now is, when the true worshippers shall worship the Father in spirit and in truth: for the Father seeketh such to worship him. God is a Spirit: and they that worship him must worship him in spirit and in truth' (John 4:23, 24).

How do you respond to a heart probing message? If, in the course of everyday conversation, a question or comment gets really close to you, reminds you of sin, secret sin, your personal sin and guilt before God, how do you react to it?

In the fourth chapter of John's Gospel our Saviour deliberately probed the heart of a fallen, guilty sinner. He exposed her adultery. That guilt before God that she tried to suppress, he deliberately stirred. She responded by defending her religion, by taking refuge in the religious traditions of her fathers and the religious ceremonies she had always observed (John 4:19, 20). Then, after plainly declaring to her that her religion was a sham and that her imaginary spiritual knowledge was utter ignorance, the Lord Jesus said, 'But the hour cometh, and now is, when the true worshippers shall worship the Father in spirit and in truth: for the Father seeketh such to worship him. God is a Spirit: and they that worship him must worship him in spirit and in truth'.

As soon as the Lord Jesus exposed her sin, this woman's conscience was aroused. She was not yet converted; but she was concerned. What a hopeful thing it is when men and women become concerned about their sin, about their souls, about God, and judgment, and eternity. That is where we find this Samaritan woman. Before this, she thought little of these things. Now, she is troubled.

The Master probed matters of the most vital importance. She was disturbed by them; but her depraved heart naturally shrank from the Saviour's barbed arrows. She fled from the penetrating truth of God. It was too probing, too personal, too troubling, too humbling. But look where she tried to hide.

She flew to the best refuge she knew. She sought refuge in religion! That is the natural refuge of the carnal mind. When the word of God first pricks the conscience, the sinner's first, most instinctive reaction is to run to his religious refuge, like a frightened rat runs to its nest in the garbage dump.

The Samaritan woman tried to take the sharp edge off the Master's words by discussing points of religious debate, denominational questions, and historical religious traditions. Such behaviour should not surprise us. It is the natural, common response of sinners when confronted with their own sin and guilt before God.

Instead of confessing her sin and asking how she might be forgiven, she said, 'Our fathers worshipped in this mountain; and ye say, that in Jerusalem is the place where men ought to worship' (v. 20).

'The carnal mind is enmity against God'. There is nothing so averse to human flesh as spiritual truth. I am not talking about that which is, as they say, 'surreal'. I am talking about that which is spiritual, that which pertains to God, the gospel of Christ. The natural mind finds the most convenient way possible of avoiding the claims of the Lord Jesus Christ in the gospel. Instead of stopping to weigh the word of God, depraved hearts run to questions about holy places, holy times, holy days, holy deeds, and holy customs, church dogma, and prophetic schemes. Men and women are willing to talk about and discuss almost any religious subject, as long as they can avoid having to deal honestly and pointedly with their own personal depravity, sin, and rebellion before God.

To her utter astonishment, the Lord Jesus informed this woman that the question she raised was irrelevant. The debate between the Jews and the Samaritans about where men ought to worship, now that Christ had come, was no longer significant. In effect, he said to her, 'Woman, believe me, that question is of no importance now, for the hour comes, yea and now is, when all the externals of religion, all the holy days, sabbath days, sacrifices, priests, laws, and ceremonies of Israel, and the temple itself, must be completely abolished and replaced by true, spiritual worship.' What a shocker that was. What a shocker it still is! All true worship is spiritual. All carnal, legal, ceremonial worship is idolatry.

In the two verses before us our Lord Jesus Christ gave a very brief, but thoroughly instructive, description of the necessity and nature of true worship.

'But the hour cometh, and now is, when the true worshippers shall worship the Father in spirit and in truth: for the Father seeketh such to worship him. God is a Spirit: and they that worship him must worship him in spirit and in truth.'

Worship Essential

Worship is essential. Where there is no worship of God, there is no spiritual life, no knowledge of God, and no salvation. All who are born of God are worshippers of God (Philippians 3:3). 'God is a Spirit: and they that worship him must worship him in spirit and in truth.' This is not an optional thing. There is no choice in this matter. There are three 'musts' in this context. All three refer to matters that are absolutely imperative. In John 3:7, our Lord said, 'Ye must be born again'. In verse 14 of chapter 3, he said, 'the Son of man must be lifted up'. Here he says, God 'must' be worshipped 'in spirit and in truth.'

The order in which these three things is given is significant. All those and only those who are born again by God the Spirit were redeemed by God the Son. And all those and only those who are redeemed and justified by Christ's blood and called by his Spirit can and will worship God the Father in spirit and in truth. It is written, 'The sacrifice of the wicked is an abomination to the Lord' (Proverbs 15:8).

Without question, the worship of God is the most important, most urgent, and most glorious action of humanity. Worship is the creature ascribing greatness and praise to the Creator. Yet, the sad fact is most of what passes for worship these days is anything but worship. That which men call worship today is designed for the pleasure, entertainment, indulgence, and gratification of the flesh, rather than for the celebration of God's excellence and praise. Most churches these days have a service even more odious than the religious exercises of previous generations. It is called 'contemporary' worship. It is well named; for in the dictionary, 'contemporary' comes right before 'contempt'.

Because true worship is essential to true Christianity, and because that which passes for worship in our day is a display of man's contempt for God, rather than a display of reverence for God, we very much need to know what true worship is. Only in the book of God can we find out what true worship is. No one can define and describe true worship except the One to whom worship is due. The One we must worship. If we would worship God, we must worship him 'after the due order' as he has prescribed.

Here in John 4:23, 24, our Lord Jesus Christ tells us five things about this business of worship. May God himself be our Teacher, as we seek to understand his doctrine in these two verses.

True And False

First, as I have already indicated, our Lord Jesus Christ here tells us that there is a true worship and a false worship. When the Samaritan woman began to talk about worship, our Lord quickly told her that she did not know anything about the matter. He said, 'Ye worship ye know not what'. In other words, he said, 'You don't have any idea what worship is'. He was, at the same time, asserting that even the worship of the Jews, in all their outward ceremonies and rituals, was no worship at all.

The worship of God in the Old Testament employed many carnal, typical, outward ordinances of divine service; but true worship, the worship of God was never merely outward and carnal, but was always inward and spiritual (Isaiah 1:2-18). The worship that is no more than an outward religious work; ritual, ceremony, formality, or service, is not worship. This was the essence of our Lord's doctrine in the Sermon on the Mount. He told us plainly that we must carefully avoid being satisfied with our religious service, or in any way making a show of religious service. Our Lord Jesus told us in Matthew chapters 5, 6, and 7, that all true worship is primarily inward. All true service to God is and must be essentially inward, not outward. Humility, faith, and repentance are inward graces, not an outward show (Matthew 5:1-12). Prayer is done in secret, not before men. Giving is to be done privately, not ostentatiously. Fasting is to be conducted without anyone being aware of it, except you and the Lord.

In the house of God there are worshippers and there are worshippers. We stand together. We sing the same hymns. We bow our heads together in prayer. We read the scriptures. We hear the same message. But there is a vast difference between us. Some gather in the house of God, endeavouring to worship God. They want to know him, hear from him, know his will, and honour him. Others have no interest in these things at all. They gather with God's saints in public worship out of a sense of duty, to soothe and pacify their consciences, to please friends or relatives, or just to save face. But they have no real interest in knowing, worshipping, honouring, and serving God.

Kinship With God

Second, true worship involves a kinship with God. In these two verses (John 4:23, 24), the Lord Jesus speaks of something that was never spoken of in reference to divine worship in the Old Testament. He speaks of men and women on earth worshipping the living God as their Father in heaven!

In the Old Testament, the Lord God was honoured as Adonai – God our Creator, the Cause and Support of All Things. He was reverenced as Jehovah – God our Saviour, our Deliverer. He was praised as El-Shaddai – God

Almighty the Lord God Omnipotent. But no one ever thought of bowing before his august throne and saying, 'Our Father which art in heaven', until the Lord Jesus taught us to pray in that manner. The Lord Jesus Christ has given us a freedom of access to God by his blood which no one ever enjoyed before he came (Hebrews 10:19-22). God the Holy Spirit has come to us as the Spirit of adoption to the sons of God in effectual calling, giving us the liberty of faith to call God our Father (Romans 8:14-17; Galatians 4:4-8). Believing on Christ, he has given us the power, the authority, and the right to be called and to call ourselves the sons of God.

'But as many as received him, to them gave he power to become the sons of God, even to them that believe on his name: Which were born, not of blood, nor of the will of the flesh, nor of the will of man, but of God' (John 1:12, 13).

We worship the Lord God as our Sovereign, our Creator, our Law Giver, and our Judge, with utmost reverence. But we also worship him as our Father. What a privilege!

'Behold, what manner of love the Father hath bestowed upon us, that we should be called the sons of God: therefore the world knoweth us not, because it knew him not. Beloved, now are we the sons of God, and it doth not yet appear what we shall be: but we know that, when he shall appear, we shall be like him; for we shall see him as he is' (1 John 3:1, 2).

> Sons we are through God's election,
> Who in Jesus Christ believe.
> By eternal destination,
> Sovereign grace we now receive!
>
> Pause, my soul! Adore and wonder!
> Ask, 'Oh why such love to me?'
> Grace hath put me in the number
> Of the Saviour's family!

> S.P.R. (Gospel Magazine 1777)

Grace Work

Worship is an inward work of the heart. It is a work, not of the body but of the heart, not of outward posture but of inward faith. It involves a kinship with God. And, third, true worship is a work of grace. Worship is a heart work, a son work, and a grace work. Our Saviour declares that those who worship God in spirit and in truth are those who have been sought out by God and caused to worship him by his grace. Our Lord's words are, 'for the Father seeketh such to worship him'.

The implication is obvious. No man will ever truly worship God until he is sought of God and taught by his grace to worship him in spirit and in truth. 'Blessed is the man whom thou choosest, and causest to approach unto thee, that he may dwell in thy courts: we shall be satisfied with the goodness of thy house, even of thy holy temple' (Psalms 65:4). In other words, worship is not something man does for God. Rather, it is something God works in men by his grace. It is the work of God's Spirit in us turning us to God. As one of the old hymn writers put it ...

> Prayer is the breath of God in man,
> Returning whence it came.

That is exactly what David said. 'Therefore thy servant hath found in his heart to pray this prayer unto thee' (2 Samuel 7:27). Worship and prayer are not things which arise from the hearts of men, but things wrought in our hearts by grace. We come together with God's saints to worship God because he has put it in our hearts to worship him.

Spiritual Worship
True worship is spiritual worship. How can I adequately say what needs to be said here? The word 'worship' comes from two English words, 'worth' and 'ship'. Worship is 'worth-ship'. It is assigning to God his true worth. If we do this, if we assign to God his true worth, we must do so in spirit, from our hearts.

The Greek word translated 'worship' means to kiss the hand, like a dog licking his master's hand. It means to fawn, couch, bow to, prostrate one's self. All these things imply an act and attitude of the heart, something inward and spiritual. Our Lord is telling us that there is no true worship, except that which takes place in the heart. Worship is not a physical, bodily function. We must never mistake acts of the body such as kneeling, making signs with our hands, rubbing beads, etc., for worship. Worship is inward, a matter of the heart, not merely carnal, outward, religious exercise. 'For bodily exercise profiteth little: but godliness is profitable unto all things, having promise of the life that now is, and of that which is to come' (1 Timothy 4:8). Worship is more than an emotional experience. It may involve weeping and/or laughing, but it is not a feeling. Worship is a spiritual, mental thing, a work of the heart.

No Images

If we would worship God, we must not use any religious images; crosses, symbols, pictures, statues or physical representations of God. Spiritual worship is simple, unadorned worship. In 2 Kings 18 we are told that the children of Israel kept the brazen serpent Moses had made in the wilderness and burned incense to it until the days of Hezekiah, who finally destroyed it, calling their cherished idol a worthless piece of brass. The use of images in the worship of God was an act of idolatry in the Old Testament (Exodus 20:3-5); and it is idolatry today. Crucifixes, crosses, pictures and images of Christ and angels have no place in the church of God, and have no place in your house or mine if we worship God.

No Holy Things

If we would worship God, we must not honour any day as a holy day, or any place as a holy place. To the believer, every day is holy and every place is holy. We call every day 'the Lord's day', and every place 'Jehovah-Shammah' (Colossians 2:8-23).

All true worship is inward, spiritual, heart worship. It is the worship of God by faith in Christ. Christ is our altar of sacrifice. Christ's blood is the laver in which we are cleansed. Christ, the bread of life, is our table of shewbread. Christ's intercession is our incense. Christ is our ark of testimony. Christ is our paschal lamb. Christ is our great high priest. Christ is God present with us! To worship God in the spirit is the worship of faith. It is calling upon him, trusting his dear Son in our hearts (Romans 10:9-13).

Why is this simple, spiritual worship such a very rare thing? Fallen man wants a god he can see and feel, a god he can show to others. Fallen man, like Cain, wants a god he can impress and obligate by his gifts and works. It is far easier to go through a form, a ceremony, a ritual, and a liturgy than it is to worship God in spirit. If we worship God in spirit, we must acknowledge, confess, and seek the forgiveness of our sins. It is impossible to traffic in spiritual worship. If we worship God in spirit, we have no idols, icons, or trinkets to sell, no priests to serve and fear, no holy places to reverence, and no rewards to win or lose.

In Truth

Fifth, if we would worship God, we must worship him in spirit and in truth. Worshipping God in truth means that we must worship him truthfully, with sincerity, honesty, and uprightness. To worship in truth is to worship without duplicity. We cannot worship God until we open our hearts before him, take off all masks, and do away with all pretence. Whether in the public assembly of God's saints, or in the quietness, stillness, and darkness of the night watches

215

upon our beds, if we would worship God, we must be deliberately naked before him (Matthew 15:8, 9).

But there is more. If we would truly worship God, we must worship him in accordance with revealed truth, as he is revealed in Christ, who is the Truth. And we must worship him according to the word of Truth (John 17:17). What does that mean? Without question, it means much, much more than I can discuss in this study. But it certainly means these two things:

If we worship God, in his house, in our assemblies for public worship, we must worship him in the way he has prescribed. Let us worship our God 'after the due order'. If we worship God in the observance of baptism, we only baptise believers, and we only baptise by immersion. If we worship God in observing the Lord's Supper, we observe the ordinance as our Lord and his disciples did, with unleavened bread and wine. In the house of God the triune Jehovah is worshipped not by waving and clapping your hands, shaking your hips and dancing, but by reading his word, singing his praise, seeking his mercy, and preaching his gospel.

If we worship God, we must worship him confessing our sins, like the publican, and trusting Christ's blood and righteousness as our Substitute. We must worship God upon an altar of his making, not ours, upon an altar of earth, without steps, an altar of free grace alone (Exodus 20:24-26). That Altar is the Lord Jesus Christ (Hebrews 13:10).

Worshipers Sought
'The Father seeketh such to worship him'. How that statement ought to fire our hearts! Does the holy, Lord God seek men and women to worship him? Indeed he does (Song of Solomon 2:14). The God of glory is seeking a people to worship him in spirit and in truth, a people to worship him upon the basis of blood atonement, by the power of his Spirit, with a heart of faith, looking to Christ. Will you worship him?

Chapter 30

Who Worships God?

'God is a Spirit: and they that worship him must worship him in spirit and in truth' (John 4:24).

In the light of that statement, here is a question that can be answered only by the word of God. It cannot be answered upon the basis of our feelings, sentiments, or emotions. It cannot be answered by creeds, confessions of faith, or religious customs. Who worships God? Only the word of God can tell us who truly worships God.

'God is a Spirit: and they that worship him must worship him in spirit and in truth.' But it is ever the nature and tendency of fallen man to pervert the worship of God. Multitudes are blessed with ordinances of divine worship. But rather than using the ordinances to worship God in spirit and in truth, they pervert them into carnal ceremonies, services, and rituals, without regard to God. Multitudes content themselves with the bodily exercise of outward worship and neglect the inward reality of spiritual worship. All men by nature prefer gaudiness to godliness!

Not Bodily Exercise

God the Holy Ghost declares, 'Bodily exercise' (the mere outward motions of divine worship) 'profiteth little: but godliness is profitable unto all things, having promise of the life that now is, and of that which is to come' (1 Timothy 4:8). You and I are impressed by, pleased with, and dedicated to, outward religion. 'But the Lord looketh on the heart' (1 Samuel 16:7). 'That which is highly esteemed among men is abomination in the sight of God' (Luke 16:15).

217

Understand what I am saying. Outward public worship and the outward service of God must never be neglected. But if outward worship is all we have, our worship is vain worship! The absence of a true heart, the absence of heart faith in Christ, and heart devotion to the glory of God makes all outward acts of religion vain worship.

'Wherefore the Lord said, Forasmuch as this people draw near me with their mouth, and with their lips do honour me, but have removed their heart far from me, and their fear toward me is taught by the precept of men: Therefore, behold, I will proceed to do a marvellous work among this people, even a marvellous work and a wonder: for the wisdom of their wise men shall perish, and the understanding of their prudent men shall be hid' (Isaiah 29:13, 14).

In Matthew 15:1-9 our Lord Jesus Christ (the Lord who spoke in Isaiah 29) applied those words to the Pharisees of his day and to all in our day who pervert the worship of God into nothing but hypocritical, outward religious service. The Pharisees added to the word of God the traditions of men, and insisted upon obedience to their traditions (Matthew 15:3). They perverted the commandment of God to suit their own self-serving, self-righteous, hypocritical religion (Matthew 15:5, 6; Mark 7:6-13).

'He answered and said unto them, Well hath Esaias prophesied of you hypocrites, as it is written, This people honoureth me with their lips, but their heart is far from me. Howbeit in vain do they worship me, teaching for doctrines the commandments of men. For laying aside the commandment of God, ye hold the tradition of men, as the washing of pots and cups: and many other such like things ye do. And he said unto them, Full well ye reject the commandment of God, that ye may keep your own tradition. For Moses said, Honour thy father and thy mother; and, Whoso curseth father or mother, let him die the death: But ye say, If a man shall say to his father or mother, It is Corban[12], that is to say, a gift, by whatsoever thou mightest be profited by me; he shall be free. And ye suffer him no more to do ought for his father or his mother; Making the word of God of none effect through your tradition, which ye have delivered: and many such like things do ye' (Mark 7:6-13).

The Lord Jesus declares that all such religion is both vain and hypocritical, an utter abomination to God!

Five Statements
Here are five statements by which holy scriptures identifies who worships God.

---

[12] Corban means a gift dedicated to God that cannot be used for any other purpose Yet, they did! They used traditions, their pretentious religious taboos, as an excuse for their hardness, but never fulfilled their claims. They would never give Corban – their vowed gift – to their needy parents; but they did not give it to God either!

Who Worships God?

1. All merely outward religion which does not involve heart worship, is vain worship. 'This people draw near to me with their mouth, and with their lips do honour me, but have removed their heart far from me.' They prayed and called upon the name of God. They professed to be the people of God. They said they believed the doctrine of God. They practised the ordinances of God. But their hearts were far removed from God; and God regarded their vain worship as an abomination, a mere form of godliness (Isaiah 1:10-18; 66:1-3).

2. All acts of divine worship, precepts of righteousness, and doctrines imposed upon the church by the traditions and customs of men are but vain worship. God says, in Isaiah 29:13, 'Their fear toward me is taught by the precept of men'! Church creeds, doctrinal confessions, and religious liturgies teach and require many things contrary to the gospel of Christ and the clearest possible instruction of holy scripture. The practice of those things required by men is not worshipping God. The observance of mass, religious holy days, infant baptism, the substitution of sprinkling or pouring water for baptism, and the keeping of sabbath days are all things spoken of in the book of God as 'will worship' (Colossians 2:8-23), not God worship.

3. All true worship is a work of the heart (John 4:23, 24; Philippians 3:3; Romans 10:9, 10). Faith is a heart work. Repentance is a heart work. Singing is a heart work. Praying is a heart work. Preaching is a heart work. Hearing is a heart work. Baptism is a heart work. Communion – the observance of the Lord's Supper – is a heart work.

It is not the bodily exercise of religious service that God requires, but godliness. God wants our hearts! 'My Son, give me thine heart.' If he has our hearts, he will accept our services of divine worship for Christ's sake. But if he does not have our hearts, God will never accept our services!

4. If we attempt to fool God with the hypocrisy of vain worship, God will leave us to the folly of vain religion. 'Therefore, behold, I will proceed to do a marvellous work among this people, even a marvellous work and a wonder: for the wisdom of their wise men shall perish, and the understanding of their prudent men shall be hid' (Isaiah 29:14).

'Therefore also now, saith the LORD, turn ye even to me with all your heart, and with fasting, and with weeping, and with mourning: And rend your heart, and not your garments, and turn unto the LORD your God: for he is gracious and merciful, slow to anger, and of great kindness, and repenteth him of the evil. Who knoweth if he will return and repent, and leave a blessing behind him; even a meat offering and a drink offering unto the LORD your God?' (Joel 2:12-14)

5. In this day of spiritual darkness, idolatry, paganism, and superstition, let us return to our God, and return to the worship of our God, in spirit and in truth. The Holy Spirit gives us a striking example of true worship in the apostle

Paul in Philippians 3:1-14. The Apostle Paul is held before us in scripture as an example of what we ought to be. His conversion, we are told, is the pattern of true conversion. His preaching is the standard of all true gospel preaching. And his worship is here held before us upon the pages of inspiration by the Spirit of God as an example of what it is to worship God in spirit and in truth.

A Delightful Exhortation
This chapter (Philippians 3) begins with a sweet, delightful exhortation (v. 1). Paul says, 'Finally, my brethren, rejoice in the Lord'. He used this word, 'rejoice', ten times in the four chapters of this short epistle. We ought to always, in the depths of our hearts and souls, rejoice in the Lord. No matter what our providential experiences and circumstances are, we always have reason to rejoice in the Lord. Here is an exhortation to joy. What a blessed command! 'Rejoice in the Lord alway: and again I say rejoice' (4:4). As we rejoice in him, we worship him.

Let all who know the Lord Jesus Christ rejoice in the greatness of his person as our all-sufficient Substitute, rejoice in the power of his blood which cleanses us from all sin, rejoice in the perfection of his righteousness which is imputed to us for justification and imparted to us in sanctification, rejoice in the abundance of his grace which is always sufficient for us, rejoice in the immutability of his love which never fails, rejoice in the rule of his providence which works all things together for our good, rejoice in the fact of his intercession which is continual and effectual on our behalf, and rejoice in the fact that your names are written in heaven.

This is the exhortation with which Paul opens this chapter, 'Rejoice in the Lord'! May God give us grace ever to do so for the glory of Christ and the good of his people.

A Serious Warning
In verse 2, the apostle gives us a serious warning. 'Beware of dogs.' He warns us here to beware of false prophets. He calls them dogs because that is what the word of God calls male prostitutes. False prophets are men who have for their own sakes prostituted the gospel of Christ and the glory of God (Deuteronomy 23:18; Isaiah 56:10, 11).

'Beware of evil workers.' This is a warning against those who teach, preach, and promote any system of man-centred, works-based, free-will religion (Matthew 7:22, 23). Man-centred, works-based, free-will religion is the single greatest evil and the single greatest cause of evil in this world. The 'good works' of religion without Christ are the most abominably evil works done in this world. Throughout the scriptures of the Old Testament and of the New, they are compared to prostitution, harlotry, sodomy and drunkenness.

They rob God of his glory. They trample underfoot the blood of Christ. They do despite to the Spirit of grace. And they gradually abase man to his lowest, most contemptible state (Romans 1:25-31).

'Evil workers', as Paul uses the term in this context, are will-worshipping Arminians, freewillers and legalists, people who teach that God's salvation depends upon man and is determined by man.

'Beware of the concision.' Those who are of the concision are men and women who cut, mutilate, and torture their bodies – doing penance, observing Lent, living in monasteries and nunneries, observing religious taboos – in hope of winning God's favour.

In a word, Paul is saying, 'Beware of Christless religion'. Beware of any religious custom, doctrine, or service that is centred in yourself and encourages you to focus attention upon yourself.

True Religion Described

In Philippians 3:3 we are given a description of true religion. Here the Holy Ghost tells us who truly worships God. This is what it is to worship God in Spirit and in truth.

'For we are the circumcision, which worship God in the spirit, and rejoice in Christ Jesus, and have no confidence in the flesh.'

True religion is not man-centred, but Christ-centred. True religion is not ceremonial, but spiritual. True religion is not a matter of creed, but of conviction. True religion is not outward, but inward. 'For we are the circumcision', we are God's true, covenant people, the Israel of God, Abraham's true children, which 'worship God in the Spirit'. We worship God as he is revealed in the scriptures, by the power of his Holy Spirit, in our spirits, and in a spiritual manner. True worship is spiritual worship, not carnal, ceremonial ritualism (John 4:23, 24). 'And rejoice in Christ Jesus', we trust the Lord Jesus Christ alone, placing all our confidence in him as our Saviour. We are complete in him (1 Corinthians 1:30, 31; Colossians 2:9, 10). 'And have no confidence in the flesh', we place absolutely no confidence in our flesh, our experiences, our emotions, or the (imaginary) excellences of our flesh. The privileges of the flesh, the feelings of the flesh, and the works of the flesh are no basis of confidence before God.

True Self-denial

In verses 4-8, Paul is set before us as an example of true self-denial. True worship involves a deliberate denial of self before God, a complete denial of any claim, any rights, or any worth before the Holy Lord God.

'Though I might also have confidence in the flesh. If any other man thinketh that he hath whereof he might trust in the flesh, I more: Circumcised the eighth day, of the stock of Israel, of the tribe of Benjamin, an Hebrew of the Hebrews; as touching the law, a Pharisee; Concerning zeal, persecuting the church; touching the righteousness which is in the law, blameless. But what things were gain to me, those I counted loss for Christ. Yea doubtless, and I count all things but loss for the excellency of the knowledge of Christ Jesus my Lord: for whom I have suffered the loss of all things, and do count them but dung.'

Self-denial is an essential aspect of saving faith. Though it increasingly comprehends all aspects of life as we grow in the grace and knowledge of our Lord Jesus Christ, self-denial begins with a denial of all personal worth and merit as a grounds of hope before God.

Here is Paul, a legalist of highest order, laying aside the filthy rags of his self-righteousness for the blessed, pure, perfect righteousness of Christ. Paul counted all his fleshly, carnal, natural privileges, all religious distinctiveness, and educational advantages, as nothing but dung before God. He placed no confidence in his flesh. He found Christ, that one Pearl of Great Price, and sold everything he had to get it (Matthew 13:45, 46). This was done on the Damascus Road when the Lord saved him (v. 7). And this was a decision he made every day, with increasing, growing commitment and consecration to Christ. He counted all things but dung for Christ.

Four Great Ambitions

Why? What was the cause of this man's self-denial, consecration, and commitment? What made this man willing to forsake everything and follow Christ? Paul was inspired, motivated, and driven to the point of utter obsession by four great ambitions of faith. He gives us those four great ambitions in verses 8-11.

'That I may win Christ'! To worship God in the Spirit is to seek Christ. What an ambition! The life of faith is the lifelong pursuit of Christ. Faith looks upon Christ as the most precious, most desirable, most lovely, most valuable Person and Object in the world. The more he is known, the more he is wanted. Therefore true faith willingly forsakes all to follow him.

Christ is the treasure hidden in the field, for which we would gladly spend all. He is the Pearl of Great Price, for which we must sell all. Jesus Christ is the 'one thing needful' who must be chosen. He is the one thing we must have. I am thankful for the many comforts of life with which I am blessed; but I must have Christ. I am thankful for my friends; but I must have Christ. I am thankful for health; but I must have Christ. I am thankful for my family; but I must have Christ. 'Yea doubtless, and I count all things loss that I may win Christ.'

'And be found in him'! (v. 9) To worship God in the Spirit is to seek to be found in Christ, 'not having mine own righteousness, which is of the law, but that which is through the faith of Christ, the righteousness which is of God by faith'.

This is the believer's standing. We are in Christ. This is Christianity. This is salvation to be in Christ, nothing less, nothing lower, nothing different. It is not partly in Christ and partly in the law, or partly in the ordinances, or partly in the church. To be saved is to be in Christ. Religion is knowing doctrines and facts. Salvation is knowing God (John 17:3; 1 John 5:20). Religion is knowing what I believe. Christianity is knowing who I believe (2 Timothy 1:12). Religion is being reformed. Salvation is being regenerated (John 3:3). Religion makes men new converts. Christianity makes us new creatures (2 Corinthians 5:17). Religion is being in the church. Salvation is being in Christ (John 15:1; Ephesians 5:30). Believers are people who are in Christ by God's eternal decree, by the Holy Spirit's operations of grace, and by personal faith. We are a people grafted into Christ by God's mighty operations of grace.

To be in Christ is to have perfect holiness before God. Our righteousness is not something we establish by performing good works, but something Christ established for us as our Representative before God. We do not make ourselves righteous by our obedience to God's law. Christ made us righteous by his obedience to the law for us (Romans 5:19). Our righteousness before God is the righteousness of God in Christ imputed to us and imparted to us by God himself. We have been made the righteousness of God in Christ.

As I stand before the holy Lord God, I want to be found in Christ. As I live in this world, when I offer any service, prayer, or sacrifice to him, when I leave this world, when I stand before his great bar of judgment, I want to be found in Christ!

'That I may know him'! (v. 10) To worship God in the Spirit is to seek to know Christ. I know that Christ is mine and I am his. Yet, I count all things but loss and dung, that I might win Christ, that I might be found in Christ, that I might know Christ. I know him; but, oh, how I want to know him! I want constantly renewed, ever increasing knowledge of and communion with the Son of God. This is the ambition of my heart. I want to know him, my God and my Saviour, my Redeemer and my Lord!

'That I may know him, and the power of his resurrection, and the fellowship of his sufferings, being made conformable unto his death' (Philippians 3:10).

I want to know him who is the great Benefactor of my soul. O that I may know him! That I may know the mysteries and glories of his person, the riches of his grace, the greatness of his salvation, the benefits of his mercies, and the depth of his love! May God give us grace never to take our eyes off of Christ! My soul, make Christ the all-consuming Object of your being! 'That I may know him!

I want to 'know him in the power of his resurrection'. The power of his resurrection declares that I am justified (Romans 4:25). The power of his resurrection gave me spiritual life (Ephesians 1:19). The power of his resurrection guarantees my resurrection (1 Corinthians 15:47-49). But I want to live every day, experimentally, walking in the knowledge of the power of his resurrection. Walking with Christ in the newness of life, I want the power of his resurrection to dominate, control, and direct my life in all things. I want to be continually made new by him.

I want 'to know him in the fellowship of his sufferings', to know my personal interest in his sufferings, and to know what he accomplished in his sufferings. As his sufferings are his glory, I want his sufferings to be my glory (Galatians 6:14). I want to know Christ and the fellowship of his sufferings to such an extent that I am ever 'being made conformable unto his death'. I want to be conformed to Christ in his death, entirely consecrated to the glory of God, perfectly submissive to the will of God, motivated by nothing but love for my God and his people.

'If by any means I might attain unto the resurrection of the dead' (vv. 11-14). To worship God in the Spirit is to seek life in, by, and with Christ. Certainly, this includes a great desire for the resurrection of our bodies at the last day. But primarily, the yearning spoken of here is a yearning for that moral, spiritual resurrection of grace that lifts us out of the death and darkness of sin. The world, the flesh, and all human life is death. In Christ there is life, real life, eternal life, a life of righteousness, peace and joy in communion with God. This is what we want. We have not yet attained it; but we are reaching for it. We want what God purposed for us in eternity and Christ purchased for us at Calvary (Ephesians 1:3-6). Every saved sinner wants to be like Christ!

These are the ambitions of our hearts, the goals we seek, the things for which we live. I pray that God will make them more and more real to me. And I pray that he will make them your heart's ambitions as well. 'That I may win him', 'And be found in him', 'That I may know him', 'If by any means I might attain unto the resurrection of the dead'.

Child of God, set your hearts upon these things, and by the grace of God you shall have them (vv. 20, 21).

'For our conversation is in heaven; from whence also we look for the Saviour, the Lord Jesus Christ: who shall change our vile body, that it may be fashioned like unto his glorious body, according to the working whereby he is able even to subdue all things unto himself.'

Worship, true worship, is not an act, or event, or ceremony. To worship God in spirit and in truth is to worship God in the totality of our lives. It is to live by faith in Christ, for the glory of God.

Chapter 31

'I that speak unto thee am he'

'The woman saith unto him, I know that Messias cometh, which is called Christ: when he is come, he will tell us all things. Jesus saith unto her, I that speak unto thee am he. And upon this came his disciples, and marvelled that he talked with the woman: yet no man said, What seekest thou? or, Why talkest thou with her? The woman then left her waterpot, and went her way into the city, and saith to the men, Come, see a man, which told me all things that ever I did: is not this the Christ? Then they went out of the city, and came unto him' (John 4:25-30).

There is a day appointed by God for the salvation of his elect, a day fixed from eternity when grace will come to the chosen sinner, an hour determined before the world began when the Good Shepherd will seek out and find his lost sheep. There is a time fixed before time began called 'the time of love', when the predestined child, the elect sinner, redeemed by the blood of Christ, must be saved. At that hour, salvation must and shall come to the soul loved of God with an everlasting love. The story of the Samaritan woman's conversion portrays this fact vividly.

> Once as the Friend of sinners dear,
> A man of sorrows sojourned here;
> Eternal love ordained it so,
> That through Samaria He must go.

But what could His dear feet incline,
Unless compelled by love divine,
From whence salvation's blessings flow,
That He must through Samaria go?

There wand'ring from the fold of God,
He saw the purchase of His blood;
And o'er this wretch to lust a slave,
Did sovereign grace her banner wave.

Herein discriminating grace
Shone with a bright, refulgent blaze:
While dead in sin ten thousands lie,
Grace brought this rebel harlot nigh!

Roused from her fond, delusive dream,
As Israel's God she worshipped Him,
Drank of that living water pure,
That shall to endless years endure.

This object of eternal love,
Ordained to fill a throne above,
Shall in the gospel annals shine,
And prove election all divine.

Jesus our Shepherd, God and King,
Thy guardian care and love we sing;
And hail that grace both rich and free,
That brings Thy wand'ring sheep to Thee.

Glory to God, till this takes place,
Bulwarks of fire and walls of grace,
Keep all His blood-bought flock secure,
Till calling proves election sure!

John Kent

Perhaps some who read these lines are in such a state of mind that you ask, perhaps you have been asking for some time, 'If God is pleased to save me, if he is pleased to grant me life and grace in Christ, how will I know? How will

I know when the Lord has saved me? How will I know that God has performed his work of grace in me?'

A Word Of Caution
While there is clearly a pattern of grace revealed in holy scripture; it is only a pattern. There are several specific things God does in and for sinners when he saves them by his grace; but our experience of grace differs widely. With some of God's elect, conversion is a climactic, revolutionary experience. With others, it is a very gradual thing. We must never attempt to judge the validity of a person's faith by the yardstick of our experience, or the validity of our faith by the yardstick of another's experience. We examine our faith by the word of God alone.

It is also a mistake to make the order in which we experience the various aspects of God's grace a matter of great concern. Our perception of things in the experience of them is often very different from reality. For example: There is no question that the new birth is the cause of faith; but we know we are born again only after we believe. Repentance and faith are so closely mingled it is impossible to distinguish one from the other, though they are separate graces.

God's Method Of Grace
As I show you what happens when God saves a sinner, while I will give you five distinct things, do not concern yourself with the order of these things, just with the reality of them. You can be certain that whenever the Lord Jesus Christ comes to save a sinner by the power and grace of his Spirit, he does for that sinner exactly what he did for the Samaritan woman in John 4.

If you are saved, you must be saved by God's work, not your own, by God's will, not your own, by God's doing, not your own (Romans 9:16). If God Almighty ever saves you by his grace, he will do five things for you and in you. If the Lord Jesus Christ ever saves you by grace, he will cross your path.

'He left Judaea, and departed again into Galilee. And he must needs go through Samaria. Then cometh he to a city of Samaria, which is called Sychar, near to the parcel of ground that Jacob gave to his son Joseph. Now Jacob's well was there. Jesus therefore, being wearied with his journey, sat thus on the well: and it was about the sixth hour. There cometh a woman of Samaria to draw water: Jesus saith unto her, Give me to drink' (John 4:3-7).

What a wonder! The Son of God came to Samaria to seek out a fallen woman from Sychar! This woman could not and would not come to Christ. He came to her! The name of God's church is Sought Out (Isaiah 62:11, 12). Salvation does not begin with man seeking God, but with God seeking man. You will never be saved, unless and until God Almighty steps in your way, crosses your path, and stops you in your mad rush for hell.

You will never have an interest in the salvation of your soul and the things of God unless the Lord God creates an interest in you. That is what our Lord did for this Samaritan woman. When she came out to Jacob's well, she had no interest in him, in the glory of God, or in eternal life. Oh, she was interested in religion, and in staying out of hell; but she had no interest in the things of God, until the Lord Jesus made her interested.

In verses 7-15, the Master got her interested in water. No doubt, she was at first only interested in water for selfish, carnal reasons. Yet, there was such spiritual truth in what the Master said that she could not put it out of her mind. I can almost hear her thinking 'Who is this man? What is this living water? Where does he have this water? How can he give it to me? I sure would like to have whatever it is he is talking about.'

Still, something else must be done. If God ever saves you, if the Lord ever has mercy on your soul, if ever the grace of God that brings salvation comes to you, the Lord God will expose your sin to you, just as he exposed this woman's sin to her.

'Jesus saith unto her, Go, call thy husband, and come hither. The woman answered and said, I have no husband. Jesus said unto her, Thou hast well said, I have no husband: For thou hast had five husbands; and he whom thou now hast is not thy husband: in that saidst thou truly. The woman saith unto him, Sir, I perceive that thou art a prophet' (John 4:16-19).

Painful as it is, and it is, you are going to have to face, deal with, and honestly confess your sin before the holy Lord God. It is painful business for God to stick his finger in your heart and rip it open; but if he never rips it open, he will never bind it up. He wounds first. Then he heals. He strips. Then he clothes. He slays. Then he makes alive. He takes away. Then he gives. He creates a thirst. Then he quenches it. He makes you hungry. Then he feeds you. He empties. Then he fills. He never does things the other way around.

I do not know whether you will ever flee to Christ for refuge or not; but I do know this, you will never flee to him for refuge, until he destroys your false refuge. I do not know what your refuge of lies is; but I know you have one; and you will not forsake it until God destroys it (Isaiah 28:14-20). Before the Lord saved this harlot, he destroyed her religious refuge (vv. 19-24). Then,

'The woman saith unto him, I know that Messias cometh, which is called Christ: when he is come, he will tell us all things. Jesus saith unto her, I that speak unto thee am he. And upon this came his disciples, and marvelled that he talked with the woman: yet no man said, What seekest thou? or, Why talkest thou with her? The woman then left her waterpot, and went her way into the city, and saith to the men, Come, see a man, which told me all things that ever I did: is not this the Christ? Then they went out of the city, and came unto him' (John 4:25-30).

228

Finally, if ever the Lord God saves you, if ever you come to know and trust the Son of God, he must reveal himself to you and in you.

Salvation comes by revelation. You cannot trust an unknown Christ. And you can never know him until he makes himself known to you (2 Corinthians 4:4-6; Galatians 1:15, 16). 'The woman saith unto him, I know that Messias cometh, which is called Christ: when he is come, he will tell us all things. Jesus saith unto her, I that speak unto thee am he.'

'I am he'

Never did the Lord Jesus, while he walked upon the earth, make himself known to anyone more clearly and fully than he did here to this Samaritan sinner. Here, Isaiah's prophecy is fulfilled. The Master declares to this woman his great name (Isaiah 52:6). When the Saviour said, 'I AM HE', he was saying to this woman, 'I am he of whom the scriptures speak'.

We must never underestimate the faith and knowledge of God's saints in the Old Testament. God's elect were saved in the Old Testament in exactly the same way they are today. God has only one way of saving sinners. That way is Christ alone, by grace alone, through faith alone. Christ was the Object of all true faith in the Old Testament, just as he is today. What amount of knowledge those Old Testament believers had, I cannot tell. It is not clearly revealed. Yet, we do know that Eve understood the promise that the Redeemer would be a man of the woman's seed (Genesis 3:15). Abel knew about blood atonement (Genesis 4). Abraham knew that the Redeemer would be God incarnate (Genesis 22:8). David clearly understood that forgiveness is sure through the blood atonement of a crucified Substitute (Psalms 22; 32; 51). Enoch even spoke plainly about the Lord's Second Advent (Jude 14). Even Job, in that which is probably the first book written in the inspired volume, describes Christ as our Redeemer and speaks of the resurrection at the last day (Job 19:25-27). Isaiah understood that the sinner's Substitute is both God and man in one person, whose work of redemption and grace must be effectual to the salvation of chosen sinners (Isaiah 7:14; 9:6-9; 52:13-53:12).

Numerous other references could be given. These are, truly, only a few; and they were randomly selected. Yet, they will suffice to make my point irrefutable. Old Testament saints knew and trusted the Lord Jesus Christ as their effectual, almighty, crucified, risen, reigning Saviour.

It is also clear, to even a casual reader of holy scripture, that the saints of the Mosaic era clearly understood and rejoiced in the gospel doctrines of God's free and sovereign grace in Christ: divine sovereignty (Psalms 115:3; 135:6; Daniel 4:35-37; Isaiah 46:9-11); total depravity (Psalms 14); unconditional election (Psalms 65:4; 2 Samuel 23:5); limited atonement (Isaiah 53:8-11); irresistible grace (Psalms 65:4; 110:3); perseverance of the saints (Psalms

23:6). In a word, God gave those saints in the Old Testament faith just as he gives us faith, by supernatural revelation, by revealing Christ to and in chosen sinners. Obviously, the Revelation of God in scripture was not as full in Job's day as it was in Moses', or in Moses' day as it was in Malachi's, or in Malachi's day as it was in John the Baptist's, or in John the Baptist's day as it was in Paul's. Yet, I must personally acknowledge that I have never begun to experience the quality of faith that Noah exhibited in building the ark, Abraham exhibited on Mount Moriah, or Moses exhibited in dealing with Pharaoh and Israel. Those men believed God! They knew, worshipped, and trusted the Lord Jesus Christ, of whom the scriptures of the Old Testament speak (John 5:39). The book of God is all about the Son of God.

When the Lord Jesus said to this Samaritan woman, 'I AM HE', he was declaring himself to be God incarnate, the great 'I AM' in human flesh. We lose much in our English translation of verse twenty-six. It would be far more accurate to translate the Master's words, 'I AM'. Young's Literal Translation translates John 4:26, 'Jesus saith to her, "I am he, who am speaking to thee".' 'I AM' was the Old Testament name by which the one true and living God, the triune Jehovah revealed himself to Moses. This was a name no scribe would write without first bathing himself. Yet, here is a man, standing in front of a sinner in need of mercy, declaring himself to be the 'I AM'!

Our Lord Jesus Christ made this claim no less than fourteen times in John's Gospel. Fourteen times he publicly took to himself this title which belongs to none but God (4:26; 6:20; 8:24, 28, 58; 13:19; 18:5). He said 'I am the bread of life' (6:35), 'I am the light of the world' (8:12; 9:5), 'I am the door' (10:7, 9), 'I am the good shepherd' (10:11, 14), 'I am the resurrection and the life' (11:25), 'I am the way, the truth, and the life' (14:6), 'I am the vine' (15:1, 5).

This name, 'I AM', is our Saviour's declaration that he is God come to save! He made himself known to this sinner as the One of whom the scriptures speak, and as God in human flesh.

When our Master said, 'I AM HE', he was declaring to this woman that he is the Messiah promised long before. The word Messiah means 'Anointed'. It means exactly the same thing as the word 'Christ'. Both the Jews and the Samaritans expected the Messiah to be a man, anointed, chosen, set apart, by God and to God, in whom all the divinely appointed offices of the Old Testament would be fulfilled: Prophet, Priest, and King. The Lord Jesus declared to this woman that he is that man, and that he is God, the God-man: the Prophet like Moses (Deuteronomy 18:18) who shows us all things, the Priest like Melchizedek who brings us to God, and the King like David who delivers us from all our enemies, rules us, protects us, and provides for us.

'The woman then left her waterpot, and went her way into the city, and saith to the men, Come, see a man, which told me all things that ever I did: is not this the Christ?'

This man, the man who died at Calvary, the man who is the Christ, the man who now sits in glory, this man who is the Saviour of the world, says to you and me 'I AM HE'! He of whom the scriptures speak. God incarnate. The I AM. The Christ. The Messiah. The Salvation of Israel!

'Lo, this is our God; we have waited for him, and he will save us: this is the LORD; we have waited for him, we will be glad and rejoice in his salvation' (Isaiah 25:9).

Chapter 32

Sychar's Sinner Saved

'And upon this came his disciples, and marvelled that he talked with the woman: yet no man said, What seekest thou? or, Why talkest thou with her? The woman then left her waterpot, and went her way into the city, and saith to the men, Come, see a man, which told me all things that ever I did: is not this the Christ? Then they went out of the city, and came unto him' (John 4:27-30).

'And upon this came his disciples, and marvelled that he talked with the woman: yet no man said, What seekest thou? Or, Why talkest thou with her?' 'And upon this'. Upon what? What is John referring to with those words? He is talking about our Lord's revelation of himself to this Samaritan woman. He had crossed her path. He had created an interest in her soul. He had exposed her sin. He exposed her to herself. He had destroyed her refuge of lies. He had just revealed himself to her. 'Jesus said unto her, I that speak unto thee am he' (v. 26). Then, we have a sad, sad picture drawn by God the Holy Spirit in verse 27! Our Lord Jesus had come to Samaria on a mission of mercy. The good Shepherd had just found one of his lost sheep. He had revealed himself to a woman of ill-repute and converted her by his almighty grace.

Shocked Disciples
The disciples had been away buying some groceries. They were totally ignorant of the conversation between the Lord Jesus and this Samaritan woman. They did not know what had happened. But when they came on the scene and saw the Lord Jesus talking to this Samaritan woman in a public

place, they were shocked by what they saw. They immediately thought, 'This doesn't look good'.

These men, saved though they were, thought to bring the Son of God before their bar and judge his actions. What brazen audacity! Yet, it is very common. Nothing in this world is more difficult for us to shake than the grave clothes of self-righteous, legal religion and all the taboos men have invented. Religious men invent a multitude of customs, traditions, and moral codes, by which they would nullify the word of God and attempt to govern the lives of others. This is exactly what these disciples did here.

They 'marvelled that he talked with the woman'. They marvelled because the Jews had very strict, well known laws regarding such behaviour. Their law (not God's law, their law) said, 'A man must not multiply discourse with a woman, even his wife, much less with his neighbour's wife'. Their religious teachers said, 'When a man talks with a woman, he is the cause of evil to himself, and ceases from the words of the law, and will at last go down into hell'. This was especially thought to be a very evil thing, if the conversation took place in public, in an inn, or in the street. This is what their religious traditions and laws required. 'Let no man talk with a woman in the streets, even with his wife, much less with another man's wife.'

These disciples presumed that what they saw was something evil. Their 'moral uprightness' made them sensitive to such things. For a preacher (teacher, rabbi, scholar, doctor of the law) to be seen talking to a woman was abhorrent. John Gill tells us, 'This is one of the six things which (were considered) a reproach to a scholar, 'to talk with a woman in the streets'. And it is even said 'Let him not talk with a woman in the street, though she is his wife, or his sister, or his daughter'.

The fact that this woman was a Samaritan only made a bad situation look worse in their eyes. 'Yet no man said', (not even Peter, who was never known for biting his tongue, openly asked the Master), 'What seekest thou? or Why talkest thou with her?'

I have said all that to say this: we need to be constantly on guard. Let us not only bridle our tongues, but also our thoughts. We ought to always put the best construction possible on the actions of others. Do not ever presume that you know what is going on with people. It may be that they are not quite as perverted as you are. John Trapp put it thus, 'All ill thoughts and sinister surmises are to be suppressed and strangled at birth'. This is exactly what our Lord Jesus teaches us in Matthew 7:1, 2.

'Judge not, that ye be not judged. For with what judgment ye judge, ye shall be judged: and with what measure ye mete, it shall be measured to you again'.

The long and short of that is this: We should never interpret the actions of another suspiciously. Love is not suspicious. It does not behave itself unseemly. Religion and self-righteousness make people suspicious and spread gossip. Love hopes for the best, believes the best, and says the best.

Mission Accomplished

'The woman then left her waterpot, and went her way into the city, and saith to the men, Come, see a man, which told me all things that ever I did: is not this the Christ? Then they went out of the city, and came unto him' (John 4:28-30).

The Lord Jesus had achieved his purpose in coming to Samaria. He always does! He had come to save a poor sinner; and it was done. How embarrassed the disciples must have been when they found out what had really taken place. This poor sinner had come to the well a fallen child of Adam. She went back to the city rejoicing in the second Adam. She came out to the well concerned only about mundane, carnal things, like water to temporarily quench her thirst. She went back with the water of life, springing up like an artesian well of life in her soul. She came out of the city foul with sin, beaten with guilt, ashamed. She went home washed, justified, and sanctified in Christ. She came down corrupt. She went back consecrated. She came out condemned. She went back free. I can almost hear her singing,

> Now I am free, there's no condemnation!
> Jesus gave me His perfect salvation.
> 'Come unto me', I heard His sweet call;
> And now He has saved me, once for all!

She came out of the city of Sychar having had five husbands, which were not husbands. She went home with one Husband who is a Husband indeed, faithful and true. This Samaritan woman was converted by the revelation of Christ to her and in her; and the evidences of her conversion are obvious.

Must Be Converted

We, too, must be converted. Conversion is always the result of the new birth, the fruit of grace. There is no salvation without it (Matthew 18:3; Jeremiah 31:19; Acts 3:19).

Have you ever thought about the great, drastic changes that take place in a new born child, radical changes, but changes that take place in the matter of just a few seconds? When a child is brought forth out of its mother's womb, eyes which have been in complete darkness before begin to see light; a body which has been snuggled up in a cosy, warm room at nearly 100 degrees, comes into a cold, cold world and must adapt to temperatures 25 or 30 degrees cooler; the umbilical cord, through which its life's blood has always flowed, is cut; a specific valve in the child's heart that had to be open in the womb must permanently shut itself by God's design, so that the used blood and fresh blood circulating through the heart do not mix; and the lungs fill with air and begin their lifelong function. Dozens of changes take place instantly. The nose, the throat, the digestive system, even the skin goes through great changes, all of which are necessary if the child is to live and be healthy.

As it is in the birth of a child, so it is in the new birth. There are changes which must and always do take place in the life of one who is born of God. These changes are evident in the Samaritan woman. There are four things revealed in these verses about this woman to which I want to direct your attention to, four marks[13] of true conversion.

A Public Confession

The first thing that is obvious in this passage is the fact that this woman made a public confession of Christ. In bygone days the first thing a doctor or nurse might do after a baby was delivered was slap it on the bottom to make it cry. The cry of the child indicated the baby was breathing. In the new birth, the first indication of life, the first evidence that the soul is breathing before God is the cry of new life, confessing Christ before men. Spiritual life is breathing before God and the 'cry of faith' is a believer's public confession of Christ.

Do you not hear this in the Samaritan woman? She said to her neighbours, 'Come, see a man, which told me all things that ever I did: is not this the Christ?'

Salvation does not come by confessing Christ before men. It must never be imagined, however, that a public confession of Christ is an optional thing. Our Lord tells us plainly that we must confess him before men; and believers do so gladly (Matthew 10:32, 33; Romans 10:9, 10). Secret disciples are always suspect disciples. One principle form of a believer's confession of Christ is the solemn ordinance of believer's baptism (Romans 6:1-6). This is a one-time confession.

Our confession of Christ is also a verbal thing. I am not talking about a show of piety. I am talking about the natural result of grace in the heart. Grace experienced, Christ revealed, makes us love him who first loved us (1 John 4:19). Believers delight to talk about him whom they love. We do so as naturally as a husband talks about his wife, or a grandmother talks about her grandchildren.

---

[13] Marks of conversion are not proof of conversion. You may have many marks of conversion without conversion; but you cannot be converted and not be changed, changed inwardly and outwardly. 'Conversion', wrote Joseph Alliene, 'is a deep work – a heart work. It goes throughout the man, throughout the mind, throughout the members, throughout the entire life.'

A Positive Change

This woman's conversion was more than lip service. It was more than a confession of Christ; it was a confession enforced and backed up by a positive change. We read in verse 28, 'The woman left her water pot'! She now had better things in her heart and greater concerns to look after. Having now the water of life in her soul, she became oblivious to that which others thought essential, to that which she thought absolutely essential just a short time before. Pastor Henry Mahan wrote,

> She had come to the well with one thing on her mind a pot of water; but now she had met Christ, tasted the living water and was so taken with him that she not only forgot the water she had come for, but left even her water pot. Once there is a clear perception of Christ to the heart, once he is revealed, known, and received as Lord and Saviour, the things of this world do not seem so important.

As we read the New Testament, we see this same thing in the lives of others. The disciples left their nets, their business, their friends, everything, for Christ. So, too, believers are brought to leave their earthly and worldly things for the sake of Christ, his gospel, his church, his kingdom, and his glory. In a word, like this Samaritan woman, saved sinners, being risen with Christ set their affection on things above, not on things on the earth (Colossians 3:1-3).

A Personal Concern

Here is another indication of this woman's conversion. Having met the Saviour she showed a personal concern for others to know him, too. Up to this point in her life, like all other people, she was concerned for herself. Previously she had known many people, and known some too well, but had never done anyone any good. She had given pleasure to many; but she had done them no good. She used them and they used her. Now, she was concerned for their souls. Her first thought seems to have been, 'I've got to tell others about the Saviour. I've got to make him known.' We read here that, 'The woman then left her waterpot, and went her way into the city, and saith to the men, Come, see a man, which told me all things that ever I did: is not this the Christ?'

Andrew and Philip, when they had found Christ themselves, told others about him and brought them to him. Levi (Matthew), the publican, once he was called by Christ, made a feast for Christ and invited many publicans and sinners to sit down with him, that they might know him as well. The Apostle Paul, once he was converted, expressed a great concern for his brethren and kinsmen according to the flesh. He wanted others to know the Saviour. Such is the nature of true grace. Those who have it want to share it. Those who know Christ want others to know him, too.

In 1866, there was a Welshman by the name of Robert J. Thomas working in China as a colporteur (a Bible and book distributor) with the Scottish Bible Society. But he had a great burden to carry the gospel into Korea. He boarded an American ship, the General Sherman, sailed from China to Pyong-yang, a large city in the northern part of Korea. As the ship neared the harbour, it was attacked by the Koreans and burned at sea. The crew and all the passengers were killed. As the ship and all aboard were sinking, Robert Thomas managed to make it to the shore. He struggled up out of the sea onto the shore with his arms filled with books. They were Bibles. He thrust the Bibles into the hands of the Koreans on shore as they clubbed him to death.

Why? He had met the Saviour. He had tasted grace. Robert J. Thomas had the same overwhelming, life-controlling fire in his soul that the Samaritan woman had. It is what Paul describes in 2 Corinthians 5:10-15.

'For we must all appear before the judgment seat of Christ; that every one may receive the things done in his body, according to that he hath done, whether it be good or bad. Knowing therefore the terror of the Lord, we persuade men; but we are made manifest unto God; and I trust also are made manifest in your consciences. For we commend not ourselves again unto you, but give you occasion to glory on our behalf, that ye may have somewhat to answer them which glory in appearance, and not in heart. For whether we be beside ourselves, it is to God: or whether we be sober, it is for your cause. For the love of Christ constraineth us; because we thus judge, that if one died for all, then were all dead: And that he died for all, that they which live should not henceforth live unto themselves, but unto him which died for them, and rose again.'

A Passionate Call
This saved Samaritan sinner went home to those she knew with a passionate call. 'Come, see a man, which told me all things that ever I did: is not this the Christ?' There was nothing half-hearted about her call. She did not say 'go', but 'Come', and she led them out to the Saviour. 'Then they went out of the city, and came unto him'. This is the concern of every saved sinner. Saved sinners want others like themselves to come to Christ (Psalms 46:8; Isaiah 1:18). Following the example of Christ himself (Matthew 11:28-30; Revelation 22:17), we call sinners to the Saviour. Come, sinner, come and welcome to the Saviour!

Chapter 33

Two Great Soul Winners

'Then they went out of the city, and came unto him' (John 4:30).

We do not hear much about soul winning these days. In fact, I do not recall ever hearing a sermon by a gospel preacher on the subject. In gospel churches, we tend to think of soul winning as an evil thing and of soul winners as ignorant Arminians. Yet, we read in Proverbs 11:30, 'The fruit of the righteous is a tree of life: and he that winneth souls is wise'.

In John chapter 4 we are given a beautifully instructive picture of the soul winner. Actually, we see two great soul winners in the chapter. First, our Lord Jesus Christ came to Samaria as the great soul winner, seeking a lost soul. Then, the sinner to whom he revealed himself immediately became a soul winner herself. Let me show you.

'And upon this came his disciples, and marvelled that he talked with the woman: yet no man said, What seekest thou? or, Why talkest thou with her? The woman then left her waterpot, and went her way into the city, and saith to the men, Come, see a man, which told me all things that ever I did: is not this the Christ? Then they went out of the city, and came unto him' (John 4:27-30).

Are you concerned about the souls of men? Are you interested in the salvation of sinners for the glory of God? Would you like to be used of God for the everlasting salvation of others?

If you have yourself experienced the grace of God in Christ, if you have found for yourself that the Lord is gracious, if you have experienced the love of God in your own soul, I know that your answer is 'yes'. You know that your family, friends, neighbours, and most implacable enemies need the Saviour. 'The one thing needful' is Christ and you know it. You want to lead others to him. Is that not so? Would you not count it your highest honour and most distinct privilege to bring a lost soul to the Son of God? Is there any believer who does not long for this? I am sure there are none.

The thing that hinders you is, perhaps, a great concern for the glory of God and the truth of God. You want to be useful to the souls of men, but you do not know how to go about the work in a manner that is consistent with the gospel of Christ. You do not want to say or do anything that would dishonour our God. And all you have ever heard about soul-winning has come from will worshippers, who are soul destroyers, not soul winners.

How many times have you asked yourself, 'How can I show the kid next door that he needs Christ?' 'How can I get my friend interested in hearing the gospel?' 'How can I minister to my mechanic?' 'What words should I use to talk about Christ to my wife, husband, son or daughter?' 'How can I minister to my neighbour?' It is the privilege and responsibility of every saved sinner to seek the salvation of other sinners.

A Tree Of Life
All who are born of God ought to be soul winners (Proverbs 11:28, 30). Some may think, 'That is strange language for one who preaches and teaches election, predestination, limited atonement, and divine sovereignty.' If you have such thoughts, you do not yet understand the glorious gospel of God's free and sovereign grace in Christ. Hear the words of Solomon. 'He that trusteth in his riches shall fall: but the righteous shall flourish as a branch ... The fruit of the righteous is a tree of life; and he that winneth souls is wise' (Proverbs 11:28, 30).

In those two verses God's saints are described as both 'a flourishing branch' (or a fruitful branch in John 15) and 'a tree of life'. In the whole course of his life, his prayers, his instruction, his example, and his influence, in the whole course of his life, the believer is 'a tree of life'. What the tree of life was in the garden and is in glory,[14] every child of God is in this wilderness: a fruitful tree (Revelation 22:2; Proverbs 10:11, 31, 32), a nourishing tree (Revelation 2:7; Proverbs 10:21), a healing tree (Proverbs 12:18; 15:4).

Without question, none but Christ can win lost souls to himself. I am fully aware of that fact, and rejoice in it. 'He only', wrote Charles Bridges, 'who purchased them by his blood, can win them to himself.' It is the Lord Jesus Christ himself, and he alone, who calls dead sinners to life by the sovereign power and omnipotent, irresistible grace of his Holy Spirit. He gives eternal life to whom he will. Repentance is a gift only he can give.

Yet, he has chosen, in great grace and condescending mercy, to use saved sinners to draw lost sinners to himself (Ephesians 3:8). This is mercy indeed.

---

[14] I do not know what the tree of life was in the garden; but the tree of life in glory is Christ himself; and it is Christ whom we are to imitate.

If Christ is made of God unto us Wisdom, then he has made us wise; and the wise man here declares, 'He that winneth souls is wise'.

This is our Lord's great commission to his church (Matthew 28:19, 20). The risen Christ has given each of us our marching orders. They are crystal clear. These orders are for every gospel church as a unit and for every believer as an individual. The souls of men are our business. Let us ever be about our Saviour's business. The righteous wife must seek to win her lost husband by living with him and before him in meekness and sobriety, reverencing him as her husband (1 Peter 3:1, 2). The believing neighbour seeks to win his unbelieving neighbour by the prayer of faith and work of love (James 5:19, 20). No one in this world, and especially none in the kingdom of God, 'liveth unto himself' (Romans 14:7). We all influence multitudes, either for good or for evil. If we are wise, we will seek by the grace of God to influence all around us for good, for the everlasting good of their immortal souls.

This is my prayer, every time I go into the home of another eternity bound sinner, or have a little time with another soul, which I must soon meet before the bar of God: 'Lord God, give me grace to influence this home, or this person for good, for eternal good.'

If we would indeed win souls to the Saviour, we must have wisdom from above. The fact is, souls are hard to be won. Their wills must be conquered. Their prejudices must be overcome. Their thoughts must be changed. In truth, the work is impossible unless he who is Wisdom both makes us wise and uses us for the salvation of others. Our labour is never in vain in the Lord; but it is nothing but vanity without him.

Still, it is our responsibility, great honour, and high privilege to engage in this work of winning souls. No work is so great and no reward so glorious as that which belongs to the wise who win souls to the Saviour (Daniel 12:3). Every soul won is a jewel for the Saviour's crown, a polished stone in his temple, a cause for joy in heaven, and a satisfaction for his soul's travail. May God give us grace to give ourselves to this business. May God give us wisdom and make us winners of souls, for the glory of Christ. For us to neglect this great work would be the height of selfish ingratitude (1 Corinthians 9:20-22; 10:31-33).

Christ The Soul Winner
The Lord Jesus Christ himself is held before us in this chapter as the great, wise Soul Winner. We read in verse four, 'And he must needs go through Samaria'. Why must he go through Samaria? The answer is given in verses 32 and 34. 'But he said unto them, I have meat to eat that ye know not of.' In verse 34, we read, 'Jesus saith unto them, My meat is to do the will of him that sent me, and to finish his work'.

In this chapter we see the Son of God, with skilful art, gracious patience, infinite love, and divine wisdom, seeking a single soul. In private, without any fanfare, without calling attention to himself in any way, he quietly, diligently went about his Father's business, seeking a lost sinner.

'His disciples marvelled that he talked with the woman.' They did? These men seem to have forgotten who they were, what they were, and where they were when the Saviour found them. Let us not be guilty of such forgetfulness (Isaiah 51:1; 1 Corinthians 6:9-11). I, too, marvel, O Lord, not that you talked with this sinner, but that you choose to speak in grace to any sinner, especially to this sinner! How we marvel that you came to save sinners, such as we are, by your precious blood, your perfect righteousness, and your matchless grace!

Yet, here the Son of God is set before us as the model, exemplary soul winner. If we would win souls, let us learn the wisdom of the art from the Master Soul Winner. Let me show you five things our Master did as he sought the salvation of this needy sinner. If we would be useful in this blessed business of winning lost sinners to the Saviour, we would be wise to seek grace from God the Holy Ghost to follow his example.

He befriended a sinner. He went to where she was, and treated her as a friend (vv. 4-6). The Lord Jesus constantly showed himself the friend of sinners. He went to the lost, the lonely, the distressed, the fallen, the perishing, the needy, the desperate, and walked among them as a friend. More than that, the holy Son of God made the most unholy of men and women perfectly comfortable in his company. He was and is the Friend of sinners!

The Lord Jesus got this sinner engaged in a conversation by asking her questions, questions about something in which she had an obvious interest. She had a water pitcher. She had come to the well. It might, therefore, be reasonably assumed that she was interested in water. So, the Master got her talking about water. He asked her for a drink of water.

Looking at this as an outside observer, it might seem a bit amusing. She was the one in need. He had come to her aid. But he asked her to do something for him. He humbled himself, that he might put himself in immediate contact with her, and compel her to give him her attention. He got her talking. The voice most people like to hear best is their own. So the Lord got this woman in a talking mood. He aroused her curiosity. No doubt, as they talked, the Samaritan woman must have begun to think, 'What an interesting man this is. How polite. How genuine.'

The Saviour talked about something relevant to the woman. It is completely useless to try to talk to people about things about which they have absolutely no interest. Of course, our Master had something on his mind other than what she perceived, and was resolved to direct her attention by the conversation; but he talked to her about water.

Nicodemus asked him about the new birth. So the Saviour talked to him about new life, a new beginning (John 3:3-7). To the man who was born blind, he talked about light, and made himself known as the Light of the world (John 9:5). To this Samaritan woman, he talked about water. He talked about her needs, needs which she (in some sense) knew she had – water (vv. 13, 14).

Notice, also, that the Lord Jesus stressed the good news. Yes, he dealt with sin. Yes, he taught her the truth about the character of God and the necessity of worshipping God in spirit and in truth. But he never got side tracked. He never got entangled with other issues. He never let her draw him into debate and argument about their different religious sects, doctrines, or practices. He had come to communicate to her the water of life. That is what he talked about – water! Living water. Refreshing water. Cleansing water. Thirst quenching water. Everlasting water.

Then, the Master pressed this woman for a decision. When she finally brought up the subject of the Messiah, whom she had been taught must come, the Master said, 'I am he'. With those words, she was forced to make a decision, either to believe his claims or to deny them. She must either bow to or rebel against the revelation of God (1 John 5:7-13).

What happened? The woman believed the testimony of God. She said, 'Is not this the Christ?' And she became a witness to the people around her.

Another Soul Winner

Once the Lord saved her, this saved sinner went about the work of wisdom as a soul winner (John 4:28-30).

'The woman then left her waterpot, and went her way into the city, and saith to the men, Come, see a man, which told me all things that ever I did: is not this the Christ? Then they went out of the city, and came unto him.'

This saved sinner became a messenger of Christ. She went to the men of the city. The Master had said to her, 'Go call thy husband, and come again'. But he did not tell her which husband to call. So she called them all. Since they were all apparently mixed in the crowd, the crowd heard her. 'Then went out the men of the city, and came unto him.'

She left her water pot. She seems to have simply forgotten it, being utterly absorbed with something more important The Lord Jesus Christ and the water of life found in him! She went to call sinners to the Saviour. I can almost hear her passionate, persuasive calls. 'Come, see a man.' 'Come, see a man who told me all things that ever I did.' 'Is not this the Christ?' Come and see!

She told others what the Saviour had done for her. She witnessed (Mark 5:18-20). The woman told all who would hear her 'how great things Jesus had done for' her. How he revealed her to herself, revealed himself to her, and graciously received her. Her testimony to those around her was very simple and clear. Since he has received me as I am, surely, he will receive you, too!

Charlotte Elliott

More than 150 years ago, there was a woman in England, who had heard the gospel all her life. She was raised in a godly home. Her brother was a preacher. But she had become an invalid before she was 33 years old; and she was angry. She was mad at God and hostile with her family, filled with anger.

One day, sitting in a church service, filled with mixed feelings of anger and despair, fightings and fears, she heard an old man preach the gospel. Right in the middle of the service, the preacher paused, seemed to point his finger directly at her, and said, 'You, miss, sitting there in the back, you can be saved right now. You don't need to do anything.'

His words were barbed arrows, shot from the bow of God to her heart. She believed the gospel. The peace of God flooded her soul. That night, Charlotte Elliott wrote these words ...

> Just as I am, without one plea,
> But that Thy blood was shed for me,
> And that Thou bidst me come to Thee,
> O Lamb of God I come.
>
> Just as I am, and waiting not
> To rid my soul of one dark blot,
> To Thee, whose blood can cleanse each spot,
> O Lamb of God I come.
>
> Just as I am, though tossed about,
> With many a conflict, many a doubt,
> Fightings and fears, within, without,
> O Lamb of God, I come.
>
> Just as I am, poor, wretched, blind,
> Sight, riches, healing of the mind,
> Yes, all I need in Thee to find,
> O Lamb of God I come.
>
> Just as I am, Thou wilt receive,
> Wilt welcome, pardon, cleanse, relieve;
> Because Thy promise I believe,
> O Lamb of God I come.

Chapter 34

The Rarest Of All Jewels

'In the mean while his disciples prayed him, saying, Master, eat. But he said unto them, I have meat to eat that ye know not of. Therefore said the disciples one to another, Hath any man brought him ought to eat? Jesus saith unto them, My meat is to do the will of him that sent me, and to finish his work' (John 4:31-34).

The rarest of all jewels must be the jewel of contentment. Everyone wants it; but few, very few possess it. What would you give to have real, lasting contentment and satisfaction? What would you give, if you could say with honesty, 'I have enough'?

There is no contentment to be found in this world. There is nothing here that can satisfy one created for eternity. All who drink from the wells of the earth shall thirst again. All who eat the bread of this world shall hunger for more bread. But there is a well with water which will quench the thirst of your soul. There is a bread, once eaten, will satisfy the deepest cravings of our immortal souls.

I pray that the Lord God will cause you this day to eat of that bread and drink of that water, that you may find satisfaction in your soul, that your conversation may be without covetousness, that you may be 'content with such things as ye have' (Hebrews 13:5). In these few verses of inspiration God the Holy Ghost shows us the rarest of all jewels. Holding the Lord Jesus Christ before us as our example he here teaches us the secret of contentment, the secret to satisfaction.

The disciples had been away buying groceries. When they returned from town and tried to get the Master to eat, he said to them, 'I have meat to eat that ye know not of ... My meat is to do the will of him that sent me, and to finish his work'. What does that mean? What is our Lord telling us here? He is telling us that satisfaction, contentment of soul, is found in doing the will of God.

If you are yet without Christ, if you are yet living in rebellion to God, in rebellion to your own conscience, in defiance of the Almighty, you will never find peace and satisfaction until you bow to Christ, until you are reconciled to God, until you believe on the Lord Jesus Christ.

If you are a believer, if you are a child of God, and still you struggle with these matters of peace, contentment, and satisfaction in your soul, the problem is your rebellion to the will of God.

I do not mean to suggest that knowing and doing the will of God will give you perfect peace, complete contentment and total satisfaction in this world. It will not. It will not, because we simply cannot do God's will perfectly, so long as we live in this body of flesh. But I do say this, if you are a child of God, you are here for a reason. God has a purpose for you to serve, a job for you to do. And the only way you will ever find contentment, peace, and satisfaction in this world is to find out what God's will is and do it with all your might. Doing what God put you here to do will give you satisfaction.

An Encouragement For Sinner
Here is an encouragement for sinners. The Lord Jesus declares, 'I have meat to eat that ye know not of ... My meat is to do the will of him that sent me, and to finish his work'. I cannot imagine a more comforting word for you if you are anxious about your soul, or a more encouraging word to you if you long for God's saving mercy and grace in Christ.

Our Lord Jesus had been seeking the salvation of one lost sinner. Once he had obtained the thing he sought, he said, 'Do you see this saved sinner? This is my Father's will; this is the meat by which I am satisfied'. Is that not what we see in his words?

Our Lord Jesus Christ here declares that the salvation of sinners is his Father's will. Sometimes people get the idea that God the Father is an austere judge, a tyrant who delights in wrath, and is bent upon the destruction of men's souls. Nothing could be further from the truth. True it is that judgment is his work; but it is his strange work. It is true that God must and will punish sin; but 'he delighteth in mercy'!

The Lord Jesus did not come here to make God merciful. He came because God is merciful. He came to make it possible for God to show mercy to sinners while maintaining strict righteousness and justice. Christ did not die to get God the Father to be gracious. Christ died because God is gracious. He did not come to get God to love, but because 'God is love' (John 3:16; Romans 5:6-8; 1 John 3:16; 4:9, 10).

If you get into the kingdom of God's dear Son, you will not come in as an intruder, but as a welcome guest. The gate of mercy is open. God himself opened it. If you get God's salvation, it is because he gives it to you. If you obtain the treasure of heaven, you will obtain it because God himself has made you his heir.

If ever you come to Christ, if ever you trust the Son of God, if ever you believe on the Lord Jesus Christ, you need not concern yourself about having violated God's decrees, overturned his purpose, or defying predestination and election. If you trust Christ, it is God's will that you trust him. He chose you to salvation. He predestinated you to be numbered among his sons and daughters. He called you by his Spirit. You were purchased by Christ's blood at Calvary. If ever you are saved, it will be because God the Father willed it. He willed it because he loved you with an everlasting love from which he can never be turned.

One of the most absurd fears a sinner ever entertained is the fear that he might believe on the Son of God and not be numbered among the elect. I rejoice to preach the glorious gospel doctrine of God's grace and glory in Christ. Electing love, absolute predestination, effectual atonement, irresistible grace, and perseverance of the saints are all great, God honouring, gospel doctrines, plainly revealed in holy scripture. But they are misunderstood and abused by many who would make them appear contrary to mercy. If these great truths appear to you to contradict the fact that the God of glory, the triune Jehovah 'delighteth in mercy', you do not understand them. All these things are true precisely because 'He delighteth in mercy'.

Be sure you understand what the book of God emphatically and universally teaches in this regard. If you desire Christ, he desired you from eternity. If you want him, he wants you. If you are hungry for him, he is the Bread of life to you. If you thirst for him, he is to you a Fountain of living water, springing up into everlasting life for you. There is no secret decree by which God forbids you to believe on his dear Son. He has not said, in some secret, hidden place, 'Seek ye me in vain'. His word is plain and clear. 'Believe on the Lord Jesus Christ, and thou shalt be saved.'

Not only is the salvation of sinners the Father's will, but the Lord Jesus Christ, the Son of God, came into this world specifically for the purpose of saving sinners (Matthew 1:21; 9:13; Mark 2:17; Luke 5:32; 1 Timothy 1:15). If Christ came to save sinners, there is no question about it, he came to save me. I qualify for his salvation, for I am a sinner. Why should I stand around and debate in my own mind or with anyone else as to whether or not he came to save me. A sick man is not reluctant to go to any physician. A poor, hungry man will not hesitate to go to a soup kitchen. A thirsty man will not pause before a bubbling well to see if it has his name upon it. Why should a sinner be reluctant about trusting Christ?

Not only is the salvation of sinners the will of God and the reason for Christ's coming, but our Saviour here declares that the great work of saving sinners is that in which he experiences the greatest delight and satisfaction. It is his meat and drink. From old eternity, he looked forward to the day when a body would be prepared for him, that he might come into the world and redeem his people from their sins. When the fulness of time was come, he ran to the work, as an eager volunteer (Hebrews 10:5-9). While he walked through this world, he was always busy about his Father's business, seeking out lost sinners.

It was alleged of him, 'This man receiveth sinners, and eateth with them'! And, blessed be his name, the allegation is true! He could have healed the leper by the mere word of his mouth, or exercise of his will, as he did the centurion's daughter. But, instead, he laid his hand on the polluted leper to let us know that he has come to be one of us, to make himself what we are, that he might make us what he is. He came here that he might be made sin, to die the just for the unjust, that he might make us the righteousness of God in him and take us to glory. Can you grasp this? The Lord Jesus Christ is a willing Saviour, the willing Saviour of helpless, ruined, lost, doomed, damned, vile sinners. His soul's delight is the salvation of sinners.

Yet, that great crowning work, the work for which all things were made, his work of suffering and death as the sinner's Substitute, that work by which our souls were effectually redeemed, was, at the same time, his greatest sorrow and agony and his greatest delight and satisfaction. This was the baptism with which he must be baptised; and he was straitened until he was immersed in it. This was the bitter cup he must drink; but he longed to drink it. Did he not say to his disciples, 'With desire I have desired to eat this passover with you before I suffer'? Even in his deepest agony, our blessed Christ had a joy before him, a joy which sustained and satisfied his holy soul, overflowing with infinite love for needy sinners. That joy set before him was and is the satisfaction of his soul in the salvation of his elect (Isaiah 53:9-11; Hebrews 12:2).

Now that he is seated upon the high throne of heaven, it is still the great delight of the Lord Jesus Christ to save sinners. If you would be saved, look away to Christ. Salvation comes by looking to Christ. Looking at your sin and hardness of heart will only drive you to despair. Look to Christ and be melted in repentance (Zechariah 12:10; Isaiah 45:22).

Peace, joy, contentment, and satisfaction come to sinners only as we look to Christ. This is the will of God revealed in the book of God. 'This is his commandment, that we should believe on the name of his Son, Jesus Christ.'

John 4:31-34 stands, first and foremost, as an encouragement for sinners. The salvation of poor, needy sinners is the will of God the Father and the work and joy of God the Son, by which he is satisfied and filled with contentment.

An Example For Saints
Here we also have an example for saints. When our Master said, 'I have meat to eat that ye know not of ... My meat is to do the will of him that sent me, and to finish his work', he set before us an example to be followed. That which gave him contentment and satisfaction on earth as a man is the thing that will give us contentment and satisfaction in this world.

If you and I are struggling with frustration, failure, doubts, fears, inadequacies, and a general sense of uselessness, it is because we are having a problem with one of the five things here exemplified in Christ. If we would have peace and satisfaction in this world, we must seek to imitate our Master in these areas.

1. The Lord Jesus always made his will subservient to his Father's will. Our Saviour did not come to do his will, but the will of him that sent him. In all things, he said, 'Not my will, thy will be done'. All our sorrows in this world spring from the root of self-will. If my will was totally subservient to my Father's will, my Father's will would always please me. Pain would have a wonderful comfort to my soul, if I did not kick so hard against it. Losses would enrich me, if I were not so covetous. Bitterness would have a wonderful sweetness, if I did not crave my own will and my own way.

2. Our Lord Jesus lived in great peace and contentment, because he always knew why he was here. He lived with a sense of urgency, pressed with great responsibility, because he knew why the Father had sent him into the world. He came on a mission, with a commission from God, as the Servant of God. He came to save his people, to build his kingdom, for the glory of God. And if we are Christ's, we are God's servants, and his mission is our mission. His commission is our commission. His work is our work. The will of God for him, is the will of God for us (John 20:21-23; Acts 1:8; 26:13-18).

3. Our Saviour's contentment and satisfaction in this world was found in doing the Father's will. He said, 'My meat is to do the will of him that sent me'. Again, he said, 'I do always those things that please him' (John 8:29). You will never find satisfaction in talking about God's will. And you will never obtain peace by debating God's will, God's word, or God's work. The Lord Jesus found his meat, his soul's food, in doing his Father's will.

I am convinced that the vast majority of what people call 'depression' arises from a lack of meaningful responsibility. I have known very, very few people in my life who were engaged in work which they perceived as meaningful, whose hands were full with a weight of responsibility, who yet struggled greatly with depression. I am neither a doctor, nor a psychiatrist or psychologist. So I will leave it to them to deal with such things. But I do know this, spiritual trouble, depression, and incessant doubtings and fears only overwhelm those who have nothing better to think about than themselves. Full hearts and full hands have no room for such worthless lumber.

Find me a person full of questions, and I will show you a person doing nothing. Find me a person constantly struggling with doubts and fears, and I will show you a person who serves no useful purpose in ministering to the souls of others. Find me a preacher who is forever in doubt of his calling, and I will show you one who should be in doubt, because he is not engaged in the work, but loitering about. Find me one who is forever questioning his election, whether or not he trusts Christ, whether he loves the Lord or no, and I will show you one who spends too much of his time thinking about himself, and too little serving the needs of others.

4. Our Redeemer's peace, contentment, and satisfaction came by his perseverance in doing his Father's will. He was not content to do the will of God a day or two, or a year or two. He was resolved to do it until he had finished it. He said, 'My meat is to do the will of him that sent me, and to finish the work.' It was this same confidence and satisfaction which sustained the apostle Paul as he came to the end of his day (2 Timothy 4:6-8). Let it be the satisfaction of our souls to do the will of God until we have finished our course.

5. The Lord Jesus made his will subservient to his Father's will. He knew why he was here, knew what his Father's will was, did the Father's will, persevered in doing the Father's will until it was done, and he did what God gave him to do with all his might, for the glory of God (John 12:27, 28).

Thank you, O my Saviour, for doing the will of God and finishing his works for us. Give me grace, blessed Redeemer, to follow your example, doing my Father's will until I have finished the work for which you have sent me into this world (Ecclesiastes 9:10; 1 Corinthians 10:31; 1 Peter 2:21-25). O Holy Spirit, make the will of God my meat and my drink. With Job of old, let me esteem my Father's will more than my necessary food (Job 23:12). Then, only then, can I possess this, the rarest of all jewels, contentment. When my will is one with his will, I shall be satisfied, not until then. That is the mark toward which I press. May God give us grace to press on. Then shall we be satisfied, when we awake in his likeness.

Chapter 35

Reaping Where Others Laboured
(Labouring For Others To Reap)

'Say not ye, There are yet four months, and then cometh harvest? behold, I say unto you, Lift up your eyes, and look on the fields; for they are white already to harvest. And he that reapeth receiveth wages, and gathereth fruit unto life eternal: that both he that soweth and he that reapeth may rejoice together. And herein is that saying true, One soweth, and another reapeth. I sent you to reap that whereon ye bestowed no labour: other men laboured, and ye are entered into their labours' (John 4:35-38).

Here are biblical motives for missions and evangelism. Any time men and women are called upon to do something unusual, to make sacrifices for a cause, they must have something to motivate them. I call upon all who are God's elect to devote their lives to the cause of Christ, to devote everything God has put in your hands to the furtherance of the gospel, the salvation of God's elect and the building of Christ's kingdom, and I call upon myself to do the same, because this is the only opportunity we have to do so.

Here in John 4:35-38, our Saviour tells us that one great motive for all evangelistic, missionary endeavour is just this – the time is now. This is the time of opportunity. The Master here tells us that we are never to think or act as if there is some future time for evangelization. He says, 'Say not ye, There are yet four months, and then cometh harvest? behold, I say unto you, Lift up your eyes, and look on the fields; for they are white already to harvest'.

I call upon all who have experienced the mercy, love, and grace of God in Christ to devote themselves anew to the business of preaching the gospel. Let

251

us indeed be his witnesses at home and abroad. Let us, like David of old (Acts 13:36), serve our generation according to the will of God. This is our mission. This is the calling, vocation, and life work of every child of God in this world. The Lord our God has left us here to serve this one purpose. He has left us here to preach the gospel, to make Christ known in the generation in which we live.

The Reasons
First, let me show you the reasons given in holy scripture for this great work. Without question, there are many more reasons and motives for evangelism and missions than I can give here. I have limited myself to just a few of the most prominent. But, after much thoughtful, prayerful consideration, I have selected seven noble reasons for this great work. Here are seven things which should constantly motivate us in the work God has given us to do.

1. The glory of God: 'Whether therefore ye eat, or drink, or whatsoever ye do, do all to the glory of God' (1 Corinthians 10:31). In the Great Commission we have our orders from our Commander-in-Chief, the Lord Jesus Christ. The orders are crystal clear, we are, every one of us who are born of God, to go forth into all the world preaching the gospel. These orders are given numerous times, in one way or another, through the scriptures. But they are specifically recorded in Matthew, Mark, Luke, John, and the Book of Acts. In each place the emphasis is different; but the orders are the same. Matthew emphasizes the authority of Christ as Lord and King; 'All power is given unto me in heaven and in earth. Go ye therefore into all the world, and preach the gospel' (Matthew 28:19, 20). Mark's emphasis is the wrath of God and salvation from it (Mark 16:15, 16). Luke presents the great commission as the fulfilling of the Old Testament scriptures (Luke 24:44-49). In John's account, the Saviour's commission is given to us in connection with his own commission from the Father. 'As my Father hath sent me into the world, so send I you' (John 20:21). In the Book of Acts, the great commission is specifically stated as the program and purpose of Christ's church and kingdom in this world (Acts 1:8).

2. The wrath of God: all who are without Christ are lost and under the wrath of God (2 Corinthians 5:10, 11). All who are ignorant of God, ignorant of Christ, ignorant of the gospel are perishing. Our sons and daughters are going to hell! Our mothers and fathers are about to meet an angry God in judgment! Our neighbours and friends are under the wrath of God! The world around us is perishing! Let us love our enemies and do good to those who spitefully use us, just as we do our own families, doing the most compassionate thing we possibly can for them. Preach the gospel to them.

3. The love of Christ: 'for the love of Christ constraineth us; because we thus judge, that if one died for all, then were all dead: And that he died for all,

that they which live should not henceforth live unto themselves, but unto him which died for them, and rose again' (2 Corinthians 5:14, 15).

4. The opportunity we have: 'Say not ye, There are yet four months, and then cometh harvest? behold, I say unto you, Lift up your eyes, and look on the fields; for they are white already to harvest' (John 4:35).

5. We ought to be motivated in the work of preaching the gospel by the opportunity which each succeeding day thrusts upon us. Do you recall our Lord's promise, when he gave the commission? He said, 'Lo! I am with you alway'! He promised us his presence; and it is his presence with us which gives us the opportunity. It is Christ's presence that makes our opportunities. It is his presence which opens doors of utterance for the gospel, and makes them effectual.

The Master speaks here in a parabolic manner. It is common for men to plough a field and sow their seed and then wait for the harvest. But our Lord here tells us that in the work of the gospel, we must never labour with the notion that the harvest is for another day. Rather, we are to labour in his vineyard in the expectation of an immediate harvest, because we are reapers where others have sowed, and others will, in turn, reap where we sow sheaves of harvests gathered from seed sown by someone else.

We cast our bread upon the waters, knowing that it shall return in due time; but while we are casting, the bread cast by someone else is returning. We go forth in the morning scattering the precious seed of the gospel, with weeping hearts; but we go forth with the joyful prospect of coming back in the evening bearing our sheaves of harvest. This is exactly what was promised in the Old Testament prophecies of this gospel age, when Messiah is present upon his throne in his kingdom (Leviticus 26:5; Psalms 126:5, 6; Amos 9:13).

6. The election of grace: the purpose of God in election and predestination assures us that our labour in the Lord is not and cannot be in vain. The apostle Paul frequently referred to God's purpose of grace in election as his motive in preaching (2 Timothy 1:1, 8-12; Titus 1:1-3).

7. The honour of service: what an honour it is that God has put the great treasure of his gospel in such earthen vessels as we are, and uses such things as we are to tell others about his wondrous, matchless, free and saving grace in Christ Jesus (Ephesians 3:8; 1 Corinthians 1:26-31).

The Rewards

Second, in verse 36, our Lord speaks plainly about the rewards which shall be given to those who serve the interests of his kingdom, to those who serve the souls of men for the glory of God by the gospel. 'And he that reapeth receiveth wages, and gathereth fruit unto life eternal: that both he that soweth and he that reapeth may rejoice together.'

The wages we shall receive are the souls of men. 'For what is our hope, or joy, or crown of rejoicing? Are not even ye in the presence of our Lord Jesus Christ at his coming?' (1 Thessalonians 2:19). And the fruit we gather is everlasting. Ours is no ordinary work. Ours is not a labour of temporary significance. Oh, no! The fruit we gather is 'unto life eternal'. Yes, what we are doing is of everlasting importance to the souls of men and of everlasting importance to the glory of the triune God!

The Reapers

Third, see what our Lord tells us about the reapers in verse 36-38. 'And he that reapeth receiveth wages, and gathereth fruit unto life eternal: that both he that soweth and he that reapeth may rejoice together. And herein is that saying true, One soweth, and another reapeth. I sent you to reap that whereon ye bestowed no labour: other men laboured, and ye are entered into their labours.'

Our Saviour here tells us several things we need to always bear in mind: first, all God's servants are one; second, it matters not whether we sow or reap as all who sow do some reaping, and all who reap do some sowing; third, he who sows and he who reaps are alike insignificant. God gives the increase!

I cannot speak for anyone else, but I consider myself a debtor. I have the medicine a dying world needs. If I were to keep it to myself, I would be guilty of the highest crime imaginable, the everlasting ruin of immortal souls!

'I am debtor both to the Greeks, and to the Barbarians; both to the wise, and to the unwise. So, as much as in me is, I am ready to preach the gospel to you that are at Rome also. For I am not ashamed of the gospel of Christ: for it is the power of God unto salvation to every one that believeth; to the Jew first, and also to the Greek. For therein is the righteousness of God revealed from faith to faith: as it is written, The just shall live by faith' (Romans 1:14-17).

Read our Lord's words again, asking God the Holy Ghost to apply them to your own heart by his grace.

'Say not ye, There are yet four months, and then cometh harvest? behold, I say unto you, Lift up your eyes, and look on the fields; for they are white already to harvest. And he that reapeth receiveth wages, and gathereth fruit unto life eternal: that both he that soweth and he that reapeth may rejoice together. And herein is that saying true, One soweth, and another reapeth. I sent you to reap that whereon ye bestowed no labour: other men laboured, and ye are entered into their labours.'

O my soul, let it never be said of me, 'The harvest is past, the summer is ended, and thou art not saved' (Jeremiah 8:20). As in nature, there is a seed time and harvest, so it is in grace. And we are told, that the Lord has given 'the appointed weeks of harvest' (Jeremiah 5:24).

Reaping Where Others Laboured
(Labouring For Others To Reap)

As the wheat ripens, it becomes more golden and weighty. The fuller and riper the grain, the more it bends toward the earth. So it is with the child of God. As he grows in the grace and knowledge of Christ, he is ripened for the garner of heaven. The more he is filled with spiritual life, the lower he becomes in his own eyes; and Christ Jesus is increasingly precious and exalted. And when the Lord signals that it is his harvest-time, the believing sinner comes to the grave 'like a shock of corn in his season' (Job 5:26).

Blessed Saviour, Lord of the harvest, carry on your work of grace in my heart; and let your gospel ever abide in my heart as good seed cast into ground made good by your grace, springing up, growing and fruitful! Oh, prepare me for the harvest! When you put forth your sickle, let me be gathered into your garner in heaven!

Chapter 36

Because Of The Woman

'And many of the Samaritans of that city believed on him for the saying of the woman, which testified, he told me all that ever I did. So when the Samaritans were come unto him, they besought him that he would tarry with them: and he abode there two days. And many more believed because of his own word; And said unto the woman, Now we believe, not because of thy saying: for we have heard him ourselves, and know that this is indeed the Christ, the Saviour of the world' (John 4:39-42).

Have you ever paused to consider the things revealed in the book of God that have come to pass because of a woman? Adam, of course, blamed the fall on the woman God gave him. And the scriptures tell us about many Jezebels and Salomes, by whom Satan has attempted to thwart the gracious purposes of God. But have you ever thought about the fact that there would be no such thing as eternal salvation, were it not for women? God forbids women to speak in the church. The New Testament strictly prohibits female preachers, deaconesses, and such. Women are not to teach or usurp authority over men in the house of God. But that does not mean God does not use women for the furtherance of the gospel and the salvation of his elect.

The fact is, no one would be saved, were it not for the many things God has done by the use of women. Our Saviour, the Lord Jesus Christ, is the Seed of woman, the Seed promised to Eve in the Garden. The Lion of the tribe of Judah came into this world because Judah's daughter-in-law, Tamar, believed God. It was a woman by the name of Rahab who brought God's Israel into the land of promise and preserved the elect nation. The Lord God raised up a woman

257

named Deborah, a prophetess, and a worshipper of God, to deliver Israel from the hand of Jabin, the King of Canaan. It was another woman, Jael, the wife of Heber, who nailed Sisera's head to the ground. It was by the faith of Ruth the Moabitess that the seed royal was preserved in a day when few believed God. And, of course, the Son of God came in the flesh through Mary's virgin womb.

Here, in the fourth chapter of John's gospel, God the Holy Ghost tells us how God saved a great multitude of Samaritans because of the testimony of a woman. He tells us that 'many of the Samaritans of that city believed on him for the saying of the woman, which testified, he told me all that ever I did'.

God's Gift

Faith in Christ is both the requirement of God and the gift of God. Wherever faith exists, it is the gift of God. Faith is not a plant that grows spontaneously in the soil of corrupt human nature. It matters not whether we are talking about little faith or great faith, it is the gift of God. If we find faith in one who was raised under the sound of the gospel by godly parents, with loving care and discipline, it is the gift of God. If faith is found in one who was raised in infidelity as an educated barbarian and has lived all the former part of his life in the most vile profligacy, his faith, too, is the gift of God. Faith is the gift of grace, the operation of God, the work of the Holy Spirit, in no way dependent upon man (Ephesians 1:19, 20; 2:8, 9; Philippians 1:29; Colossians 1:12).

I take great encouragement from this fact. If faith in Christ is, in all cases, God's gift, we should never be selective in the work of the ministry[15]. Our Lord gave us no such example and no such commission. He told us plainly, to go into all the world and preach the gospel to every creature, beginning in Jerusalem and Samaria. Had our Saviour carefully studied a map of Palestine, he probably could not have found a more unlikely place in the entire country from which he might expect to find men and women who would believe the gospel and become his disciples.

Samaria was as unlikely a place as any in which we might expect to find people chosen of God to be made followers of the Lord Jesus. When the Lord Jesus first came there, he found the great evil of racial prejudice against him. The Samaritans despised and would never trust a Jew. They would not even listen to a Jew. Yes, it is true, the Jews had no dealings with the Samaritans. Yet, the Samaritans reciprocated the feeling, and had no dealings with the Jews.

Still, it was from among the Samaritans, a race of mongrels whose faith was a mongrel faith, that the Lord Jesus gathered his elect in larger numbers

---

[15] The world's way to build churches, the way of all denominations, is first to get some surveys, find out where the upwardly mobile, prosperous, educated part of society is moving and what they want.

than anywhere else. Judging by the events of John 4, we would always be wise to go the opposite way of the world. We ought always go first to those places and those people where there seems to be the least likelihood of conversions. God's thoughts are not our thoughts. God's ways are not our ways. But his thoughts are always right and his ways always best. When Paul wanted to go preach the gospel in Bithynia, God would not allow it. He had planned and purposed the salvation of some folks down in a place called Philippi (Acts 16).

If we ever truly learn that faith in Christ is the gift, work, and operation of God, and a supernatural thing, it will have a profound effect. It will alter everything. We will stop trying to figure out how to make the gospel effectual, and just preach it. We will quit trying to determine where God is likely to work, and serve him where we are. We will cease trying to determine who is likely to be saved, and preach the gospel to anyone whose ear we can get. We will quit trying to make the gospel politically correct, socially palatable, and culturally relative, and just preach it.

I say to the preachers of this generation, who seem hell-bent on compromising the gospel in the name of seeing sinners converted, compromise accomplishes nothing! Any converts gained by compromise are twofold more the children of hell than they were before. Faith is God's gift, God's work, God's operation. And it is an operation performed, a work accomplished, and a gift bestowed through the preaching of the gospel (Romans 10:17).

You and I may and must go, feeble as we are, useless as we are, and tell sinners about the sinners' Saviour. We may and must scatter the precious seed of the gospel. The hand that sows the seed is meaningless. Life is in the seed, not in the hand that sows it. In spiritual matters, not even the soil matters, it is the grace of God that makes the soil rich and fertile. Until grace comes, all is alike barren, empty and desolate, but God can make sown seed fruitful anywhere. He can cause it to spring up in everlasting life anywhere. He can make it spring up like a root out of a dry ground. As of old, he brought water out of the rock, and oil out of the flinty rock, so can he bring a harvest to his glory where everything is utterly barren. If this is God's work, let us have no doubts regarding it, let us have no despondency concerning it. Let us, rather, continually put ourselves into his hands, praying that he will use us anywhere he pleases. He knows what is best and always does it. Let him do what he will.

God's Instrument
In verse 39, the Holy Spirit shows us the instrument God used to save his elect in Samaria. We are specifically told that God used a harlot, a harlot saved by free-grace, to carry the gospel to the men of Samaria. 'Many of the Samaritans of that city believed on him for the saying of the woman, which testified, he told me all that ever I did'.

How I love and rejoice in God's great, condescending goodness and grace! The objects of his grace were Samaritans. These Samaritans were not just sinners, they were the most despised sinners, a mixed breed with a mixed religion. The only thing in the world that ranked lower than dogs, publicans, and women in the minds of Jewish people in that day was a Samaritan. The fact is God's elect are always those whom we are least likely to choose (1 Samuel 16:12). Not only is it true that God's elect are the most unlikely, it is also a demonstrated fact that God uses the most unlikely instruments for the saving of his elect and the building of his kingdom (1 Corinthians 1:26-29).

The message of grace was carried to Samaria by a harlot. She spoke was the instrument God used to bring many of his elect to life and faith in Christ. God Almighty can make the weakest of instruments mighty to pull down the strong holds of Satan. That simply means that God Almighty can use such things as you and me for the salvation of sinners.

The message this old harlot delivered was no more and no less than the testimony of her experience. She told her neighbours what she knew, and urged them to see for themselves whether or not she knew what she was talking about. 'The woman then left her waterpot, and went her way into the city, and saith to the men, Come, see a man, which told me all things that ever I did: is not this the Christ?' (John 4:28, 29).

We see here a clear display of God's great and glorious sovereignty. Wherever you see grace exercised, you see sovereignty manifested. You do not have to look for it. You just have to open your eyes to see it. Many were converted, but not all (Acts 13:48; Matthew 22:14). Those converted were idolatrous Samaritans, not enlightened Jews. And they were converted, not by seeing miracles performed, but by the mere word of grace.

'My thoughts are not your thoughts, neither are your ways my ways, saith the LORD. For as the heavens are higher than the earth, so are my ways higher than your ways, and my thoughts than your thoughts' (Isaiah 55:8, 9).

Clinging To Christ
In verse 40, we see this fact, needy sinners hang on to Christ. Those who experience God's saving grace in Christ will be found clinging to Christ until they are with him in glory. 'The righteous shall hold on his way' (Job 17:9).

'So when the Samaritans were come unto him, they besought him that he would tarry with them: and he abode there two days.' That one sentence contains volumes of practical, spiritual instruction for our souls. The desire of the Samaritans and our Lord's compliance with it shows the willingness of Christ to abide with and meet the needs of those who want him. The Gergesenes prayed for the Lord to depart from them (Matthew 8:34). The Samaritans prayed him to tarry with them. Both got what they wanted! What blessings those two disciples would have missed on the Emmaus road had they not said to the Lord Jesus as he was about to leave them, 'Abide with us' (Luke 24:29). If we do not have Christ abiding with us it is because we do not ask him, and because we are willing to be without him (Song of Solomon 3:5).

Experiences Differ
I remind you, once more, we do not all experience grace the same way. The needs are the same in us all. The grace we experience is the same and the salvation is the same, but the experiences of God's elect in grace and salvation vary greatly. We read in verse 41 'And many more believed because of his own word'. Some of the Samaritans were converted by the woman's witness. Others were converted by the preaching of Christ himself. Some appear to have been converted immediately. Others were converted gradually, over the course of the two days of our Lord's ministry in Sychar.

I call your attention to this to remind you that we must never try to put God in our little box. He just will not fit! God saves his people according to his own pleasure and will; and he always does it in such a way that no man can say, 'There, I did that. I am responsible for the grace this or that person enjoys.'

Hell must hoot with laughter while men who profess to be gospel preachers bloviate about theological trivia to immortal souls living but a breath from eternity! While preachers and churches weigh arguments and take sides, fussing and fighting about how a person comes to Christ, sinners are going to hell! What folly! What madness! I do not care how you come, when you came, or where you were at the time. I am concerned for only this one thing, do you trust Christ?

Same Faith
Every believer's faith is the same. All who are born of God believe the same thing and have the same faith. In all matters of 'the faith once delivered to the saints', we all see 'eye to eye'. Every gospel preacher has the same message. Every saved sinner has the same faith. Is that not what verse 42 tells us?

'And said unto the woman, Now we believe, not because of thy saying: for we have heard him ourselves, and know that this is indeed the Christ, the Saviour of the world.'

Sooner or later, every saved sinner confesses faith in the Lord Jesus Christ. It may take some, like Nicodemus and Joseph of Arimathaea, a while to openly do so, but all who trust Christ will confess him before men. Believers identify themselves with the Saviour (Romans 10:9, 10).

Those men of Samaria, once they were converted, said, 'Now we believe'. In those words they acknowledged that before this, they were unbelievers. Religious? Yes, but unbelievers. Bible believers? Yes. They believed the same

Bible the Jews did. But they did not know God. Moral? Sure, but lost unbelievers, nonetheless. These men here repented of their former religion and abandoned it forever. They came out of Babylon!

'We believe, not because of thy saying'. The Samaritans acknowledged their faith was not based on, and did not arise from, the words and arguments of a mere mortal. Our faith does not stand in the wisdom of men, but in the power of God. 'We have heard him ourselves'. Faith in Christ is the result of divine revelation. It is a matter of personal experience (1 John 1:1-3; Galatians 1:11, 12). 'And know that this is indeed the Christ'. Those words might better be translated, 'We know that this is truly the Christ', or, 'We know that this is the true Christ'. Both the Jews and the Samaritans looked for and believed in a 'christ', a messiah; but both looked for a political Saviour, a moral reformer, a false 'christ'. All God's people know, own, acknowledge, trust, love, and worship the true Christ.

These two things are always joined together. When God the Holy Ghost humbles the soul for sin, he graciously makes the sinner know his need of a Saviour, so that self-abhorring and Christ exalting always go together. What did Job say when he saw God in Christ? 'Behold I am vile, what shall I answer thee: I will lay my hand upon my mouth'! (Job 40:4; 42:5, 6). What did Isaiah say when he saw the glory of Christ? 'Woe is me, I am undone; for I am a man of unclean lips; mine eyes have seen the King, the Lord of hosts' (Isaiah 6:5; John 12:41). What did David say? 'Enter not into judgment with thy servant: for in thy sight shall no man living be justified' (Psalms 143:2). What did Paul say? 'O wretched man that I am' (Romans 7:24). If ' God the Holy Spirit opens to you your own vileness and Christ's fulness, you will respond the same way!

This one and only true Christ is 'the Saviour of the world'! He is the only Saviour of the world and the effectual Saviour of the world, the Saviour of God's elect in all the world. Do you know him? Have you met the Lord God of the Hebrews, as this woman and these Samaritans did? Have you seen your sin exceeding sinful? Have you seen Christ exceeding precious? If you have met the Lord Jesus Christ by the saving revelation of his Spirit, in the saving experience of his grace, then you know him as he is: the Christ of God, the Sent One of God, and One with God. Now, you can truly say with holy men of old, 'We believe and are sure that thou art Christ, the Son of the living God' (John 6:69).

Nothing short of this knowledge of yourself and of the Lord Jesus Christ can enable you, as this woman and these Samaritans did, to believe on him unto life everlasting. May God the Holy Ghost give you life in his Christ! May he give you grace, in this Christ-despising day and generation, to know the Lord Jesus and to believe on him for life and salvation, as he did this woman and these Samaritans!

Chapter 37

Just For Certain Ones

'Now after two days he departed thence, and went into Galilee. For Jesus himself testified, that a prophet hath no honour in his own country. Then when he was come into Galilee, the Galileans received him, having seen all the things that he did at Jerusalem at the feast: for they also went unto the feast. So Jesus came again into Cana of Galilee, where he made the water wine. And there was a certain nobleman, whose son was sick at Capernaum. When he heard that Jesus was come out of Judaea into Galilee, he went unto him, and besought him that he would come down, and heal his son: for he was at the point of death. Then said Jesus unto him, Except ye see signs and wonders, ye will not believe. The nobleman saith unto him, Sir, come down ere my child die. Jesus saith unto him, Go thy way; thy son liveth. And the man believed the word that Jesus had spoken unto him, and he went his way. And as he was now going down, his servants met him, and told him, saying, Thy son liveth. Then inquired he of them the hour when he began to amend. And they said unto him, Yesterday at the seventh hour the fever left him. So the father knew that it was at the same hour, in the which Jesus said unto him, Thy son liveth: and himself believed, and his whole house. This is again the second miracle that Jesus did, when he was come out of Judaea into Galilee' (John 4:43-54).

Grace is not for everybody, but just for certain ones. If you read the Bible with your eyes open, that fact cannot be missed. It is as plain as the nose on your face. We read in Matthew 9:18 of 'a certain ruler' by the name of Jairus to whom the Lord Jesus was merciful. He was in desperate need. His daughter was dead. No one could help him, but the Lord Jesus. As the Saviour was going

263

to Jairus' house, he was detained by 'a certain woman', who had been plagued with an issue of blood for twelve years (Mark 5:25). How great her need! How desperate she was! She had spent all her living on physicians of no value, and only grew worse. The only hope she had was that the Lord Jesus would be gracious to her.

Then, there was 'a certain man' whose son was a lunatic (Matthew 17:14-21), who came kneeling before the Saviour, crying for mercy for his son. Who would not pity this poor man? How desperately he needed mercy! His boy was grievously vexed of the Devil. Then there was 'a certain woman' (Mark 7:25), a Syrophenician, a Gentile, whose young daughter was possessed of an unclean spirit. She had no right to expect anything from the King of Israel. She was a Gentile dog. But, because her need was desperate, because the only hope she had was the grace of Christ, she took her place at his feet, under his table, as his dog. That poor, desperately needy soul would be satisfied with any crumb of mercy that he might toss on the floor in her direction.

There was 'a certain centurion's servant' (Luke 7:2), who was at the point of death. 'A certain man' (Luke 8:27) dwelling among the tombs, possessed by a legion of devils, a wild man. How desperate was his need! 'A certain man' (Luke 14:2) had the dropsy. We read of 'a certain beggar' (Luke 16:20) named Lazarus. As the Lord Jesus came into Jericho there was 'a certain blind man' (Luke 18:35) sitting by the roadside begging.

In the parable of the Good Samaritan (Luke 10) our Lord Jesus describes all those whom he came to save under the image of 'a certain man' who, going down from Jerusalem to Jericho, fell among thieves, who stripped him, robbed him, wounded him, and left him half dead in desperate need. I repeat grace is not for everybody, but just for certain ones. Grace is for poor sinners in desperate need of grace, sinners who must have the mercy of God, who must have grace, who must have Christ.

> Leprous souls, unsound and filthy,
> Come to Jesus as you are:
> 'Tis the sick man, not the healthy,
> Needs the great Physician's care.
>
> O beware of trust ill-grounded
> 'Tis but fancied faith at most:
> To be cured and not be wounded,
> Is to be found before you're lost.
>
> Joseph Hart

'Now after two days he departed thence, and went into Galilee'. If you look back to the beginning of this chapter (vv. 1-3), you will see that our Saviour was on his way to Galilee, when he was detained for two days in Samaria. He was detained there because the time had come for the salvation of many of God's elect among the Samaritans. The Lord Jesus spent two wonderful days in Samaria, raining mercy from heaven and gathering flowers of grace. Now, seven great lessons are stamped out in bold letters in these last twelve verses of John 4. May God the Holy Ghost write them upon our hearts and fix them in our memories, that we may use them continually as we journey through this world of time and trouble.

Prophets And Honour
The first lesson taught here is about prophets and honour. God's prophets do not seek or want the honour of the world; but none should be honoured more by men than those men who faithfully minister to the needs of their immortal souls. Yet, our Lord Jesus testified repeatedly 'that a prophet hath no honour in his own country' (v. 44).

Our Saviour went back to Galilee, but not to Nazareth, his home, where he was despised and rejected. Rather, he went back to Cana, where he performed his first miracle, where men and women, 'having seen all the things that he did', received him. The people of Nazareth despised God's word and lost it forever. In Cana of Galilee, where the Lord Jesus began to show forth his glory by making the water wine, needy souls believed him and received God's word. Here John tells us that our Saviour returned to that place where he was honoured as God's Messenger, as God's Prophet. And here, again, we are taught that prophets, gospel preachers, ought to be highly honoured because they are God's servants. They should be honoured because of the gospel they preach. As God the Holy Ghost puts it, they should be highly esteemed in love for their work's sake (1 Thessalonians 5:12, 13; 1 Timothy 5:17).

Though God's prophets should be highly esteemed and honoured, they are more commonly held in contempt than honoured, especially by those of their own country and kin (Luke 4:24; Matthew 13:57). Joseph, when he began to be a prophet, was hated by his brothers. David's brothers looked upon him with utter disdain (1 Samuel 17:28). Jeremiah was maligned by the men of Anathoth (Jeremiah 11:21). Paul was despised by his countrymen, the Jews. And our Lord's near kinsmen spoke of him with contempt (John 7:5). His family friends said, 'He is beside himself' (Mark 3:21).

Men do not like to receive instruction from their peers, let alone reproof; and they are insulted by the instruction and reproof of one they consider less than a peer. Matthew Henry rightly observed, 'Desire of novelty and of that which is farfetched and dear bought, and seems to drop out of the sky to them, makes them despise those' they know well. Proud religious men love titles of honour, but despise truth. Proud well-educated men love academic degrees, but despise dogmatism. Proud unlearned men love higher education, but despise heavenly enlightenment.

Look at what we are told about these Galileans, these country folk, these hill-billies, these redneck hicks from Galilee. In verse 45, the Spirit of God tells us that they received the Lord Jesus, welcomed him, believed him, and cheerfully embraced his doctrine. The reason given is that the Galileans had seen all the things the Saviour did at Jerusalem.

They went up to Jerusalem at the feast of the Passover. The Galileans lived a long distance from Jerusalem. Their road to Jerusalem took them straight through Samaria; and no Jew wanted to walk through Samaria. Yet, in obedience to God's command, they went up to the feast; and there they became acquainted with the Lord Jesus. At Jerusalem, they saw the Saviour's miracles, his wondrous works.

Things Made
Second, we are reminded in verse 46 that our Lord Jesus' first miracle was performed in Cana of Galilee, and that he 'made the water wine'. There is a lesson here about things our God transforms, things he makes what they were not before, things transformed entirely. We are told here that our Saviour 'made the water wine'. He did not make the water look like wine. He 'made the water wine'. He did not make the water taste like wine. He 'made the water wine'. He did not make the water appear to be wine. He 'made the water wine'. He did not treat the water as though it were wine. He 'made the water wine'. And he did not make the water bear the consequences of being wine. He 'made the water wine'.

The word 'made' refers to a single act and means 'caused to be' or 'caused to become'. It refers to a complete transformation of something. This is exactly the same word used in the first part of 2 Corinthians 5:21, where we are told that Christ was 'made sin for us, that we might be made the righteousness of God in him'. I want you to see something here. The Lord Jesus was made (caused to be, caused to become) sin for us. When he was made sin, our sin was imputed to him, and he bore all the guilt of our sins, as our Substitute. Otherwise, the Lord God could never have punished him for our sins (Proverbs 17:15).

The word translated 'made' in the second part of 2 Corinthians 5:21 is another word altogether. When the Holy Ghost speaks of God making us righteous as the result of Christ being 'made sin', the word translated 'made' means 'to generate', 'to cause to come into being', 'to finish', and 'to fulfil'. Thus, like the water in Cana of Galilee, our Lord Jesus was made sin that he might be made a curse (Galatians 3:13) for us and die in our place. As the result of that, all for whom he died are generated to righteousness by grace, born again as righteous ones, made new creatures in Christ (2 Corinthians 5:17-21).

Faith And The Word

Third, we have before us a very important lesson about true faith and the word of God. Saving faith involves hearing, seeing, and believing; and that faith is God's work and God's gift.

The Galileans believed because they saw all the things Christ did at Jerusalem. If ever you come to trust the Lord Jesus, it will be because God the Holy Spirit has caused you to see all the things Christ did at Jerusalem, when he laid down his life for his sheep. You will be caused to see, by divine revelation, that the Lord Jesus Christ satisfied justice by his substitutionary death, put away our sins by the sacrifice of himself, brought in everlasting righteousness by his obedience as our Representative and Surety, saved his people from their sins, redeemed his elect, and glorified God

And this certain nobleman came to the Saviour for mercy, because he 'heard that Jesus was come'. 'Faith cometh by hearing, and hearing by the word of God' (Romans 10:17; 1 Peter 1:23-25). This fact needs to be emphasized. Faith in Christ comes by hearing the word of God preached. This faith in Christ is created in the hearts of chosen, redeemed sinners by God the Holy Ghost, by the instrumentality of gospel preaching (1 Peter 1:25). Did you notice that our Saviour said to this nobleman, 'Except ye see sign and wonders, ye will not believe' (v. 48). He could not believe because he would not believe; and he would not believe because he could not believe. Yet, when the Lord Jesus said to him, 'Go thy way; thy son liveth ... The man believed the word that Jesus had spoken' (v. 50). The word spoken came home to his heart with divine, irresistible power, causing him to believe.

There is something else taught in this passage by the Spirit of God that is commonly overlooked. I do not want you to miss it. It is a sweet, blessed thing to learn. Our Saviour's word is as good as his presence. The Lord Jesus did not go down to Capernaum to see the nobleman's sick son, but only spoke the word, 'Thy son liveth'. Omnipotent power went with that short sentence. That very hour the boy began to get better. Christ spoke, and the cure was done. Christ commanded, and the deadly disease was halted.

That fact is full of comfort. It gives enormous value to every promise of mercy, grace, and peace, which ever fell from Christ's lips. If we build our hope upon the Saviour's word, we are built upon a Rock that he has exalted above his very name (Psalms 138:2).

What Christ has said, he is able to do. What he has undertaken, he will perform. What he has promised, he will make good. The sinner who rests his soul upon the word of the Lord Jesus is safe to all eternity. He could not be safer, if he saw his name written in the book of life with his own eyes. The Lord Jesus Christ has said, 'him that cometh unto me, I will in no wise cast out'. I have come, and he will never cast me out. In all earthly things seeing is believing; but in gospel matters believing is seeing!

Parents And Children
Read John 4:43-54 again, and see a fourth lesson. It is a lesson about parents and children, a lesson about parenting. Let all who are parents do as this nobleman did. Flee away to the Lord Jesus in earnest, importunate prayer, carrying your little ones, dead in trespasses and in sins, to the Saviour for mercy. There is something that stands out here and throughout the New Testament that ought to be encouraging to every mother and father. Never once did a mother or father bring the needs of a child to the Saviour who did not obtain for his child the mercy he sought.

O believing parent of soul-sick children, bring your sick darlings to the Lord Jesus. Cast them at his feet and beg his mercy for them!

Providence And Grace
Fifth, there is a lesson here about providence and grace. As the word of Christ was proved to the nobleman by the witness of his servants, so God's providence often proves his word. O that we had eyes to see it! As the sickness of the nobleman's son brought him to the Saviour, so God's afflictive providences are often the means by which he hedges about his elect and sweetly forces them into the Saviour's arms.

We recognise that judgment never produces repentance. Yet, the scriptures do teach, and teach very clearly, that our God graciously arranges all the affairs of providence to graciously compel chosen sinners to seek his mercy. That is exactly what we read in Psalms 107:1-43.

What benefits affliction often bring on our souls! Anxiety about his son brought this nobleman to Christ in order to obtain help in time of need. Once in the Saviour's company he learned a lesson of priceless value. In the end, 'he believed, and his whole house'. All this, remember, was brought about as a result of the son's sickness.

Affliction is one of God's medicines. By adversity, the Lord often teaches us things that cannot be learned any other way. He will not hesitate to burn your barley fields to get you; and if he does, you will thank him for burning your fields. Thousands have ruined themselves only to be healed by Christ. Untold multitudes have learned grace by the things they have suffered, and obedience by the rod of sorrow.

Let us beware of murmuring in times of trouble. May God settle it firmly in our hearts, that there is a needs-be for every tear and a message from God in every sorrow that falls upon us. J. C. Ryle rightly observed, 'There are no lessons so useful as those learned in the school of affliction. There is no commentary that opens up the Bible so much as sickness and sorrow.' The resurrection morning will prove that all our losses were, in reality, eternal gains (Hebrews 12:11; 1 Peter 1:3-7).

'Oh that men would praise the LORD for his goodness, and for his wonderful works to the children of men ... The righteous shall see it, and rejoice: and all iniquity shall stop her mouth. Whoso is wise, and will observe these things, even they shall understand the lovingkindness of the LORD' (Psalms 107:31, 42, 43).

Riches And Sorrow

Sixth, we see in this passage that rich noblemen have the same sorrows as poor nobodies. This rich nobleman was in great pain. His darling son was dying. His money did not help. His noble standing in society gave him no comfort. He was born into nobility and rich beyond imagination; but his son lay dying; and he could not do anything to help his dying son.

Wealth does not bring happiness. Someone once said, 'Silks and satins often cover very heavy hearts'. Gold and silver cannot prevent pain, trouble, and sorrow; and cannot make them more bearable. Those who live high often sleep little. The higher the tree, the more it is shaken in the storm. The broader its branches, the bigger target it is for the strike of the lightning bolt. David was a happier man when he kept his father's sheep at Bethlehem, than when he dwelt as a king at Jerusalem and ruled the twelve tribes of Israel.

Wealth and distinction are not things to be sought. If God puts these things in your hands, you have a very great responsibility to use them for good; but do not seek them. Seek grace. Seek mercy. Seek Christ. Seek usefulness. But do not seek wealth. Do not seek honour (Colossians 3:1-3).

Death And Age

Seventh, we have before us a very sobering lesson about death and age. Death does not wait for old age. Sickness and death come to the young as well as to the old. Here is a son sick unto death and a helpless, healthy father watching. The boy is going to the grave. The father is about to bury the son.

The lesson is one we are slow to learn. We all shut our eyes to plain facts, and speak and act as if young people do not die. Yet, the grave-markers in every cemetery tell a different story. The first grave that ever was dug on this earth was that of a young man. The first person who ever died was not a father, but a son. Aaron lost two sons at once. David, the man after God's own heart, lived long enough to see three children buried. Job was deprived of all his children in one day.

These things were carefully recorded for our learning. They stand as blazing beacons, saying to all, 'Prepare to meet thy God! Tomorrow thou shalt die'!

Chapter 38

The Angel That Troubles The Water

'After this there was a feast of the Jews; and Jesus went up to Jerusalem. Now there is at Jerusalem by the sheep market a pool, which is called in the Hebrew tongue Bethesda, having five porches. In these lay a great multitude of impotent folk, of blind, halt, withered, waiting for the moving of the water. For an angel went down at a certain season into the pool, and troubled the water: whosoever then first after the troubling of the water stepped in was made whole of whatsoever disease he had. And a certain man was there, which had an infirmity thirty and eight years. When Jesus saw him lie, and knew that he had been now a long time in that case, he saith unto him, Wilt thou be made whole? The impotent man answered him, Sir, I have no man, when the water is troubled, to put me into the pool: but while I am coming, another steppeth down before me. Jesus saith unto him, Rise, take up thy bed, and walk. And immediately the man was made whole, and took up his bed, and walked: and on the same day was the sabbath. The Jews therefore said unto him that was cured, It is the sabbath day: it is not lawful for thee to carry thy bed. He answered them, he that made me whole, the same said unto me, Take up thy bed, and walk. Then asked they him, What man is that which said unto thee, Take up thy bed, and walk? And he that was healed wist not who it was: for Jesus had conveyed himself away, a multitude being in that place. Afterward Jesus findeth him in the temple, and said unto him, Behold, thou art made whole: sin no more, lest a worse thing come unto thee. The man departed, and told the Jews that it was Jesus, which had made him whole. And therefore did the Jews persecute Jesus, and sought to slay him, because he had done these things on the sabbath day' (John 5:1-16).

One of the many great names by which God our Saviour identifies himself is Jehovah-rophe, 'the Lord that healeth thee'. After God had so graciously delivered the children of Israel across the Red Sea, miraculously opening a path for them in the sea and then drowning Pharaoh and the armies of Egypt in the depths of the sea, he brought Israel into the wilderness of Shur, where for three days they wandered without water. The scorching sun beat down upon them. The desert sands scalded their feet. Their cattle were perishing. Their children's tongues were swollen. Their lips were parched. They had roamed for three days in the barren wilderness without water. Then, at last, they came to the plentiful fountains of Marah. When they saw the waters of Marah, how their hearts must have rejoiced in hope and expectation. As they approached Marah, they could almost taste the water. They could almost feel the cool, refreshing water in their mouths. But when they got there, the waters were bitter and they could not drink them! Can you imagine the frustration and disappointment those men and women must have felt?

Immediately, they turned upon Moses, and began to murmur and complain. Actually, they turned upon the Lord God who had brought them to this place. Though the Lord had led them by the fiery and cloudy pillar, though he was with them, though he had miraculously and graciously delivered them from the bondage of Egypt and promised to do them good, they could not see him. All they could see, all they could think about, was the bitter waters before them and the thirst within them. Because they saw nothing good in God's providence, they despised his providence.

Do you know anyone like those Israelites in the wilderness? If we are honest, I am afraid we all must see ourselves in those grumbling people. When they should have remembered God's goodness, they thought only of their troubles. When they should have looked to their merciful Deliverer, they looked only upon Marah's bitter waters. When they should have prayed, they murmured. When they should have believed, they grumbled. 'But God, being full of compassion, forgave their iniquity, and destroyed them not ... For he remembered that they were but flesh' (Psalms 78:38, 39).

Remember, it was God who brought Israel to Marah. He brought them here to teach them and to make himself known to them. And he did it to teach us and make himself known to us. 'All these things happened unto them for ensamples: and they are written for our admonition' (1 Corinthians 10:11). We read, in Exodus 15:25 and 26, that Moses 'cried unto the Lord; and the Lord showed him a tree, which when he had cast into the waters, the waters were made sweet: there he made for them a statute and an ordinance, and there he proved them, And said, if thou wilt diligently hearken to the voice of the Lord thy God, and wilt do that which is right in his sight, and wilt give ear to his commandments, and keep all his statutes, I will put none of these diseases upon thee, which I have brought upon the Egyptians: for I am the LORD that healeth thee.'

Here in John's Gospel we see another pool of water, a pool called Bethesda, which means, 'house of mercy'. To this pool Jehovah-rophe, Jehovah our Healer, came to perform one of his great, memorable acts of mercy upon a poor, impotent sinner he saw lying by the pool.

When I read this story, I feel like Moses must have felt when he saw the Lord in the burning bush, and said, 'I will now turn aside and see this great sight'. Everything in this story is highly significant. Everything written here is designed of God to teach us spiritual things relating to Christ, the gospel of God's free grace, and our salvation in and by him.

The Healing Pool
The first thing that demands our attention is the healing pool that is described for us by God the Holy Spirit. We are told in verse 1 that our Lord Jesus had gone up to Jerusalem to keep one of the annual feasts of the Jews. We are not told which feast this was, because it is not important. Our blessed Saviour went up to Jerusalem in compliance with the law of Moses, because he had come to obey, fulfil, and finish the law as our covenant Surety and Representative.

In Jerusalem near the sheep gate, here called 'the sheep market', there was a pool with five porches called Bethesda. This Pool of Bethesda was near the brook Cedron, which ran by Gethsemane (John 18:1). This sheep gate was sanctified in the days of Nehemiah (Nehemiah 3:1, 32; 12:39), and is mentioned by Jeremiah as a place of significance in Jeremiah 31 (vv. 38, 39). Right by this sheep gate, or sheep fold, stood the Pool of Bethesda.

The name of this pool, 'Bethesda', means 'house of mercy', or 'house of grace'. Apparently, it was given this name because many had been healed of their infirmities by its waters, when 'an angel went down at a certain season into the pool, and troubled the water'. Many suggest that John was simply relating a Jewish superstition. The Jews gradually became more and more superstitious, as they became wrapped up in carnal ordinances of outward religious ceremony and ignored the message of those ceremonies and the instruction of God's word. They actually believed that the blood of their sacrifices mixed with the water of Bethesda's pool gave the waters miraculous, healing power. Others attempt to destroy the faith of Christ by trying to prove that the waters had certain minerals in them that gave them some healing efficacy. But the Spirit of God inspired John to write as he did, telling us both of this Pool of Bethesda and the angel that troubled the water, making its waters effectual for healing at specific times.

What does this Pool of Bethesda represent? Remember, the name 'Bethesda' means 'house of mercy'. Without question, it is symbolic of something connected with the mercy, grace, and goodness of God bestowed upon sinners in the saving operations of his grace.

Perhaps the Pool of Bethesda refers to God's appointed means of grace, the divinely appointed means he uses to save his elect: The worship of God and the preaching of the gospel in his house. In the house of God the free, sovereign, rich, and abundant grace and mercy of God in, by, and through Christ is proclaimed as the only ground and foundation of a sinner's hope. Here the mercy of God, as it is displayed in the covenant of grace, in the mission of Christ, and redemption accomplished by him is preached. Here, in the house of mercy, the mercy of God in redemption, regeneration, and in the forgiveness of sin is published abroad to sinners. And here, in the house of grace, the whole of salvation, from first to last, is held forth for the relief of poor, helpless souls.

Whether the Pool of Bethesda has reference to the place of divine worship, I do not know. But in Zechariah 13:1, we see a fountain to which it most definitely does have reference, the fountain of Christ's precious blood, opened for polluted sinners, the fountain in which we are washed and cleansed from all sin. This fountain cures all diseases. It is opened in the house of mercy by the preaching of the gospel. The gospel itself is compared to a fountain of waters (Isaiah 4:1; Zechariah 14:8; Joel 3:18).

It is not insignificant that this Pool of Bethesda was by the Sheep Gate, or the Sheep Fold that the Lord God had sanctified. This much is certain: Christ is found wherever his sheep are found. Those the Father has given him, the sheep for whom he died, he must bring in. Wherever they are found, there he sends his word; and by his word he gathers them in and heals them (Psalms 107:20).

The Spirit of God tells us that there were five porches, five large, covered porches adjoined to and surrounding the Pool of Bethesda. John Gill suggested that these five porches might be intended to refer to the law, the five books of the law written by Moses, telling us that there is no grace, no mercy, and no salvation in the works of the law. If we would be saved, we must get off the hard, cold slab of death in the law and into the living waters of grace in Christ (Romans 9:30-10:4; Galatians 2:16, 21; 3:21; 5:1-4).

The Impotent Multitude
Second, the impotent multitude laying on those five porches, waiting for the moving of the water, portray vividly poor, lost sinners in the house of God (v. 3). Notice the words used by the Spirit of God to describe our lost and ruined condition, since the sin and fall of our father Adam.

1. Impotent: that is a pretty good way to describe fallen man. He is impotent before the law. Enfeebled by sin, man can do nothing to save himself. We are, by nature, impotent, as impotent as any dead man in the grave. He has neither the power to redeem himself, nor to regenerate himself, nor even to choose to be redeemed and regenerated.

2. Blind: fallen man, dead in trespasses and in sins, is as blind as he is impotent. He is ignorant of, and blind to, everything that is spiritual; himself, God, his Son, his righteousness, his grace, his salvation.

3. Halt: as the sinner is impotent and blind, he is also 'halt', lame on both his feet. This word, 'halt' (lame), is used in reference to people hesitating about the things of God, halting between two opinions. It is sometimes used to speak of the infirmities of God's saints, and our faltering and failure in spiritual matters. It refers to the incapacity of man to walk. We cannot come to Christ for grace and life. We cannot walk by faith in him, except God himself turn us, and draw us, and bring us.

4. Withered: the word means 'dried up'! That is us. Dried up! What a pitiful looking crowd that must have been! There is one with an arm all twisted and dried up. There is another whose legs are withered. There is one who looks as if there is no moisture left in his muscles, or in his body at all. Destitute of grace and destitute of hope, without God, without Christ, poor, lost sinners are withered, dried up!

5. Waiting: these poor souls, impotent, blind, halt, and withered were waiting for the moving of the water. They were laying there because someone had informed them that on certain, specific days God sent an angel from heaven to move the water in that pool, and that the first person in the water, as it was stirred by the angel, would be healed. There they lay, waiting at Wisdom's gates, watching at the posts of her doors.

The Angel That Troubles

Now, third, look at this angel that troubled the water. I cannot speak with certainty about this, because the scriptures do not, but it appears that the Pool of Bethesda was a standing miracle in Jerusalem. It was specifically intended, by the grace of God, to be a standing witness to his mercy during those dark days of silence, between Malachi and the coming of the Lord Jesus Christ, those silent years in which the Lord removed the Spirit of prophecy, when Urim and Thummim were not, and the Shekinah was not seen in his house.

The Pool of Bethesda was a standing witness that the Lord had 'not cast away his people whom he foreknew'. Therefore, the impotent folk; blind, halt, and withered, were brought here to wait for the angel of God to trouble the water, just as poor sinners were taught of God to wait for Christ. As our blessed Lord Jesus was the fountain to be opened in that day to the house of David and

275

to the inhabitants of Jerusalem for sin and uncleanness, the pool of Bethesda shadowed forth his coming.

When the Son of God came here and performed the miracle of mercy recorded upon this page of holy scripture, and performed it without the use of Bethesda's waters, he said to the man, to the multitude who waited for the angel to trouble the water, and to the Pharisees who stood by, 'I am the Fountain opened for sin and uncleanness. I am the Water of Life. I am the Angel that heals. My name is Jehovah-rophe.' 'I am the Lord that healeth thee'! In this day of mercy 'the Lord bindeth up the breach of his people, and healeth the stroke of their wound' (Exodus 15:26; Isaiah 30:26). And now, since he has come, of whom the pool gave witness, since the Substance has appeared, the shadow has been taken away. Never again do we hear or read any mention of the Pool of Bethesda and its healing waters.

Yet, there is a striking parallel between the Pool of Bethesda and the ministry of the word in the house of God. Gospel churches are the Bethesdas, houses of mercy, of this gospel day. But, as in the story before us, we must wait for the decent of the Angel of God, Christ the Almighty Angel of the Covenant, to give healing power and saving efficacy to the gospel we preach, the water of the word.

There was a certain season when the angel went down and troubled the water in Bethesda's pool. Some suggest that it was during the divinely appointed feast days in Jerusalem. Others suggest that it was on the sabbath, the divinely appointed day of worship. Whatever the case may have been, there are certain seasons when the Angel of God, the Lord Jesus Christ, comes to our gospel Bethesdas to trouble the water. At the appointed hour of public worship, wherever two or three are gathered together in his name, Christ comes to stir the water (Matthew 18:20; 1 Corinthians 3:16). At the appointed time of love, when the chosen, redeemed sinner must be called, the Angel of the Covenant comes to bring all the blessings of the Covenant to his chosen.

The troubling, the stirring, agitation, and shaking of the water speaks of the Lord Jesus pouring out his Spirit upon us in the house of God, causing his word to run swiftly, to go forth to the hearts of chosen, redeemed sinners in saving power and efficacy. The Angel who troubles the water is the One who heals the needy soul, Christ our Saviour. John Gill made the following instructive observation,

> The Spirit of God, who moved upon the face of the waters in the first creation, in and by the ministry of the word, troubles the minds of men. And whilst the prophet prophesies, (He) causes a shaking among the dry bones, which is done at certain seasons; for as there are certain seasons for the preaching of the gospel,

so there is more especially a fixed, settled, and appointed one, for the conversion of God's elect; who are called according to purpose, and at the time the Lord has appointed. And whoever now, upon the preaching of the gospel, are enabled to step forth and come to Christ, and believe in him, are cured of all their soul maladies and diseases, be they what they will. All their iniquities are pardoned, their persons justified, and they are saved in Christ, with an everlasting salvation. And as this cure was not owing to any natural virtue in the water, nor even to the angel's troubling it, but to a supernatural power; so the conversion of a sinner is owing, not to ministers, and to the word and ordinances as administered by them, but to the superior power of the grace of God, and which is exerted in his time, and on whom he pleases.

But there are two very great differences between the Pool of Bethesda and our gospel Bethesdas. Here is great mercy. First, the grace of our Lord Jesus Christ proclaimed in the house of God is not limited to one poor, impotent soul. The gospel invitation is issued to all who will hear his voice; and he assures all who come to him, 'him that cometh unto me I will in no wise cast out'! And second, the salvation of God does not wait for sinners to step into the Water of Grace. He who is God's salvation comes to poor, impotent sinners, blind, halt, and withered. He binds up our wounds and pours in the oil of his Spirit and the wine of his grace, and makes the impotent whole.

The Patient Healed
Christ is the great Physician, the Angel that troubles the water. Fourth, we have before us the poor patient he healed, the impotent man; blind, halt, and withered. He was impotent; and he had been that way for a long, long time, thirty-eight years. He was a certain man, sovereignly chosen, distinctly elected. He was under the watchful eye of the Son of God, 'Jesus saw him'. He had no ability of his own, and had no one to help him; but he was effectually called. 'Rise, take up thy bed, and walk'. That is a command; and with the command came the power to obey.

'And a certain man was there, which had an infirmity thirty and eight years. When Jesus saw him lie, and knew that he had been now a long time in that case, he saith unto him, Wilt thou be made whole? The impotent man answered him, Sir, I have no man, when the water is troubled, to put me into the pool: but while I am coming, another steppeth down before me. Jesus saith unto him, Rise, take up thy bed, and walk. And immediately the man was made whole, and took up his bed, and walked: and on the same day was the sabbath.'

The Day Of Healing
Fifth, we are told that the day of this man's healing was the sabbath day. How often we read of our Lord performing works of mercy and healing needy souls on the sabbath day (Matthew 12:1-12; Luke 13:11, 12; 14:1-4; John 9:1-16). The sabbath day is the day Christ gives us rest from our sin, from our curse, and from our labour (Matthew 11:28-30). We observe no carnal, legal sabbath. Ours is a sabbath of faith. Trusting Christ, we have rest. Trusting him, we keep the sabbath (Hebrews 4:4-11).

Sin No More
It would be irresponsible of me to conclude the study of this portion of holy scripture without answering the question that immediately pops into our minds when we read verses 10-16.

'The Jews therefore said unto him that was cured, It is the sabbath day: it is not lawful for thee to carry thy bed. He answered them, he that made me whole, the same said unto me, Take up thy bed, and walk. Then asked they him, What man is that which said unto thee, Take up thy bed, and walk? And he that was healed wist not who it was: for Jesus had conveyed himself away, a multitude being in that place. Afterward Jesus findeth him in the temple, and said unto him, Behold, thou art made whole: sin no more, lest a worse thing come unto thee. The man departed, and told the Jews that it was Jesus, which had made him whole. And therefore did the Jews persecute Jesus, and sought to slay him, because he had done these things on the sabbath day.'

What did our Saviour mean when he said to this man he had healed, 'Behold, thou art made whole: sin no more, lest a worse thing come unto thee'? He assured him that he was one time, with finality made whole. Then he said, 'sin no more, lest a worse thing come unto thee'. Did the Master mean to imply that if he sinned again he might be made unwhole again? No. Did the Lord Jesus mean by this that saved sinners might lose their salvation, if they do not live right? Of course not! Did the Saviour here imply that it is possible for us to live in this world without sinning? You know better!

What do these words mean? 'Sin no more, lest a worse thing come unto thee'. Read the command like this: 'Cease from sin, lest a worse thing come upon you' and turn to 1 Peter 4, where we see exactly what our Lord meant.

'Forasmuch then as Christ hath suffered for us in the flesh, arm yourselves likewise with the same mind: for he that hath suffered in the flesh hath ceased from sin; That he no longer should live the rest of his time in the flesh to the lusts of men, but to the will of God. For the time past of our life may suffice us to have wrought the will of the Gentiles, when we walked in lasciviousness, lusts, excess of wine, revellings, banquetings, and abominable idolatries:

Wherein they think it strange that ye run not with them to the same excess of riot, speaking evil of you.'

If the Lord Jesus has made you whole, he has redeemed you by the sacrifice of himself. He bore your sins in his own body on the tree as your Substitute. When he did, he died to sin, and you died in him. Now, you must reckon yourself dead indeed unto sin, and alive unto God by Christ, in Christ and with Christ (Romans 6:11). Cease from sin. Trusting Christ live in freedom; free from guilt, free from fear, free from the world. And live unto him that died for you and rose again (1 Corinthians 6:19, 20). Live unto God, to the will of God and the glory of God, ever looking to Christ, living in the sweet and blessed 'joy of faith'.

'Behold, thou art made whole: sin no more, lest a worse thing come unto thee'. God's grace and God's salvation are not bestowed by our merit and cannot be destroyed by our demerit. Yet, we can bring much sorrow upon ourselves by reverting to a sense of guilt, living in the apprehension of death. Though you cannot forfeit God's grace by something you do, you may bring upon yourself something much worse than any impotence of the body. Though you cannot, when justified freely by his grace, lose God's favour, you may bring yourself under great sorrow of heart by wilful sin, causing the Lord God to hide his face from you. When the arrows of the Almighty are in you and the terrors of God set themselves in array against you (Job 6:4), that is far worse than any calamity of the body (Psalms 32:3, 4; 51:4-12; 88:9, 12, 14-18).

Has the Saviour made you whole? If he has, cease from sin and live unto God by him. 'I beseech you therefore, by the mercies of God, that ye present your bodies a living sacrifice, holy, acceptable unto God, which is your reasonable service. And be not conformed to this world: but be ye transformed by the renewing of your mind, that ye may prove what is that good, and acceptable, and perfect, will of God' (Romans 12:1, 2).

Chapter 39

'Because he is the Son of man'

'But Jesus answered them, My Father worketh hitherto, and I work. Therefore the Jews sought the more to kill him, because he not only had broken the sabbath, but said also that God was his Father, making himself equal with God. Then answered Jesus and said unto them, Verily, verily, I say unto you, The Son can do nothing of himself, but what he seeth the Father do: for what things soever he doeth, these also doeth the Son likewise. For the Father loveth the Son, and sheweth him all things that himself doeth: and he will shew him greater works than these, that ye may marvel. For as the Father raiseth up the dead, and quickeneth them; even so the Son quickeneth whom he will. For the Father judgeth no man, but hath committed all judgment unto the Son: That all men should honour the Son, even as they honour the Father. He that honoureth not the Son honoureth not the Father which hath sent him. Verily, verily, I say unto you, he that heareth my word, and believeth on him that sent me, hath everlasting life, and shall not come into condemnation; but is passed from death unto life. Verily, verily, I say unto you, the hour is coming, and now is, when the dead shall hear the voice of the Son of God: and they that hear shall live. For as the Father hath life in himself; so hath he given to the Son to have life in himself; and hath given him authority to execute judgment also, because he is the Son of man' (John 5:17-27).

After the sin and fall of our father Adam, before the fallen pair were driven from the garden, the Lord God promised a man whom he would send to be the Saviour of fallen men, a man who would come to crush the serpent's head, a man who would make restitution to God for men and restore that which he took not away (Genesis 3:15).

Abraham understood that this man would be God incarnate, God in our flesh, God in our nature. He told his son Isaac that God himself would be the sacrifice by whom sin would be put away, the sacrifice by whom fallen man would be brought back to God (Genesis 22:8).

Throughout the Old Testament era, believing sinners looked for the coming of one man, who was known as 'the Son of man' (Psalms 80:17; Daniel 7:13, 14). That man is the God-Man, the Man-God, whom we worship, Jesus Christ the Lord.

We have before us one of the deepest, most solemn and profound passages to be found in the entire volume of sacred scripture. Here the Lord Jesus asserts his own divinity in words so plain that even the unbelieving Jews understood him clearly. He declares his own eternal power and Godhead with such distinct clarity that his words cannot be misunderstood, except by those who wilfully reject the word of God as the word of God. In these verses the Son of man, the man Christ Jesus, states both his own divine nature and his complete, eternal union with God.

Yet, it is in this portion of scripture that our Lord Jesus speaks most plainly of himself as that Man who is 'the Son of man', Jehovah's righteous Servant. In fact, the very words used here by our Saviour to declare his Godhead are the words by which he reveals himself as 'the Son of man'. Truly, there is much in the verses before us that our puny brains simply cannot comprehend. Of the things here spoken by our Saviour and recorded by divine inspiration for our learning, we must confess, 'Such knowledge is too wonderful for me; it is high, I cannot attain unto it' (Psalms 139:6).

Here our Lord Jesus Christ holds before us seven glaring declarations of his eternal Godhead. Yet, the things he here asserts are all said to be true of him in his office capacity as our God-man Mediator, 'because he is the Son of man'. Here the words of the psalmist are fulfilled, 'his glory is great in thy salvation: honour and majesty hast thou laid upon him' (Psalms 21:5). Nowhere is the dignity of his character, the greatness of his being, and the glory he possesses more fully displayed than in these seven things.

His Redemptive Works

First, our blessed Saviour declares that he is one with the Father in his wondrous, redemptive works. 'But Jesus answered them, My Father worketh hitherto, and I work' (v. 17). This work of redemption, the complete salvation of God's elect, was begun and finished by the triune Jehovah, our great God, before the world began (Romans 8:28-30; Ephesians 1:3-6). It is written, 'the works were finished from the foundation of the world' (Hebrews 4:3).

282

'Because he is the Son of man'

Though fully accomplished in the decree and purpose of God from eternity, our Lord Jesus engaged himself as our Surety to perform all the great works of redemption for us and in us in time, bringing to the light in the sweet experience of grace what was done in eternity in the purpose of grace (2 Timothy 1:9, 10). In all his wondrous, redemptive works the triune God is one. The works of the Father are the works of the Son; and the works of the Son are the works of the Father (John 9:4; 14:10). The Jews standing before him understood exactly what the Lord Jesus was saying.

'Therefore the Jews sought the more to kill him, because he not only had broken the sabbath, but said also that God was his Father, making himself equal with God' (v. 18). These Jews were horrified that the Lord Jesus had healed a man on the sabbath. So, being the typical legalists they were, they tried to kill him on the sabbath day for healing on the sabbath day. Would to God I could get the ear of every child of God in this world whom religious legalists seek to bind in legal shackles, whose souls they would murder with law works if they could. I would tell them that all healing is in the Sabbath. Christ is our Sabbath. We rest in him! Pastor John Chapman wrote,

'Natural men will do anything and everything except rest in Christ and the believer has to labour to do it because of remaining sin. "There remaineth therefore a rest to the people of God. For he that is entered into his rest, he also hath ceased from his own works, as God did from his. Let us labour therefore to enter into that rest, lest any man fall after the same example of unbelief"' (Hebrews 4:9-11).

'Therefore the Jews sought the more to kill him, because he not only had broken the sabbath, but said also that God was his Father, making himself equal with God'. I repeat; these men understood exactly what the Lord Jesus said. They sought to kill him for declaring that he is God (John 10:30-33; 19:7).

In his work our Lord Jesus is one with the Father. Yet, his great, redemptive work is a work performed in obedience to his Father (John 10:15-18), 'because he is the Son of man', our Surety, Mediator, and Substitute, Jehovah's Righteous Servant.

His Will And Purpose
Second, God the Father and God the Son are one in will and purpose (v. 19). Remember, our Saviour is specifically talking to religious legalists and self-righteous zealots who were trying to murder him. 'Then answered Jesus and said unto them, Verily, verily, I say unto you, The Son can do nothing of himself, but what he seeth the Father do: for what things soever he doeth, these also doeth the Son likewise'. This does not imply a restriction or limitation placed upon his power by his incarnation. Rather, our Saviour is declaring

283

simply that he never does anything independently of his Father. Everything he does he does in pursuance of his covenant engagements as our Surety.

We must never imagine that the incarnation of God the Son placed limitations upon him. Assuming our nature enabled him to do what he never could have done otherwise. Only by becoming one of us, only by the Word being made flesh, only by the Son of God becoming the Son of man could he bring in righteousness for us by his obedience to the law, be made sin for us, bearing our sins in his own body on the tree, suffer death as our Substitute, satisfy divine justice, put away sin, put all things under the feet of man and be a merciful and faithful High Priest who is touched with the feeling of our infirmities.

He who is our Saviour is one with the Father in everything he does. The will of the Father is the will of the Son; and the will of the Son is the will of the Father. The work of the Son is the work of the Father; and the work of the Father is the work of the Son. 'Because he is the Son of man'!

In all that our Saviour here declares, he is identifying himself as the one and only Mediator between God and men, the Man Christ Jesus. He is showing us his character, authority, and power as the Man-God, the God-Man, our Mediator. These things show him to be God, but more than God: God in human flesh, God and man fully united in one person. He is fully God and fully man, 'because he is the Son of man'!

His Perfect Knowledge
Third, the same thing is true with regard to our Saviour's knowledge. In knowledge he is one with the Father. 'For the Father loveth the Son, and showeth him all things that himself doeth: and he will show him greater works than these, that ye may marvel' (v. 20). If the Son knows all things that the Father does, he is one with the Father. As there is no lack of omnipotence in him, there is no lack of omniscience in him. No mere creature is capable of knowing and understanding all the ways and works of God (Romans 11:33-36). Yet, the knowledge spoken of here is a knowledge conveyed to him as the Son of man, the man-God, our Mediator. All that the Son beheld the Father do in his eternal decree, he knows and he performs in time, 'because he is the Son of man' (Proverbs 8:22-31).

Then, the Lord Jesus asserted that the Father would reveal greater things than the healing of impotent folk, things that would cause even the unbelieving to marvel (John 6:61, 62; 2 Timothy 1:10).

It is by his perfect knowledge as Jehovah's righteous Servant, 'because he is the Son of man', that the Lord Jesus justifies his elect (Isaiah 53:12). By the knowledge of his Father's will and his fulfilment of it for the salvation of his elect (Hebrews 10:5-9), the Lord Jesus justifies all who trust him.

His Glorious Sovereignty
Fourth, the Father and the Son are one in glorious sovereignty. 'For as the Father raiseth up the dead, and quickeneth them; even so the Son quickeneth whom he will' (v. 21). Here, our Lord Jesus, the Man-God our Mediator, lays claim to divine sovereignty. When he healed a lame man, he did not heal all the impotent folk, but singled out one identified only as 'a certain man', and made him whole. The Son, like the Father, gives life to whom he will. Nothing more need be said. That ends the matter. God's absolute sovereignty is not a fine point of theology to be debated in the coffee shop, but a glorious revelation of grace to be proclaimed from the house-top, believed in the heart, and rejoiced over in the soul (Exodus 33:18, 19; Romans 9:13-16).

His Rightful Honour
Fifth, the Lord Jesus Christ is one with the Father in worship, praise, and honour, 'because he is the Son of man'.

'For the Father judgeth no man, but hath committed all judgment unto the Son: That all men should honour the Son, even as they honour the Father. He that honoureth not the Son honoureth not the Father which hath sent him' (vv. 22, 23).

The Father is the one we might most naturally expect to be the Judge. He has been sinned against, wronged, and his claims denied; but the Father has committed all judgment of Satan, of men, and of this world to the Son, 'because he hath appointed a day, in the which he will judge the world in righteousness by that man whom he hath ordained; whereof he hath given assurance unto all men, in that he hath raised him from the dead' (Acts 17:31). The reason for this is 'that all should honour the Son even as they honour the Father', 'because he is the Son of man' (Colossians 1:14-18).

His Saving Power
Sixth, the Son is one with the Father in his saving power, snatching poor sinners from the jaws of death and bringing them into the joys of life. That is a work none can perform, but God alone.

'Verily, verily, I say unto you, he that heareth my word, and believeth on him that sent me, hath everlasting life, and shall not come into condemnation; but is passed from death unto life. Verily, verily, I say unto you, the hour is coming, and now is, when the dead shall hear the voice of the Son of God: and they that hear shall live. For as the Father hath life in himself; so hath he given to the Son to have life in himself' (vv. 24-26).

All who believe on the Lord Jesus Christ were once dead in trespasses and in sins. They have been called by the voice of the Lord Jesus Christ, the Son of God. And being called by his irresistible, effectual, omnipotent, life-giving voice, we now live. Faith in Christ is the evidence of life, the result of having passed from death unto life. The life Christ gives is everlasting life. If we have everlasting life, we shall not come into condemnation. 'Because he is the Son of man', he has life in himself; and the life he has in himself is the gift of life for his elect.

His Execution Of Judgment

Seventh, the Son is one with the Father in judicial power and authority, in the execution of judgment at the last day. 'And hath given him authority to execute judgment also, because he is the Son of man' (v. 27). God the Father, the triune Jehovah, gave his Son, the Lord Jesus Christ, the power and authority to execute all judgment, 'because he is the Son of man', because he took our nature into union with himself to save his people from their sins.

He who is to be the final judge of the quick and dead, is now, and will be then, our Brother, our Head, our Surety, our Advocate, and our Husband. Oh, how precious the thought! All judgment is committed to him who was judged in our stead upon Calvary's cursed tree!

It was because the Son of God took our flesh and walked this earth as man that he was despised, rejected, and crucified. Because he became one of us, his divine glory was denied and disowned! Therefore, the despised one shall have the place of supreme honour and authority. All will be compelled to bow the knee to him and confess that he is Lord to the glory of God the Father (Acts 2:36; Philippians 2:5-11; Matthew 28:18; John 17:1, 2; Isaiah 45:20-25). All this honour and glory, all this authority and power has been and is heaped upon the Lord Jesus Christ, 'because he is the Son of man', because he is our Mediator. It is his to have life in himself, and his to communicate life to whom he will. It is his to save or to destroy. It is his to deliver us from going down into the pit, or to cast us into the pit. It is all his, for his people! How this ought to endear him to our souls!

Chapter 40

'according to their works'

'For the Father judgeth no man, but hath committed all judgment unto the Son ... And hath given him authority to execute judgment also, because he is the Son of man. Marvel not at this: for the hour is coming, in the which all that are in the graves shall hear his voice, And shall come forth; they that have done good, unto the resurrection of life; and they that have done evil, unto the resurrection of damnation' (John 5:22-29).

What do we deserve from God? If God deals with us fairly in justice, as he most surely will, what shall be our everlasting portion? The book of God declares plainly and repeatedly that all shall be judged in the last day 'according to their works'. So, what shall your everlasting portion be? What shall my portion be after the judgment? Everlasting life, or everlasting damnation?

Of this you can be sure, every one of us will receive from the holy Lord God exactly what we deserve. Because the righteous Lord loves righteousness, he always deals with all moral creatures upon the basis of strict righteousness, both in the execution of his wrath and in the exercise of his grace (Psalms 11:7). The Judge of all the earth must and shall do right (Genesis 18:25).

If God sends you to hell, he will do so upon the grounds of absolute, unquestionable righteousness. If he is pleased to bring you into the everlasting bliss and glory of heaven, he will do so upon the grounds of absolute, unquestionable righteousness. The holy Lord God will never violate, or even bend his holy law. He will not compromise his justice (2 Corinthians 5:10, 11; Revelation 20:11-15). And when he gets done with us, every creature in heaven, earth, and hell will declare, 'Even so, Lord God Almighty, true and righteous are thy judgments' (Revelation 16:7).

In Romans 14:10 and again in 2 Corinthians 5:10 this judgment seat before which we shall all soon stand is called 'the judgment seat of Christ'. In Revelation 20 God the Holy Spirit describes that awesome, glorious throne of judgment before which we all must appear in the last day as, 'a great white throne', to set forth the power, holiness, and sovereignty of the One who sits upon it. It is called 'great' because it is the throne of the omnipotent God. It is called 'white' because it is pure, spotless, righteous, and just. Nothing proceeds from this throne but justice and truth. It is called a 'throne' because the Judge who sits upon it, before whom we all must stand, is the holy, sovereign Lord God. In the last day, when all that are in the grave have been resurrected, when time shall be no more, we all must appear before this august, great, white throne to be judged of God, to be judged according to the strict and exact righteousness and justice of the thrice holy God, and judged 'according to their works'.

Yet, while the word of God constantly warns the wicked of the terror of divine judgment and the everlasting wrath of God, the day of judgment is never described as a terror to the believer, or even a thing to be dreaded by us. Rather, for the believer, the day of judgment is always set forth as a matter of anticipated joy and glory.

On this earth, God's saints are constantly misjudged. His servants are maligned and slandered by reprobate men. But in that last great day, God Almighty will vindicate his people, and he will vindicate his servants (1 Corinthians 4:3-5). I am not dreading that day. I am looking forward to it! And I do so with peace. If, as a believer, a sinner saved by God's free and sovereign grace, through the sin-atoning blood and imputed righteousness of the Lord Jesus Christ, you understand what the Bible teaches about that great day, you will look forward to it, too. Let us see what the Bible teaches about the great white throne judgment.

A Gospel Revelation
First, here is a gospel revelation. The Lord Jesus Christ is coming again. Do not concern yourself about the signs of the times and those things that men imagine are indications of the last days. There is very little, if anything, of spiritual value to be gained by studying all the books ever written on prophetic issues. They all have to be rewritten as soon as the predicted events have failed to come to pass. We are never commanded to look for signs of our Lord's coming. We are commanded to be looking for him to come. Get this one blessed fact fixed in your mind: Jesus Christ, our Lord, our Saviour, the Son of God, is coming again!

The Son of God is personally coming again to this earth.

'And when he had spoken these things, while they beheld, he was taken up; and a cloud received him out of their sight. And while they looked stedfastly toward heaven as he went up, behold, two men stood by them in white apparel; Which also said, Ye men of Galilee, why stand ye gazing up into heaven? this same Jesus, which is taken up from you into heaven, shall so come in like manner as ye have seen him go into heaven' (Acts 1:9-11).

That very same God-man who was born at Bethlehem, who lived as our Representative, and died as our sin-atoning Substitute on the cross, is coming to this earth again. He said, 'I will come again'! (John 14:3). The Apostle Paul wrote, 'The Lord himself shall descend from heaven' (1 Thessalonians 4:16). He said, 'The Lord Jesus shall be revealed from heaven' (2 Thessalonians 1:7). And so it shall be. He came once in weakness. He is coming again in power. He came once in humiliation. He is coming again in glory. He came once to be despised. He is coming again to be admired. He came once to suffer and die. He is coming again to conquer.

'I know that my redeemer liveth, and that he shall stand at the latter day upon the earth: And though after my skin worms destroy this body, yet in my flesh shall I see God: Whom I shall see for myself, and mine eyes shall behold, and not another; though my reins be consumed within me' (Job 19:25-27).

The second coming of Christ will be sudden, unannounced, unexpected, and climactic. 'The day of the Lord will come as a thief in the night' (1 Thessalonians 5:2). Our Lord said, 'I will come on thee as a thief, and thou shalt not know what hour I will come upon thee' (Revelation 3:3). The Lord does not tell us to look for the tribulation, or the regathering of Israel, or the rebuilding of a Jewish temple. He tells us to look for him. If you look for signs, and times, and seasons, you will be shocked when Christ comes. The only thing mentioned in the word of God that will announce the Lord's coming will be 'a shout, the voice of the archangel and the trump of God' (1 Thessalonians 4:16).

No man knows the day or hour of our Lord's coming; and that is best (Matthew 24:36; Mark 13:32; Acts 1:7). If we knew the day or hour, we would become irresponsible and negligent with regard to our daily duties. Do not seek to know when Christ is coming. Be content with his promise, and wait for his appearing.

Our Lord Jesus may appear at any moment. 'Behold, he cometh'! (Revelation 1:7). Look for him upon the tiptoe of faith and expectation. All will be taken by surprise, except those who are expecting him to appear. Like those Thessalonians who believed God, we must constantly 'wait for his Son from heaven' (1 Thessalonians 1:10). Faith is ever 'looking for that blessed hope and the glorious appearing of the great God and our Saviour Jesus Christ' (Titus 2:13). Christ is coming now. John said, 'Behold, he cometh'! That means he is on his way right now. Ever since he went up to heaven yesterday (a thousand years with him is but a day!) he has been on his way back to fetch his bride up to heaven. Every event of providence is but the footstep of our Saviour coming for us! Soon he shall appear. When the Son of God appears, he will bring with him a crown of righteousness, immortality, and life for all who love him and look for his appearing. 'Henceforth there is laid up for me a crown of righteousness, which the Lord, the righteous judge, shall give me at that day: and not to me only, but unto all them also that love his appearing' (2 Timothy 4:8). 'Blessed is the man that endureth temptation: for when he is tried, he shall receive the crown of life, which the Lord hath promised to them that love him (James 1:12).

A General Resurrection
Second, when Christ comes, there will be a great, general resurrection of all who have ever lived upon the earth. 'And the sea gave up the dead which were in it; and death and hell delivered up the dead which were in them: and they were judged every man according to their works' (Revelation 20:13).

'Marvel not at this: for the hour is coming, in the which all that are in the graves shall hear his voice, And shall come forth; they that have done good, unto the resurrection of life; and they that have done evil, unto the resurrection of damnation' (John 5:28, 29).

I do not offer any argument or proof for these things. I am simply declaring to you the plain facts, as they are revealed in holy scripture. Those who rebel against them, mock them, despise them, or ignore them do so to their own eternal ruin. But I assure you that the Son of God is coming again; and when he comes there will be a resurrection of the dead.

First, all who have died in faith shall be raised from the grave. All will be raised. But the saints of God will have distinct priority in the resurrection. 'The dead in Christ shall rise first'. The bodies of God's saints shall be raised from their graves and reunited with their souls: all the Old Testament saints, all the martyrs, all our brothers and sisters who 'sleep in Jesus' (1 Thessalonians 4:13-18). Then, immediately after the sleeping saints arise, all believers living upon the earth shall be changed and caught up to meet the Lord in the air (1 Corinthians 15:51-58). As our Lord descends in the brilliant glory of his second advent, we shall go out to meet him and return with him, as he comes with all his saints to burn up the earth, destroy the wicked, and make all things new. What a day that will be!

Then, after the Son of God has gathered all the ransomed bodies of his elect from the earth, after he has destroyed all the wicked with the brightness of his coming, all the wicked shall be raised. Yes, there is a resurrection for the wicked, too. But, for those who believe not, there is no music in the resurrection. The Lord himself shall issue a summons they will not be able to resist.

You, unbeliever, will stand in terror before him whose grace you have despised, against whom you have sinned. Your body and soul now united in sin shall be united in horror. I have no word of comfort for you who will not bow to the claims of Christ. If you die without Christ, you die without hope and without peace. Your resurrection shall be a resurrection of damnation!

A Great Reckoning
Thirdly, immediately after the resurrection, we must all be judged by God according to the record of our works (2 Corinthians 5:10, 11; Hebrews 9:27; Revelation 20:12, 13). The Judge before whom we must stand is the God-man, whom we have crucified. 'For the Father judgeth no man, but hath committed all judgment unto the Son'. 'Because he hath appointed a day, in the which he will judge the world in righteousness by that man whom he hath ordained; whereof he hath given assurance unto all men, in that he hath raised him from the dead' (Acts 17:31). 'We must all appear before the judgment seat of Christ; that every one may receive the things done in his body, according to that he hath done, whether it be good or bad' (2 Corinthians 5:10).

We will be judged out of the books, according to the record of God's strict justice. When the books are opened, what shocks of terror will seize the hearts and souls of those who have no righteousness and no atonement before the holy Lord God! With the opening of the books, every crime, every offence, every sin you have ever committed in mind, in heart, and in deed shall be exposed! This is what Daniel saw in his prophetic vision. 'Judgment was set; and the books were opened' (Daniel 7:10).

I realise that this is figurative language. God does not need books to remember man's sins. However, as John Gill wrote, 'This judgment out of the books, and according to works, is designed to show with what accuracy and exactness, with what justice and equity, it will be executed, in allusion to statute-books in courts of judicature.'

In the scriptures God is often represented as writing and keeping books. And according to these books, we all shall be judged. What are the books? They are, the book of divine omniscience (Malachi 3:5), the book of divine remembrance (Malachi 3:16), the book of creation (Romans 1:18-20), the book of God's providence (Romans 2:4, 5), the book of God's holy law (Romans 2:12). This book of the law has two tables. The first table contains all the sins of men against God (Exodus 20:3-11). The second table contains all the sins of men against one another (Exodus 20:12-17). Then there is the book of the gospel (Romans 2:16) and the book of conscience (Romans 2:15).

But, blessed be God, there are some against whom no crimes, no sins, no offences can be found, not even by the omniscient eye of God himself! 'In those days, and in that time, saith the LORD, the iniquity of Israel shall be sought for, and there shall be none; and the sins of Judah, and they shall not be found: for I will pardon them whom I reserve' (Jeremiah 50:20).

Their names are found in another book, a book which God himself wrote and sealed before the worlds were made. It is the Lamb's book of life (Revelation 13:8; 17:8). In this book there is a record of divine election. In this book there is the name of a divine Surety. In this book there is a record of perfect righteousness (Jeremiah 23:6; cf. 33:16). In this book there is a record of complete satisfaction and blood atonement. And in this book there is the promise of eternal life.

The question is often raised, 'Will God judge his elect for their sins and failures committed after they were saved, and expose them in the day of judgment?' The only reason that question is ever raised is because many try to retain the threat and fear of the Roman doctrine of purgatory, by which they hope to hold over God's saints the whip and terror of the law.

There is absolutely no sense in which you who trust the Lord Jesus Christ shall ever be made to pay for your sins. Our sins were imputed to Christ and shall never be imputed to us again (Romans 4:8). Christ paid our debt to God's law and justice; and God will never require us to pay. God who has blotted out our transgressions will never write them again. He who covered our sins will never uncover them. The perfect righteousness of Christ has been imputed to us. On the day of judgment, God's elect are never represented as having done any evil, but only good (Matthew 25:31-40). The day of judgment will be a day of glory and bliss for Christ and his people, not a day of mourning and sorrow. It will be a marriage supper. Christ will glory in his Church. God will display the glory of his grace in us. We will glory in our great and glorious, triune God, Father, Son, and Holy Ghost.

A Just Reward
Fourth, those who are found perfectly righteous, righteous according to the records of God himself, shall enter into eternal life and inherit everlasting glory with Christ. They that have done good, nothing but good, perfect good, without any spot of sin, wrinkle of iniquity, or trace of transgression, shall enter into everlasting life. It is written 'He that is unjust, let him be unjust still: and he which is filthy, let him be filthy still: and he that is righteous, let him be righteous still: and he that is holy, let him be holy still' (Revelation 22:11).

Who are these perfectly righteous ones? None are so by nature and none by works of their own. But all God's elect, every redeemed sinner, all who are born of God, all who believe on the Lord Jesus Christ are made righteous by

God's free, justifying, sanctifying grace. The righteousness of God in Christ is ours, imputed to us in justification and imparted to us in sanctification; and sin can never be imputed to us (2 Corinthians 5:21; Colossians 1:27; Romans 4:8; 8:1, 32-34).

Though there shall be degrees of punishment for the wicked in hell, because there are degrees of wickedness, there shall be no degrees of reward and glory among the saints in heaven, because there are no degrees of redemption and righteousness. Heaven was earned and purchased for all God's elect by Christ. We were predestined to and obtained our inheritance from eternity (Ephesians 1:11). Christ has taken possession of heaven's glory as our forerunner (Hebrews 6:20). We are heirs of God and joint-heirs with Jesus Christ (Romans 8:17). Our Saviour gave all the glory he earned as our Mediator to all his elect (John 17:5, 20). In Christ every believer is worthy of heaven's glory (Colossians 1:12). Glorification is but the consummation of salvation; and salvation is by grace alone.

That means that no part of heaven's bliss and glory is the reward of our works, but all the reward of God's free grace in Christ! All spiritual blessings are ours from eternity in Christ (Ephesians 1:3). And that with which God blessed us in Christ before the world began he will not take from us when this world is no more (Romans 11:29). God will do all that is necessary to bring us to Heaven, and when we get there he will say to us, 'Well done good and faithful servant'!

A Just Retribution
Fifth, I must warn you, if you are yet without Christ, if you will not trust Christ, you must be forever damned. All who are found guilty of sin in that great and terrible day of judgment shall be cast into the lake of fire and there be made to suffer the unmitigated wrath of Almighty God forever!

One by one the Lord God will call the wicked before his throne and judge them. As he says to you, 'Depart ye cursed'! He will say to his holy angels, 'Take him! Bind him! Cast him into outer darkness'! There will be no mercy for you. There will be no pity for you. There will be no sorrow for you. There will be no hope for you. There will be no end for you!

To hell you deserve to go. To hell you must go. To hell you will go. Unless you flee to Christ and take refuge in him, in that great day the wrath of God shall seize you and destroy you forever! I beseech you now, by the mercies of God, be reconciled to God by trusting his darling Son. 'Knowing therefore the terror of the Lord, we persuade men'. Come to Christ now. Eternity is before you! Behold his infinite love (2 Corinthians 5:14, 15). Behold his finished atonement (2 Corinthians 5:21). Behold his amazing, almighty, saving grace (2 Corinthians 5:17-21).

293

In that great and terrible day I hope to be found in Christ, not having my own righteousness, but having his righteousness. How will it be for you in that day?

Chapter 41

'the first resurrection'

'Verily, verily, I say unto you, The hour is coming, and now is, when the dead shall hear the voice of the Son of God: and they that hear shall live' (John 5:25).

God the Holy Spirit declares in Revelation 20:6, 'Blessed and holy is he that hath part in the first resurrection: on such the second death hath no power'. This work of God the Holy Spirit is described in the latter part of Ephesians 1 and in the first ten verses of Ephesians 2. The first resurrection is the new birth. Salvation is nothing less than the resurrection of our souls, a resurrection from spiritual death to spiritual life in Christ. It is a resurrection to life accomplished in us by the omnipotent mercy, effectual grace, and irresistible power of God our Saviour. This first resurrection, the new birth, is what our Lord Jesus speaks of in John 5:25. 'Verily, verily, I say unto you, The hour is coming, and now is, when the dead shall hear the voice of the Son of God: and they that hear shall live'.

The Condition Of The Sinner
First, our Saviour here speaks about the condition of every sinner. Every child of Adam is born 'dead', spiritually dead, 'dead in trespasses and in sins'.

'And you hath he quickened, who were dead in trespasses and sins: Wherein in time past ye walked according to the course of this world, according to the prince of the power of the air, the spirit that now worketh in the children of disobedience: Among whom also we all had our conversation in times past in the lusts of our flesh, fulfilling the desires of the flesh and of the mind; and were by nature the children of wrath, even as others. But God, who is rich in mercy, for his great love wherewith he loved us, Even when we were dead in sins, hath quickened us together with Christ, (by grace ye are saved)' (Ephesians 2:1-5).

'Buried with him in baptism, wherein also ye are risen with him through the faith of the operation of God, who hath raised him from the dead. And you, being dead in your sins and the uncircumcision of your flesh, hath he quickened together with him, having forgiven you all trespasses' (Colossians 2:12, 13).

Fallen man is not sick, wounded, or unconscious. He is dead. He is spiritually dead, incapable of motion, feeling, work, or even response. He is dead. He does not need revival. He needs life. He does not need reforming. He needs life. He does not need help. He needs life. He does not need religion. He needs life.

What is this spiritual death? Death is separation. Physical death is the separation of the soul from the body. You know what it is for the body to be dead physically. That body lying on that hard, cold slab in the morgue waiting to be embalmed is dead. The soul has departed and has left the body insensible and incapable of preserving itself. The soul was like salt to the body. As soon as the soul is gone, the body begins to decay and return to the dust. Very soon it putrefies and becomes utterly obnoxious. Who wants to look upon a dead body, after it has been in the grave for even a short time?

Spiritual death is the separation of the soul from God. In Genesis 2:17 the Lord God told Adam that in the day he ate of the forbidden fruit he would 'surely die'. But, when Adam ate of the fruit, he did not die physically. His physical death did not occur until hundreds of years later. The Lord must have had something else in mind, when he said, 'In the day thou eatest thereof thou shalt surely die'. He did indeed. He was referring to spiritual death, for 'in Adam all die' (Romans 5:12).

This spiritual death, this separation from God is exactly what we see in Genesis 3:8. When Adam and Eve heard the voice of the Lord, they 'hid themselves from the presence of the LORD God'. The fellowship had been broken. They were spiritually dead. God and man were separated by sin. A wall of death stood between the fallen pair and God their Maker.

When hanging on the cross as our Substitute, bearing our sins in his own body on the tree, the Lord Jesus was forsaken of God, separated from God in death, when he was made sin for us. Though he is himself our God, when he was made sin, he suffered the consequence of our guilt that he made his own, and cried in agony no man can comprehend, 'My God, my God, Why hast thou forsaken me?' (Mark 15:33, 34).

Man without Christ is spiritually dead. Paul describes it as 'being alienated from the life of God' in Ephesians 4:18. Fallen man, like Adam in the garden hiding from God, is isolated from God. He hides from God, hides from his presence, and hides from his voice (Genesis 3:8-10).

The dead have none of the senses of the living. The dead cannot hear, or see, or feel, or taste, or smell. Those who are dead cannot hear the gospel, see the kingdom of God, feel the Saviour's love, taste the sweet morsels of his grace, or smell the sweet fragrance of his sacrifice. The dead cannot enter the kingdom of God. Fallen man is dead. Pity him. He is dead. Dead to all things spiritual, dead to all things divine, dead to all things eternal, dead to holiness, dead to truth, dead to all his soul's needs!

In the new birth, in the first resurrection, this spiritual death is reversed. The dead hear the voice of the Son of God, and they that hear his voice live, live by the power of that voice!

We were spiritually dead, incapable of saving ourselves, incapable of even perceiving, let alone receiving eternal life, incapable of even knowing our need of life, until the Lord Jesus came and gave us life by his almighty grace (Titus 3:5-7; Ezekiel 16:6-8; 37:1-14).

The book of Revelation speaks of the 'second death' (Revelation 2:11; 21:8) the final, everlasting, conscious separation of lost sinners from God. Only those who have never experienced new life in Christ will partake of the second death. It is written, 'Blessed and holy is he that hath part in the first resurrection: on such the second death hath no power, but they shall be priests of God and of Christ, and shall reign with him a thousand years' (Revelation 20:6).

The Command Of The Saviour
But, blessed be God, there is hope for the dead. Hear our Saviour's words. 'Verily, verily, I say unto you, The hour is coming, and now is, when the dead shall hear the voice of the Son of God: and they that hear shall live.'

There is hope, not in the dead, but for the dead. Hope is found in the command (not invitation, not offer, but command) of the Saviour. Our Lord Jesus declares, 'The dead shall hear the voice of the Son of God'. He initiates the call, not the preacher, or the parent, or the personal worker. The God who said, 'Let there be light', also says, 'Let there be life', and there is life. When he speaks, it is done.

What power there is in the voice of the Son of God! In the picture of our risen and glorified Lord, drawn by the pen of inspiration in the first chapter of the Revelation, after speaking of his incomparable figure, glowing and shining above the brightness of the sun, John says, 'Out of his mouth proceeded a sharp two-edged sword'. In Hebrews 4, we read,

'For the word of God is quick, and powerful, and sharper than any twoedged sword, piercing even to the dividing asunder of soul and spirit, and of the joints and marrow, and is a discerner of the thoughts and intents of the heart. Neither is there any creature that is not manifest in his sight: but all things are naked and opened unto the eyes of him with whom we have to do'.

Christ's voice, the voice of him who is the Word of God, is an omnipotent, life-giving voice. It was his voice that said to the paralyzed man, 'Arise, and take up thy bed, and go thy way'! When the centurion of Capernaum sought him out and said to him, 'My servant is sick. Just speak the word and he'll be healed'. The Lord said, 'No, I will go with you and lay my hands upon the servant'. The centurion said, 'That's not necessary, not at all. You just speak, you just say the word, and my servant will be healed' And the all-powerful, omnipotent voice of Christ healed the centurion's servant. 'Ephphatha', he said in Decapolis, and the deaf and the dumb could hear and speak. 'Talitha cumi', he said to the daughter of Jairus, and the young maiden awakened from the dead. He stopped the funeral procession in Nain, as the poor widow was going out to bury her son, and, speaking to the young man on the bier, he brought the dead to life. He simply spoke the words, 'Lazarus, come forth', and, Lazarus, bound in his grave clothes, stepped out of the sepulchre full of life. The omnipotent, all-powerful voice of the Son of God will be heard and the very dead shall come to life.

'The hour is coming, and now is when the dead shall hear the voice of the Son of God'. Our Lord Jesus Christ is in scripture, especially in the Gospel of John, called 'the Word'. Here his voice is spoken of, but what is a voice apart from the person that utters it? What is the word he speaks by which dead men are brought to life? Is not Jesus Christ himself the Word of God to man? The distinct, articulate manifestation of deity is Jesus Christ. 'No man hath seen God at any time; the only begotten Son, which is in the bosom of the Father, he hath declared him' (John 1:18).

Behold the Christ of God and hear his voice in the incarnation (John 1:14), in his life of obedience (Jeremiah 23:6), in his sin-atoning sacrifice (Romans 8:1), in his triumphant resurrection (Colossians 2:15), in his glorious ascension (Psalms 68:19, 20), and in his heavenly intercession (Romans 8:32-39).

'The hour is coming, and now is, when the dead shall hear.' I have told you what they will hear; they will hear the word; but who will speak it? Who is it that alone can speak it with life-giving power? 'When the dead shall hear the voice of the Son of God, they that hear shall live.' Whenever any dead soul is made to live, it is through the word preached, but it is not through the voice of the preacher. Preachers are instruments, nothing more. The voice that makes dead souls live is the voice of Christ Jesus. And the voice of the Son of God, by which the word of God comes in life-giving, omnipotent, irresistible power, is God the Holy Spirit. 'It is the spirit that quickeneth; the flesh profiteth nothing: the words that I speak unto you, they are spirit, and they are life' (John 6:63).

The gospel preached must be brought home to the hearts and consciences of chosen, redeemed sinners, effectually applied by God the Holy Ghost. It is through the Holy Spirit that the voice of Christ is heard in the soul (Hebrews 9:12-14).

What, then, can we do with sinners, if we cannot make them hear? We can pull our Master's sleeves, and say to him, 'Blessed Lord Jesus, speak the word, speak the word'! When I come into the pulpit the prayer that rises to my heart is always this, 'Lord Jesus, speak your word to the hearts of chosen, redeemed sinners through this worthless, empty, dirty, broken pipe'! It is by this means that lost, ruined, helpless, dead sinners are made to live (1 Peter 1:18-25).

> Oh! let the dead now hear thy voice,
> Bid, Lord, thy banished ones rejoice;
> Their beauty this, their glorious dress,
> Jesus, the Lord, our righteousness.

> Nicholaus Ludwig von Zinzendorf

The Certainty Of Success
Third, our Lord Jesus here assures us of the certainty of his success in causing the dead to hear his voice. 'Verily, verily, I say unto you, The hour is coming, and now is, when the dead shall hear the voice of the Son of God: and they that hear shall live.'

'They that hear shall live'! What a good word that word 'shall' is! It is a declaration of absolute certainty. When the Lord speaks to the dead sinner, the dead comes to life by the force of irresistible omnipotence. He does not woo or entice the dead. He draws him to himself by sovereign power; and the dead are made to live. The fruit of this life that the Son of God gives is conviction (John 16:8-11). The fruit of this life that the Son of God gives is faith (John 3:36). The fruit of this life that the Son of God gives is repentance (1 Thessalonians 1:4-10). This is the first resurrection. 'Blessed and holy is he that hath part in the first resurrection: on such the second death hath no power, but they shall be priests of God and of Christ, and shall reign with him a thousand years.'

Chapter 42

Five Reasons For Trusting Christ

'I can of mine own self do nothing: as I hear, I judge: and my judgment is just; because I seek not mine own will, but the will of the Father which hath sent me. If I bear witness of myself, my witness is not true. There is another that beareth witness of me; and I know that the witness which he witnesseth of me is true. Ye sent unto John, and he bare witness unto the truth. But I receive not testimony from man: but these things I say, that ye might be saved. He was a burning and a shining light: and ye were willing for a season to rejoice in his light. But I have greater witness than that of John: for the works which the Father hath given me to finish, the same works that I do, bear witness of me, that the Father hath sent me. And the Father himself, which hath sent me, hath borne witness of me. Ye have neither heard his voice at any time, nor seen his shape. And ye have not his word abiding in you: for whom he hath sent, him ye believe not. Search the scriptures; for in them ye think ye have eternal life: and they are they which testify of me. And ye will not come to me, that ye might have life. I receive not honour from men. But I know you, that ye have not the love of God in you. I am come in my Father's name, and ye receive me not: if another shall come in his own name, him ye will receive. How can ye believe, which receive honour one of another, and seek not the honour that cometh from God only? Do not think that I will accuse you to the Father: there is one that accuseth you, even Moses, in whom ye trust. For had ye believed Moses, ye would have believed me: for he wrote of me. But if ye believe not his writings, how shall ye believe my words?' (John 5:30-47).

God the Holy Spirit declares, 'Whosoever believeth that Jesus is the Christ is born of God' (1 John 5:1). My prayer and heart's desire to God for you who read these words is that you might believe that Jesus is the Christ, that you might trust the Lord Jesus Christ. Our faith says, 'We believe and are sure that thou art the Christ, the Son of the living God' (John 6:69). We believe that Jesus of Nazareth is the Christ, the Messiah, promised by God in all the Old Testament prophets. Peter's confession, 'Thou art the Christ, the Son of the living God' (Matthew 16:16), is the foundation of Christianity, the foundation upon which the church of God is built, and the foundation of the gospel. This is the foundation upon which we are built and the foundation upon which we build.

If I call upon you and urge you to trust Christ, to trust your immortal soul to him, to trust his blood, his righteousness, his grace, his intercession, to trust Christ alone for your everlasting salvation, if I persuade you to believe on the Lord Jesus Christ, it is only reasonable that you should say to me, 'Pastor, you are going to have to give me some reasons why I should trust him. You are going to have to convince me that I can and should trust Christ.' I hope you have that attitude. And I pray that God the Holy Spirit will enable you to receive what he has written in his word and give you faith in the Lord Jesus. Here in John 5:30-47 the Lord Jesus himself is speaking. He is speaking to the Jews and their religious leaders, the Pharisees. As he does, he sets before us five reasons for trusting him. The Jews refused still to believe him. The Pharisees refused still to believe him. Will you believe on the Son of God?

The Saviour had just performed a miracle at the pool of Bethesda, healing the impotent man, by which he showed himself to be the Messiah, the Christ of God (vv. 1-9). He declared himself God, one with the Father, a man equal with God (vv. 17, 18). Rather than believing him, these Jews sought to kill him, accusing him of blasphemy; but the Lord Jesus pressed his claims upon them more fully, declaring that everything he had done was the work of God and that the Father had given him all authority and power as the Messiah, the Son of man, the incarnate God (vv. 19-29).

He declared plainly that he and he alone had it in his power, as the Christ of God, to give eternal life to whom he will, and that in the last day he would both raise the dead and execute judgment upon the righteous and the wicked as the Christ.

Having made such assertions, our Master now gives five witnesses to himself. By these five witnesses, he shows irrefutably that he is the Christ promised in the Old Testament scriptures. As Paul reasoned with the people of Thessalonica out of the scriptures, 'Opening and alleging, that Christ must needs have suffered, and risen again from the dead; and that this Jesus, whom I preach unto you, is Christ' (Acts 17:2, 3), in this study of John 5, I want to reason with you out of the scriptures, and give you five reasons for trusting Christ. I will give you these five reasons in the witnesses to which the Lord Jesus himself pointed in this passage.

In verse 30 the Saviour openly declares that he is God the Son, one with, and equal with God the Father, in all things working the works of God. 'I can of mine own self do nothing: as I hear, I judge: and my judgment is just; because I seek not mine own will, but the will of the Father which hath sent me.' The Son cannot act independently of the Father, or the Father of the Son. He who is the Christ, the Son of God, is in all things (in will, in work, in word, and in his Person) in complete union with the Father.

Then, in the next verse he asserts 'If I bear witness of myself, my witness is not true'. But in John 8:14 we read just the opposite of this. There the Lord Jesus says, 'Though I bear record of myself, my record is true'. But there is no contradiction. Here in John 5:31, he is speaking in reference to the law of God which required two or three witnesses for anything to be established. According to the law, no man can be a witness in his own cause. The words of men do need confirmation, but not so the Son of God. However, Christ came to 'fulfil all righteousness' and to do all that he did 'according to the scriptures' (Deuteronomy 19:15; Matthew 18:15). The law required two or three witnesses for anything to be established. So our Lord Jesus, to establish his claims as the Christ of God, the Messiah, gives five undeniable witnesses to his deity and his mission as the Messiah.

John The Baptist
The first witness our Saviour calls to himself is John the Baptist (vv. 32-35). John the Baptist was that one of whom Malachi spoke, calling him Elijah, the forerunner and herald of the Christ (Malachi 4:5, 6; Matthew 11:14, 15). The Lord Jesus reminded these Jews that John the Baptist bore faithful witness to both his person and his work, when they sent messengers to ask him who he was (John 1:20-29).

'There is another that beareth witness of me; and I know that the witness which he witnesseth of me is true. Ye sent unto John, and he bare witness unto the truth. But I receive not testimony from man: but these things I say, that ye might be saved. He was a burning and a shining light: and ye were willing for a season to rejoice in his light' (vv. 32-35).

'But I receive not testimony from man' (v. 34). He was not appealing to the witness of John for a confirmation of his own words and works, but he appealed to John's testimony to them. John was sent of God to arouse men's attention and to produce in them a sense of their deep need for the One who was to come. John was indeed a famous light, burning with knowledge of and love for the truth. For a while they pretended great affection for him; but when they saw that John's one purpose was to bear witness of Christ the Lamb, they turned away from him; for they looked for a more splendid and glorious Messiah than the one Christ appeared to be. They despised John, the messenger, because they hated and despised Christ, the Message.

I call upon you to trust Christ, because he is that One to whom John the Baptist gave witness. John went before his face to prepare his ways (Matthew 11:14, 15; Luke 1:76-79).

His Own Works
In verse 36 the Lord Jesus calls for his own works to bear witness of him. 'But I have greater witness than that of John: for the works which the Father hath given me to finish, the same works that I do, bear witness of me, that the Father hath sent me.' Is it not a wonderful thing to realise that the Lord Jesus looked upon the works his Father gave him to perform for us as his Father's gift to him? (John 17:4). He calls the redemption of our souls the 'joy set before him' (Hebrews 12:2).

Our Saviour's mighty works, which he performed while walking through this earth, bore unmistakable witness to who he is and what he came to do. He frequently appealed to his works as affording divine testimony to himself (John 10:25, 38; 14:11; 15:24). He caused the blind to see, the lame to walk, the deaf to hear, the dumb to speak, the lepers to be cleansed, and the dead to be raised to life (Luke 7:19-22)

J. C. Ryle calls attention to five things about our Lord's miracles: (1) Their number. They were very many. (2) Their greatness. They were mighty, supernatural works. (3) Their public nature. They were not done secretly, but publicly for all to behold. (4) Their nature. They were always works of love, mercy, and compassion. They were not just exhibitions of power, but were works beneficial to men. (5) Their direct appeal to man's senses. They were real, visible, and would bear any examination.

Obviously, our Lord Jesus spoke these words for the benefit of future generations, for he speaks of the works the Father gave him to finish as works that bore witness to him as the Sent One of God (Matthew 1:21). May God give you grace to behold the works he has finished, and trust him. He finished the law. He finished the prophecies. He finished the sacrifices. He finished righteousness. He finished sin. He finished death (Hebrews 10:11, 12).

I call upon you to trust the Lord Jesus Christ because he has finished the work the Father gave him to accomplish as the covenant Surety and Saviour of his people. He has saved his people from their sins by the sacrifice of himself.

God The Father

Third, our Saviour declares that his Father is his witness. 'And the Father himself, which hath sent me, hath borne witness of me' (v. 37). At his baptism, upon the Mount of Transfiguration, and in the totality of the book of inspiration, the Father bears witness of the Lord Jesus, as his Son, as our Mediator, and as the Christ (Matthew 3:17; 17:5; 1 John 5:7-10).

Though the Father bears witness of him, the Lord Jesus said to these Jews, and to all who refuse to trust him, 'Ye have neither heard his voice at any time, nor seen his shape. And ye have not his word abiding in you: for whom he hath sent, him ye believe not' (vv. 37, 38). You have not heard his voice. You have not seen him who is the image of the invisible God, the Revelation of God. You do not have his word in you. You may have it memorized; but it is not in you.

None are so blind as those who will not see. None are so deaf as those who will not hear. Will you hear the voice of God who spoke from heaven? I call on you to trust the Son of God, because God the Father has borne witness of him with his own voice. Every voice heard from heaven throughout the Old Testament dispensation, from the Garden of Eden to the Incarnation, was the voice of God identifying him.

The Scriptures

The fourth witness to our Saviour is the volume of Old Testament scripture. All the Old Testament speaks of Christ. 'Search the scriptures; for in them ye think ye have eternal life: and they are they which testify of me' (v. 39). Look at this verse line by line.

'Search the scriptures'. This refers to the Old Testament. The New Testament was not yet written. Yet, what is here said of the Old Testament may (and should) be applied to the New. All the Old Testament scriptures were given by divine inspiration. They were frequently referred to and appealed to by our Saviour and his apostles as the only standard and basis for all true doctrine and the solitary authority for all things in the worship of God. Therefore, we are here commanded to 'search the scriptures', to diligently examine the book of God, if we would know the mind and will of God. Test all doctrine by the scriptures. Test every ordinance of religion by the scriptures.

Like the churches and the religious world around us, the Jews had the scriptures, the sacred oracles of God, in their possession. They read them and expounded them every sabbath day in their synagogues. They brought their children up, teaching them the scriptures. But they had no knowledge of the message of holy scripture.

Look at the next line. 'For in them ye think ye have eternal life'. The Jews of our Lord's day, like religionists today, presumed that by learning the letter of the scriptures and practicing the ordinances of divine worship they obtained and would inherit eternal life. They adored the scriptures, but despised the Saviour of whom the scriptures spoke. They reverenced the written word, but despised the living Word revealed by it. They made idols of ordinances, and refused to worship him portrayed in the ordinances.

Sadly, in our day, multitudes, who profess to be worshippers of God, read every dime-store novel and piece of fiction they can find, while the book of God lays gathering dust from Sunday to Sunday beside the coat they wear to church. In the 1600s the French reformer, Pierre Du Moulin, wrote of his countrymen, 'While they burned us for reading the scriptures, we burned with zeal to be reading from them. Now with our liberty is bred also negligence and disesteem of God's word.' Is that not the case with us?

'And they are they which testify of me'! 'The babe of Bethlehem', John Trapp said, 'is bound up in these swathing bands.' All the book of God speaks of Christ; but our Lord Jesus here specifically declares that the Old Testament scriptures testify of him. In the Old Testament scriptures we read that this man, Christ Jesus is Jehovah, the Son of God, God, and the Mighty God. Is the Prophet, Priest and King of his people. Would be born of a virgin, born in Bethlehem, and born of the tribe of Judah. Would perform miracles of mercy upon the bodies of men. Would be betrayed by a friend and sold for thirty pieces of silver. Would be scourged, beaten, spit upon, and mocked. Would be despised and rejected of men and nailed upon the cursed tree between two thieves as our Substitute (Psalms 22; Isaiah 53), and that men would cast lots for his vesture. He would be buried, rise from the dead the third day, and ascend up into heaven. He would make intercession for transgressors as our Advocate and High Priest, will come again, make all things new, and sit in judgment over all nations.

I call upon you to trust the Lord Jesus, because he is the One to whom all the scriptures bear witness.

Moses And The Law
Then, in verses 45-47 our Lord Jesus points to Moses and the law as a fifth witness to him.

'And ye will not come to me, that ye might have life. I receive not honour from men. But I know you, that ye have not the love of God in you. I am come in my Father's name, and ye receive me not: if another shall come in his own name, him ye will receive. How can ye believe, which receive honour one of another, and seek not the honour that cometh from God only? Do not think that I will accuse you to the Father: there is one that accuseth you, even Moses, in whom ye trust. For had ye believed Moses, ye would have believed me: for he wrote of me. But if ye believe not his writings, how shall ye believe my words?'

The Jews claimed to believe Moses and claimed to love the law of God given by his hand. But everything Moses wrote, every prophecy, every precept, every promise, every pattern, every picture of the law, pointed to Christ (John 1:45; Hebrews 8:1; 10:1-4).

I call upon you to come to Christ, to trust the Son of God, because it is most reasonable for you to do so. These five witnesses should convince any reasonable person to trust Christ.

But it was not a lack of evidence that kept these Jews from believing on the Lord Jesus; and it is not a lack of evidence that keeps sinners from trusting him today. That which keeps sinners from Christ is the depravity of their hearts and the perversity of their wills. That which keeps the sinner from faith in Christ is his obstinate, depraved heart, that heart that is unwilling to acknowledge his need of Christ and incapable of trusting him, because of the enmity that is in him against God.

So I finish this study with the prayer that God, the God of all grace, will be pleased to do for you what you cannot and will not do for yourself. May he pour out his Spirit upon you, give you life in Christ, and cause you to trust him!

Chapter 43

Why Don't People Come To Christ?

'Search the scriptures; for in them ye think ye have eternal life: and they are they which testify of me. And ye will not come to me, that ye might have life' (John 5:39, 40).

Faith in Christ is set before us in many different ways in scripture. Faith is looking to Christ. 'Look unto me, and be ye saved, all the ends of the earth: for I am God, and there is none else' (Isaiah 45:22). 'Behold, as the eyes of servants look unto the hand of their masters, and as the eyes of a maiden unto the hand of her mistress; so our eyes wait upon the LORD our God, until that he have mercy upon us' (Psalms 123:2). Faith is trusting Christ, as a son trusts his father. 'O LORD of hosts, blessed is the man that trusteth in thee' (Psalms 84:12). Faith is seeking Christ, as a man seeks something he has lost. Faith is laying hold of Christ, as a drowning man lays hold of a life-line. Saving faith is described in scripture as coming to Christ. The Lord Jesus is able to save to the uttermost all them that come to God by him. Believers are described by Peter as a people coming to the Saviour. 'To whom coming, as unto a living stone, disallowed indeed of men, but chosen of God, and precious' (1 Peter 2:4).

How often poor, needy sinners came to Christ, or were brought to him in desperate need, while he walked on the earth. And as often as a needy soul came to our omnipotent, ever-gracious, all-merciful Saviour, he obtained the healing power and saving mercy he needed (Matthew 8:1-3; 9:1-8, 20-22, 18-26, 27-31). Salvation is obtained by coming to Christ. The Lord Jesus is able to save all who come to God by him. The Lord Jesus has promised that he will save all who come to him. (Matthew 11:28; John 6:37; John 7:37, 38). And in the Gospel narratives every poor sinner who came to Christ obtained the salvation he sought.

In John 5:39, 40 our Lord Jesus is talking to religious people, people who went to church every week, people who read and studied the Bible. He says, 'Search the scriptures; for in them ye think ye have eternal life: and they are they which testify of me. And ye will not come to me, that ye might have life.' These were Bible-thumping, conservative, religious, church going people, people who read, memorized, and studied the word of God. Yet, our Saviour said to these religious people, 'Search the scriptures; for in them ye think ye have eternal life: and they are they which testify of me. And ye will not come to me, that ye might have life.'

Throughout the word of God, there is a clear-cut message of redemption, through the blood of Calvary's cross. There is absolutely no salvation from sin, except through the substitutionary death of the Lord Jesus Christ, our Saviour. Like these Pharisees, many who state their belief in a supreme being, in a divinely inspired Bible, and even in an eternal heaven and burning hell, yet perish in their sins without hope and without God. For the word of God clearly says, 'without shedding of blood, (there) is no remission' of sins (Hebrews 9:22).

Christ is 'the Way', all without him are lost, wandering in the wilderness of sin. Christ is 'the Truth', men and women without him live a lie. Christ is 'the Life', all without him are dead in trespasses and in sins. Christ is 'the Light', all without him are in utter darkness. Christ is 'the Vine', those who are without him are withered branches to be cast into the fire. Christ is 'the Rock', if you are without him, you will be carried away by the flood of judgment. Christ is 'the Bread' and 'Water of Life', if you are without him, you must hunger and thirst throughout eternity.

When these truths are so plainly written in the word of God, and when they are faithfully preached day after day from the pulpit, the radio, television, the printed page, and the internet, I cannot help asking, 'Why don't people come to Christ?' If Christ is able to save, if salvation is to be had by coming to Christ, if the Lord Jesus promises to save all who come to him, and if all who ever came to the Lord Jesus Christ obtained salvation by him, in him, and with him, why don't you come to him? Why do people continue to live in unrest, unhappiness, and sin, when to come to Christ means rest, joy, and salvation from sin? To find the answer to this question, we must go to the scriptures.

The Son of God declares, 'And ye will not come to me, that ye might have life'. Let me show you from the book of God why it is that people will not come to Christ. If you do not come to my Saviour, if you do not trust the Lord

Why Don't People Come To Christ?

Jesus as your only, able, and all-sufficient Saviour, it is because of these five facts revealed in the word of God.

Spiritually Blind

First, the word of God shows us plainly that all the sons and daughters of our father Adam are spiritually blind. Yes, man's problem is that he is blind, so blind that unless and until he is born again, he cannot see the kingdom of God. He cannot see, discern, or understand anything spiritual.

Men do not come to Christ because they are spiritually blind and the gospel is hid from them. Paul says, 'If our gospel be hid, it is hid to them that are lost: In whom the god of this world hath blinded the minds of them which believe not, lest the light of the glorious gospel of Christ should shine unto them' (2 Corinthians 4:3, 4). A blind man has no appreciation for the beautiful scenery of the Great Smokey Mountains. A deaf man has no appreciation for the glorious music of the symphony orchestra. And the spiritually blind sinner, the person who has no spiritual eyes to see, receive, and rejoice in spiritual things cannot see the kingdom of God. The things of God are foolishness to him. All mankind are in a lost and perishing condition through sin. Every child born into this world is conceived in sin, born in sin, and brought forth in iniquity; each one goes forth from the womb speaking lies.

Blessed be his name, God will save a multitude no man can number! Some have been chosen and redeemed, and shall be saved out of every tribe, tongue, and nation. God the Father chose them in eternity. God the Son redeemed them at Calvary. God the Spirit will call them irresistibly and effectually. God will save all his elect, but the rest will be lost forever, never seeing the truth, never knowing God, without Christ, because their eyes are blind and they are given over to a reprobate mind to continue in those things that are not convenient (Romans 1:28). Every vessel of mercy shall be prepared unto glory and every vessel of wrath fitted for destruction, according to God's eternal, unalterable, sovereign purpose (Romans 9:11-28). This is both a matter of divine justice and a matter of divine sovereignty (John 5:40; 10:25, 26).

The Church of Christ must not cease from its labour until it has preached the gospel to every creature. We must give ourselves to missions, evangelism, and witnessing, thereby fulfilling the great commission of our Saviour. But we will not add one name to the Book of Life of the Lamb slain from the foundation of the world. And all our labours, our most fervent and faithful labours are less than vanity, without the blessing of God the Holy Spirit. Let us ever pray that he will bless our labours, ours and those of our brethren around the world, to the salvation and consolation of God's elect. He alone can take the things of Christ and show them to men. He alone can give sinners eyes to behold and hearts to believe the gospel (John 16:8-11).

311

All the tricks, gimmicks, pleadings, and begging of churches and preachers to get lost men and women to make decisions and professions are useless, worse than useless; it is a mockery of God and a mockery of men's souls!

Unless God the Holy Spirit performs a divine operation on their blinded minds, and opens their eyes to receive God's truth, blind sinners shall remain blind. None but God the Holy Spirit can 'lead men to Christ'. Only God the Father can 'draw men to the Son'. Sinners will not and cannot come to Christ of their own accord, because they are blind and cannot see their condition and their need of Christ. Natural men do not see that they are wicked and that 'God is angry with the wicked every day' (Psalms 7:11). They do not know the plague of their hearts. They cannot understand that salvation is in the blood of Christ. The preaching of the cross is foolishness to them. All of these glorious truths are revealed and known only by the work and power and operation of God the Holy Spirit through the preaching of the gospel.

We must preach, yes, but we must wait upon the Spirit to convict and convert. The emphasis today is not upon the faithful preaching of all the word of God, but it is placed upon getting sinners to 'make a decision', teaching them to say 'the sinner's prayer', and pressing men to 'accept Christ', all terms that never appear in the word of God. Nowhere in the Bible do we find God's preachers going around begging the wicked to 'decide for Christ' and 'accept Jesus'. Not once! In the Bible you find God's prophets delivering 'the burden of the word of the Lord', condemning sin, calling sinners to repentance, holding their feet to the fire until, smarting under the pricks of the Spirit, they cried, 'What must we do to be saved?'

The knowledge of these truths does not lead to fatalism, nor to an anti-evangelistic spirit, but will lead us to properly emphasize all Bible doctrine and will correct those unbiblical methods so often used to enlist great numbers of unsaved church members, who have made a decision for Christ, but who have never been born of the Spirit, to make, in turn, proselytes of others. In the mad race for numbers and praise from men, churches around the world put on shows and employ all the tricks of snake-oil salesmen to get more people on the church roll and make them feel secure until they wake up in hell, forever lost!

When these modern deceivers of men's souls have compassed land and sea to make one disciple or a million disciples, they have done nothing for the benefit of any, but only make them twofold more the children of hell. As a result of all the religious carnival acts in them, the churches of this reprobate age are filled with sinners who are trying to live the Christian life without Christ, who are trying to act holy without having holiness, and who are 'the blind' trying to 'lead the blind'.

It is time for preachers and churches to start being honest. It is a sin against God and sinners to trick and talk men into professions without faith, and decisions without regeneration. The Lord Jesus said,

'And ye will not come to me, that ye might have life' (John 5:40). 'All that the Father giveth me shall come to me; and him that cometh to me I will in no wise cast out. For I came down from heaven, not to do mine own will, but the will of him that sent me. And this is the Father's will which hath sent me, that of all which he hath given me I should lose nothing, but should raise it up again at the last day. And this is the will of him that sent me, that every one which seeth the Son, and believeth on him, may have everlasting life: and I will raise him up at the last day. The Jews then murmured at him, because he said, I am the bread which came down from heaven. And they said, Is not this Jesus, the son of Joseph, whose father and mother we know? how is it then that he saith, I came down from heaven? Jesus therefore answered and said unto them, Murmur not among yourselves. No man can come to me, except the Father which hath sent me draw him: and I will raise him up at the last day' (John 6:37-44).

Spiritually Dead

Why don't people come to Christ? You will not come because you are spiritually blind; and, second, you will not come because you are spiritually dead. Men do not come to Christ because they are dead in trespasses and sins and must be quickened by God's Spirit. In the heart of man there dwells no good thing. In the soul of man there is no spiritual life. In the mind of man there is no longing for God, or seeking after God.

Men out of Christ are dead. They are just as dead and helpless spiritually as a corpse is helpless physically. I would as soon expect a dead man to get out of his casket, go into the kitchen and get himself a drink of water as expect a sinner to rise out of his sins and come to Christ who is the Water of Life, without the quickening, regenerating work of the Holy Spirit.

If a man is ever saved from sin, he must first be effectually quickened by the Spirit of God. Paul in writing to the Ephesians calls our attention to the fact that we were 'quickened' to life (Ephesians 2:1) by the Spirit. God does not perform this effectual work of the Spirit in the hearts of all men, but only in the hearts of those he has purposed to save. He saves men on purpose. There are no accidents with God.

This talk of 'God has done his part, now you must do your part' completely destroys salvation by pure, free, grace, making it to depend on the works of man, which is no more grace but works. Man made his decision in Eden. He chose to disobey God and serve Satan. That decision still controls the hearts of unregenerate men. Now God is calling his people out of every nation under heaven, the people redeemed by the precious blood of his dear Son. God does not tell us that the destiny of any man rests upon our success as soul-winners; but he has sent us out, telling us to preach the gospel to every creature. The work of regeneration is in his hands, the hands of the Spirit's omnipotent grace!

I suppose every preacher in the country has a sermon on the words of Pilate, 'What shall I do then with Jesus which is called Christ?' (Matthew 27:22). They use it to try and prove to the sinner that the salvation of his soul rests entirely in his deciding for Jesus. But very few preachers are fair enough to preach on the reply the Lord Jesus made to these words of Pilate. He said to Pilate, 'thou couldst have no power at all against me, except it were given thee from above' (John 19:10).

There you have it, sinner, we are in the hands of a God who does as he pleases and he is responsible to and answerable to no man for his actions. He said to Moses, 'I will make all my goodness pass before thee, and will be gracious to whom I will be gracious, and will show mercy on whom I will show mercy' (Exodus 33:19).

Spiritual Enmity
Why don't people come to Christ? They are spiritually blind. They are spiritually dead. And, third, their hearts are filled with enmity against God. Sinners, whose hearts are enmity against God, are filled with spiritual enmity toward the gospel, and are violently opposed to God's terms of salvation. People despise the fact that God declares them to be doomed, damned, dead sinners, without any ability before him. That is the doctrine of total depravity. Men hate the fact that salvation is by the will and choice of God alone. That is the doctrine of unconditional election. Oh, how men hate the fact that salvation comes to sinners by the merit of Christ's effectual redemption. That is the sweet doctrine of limited atonement. Sinners everywhere despise being told that salvation comes only by the effectual call of God the Holy Spirit. That is the doctrine of irresistible grace. And sinners hate being told that salvation's security is completely assured to all who trust Christ because, and only because we are preserved and kept by grace. That is the doctrine of the perseverance of the saints.

Sinners refuse to come to Christ because of his terms of salvation. The average man would be willing to accept a salvation from the fires of hell if he could have it and keep the reins of his life in his own hands; but that will never happen. The Son of God demands that we surrender to him as our Lord. Faith in Christ is nothing less than the surrender of myself to him (Luke 14:25-33).

There are two kinds of faith. There is a faith that centres in me, and what I can get from God. And there is a faith that centres in God and his glory. If my faith is primarily concerned with me, and what I want, then the object of my faith is me. I really worship myself. If my faith is primarily concerned with God and his glory, then God is the Object of my faith. I worship him.

Martin Luther once defined salvation as 'the realisation of God's will and purpose, whatever it might be, rather than the satisfaction of human need.' He saw that true faith is not seeking something from God, but bowing to the rule of God. Calvin said, 'True faith is having confidence in God, regardless of profit or loss.' It is the heart's willing affirmation of God's right to be God. This is the one issue between God and man.

Sinners will not come to Christ because they hate his terms and will not submit to them. They will not lay down their weapons of warfare and their arms of rebellion, until the Spirit of God has laid bare their hearts, stripped them of their self-righteous rags, and destroyed all their false foundations.

Another Refuge
Isaiah 28:14-20 gives us a fourth reason why sinners will not come to Christ. If you are yet without Christ, if you still harden your heart and will not hear his voice, you choose not to trust the Son of God because you have another refuge.

'Wherefore hear the word of the LORD, ye scornful men, that rule this people which is in Jerusalem. Because ye have said, We have made a covenant with death, and with hell are we at agreement; when the overflowing scourge shall pass through, it shall not come unto us: for we have made lies our refuge, and under falsehood have we hid ourselves' (Isaiah 28:14, 15).

What is your refuge? Where are you hiding? What is your covenant with death? Is it your good works? Is it your decision for Jesus? Is it your religious experience? There is only one refuge for our souls; and that Refuge is the one God himself has provided for sinners, Jesus Christ the Lord; his blood, his righteousness, his grace! 'Therefore thus saith the Lord GOD, Behold, I lay in Zion for a foundation a stone, a tried stone, a precious corner stone, a sure foundation: he that believeth shall not make haste' (Isaiah 28:16). God give us some preachers today who will rout sinners out of their refuge of lies and exalt the God of the Bible!

'Judgment also will I lay to the line, and righteousness to the plummet: and the hail shall sweep away the refuge of lies, and the waters shall overflow the hiding place. And your covenant with death shall be disannulled, and your agreement with hell shall not stand; when the overflowing scourge shall pass through, then ye shall be trodden down by it. From the time that it goeth forth it shall take you: for morning by morning shall it pass over, by day and by night: and it shall be a vexation only to understand the report. For the bed is shorter than that a man can stretch himself on it: and the covering narrower than that he can wrap himself in it' (Isaiah 28:17-20).

Without Grace

Here's the fifth reason why sinners will not come to Christ. Sinners who will not come to Christ will not come because they are without grace. Our Saviour says in John 5:40, 'And ye will not come to me, that ye might have life'. In chapter 6, verse 44 our Saviour is still talking to these self-righteous Pharisees, these religious hypocrites. He tells us plainly that the reason men and women will not come to Christ is that they cannot come. 'No man can come to me, except the Father which hath sent me draw him: and I will raise him up at the last day.'

Those who will not come are to be blamed for their obstinate, wilful unbelief. It is the perversity, the depravity, the bondage of man's will to his nature that keeps him from Christ. Men will not come because they hate God. They will not come because they love sin. They will not come because they do not want to come.

Still, when all is said and done, the reason why sinners do not come to Christ is this. They who refuse to trust the Son of God are yet without grace. If you now come to Christ, your coming is proof that you have been given grace to come. If you do not come, it is because God Almighty has left you alone, and you are without grace (1 Peter 2:3-10). If you believe on the Son of God, it is because God has saved you by his grace (Ephesians 2:8, 9).

Chapter 44

Calculating Without Christ

'After these things Jesus went over the sea of Galilee, which is the sea of Tiberias. And a great multitude followed him, because they saw his miracles which he did on them that were diseased. And Jesus went up into a mountain, and there he sat with his disciples. And the passover, a feast of the Jews, was nigh. When Jesus then lifted up his eyes, and saw a great company come unto him, he saith unto Philip, Whence shall we buy bread, that these may eat? And this he said to prove him: for he himself knew what he would do. Philip answered him, Two hundred pennyworth of bread is not sufficient for them, that every one of them may take a little. One of his disciples, Andrew, Simon Peter's brother, saith unto him, There is a lad here, which hath five barley loaves, and two small fishes: but what are they among so many? And Jesus said, Make the men sit down. Now there was much grass in the place. So the men sat down, in number about five thousand. And Jesus took the loaves; and when he had given thanks, he distributed to the disciples, and the disciples to them that were set down; and likewise of the fishes as much as they would. When they were filled, he said unto his disciples, Gather up the fragments that remain, that nothing be lost. Therefore they gathered them together, and filled twelve baskets with the fragments of the five barley loaves, which remained over and above unto them that had eaten. Then those men, when they had seen the miracle that Jesus did, said, This is of a truth that prophet that should come into the world' (John 6:1-14).

Of all miracles performed by our Lord Jesus, the feeding of the five thousand is the only one recorded by each of the four Evangelists (Matthew 14:13-21;

Mark 6:32-44; Luke 9:10-17; John 6:1-14). Of all the great works our Saviour performed, none was done so publicly and before so many witnesses as the feeding of the five thousand. There must be something about that great miracle that is unique and of special importance.

'After these things' (v. 1). 'These things' refers to those things mentioned in chapter 5; the healing of the impotent man, the persecution by the Jews because the Lord Jesus had performed that miracle of mercy on their sabbath day, and his lengthy discourse on his deity, power, and mission as the Son of man, the Messiah, the God-man Mediator. After all those things, because they believed him not, our Saviour left Jerusalem and went over the Sea of Galilee. He left them to themselves, left them to be damned, believing a lie and clinging to their religious traditions. What a warning this ought to be to every religious ritualist!

Though he left Jerusalem, a great multitude followed him, 'because they saw his miracles' (v. 2). Like countless others in every age, these poor souls loved excitement and found gratification in wonders; but they totally failed to perceive the Saviour's doctrine. They did not trust him as the Son of God, the Saviour of sinners, and the promised Messiah (John 2:23-25; 6:25, 26). We see the same thing today. People everywhere follow clever evangelists, fake healers, miracle workers, and religious showmen, but few are interested in Christ the Redeemer, the Saviour of poor, needy sinners.

In verses 3 and 4 our Lord withdrew himself, even from the crowd that followed him across the Sea of Galilee. Weary with their unbelief, weary with their self-righteousness and empty traditions, he took his disciples up into a quiet, secluded place. The Passover was at hand; and John notes that the Lord's Passover had degenerated into 'a feast of the Jews'. Though the Passover was near, 'the Lamb of God' who was in their midst was unknown and unwanted.

Tender Care
First, I call your attention to our Saviour's tender care for the needs of men. After a while, the Lord Jesus came down from the mountain; and the great multitude that had followed him was still there. Matthew tells us, 'He had compassion on them and healed their sick' (Matthew 14:14, 15). The Master then put Philip to a strong test. He knew what he was going to do (v. 6); but to test Philip's faith, he asked him, 'Whence shall we buy bread, that these may eat?'

Philip was a man much like you and me. He looked at the crowd, saw the need, and began to calculate. He said, 'We don't have enough money to buy a little snack for this many people, let alone to feed them. Two hundred pennyworth of bread would only give each one a little to eat'.

318

What a sad portrait Philip is of us in this trial! How often in our daily trials and difficult situations we start to calculate the need, and draw back. How often when seeing a work to be done for Christ and the souls of men we start calculating the need, and draw back. Philip began to calculate his own resources and abilities to accomplish the task of feeding this huge crowd, and said, 'Lord, we can't do it'. Imagine talking of 'little' in the presence of infinite power and riches! What is our feebleness compared to his power? What is our emptiness compared to his fulness? Instead of looking to him, Philip, like us, looked to himself and his own strength.

Unbelief is a horribly infectious thing. In verses 8 and 9 Andrew, who had been a disciple longer than any of the others, said the same thing; and all the others agreed (Mark 6:37). Andrew, Philip and all the rest of the disciples seem to have forgotten what they had seen, and heard, and learned. They all seem to have been temporarily blinded to the glory and power of Christ. 'There is a boy here with five pieces of bread and two little fish, but we can't feed all these people with that'! There is just one problem with their calculations: They were calculating without Christ! (Psalms 78:19-22). 'Is any thing too hard for the LORD?' (Genesis 18:14).

> The birds without barn or storehouse are fed;
> From them let us learn to trust for our bread.
> His saints what is fitting shall ne'er be denied,
> So long as 'tis written 'The Lord will provide'.
>
> No strength of our own, nor goodness we claim;
> Yet, since we have known the Saviour's great name,
> In this our strong tower for safety we hide,
> The Lord is our power; 'The Lord will provide'!
>
> John Newton

If our Lord Jesus was moved with compassion upon these multitudes, many of whom he knew were not his own, and so moved that he performed an astounding miracle to provide for the needs of their bodies, shall he not, without a doubt, provide for every need of our souls and our bodies? My brother, my sister, let nothing tempt you, let nothing tempt me, to be cast down with fear and unbelieving! As Hawker put it, 'Both your bread that perisheth with using, and that which endureth to everlasting life, shall be given, and your water sure'. It is written, 'He shall dwell on high: his place of defence shall be the munitions of rocks: bread shall be given him; his waters shall be sure'

319

(Isaiah 33:16). 'My God shall supply all your need according to his riches in glory by Christ Jesus' (Philippians 4:19).

Disciples Used

Second, notice that our Lord Jesus chose to use these same disciples to feed the crowd. How patient the Lord was with his unbelieving disciples! There was not even a hint of rebuke (Psalms 103:13, 14). The Lord Jesus simply said, 'Make the men sit down' (v. 10), and proceeded to perform another miracle using those poor, weak, unbelieving disciples, just as though they had believed him perfectly and unhesitatingly. Mark tells us they sat down by companies in ranks by hundreds and fifties (Mark 6:39, 40). I see four things here.

1. The Lord Jesus told the disciples to seat these people in an orderly manner, because our God is a God of order (1 Corinthians 14:33).

2. Not only that, our Lord required these people to be seated, because the activities of the flesh must come to an end, if we are to be fed the Bread of Life (Psalms 23:2).

3. Our great and gracious God and Saviour does not need, but he condescends to use such insignificant, weak, and worthless things as we are to perform his great works in this world (John 11:39; 1 Corinthians 1:26-29; 1 Peter 1:23-25).

4. He even accepts and uses the most insignificant gifts we might put into his hands. We read in verse 11 that 'Jesus took the loaves'. He did not scorn the loaves because they were few nor the fish because they were small. God uses small and weak things.

Distributing Bread

Third, in verses 11 and 12 we see that the work of God's servants in this world is distributing bread to hungry souls.

'And Jesus took the loaves; and when he had given thanks, he distributed to the disciples, and the disciples to them that were set down; and likewise of the fishes as much as they would. When they were filled, he said unto his disciples, Gather up the fragments that remain, that nothing be lost.'

The Lord Jesus 'took the loaves' and the fish. He gave 'thanks'. Thus, he teaches us to acknowledge God as the Giver of every good gift and to own him as the one who provides all things. He distributed to the disciples. The disciples distributed to the people. What a clear picture this is of the way God uses men to perform his wonders of grace in this world. Let us never despise the means he uses (Ephesians 4:10-13; 2 Corinthians 4:7; 2 Corinthians 5:18-21).

The disciples did not make the loaves and fish increase and multiply; but they increased and multiplied. By a strange, heavenly kind of arithmetic, they were multiplied by division and increased by subtraction. God's gifts grow in the hands of those who use them for the benefit of others, especially for the benefit of his people. It was the Saviour's almighty power that provided an unfailing supply of food. It was the work of his disciples to receive humbly, and distribute faithfully.

That is a very vivid picture of the work every gospel preacher is meant to do. The preacher is not a mediator between God and man. The pastor has no power to put away sin, or impart grace. The preacher's work is to receive the Bread of Life, which his Master provides, and to distribute it among the souls among whom he labours. He cannot make men value the Bread, or receive it. He cannot make the Bread effectual, beneficial, and saving. He cannot cause the Bread to meet any need, or compel anyone to eat it. That is God's work, not the preacher's. Preachers are not responsible for those things.

The whole work of the gospel ministry is the faithful distribution of the Bread of Life. The preacher must seek the Bread by earnest prayer and diligent study. Deacons were ordained in the church so that God's preachers might devote themselves to seeking the Bread of Life and have no concern about earthly bread (Acts 6). The preacher must faithfully distribute the Bread among hungry souls.

Divine Omnipotence
Fourth, this miracle stands before us as an undeniable display of divine omnipotence. We see our Lord Jesus feeding five thousand men with 'five barley loaves and two small fish'. When the day was over, 'twelve baskets of fragments' remained after all those thousands had eaten all they could hold. Nothing less than the creative omnipotence of the Almighty God could have performed this great miracle. This man, the God-man, called food into existence that did not exist before. In healing the sick and raising the dead, he mended and restored that which had previously existed. Here something had to be created which had no prior existence.

This miracle ought to be especially instructive and encouraging to all who seek to do good to immortal souls. It shows us that the Lord Jesus Christ is God, 'able to save to the uttermost'. He has all power over dead hearts. Not only can he mend that which is broken, build that which is cast down, heal that which is sick, and strengthen that which is weak, he can do and does greater things than these. He calls into being that which was not before (2 Corinthians 5:17), and calls it out of nothing! With a Saviour who, by his Spirit, can create a new heart, nothing is impossible!

All Filled
Fifth, look at verse 12. The Spirit of God tells us that, 'They were filled'. All those thousands of people, when fed by the miraculous power and grace of the

Son of God, were filled. When the Lord Jesus feeds us, he fills us with grace and satisfies our souls with fatness (Colossians 2:9, 10). His grace is all-sufficient grace (Romans 5:20, 21; 2 Corinthians 12:1-10).

Nothing Lost
Sixth, take notice of the fact that our Saviour required his disciples to 'Gather up the fragments that remain, that nothing be lost'. When they did, they had twelve heaping baskets full of leftovers (vv. 12, 13). There was abundance for all, and the boy had twelve baskets to take home. The liberal soul is made fat (Proverbs 11:25).

I am certain that our Saviour's intention here was not merely to teach us to be frugal with our earthly goods. No, his instruction is far more needful. He required this gathering up of the fragments to teach us that we must take great care not to lose by our neglect the bounties of the gospel (Hebrews 2:1-4). Let us take care that we do not lose that which God has given us. Let us never be moved away from the hope of the gospel. Let us never be turned aside from the simplicity that is in Christ. Let us never be entangled with the yoke of bondage and the works of the law.

Come, hungry soul, and eat this Bread. Eat this Bread and live forever (John 6:47-50, 53-58).

'Verily, verily, I say unto you, he that believeth on me hath everlasting life. I am that bread of life. Your fathers did eat manna in the wilderness, and are dead. This is the bread which cometh down from heaven, that a man may eat thereof, and not die ... Then Jesus said unto them, Verily, verily, I say unto you, Except ye eat the flesh of the Son of man, and drink his blood, ye have no life in you. Whoso eateth my flesh, and drinketh my blood, hath eternal life; and I will raise him up at the last day. For my flesh is meat indeed, and my blood is drink indeed. He that eateth my flesh, and drinketh my blood, dwelleth in me, and I in him. As the living Father hath sent me, and I live by the Father: so he that eateth me, even he shall live by me. This is that bread which came down from heaven: not as your fathers did eat manna, and are dead: he that eateth of this bread shall live for ever' (John 6:47-50, 53-58).

Chapter 45

Alone In The Dark

'When Jesus then lifted up his eyes, and saw a great company come unto him, he saith unto Philip, Whence shall we buy bread, that these may eat? And this he said to prove him: for he himself knew what he would do. Philip answered him, Two hundred pennyworth of bread is not sufficient for them, that every one of them may take a little. One of his disciples, Andrew, Simon Peter's brother, saith unto him, There is a lad here, which hath five barley loaves, and two small fishes: but what are they among so many? And Jesus said, Make the men sit down. Now there was much grass in the place. So the men sat down, in number about five thousand. And Jesus took the loaves; and when he had given thanks, he distributed to the disciples, and the disciples to them that were set down; and likewise of the fishes as much as they would. When they were filled, he said unto his disciples, Gather up the fragments that remain, that nothing be lost. Therefore they gathered them together, and filled twelve baskets with the fragments of the five barley loaves, which remained over and above unto them that had eaten. Then those men, when they had seen the miracle that Jesus did, said, This is of a truth that prophet that should come into the world. When Jesus therefore perceived that they would come and take him by force, to make him a king, he departed again into a mountain himself alone. And when even was now come, his disciples went down unto the sea, And entered into a ship, and went over the sea toward Capernaum. And it was now dark, and Jesus was not come to them. And the sea arose by reason of a great wind that blew. So when they had rowed about five and twenty or thirty furlongs, they see Jesus walking on the sea, and drawing nigh unto the ship: and they were afraid. But he saith unto them, It is I; be not afraid. Then they willingly received him into the ship: and immediately the ship was at the land whither they went' (John 6:5-21).

When I was young, boys were taught never to show fear. If a boy let another boy know he was afraid, he would never hear the end of it. But not showing fear and not having fear are two different things. I tried never to show it, but of all the things that caused me fear when I was a boy, other than the thought of my mother with a belt, nothing compared with being alone in the dark.

In these verses the Apostle John was inspired by God the Holy Spirit to record two of our Lord's great miracles. At first reading, they might appear to be unrelated; but that is not the case. In fact, if you read the word of God carefully, you will see that it was written with a very specific order. The things that happened were brought to pass with very precise order; and our Lord's miracles were both performed and recorded in that precise order to teach us specific aspects of his greatness and his grace. In verses 5-14 the Lord Jesus took five loaves and two small fish from the hands of a boy and fed 5000 men. In verses 15-21 we see the Lord Jesus walking across the troubled, storm tossed sea to his disciples. In the first miracle the Lord Jesus used a huge crowd of hungry people to prove Philip and the other disciples. In the second miracle the Son of God sent his disciples sailing directly into a storm, that he might prove them. Like these disciples, you and I must have our proving times.

We all have our proving times. Our proving times are seasons appointed by the Lord himself in which he proves himself to us and proves us to ourselves. These are times of trial and adversity, times that call for and demand faith, and more. These proving times are times in which the Lord God graciously works faith in us, forcing us into his omnipotent arms of mercy, compelling us to do what we will never otherwise do, compelling us to cast all our care on him who cares for us. What a proving time it was for Abraham at Moriah! What a proving time all those years were for Jacob, when he thought Joseph was dead! What a proving time Job endured when the Lord turned Satan upon him! What a proving time Peter had when the Lord Jesus permitted Satan to sift him as wheat!

What are we to learn from these two miracles, from these two proving times? What lessons do these two miracles hold for you and me? Why are they here recorded as they are, by the finger of God, for our learning and our admonition?

The Lord Knows
First, learn this and remember it. The Lord God, our great Saviour, always knows what he will do.

'When Jesus then lifted up his eyes, and saw a great company come unto him, he saith unto Philip, Whence shall we buy bread, that these may eat? And this he said to prove him: for he himself knew what he would do' (vv. 5, 6).

Alone In The Dark

We are often caught off guard. Nothing ever catches him off guard. We are often taken by surprise. Nothing ever catches him by surprise. We are often unprepared. He is never unprepared. Our great God and Saviour always knows what he will do. He knew what he would do before Lucifer fell, before Adam sinned, and before we went astray from the womb. He knows what he will do for poor, lost sinners chosen of God before all worlds, loved by him with an everlasting love, and redeemed by his precious blood. Child of God, he knows what he will do for you.

> He knows: let this my comfort be;
> He knows the path designed for me;
> A healing balm for all my woes
> O blessed thought! My Saviour knows!
>
> The thorns that pierce my weary feet;
> The lowering clouds, the storms that beat;
> And then, with bliss of calm repose,
> O blessed thought! My Saviour knows!
>
> He knows: let this suffice for me;
> He knows the end I cannot see;
> Then let my anxious heart be still,
> And patient, wait my Saviour's will.
>
> My prayer for strength to Him is known,
> Though breathed in secret and alone;
> The weary heart, the tear that flows,
> O blessed thought! My Saviour knows!
>
> Frances Crosby

The things our Saviour knew he would do in these two miracles are the very things he is constantly doing with us and for us. He was about to show his disciples their utter insufficiency (John 15:5). And he was about to show them his all-sufficiency (2 Corinthians 12:7-10). Gideon's army was a mighty one indeed when it was reduced to an army of 300 men too scared to get a drink of water. And I assure you that before ever the Lord Jesus causes the light of his grace to shine upon you, he will fill you with the darkness of his terror.

Nothing Lost

Second, when the Lord Jesus tries and proves us, though he sift us as wheat and refine us as silver, nothing shall be lost by the trial, and much gained. These very disciples whom the Master proved were required to 'Gather up the fragments that remained, that nothing be lost' (v. 12); and they gathered up twelve baskets of fragments! Israel lost nothing by their four hundred years in Egypt; and they spoiled the Egyptians when they came out of the land of bondage. Job lost nothing, but gained much by his great trials. Shadrach, Meshach, and Abednego lost nothing in the fiery furnace. Peter lost nothing by Satan sifting him. And our Saviour asks all who forsake all and follow him, 'Lacked ye anything?' And all must acknowledge, 'Nothing' (Luke 22:35).

'But now thus saith the LORD that created thee, O Jacob, and he that formed thee, O Israel, Fear not: for I have redeemed thee, I have called thee by thy name; thou art mine. When thou passest through the waters, I will be with thee; and through the rivers, they shall not overflow thee: when thou walkest through the fire, thou shalt not be burned; neither shall the flame kindle upon thee. For I am the LORD thy God, the Holy One of Israel, thy Saviour: I gave Egypt for thy ransom, Ethiopia and Seba for thee. Since thou wast precious in my sight, thou hast been honourable, and I have loved thee: therefore will I give men for thee, and people for thy life. Fear not: for I am with thee: I will bring thy seed from the east, and gather thee from the west' (Isaiah 43:1-5).

After our Lord Jesus performed this great miracle, those who saw what he had done said, 'Surely this is the Messiah, that Prophet' (v. 14; John 1:21; Deuteronomy 18:15). Like all of Israel, they were looking for a leader, a king, a Messiah to lead them in a successful revolt against the hated Romans (Acts 5:36, 37). They did not understand that the Messiah's kingdom is a spiritual kingdom, a kingdom not of this world (John 18:36), but within us. They did not know the meaning of the sacrifices and the atonement portraying the Messiah's redemptive work. But they were expecting the Messiah.

Do not be misled by those who talk of Christ the Prophet and King, but who despise his cross. Our Lord immediately withdrew from these ambitious men who wanted to make him king over a nation of unbelievers. He came to save sinners, to redeem a people for his glory, to call out of every nation a holy people to reign forever with him in a new heaven and a new earth (Titus 2:14; 1 Peter 2:9, 10). These Jews had professed with their lips Christ as that Prophet, and would by force make him King; but there is another office, which comes in between these. Christ must officiate as Priest, offering himself as a sacrifice for sin. Besides, he needed not to be made king by them; he is the King (Revelation 19:16).

Nights Alone In The Dark

Here's the third lesson. While living in this world, we will have, and must have our nights alone.

'And when even was now come, his disciples went down unto the sea, And entered into a ship, and went over the sea toward Capernaum. And it was now dark, and Jesus was not come to them' (vv. 16, 17).

Oh, blessed is the sinner whom the Son of God sweetly forces to be shut up alone in the darkness of his guilt and sin (John 8:1-8). Matthew tells (Matthew 14:22, 23) us that the disciples boarded this ship and set sail for the other side, because the Lord Jesus told them to do so. They looked for the Master on every boat that passed; but he did not come to them. Then, it got dark; and he still had not come to them. There they were in the middle of the sea, because they were obeying him; but he had not come to them. They were alone in the dark.

Then, a terrible storm arose (v. 18). They manned the oars and rowed hard against the storm; but these experienced seamen knew they were getting nowhere. The darkness was thick. The storm was great. The winds were strong. And they were alone in the dark. They were the Lord's servants; but the Lord was not with them. They were doing what the Lord told them to do; but he had not come to them. They had twelve baskets of food in the boat with them; but they couldn't eat a bite.

Every lost sinner's life is one long, starless night. But the believer has his night too. We have our nights of trial, adversity, and pain. We have our nights of emptiness, desolation, and woe. We have our nights of sorrow, bereavement, and heartache.

The Church of God has her night. She is 'not of the night', but she has 'nights'. Darkness, tempest, and dangers are all around us. 'Famine, and nakedness, and peril, and sword' continually assail us (Job 30:26; Micah 7:8; Isaiah 50:10).

How dark the night is when the Lord Jesus is not with us! When he appears to have abandoned us!

> How tedious and tasteless the hours,
> When Jesus no longer I see;
> Sweet prospects, sweet birds, and sweet flowers,
> Have lost all their sweetness with me!
> The mid-summer sun shines but dim,
> The fields strive in vain to look gay;
> But when I am happy in Him,
> December's as pleasant as May.

His name yields the richest perfume,
And sweeter than music His voice;
His presence disperses my gloom,
And makes all within me rejoice!
I should, were He always thus nigh,
Have nothing to wish or to fear;
No mortal so happy as I,
My summer would last all the year.

Content with beholding His face,
My all to His pleasure resigned;
No changes of season or place,
Would make any change in my mind.
While blessed with a sense of His love,
A palace a toy would appear;
And prisons would palaces prove,
If Jesus would dwell with me there.

Dear Lord, if indeed I am Thine,
If Thou art my sun and my song;
Say, why do I languish and pine,
And why are my winters so long?
O drive these dark clouds from my sky,
Thy soul-cheering presence restore;
Or take me unto Thee on high,
Where winter and clouds are no more.

John Newton

Does darkness engulf you? Does danger seem to roar around you? Has desertion withered you? Things are not as they appear. Child of God, the Saviour is with you! The night has not come because of some evil you have done; but to make you know, again, by experience, your utter insufficiency and Christ's all-sufficiency. These night seasons, alone in the dark, make us conscious of our need. The Saviour's mercy, love, and grace are unchanged!

If ever it should come to pass
That one sheep of Christ should fall away;
My fickle, feeble soul, alas!
Would fall a thousand times a day.

These night seasons are not wasted seasons. In fact, in the word of God we find that for God's saints these night seasons are very profitable seasons for our souls. In the darkness of night the Lord God has given stars for light (Jeremiah 31:35; Revelation 1:20). In the night season, when we find ourselves in the dark alone, we are compelled to seek the Saviour (Song of Solomon 3:1-5). The night of darkness is the time when the sweetest revelations of the Saviour come (Daniel 7:2, 9; Zechariah 1:8). Nicodemus came to the Saviour by night; and we do, too. In the darkness of the night, the Lord God our Saviour will appear for our glorious defence.

'And the LORD will create upon every dwelling place of mount Zion, and upon her assemblies, a cloud and smoke by day, and the shining of a flaming fire by night: for upon all the glory shall be a defence. And there shall be a tabernacle for a shadow in the daytime from the heat, and for a place of refuge, and for a covert from storm and from rain' (Isaiah 4:5, 6).

Christ Comes In The Darkness
Fourth, the Lord Jesus will come to you in the night of your storm, and come to you in such a way as he could not otherwise appear.

'And entered into a ship, and went over the sea toward Capernaum. And it was now dark, and Jesus was not come to them. And the sea arose by reason of a great wind that blew. So when they had rowed about five and twenty or thirty furlongs, they see Jesus walking on the sea, and drawing nigh unto the ship: and they were afraid. But he saith unto them, It is I; be not afraid' (vv. 17-20).

The Lord's disciples were in the midst of a terrible storm, in the middle of a dark, dark night. They were toiling hard with trouble; but everything appeared to be contrary to them. In those circumstances, our all-glorious, ever-gracious Saviour came to his troubled friends walking upon the sea that caused them so much trouble. They were afraid, terrified. They thought they saw a ghost! As he approached their little, storm-tossed boat, he said, 'Be of good cheer: it is I; be not afraid'. Then, 'he went up unto them into the ship, and the wind ceased' (Mark 6:45-51).

This is written in the book of God for you and me, 'that we through patience and comfort of the scriptures might have hope' (Romans 15:4). The Lord Jesus will graciously step into your storm-tossed life and cause the winds that appear to be so contrary to you today to be calm.

Remember, it was the Lord Jesus who sent his friends into the storm, who sent them away from himself (Mark 6:45, 46). He seems to have done so specifically that he might come to them when they desperately needed him, speak these words to them, and make himself known to them in a way that was not otherwise possible. Surely, that is the case with you. Listen, then, to the voice of your tender, omnipotent Saviour in the midst of your storm. 'Be of good cheer: it is I; be not afraid'.

'It is I' who raised the tempest in your soul, and will control it. 'It is I' who sent your affliction, and will be with you in it. 'It is I' who kindled the furnace, and will watch the flames, and bring you through it. 'It is I' who formed your burden, who carved your cross, and who will strengthen you to bear it. 'It is I' who mixed your cup of grief, and will enable you to drink it with meek submission to your Father's will. 'It is I' who took from you your strength and health, your peace and tranquillity. 'It is I' who made the light darkness about you and raised the contrary winds. 'It is I' who have done all these things, not against you, but for you, not to hurt you, but to do you good. I make the clouds my chariot, and clothe myself with the tempest as with a garment. The night hour is my time of coming to you. The dark, surging waves and billows are the pavement upon which I walk to you. Take courage! 'It is I'. Don't be afraid. 'It is I', your Friend, your Brother, your God, your Saviour! I am causing all the circumstances of your life to work together for your good. 'It is I' who brought this storm that assails you. Your affliction did not spring out of the ground, but came down from above, a heaven sent blessing, as an angel of light clothed in a robe of darkness. Cowper's hymn describes God's ways so well. We need often to be reminded that,

God moves in a mysterious way
His wonders to perform.
He plants His footsteps in the sea,
And rides upon the storm.

Deep, in unfathomable mines
Of never failing skill,
He treasures up His bright designs,
And works His sovereign will.

Ye fearful saints, fresh courage take,
The clouds you so much dread
Are big with mercy and will break
In blessings on your head.

Judge not the Lord by feeble sense,
But trust Him for His grace.
Behind the frowning providence
He hides a smiling face.

Alone In The Dark

His purposes will ripen fast,
Unfolding every hour.
The bud may have a bitter taste,
But sweet will be the flower!

William Cowper

He who loves you with an everlasting love has sent the storm, in love for your soul, not in anger. Be assured, my brother, be assured, my sister, your trial will not be forever. It will not always cast you down. 'It is I' who ordered, arranged, and controls it. In every stormy wind, in every dark night, in every lonely hour, in every rising fear may God the Holy Spirit give us grace to hear our Saviour's voice saying to us, 'Be of good cheer: it is I; be not afraid'.

Poor sinner, do you despair of life? Has guilt shut you up alone in darkness before God. If the Lord has stripped you, he will clothe you. If he has emptied you, he will fill you. If he wounds, he will heal. If he kills, he will make alive. If you know your need of him, come to him for mercy, for he has come to you with mercy. If now you seek his mercy, your cry for mercy is but the answer to mercy already bestowed.

Christ In The Ship
Fifth, as soon as the Saviour comes, the troubled soul receives him willingly into the ship; and immediately the ship lands in its desired haven. 'Then they willingly received him into the ship: and immediately the ship was at the land whither they went' (v. 21).

This language seems to indicate that a miracle of grace was immediately wrought. They were instantaneously saved from their danger. The desire of their hearts was fully met, and immediately! Instantly, they arrived at the longed-for haven of rest. As soon as Christ is willingly received into your ship, that reception of the Saviour is always accompanied with deliverance and rest (Matthew 11:28-30). Instant salvation is the gift of him who saves to the uttermost.

When the disciples got to about the middle of the lake, they seemed to be beaten. They could do nothing. But what they could not do, the Lord Jesus immediately did when he got into their ship. 'Not by works of righteousness which we have done, but according to his mercy he saved us'.

'They that go down to the sea in ships, that do business in great waters; These see the works of the LORD, and his wonders in the deep. For he commandeth, and raiseth the stormy wind, which lifteth up the waves thereof.

They mount up to the heaven, they go down again to the depths: their soul is melted because of trouble. They reel to and fro, and stagger like a drunken man, and are at their wits' end. Then they cry unto the LORD in their trouble, and he bringeth them out of their distresses. He maketh the storm a calm, so that the waves thereof are still. Then are they glad because they be quiet; so he bringeth them unto their desired haven. Oh that men would praise the LORD for his goodness, and for his wonderful works to the children of men' (Psalms 107:23-31).

Blessed is that night of darkness that introduces us more fully into the fellowship of and knowledge of our Lord Jesus Christ! And blessed be his name forever, there is a day coming, the long, eternal day of glory is at hand! 'So shall we ever be with the Lord'! If his presence made night not only endurable but even pleasant for these disciples, what joy his presence will make for us in that coming day!

There is coming a day when no heartaches shall come
No more clouds in the sky, no more tears to dim the eye.
All is peace forevermore on that happy golden shore,
What a day, glorious day that will be.

There'll be no sorrow there, no more burdens to bear,
No more sickness, no pain, no more parting over there;
And forever I will be with the One who died for me,
What a day, glorious day that will be.

What a day that will be when my Jesus I shall see,
And I look upon His face, the One who saved me by His grace;
When He takes me by the hand and leads me through the Promised Land,
What a day, glorious day that will be.

Jim Hill

Chapter 46

The Work God Requires

'The day following, when the people which stood on the other side of the sea saw that there was none other boat there, save that one whereinto his disciples were entered, and that Jesus went not with his disciples into the boat, but that his disciples were gone away alone; (Howbeit there came other boats from Tiberias nigh unto the place where they did eat bread, after that the Lord had given thanks:) When the people therefore saw that Jesus was not there, neither his disciples, they also took shipping, and came to Capernaum, seeking for Jesus. And when they had found him on the other side of the sea, they said unto him, Rabbi, when camest thou hither? Jesus answered them and said, Verily, verily, I say unto you, Ye seek me, not because ye saw the miracles, but because ye did eat of the loaves, and were filled. Labour not for the meat which perisheth, but for that meat which endureth unto everlasting life, which the Son of man shall give unto you: for him hath God the Father sealed. Then said they unto him, What shall we do, that we might work the works of God? Jesus answered and said unto them, This is the work of God, that ye believe on him whom he hath sent' (John 6:22-29).

The Jewish Talmud states that, 'The whole law was given to Moses at Sinai in 613 precepts'. It was summarized and given to the children of Israel in Ten Commandments (Exodus 20:1-17). Those Ten Commandments are holy, just and good. They reveal something of the character of God and show us our sin. Those Ten Commandments identify sin for us and show us our need of a Saviour, a Mediator, a Substitute, a Redeemer and Representative: One who can stand between man and God, to meet the demands of God for us and satisfy our needs before God as men. That Mediator is Christ, the Son of God.

Isaiah, writing by divine inspiration, reduced all the commandants to six, promising that all who (1) walk righteously, (2) speak uprightly, (3) despise the gain of oppression, (4) refuse to be bribed, (5) despise the shedding of blood, and (6) turn away from evil 'shall dwell on high' (Isaiah 33:15, 16). The Prophet Micah reduced all the commandments to just three (Micah 6:8). And during the days of his earthly ministry, our Lord Jesus Christ declared that all the commandments could be reduced to just two (Matthew 22:37-40).

The six hundred and thirteen precepts of the law, when reduced to their essence, require but two things from us: that we love God and that we love one another perfectly. Yet, these two great and good commandments condemn us all. Not one of us loves God or his neighbour perfectly. Still, hope is not gone. We can yet fulfil the law of God completely and perfectly. We can do all that God requires of man, if we keep the one commandment to which God promises eternal life. Are you interested in the one work which God requires of men and women, the one work by which sinners fulfil all the law of God? Our Lord Jesus states it plainly in verse twenty-nine. 'This is the work of God, that ye believe on him whom he hath sent.'

Our Lord Jesus knows the thoughts of every man's heart; and he knew the thoughts of these people who pretended to honour him. He knew their secret motives. Commenting on verses 22-26, J. C. Ryle wrote,

> Let us be real, true, and sincere in our religion, whatever else we are. The sinfulness of hypocrisy is very great, but its folly is greater still. It is not hard to deceive ministers, relatives, and friends. A little decent outward profession will often go a long way. But it is impossible to deceive Christ. 'His eyes are as a flame of fire' (Revelation 1:14). He sees us through and through. Happy are those who can say, 'Lord, thou knowest all things; thou knowest that I love thee' (John 21:17).

'Labour not for the meat which perisheth, but for that meat which endureth unto everlasting life, which the Son of man shall give unto you: for him hath God the Father sealed' (v. 27). What our Lord forbids here is not labour and care with regard to material things. The Lord God nowhere promotes sloth and idleness, and nowhere encourages indifference with regard to our earthly responsibilities. What he does forbid is excessive care for material things. Rather than devoting ourselves to that which is marked for destruction, the Lord Jesus here instructs us to seek him, to set our hearts on him, to devote ourselves to the pursuit of everlasting life, to live not for time but for eternity. This life everlasting is that which is the gift of the Christ, our God-man Mediator, 'the Son of man'. This Mediator, this Son of man, the Lord Jesus Christ, is that One that 'God the Father sealed', stamped with his royal signet, marked for security, and kept secret.

'Then said they unto him, What shall we do, that we might work the works of God?' (v. 28) We love works; don't we? Give us something to do; and we'll do it! That is the religion of man, the religion of the world, your religion, and my religion by nature. We all want to weave a web of righteousness of our own spinning, spinning a thread from our own entrails by which we might climb up to heaven. No man wants salvation free of cost.

Martin Luther was exactly right when he called works religion 'the devil's faeces'. Those who seek to be saved by works, he called 'the devil's martyrs', because they take great pains to go to hell.

'Jesus answered and said unto them, This is the work of God, that ye believe on him whom he hath sent' (v. 29). Did you read that right? 'This is the work of God', the one and only work that God requires of you and me, 'that ye believe on him whom he hath sent'. This is the work God requires, the work God performs, and the work God accepts. We read in 1 John 3:23, 'This is his commandment, that we should believe on the name of his Son Jesus Christ'. Faith in Christ is what God requires of man!

Four Things About Faith

I do not claim to know a lot about faith. I feel like the centurion who said, 'Lord, I believe, help thou my unbelief'. But I am very interested in this subject, and you ought to be. The word of God has a lot to say about faith.

Our Lord said, 'If thou canst believe, all things are possible to him that believeth' (Mark 9:23). 'If ye had faith as a grain of a mustard seed, ye might say to this sycamore tree, Be thou plucked up by the root, and be thou planted in the sea; and it should obey you' (Luke 17:6). 'If thou wouldest believe, thou shouldst see the glory of God' (John 11:40). He once said to a harlot, 'Thy faith hath saved thee'! (Luke 7:50). 'When he saw' the faith of four men who brought a sick friend to him, he said to the one they brought to him, 'Man, thy sins are forgiven thee' (Luke 5:20).

Paul wrote, 'Being justified, by faith we have peace with God' (Romans 5:1). He also said, 'By grace are ye saved through faith' (Ephesians 2:8). The word of God highly exalts faith! Here are four things revealed in the word of God about faith in Christ:

Faith Is The Foundation Grace

While love is the greatest of all graces and hope is the grace of comfort and expectation, faith is the foundation grace from which both love and hope spring (John 3:36; Mark 16:15, 16; Romans 10:11-15). The first evidence of life in the soul is faith. Faith in Christ is the proof that we have life. Believing on Christ we have been delivered from penal death in justification and spiritual death in regeneration.

No form of works, no religious profession, no amount of knowledge, no feelings and emotions can assure me that I am both absolved of guilt and born of God, but faith does (1 John 5:1).

As faith is the first evidence of life in the soul, so all true, spiritual life is sustained by faith. The child of God does not trust his emotions or his devotions, his feelings or his doings. He looks to Christ. 'The just shall live by his faith'! Spurgeon said, 'Hearty belief in God, his Son, his promises, his grace is the soul's life, neither can anything take its place. "Believe and live" is the standing precept both for saint and sinner.' John Flavel wrote, 'The soul is the life of the body. Faith is the life of the soul. Christ is the life of faith.'

Faith is the foundation grace. If you do not have faith in Christ, you do not have life. You are yet in your sins. The wrath of God is upon you.

This Faith Is The Gift Of God

You may believe many things. And there may be many types of faith in man. But saving faith, that faith that unites a sinner to Christ in a living, indissoluble union is the gift of God (Ephesians 2:8, 9). It is not the product of the flesh (John 1:12, 13; Philippians 1:29; Ephesians 1:19; Colossians 2:12).

Sinners Are Justified By Faith Alone

Faith is not the cause of justification. That is the grace of God. Faith is not the basis of justification. That is the blood of Christ. But faith is the voice of justification. Faith is the means by which we receive justification and by which God declares justification in the heart (Romans 4:25-5:11; Galatians 2:16).

True, Saving Faith Is A Growing Grace

Everything that is alive grows. If our faith is the dead faith of religious profession and doctrinal orthodoxy, it does not grow and increase. But if our faith is a living thing, it grows. 'Your faith groweth exceedingly' (2 Thessalonians 1:3). Believers 'grow in the grace and knowledge of our Lord Jesus Christ' (2 Peter 3:18). As faith grows assurance grows. As faith grows love for Christ and one another grows. As faith grows rest and peace increase. The more we grow in the faith of our Lord Jesus Christ the less concern we have for life, the less interest we have in the world, and the less fretful we are in trials!

There are many imitators of faith, many kinds of false faith that cannot save. False faith can do much to impress men and to impress us with ourselves. 'Thou believest that there is one God; thou doest well: the devils also believe, and tremble' (James 2:19). Even a casual reading of holy scripture reveals that false faith may be greatly enlightened and have great knowledge (Hebrews 6:4), excites the affections of the stony ground hearer, reforms the outward life and makes people religious Pharisees, speaks well of Christ as Nicodemus did in John 3, confesses sin with great sorrow like Judas.

False faith may humble itself in sackcloth and ashes with Ahab, repent like Esau, do religious works with diligence, be very generous as Ananias and Sapphira were, tremble at the word of God with Felix, experience much in religion (Hebrews 6:1-4), enjoy great religious privileges like Lot's wife, preach, perform miracles, and cast out demons (Matthew 7:23), attain high office in the church with Diotrephes, walk with great preachers as Demas walked with Paul, be peaceful and secure like the five foolish virgins and even persevere and hold out until the day of judgment (Matthew 7:22, 23).

Three Questions
What is saving faith? I cannot give you a plan or a blueprint and say, 'Follow this, do that, say the other, and you will have faith.' Anyone who tells you how you can obtain faith knows nothing about faith. The gift of faith is God's sovereign prerogative. God the Holy Spirit gives faith to chosen, redeemed sinners through the preaching of the gospel (Romans 10:17; 1 Peter 1:23-25). And saving faith has three characteristics (2 Timothy 1:12).

Knowledge
'I know whom I have believed'. A man cannot believe what he does not know. You cannot trust an unknown, unrevealed Saviour (John 20:30, 31). No one has faith in Christ until he knows something of the Bible, something about the character of God, something about his own depravity, guilt, and sin, and something of the person and work of Christ. You cannot trust Christ until you know who he is, what he accomplished at Calvary, and where he is now. Saving faith is not a leap in the dark. Saving faith is based upon revealed truth and knowledge (Romans 10:13, 14). But there is more to faith than knowledge. There must also be a …

Persuasion
'I am persuaded'. Paul said, I know what God has revealed, and I am persuaded that it is true. I not only read the scriptures and understand what they say about

the person and work of Christ, but I give full consent and agreement to them. It is impossible for anyone to have saving faith in the Lord Jesus Christ who puts a question mark on the word of God. Still, there is something more to saving faith than knowledge, or even persuasion. Many, I fear, are persuaded of gospel truth who do not have faith in Christ. This third, vital element of faith is missing in them.

Commitment

'I know whom I have believed and am persuaded that he is able to keep that which I have committed unto him against that day.' Paul committed himself to Christ. He trusted to Christ all the affairs of his life and trusted Christ alone for his everlasting acceptance with God.

> My life, my love I give to thee,
> Thou Lamb of God Who died for me;
> O may I ever faithful be,
> My Saviour and my God!

> Ralph Erskine Hudson

'Believe on the Lord Jesus Christ, and thou shalt be saved' (Acts 16:31). Thomas Brooks wrote, 'He that believeth on Christ shall be saved, be his sins never so many. He that believeth not on Christ must be damned, be his sins never so few.' 'He that believeth on the Son (of God) hath everlasting life: and he that believeth not the Son shall not see life; but the wrath of God abideth on him' (John 3:36).

Why is faith in Christ necessary? Much could and should be said in this regard. But for the sake of brevity, let me just give you three reasons for the necessity of faith, three reasons why we must trust the Lord Jesus Christ.

The only way fallen men and women can ever please the holy Lord God is by faith in Christ (Hebrews 11:6; Romans 3:31; 8:1-4). No sinner has ever pleased God, except by faith in Christ; and every sinner who trusts the Lord Jesus pleases God and fulfils all the law of God.

There is no true humility apart from faith. Grace is for the humble. God gives grace to the humble and resists the proud. But the only humble person in the world is the one who believes on the Lord Jesus Christ. Everyone else has something to claim as a ground of merit before God, or imagines that he does. Believers are truly humble. We need a Saviour and know it. We come to Christ with empty hands, trusting him for everything. We receive Christ and the grace of God in him as a gift, not a wage or reward. We trust Christ alone for our total, everlasting acceptance with God (1 Corinthians 1:30, 31)

> Nothing in my hands I bring,
> Simply to Thy cross I cling.
> Naked come to Thee for dress,
> Helpless look to Thee for grace!

> Augustus Montague Toplady

Faith in Christ is necessary, because there is no other way for a sinner to come to God and be saved (Romans 4:16). Christ alone is the Way (John 14:6). Christ alone is the Door (John 10:9). We cannot be saved any other way (Acts 4:12).

Do you have this saving faith in Christ? Do I? This question is vital. It must not be passed over lightly (2 Corinthians 13:5). Find the answer to this question and you will make your calling and election sure. Do you have faith in the Lord Jesus Christ? I cannot answer that question for you. You must answer for yourself. But this much I know: he who has saving faith experiences the power and grace of God in his Son. Faith is more than doctrine! Faith involves personal experience; and the experience is a growing experience.

He who has faith in Christ has great, high esteem for the Lord Jesus Christ, the Son of God. 'Unto you therefore which believe he is precious' (1 Peter 2:7). His blood is precious blood. His righteousness is precious to all who have no other righteousness but his. All who have faith in Christ renounce and continue to renounce all personal righteousness, knowing that all their righteousnesses are filthy rags! His very name is precious to all who know him, for his name reveals who he is.

'Then said they unto him, What shall we do, that we might work the works of God? Jesus answered and said unto them, This is the work of God, that ye believe on him whom he hath sent.' This is the work God requires, the work God performs, the work God gives. 'This is the work of God, that ye believe on him whom he hath sent'!

Chapter 47

Some Things That Are Sealed

'Labour not for the meat which perisheth, but for that meat which endureth unto everlasting life, which the Son of man shall give unto you: for him hath God the Father sealed' (John 6:27).

I have gone through the book of God many times marking those things we are told God has sealed. Every time I look at these things, I am both instructed in the things of God and blessed in my soul. May God the Holy Spirit be pleased to open the scriptures to our hearts by his grace and reveal these things that are sealed to us in the fresh experience of his grace.

A Sealed Saviour
'Labour not for the meat which perisheth, but for that meat which endureth unto everlasting life, which the Son of man shall give unto you: for him hath God the Father sealed.' The Lord Jesus here declares that he, as the Son of man, that One who gives everlasting life to all who trust him, is a sealed Saviour. 'For him hath God the Father sealed.' What does that mean?

The word that is translated 'sealed' throughout the New Testament means 'stamped for security, preserved, or kept secret'. Really, the sentence might be more correctly translated, 'him hath the Father sealed, God'. If that is the case, John is telling here the same thing Peter announced on the Day of Pentecost (Acts 2:22, 23). God the Father has demonstrated beyond question that this Man is God.

This is one of those many, precious places in holy scripture in which we see, in very few words, a huge volume of sacred theology. Here, in just seven words our Lord Jesus declares that all three persons of the triune Godhead concur and co-operate in the great work of redemption and grace by Christ Jesus. I fully agree with Robert Hawker, when he said,

'No doubt, all scripture is blessed, being given by inspiration of God; but there is a peculiar blessedness in these sweet portions, which at one view, represent the Holy Three in One, unitedly engaged in the sinner's redemption.'

Who could be the 'him' here spoken of, if not the Lord Jesus? Who, other than God the Father, could seal him? With whom was Christ sealed and anointed, except God the Holy Spirit? Who, but God, could give such a full, instructive and blessed testimony to the glorious foundation-truth of the whole Bible in just seven words? 'For him hath God the Father sealed.'

Let us ever behold, as the warrant of our faith, the divine authority of the Lord Jesus Christ, the Son of man, our Mediator. He (and he alone) is infinitely suited for our poor souls' needs in every state and every circumstance. The validity of all his gracious acts and deeds as our Substitute is founded in this: 'For him hath God the Father sealed', marked and stamped from eternity, by his choice, appointment, and decree, as the Lamb slain and accepted from the foundation of the world, and marked and stamped in time by his Spirit.

By the Spirit of prophecy (Acts 10:43).
By the Spirit of his anointing (his baptism).
By the Spirit he has given (Galatians 3:13, 14; Acts 2).
By the Spirit of revelation (John 16).

It was the Spirit of Jehovah that was upon him, when he was anointed to 'preach the gospel to the poor, to heal the broken hearted, to give deliverance to the captive, and the restoring of sight to the blind, to set at liberty them that are bruised, and to proclaim the acceptable year of the Lord.'

This great Saviour, whom God the Father has sealed, is thus held forth and recommended by the great seal of heaven to every poor sinner who knows his need of salvation. Every act of his love, every word of his lips, every deed of his hands, every work of his grace proclaims the Lord Jesus as 'him whom God the Father hath sealed'! Help poor sinners, O Lord God, by your blessed Spirit, to receive Christ the Saviour as the One sealed by God, and to rest in nothing short of being sealed by your Spirit.

In every act of faith, in every tendency of our souls let us live unto our blessed Saviour, with those same earnest longings of the church, when she cried out, 'Set me as a seal upon thy heart, as a seal upon thine arm; for love is strong as death; jealousy is cruel as the grave; the coals thereof are coals of fire, which hath a most vehement flame.'

A Sealed Book

First, we have a sealed Saviour. In Revelation 5 we are told about a sealed book (Revelation 5:1-7).

'And I saw in the right hand of him that sat on the throne a book written within and on the backside, sealed with seven seals. And I saw a strong angel proclaiming with a loud voice, Who is worthy to open the book, and to loose the seals thereof? And no man in heaven, nor in earth, neither under the earth, was able to open the book, neither to look thereon. And I wept much, because no man was found worthy to open and to read the book, neither to look thereon. And one of the elders saith unto me, Weep not: behold, the Lion of the tribe of Juda, the Root of David, hath prevailed to open the book, and to loose the seven seals thereof. And I beheld, and, lo, in the midst of the throne and of the four beasts, and in the midst of the elders, stood a Lamb as it had been slain, having seven horns and seven eyes, which are the seven Spirits of God sent forth into all the earth. And he came and took the book out of the right hand of him that sat upon the throne.'

The book John saw is the book of God's eternal decrees. It represents God's eternal purpose of grace in sovereign predestination, which includes all things. It is to this book that our great Surety referred when he said, 'Lo, I come: in the volume of the book it is written of me, I delight to do thy will, O my God' (Psalms 40:7, 8; Hebrews 10:5-10).

William Hendriksen said of this book, 'It symbolises God's purpose with respect to the entire universe throughout history, and concerning all creatures in all ages and unto all eternity.'

The Lord our God is a God of purpose, eternal, unalterable, purpose (Isaiah 46:9-11). The object of God's eternal purpose of grace in predestination is the salvation of his elect (Romans 8:28-30). Everything that comes to pass in time was purposed by God in eternity (Romans 11:36). And the object of God in all that he does is the effectual accomplishment of the everlasting salvation of his elect.

In election, God chose a people whom he would save. In predestination, he sovereignly ordained all things that come to pass to secure the salvation of his chosen. And in providence, he accomplishes in time what he purposed from eternity.

As John saw it, the book of God was closed, a mystery sealed with seven seals. The seven seals do not represent an imaginary 'seven dispensations' of time. The writing within and on the back and the seven seals simply means that God's purpose is full, complete, perfect, and unalterable. Nothing can be added to it. Nothing can be taken from it. The seven seals also tell us that God's purpose of grace is unknown, unrevealed, a secret known only to God, until Christ reveals it.

A Sealed People

In Revelation 7 we read about a sealed people. There is a vast multitude of people in this world called 'the elect', a people chosen in eternity and redeemed at Calvary, who must be sealed by the Spirit of grace (Revelation 7:1-4).

'And after these things I saw four angels standing on the four corners of the earth, holding the four winds of the earth, that the wind should not blow on the earth, nor on the sea, nor on any tree. And I saw another angel ascending from the east, having the seal of the living God: and he cried with a loud voice to the four angels, to whom it was given to hurt the earth and the sea, Saying, Hurt not the earth, neither the sea, nor the trees, till we have sealed the servants of our God in their foreheads. And I heard the number of them which were sealed: and there were sealed an hundred and forty and four thousand of all the tribes of the children of Israel.'

'The Lord is not slack concerning his promise, as some men count slackness; but is longsuffering to us-ward, not willing that any should perish, but that all should come to repentance' (2 Peter 3:9).

'After this I beheld, and, lo, a great multitude, which no man could number, of all nations, and kindreds, and people, and tongues, stood before the throne, and before the Lamb, clothed with white robes, and palms in their hands; And cried with a loud voice, saying, Salvation to our God which sitteth upon the throne, and unto the Lamb. And all the angels stood round about the throne, and about the elders and the four beasts, and fell before the throne on their faces, and worshipped God, Saying, Amen: Blessing, and glory, and wisdom, and thanksgiving, and honour, and power, and might, be unto our God for ever and ever. Amen' (Revelation 7:9-12).

When God saves a sinner, that sinner is sealed by the Holy Spirit, marked as God's own, secretly preserved and kept by God the Holy Spirit (Ephesians 1:12-14; 4:30). It is this sealing of the Spirit that was symbolised in the Old Testament rite of circumcision. The sealing of the Spirit is that circumcision of the heart that is made without hands (Romans 2:29; Colossians 2:11, 12).

We would be wise to make Ephesians 4:30 the motto of our daily walk. Is God the Holy Spirit grieved when a child of God forgets the Lord Jesus, and by indulgence in any sin, loses sight of those sufferings which he endured because of sin? Yes, he is grieved, communion with God the Father is interrupted, and all the agonies and bloody sweat of our dear Saviour are forgotten, when any ransomed soul lives a loose and careless life.

Shall I grieve the Holy Spirit, my divine Keeper, by the allowance of wickedness? God forbid! Would you grieve for me, O Lord, at such a sight? Can it be possible that a poor worm of the earth, such as I am, should excite such regard and attention? Such considerations should be enough to keep us from evil. Yet, we will run eagerly after the poisonous ooze of our own depraved hearts, except the Lord Jesus himself keep us from the evil by his blessed Holy Spirit!

Blessed, ever-gracious Lord, withdraw not your restraining influences; leave us not for a moment to ourselves! If you keep us, we shall be well kept! Blessed Son of God, 'Cast me not away from thy presence; and take not thy Holy Spirit from me'! Let me not grieve him by whom I am sealed unto the day of redemption! (Psalms 51:11).

God's church in this world is a sealed fountain. 'A garden enclosed is my sister, my spouse; a spring shut up, a fountain sealed' (Song of Solomon 4:12-15). The church of Christ is a garden flourishing with good works, works done for him, works which he has created in us. She is a garden planted by his grace and watered by his Spirit, so thoroughly and effectually watered that she has become herself a fragrant, fruitful fountain of gardens and living waters, with streams flowing out of her into all the world to refresh the earth. That is the picture drawn in the Song of Solomon 4:12-15. 'A garden enclosed is my sister, my spouse; a spring shut up, a fountain sealed. Thy plants are an orchard of pomegranates, with pleasant fruits; camphire, with spikenard, Spikenard and saffron; calamus and cinnamon, with all trees of frankincense; myrrh and aloes, with all the chief spices: A fountain of gardens, a well of living waters, and streams from Lebanon.'

Our works, the works of God's church, those works performed for Christ are never counted by us as being worthy of anything. We know that if we did all things perfectly, we would only have done what we should have done. We constantly repent even of our best, noblest, most righteous works, because 'all our righteousnesses are filthy rags' before the holy Lord God. But he whom we love and serve looks upon our puny works as his pleasant fruits. They are rich, sweet fragrances; the smell of which ravishes his heart. They are works of faith and love. They are works produced by him and honoured by him (Ephesians 2:10). That which is done by faith in Christ, arising from a heart of love for him, is honoured and accepted by him. Let us ever rest in his love and walk in communion with him. And let us faithfully serve our Redeemer who loved us and gave himself for us.

A Sealed Vision
In Isaiah 29 we learn that there are many in this world to whom the gospel of Christ and the word of God is a sealed vision.

'Stay yourselves, and wonder; cry ye out, and cry: they are drunken, but not with wine; they stagger, but not with strong drink. For the LORD hath poured out upon you the spirit of deep sleep, and hath closed your eyes: the prophets and your rulers, the seers hath he covered. And the vision of all is become unto you as the words of a book that is sealed, which men deliver to one that is learned, saying, Read this, I pray thee: and he saith, I cannot; for it is sealed: And the book is delivered to him that is not learned, saying, Read this, I pray thee: and he saith, I am not learned' (Isaiah 29:9-12).

To every sinner left to himself, not being taught of God, the book of God is a sealed vision, because 'the natural man receiveth not the things of the Spirit of God: for they are foolishness unto him: neither can he know them, because they are spiritually discerned' (1 Corinthians 2:14).

A Sealed Vengeance
In Deuteronomy 32 we see a fifth thing that is sealed. In this place the word translated sealed is, of course, a Hebrew word; and the meaning is slightly different. The word means 'closed up, ended, stopped'. In this chapter the Lord God warns the ungodly, those who, because they have no understanding, do not trust Christ and do not worship God, that the vengeance and wrath that he shall execute upon them is a sealed vengeance for the time appointed. Sinners, be warned, you shall not escape the vengeance of God, except you take refuge in Christ.

'Is not this laid up in store with me, and sealed up among my treasures? To me belongeth vengeance, and recompense; their foot shall slide in due time: for the day of their calamity is at hand, and the things that shall come upon them make haste' (Deuteronomy 32:34, 35).

'Because sentence against an evil work is not executed speedily, therefore the heart of the sons of men is fully set in them to do evil' (Ecclesiastes 8:11).

A Sealed Bag
All who are taught of God come to Christ and live by him (John 6:45). And all who come to Christ find, as they come to him, that their sins are in a bag cast behind God's back into the depths of the sea of infinite forgetfulness. So, the sixth thing described in the scriptures as a sealed thing is a sealed bag (Job 14:17).

'If a man die, shall he live again? all the days of my appointed time will I wait, till my change come. Thou shalt call, and I will answer thee: thou wilt have a desire to the work of thine hands. For now thou numberest my steps: dost thou not watch over my sin? My transgression is sealed up in a bag, and thou sewest up mine iniquity' (Job 14:14-17).

In ancient times when men died at sea, their bodies were placed in a weighted bag, which was sewn together and sealed. Then, they were cast into the depths of the sea. That is what God has done with our sins. They are cast 'into the depths of the sea'. When Christ died, by his one sacrifice for our sins, which were made to be his, he put away all our sins. They were buried in the sea of God's infinite forgiveness, put away, never to be brought up again. God Almighty will never charge us with sin, impute sin to us, remember our sins against us, or treat us any the less graciously because of our sin. That is forgiveness! 'Blessed is the man to whom the Lord will not impute sin.'

When Job asks, in verse 16, 'Dost thou not watch over my sin?' the obvious answer is, 'Yes'. And if he finds any, we are forever damned; but that cannot be, because he has cast them away in a sealed bag (Jeremiah 50:20).

A Seal Desired

The seventh thing is a seal desired. 'Set me as a seal upon thine heart, as a seal upon thine arm: for love is strong as death; jealousy is cruel as the grave: the coals thereof are coals of fire, which hath a most vehement flame' (Song of Solomon 8:6). This is a prayer which arises from the earnest hearts of God's believing children. Yet, it is a prayer any sinner desiring mercy, grace, and salvation might make at the throne of grace. 'Set me as a seal upon thine heart, as a seal upon thine arm'. The allusion here is to the high priest in Israel. The prayer is really twofold: We long to know that we have an interest in the love of Christ's heart; and we long to experience the power of his arm (Exodus 28:12, 29, 30, 36-38).

Believers know the meaning of this prayer by personal experience. It is the longing, the desire of a sinner seeking grace to know that his name is engraved upon the Saviour's heart. In the language of the psalmist, we say to the Lord Jesus, 'Say unto my soul, I am thy salvation'. I desire an interest in your love; but I want more. I want to know that I have an interest in your love. Write my name in your heart, and engrave it as a signet upon your heart, so that I may see it and know it.

Without question, there are many whose names are written on our Lord's heart who do not yet know it. Christ has loved them from all eternity. His heart has been set upon them from everlasting. But they have not yet seen the signet with their names written upon it. In all of his work our great High Priest bears the names that are upon his heart.

For them he makes intercession (John 17:9, 20; 1 John 2:1, 2). He bore their sins in his body upon the cursed tree (1 Peter 2:24; 3:18). He endured all the unmitigated wrath and horrid fury of divine judgment to the full satisfaction of justice for them (Isaiah 53:9-11). He made atonement for them, putting away their sins by the sacrifice of himself (Hebrews 9:26). He obtained eternal redemption for them by the merit of his blood (Hebrews 9:12). Upon them he pronounces the blessing of God (Numbers 6:24-27; Ephesians 1:3-6).

We want to know by personal experience the power of our Saviour's arm. We want always to see and know that our Redeemer's heart and hand are eternally engaged for us, engaged to accomplish our everlasting salvation. This is our souls' desire. We want to know and be assured that the Lord Jesus Christ is our High Priest, our Advocate, our sin-atoning Mediator before God. If we can know we have a place in his heart of love and that his arm is set to do us good, we want no more. All is well with our souls. His arm preserves us, protects us, and provides for us. This is the prayer we make. What more could we desire than this? 'Set me as a seal upon thine heart, as a seal upon thine arm'.

Four Pleas
Anytime we go to God in prayer, it is wise to not only make our request known to him, but also to offer a plea, an argument, a reason why he should grant the thing we ask. Be sure that you understand this: The only grounds upon which we can appeal to God for mercy are to be found in God himself (see Psalms 51:1-5). Our hope, our basis of appeal with God must be found in him.

Do you see how the spouse here urges her request? She says, 'Make me to know your love for me, because I know this concerning your love: It is as strong as death. It is as firm as the grave. It is as intense as fire. And it is as unquenchable as eternity. With these four pleas, we back up and press our suit for mercy.

1. Show me your love, for your love is strong as death. 'Love is strong as death'. The love of Christ is as irresistible as death; and the love of Christ triumphed over death for us. As death refuses to give up its victims, so the love of Christ refuses to give up its captives. Nothing shall ever cause the Son of God to cease from loving his people or ever let them go.

2. Show me your love, for your love is as firm as the grave. 'Jealousy is cruel as the grave'. These words would be more accurately translated, 'Jealousy is as hard as hell'. Our Lord is jealous over his people. He will not allow those he loves to be taken from him. You will more likely see the gates of hell opened, the fires of hell quenched, and the spirits of the damned set free than see the Son of God lose one of those who are engraved upon his heart (Romans 8:28-39). Those God has chosen he will never cast away. Those Christ has redeemed he will never sell. Those he has justified he will never condemn. Those he has found he will never lose. Those he has loved he will never hate.

3. Show me your love, for your love is as intense as fire. 'The coals thereof are coals of fire, which hath a most vehement flame'. These words seem to allude to that fire which always burned at the altar and never went out. Those coals of fire were always kept burning in the typical Levitical dispensation. The flame was originally kindled by God. It was the work of the priests to perpetually feed it with the sacred fuel. The love of Christ is like the coals of that altar which never went out, and more. The love of Christ for his own elect

is vehement, blazing, an intense love that never diminishes. The only cause of his love for us is in himself. There is nothing, no form of love to compare with his love. And the love of Christ for his elect is free, sovereign, eternal, saving, immutable love.

4. Show me your love, for your love is as unquenchable as eternity. 'Many waters cannot quench love, neither can the floods drown it' (Romans 8:37-39). No other love is really unquenchable, but our Saviour's love is. His love is eternal and everlasting, immutable and unalterable. The love of Christ is infinitely beyond that of a father or a mother, or a brother or a sister, or a husband or a wife. The love of Christ is the one and only love that passes knowledge, the one love that nothing in heaven, or earth, or hell is able to extinguish or cool, the one love whose dimensions are beyond all measure (Ephesians 3:14-19).

Unquenchable Love
Our Redeemer's love is here compared to fire that cannot be quenched. As such it is affirmed that 'waters', 'many waters' cannot quench it. Christ's love for us is something the floods cannot drown (Psalms 69:15; 93:3). The waters of God's wrath could not quench the love of Christ for his people. 'Having loved his own which were in the world, he loved them to the end.' It was our Saviour's matchless love for us that made him willing to endure all the horror of God's wrath in our stead.

The waters of shame and suffering sought to quench and drown it. They would have hindered its outflow, and come, like Peter, between the Saviour and the cross; but his love refused to be quenched on its way to Calvary. Herein was love! It leaped over all the barriers in its way. It refused to be extinguished or drowned. Its fire would not be quenched. Its life could not be drowned (Psalms 69:1-7).

The waters of death sought to quench it. The waves and billows of death went over the great Lover of our souls. The grave sought to cool and quench his love; but his love proved itself stronger than death. Neither death nor the grave could alter or weaken his love for us. It came out of both death and the grave as strong as before. Love defied death, and overcame it.

Even the floods of our sins could not quench the love of Christ for us. The waters of our unworthiness could not quench nor drown the love of Christ for our souls. Love is usually attracted to that which is loveable. When something ugly, unlovely, unattractive comes, love, so called, withdraws from its object. Not so here. All our unfitness and unloveableness could not quench nor drown the love of Christ. It clings to the unlovely, and refuses to be torn away.

The waters of our long rejection sought to quench it. Though the gospel showed us that personal unworthiness could not arrest the love of Christ, we continued to reject him and his love. We continued to hate him and despise his love. Yet, his love for us rose above our enmity to him, rose above our unbelief, and survived our hardness. In spite of everything we are and have done, his love was unquenched.

Though he has saved us by his matchless grace, the waters of our daily inconsistency seek to quench his love, but, blessed be his name, without success! Even after experiencing his adorable grace, we are constantly spurning his unspurnable love! What inconsistencies, coldness, lukewarmness, unbelief, worldliness, hardness, and utter ungodliness daily flows from us against the Saviour's love like a mighty flood to quench its fire and drown its life! Yet it survives all; it remains unquenched, unquenchable, and unchanged!

All these evils in us are like 'waters', 'many waters', like 'floods', torrents of sin, waves and billows of evil, all constantly labouring to quench and drown the love of Christ! They would annihilate any other love, any love less than his. But our Saviour's love is unchangeable and everlasting.

> I ask my dying Saviour dear
> To set me on His heart;
> And if my Jesus fix me there,
> Nor life, nor death shall part.
>
> As Aaron bore upon His breast
> The names of Jacob's sons,
> So bear my name among the rest
> Of Thy dear chosen ones.
>
> But seal me also with Thine arm,
> Or yet I am not right.
> I need Thy love to ward off harm,
> And need Thy shoulder's might.
>
> This double seal makes all things sure,
> And keeps me safe and well;
> Thy heart and shoulder will secure
> From all the host of hell.
>
> John Berridge

Chapter 48

Three Pearls Strung Together

'They said therefore unto him, What sign shewest thou then, that we may see, and believe thee? what dost thou work? Our fathers did eat manna in the desert; as it is written, he gave them bread from heaven to eat. Then Jesus said unto them, Verily, verily, I say unto you, Moses gave you not that bread from heaven; but my Father giveth you the true bread from heaven. For the bread of God is he which cometh down from heaven, and giveth life unto the world. Then said they unto him, Lord, evermore give us this bread. And Jesus said unto them, I am the bread of life: he that cometh to me shall never hunger; and he that believeth on me shall never thirst. But I said unto you, That ye also have seen me, and believe not. All that the Father giveth me shall come to me; and him that cometh to me I will in no wise cast out. For I came down from heaven, not to do mine own will, but the will of him that sent me. And this is the Father's will which hath sent me, that of all which he hath given me I should lose nothing, but should raise it up again at the last day. And this is the will of him that sent me, that every one which seeth the Son, and believeth on him, may have everlasting life: and I will raise him up at the last day' (John 6:30-40).

One of the glories of the gospel is its simplicity. It is so simple, and presented in such simple language, and is illustrated by such simple pictures that proud men who think they are wise stumble over the obvious and go to hell, while studying that which they think is profound. That was the problem the Jews in John 6 were having with the doctrine of Christ. Those standing before our Lord Jesus were Pharisees and the disciples of the Pharisees. They asked the Lord

Jesus what they had to do to do the works of God (v. 28), and he told them. 'This is the work of God, that ye believe on him whom he hath sent' (v. 29). Then, in verse 30 they asked him for a sign. 'They said therefore unto him, What sign shewest thou then, that we may see, and believe thee? what dost thou work?' Before he even answered them, those proud Jews started to brag about their ancestors and Moses' feeding them in the wilderness (v. 31).

Our Master seized the opportunity to declare that he is the Bread of Life, represented in the manna God sent down from heaven, to declare the purpose for which he came into the world, and to declare the certainty of his success in accomplishing his Father's will, which is the everlasting salvation of all his elect (vv. 32-40).

Here are three of our Lord's great sayings, strung together like pearls on a necklace. Each statement is as sweet as it is simple and as precious as it is profound. All three taken together form a deep mine of revealed truth, in which we find ore more precious than gold.

About Himself

Here is the first pearl. The Lord Jesus makes a statement about himself. He says in verse 35, 'I am the bread of life, he that cometh to me shall never hunger, and he that believeth on me shall never thirst'.

The Bread of God is the Lord Jesus Christ, whom the Father sent to redeem us from the curse of the law and death by sin. That typical bread had no power against even physical death. All who ate that bread in the wilderness died; but Christ is the true bread. He bestows eternal life. He says, 'I am the Bread of Life'. He is the great God, Jehovah, the 'I AM'! He is the Bread that came down from God. He is the Bread that gives spiritual and eternal life. And he is the Bread that nourishes and sustains that life.

Our Lord would have us know that he himself is the appointed and necessary food for man's soul. The soul of every man is naturally starving and famishing because of sin. Christ is given by God the Father to be the Satisfier, the Reliever, and the Physician of man's spiritual need. In him and his mediatorial offices, in him and his atoning death, in him and his priesthood, in him and his grace, love, and power, in him alone empty souls find their needs supplied. In him alone there is life. He is 'the Bread of life'.

Bread is used in scripture to represent food that is necessary, the food that sustains life, and the food that satisfies hunger. That is Christ our Saviour. We must have him, or we will die in our sins.

Bread is food that suits all. Some cannot eat meat, and some cannot eat vegetables. But all like bread. It is food both for the rich and the poor. So is it with Christ. He is just the Saviour that meets the needs of every class.

Bread is food we need daily. Other foods we may eat only occasionally. But we want bread every morning and evening in our lives. So is it with Christ. There is never a day in our lives that we do not need his blood, his righteousness, his intercession, and his grace. Well may he be called, 'The Bread of Life'!

Jesus of Nazareth is the Christ, the Messiah, whom God sent into the world, to quicken those that are dead in trespasses and sins (Ephesians 2:1), and to give eternal life 'to as many as the Father hath given him'. If we would have this life, we must come unto him. We must eat this Bread.

Do you know anything of spiritual hunger? Do I? Do we feel anything of craving and emptiness in conscience, heart, and affections? Let us distinctly understand that Christ alone can relieve and supply us, and that it is his office and work to do so. We must come to him by faith. We must believe on him. We must commit our souls into his hands. So coming, he pledges his royal word that we shall find lasting satisfaction both for time and eternity in him. It is written, 'He that cometh to me shall never hunger, and he that believeth on me shall never thirst.'

About His People
Here is the second pearl. Our blessed Saviour makes a statement about his people. In verse 37 the Son of God makes a broad, unconditional, unqualified, completely unguarded promise. 'him that cometh to me I will in no wise cast out'. What a great promise that is!

What do those words 'cometh to me' mean? They refer to that movement of the soul that takes place when a sinner, feeling his sins, and finding out that he cannot save himself, hears of Christ, applies to Christ, trusts in Christ, lays hold on Christ, and leans all the weight of his immortal soul on Christ, trusting Christ alone for his complete salvation. When that happens, a man is said, in scripture language, to 'come' to Christ. Coming to Christ is believing on Christ.

What did our Lord mean by saying, 'I will in no wise cast him out'? He meant that he will not refuse to save anyone who comes to him, no matter what he may have been. Your past sins may have been very many and very great. Your present sins may be very many and very great. Your weakness and infirmity may be very great. But if you come to Christ by faith, Christ promises to embrace you and promises to keep embracing you forever! He will receive you graciously, pardon you freely, place you in the number of his dear children, and give you everlasting life. He will receive all who come to him; and he will never cast out any who come for any reason or upon any condition.

'I will in no wise cast him out'! These are golden words indeed! They have softened many a dying pillow, and calmed many a troubled conscience. Let them sink down deeply into our hearts, and abide there continually. A day will come when flesh and heart shall fail, and the world can help us no more. Happy shall we be in that day, if the Spirit witnesses with our spirit that we have come to Christ.

About God's Will

Here is the third pearl. Our Lord Jesus, in verse 40, gives us a very clear statement about the will of God, a statement by which he clearly reveals the will of God. Three times in verses 38-40 our Saviour speaks of the will of God, our Heavenly Father.

'For I came down from heaven, not to do mine own will, but the will of him that sent me. And this is the Father's will which hath sent me, that of all which he hath given me I should lose nothing, but should raise it up again at the last day. And this is the will of him that sent me, that every one which seeth the Son, and believeth on him, may have everlasting life: and I will raise him up at the last day.'

He tells us that he was sent to do the will of God (v. 38). We know what this purpose is from Matthew 1:21 and Hebrews 10:1-14; where the Holy Spirit identifies the will of God as the salvation of his people.

The Son of God came into this world in our flesh to do the Father's will. The will of the Father and the will of the Son are one. 'I and my Father are one' (John 10:30). But the Son is speaking here as Jehovah's Servant (Isaiah 42:1-4). The design of God in redemption is to have a new heaven and a new earth wherein righteousness dwells perfectly and forever, to have a holy people, all like Christ, to populate that new creation, and to judge and destroy all things contrary to himself. This Christ came to do; and this he shall do (Isaiah 53:10, 11).

Our Saviour tells us that it is his Father's will that he lose none of those who were given and trusted to him, and for whom he was trusted in the everlasting covenant (v. 39).

The Lord Jesus speaks of a definite company of people who have been given to him by the Father in an everlasting covenant of grace. He refers to this blessed company six times in John 17 (see verses 2, 6, 9, 11, 12, 24). Each one that the Father gave to the Son in eternity past comes to him in time as a lost sinner to be saved. He will never forget them, forsake them, nor cast them out (John 10:24-30).

Eternal election and eternal predestination guarantee eternal preservation. Our Saviour declares that it is the sovereign will of God that all elected by the Father, redeemed by the Son, and called by the Spirit shall be raised from the grave to eternal glory, and that not one shall be lost. Our salvation, security, and resurrection rest not upon anything in us or anything done by us, but entirely upon the Father's choice, the Son's obedience and sacrifice, and the Spirit's operations of grace (Philippians 3:10, 11, 20, 21).

The Lord Jesus declares that 'every one which seeth the Son, and believeth on him, may have everlasting life: and I will raise him up at the last day' (v. 40).

This verse speaks of the same people referred to in the previous verses: God's elect. But election alone is not salvation. Election is unto salvation. Christ was the Lamb slain from the foundation of the world. Yet, he must come to earth and die, if we are to be saved. Even so, the elect were chosen to life in eternity; but they must be saved in the experience of grace in time. All the chosen must hear the gospel (Romans 10:17; 1 Peter 1:23-25). Each one must have Christ revealed to him. Each must see Christ for himself by faith as his righteousness, sanctification, and redemption. Each must believe on the Lord Jesus Christ with a sincere heart (John 3:18, 36: Romans 10:13-17; 1 Thessalonians 1:4-6). And all this great host of sinners, chosen, redeemed, and called, shall be preserved through all the events of providence, trials of faith, temptations of Satan, and their countless falls, and shall be raised up in glory at the last day (Jude 24, 25; Philippians 3:20, 21). Because this is the will of God!

Our blessed Saviour, the Lord Jesus Christ, will never allow any soul that comes to him to be lost and cast away. He will keep us safe in grace and unto glory, in spite of the world, the flesh, and the devil. Not one bone of his mystical body shall ever be broken. Not one lamb of his flock shall ever be left behind in the wilderness. He will raise to glory, in the last day, the whole flock entrusted to his charge; and not one shall be found missing.

'For our conversation is in heaven; from whence also we look for the Saviour, the Lord Jesus Christ: Who shall change our vile body, that it may be fashioned like unto his glorious body, according to the working whereby he is able even to subdue all things unto himself' (Philippians 3:20, 21).

'Now unto him that is able to keep you from falling, and to present you faultless before the presence of his glory with exceeding joy, To the only wise God our Saviour, be glory and majesty, dominion and power, both now and for ever. Amen' (Jude 24, 25).

Chapter 49

Freewill Crushed, Free Grace Exalted

'The Jews then murmured at him, because he said, I am the bread which came down from heaven. And they said, Is not this Jesus, the son of Joseph, whose father and mother we know? how is it then that he saith, I came down from heaven? Jesus therefore answered and said unto them, Murmur not among yourselves. No man can come to me, except the Father which hath sent me draw him: and I will raise him up at the last day. It is written in the prophets, And they shall be all taught of God. Every man therefore that hath heard, and hath learned of the Father, cometh unto me. Not that any man hath seen the Father, save he which is of God, he hath seen the Father. Verily, verily, I say unto you, he that believeth on me hath everlasting life. I am that bread of life. Your fathers did eat manna in the wilderness, and are dead. This is the bread which cometh down from heaven, that a man may eat thereof, and not die. I am the living bread which came down from heaven: if any man eat of this bread, he shall live for ever: and the bread that I will give is my flesh, which I will give for the life of the world' (John 6:41-51).

There is a hideously ugly monster, a beast that has risen up in the world, whose hide I would like to see nailed to the wall in every church building in the world. This beast has been around for a long, long time. We read about him in the Book of Revelation (Revelation 11:7; 13:1-4, 11, 12, 14, 15, 17, 18; 14:9-11; 15:2; 16:2, 10, 13; 17:3, 7, 8, 11-13, 16, 17; 19:19, 20; 20:4, 10). He arose from the sea, the pagan, idolatrous, Gentile world. He has many names; but his name is always 'Blasphemy'. He always ascribes to man the work of God. He is found in every part of the world, having 'seven heads'. He is very powerful, having 'ten horns'. He is found in high places, wearing 'ten crowns'. He is deceitful, like a leopard. He is destructive, walking through the forests of darkness with the feet of a bear. He is furious, devouring with the mouth of a lion. Multitudes have perished by him. But his number is 'the number of a man' 666, assuring us that he shall meet with frustration, failure, and defeat.

This beast must be slain. And he will be slain, not by might, nor by power, but by the Spirit of God. He will be slain by the preaching of the gospel.

Though the Philistines propped him up again and again Dagon their god fell on his face before the ark of God, with his hands broken off his arms and his head broken off his body. So, too, free-will must fall before our Saviour. As the ark of God was exalted as Dagon lay in the dirt before it, so when Christ is exalted, free-will will be laid in the dirt before him. As Dagon and the ark of God could not abide in the same house, so free-will and free grace cannot abide together. One or the other must be pushed out of the house. In the house of God faithful men make it their business to push free-will out of the house, to throw it in the dirt before our God, trample it beneath our feet, and cast it out.

Idolatry

Nothing in all the world is more foolish, more debasing to humanity, more dishonouring to God, and more assuredly damning to the souls of men than idolatry. It is pathetic to see men and women worship gods that other men have made, dumb gods, made by the hands of ignorant men. Idolatry is hideously evil (Psalms 115:4-8). But the most abominable form of idolatry in the world is that which Paul calls 'will worship', the worship of yourself (Colossians 2:23). Those who attribute salvation in whole or in part to the will, work, or worth of man are the most abominably evil idolaters in the world, for they worship themselves. Free-willism is the worship of self. Legalism is the worship of self. Freewill works religion makes man his own Saviour, for it makes the will, work, or worth of man the determining factor in salvation.

If your salvation, in whole or in part, is looked upon by you as something that is dependent upon or determined by your will or your works, you are a lost, Christless soul, an idolater. You may talk about God and grace, Christ and redemption, the Holy Spirit and regeneration; but you really worship yourself. You trust in your own decision. Your confidence is in your personal goodness. Your peace is derived not from what Christ has done, but from what you have done. Redemption is something accomplished for us altogether outside ourselves. Our hope is outside of us, not in our experience, but in God's Son. But in your opinion the thing that separates you from the damned is not the will of God, the work of Christ, and the call of the Spirit, but your own will, your own work, and your own worth. If I have described you and your religion,

I want to go directly into the dark, idolatrous chambers of your heart and destroy your gods.

Gospel truths of the greatest magnitude and importance follow each other in rapid succession in this chapter. I am sure that there is much more in the chapter than has yet been declared; but I call your attention to just five things in these verses.

A Gin to Entrap

First, we see the fulfilment of Isaiah's prophecy in verses 41 and 42. Isaiah prophesied that the Lord Jesus, that one who would be born of a virgin, the Messiah, would be to many a gin and a snare, a stone of stumbling and a rock of offence (Isaiah 8:14, 15); and so it has come to pass (vv. 41, 42). He who is our Saviour, the Sanctuary in whom we take refuge and hide, is to others a gin and a snare, by which their souls are snared, entrapped, and carried away to hell (Romans 9:30-10:4; 1 Peter 2:7, 8).

Because he very simply and very plainly declared himself to them, because he said in no uncertain terms, 'I am the bread which came down from heaven', because he said, 'I am the Christ', the Jews began to murmur. They stumbled at that which rejoices the hearts of God's elect. They murmured against the very thing we find most delightful. Why? What is the difference between them and us? It is the difference God has made by his distinguishing grace (1 Corinthians 4:7).

Our Lord's humiliation, the very fact that he made himself of no reputation, while he was upon earth, is a stumbling-block to many. Like these Jews, multitudes today say, 'Is not this Jesus, the son of Joseph, whose father and mother we know? How is it then that he says, I came down from heaven?' Had our Lord come as a conquering king, with wealth and honours to bestow on his followers and mighty armies in his train, they would have been willing enough to receive him. But a poor, lowly, suffering Messiah was an offence to them. Their pride refused to believe that such a one was sent from God.

That should not surprise us. It is human nature showing itself in its true colours. We see the same thing in the days of the Apostles. Christ crucified was 'to the Jews a stumbling-block, and to the Greeks foolishness' (1 Corinthians 1:23). The cross of Christ was an offence to many wherever the gospel was preached in that day; and the same thing is true today. The offence of the cross has not ceased. There are multitudes of religious people who despise the distinctive doctrine of the gospel, because the doctrine of the cross is humbling to man. Most everyone approves of Christ's exemplary service to others; but they despise the expiation of sin by his blood. They love to talk about what they call his 'moral principles', but they cannot tolerate blood atonement, penal substitution and the satisfaction of justice by his sacrifice. His self-denial they admire; but his doctrine they despise.

Speak to the religionists of this world about Christ's blood, about Christ being made sin for us, about Christ's death being the corner-stone of our hope, about his poverty being our riches, about his obedience being our righteousness, about his death being our life, and you will discover that they hate these things with a deadly hatred; and they will show their hatred for you, if you dare assert these truths. The offence of the cross is not yet ceased.

Human Inability

Second, our Lord plainly declares in verse 44 the utter inability of man; man's complete helplessness and inability to believe on him. 'No man can come unto me, except the Father which hath sent me draw him'. Until the Father draws the heart of man by his grace, man will not believe.

It is too obvious to need comment that coming to Christ is merely another word for believing on Christ. It is not a physical but a spiritual coming to Christ that is necessary and saving. But this coming is impossible to man. Our Saviour says, 'No man can come unto me'. That is to say, 'No man has the ability to come unto me'. No man in his natural state can come to Christ, 'Because the carnal mind is enmity against God: for it is not subject to the law of God, neither indeed can be' (Romans 8:7).

Fallen man has neither the power nor the will to come to Christ. Man is dead in trespasses and in sins. He has no power to give himself life. He is spiritually impotent. Blind, he sees no need to come to Christ. Walking in darkness, he cannot know the way. Unregenerate, his heart is set on other things.

Men boast and brag about their will. Men everywhere; papists, pagans and Pentecostals, Buddhists, Brahmans and Baptist, Methodists, Moravians and Mennonites all love to talk about man's 'free will'. All defend the doctrine of man's 'free will'. Even atheistic philosophers defend the blasphemous notion of 'free will'.

But our Lord makes it plain that man's problem is his will. What is man's inability? It is not a physical inability that keeps sinners from Christ. It is not a moral inability that keeps them from coming to the Lord Jesus. It is the very will of man that keeps him from the Saviour. It is his corrupt will that holds him in bondage. Sinners cannot come because they will not come; and they will not come because they cannot come.

No man can come to Christ by nature because faith is the gift and operation of God the Holy Spirit. A new nature must be put in you, or you cannot come. A new heart must be put in you, or you cannot come. A new creation must be performed in your soul by God the Creator, or you cannot come. Unto you it must be given by God the Holy Spirit to believe on Jesus Christ, or you cannot come (Ephesians 2:8, 9; Colossians 2:10-15).

Yet, inability is no excuse for unbelief. The fact is sinners do not come to Christ because they do not want to come to him. You are responsible for your own soul. Your inability to come to Christ does not make you any less responsible. If you are lost at last, it will be your own fault. If you go to hell, you will go to hell, as our Saviour said, because 'Ye will not come to me that ye might have life' (John 5:40). Your blood will be on your own head.

Divine Efficacy
Third, our Lord sets before us the divine efficacy of God's free, sovereign, saving grace in him. He shows us this great efficacy in three things: the drawing of the Father (v. 44), the teaching of the Father (v. 45), the revelation of the Father (v. 46).

If ever you are saved, if ever you come to Christ, you must be drawn to him by God's sovereign, irresistible grace, drawn to him by the irresistible force of his grace. 'No man can come to me, except the Father which hath sent me draw him: and I will raise him up at the last day (v. 44). Oh, what a blessed 'except'! 'No man can come to me, except the Father which hath sent me draw him'! And if the Father draws you to the Saviour, you will come to him. We know that because he says, 'and I will raise him up at the last day'!

The word 'draw' suggests the idea of someone drawing water out of a well. No one begs and pleads for the water to get into the bucket! No, if you go to the well to get water, you reach down and, by an act of your own strength, you act upon the water, dipping the bucket in and pulling the water up to yourself. In the same way, sinners are drawn to Christ. God sends his Spirit to the chosen, redeemed sinner. God performs a work on and in the poor, lost, spiritually dead sinner called 'regeneration', or 'the new birth'. And God graciously draws the object of his mercy to Christ.

This word 'draw' is used in a few other places in the New Testament. Everywhere it is used, we see the same thing. It implies force and coercion. It never implies or suggests an invitation or even an urging. In Acts 16:19 those who were enriched by the demon-possessed girl 'caught Paul and Silas and drew them into the marketplace unto the rulers'. In Acts 21:30 the Jews 'took Paul, and drew him out of the temple ... and ... went about to kill him'. They were not begging and pleading with Paul. They drew him. They forcibly dragged him. In James 2:6 we are warned to beware of rich men who draw believers before the judgment seats. Again, the word does not suggest an invitation, but an irresistible force. God the Holy Spirit effectively and successfully draws the chosen, redeemed sinner to Christ. There are no exceptions. The call of God is always irresistible, effectual, and saving.

Look at verse 45. If you are saved, you must be taught of God; and all who are taught of God come to Christ and are saved by Christ. 'It is written in the prophets, And they shall be all taught of God. Every man therefore that hath heard, and hath learned of the Father, cometh unto me'. Read Isaiah 54:13, Jeremiah 31:34 and in Micah 4:2.

'They shall be all taught of God'. All who are ordained to eternal life, all who were given to Christ and are chosen in him, all for whom he died and obtained eternal redemption, all the children of God by special adoption and grace, sooner or later, shall be taught of God. Read on. 'Every man therefore that hath heard, and hath learned of the Father, cometh unto me'. God's teaching is always effectual. Our Lord did not say, 'Every man that hath heard and learned of the preacher comes unto me.' He said, 'Every man that hath heard and learned of the Father cometh unto me.'

Everyone who hears the voice of the Father's mercy, love, and grace in the gospel learns of him the way of life and peace and salvation by Christ. All who are taught of God, by the sweet force of his grace, come to Christ. Every sinner who is taught of God, hearing his declarations and promises of grace in Christ, ventures his soul on Christ and commits it to him, trusting him, relying on his person, his blood, his righteousness and his sacrifice, for peace, pardon, justification, atonement, acceptance with God, righteousness, sanctification, and eternal life.

If ever you come to Christ, it will be because he, as the God-man Mediator, has become the revelation of God, the word of God to you. 'Not that any man hath seen the Father, save he which is of God, he hath seen the Father' (v. 46). The hymn writer says,

A form of words, though e'er so sound,
Can never save a soul;
The Holy Ghost must give the wound,
And make the wounded whole.

Though God's election is a truth,
Small comfort there I see,
Till I am told by God's own mouth,
That He has chosen me.

That Christ is God I can avouch,
And for His people cares,
Since I have prayed to Him as such,
And He has heard my prayers.

That sinners black as hell, by Christ
Are saved, I know full well;
For I His mercy have not missed,
And I am as black as hell.

Thus, Christians glorify the Lord,
His Spirit joins with ours,
In bearing witness to His Word,
With all His saving powers.

Joseph Hart

Faith's Assurance

In verse 47, our blessed Saviour gives a word of sweet assurance to faith. Here it is. 'Verily, verily, I say unto you, he that believeth on me hath everlasting life.' If you find yourself believing on the Lord Jesus, you already possess eternal life. Faith does not cause you to have it. Faith is the assurance that you have it, the assurance that you are chosen of God, redeemed by Christ, called by the Spirit, taught of God, and born again (Hebrews 11:1; 1 John 5:1).

This salvation is a present thing, a present possession that lasts forever and can never be taken away, lost, or destroyed. 'Verily, verily, I say unto you, he that believeth on me hath everlasting life.'

Many seem to think that forgiveness and acceptance with God are things which we cannot attain in this life, that they are things which are to be earned by a long course of mourning and anguish, things we may receive at the bar of God at last, but must never hope to enjoy in this world. That is horribly wrong. Our Saviour says, 'Verily, verily, I say unto you, he that believeth on me hath everlasting life'! If you believe on the Lord Jesus Christ, your name is in the book of life, your sins are blotted out, and you have a clear title to heaven. Neither Satan, nor hell, nor even you can alter or overthrow the work of God! 'He that believeth on the Son hath everlasting life: and he that believeth not the Son shall not see life; but the wrath of God abideth on him' (John 3:36).

Bread For The Hungry

Then, lastly, our blessed Saviour, by the most simple picture imaginable, declares himself to be the Bread of Life, living bread for hungry souls.

'I am that bread of life. Your fathers did eat manna in the wilderness, and are dead. This is the bread which cometh down from heaven, that a man may eat thereof, and not die. I am the living bread which came down from heaven:

if any man eat of this bread, he shall live for ever: and the bread that I will give is my flesh, which I will give for the life of the world' (vv. 48-51).

Salvation is to be had only by feeding on Christ, only by trusting his obedience unto death as our Substitute; and that is exactly how we must live upon him. 'As ye have therefore received Christ Jesus the Lord, so walk ye in him' (Colossians 2:6). As bread is the staff of life for the body, so Christ, the Bread of Heaven, is the life of the soul. And, as the body cannot subsist without daily food, so neither can the soul subsist without Christ, the Bread of Life. 'Lord, evermore give us this bread'!

Chapter 50

A Hard Saying Or Sweet Bread To Eat?

'I am that bread of life. Your fathers did eat manna in the wilderness, and are dead. This is the bread which cometh down from heaven, that a man may eat thereof, and not die. I am the living bread which came down from heaven: if any man eat of this bread, he shall live for ever: and the bread that I will give is my flesh, which I will give for the life of the world. The Jews therefore strove among themselves, saying, How can this man give us his flesh to eat? Then Jesus said unto them, Verily, verily, I say unto you, Except ye eat the flesh of the Son of man, and drink his blood, ye have no life in you. Whoso eateth my flesh, and drinketh my blood, hath eternal life; and I will raise him up at the last day. For my flesh is meat indeed, and my blood is drink indeed. He that eateth my flesh, and drinketh my blood, dwelleth in me, and I in him. As the living Father hath sent me, and I live by the Father: so he that eateth me, even he shall live by me. This is that bread which came down from heaven: not as your fathers did eat manna, and are dead: he that eateth of this bread shall live for ever. These things said he in the synagogue, as he taught in Capernaum. Many therefore of his disciples, when they had heard this, said, This is an hard saying; who can hear it?' (John 6:48-60).

In the sixth chapter of John's Gospel, after feeding five thousand men with five loaves of bread and two small fish, our Lord Jesus amassed a huge following. The multitude that followed him did not trust him. They were not converted. They just wanted more religious excitement. They wanted to see more miracles. And they wanted more free bread (v. 26).

In verses 27-36 the Lord Jesus taught these men and women the necessity of faith, the necessity of trusting him. Then he proclaimed to them, and proclaims to us, the blessed freeness and certainty of everlasting salvation to all who trust him (vv. 37-40).

In verses 44-47 the Master declares the utter inability of man and the blessed, sovereign efficacy of God's free, saving grace. Then, beginning in verse 48 the Lord Jesus declares himself to be the Bread of Life and explains that faith in him, trusting him, is like eating bread and living by the bread eaten.

After all that, after seeing the miracle, after eating the loaves and fish, after hearing the Saviour's discourse about the necessity of faith, the freeness and certainty of God's salvation, the inability of man and the efficacy of God's saving grace, after the Lord Jesus uses the simple eating of bread to illustrate what faith is, we read in verse 60 'Many therefore of his disciples, when they had heard this, said, This is an hard saying; who can hear it?'

Here are five statements that will summarize our Lord's doctrine in our text. These five things to the unbelieving are hard, offensive things. To the believer, they are sweet, delightful things.

Jesus Christ Our Saviour Is God
We see this very clearly stated in verse 48, where the Lord Jesus says, 'I am the bread of life'. With those two words, 'I am', he points us back to Exodus 3:13, 14, where Moses asked the Lord God, who spoke to him out of the bush, 'What is thy name?' The answer was, 'I AM'. When our Saviour said, 'I am that bread of life', he used the title 'I am' to identify himself as the great Jehovah, who appeared to Moses in the bush, plainly asserting his eternal deity.

Remember, the purpose of John's Gospel is to show us the glorious divinity of our blessed Saviour (John 1:1-3; 14:9). It should not be surprising to us that John was inspired to record our Lord's use of 'I am' throughout this gospel narrative to identify himself as God (John 6:35, 48-58; 8:12; 10:9, 11, 14-16, 36; 11:25; 13:19; 14:6-9; 15:1-10; 18:37, 49; 19:19-22).

'I am the bread of life' (6:35, 48-58). 'If any man eat of this bread, he shall live forever'. Christ is the true and only Bread that not only gives, but also upholds and maintains spiritual, eternal life. He is the Bread which every sinner needs and without which all will perish.

'I am the light of the world' (8:12). He who follows Christ, the Light, no longer walks in the darkness of tradition, superstition, idolatry, and sin, but rather walks in the light of the knowledge of the glory of God.

'I am the door' (10:9). Christ is the only Door of entrance into the kingdom of God. He is the Door of the sheep. And all who enter in by him shall be saved.

'I am the good shepherd' (10:11, 14-16). The good Shepherd gave his life for his sheep, knows his sheep, gathers his sheep, and keeps his sheep.

'I am the Son of God' (10:36). Thus the man Christ Jesus asserted his divinity, his eternality, the plurality of Persons in the Godhead, and the unity of the divine Persons; and the Jews to whom he spoke understood him perfectly (10:33).

'I am the resurrection' (11:25). Those who believe on him shall never die.

'I am he' (13:19). He of whom the prophets spoke, whose name is I AM, who came to save his people (18:49).

'I am the way'. Without him we cannot come to God.

'I am the truth'. Without him we cannot know God.

'I am the life' (14:6). Without him we cannot live before God.

'I am the vine' (15:1-10). We are the branches. The branches bear fruit of the Vine. But in order to bear fruit, they must be pruned and must abide in the Vine.

'I am king' (18:37; 19:19-22). He is King everywhere, over all things, forever. He must reign! The Father decreed it. He deserves it. And all his saints desire it and delight in it.

Jesus Christ is God our Saviour, Jehovah incarnate, over all God, blessed forever!

Christ Is The Bread By Which We Live

'Your fathers did eat manna in the wilderness, and are dead' (v. 49). The manna in the wilderness was typical of and portrayed Christ, just as the Rock which gave forth water was a type of Christ (1 Corinthians 10:4). Neither the manna nor the water that flowed from that Rock had any saving benefit or efficacy, even to give or maintain physical life, let alone spiritual, eternal life. Those who ate the manna and drank the water died physically; and, evidently, many perished eternally, though they ate that bread and drank water out of the rock, for they entered not into Canaan (Hebrews 3:17-19).

Christ is the Bread of God. The Bread that comes from God and the Bread that satisfies God (Matthew 3:17; 17:5). He is the Bread given by God, the gift of God (1 Corinthians 9:15). He is the living Bread and the Bread of Life. He is Life; and he gives life; and we live by him. He is sweet Bread and satisfying Bread. (John 6:32-35).

Before We Could Live, Christ Had To Die

'This is the bread which cometh down from heaven, that a man may eat thereof, and not die' (v. 50). If a man eats of the Bread of Life, he has life eternal. He shall never die. Eating Christ, the Bread of Life, is believing on him, receiving him by faith. Believing on Christ is expressed by eating, because eating is the reception of food into our bodies for the sustenance of physical life; so receiving Christ by faith is drawing life from him.

We do not get life by eating bread; but we draw from the bread we eat that by which life is sustained, by which we grow, by which we are nourished, and by which we are strengthened. So it is with spiritual, eternal life. We do not get life by faith in Christ. Faith is the result of life. But we draw life from Christ by faith. Faith is believing on the Son of God, trusting the Lord Jesus, entering in by Christ the Door, coming to Christ the Lamb, bowing to Christ the King, laying hold on Christ our Hope, eating Christ the Bread of Life, drinking from Christ the Fountain, building on Christ the Foundation, looking to Christ the Saviour. But we could never draw life from Christ had he not first died as our Substitute. He became to us living Bread by dying in our stead, 'I am the living bread which came down from heaven: if any man eat of this bread, he shall live for ever: and the bread that I will give is my flesh, which I will give for the life of the world' (v. 51).

Bread is made from the flour of corn, rye, barley, wheat, or some other grain. The grain has to be thrashed and sifted, ground and sifted, sifted and kneaded, and baked before it is suitable food for the table. Thus, 'It behoved Christ to suffer' (Luke 24:46).

He who is our Saviour, the life-giving Bread of God, is the Lamb of God slain from the foundation of the world, by whom we live. The 'flesh and blood of the Son of man' refer to the sacrifice of his own body upon the cursed tree, when he died for his elect. Those words speak of the atonement made by his obedience unto death, the satisfaction made by his sufferings as our Substitute, the redemption accomplished by his enduring the penalty of the law and justice of God for our sins in his own body on the tree. It is only by the crucified Lamb of God that we have redemption, the forgiveness of sins and eternal life (Hebrews 10:18-22).

Faith Is A Spiritual Act Of The Heart
Faith in Christ is an intensely personal thing, a spiritual act of the heart. It is written, 'With the heart man believeth unto righteousness' (Romans 10:9-13). But these Jews, like Nicodemus, were trying to interpret spiritual things in a carnal sense (John 3:4). 'The Jews therefore strove among themselves, saying, How can this man give us his flesh to eat?' (v. 52).

Multitudes there are today who, like those Jews at Capernaum, vainly seek to make faith in Christ and the worship of God carnal things. Multitudes ignorantly imagine that eternal life can be obtained by carnal means. Papists teach that our Lord is here, in this passage, talking about eating the bread and wine of what they call 'the Eucharist', or 'holy communion', which by some religious mumbo jumbo is transformed into the body and blood of Christ.

Many Protestants, who vigorously denounce the heresies of Rome, teach essentially the same heresy, telling men that they spiritually eat and drink the body and blood of Christ in what they call the 'sacrament' of the Lord's Supper. Religious fundamentalists make salvation to be nothing more than a logical decision, repeating a scripted prayer, walking a church aisle, or saying, 'I believe in Jesus'.

Man tries hard to make religion a matter of forms and ceremonies, of doing and performing, of sacraments and ordinances, of sight and of sense. Fallen man despises that which is truly spiritual, that which makes the heart the principal thing. Man labours to keep everything on his own level; carnal, fleshly, material, earthly. Ever beware of the influence of Rome. It is always evil. It is never good. Baptism and the Lord's Supper are ordinances of God, prescribed and instituted by our Saviour. They are blessed, blessed means of worship; but they are not 'sacraments'. They are not means of grace.

The 'eating and drinking', without which there is no life in us, is the believing reception of Christ and his sacrifice, which takes place when a sinner trusts Christ crucified as his Saviour. It is an inward and spiritual act of the heart and has nothing to do with the body. Whenever a sinner, feeling his own guilt and sin, lays hold on Christ, trusting his righteousness and his sin-atoning blood, he 'eats the flesh of the Son of man, and drinks his blood'. His soul feeds on Christ's sacrifice by faith, just as his body would feed on bread. Believing, we 'eat'. Believing, we 'drink'. And that which we eat and drink, and from which we benefit, is the atonement made for our sins by Christ's death in our room and stead on Calvary. We eat his flesh, the righteousness of the incarnate God our Saviour. We drink his blood, his justice-satisfying, sin-atoning blood. And, just as believer's baptism portrays the fulfilment of all righteousness by the obedience of Christ, the Lord's Supper portrays our faith in the obedience of Christ as our Mediator unto death.

'Then Jesus said unto them, Verily, verily, I say unto you, Except ye eat the flesh of the Son of man, and drink his blood, ye have no life in you. Whoso eateth my flesh, and drinketh my blood, hath eternal life; and I will raise him up at the last day' (John 6:53, 54).

The decree of God in predestination does not make the work of God in time meaningless, but guarantees that it shall be done. And that which God did in eternity does not make his work in time unnecessary. What God did in eternity simply made certain that it would come to pass in time. Though our Lord Jesus is the Lamb slain from the foundation of the world, still he had to come to earth and die. The decrees of God do not make the accomplishments of Christ in time unnecessary. Even so, while Christ has been given a people and has redeemed them by his life and death, a people saved by him from eternity

(Romans 8:29), they must hear the gospel and believe (John 6:37-44; Romans 10:13-15). Christ must be received and believed or you will have no life!

You must trust the Son of God. Just as no one can eat and drink for you, no one can believe for you. You must believe on the Lord Jesus Christ. 'Just as there was no safety for the Israelite in Egypt who did not eat the passover-lamb, in the night when the first-born were slain, so there is no life for the sinner who does not eat the flesh of Christ and drink his blood' says J. C. Ryle.

Trusting Christ, I have eternal life now; and I shall have it forever in resurrection glory. 'Whosoever believeth that Jesus is the Christ is born of God' (1 John 5:1). It is not how much faith I have, but whom I believe that matters. That is exactly what our Saviour tells us in verse 55. 'For my flesh is meat indeed, and my blood is drink indeed.'

Paul said, 'I know whom I have believed'. It is not just eating that nourishes a man. You get nourishment only if you eat the right food. If you eat poison, you will die. The same thing is true spiritually. Christ's flesh, his obedience, is true life-giving meat; and his blood, his death, is saving, cleansing blood. It is not what I think of myself that matters, or even what you think of me. It is, 'What think ye of Christ?' That's the only thing that matters. It is not my standing before you that gives me peace, but my standing in Christ. He is able to present us faultless before the presence of his glory. It is not my ability to keep the law that determines my eternal destiny, but Christ's fulfilment of the law for me. 'Christ is the end of the law for righteousness to everyone that believeth'! It is not my being free from sin that gives me free access to God, but Christ's being free from sin. And in him, I am free from sin (1 Peter 4:1, 2). It is not my mourning, groaning, and suffering under the load of sin that appeases and satisfies a holy God, but the fact that Christ groaned and suffered under the weight of my guilt and sin. 'For Christ also hath once suffered for sins, the just for the unjust, that he might bring us to God, being put to death in the flesh, but quickened by the Spirit' (1 Peter 3:18). I am not accepted by my best effort. I am 'accepted in the Beloved'! And it is not my ability to keep myself that sustains me in faith, and grace, and hope, but his ability to keep me. 'We are kept by the power of God through faith'! 'He is able to keep you from falling'!

The life we live by faith in Christ is a life that is inseparable from Christ's own life.

'He that eateth my flesh, and drinketh my blood, dwelleth in me, and I in him. As the living Father hath sent me, and I live by the Father: so he that eateth me, even he shall live by me. This is that bread which came down from heaven: not as your fathers did eat manna, and are dead: he that eateth of this bread shall live for ever. These things said he in the synagogue, as he taught in Capernaum' (John 6:56-59).

A Hard Saying Or Sweet Bread To Eat?

Our blessed Saviour here declares that the life we have in him is a living, vital union with him (John 15:1-5). Just as Christ the God-man, our Surety, our Mediator lives by the Father, beside the Father, and with the Father, we live by Christ, beside Christ, and with Christ. Just as Christ cannot be separated from the Father, we cannot be separated from the Saviour. We dwell in him; and he dwells in us.

God's elect enjoy the most intimate union, communion, and fellowship possible with Christ (Galatians 2:20). His existence, fulness, and completion as our Mediator is inseparable from ours (Colossians 2:10); and our existence is inseparable from his. He partook of our nature; and we are made partakers of his nature. 'Partakers of the divine nature'! He has his being with us from eternity; and we have our being with him from eternity. As the Father and Son are one, we are one in the Son. 'I in them, and thou in me, that they may be made perfect in one; and that the world may know that thou hast sent me, and hast loved them, as thou hast loved me' (John 17:23). What he has done, we have done. What he has, we have. And where he is, we are!

'Many therefore of his disciples, when they had heard this, said, This is an hard saying; who can hear it?' (v. 60). To some who hear it the very simplicity of the gospel is 'a hard saying'. But to others the message preached, the Christ proclaimed, is sweet Bread for the soul, sweet Bread to eat. May God the Holy Spirit make Christ our Saviour the Bread of Life to you. O Holy Spirit, cause sinners here to hunger for Christ; and feed every hungry soul with the Bread of Life.

Chapter 51

'From that time'

'Many therefore of his disciples, when they had heard this, said, This is an hard saying; who can hear it? When Jesus knew in himself that his disciples murmured at it, he said unto them, Doth this offend you? What and if ye shall see the Son of man ascend up where he was before? It is the spirit that quickeneth; the flesh profiteth nothing: the words that I speak unto you, they are spirit, and they are life. But there are some of you that believe not. For Jesus knew from the beginning who they were that believed not, and who should betray him. And he said, Therefore said I unto you, that no man can come unto me, except it were given unto him of my Father. From that time many of his disciples went back, and walked no more with him. Then said Jesus unto the twelve, Will ye also go away? Then Simon Peter answered him, Lord, to whom shall we go? thou hast the words of eternal life. And we believe and are sure that thou art that Christ, the Son of the living God. Jesus answered them, Have not I chosen you twelve, and one of you is a devil? He spake of Judas Iscariot the son of Simon: for he it was that should betray him, being one of the twelve' (John 6:60-71).

'From that time many of his disciples went back, and walked no more with him' (v. 66). Note those words, 'From that time'. This was a time of great importance in the history of our Lord's earthly ministry. It was a time when the vast majority of those who had been following our Lord forsook him. They wanted a miracle, but not a master. They wanted a wonder-worker, but not a sovereign Saviour. This was a time of great importance to the Jewish nation. God's Messiah had come. The law and the prophets were being fulfilled before their very eyes. God himself assumed human flesh and dwelt among men. But he was despised, rejected, and hung up to die upon a cross. Therefore, God removed all light from that nation, left it desolate, and destroyed it. And this proved to be a time of great importance to the church and kingdom of our Lord Jesus Christ. Her first real trial had come. Just when she began to gain some influence and respectability among men, many who had joined themselves to her forsook her. 'From that time many of his disciples went back, and walked no more with him'. What was this time?

It was a time of declaration. Our Lord plainly declared the gospel to these men. He had told them many spiritual truths concerning himself and his kingdom. They were confused and offended by his doctrine. So many turned away and walked no more with him. He had declared God's eternal purpose of grace (vv. 37-40). He had declared his own deity (v. 46). He had declared his divine sovereignty (v. 63). He had declared man's inability (vv. 44, 63, 65). He had declared that salvation is the work of God alone: election by God the Father, redemption by God the Son, and regeneration by God the Holy Spirit. He had declared that salvation comes by divine revelation.

Salvation is the gift of God. It is not what man does for God that saves his soul, but what God does for man. God alone can make you a new creature in Christ. God alone can give life to dead sinners. God alone can make you an heir of eternal glory.

This was a time of decision (vv. 53, 54). These men must choose Christ and feed upon him, or they must choose the dry husks of empty ritualism and Judaism and drink from the polluted cistern of self-righteousness.

This was a time of defection (v. 66). Many of those who had followed Christ and professed to be his disciples forsook him. They went back to their old companions, to their own hearts' lusts. They went back to their old, empty religion. They went back, and walked no more with the Lord Jesus. There are many who follow Christ for a while, and afterwards turn away from him; but there are some who, clinging to Christ with a steadfast faith, cannot leave him; and the only difference between the two is the free, sovereign, distinguishing love, mercy and grace of God. There are some very obvious lessons in the passage we have before us. Yet, obvious as they are, they are lessons that are missed altogether by most. So, read what is before you carefully, with your Bible open before you, and ask God the Holy Spirit to teach you.

The Doctrine Of Christ Is Offensive To Lost Men
Both the religious and the irreligious are offended by the doctrine of Christ, specifically by the doctrine he taught in this sixth chapter of John's Gospel. We do not have to guess what that doctrine is (vv. 60-65). It is the doctrine of

salvation finished by Christ. Our Lord Jesus ascended up to heaven because he had finished his work. He had finished all he came to finish.

Another thing that offends men is the doctrine our Saviour proclaimed in verse 63, the blessed declaration of the fact that salvation can be obtained only by God's sovereign, quickening Spirit. In every place there are some who believe and some who believe not; and the determination is altogether God's work. The matter is determined from eternity by God's decree in election (Acts 13:48; John 10:25), by Christ's accomplishments in redemption (Galatians 3:13, 14), and by the Holy Spirit's effectual, irresistible grace and quickening power.

'It is the spirit that quickeneth; the flesh profiteth nothing: the words that I speak unto you, they are spirit, and they are life.' It was the Spirit that quickened the dead body of our crucified Substitute. His flesh did not quicken itself to life. It is the Spirit that makes the word preached to have quickening power. 'The flesh profiteth nothing'! It is the Spirit that quickens the dead sinner. 'The flesh profiteth nothing'!

Another thing taught by our Saviour is so offensive to proud man that none can or will receive it, as our Saviour here declares it, except they be taught of God and quickened by the Spirit. That is the doctrine of man's utter inability in all things spiritual (vv. 63-65). No man can believe, except the Spirit quicken him. No man can understand the things of God, except the Spirit quicken him. No man can revive his languishing soul, except the Spirit quicken him. No man can keep himself from evil, except the Spirit quicken him. No man can restore himself when fallen, except the Spirit quicken him. 'The flesh profiteth nothing'!

Many Who Seem To Be Christ's Disciples Go Back

'From that time many of his disciples went back, and walked no more with him.' Many follow Christ for a time, but stumble when they hear that salvation involves a personal union of faith with Christ. Many in this passage were following Christ. They were evidently much taken with him. They called him a prophet. They wanted to make him a king. They followed him across the sea. Yet, when he told them that he is the Bread of Heaven, they murmured. When he told them that they must eat his flesh and drink his blood to have eternal life, they said, 'This is a hard saying', and it was for this reason they turned back, and walked no more with Jesus.

So it is now. Many there are who are much taken with Christ. They have some anxiety about their souls. They like to hear good sermons. But when they are pressed with the claims of the Son of God, when they are pressed to eat his flesh and drink his blood, they say, 'That is a hard saying, who can hear it?'

Many follow Christ for a time; but when they are told that Christ must dwell in them, they stumble and fall. They go back, and walk no more with him. So it was here. The multitude that followed Christ was pleased with a great many things he did and said. When he fed them with the five barley loaves and the two fish, they said, 'Lord, it is good for us to be here ... This is in truth that prophet that should come into the world'. And when the Lord Jesus told them of bread from heaven that would give life, they said most devoutly: 'Lord, evermore give us this bread'. But, when Christ said, 'He that eateth my flesh, and drinketh my blood, dwelleth in me, and I in him', they were offended. When he told them that he would be their life, and would dwell in them, they said, 'It is a hard saying, who can hear it?' They believed not. They went back, and walked no more with him.

It is so with many today. They cannot grasp how a man can be made a new creature. So they are stumbled by it. They are stumbled by the fact that all who are born of God are made partakers of the divine nature. They laugh and poke fun at the doctrine, stumbling down to hell in proud rebellion. When the Saviour says, 'Ye must be born again ... he that eateth me, even he shall live by me', they say, 'This is a hard saying, who can hear it?' Many profess that they will follow Christ; but when they are plainly told that they must be drawn to Christ, that salvation is altogether by God's free grace, they are offended.

How many there are who receive the word as seed sown upon stony ground where it is quickly scorched out by the sun of adversity, or among thorns where it is choked out by the weeds of earthly care, the care of this world and the deceitfulness of riches!

Though many go back, blessed be God, those who are Christ's cannot go back, because the Saviour will not let us go back (vv. 67-69).

'Then said Jesus unto the twelve, Will ye also go away? Then Simon Peter answered him, Lord, to whom shall we go? thou hast the words of eternal life. And we believe and are sure that thou art that Christ, the Son of the living God' (vv. 67-69)

True believers never quit the Saviour. They cannot go back, because they are the objects of special love. When the crowd went away the Saviour did not go after them. He spoke not a word. But when his own believing disciples thought themselves in danger of being led away, he speaks to them. 'Will ye also go away?' Will you whom I have chosen, you whom I have washed, you whom I have sanctified and filled with hopes of glory, 'will ye also go, away?' Oh, how graciously Christ watches over his own! He is walking in the midst of the seven golden candlesticks, and his word is, 'I know thy works'.

True believers cannot forsake Christ because they are heirs of an everlasting covenant that cannot be broken (Jeremiah 31:3, 31-34; 32:38-41). They cannot be lost because they are God's elect. They cannot perish because

Christ purchased them. They cannot go back because they are kept by God's power and grace. They cannot go back because they are sealed by the Spirit. They cannot go back because God, who gives us eternal life and sustains it, cannot change.

Eternal life is the gift of God. Eternal life comes to men as a matter of free grace. Man does not have eternal life by nature. Eternal life does not evolve from man's sinful heart by some mysterious process of 'spiritual evolution'. It is given to men graciously. It is performed in the heart by the power of God's sovereign grace. The very word 'gift' forbids the idea that eternal life comes to men as a matter of debt or reward. 'The gift of God is eternal life'. There was nothing in our hearts or conduct which caused God to bestow eternal life upon us (Jeremiah 31:3; Romans 8:30; Ephesians 2:1-4). And there is nothing in the believer's heart or conduct which can cause God to take away his gift of eternal life (Isaiah 54:10; Psalms 89:30-36).

R. L. Dabney wrote, 'God was not induced to bestow his renewing grace in the first instance by anything which he saw meritorious and attractive in repenting sinners; and therefore the subsequent absence of everything good in them would be no new motive to God for withdrawing his grace.'

It is contrary to the nature and character of God to take away his gifts so freely bestowed (Romans 11:29). This gift of eternal life is a gift freely bestowed, in no way dependent upon the contingencies of this present, mortal existence. If we acknowledge that eternal life is entirely the gift of God, in no way earned by or dependent upon the goodness of man, it must be concluded that those to whom eternal life is given are eternally secure in Christ (Ecclesiastes 3:14).

Any child who has not been blinded by religious error must recognise that eternal life must of necessity be eternal. I realise that 'eternal life' refers more to the quality of the believer's life union with Christ than it does to the duration of his life. But it certainly implies a life of eternal duration. When our Lord says, 'eternal', he means eternal. How can life be eternal if it comes to an end? If I have received from God the gift of eternal life, it is not possible for me, by any act of mine, or upon any grounds, to lose it and perish. 'The gift of God is eternal life'.

That which is born of God, the new nature created in us by the power of God, cannot sin and cannot die (1 John 3:5-9).

The believer's life must be eternal because it is a life in union with Christ. We who believe are so really and truly joined to Christ that we cannot possibly perish, unless he also perishes. We are truly one with Christ. He says, 'Because I live, ye shall live also'. This union between Christ and his people is an immutable, indissoluble union. We are married to Christ (Hosea 2:19, 20; Ephesians 5:30). We are members of Christ's body, the church (Ephesians

1:23). Can you imagine Christ with a maimed body? Perish the thought! Yet, his body would not be complete if so much as one member were lost.

The believer's life in Christ must be a life of eternal duration, because we are preserved in life by the power and grace of God the Holy Spirit (Ephesians 1:14; 4:30). The Holy Spirit was sent into the world both to call and to preserve God's elect. He is the Giver of life and the Preserver of life. The Spirit of God is the seal of the new covenant. That seal is a mark of ownership. A seal is that which keeps something legally secure. A seal suggests permanent freshness. A seal means everything is okay!

The True Believer Cannot Go Back
The true believer cannot go back because we have none to go to but Christ. 'Thou hast the words of eternal life.' To unconverted minds the words of Christ are hard sayings. To his own they are tried and proven words, words of eternal life. The very thing that drives the world away from Christ draws his own disciples closer and closer to him. The world is offended when Christ says we must eat his flesh. That is a word of eternal life to the believer. The religionist goes away when he hears of Christ dwelling in the soul. The believer draws nearer and says, Lord, evermore dwell in me. The will-worshipper walks no more with him when he hears that salvation is altogether by grace. Believers bow in the dust and bless God, who alone makes him to differ from the reprobate. 'Lord, to whom shall we go? Thou hast the words of eternal life.'

'We believe and are sure that thou art that Christ, the Son of the living God.' It is this confident conviction that he is our divine Saviour that rivets the believing soul to Christ. If Christ were only a man like ourselves, how could he be a Surety for us? But we believe and are sure that he is the Son of the living God. We therefore know he is a sufficient Surety for us. To whom else can we go for pardon?

If Christ were only a man like ourselves, how could he dwell in us or give the Spirit to abide with us forever? But we believe and are sure that he is that Christ, the Son of the living God. Therefore we know he is able to dwell in us and put his Spirit in us forever. To whom, then, can we go for a new heart but unto Christ?

Have you thus been taught of God? Then blessed are you, 'for flesh and blood hath not revealed it unto you, but my Father which is in heaven.'

Salvation Is Altogether The Result Of Our Saviour's Choice
'Jesus answered them, Have not I chosen you twelve, and one of you is a devil? He spake of Judas Iscariot the son of Simon: for he it was that should betray him, being one of the twelve' (vv. 70, 71). 'Ye have not chosen me, but I have chosen you, and ordained you, that ye should go and bring forth fruit, and that

your fruit should remain: that whatsoever ye shall ask of the Father in my name, he may give it you' (John 15:16).

Even the most evil deeds performed by men under the influence of hell itself are ordained and overruled by our great God for the salvation of his elect.

'Jesus answered them, Have not I chosen you twelve, and one of you is a devil? He spake of Judas Iscariot the son of Simon: for he it was that should betray him, being one of the twelve' (vv. 70, 71).

'Him, being delivered by the determinate counsel and foreknowledge of God, ye have taken, and by wicked hands have crucified and slain' (Acts 2:23).

'Surely the wrath of man shall praise thee: the remainder of wrath shalt thou restrain' (Psalms 76:10).

Let the Arminians, work-mongers, and will-worshippers of the world hoot and holler all they will; these things cannot be gainsaid. Those who denounce them denounce the word of God. Those who despise them despise the God who reveals them, performs them, and attaches his glory to them (Ephesians 1:3-14). All who are taught of God believe God.

Chapter 52

'Doth this offend you?'

'These things said he in the synagogue, as he taught in Capernaum. Many therefore of his disciples, when they had heard this, said, This is an hard saying; who can hear it? When Jesus knew in himself that his disciples murmured at it, he said unto them, Doth this offend you?' (John 6:59-61).

John 6 is a record of the running controversy between the Lord Jesus Christ and lost religionists who wanted to eat the bread he alone could provide, but hated the doctrine he taught. After our Lord performed that great miracle of feeding 5,000 men with just five barley loaves and two small fish, the people began to flock to him in droves. But when he began to teach them the word of God, when he began to preach to them the doctrine of the gospel, they were offended. His doctrine was a stumbling stone and a rock of offence to lost religious people in that day; and things have not changed. The doctrine of Christ is still offensive to lost, religious men and women.

We read in the scriptures that when the Lord Jesus preached, the people who heard him became so enraged that they picked up rocks and tried to stone him to death. And I tell you plainly that any man who dares to preach the gospel of Christ today, as the Master himself preached it, will meet with the same response among unregenerate religious people.

In this chapter our Lord began his sermon in verse 26, where he rebuked the Jews, telling them that the only reason they followed him was that they wanted to see more miracles and eat more bread. The message ends in verse

58 with the promise of life eternal to all who trust the Lord Jesus Christ. After he brought his message, the people who heard him began to murmur. They said that teaching is too hard. 'This is a hard saying, who can hear it?' The Lord Jesus answered their quibbles by saying, 'Doth this offend you?' Then he went on preaching, re-emphasising what he had said before. He wanted to make sure they heard what he was saying (vv. 62-65).

When he got done, the whole crowd left him, all 5,000 men, their wives, and their children. Our Lord Jesus Christ was not a crowd pleaser. Then he turned to the twelve disciples who remained with him and said, 'Will ye also go away?' They stayed, but the crowd left. The crowd was offended by the gospel. Every god they worshipped, every altar they cherished, every hope they clung to was being destroyed by Christ's doctrine. They said, 'We've heard enough of that. We will not listen to it anymore.' And they walked away from the gospel and went to hell, clinging to the traditions of their Christless religion.

The gospel of the grace of God is just as offensive to unregenerate men and women today as it was to these people in John 6. It offended people then; and it offends people now. There is no way to make the gospel inoffensive without denying it altogether. The gospel of the grace of God will either bring people to Christ in repentance and faith, or drive them away from him in obstinate rebellion. It will either save those who hear it, or it will condemn them. But, blessed be God, the preaching of his free and sovereign grace in Christ will accomplish the purpose whereunto he sends it (2 Corinthians 2:14-16; Isaiah 55:11).

Seven Truths
I want to show you the doctrine of Christ, as it was preached by the Lord Jesus Christ himself in the Gospel of John. Later on, in his second Epistle, John wrote, 'Whosoever transgresseth, and abideth not in the doctrine of Christ, hath not God. He that abideth in the doctrine of Christ, he hath both the Father and the Son' (2 John 9).

Here are seven great foundation truths of the gospel, which fell from the lips of the blessed Saviour himself. It cannot be denied that these seven things are the doctrine of Christ. They were taught by him. John heard them. And being inspired by the Spirit of God to do so, he wrote them down for our learning and admonition. They are offensive to the world, but they are honouring to God and full of comfort and joy for his people. Here are seven things the Son of God taught when he walked and preached among men. And that which he taught, all who are his messengers in every generation faithfully teach as well.

1. Divine Sovereignty

Our Lord Jesus Christ preached the glorious sovereignty of God in the exercise of his grace.

'All that the Father giveth me shall come to me; and him that cometh to me I will in no wise cast out. For I came down from heaven, not to do mine own will, but the will of him that sent me. And this is the Father's will which hath sent me, that of all which he hath given me I should lose nothing, but should raise it up again at the last day. And this is the will of him that sent me, that every one which seeth the Son, and believeth on him, may have everlasting life: and I will raise him up at the last day' (John 6:37-40).

Here we see God in his sovereignty. We see God's will being done in the world. The Lord Jesus tells us that he came down here, appointed, delegated, set apart, and sent of God to accomplish his sovereign will. When the Lord Jesus Christ preached, he preached God on the throne as an absolute sovereign, who always does what seems good in his sight.

I know that men hate God's sovereignty. It offends them. It makes all men and women paupers before the great and glorious Lord God, who does what he pleases, when he pleases, with whom he pleases. 'None can stay his hand, or say unto him, what doest thou?' (See Isaiah 14:24, 26 and 27.) Anytime a preacher dares take the crown off man's head and puts it where it belongs, on God's head, the fur begins to fly. You can count on it. But every man who is called of God to preach the gospel will do just that, regardless of cost or consequence.

When I declare that God is sovereign, I mean that God really is God. Everything is determined by him, everything depends upon him, and everything is absolutely governed by him. The will and purpose of God is absolute and irresistible. God's will determines all things and rules all things. Everything depends upon the will of God. Christ died by the will of God (Acts 2:23, Hebrews 10:1-14). Paul tells us that God 'worketh all things after the counsel of his own will' (Ephesians 1:11). James says, 'If the Lord will, we will live and do this or that' (James 4:15). John tells us, regarding the kings, princes, and nations of the world that 'God hath put in their hearts to fulfil his will' (Revelation 17:17). When Paul wrote to the Corinthians, he said, 'I will come to you shortly, if the Lord will' (1 Corinthians 4:19).

And when I say that God is sovereign, I am telling you that God Almighty always saves sinners on his terms (Isaiah 45:22). If you are saved, you are saved because it pleased the Lord to save you. 'It pleased the Lord' to make you his people (1 Samuel 12:22). 'It pleased the Lord' to bruise his Son in the place of his people (Isaiah 53:9). 'It pleased the Lord' to put all the fulness of grace and glory in Christ (Colossians 1:18). 'It pleased the Lord' to reveal his

Son in you (Galatians 1:15). 'It pleased the Lord' to save sinners by the preaching of the gospel (1 Corinthians 1:21).

Seminaries and Bible colleges deny God's sovereignty. Preachers everywhere oppose it. Men who hate God hate it. But the Son of God preached it! 'Doth this offend you?' It offends you only if you want to be God yourself.

2. Total Depravity
Remember, I am showing you the doctrine of Christ specifically as the Apostle John was inspired by God the Holy Spirit to present it in his gospel narrative. Here in the Gospel of John, specifically in this sixth chapter, we see the Lord Jesus Christ openly preaching the total depravity and inability of man (John 6:44). He's preaching to lost people about divine sovereignty, total depravity, election, and limited atonement!

'No man can come to me, except the Father which hath sent me draw him: and I will raise him up at the last day' (John 6:44).

'When Jesus knew in himself that his disciples murmured at it, he said unto them, Doth this offend you? What and if ye shall see the Son of man ascend up where he was before? It is the spirit that quickeneth; the flesh profiteth nothing: the words that I speak unto you, they are spirit, and they are life. But there are some of you that believe not. For Jesus knew from the beginning who they were that believed not, and who should betray him. And he said, Therefore said I unto you, that no man can come unto me, except it were given unto him of my Father' (John 6:61-65).

Our Lord preached God on the throne and man in the dust. He preached God exalted and man abased, God high and man low. Man was not always low; but sin has made him so. Ever since our father Adam fell in the garden, the sons of Adam have been wallowing in the mire of depravity. And Christ preached it that way. He said, 'No man can come to me, except the Father which hath sent me draw him'. My Lord put man in a spiritual grave, unable to rise by his own strength, declared him an impotent thing on a cripple's bed, unable to walk, and on a blind man's stool, unable to see.

Men and women everywhere tell us we should not teach and preach these things because they offend people. I am fully aware of that, but I would rather offend man than offend God. And when we preach and teach these glorious doctrines plainly and openly we are following a good example. This is the doctrine of Christ. Is it not?

To preach free-willism and decisionism is to deceive the souls of men. Man can no more save himself than the demons of hell could save themselves. No man can ever be saved except by the omnipotent mercy, irresistible grace, and sovereign will of God. 'Salvation is of the Lord' in its planning, in its purchase, in its performance, in its preservation, and in its perfection.

'Doth this offend you?' If it does, it offends you only because you think you are good.

3. Unconditional Election
The Lord Jesus Christ preached God's free, sovereign, eternal, unconditional election of certain individuals to salvation and eternal life in Christ. We just read that in verses 64 and 65. Because he knew from the beginning that they would believe not, the Saviour says, 'Therefore said I unto you, No man can come unto me except it were given unto him of my Father'. It is the Son of God who said, 'Ye have not chosen me, but I have chosen you, and ordained you, that ye should go and bring forth fruit, and that your fruit should remain: that whatsoever ye shall ask of the Father in my name, he may give it you' (John 15:16).

Election is a humbling doctrine, for it takes salvation completely out of man's hands. 'Ye have not chosen me'. Election is a clearly revealed and very prominent Bible doctrine. (Ephesians 1:3-6; 2 Thessalonians 2:13, 14). And election is a most blessed and comforting doctrine. It is our election that secures us from the delusions of antichrist (2 Thessalonians 2).

4. Blood Atonement
Our Saviour preached blood atonement (John 6:54-57). People in his day resented the preaching of blood atonement as much as they do in our day. But he still preached it. The Son of God preached redemption by the blood (John 3:14-16), God's blood (Acts 20:28), holy blood (Exodus 30:10), precious blood (1 Peter 1:18-20), God's spilt blood (Zechariah 13:7), saving blood (Romans 5:9), effectual, sin-atoning blood (Hebrews 1:3; 9:12).

And the Son of God preached that his blood effectually made atonement for and redeemed a particular people called his sheep (John 10:11, 15, 25). The Lord Jesus Christ did not shed his blood in vain (Galatians 2:21). Our Redeemer preached salvation by blood atonement. Nothing but the blood could satisfy the justice of a holy God. Nothing but the blood can wash away my sin. There is no hope for sinners outside of the precious blood of Christ.

'Doth this offend you?' If it does, it offends you only because you have some other hope, only because you have made for yourself a 'refuge of lies'.

5. Effectual Calling
The Son of God preached the effectual call of God the Holy Spirit. 'It is the spirit that quickeneth; the flesh profiteth nothing: the words that I speak unto you, they are spirit, and they are life' (John 6:63). We preach the gospel to all who hear us, calling all to Christ. But that general call of the gospel is of no benefit to any who hear the word preached, except it be made effectual in the

heart by God the Holy Spirit in the powerful, irresistible call that brings chosen, redeemed sinners to the Saviour (Psalms 65:4; 110:3).

All who are privileged to hear the gospel preached are called externally by the preaching of the gospel; but those who are saved, 'the called', have been called internally, effectually, and irresistibly by God the Holy Spirit. 'The called' are like the Thessalonian saints. Their election, redemption, and calling are made manifest by the fact that the word of God has come to them, not in word only, but in the power of the Holy Ghost[16]. Salvation comes to chosen, redeemed sinners in the experience of grace by the almighty, irresistible, effectual call of God the Holy Spirit.

It is this call of which David sang, when he said, 'Blessed is the man whom thou choosest, and causest to approach unto thee.' This is the call the Apostle Paul was talking about when he said, 'God separated me from my mother's womb, called me by his grace, and revealed his Son in me.' Paul was talking about this internal, effectual call when he wrote to Timothy. God 'hath saved us, and called us with an holy calling, not according to our works, but according to his own purpose and grace, which was given us in Christ Jesus before the world began, But is now made manifest by the appearing of our Saviour Jesus Christ, who hath abolished death, and hath brought life and immortality to light through the gospel: Whereunto I am appointed a preacher, and an apostle, and a teacher of the Gentiles' (2 Timothy 1:9-11).

'Doth this offend you?' If it does, it offends you only because you have never been called.

6. Certain Perseverance
And our Lord Jesus Christ preached the preservation and perseverance of every believer (John 10:27-30). Sheep are weak, helpless, defenceless creatures. They have no strength to withstand their enemies. If they are lost, they cannot find their way home again. If sick, they cannot fight off their disease. If threatened, they cannot run fast enough to escape danger. If attacked, they cannot defend themselves.

The only security sheep have is in their shepherd. If their shepherd is wise, good, and strong, they are secure. If the sheep survive, if they live and flourish, the honour belongs to the shepherd. If the sheep perish, the blame belongs to the shepherd. It is the shepherd's responsibility to keep the sheep. Knowing these things, those who are the Lord's sheep rejoice to hear him say, 'My sheep hear my voice, and I know them, and they follow me: And I give unto them eternal life; and they shall never perish, neither shall any man pluck them out

---

[16] I remind you, there is no effectual call of grace apart from the preaching of the gospel. Yet, the preaching of the gospel will never produce life and faith in Christ without the effectual call of God the Holy Spirit.

---

of my hand. My Father, which gave them me, is greater than all; and no man is able to pluck them out of my Father's hand. I and my Father are one.'

The doctrine of our Lord in this text is very plain and obvious. We who believe are Christ's sheep, we are weak, helpless, defenceless creatures. And the Lord Jesus Christ, the Son of God, is our Shepherd, he is wise, good, and strong. Because Christ is our Shepherd, we are secure in him. This is what the Son of God, our dear Shepherd, says concerning all his sheep. 'They shall never perish'! With those words, the Son of God declares the absolute, infallible, unwavering security of God's elect in himself.

> Once in Christ, in Christ forever,
> Nothing from Him our souls can sever!

'Doth this offend you'? If it does, it offends you only because you think you can save yourself.

7. Salvation Full And Free

The Lord Jesus Christ preached salvation full and free to all who believe, to all who trust him.

'For God so loved the world, that he gave his only begotten Son, that whosoever believeth in him should not perish, but have everlasting life. For God sent not his Son into the world to condemn the world; but that the world through him might be saved. He that believeth on him is not condemned: but he that believeth not is condemned already, because he hath not believed in the name of the only begotten Son of God' (John 3:16-18).

'He that believeth on the Son hath everlasting life: and he that believeth not the Son shall not see life; but the wrath of God abideth on him' (John 3:36).

'All that the Father giveth me shall come to me; and him that cometh to me I will in no wise cast out' (John 6:37).

Salvation is in Christ. Salvation in Christ is free. This salvation that is in Christ is unconditional. It is everlasting, eternal salvation. The Son of God says, 'him that cometh unto me I will in no wise cast out'.

'Doth this offend you?' If it does, it offends you only because you refuse to be saved by free grace alone.

Do Not Assist Those Who Oppose Christ

This is the doctrine of Christ. If it offends you, it offends you because you do not know or trust the Lord Jesus Christ. If Christ's doctrine is your doctrine, be certain, child of God, that you do not assist those who oppose his doctrine in any way.

'Whosoever transgresseth, and abideth not in the doctrine of Christ, hath not God. He that abideth in the doctrine of Christ, he hath both the Father and the Son. If there come any unto you, and bring not this doctrine, receive him not into your house, neither bid him God speed: For he that biddeth him God speed is partaker of his evil deeds' (2 John 9-11).

Chapter 53

Why Is Christ Hated So?

'After these things Jesus walked in Galilee: for he would not walk in Jewry, because the Jews sought to kill him. Now the Jews' feast of tabernacles was at hand. His brethren therefore said unto him, Depart hence, and go into Judaea, that thy disciples also may see the works that thou doest. For there is no man that doeth any thing in secret, and he himself seeketh to be known openly. If thou do these things, shew thyself to the world. For neither did his brethren believe in him. Then Jesus said unto them, My time is not yet come: but your time is alway ready. The world cannot hate you; but me it hateth, because I testify of it, that the works thereof are evil. Go ye up unto this feast: I go not up yet unto this feast; for my time is not yet full come. When he had said these words unto them, he abode still in Galilee. But when his brethren were gone up, then went he also up unto the feast, not openly, but as it were in secret. Then the Jews sought him at the feast, and said, Where is he? And there was much murmuring among the people concerning him: for some said, he is a good man: others said, Nay; but he deceiveth the people. Howbeit no man spake openly of him for fear of the Jews' (John 7:1-13).

The fact that our Lord Jesus Christ, while he walked through this world, was utterly hated by men is obvious. As soon as opportunity was given them, the princes of this world crucified the Lord of glory. Why? Why was Christ so hated? Why is the Son of God so hated today? The answer to that question is found in these thirteen verses of holy scripture.

This chapter opens with John's declaration that the Jews sought to kill the Lord Jesus. He was so hated, so viciously despised that the Jews, that is the religious leaders among the Jews; the scribes, the Pharisees, the Sadducees, the priests, the elders, etc., were looking for a way to murder him, without appearing to have done anything contrary to the law of God.

The Jews' Feast
The first thing that is obvious in this passage is the fact that multitudes have a form of godliness who have no knowledge of God. Multitudes are religious, but lost. We read in verse 2 'Now the Jews' feast of tabernacles was at hand'.

What scathing words of condemnation those are! The divinely ordained Feast of Tabernacles is here referred to by the Spirit of God as 'the Jews' Feast of Tabernacles'! This blessed ordinance of divine worship had so degenerated that it was no longer observed as an ordinance of divine worship, but as a custom of Jewish religious tradition.

The Feast of Tabernacles was a feast God commanded the children of Israel to keep on the 15th day of the seventh month of every year to celebrate his goodness to his people. After they had gathered in the fruits of the land, they were to dwell in tents for seven days in remembrance of the forty years spent in the wilderness (Leviticus 23:34-36, 39-44). The feast was the grand harvest festival, when the Lord of harvest was praised for his mercies.

This Feast of Tabernacles was a time when Israel was reminded that they dwelt in booths in the wilderness and God dwelt with them in the cloudy and fiery pillar. But it spoke of more than that. It foreshadowed that time when God came here and tabernacled in human flesh that he might at last bring God and man together in eternal glory and perfect fellowship, with sin and every evil consequence of it expiated, put away, purged, gone, and forgotten forever (Psalms 72:16-19; John 1:14; Revelation 21:1-7).

How sad, how horribly, horribly sad it is to see multitudes today doing exactly what the Jews in our Lord's day had done, clinging to a form of godliness, while denying the power thereof, clinging to outward ceremonies, while despising spiritual worship! Public worship is meaningless, unless it involves heart worship. Baptism is an empty ritual, unless you are baptised into Christ. The Lord's Supper is a worthless ceremony, unless Christ is held in the memory of the heart.

Let us ever seek grace from God the Holy Spirit to pray with the spirit and pray with the understanding also, to sing with the spirit and sing with the understanding also, to read with the spirit and read with the understanding also, to hear with the spirit and hear with the understanding also, to worship with the spirit and worship with the understanding also.

Impossible Faith

Second, we see in our Saviour's brethren a glaring declaration of the fact that it is impossible for anyone to believe on the Son of God except by the call, gift, operation, and power of God the Holy Spirit. So obstinate, so desperately wicked, so great is the hardness and unbelief of human nature that we are plainly told, 'Neither did his brethren believe in him' (v. 5). Holy and harmless and blameless as he was in life, our Lord's nearest relatives, according to the flesh, did not receive him as the Messiah, did not trust him as their Saviour, and did not worship him as the God-man Mediator. It was bad enough that his own people, 'the Jews sought to kill him'. But it was even worse that 'his brethren did not believe in him'.

These 'brethren' (vv. 3-5) were our Saviour's earthly kinsmen (Matthew 12:46, 47; 13:55). These 'brethren' urged the Lord Jesus to go to Jerusalem, the centre of Judaism, and let his followers there see the mighty works and miracles he could perform. They thought that the Feast of Tabernacles would be a good time for him to demonstrate his powers, since multitudes of Jews would be in Jerusalem for the feast.

'His brethren' wanted the Lord Jesus to obtain fame, but cared nothing for the glory of God. They thought his fame would be to their advantage. They said, 'If you want fame and notoriety you have got to put yourself in the limelight. Go to Jerusalem. Nobody will ever know who you are, if you only preach in these small country villages. You have got to go to Jerusalem and there 'shew thyself unto the world'' (v. 4). These are the same 'his brethren' who said in Mark 3:21, 'He is beside himself'!

The fact is, with men, faith in Christ is an utter impossibility. So hard, so depraved is the heart of fallen man that our Lord's own kinsmen, though they lived constantly in his company, observed his day by day conduct, watched perfection live before them, saw his miracles and heard every word he spoke, did not believe in him. His own kinsmen did not believe! The fact is earthly relations cannot secure God's grace. Grace does not run in any family. Faith comes only by divine revelation. Faith is the gift of God, the fruit and the result of divine operations. Faith is born in the new-born soul in regeneration, brought forth by the effectual call of God the Holy Spirit, and is exercised by the Spirit of God in the heaven born soul.

The mere possession of spiritual advantages and privileges has no saving efficacy. All is useless without the irresistible grace and power of God the Holy Spirit. In John 6 our Lord Jesus said, 'No man can come to me, except the Father which hath sent me draw him ... no man can come unto me, except it were given unto him of my Father' (John 6:44, 65).

We often hear people assigning blame to preachers and preachers assigning blame to church members for the lack of conversions in a place, as though we might be able to increase the number of God's elect if we just did things differently. Do not be so foolish! Salvation is God's prerogative. 'Salvation is of the Lord'!

His Time

Third, we are reminded that everything comes to pass at God's appointed time. 'To every thing there is a season, and a time to every purpose under the heaven' (Ecclesiastes 3:1). Without question, everything connected with the incarnation, life, obedience, death, and resurrection of our Lord Jesus Christ was accomplished at his own divinely appointed time.

'Then Jesus said unto them, My time is not yet come: but your time is alway ready. The world cannot hate you; but me it hateth, because I testify of it, that the works thereof are evil. Go ye up unto this feast: I go not up yet unto this feast: for my time is not yet full come' (vv. 6-8).

The Lord Jesus refused to go up to the feast with his brethren at this particular time because the time or hour was not yet come for him to publicly display his miracles in Jerusalem, to have a head-on confrontation with the religious leaders, to reveal himself as the Messiah and King, and so to stir up their enmity and fears of him, which would lead them to crucify him in open shame. He said to these brethren, 'Your time is always ready', or anytime is suitable for you; for you are of the world, and the world does not hate you. They had in mind, like everyone else, an earthly kingdom, great favour, and the applause of the world. But our Lord came to redeem a people, to condemn the social, political, and religious world in general. Therefore, he incurred the wrath of all. When the appointed time came, he showed himself and accomplished his death at Jerusalem (Romans 5:6-8). And everything connected with the salvation of his people is accomplished at his own appointed time of love (Galatians 4:4-6).

The World's Hatred

Fourth, our Lord Jesus tells us plainly in verse seven that he was hated by the world in which he lived simply because he showed that its works are evil. 'The world cannot hate you; but me it hateth, because I testify of it, that the works thereof are evil.'

He says to 'his brethren', his own kinsmen after the flesh, 'The world cannot hate you'. That makes it obvious that he is talking to men who are themselves very religious. They are discussing religious, theological, prophetic issues in this chapter. These are not drunks, profligate and morally degenerate derelicts. These men were, themselves, upstanding, conservative religious people. Yet, he says to them, 'The world cannot hate you'.

Obviously, 'the world' in this context refers to the religious people of this world, or the religion of this world. He is referring to the self-righteous, works religion that is embraced, promoted, loved, and, to a greater or lesser degree, practiced by men everywhere. It may be called Islam, or Judaism, or Christianity, Animism, or Hinduism, or Atheism; but it is the religion of the world. It is embraced by men and women everywhere. And they are enraged when it is shown to be evil (Proverbs 14:12; 16:25).

Our Saviour here declares that the reason the world hated him so was 'because I testify of it, that the works thereof are evil'. And that which was true then is true today. It was so even from the beginning. Those things that men call good works, by which they hope they have God's favour, our God and Saviour declares to be evil. That was the reason Cain murdered Abel.

The fact is, as John Calvin put it, 'The Gospel cannot be faithfully preached without summoning the whole world, as guilty, to the judgment-seat of God, that flesh and blood may thus be crushed and reduced to nothing.'

Exactly how did the Lord Jesus testify against these men, that their works were evil? He healed a man on the sabbath day, declaring that their sabbath observance was useless. He refused to practice their customs, refused to publicly wash his hands before eating, declaring that their religious customs were worthless human inventions. By his actions as well as his doctrine, the Lord Jesus exposed all their religious activity to be nothing but self-serving hypocrisy.

He preached the gospel. He preached the necessity of a turning of men to God by God and their necessary repentance. He preached the necessity of perfect righteousness, the necessity of complete atonement, the necessity of the new birth, and the necessity of divine preservation. All these things asserted plainly that religion without grace, religious activity without God the Holy Spirit, religious knowledge without faith in Christ is damning.

The world loves religion. It will embrace and be tolerant of every form of religion. It will demand respect for all religions, except the gospel of Christ. That, the world cannot receive. The gospel puts all sinners upon the same level, in the dust of humiliation. The gospel puts all men in the hands of God. The gospel makes salvation God's work alone. The gospel strips man of all pride, honour, and distinction. And the gospel puts the crown on the head of the triune Jehovah where it belongs.

Dividing Opinions

Fifth, we see in verses 10-13 that men everywhere are divided from one another by three very strong opinions about the Lord Jesus Christ.

'But when his brethren were gone up, then went he also up unto the feast, not openly, but as it were in secret. Then the Jews sought him at the feast, and said, Where is he? And there was much murmuring among the people concerning him: for some said, he is a good man: others said, Nay; but he deceiveth the people. Howbeit no man spake openly of him for fear of the Jews.'

Some say that Jesus was a good man. Others say he was a deceiver of men. Those two groups of people will always find some way or other to get along, like conservative and liberal politicians. But the third group they will not embrace. Believers know and are sure that Jesus is the Christ, the Son of the living God, the only Saviour of fallen men. 'What think ye of Christ?'

> Though all the world my choice deride,
> Yet Jesus shall my portion be;
> For I am pleased with none beside;
> The fairest of the fair is He.

> Gerhardt Tersteegen

Chapter 54

'Where is he?'

'Then the Jews sought him at the feast, and said, Where is he?' (John 7:11).

Some sought to take him and kill him. Others sought to take him and make him a king. Some sought to see his miracles. Others sought to hear his doctrine. Some sought him out of curiosity. Others sought him out of need. Everyone knew that the Lord Jesus would be in Jerusalem during the Feast of Tabernacles. It was both his custom and his duty as an Israelite to come at this time to the house of God to worship God. Therefore everyone expected him to be there. Throughout the days of the feast, there was a murmuring about him. It seems that everyone at the feast was asking one question 'Where is he?'

When Elisha took up Elijah's mantle, he cried, 'Where is the God of Elijah?' (2 Kings 2:14). In his time of great trial, in the midst of his groaning and heaviness of heart, Job cried, 'Oh that I knew where I might find him! That I might come even to his seat'! (Job 23:3).

There are appointed places where the Lord Jesus Christ may be found by those who seek him with all their hearts. If you really want to find him, there are places where he may be found.

The Question Of Many

First, this is a question asked by many people, from different circumstances, and for different reasons. Our text specifically tells us that the Jews asked, 'Where is he?' But this is a question that has often been asked by numerous people throughout the ages of Christianity. In the days of his manhood upon

395

this earth, many frequently asked where he was, because they hated him and wanted to kill him.

You will remember that King Herod asked this question of the wise men, when our Saviour first came into the world. He pretended that he wanted to worship him; but he really wanted to destroy him (Matthew 2:1-13).

There have been multitudes, like Herod, who sought to destroy Christ, that is to destroy his people, his gospel, and his cause in this world, while pretending that they worship him. Opposition and persecution arises from many quarters; but it is never so dangerous as when it comes from those who pretend that they are the Lord's disciples. The persecutions of the papists, the heresies of freewillers and work-mongers, the slanders of false brethren are all assaults upon Christ, attempts to rid the world of him and his influence. Infidels, who sneeringly denying our Lord's very existence, taunt and deride his people, saying, 'Where is he?' 'They are scoffers, walking after their own lusts, And saying, Where is the promise of his coming? for since the fathers fell asleep, all things continue as they were from the beginning of the creation' (2 Peter 3:3, 4).

This is a question that is sometimes asked by fearful, trembling believers. God's saints are sometimes so overcome with trials and troubles, with heartache and grief, that they question his presence, his power, his promises, and his providence. In such times of weakness, our hearts cry, 'Where is he?' Job certainly did (Job 23:8, 9), so did David (Psalms 22:1). We ought never to doubt our God and Saviour. He is worthy of implicit trust and confidence. But we are often like the disciples in their little boat on the storm-tossed sea, crying, 'Master, carest thou not that we perish?' (Mark 4:38).

Penitent sinners humbly seek the Lord Jesus Christ, asking, 'Where is he?' that they may come to him, confess their sin to him, and obtain mercy from him. 'When thou saidst, Seek ye my face; my heart said unto thee, Thy face, LORD, will I seek' (Psalms 27:8). 'With my soul have I desired thee in the night; yea, with my spirit within me will I seek thee early: for when thy judgments are in the earth, the inhabitants of the world will learn righteousness' (Isaiah 26:9).

All who trust Christ seek him with all their hearts. Believers are men and women who live in the pursuit of the Lord Jesus Christ (2 Corinthians 5:9; Philippians 3:7-14). Those who love the Lord earnestly seek him (Song of Solomon 3:3). When our Beloved has withdrawn himself from us and hides his face from us because of our sinful neglect of him or disobedience to him, once we are made to bitterly lament our sin and his absence, we crave his return. Our hearts pine for communion with him. We ache for his manifest presence with us.

And we know, we are graciously made to know, that we pine for our Beloved only because he graciously causes us to pine for him (Song of Solomon 5:2-8).

The soul that thirsts for Christ, longing to behold his glory, anxiously looking for his second coming, cries 'Where is he?' When we hear our Saviour say, 'Surely I come quickly. Amen', our hearts respond, 'Even so, come, Lord Jesus' (Revelation 22:20).

Answered By Scripture
Second, this question, 'Where is he?' is answered plainly in the book of God. This is not something about which God leaves us to guess. Where is Christ to be found? If we turn to the pages of holy scripture to discover the answer to this question, we will find that it is answered very clearly. Do you ask, 'Where is he?' Search the scriptures, and you will discover.

He is in the bosom of the Father (John 1:18). Christ is the centre of heaven. Here is the glory of glory (Revelation 4 and 5). He is the Lamb in the midst of the throne. 'Where is he?' he is seated upon the throne of universal dominion. There he sits in the serenity of total sovereignty. There he reigns and must reign, until he has made all his foes his footstool. Jesus Christ is Lord of all forever (John 17:2; Romans 14:9; 1 Corinthians 15:24-28). He is at the right hand of the majesty on high, in the place of representation and advocacy as our great High Priest (Romans 8:27, 34; 1 John 2:1, 2). The Lord Jesus Christ is on the throne of grace, dispensing mercy to helpless, guilty, needy sinners. The Son of God is within the reach of needy sinners like you and me. He is God accessible to all who seek him (Hebrews 4:15, 16).

Answered By Experience
Third, this is a question that must be answered by experience. 'Where is he?'

Let me tell you what I know by the sweet experience of his grace. Are you yet without Christ? I pray that God has aroused an interest in your soul. I hope you are interested in the answer to this question, 'Where is he?' If you are interested in the answer, I want to give the testimony of a needy soul who has 'found him whom my soul loveth'. I have found him at the mercy-seat when, in the closet of my heart, I have cried to him in secret prayer (Isaiah 65:24). I have found him in his word, when I have opened the book of God seeking him (John 5:39; Luke 24:44-47). I have found him in the assemblies of his people, where he promised to meet his own (Matthew 18:20). I have found him at his table in the bread and wine of the Lord's Supper.

I find him in the field of service, as I have sought to do his bidding (Matthew 28:18-20). As we serve the interests of his kingdom, his people, his gospel, and his glory, as we seek to do his will and honour his name, as we endeavour to serve the souls of men, as we try to serve our generation by the will of God, our Saviour says, 'I am with you always'! And he is! He is with us in sympathy. He is with us to guide us. He is with us to strengthen us. He is with us to protect us. And he is with us to make our way prosperous and successful, according to the will of God.

I have found him in every fiery furnace of trial, in every lion's den of persecution, in every storm of difficulty, and in every river of woe to which I have been exposed. I have been a lot of places. I have experienced a lot of things. I have known a few troubles along the way. But I have never been in any place of need without him who is my Rock and my Salvation (Isaiah 43:1-5). I have always found the Lord Jesus Christ to be a God at hand (Philippians 4:4-7). Christ is always near us. Christ is always with us. Christ is always in us (Colossians 1:27).

A Personal Question
Fourth, I want you to make this a very personal question. 'Where is he' in relation to me? Is he in you? If Christ is in you, then you are in him and in him you are worthy before God (Colossians 1:12), 'counted worthy of the kingdom of God' (2 Thessalonians 1:5). This is the issue to be settled. Is Jesus Christ in you? Is Christ alone at the foundation of your hope, at the ground of your faith? Is he at the root of your joys? Is Jesus Christ king upon the throne of your heart? Is his presence in you manifest in your spirit, attitude, words, and actions? Is Christ before you as the goal of your life, the hope of your soul, the end of your journey, the prize of heaven toward whom you are pressing?

'Where is he?' Our Master is always at home; but he does not always meet his family in the same room. Sometimes we meet him in the closet of prayer. At other times he meets us in the great assembly hall of his palace, the house of public worship. We meet him on his porch, beholding his wonders in morning and evening meditations. Reading the Bible, I meet him in his library. As I labour in his vineyard, I commune with him in his garden. When my heart is lively and filled with hopeful expectation, he walks with me on the housetop. When my spirits sink, he meets me in the cellar, takes me by the hand, and leads me up the stairs. Every room in his house is good. Wherever he meets me, I rejoice. But the best room in the house is that in which he spreads his table before me and makes himself to be Bread and Wine to my soul, 'a feast of fat things' (Isaiah 25:6) to my soul! Let it be the ever increasing desire of our hearts, while we live in this world, to find him and live upon him and walk with him!

Chapter 55

Temple Doctrine

'Now about the midst of the feast Jesus went up into the temple, and taught. And the Jews marvelled, saying, How knoweth this man letters, having never learned? Jesus answered them, and said, My doctrine is not mine, but his that sent me. If any man will do his will, he shall know of the doctrine, whether it be of God, or whether I speak of myself. He that speaketh of himself seeketh his own glory: but he that seeketh his glory that sent him, the same is true, and no unrighteousness is in him. Did not Moses give you the law, and yet none of you keepeth the law? Why go ye about to kill me? The people answered and said, Thou hast a devil: who goeth about to kill thee? Jesus answered and said unto them, I have done one work, and ye all marvel. Moses therefore gave unto you circumcision; (not because it is of Moses, but of the fathers;) and ye on the sabbath day circumcise a man. If a man on the sabbath day receive circumcision, that the law of Moses should not be broken; are ye angry at me, because I have made a man every whit whole on the sabbath day? Judge not according to the appearance, but judge righteous judgment. Then said some of them of Jerusalem, Is not this he, whom they seek to kill? But, lo, he speaketh boldly, and they say nothing unto him. Do the rulers know indeed that this is the very Christ? Howbeit we know this man whence he is: but when Christ cometh, no man knoweth whence he is. Then cried Jesus in the temple as he taught, saying, Ye both know me, and ye know whence I am: and I am not come of myself, but he that sent me is true, whom ye know not. But I know him: for I am from him, and he hath sent me. Then they sought to take him: but no man laid hands on him, because his hour was not yet come. And many of the people believed on him, and said, When Christ cometh, will he do more miracles than these which this man hath done? The Pharisees heard that the people murmured such things concerning him; and the Pharisees and the chief priests sent officers to take him. Then said Jesus unto them, Yet a little while am I with you, and then I go unto him that sent me. Ye shall seek me, and shall not find me: and where I am, thither ye cannot come. Then said the Jews among themselves, Whither will he go, that we shall not find him? will he go unto the dispersed among the Gentiles, and teach the Gentiles? What manner of saying is this that he said, Ye shall seek me, and shall not find me: and where I am, thither ye cannot come?' (John 7:14-36).

In the midst of the Feast of Tabernacles, the Lord Jesus went up into the Temple at Jerusalem and taught. Here, in John 7:14-36, we read the doctrine he taught. Would to God that in every place where men and women claim to worship God today such doctrine were taught. Robert Hawker observed,

> It is very blessed to behold Christ going up to keep this ordinance, in fulfilling the whole law. And we have abundant reason to bless him that he did, for the Church would have lost this divine Sermon, which this chapter records, had he not gone there. Yea, indeed, as this was the last public preaching of Jesus, at the feast of tabernacles, it merits the attention of his people the more, as being decisive to the great points of his doctrine.

May God the Holy Spirit graciously teach us our Saviour's doctrine. Here are seven decisive points of doctrine to be observed in this passage.

1. If you go to hell, it will be entirely your own fault (vv. 16, 17). Man's will and works have nothing to do with salvation. That is all God's work alone. But if you perish, it will be altogether because of your will and your work. 'The wages of sin is death; but the gift of God is eternal life through Jesus Christ our Lord.' That is precisely the doctrine our Lord Jesus declared in John 7:16, 17. Faith in Christ is the gift of God; but unbelief is a choice of man, a decision of the will, a deliberate act of obstinate rebellion to God. The Son of God here tells us plainly that if you will do God's will, you will know his doctrine. But, our Saviour says, 'Ye will not believe' (Luke 22:67). 'And ye will not come to me, that ye might have life' (John 5:40).

2. Any preacher who exalts and promotes himself is not God's servant (v. 18). 'He that speaketh of himself seeketh his own glory: but he that seeketh his glory that sent him, the same is true, and no unrighteousness is in him.' Multitudes, like Diotrephes, fill the pulpits of churches in every place, who, craving the honour of men and loving to have pre-eminence, exalt themselves.

Such men are crafty, self-serving users of men. Our Lord Jesus was not such a preacher; and those who serve him are not such (2 Corinthians 4:5).

That man who is called of God is deeply sensible of his Saviour's majesty and his own infirmity. He sees in himself nothing but sin, unworthiness, and insufficiency. He knows that he is less than nothing (Ephesians 3:8; 1 Corinthians 15:9). But that man who knows that he is not motivated by Christ, that he is not led by the Spirit of God, that he has no regard for the glory of God, tries to cover his defects by exalting his name. Like the scribes and Pharisees of old, he seeks the praise of men.

God's servants do not exalt themselves. They exalt the triune God, uplifting the crucified Christ, crying, 'Behold the Lamb of God'!

3. Any religion that destroys mercy and compassion is false religion (vv. 19-23). The scribes and Pharisees, the religious rulers at the feast in Jerusalem, were still stewing over the fact that our Lord Jesus had healed the impotent man (John 5:1-8) on the sabbath day. Those same men were very strict about circumcising a child on the eighth day, even if the procedure had to be done on the sabbath. They did not mind cutting an infant on the Sabbath; but they despised the Lord Jesus because, as he puts it, 'I have made a man every whit whole on the sabbath day' (v. 23). 'And therefore did the Jews persecute Jesus, and sought to slay him, because he had done these things on the sabbath day' (John 5:16).

God's servants are more interested in caring for the souls of men than in defending a creed. They are more concerned about helping sinners than disciplining them. They prefer compassion to confessions, and are more interested in knowing, trusting, serving, and worshipping the Lord Jesus than they are in the opinions of men about them and their work.

4. Our judgment concerning other people and their actions should never be rash and hasty, but cautious and righteous (v. 24). 'Judge not according to the appearance, but judge righteous judgment.' We must not judge by appearance. The wise man says, 'It is not good to have respect of person in judgment' (Proverbs 24:23). 'Judge righteously between every man and his brother ... Ye shall not have respect of persons in judgment' (Deuteronomy 1:16, 17). 'My brethren, have not the faith of our Lord Jesus Christ, the Lord of glory, with respect of persons' (James 2:1).

We are all far too quick to censure others. To the eye of man, seeing a child circumcised on the sabbath day might appear evil; but it was not. God commanded it. Neither was it evil to heal a man on the sabbath. Mercy is never wrong! Let us judge things rightly. Always judge the actions of others with the greatest lenience possible. If we must be severe, we should be severe in judging ourselves and our own actions. 'First cast out the beam out of thine own eye;

and then shalt thou see clearly to cast out the mote out of thy brother's eye' (Matthew 7:5).

5. Unbelief is a wilful, deliberate denial of that which men know; yet no man can believe on the Son of God except he be taught of God (vv. 25-29). These men knew what they were doing. They had heard the Saviour's words. They saw his miracles. They knew that he was, after the flesh, of the royal seed of David. Yet, they wilfully shut their eyes to the things they knew, because they had no spiritual knowledge. Their heads were full of facts; but they did not know God. 'Willingly ignorant' (2 Peter 3:5) men and women shut their eyes against the plainest facts and most undeniable doctrines, because they will not bow to, and trust, the crucified Christ as their Lord and Saviour. Men will not believe what they do not want to believe (John 6:44-47). So they 'hold', they hold down and suppress, 'the truth in unrighteousness'.

6. Our great God and heavenly Father rules and overrules all things, even the will of man, to accomplish his own will (v. 30). So magnificently wise and great is our God that he even rules the very thoughts of his enemies, ever using them only as he will, for the accomplishment of his great saving purposes of grace in the redemption of our souls. 'Then they sought to take him: but no man laid hands on him, because his hour was not yet come.'

All our Lord's sufferings were voluntary, of his own will. He did not go to the cross because he could not help it. He did not die because he could not prevent his death. Neither Jew nor Gentile, Pharisee nor Sadducee, Annas nor Caiaphas, Herod nor Pontius Pilate, could have injured him, except power had been given them from above. All that they did was done under the control and by the decree of God (Acts 2:23). The crucifixion was purposed in the eternal counsels of the trinity. The sufferings and death of our Lord Jesus could not begin until the very hour which God had appointed before the world was made.

This is a great mystery. But it is a blessed revelation of divine truth. It is full of sweet, pleasant, and unspeakable comfort to God's saints. Let us never forget that we live in a world ruled by our God. Our heavenly Father overrules all times and events; and nothing can happen but by God's will, purpose, and decree. The very hairs of our heads are all numbered. Neither sorrow nor sickness, nor poverty, nor persecution can touch his elect, unless God has ordained it as an instrument to help his chosen. Our times are in God's hands (Psalms 31:15). All is well!

7. When God shuts the door, it cannot be opened (vv. 31-34). To some the preaching of the gospel is 'the savour of life unto life', to others 'of death unto death'. If God opens the door, none can shut it; and if God shuts the door, none can open it. Oh, may he be pleased to open to you the Door Christ Jesus and sweetly force you in. God help you now. Oh, may he sweetly force you by irresistible grace to come to Christ and be saved.

Chapter 56

Are You Thirsty?

'In the last day, that great day of the feast, Jesus stood and cried, saying, If any man thirst, let him come unto me, and drink. He that believeth on me, as the scripture hath said, out of his belly shall flow rivers of living water. (But this spake he of the Spirit, which they that believe on him should receive: for the Holy Ghost was not yet given; because that Jesus was not yet glorified)' (John 7:37-39).

By the time our Lord Jesus came into this world the Jews' religion had degenerated into nothing but an outward form, bearing very little resemblance to the worship God established by the hand of Moses when he gave his servant the Pattern of the tabernacle. They retained much of the outward form, the holy days and the great holy convocations required by the law. But they knew nothing of spiritual worship, and really cared nothing for the meaning of the ordinances they practiced. They retained what they wanted, observed what they enjoyed, and practiced that by which they could gain something. Everything else in the book of God they ignored. Much like most religious people today.

In addition to that mockery of God, the Jews had more religious traditions and customs of human invention than a dog has fleas. Let me tell you about one of them.

During the Feast of Tabernacles, on the eighth day of the feast, which was the last day of the feast, that which they considered 'the great day of the feast', they read the last section of the law. Then, as the climactic act of their feast, they observed a very solemn ceremony, a ceremony altogether of their own invention. I presume they thought it made the worship of God more appealing.

John Trapp tells us that in a great procession the people would parade down to the river Shiloh, perhaps a reference to the spring of Gihon, with buckets, and bring water up to the temple. The priests would take their buckets of water and pour them out on the altar. As they did, the people would sing, 'With joy shall ye draw water out of the wells of salvation' (Isaiah 12:3).

That is exactly where we are in John 7:37-39. The Jews had been up to the Feast of Tabernacles at Jerusalem. They had been there for eight days. They had gone through all the rites and ceremonies of their now empty religion. They had done all that they knew to do. They had done all that their religious leaders told them to do. But their religion had left them thirsty. Now, they were going home, going home just as empty and thirsty as they were when they came up to the feast. As they were leaving the temple, the Lord Jesus stepped up on a high place where he could be seen and heard by all, and cried with a loud voice, 'If any man thirst, let him come unto me, and drink. He that believeth on me, as the scripture hath said, out of his belly shall flow rivers of living water.'

Are you thirsty? Has your religion left you thirsty? Come to Christ. Drink of the life-giving Fountain; and thirst no more.

The Thirst

The Lord Jesus says, 'If any man thirst'. The thirst he speaks of is a spiritual thirst, a thirst in your soul, a thirst in the heart. It is an anxiety of soul arising from conviction of sin, a desire of pardon arising from a sense of guilt, a longing after peace of conscience arising from a dread of judgment. Do you feel your guilt, your sins, your iniquity? Do you want forgiveness? Are you sensible of your soul's need? Do you want help and relief? If so, this is the Saviour's word to you.

'If any man thirst'. The Jews who heard Peter preach on the day of Pentecost, and were 'pricked in their hearts', were thirsty. The Philippian jailer who cried to Paul and Silas, 'What must I do to be saved?' was thirsty. Are you thirsty? Few people are.

Many there are who thirst after every vain thing; but few thirst for Christ. Few thirst for mercy. Few thirst for God's salvation. Are you thirsty? Blessed are those who know something by experience of this spiritual 'thirst'. The beginning of all true Christianity is to discover that we are guilty, empty, needy sinners. Until we know that we are lost, we cannot be saved. The very first step toward heaven is to be thoroughly convinced that we deserve hell. That sense of sin, which sometimes alarms a man and makes him think his own case is hopelessly desperate, is a good sign. It is in fact an indication of God given life wrought in the soul (Matthew 5:1-6).

How broad, how inclusive these words are! 'If any man thirst'! The gospel of Christ is for 'any man'. It matters not who you are, what you have been, or what you have done. The Lord Jesus says, 'If any man thirst let him come'! If you are thirsty, the invitation is for you. No other qualification is required. Are you thirsty? Our Lord Jesus does not say a word here about repentance that must be experienced, amendments that must be made, preparations for grace that must be experienced, knowledge that must be gained, or works that must be done.

Are you thirsty? Do you feel the weight of your sins pressing you down to hell? Do you thirst for peace, pardon, forgiveness, righteousness, acceptance with God? If so, this is a word from God for you.

Come And Drink

'If any man thirst, let him come unto me and drink.' Here is the Fountain of Life, the Fountain opened for sin and uncleanness, the smitten Rock that gushes forth rivers of living waters, the Well of Salvation, stretching forth his hands to poor, needy sinners, calling thirsty souls to come to him and drink. Christ is the Supplier of all spiritual necessities. Christ is the Reliever of all spiritual needs. He calls all who feel the heavy burden of sin to come to him and find relief.

Those words, 'let him come unto me', are very simple and easily understood. But they settle a mighty question, which all the wisdom of Greek and Roman philosophers could never settle. They tell us how man can have peace with God. They tell us that peace is to be had in Christ by trusting in him as our Mediator and Substitute.

To 'come' to Christ is to believe on him; and to 'believe' on him is to come. There is no other way to obtain peace. Salvation is to be had by casting your soul upon Christ, committing yourself to Christ, coming to Christ. Through believing on the Son of God, and in coming to the Lord Jesus, we receive the adoption of children and free and full justification as the sons of God (John 1:12, 13; 6:35, 37; Romans 4:25-5:11).

The saints of God in every age have been and are men and women who drink of this fountain by faith and find relief. They have experienced this thirst of soul and the relief of Christ quenching their souls' thirst. They felt their guilt and emptiness and thirsted for deliverance. They heard of a full supply of pardon, mercy, and grace in Christ crucified for all who trust him. They believe the good news. They cast aside all confidence in their own goodness and worthiness and come to Christ by faith. In coming they have found relief. In coming daily they live. In coming they hope to die.

'If any man thirst, let him come unto me and drink.' 'Drink'! What a great word that is! The Son of God says to thirsty sinners, 'Come unto me and drink'! He says, 'Come to me and freely take from me everything your soul needs; mercy, grace, pardon, peace, strength, wisdom, righteousness, sanctification, redemption'! Christ is the Fountain of Life. Drink from the Fountain! Bathe in the Fountain! Swim in the Fountain!

The Promise Of Life

In verse 37 the Lord Jesus promises life to all who come and drink. But there is more here than the promise of life. The Lord Jesus promises that every thirsty sinner who comes to him shall have life in a river of life in himself. 'He that believeth on me, as the scripture hath said, out of his belly shall flow rivers of living water.' All who come to Christ by faith shall find in him abundant satisfaction for themselves. And the believing sinner becomes a fountain of life to others. Being blessed of God, the believing sinner is made an instrumental source of blessing to others. What a Fountain of Life Christ is in our souls! 'Christ in you', the Spirit of God declares, is 'the hope of glory'!

What peace and hope, what comfort and joy, what riches of grace and mercy and love we find in our dear Saviour! In him we find grace according to our need, and strength according to our days. In myself I find nothing but disappointed; but I have never been disappointed in Christ.

I cannot tell you what a blessing my God has made other saved sinners to be to me. I constantly find the sweet waters of life flowing to my soul from God's saints. Their love engaged for my help, their quickness to forgive my offences, their readiness to supply the needs of others, their eagerness to see sinners come to know the Saviour, and their zeal for the gospel, for the glory of God and for the kingdom of God are all as rivers of living waters to my soul, ever refreshing, reviving, and invigorating.

Only in the day of judgment, when all things are revealed, will we know the good that God has done by each believer, once the rivers of living water start flowing out of his belly. Some do good while they live, by their tongues, like the Apostles and first preachers of the gospel. Others do good when they are dying, like Stephen and the penitent thief. And others do good after they have been dead many years, like Bunyan, Gill, Spurgeon, Hawker, etc..

When I read, 'He that believeth on me, as the scripture hath said, out of his belly shall flow rivers of living water', I thought, 'I don't recall a passage that says that'. So I took down a concordance and started looking for the place in which the scriptures say that, and discovered that my memory had not failed me. The scriptures do not say that anywhere; but the scriptures do declare it everywhere (Isaiah 12:3; 35:6, 7; 41:18; 44:18; 55:1; Zechariah 14:8, 16).

Are You Thirsty?

A Difficulty Cleared

I am reluctant to mention it, but there is a difficulty in our text that needs to be cleared. Look at verse 39. (But this spake he of the Spirit, which they that believe on him should receive: for the Holy Ghost was not yet given; because that Jesus was not yet glorified.)

Obviously, the Holy Spirit existed before the Lord Jesus was glorified. He is the eternal God, the third Person in the triune Godhead (1 John 5:7).

Equally obvious is the fact that in the Old Testament, God the Holy Spirit regenerated, called, sanctified, guided, and preserved chosen, redeemed sinners, just as he does today. Without the Spirit of God there is no spiritual life. Without him there is no faith in Christ. Without him there is no union with Christ. Yet, God's saints of old enjoyed those sweet blessings of grace just as we do. Noah found grace in the eyes of the Lord. Enoch walked in sweet communion with God and spoke by the Spirit of prophecy. Abraham believed God. David cried, 'Take not thy Holy Spirit from me'!

What, then, is the meaning of John's words in verse 39? In what sense was the Holy Spirit not yet given because Christ was not yet glorified? He was not yet given to the Gentiles as the manifest, inaugural gift of the enthroned Messiah. It was, as our Saviour said in John 16, expedient for us that he return to the Father, that the blessing of Abraham, the promise of the Spirit might gush forth from heaven upon chosen sinners of every nation, kindred, tribe, and tongue in all his life-giving power. The gift of the Spirit is God's declaration of redemption accomplished, Christ enthroned, salvation finished, the Surety accepted, and the covenant fulfilled (Psalms 68:18, 19).

Are you thirsty? Come to Christ the Saviour and drink away the thirst of your soul!

> Come, ye sinners, poor and wretched,
> Weak and wounded, sick and sore;
> Jesus ready stands to save you,
> Full of pity, love and power:
> He is able, He is able,
> He is willing: doubt no more.
>
> Ho! Ye thirsty, come and welcome;
> God's free bounty glorify;
> True belief and true repentance,
> Every grace that brings us nigh,
> Without money, Without money,
> Come to Jesus Christ and buy.

407

Let not conscience make you linger,
Nor of fitness fondly dream;
All the fitness He requireth
Is to feel your need of Him:
This He gives you; This He gives you;
'Tis the Spirit's rising beam.

Come, ye weary heavy laden,
Bruised and mangled by the fall;
If you tarry till you're better,
You will never come at all;
Not the righteous, Not the righteous,
Sinners Jesus came to call.

View him grov'ling in the garden,
Lo! Your Maker prostrate lies;
On the bloody tree behold Him!
Hear him cry before He dies,
'It is finished'! 'It is finished'!
Sinner, will not this suffice?

Lo! Th' incarnate God ascended,
Pleads the merit of His blood;
Venture on Him, venture wholly,
Let no other trust intrude:
None but Jesus, None but Jesus,
Can do helpless sinners good.

Saints and angels, joined in concert,
Sing the praises of the Lamb;
While the blissful seats of heaven
Sweetly echo with His name.
Hallelujah! Hallelujah!
Sinners here may sing the same.

Joseph Hart

Chapter 57

Christ, The Cause Of Division

'Many of the people therefore, when they heard this saying, said, Of a truth this is the Prophet. Others said, This is the Christ. But some said, Shall Christ come out of Galilee? Hath not the scripture said, That Christ cometh of the seed of David, and out of the town of Bethlehem, where David was? So there was a division among the people because of him. And some of them would have taken him; but no man laid hands on him. Then came the officers to the chief priests and Pharisees; and they said unto them, Why have ye not brought him? The officers answered, Never man spake like this man. Then answered them the Pharisees, Are ye also deceived? Have any of the rulers or of the Pharisees believed on him? But this people who knoweth not the law are cursed. Nicodemus saith unto them, (he that came to Jesus by night, being one of them,) Doth our law judge any man, before it hear him, and know what he doeth? They answered and said unto him, Art thou also of Galilee? Search, and look: for out of Galilee ariseth no prophet. And every man went unto his own house' (John 7:40-53).

What horrible divisions there are among men! Since the days of Noah, men have been dividing into groups. It seems that man, by nature, prefers strife to unity, conflict to communion, and war to peace. Men and women everywhere look for excuses to quarrel. How easily even families, husbands and wives, brothers and sisters, children and parents are divided from one another! How sad! How very, very sad!

Even among those who are brothers and sisters in Christ, divisions often come. Paul and Barnabas were both true servants of God, brothers in Christ and co-labourers in the gospel. Both were loved of God, redeemed by Christ, and indwelt by God the Holy Spirit. Both were used greatly by God for the furtherance of the gospel and the glory of Christ. Yet, Paul and Barnabas fell into strife and were divided from one another!

What is the cause of strife and division among men? What causes strife in your home? What is the cause of strife among brethren? This is what the book of God says: 'Only by pride cometh contention' (Proverbs 13:10). Pride of race, pride of place, and pride of face are the things that raise contention. Nosey busybodies cause divisions. Idle gossips, with their slandering tongues, cause strife. Hear what God says about this matter.

'A wrathful man stirreth up strife' (Proverbs 15:18). 'He that covereth a transgression seeketh love; but he that repeateth a matter separateth very friends' (Proverbs 17:9). 'A froward man soweth strife: and a whisperer separateth chief friends' (Proverbs 16:28). 'He loveth transgression that loveth strife' (Proverbs 17:19). 'Where no wood is, there the fire goeth out: so where there is no talebearer, the strife ceaseth. As coals are to burning coals, and wood to fire; so is a contentious man to kindle strife' (Proverbs 26:20, 21). 'He that is of a proud heart stirreth up strife' (Proverbs 28:25). 'An angry man stirreth up strife' (Proverbs 29:22). 'The forcing of wrath bringeth forth strife' (Proverbs 30:33).

May God teach me kindness and give me grace to use my influence and energy to promote others and promote peace. Spirit of God, keep me from grieving you by that corrupt communication, bitterness, anger, wrath, and evil speaking that injures others and causes strife. 'Blessed are the peacemakers: for they shall be called the children of God' (Matthew 5:9). I want to be a peacemaker. Don't you?

But, having said all that, I hasten to say that not all strife is evil and not all peace is good. Division is not always evil; and unity is not always good. A united mob of rebels is still a mob of rebels. A peaceful cemetery is still a cemetery.

Here in John 7 we will read about a strife that cannot be avoided, if we are faithful to our God and faithful witnesses of Christ. Christ himself is often the cause of great division among men. Why was John inspired by God the Holy Spirit to record these things? Why does he tell us about this division of men that arose because of the Lord Jesus? What are we to learn from this passage? Four things are obvious. May God the Holy Spirit teach us these four things.

Useless Knowledge
First, there is a vast difference between religious knowledge and spiritual knowledge. Religious knowledge without faith in Christ is useless, damning

knowledge. Spiritual knowledge is the gift of God, the gift and accompaniment of saving grace. Religious knowledge is but the acquirement of the flesh.

We are told that some of our Lord's hearers knew clearly where Christ was to be born. They were obviously very familiar with many facts recorded in scripture. They knew the prophets. They knew that the Messiah would be of David's seed. They knew that he would be born in Bethlehem. They knew that the time for his coming was then at hand.

Yet, the eyes of their understanding were not enlightened. They groped about in utter darkness. The Christ, the Messiah was standing before them; and they could not see him! He was standing in their midst; and they were debating about places, family trees, and dates. Christ was in their midst; but they did not know him, believe him, receive him, trust him, or obey him.

Without question, where there is no knowledge there is no faith. 'Faith comes by hearing and hearing by the word of God.' Faith is not a leap in the dark. An 'unknown God' can never be the object of true worship, worship in spirit and in truth. You cannot know, trust, love, and worship an unknown God. But spiritual, saving knowledge is not something that can be acquired by human effort.

Many in our day, like these men in John 7, know the words of scripture well who have not a clue what those words teach. Many know the facts of scripture history who have no idea what those facts recorded mean, what they are intended to teach. Many know the doctrine of Christ who do not know Christ. Salvation is knowing Christ (John 17:3). Salvation is not knowing about Christ, but knowing Christ. It is not knowing what he taught, but knowing him! Eternal life is not knowing what Christ did, but knowing Christ (Jeremiah 9:23, 24).

The very devils know the scriptures better than you or me; but they are devils still. They are unaffected by what they know. And many men and women are just like them. They are familiar with the letter of scripture, and are able to quote scores of texts. They reason, argue, and debate about theological theory; and they are dead in trespasses and sins.

Saving knowledge is heart-knowledge. Sunday School teachers cannot convey it. Preachers cannot bestow it. Parents cannot give it. Heart-knowledge comes when Christ is revealed in you (Galatians 1:15). Heart-knowledge is bestowed when Christ is formed in you in the new birth. When Christ is in you, you have the mind of Christ. Until then, you have no spiritual knowledge (1 Corinthians 2:12-16).

Saving, spiritual knowledge, that knowledge that comes by the new creation of grace, causes the heaven born soul to know the plague of his own heart, the guilt of sin, the righteousness of God in Christ, and the accomplishment of redemption by Christ (John 16:7-11).

411

This is the highest degree of knowledge to which any mortal can attain. If you have it, it is God's gift; and you have eternal life. If you lack this saving knowledge that causes poor, needy sinners to cast all hope upon Christ, then all your learning and wisdom, all your knowledge and skill in religious things is but darkness and delusion.

Preaching With Authority

Second, our Master is held before us in this passage as the example to be followed by all preachers. He shows us what it is to preach with authority. We are told that even the officers of the chief priests who were sent to arrest him were struck with awe and were amazed by his preaching. They said, 'Never man spoke like this man' (v. 46). That is exactly what we are told people said about our Saviour when he finished preaching the Sermon on the Mount (Matthew 7:28, 29).

Our Lord's authority in preaching was not in the loudness of his voice, or the oratorical skills he displayed. He obviously displayed none. It was not the authority of learning, or the authority of bombastic theatrics. Our Master's authority in preaching was the confidence with which he spoke the things of God. He believed; therefore, he spoke. His authority was displayed in the simplicity with which he spoke the truth of God. Authoritative preaching needs nothing to cover it, no hedges to hide behind, no hidden meaning to which one can retreat. Our Master's authority in preaching was the fact that he preached to the hearts of men.

God give me grace to be such a preacher (1 Corinthians 2:1-5). May God raise up many to preach with such heavenly authority in this generation.

A Gradual Work

Third, we see in the example of Nicodemus that the work of God's Spirit in converting a sinner is often a gradual work. We are told that Nicodemus stood up in the council of our Lord's enemies and mildly pleaded that he deserved fair dealing. 'Doth our law judge any man, before it hear him, and know what he doeth?' (v. 51).

Nicodemus is the man who eighteen months earlier came to our Lord by night. Yet, here he is, still content to be numbered among the Sanhedrin. Still, he appears to have been, even now, a disciple, a secret disciple forced to identify himself with his Saviour. Obviously, I cannot speak with certainty about him; but that appears to be the case. Though he does not speak boldly, he does speak up in the Master's defence. Soon, this same man would openly identify himself with the despised Nazarene, and would do so at a time when very few would. He was soon to come with Joseph of Arimathaea to seek permission from Pilate to prepare our Lord's dead body for burial. He did so, remember, when all the Lord's chosen apostles had forsaken him and fled (John 19:38, 39).

The work of the Spirit does not always proceed with the same speed in the hearts and lives of chosen sinners. In some cases God's work of grace may appear to be very slow, though real and true. We are often too quick to condemn some as graceless, because their experience does not exactly tally with our own. We should never set ourselves up as judges who can tell who is saved and who is lost. We should always be content to leave every man and every woman to stand or fall before his Master. They do not stand or fall before you and me. Because we judge everything by outward appearance, we always judge wrong. Some I once thought to be strong examples of faith and faithfulness proved to be reprobate in the end. Others I thought had proved themselves reprobate have proved themselves faithful. You cannot tell wheat from tares until harvest time. At harvest time the tares stand straight and tall. The wheat bows its head.

Division Because Of Christ
Fourth, we are plainly told that our Lord Jesus Christ is the cause of division among men. 'So there was a division among the people because of him' (v. 43). He who is the Prince of Peace is the greatest divider of men the world has ever known.

There was a division among the unbelieving people here because of him. Some said he was a prophet. Others said he was a deceiver. Still others acknowledged his claims, but still did not trust him. A few became his disciples, trusting him and following him.

There was a division of believers from unbelievers because of the Lord Jesus. There always is. This is a great and wide division. The more clearly it is seen the better. It is a division that must be maintained. Those who believed and those who believed not could not walk together. Eventually, Nicodemus was forced to separate himself from his lifelong friends, because he belonged to Christ. The same will be true of you and of me, if we belong to the Son of God.

In Revelation 18:4 we have a command from the lips of our Lord Jesus Christ. This is the command our Lord gives to his people in every age. 'Come out of her, my people, that ye be not partakers of her sins, and that ye receive not of her plagues.'

Babylon is God's name for all false religion. It is any religion and all religions which declare that salvation is ultimately dependent upon, decided by, or determined by man. Babylon is the religion of man. Babylon is the religion of the world. From Babylon we must come out, 'and deliver every man his soul' (Jeremiah 51:6). We are given the same command, only in broader terms, in 2 Corinthians 6:14-18.

It is the responsibility of God's people in every age to thoroughly and distinctly separate themselves from false, apostate religion. As God commanded Lot to come out of Sodom, so he commands us to come out of Babylon. But, like Bro. Lot, we are all reluctant to do so. Our flesh is opposed to distinct separation. The religion of Babylon is so appealing and gratifying to our flesh that we will not leave it unless God lays hold of our hearts by the hand of his omnipotent grace and brings us out, even as the angel laid hold of Lot and brought him out of his beloved and cherished Sodom. May the Lord God be pleased to lay hold of our hearts and bring us altogether out of Babylon.

The Greek word translated 'division' in John 7:43 is schism. It is used to identify a violent split, a split involving fierce contention. This cleavage caused by Christ divides the dearest friends and relatives. It is the deepest, the most painful, the most real, and the most permanent separation of men in the world. Yet, when faith comes and the separation is made, unity is produced that can never be dissolved or broken. Union with Christ gives us union with one another. In Christ all who are born of God are one: one body, one family, one kingdom, one church (Ephesians 2:11-22). In Christ Jesus nationalities are blended. Calvary heals Babel. Personal peculiarities cease to divide. Position, rank, and wealth bow before the uniting influence of grace. All God's elect in all the changing ages of time are one in Christ Jesus. All the saints in heaven and on earth are one in him (Colossians 3:1-3, 10-15).

Chapter 58

'none but the woman'

'Jesus went unto the mount of Olives. And early in the morning he came again into the temple, and all the people came unto him; and he sat down, and taught them. And the scribes and Pharisees brought unto him a woman taken in adultery; and when they had set her in the midst, They say unto him, Master, this woman was taken in adultery, in the very act. Now Moses in the law commanded us, that such should be stoned: but what sayest thou? This they said, tempting him, that they might have to accuse him. But Jesus stooped down, and with his finger wrote on the ground, as though he heard them not. So when they continued asking him, he lifted up himself, and said unto them, he that is without sin among you, let him first cast a stone at her. And again he stooped down, and wrote on the ground. And they which heard it, being convicted by their own conscience, went out one by one, beginning at the eldest, even unto the last: and Jesus was left alone, and the woman standing in the midst. When Jesus had lifted up himself, and saw none but the woman, he said unto her, Woman, where are those thine accusers? hath no man condemned thee? She said, No man, Lord. And Jesus said unto her, Neither do I condemn thee: go, and sin no more. Then spake Jesus again unto them, saying, I am the light of the world: he that followeth me shall not walk in darkness, but shall have the light of life' (John 8:1-12).

When the Feast of Tabernacles was over, we are told that 'every man went unto his own house' (John 7:53); but, though 'the foxes have holes, and the birds of the air have nests; the Son of man had not where to lay his head' (Matthew 8:20). So we read in John 8:1 that 'Jesus went unto the mount of

415

Olives'. How our Saviour loved to go to the Mount of Olives and pray in the Garden of Gethsemane! He went there often to spend the night alone with his Father and our Father, his God and our God (Luke 22:39). This was a place to which he went so regularly that when Judas betrayed him and led a band of soldiers to arrest him, the betrayer knew exactly where the Master would be (John 18:1, 2).

You will remember that David, the great type of Christ, ascended the Mount of Olives barefooted and sorrowful (2 Samuel 15:23). Here, in the Garden of Gethsemane, our Lord Jesus knew he must soon encounter the prince of darkness. Knowing that here, in Gethsemane, he would soon sweat blood in anticipation of being made sin for us, knowing that here he would soon be betrayed, arrested and carried away to the cursed tree to be crucified for us, our blessed Saviour made the Mount of Olives and its garden, Gethsemane, his favourite spot of ground. Truly, this place was to him, sacred ground, hallowed by his own precious blood! How sacred Gethsemane's memory ought to be to us!

'Jesus went unto the mount of Olives. And early in the morning he came again into the temple, and all the people came unto him; and he sat down, and taught them' (vv. 1, 2). He prayed in Gethsemane by night and preached in the temple by day. His time seemed to be divided only by these two things: prayer and preaching. So it should be with all who preach the gospel (Acts 6:2). If we would serve the souls of men, if we would serve the cause of God's glory in this generation, if we would be useful, let every gospel preacher devote himself to prayer and preaching. May God the Holy Spirit raise up pastors for his people who are addicted to prayer, study and preaching! What might we expect, if he were to do such a thing?

While our Lord Jesus was at the Feast of Tabernacles he infuriated the self-righteous scribes and Pharisees who were the exalted, highly praised leaders of Israel. Throughout the week, all during the feast, they tried to find some reason to kill him, or at least to discredit him. At last, they hatched a scheme that they thought would surely work. They laid a trap for an unsuspecting woman. One of them seduced her into the act of adultery. While he lay in his tent with this woman, his friends were posted outside the tent door watching to catch her in the very act of adultery.

On the day after the feast, our Lord came to the temple early in the morning. As he sat down and began to preach, the people gathered around to hear his words. While he was preaching, the scribes and Pharisees broke in and sat this woman in the middle of the crowd and said, 'Master, this woman was taken in adultery, in the very act. Now Moses in the law commanded us, that such should be stoned: but what sayest thou?' Those poor, ignorant men thought they had surprised the Saviour. They thought, 'We've got you now'! I can see the smug grin on their faces. Can't you? They had no idea that the Lord Jesus had been praying for this woman all night. I can almost see the beaming smile of his heart, as the Pharisees bring the object of the Saviour's love to him. They brought her to him, they thought, to have her killed. They had no idea that the Lord Jesus had used them to bring her to him to have her saved by his grace!

Those proud fools thought they had laid a trap from which the Lord Jesus could not escape. They reasoned within themselves that there is no way possible for this woman to be forgiven, without the law being broken. If Christ forgave the woman, they would accuse him of dishonouring the law. If he commanded the woman to be stoned, they would accuse him of falsely pretending to be merciful and compassionate. They thought that the Lord Jesus would have to relinquish justice, or that he would have to refuse mercy.

With devilish insight, these self-righteous men had hit upon the problem of all problems in respect to the relationship of a sinful man to a holy God. The problem is this: how can God show love, mercy, and grace to a sinner and still be just, holy and true? How can God be both just and the justifier of the ungodly? How can a man be just with God? From a human point of view, and in the minds of self-righteous religionists, the problem was unsolvable. But that which with men is impossible, is possible with God.

In this passage of scripture we have a vivid picture of our Lord's compassion, mercy and grace upon sinners. He said, 'I came not to call the righteous, but sinners to repentance', and that is what he did. The self-righteous Pharisees went away confounded; and the poor guilty sinner was accepted, pardoned and justified. Here are five very important lessons for us to learn from this story of the woman taken in adultery.

Self-righteousness

First, we see, in the actions and attitude of these scribes and Pharisees, the terrible evil of self-righteousness. The real evil revealed in this passage is not adultery, but self-righteousness. The real culprits were these proud, religious hypocrites, the Pharisees, not this woman. These Pharisees were very proud of their pretended righteousness and morality, though in reality they were the vilest of men. They were not without guilt in this matter.

Without question, self-righteousness is the most terrible of all sins. It is more offensive and abominable in the sight of God than any other crime. Murder is a terrible crime; but I would rather be charged with murder before the law of God than with self-righteousness. Stealing is a dreadful offence; but I would rather be charged with stealing before the bar of divine justice than with self-righteousness. Adultery is a loathsome evil; but I would rather stand before God as an adulterer than as a self-righteous man. Lying is a fearful breach of God's holy law; but I would rather appear before God guilty of lying than to appear before him guilty of self-righteousness.

This is no new sin. Ever since man became sinful, he has professed to be righteous. Self-righteousness is the most difficult sin we have to deal with. Anger, wrath, envy, hatred, and lusts may be overcome, because they are easily identified. But pride and self-righteousness are most well covered. Those who have the most of these are the least aware of them.

Self-righteousness flourishes and grows best among devoutly religious people. There it is watered by prayer, cultivated by religious profession, and fertilised by religious ceremony (Matthew 6:1-4, 5-8, 16-18). I fear that most of our public praying, most of our religious works, most of what we think is assurance of salvation and evidence of grace, most of what we imagine is righteousness is nothing but self-righteous. All of our hurt feelings are manifestations of self-righteous (Matthew 6:1-8, 16-18).

The wrath of God burns most intensely against self-righteousness; and the hottest place in hell is reserved for the self-righteous (Luke 20:46, 47). Self-righteousness hates the grace of God. Self-righteousness is at the root of all gossip, slander, and persecution. Love covers sin. Self-righteousness exposes it. These Pharisees were not interested in honouring the law of God. They were interested in their own honour. They had no regard for this woman. They hated Christ because he exposed the evil of their hearts. They hated the doctrine of Christ, salvation by grace alone. They were using this woman for their own purposes. They no regard for her at all. They could not have cared less whether she lived or died. They had no regard for Moses and the law either. They were just using the law and Moses' name for their own designs. That is always true of Pharisees. They are religious zealots who care for nothing but themselves!

Self-righteousness is the most deadly of all sins. It most effectually bars a man from any hope of salvation. It makes God a liar (1 John 1:10). It blasphemes God. It rejects the righteousness of God in Christ. Self-righteousness is the most loathsome form of idolatry. It is the worship of self.

That is the first obvious thing to be learned from this story. Self-righteousness is a terrible evil. 'Beware of the leaven of the scribes and Pharisees'! It is self-righteousness (Luke 16:15).

Strict Justice
The second thing we see in this passage is the utter severity of God's holy law. The law of God is unbending, unrelenting, uncompromising in its strict justice. There is no question that the law of God required that this woman be put to death (Deuteronomy 22:22-24; Leviticus 20:10). It is written in the law, 'The soul that sinneth, it shall die' (Ezekiel 18:20).

The law of God is perfectly clear and utterly severe. There are no exceptions, no excuses, no extenuating circumstances to be considered. There is no room for pardon. There are no grounds for amnesty. 'The soul that sinneth, it shall die'! The law does not take into consideration the sinner's age, only his guilt. The law does not take into consideration the sinner's ability or lack of ability, only his guilt. The law does not take into consideration the sinner's environment, only his guilt. The law does not take into consideration the sinner's intelligence or ignorance, only his guilt.

One breach of God's holy law, one transgression, one act of sin is ground enough for our punishment. Any lack of conformity to the holy law of God, in thought, in word, or in deed demands eternal damnation. Sin is an evil committed against the infinite God, demanding infinite satisfaction, or eternal punishment. We are guilty; and we must die. The law of God demands it. 'The soul that sinneth, it shall die'. The law of God will not allow leniency. The law will not allow mercy. The law will not allow pardon. The law will not allow forgiveness. The law of God is utterly, inflexibly severe. Wherever sin is found, it must be punished. 'Now we know that what things soever the law saith, it saith to them who are under the law: that every mouth may be stopped, and all the world may become guilty before God. Therefore by the deeds of the law there shall no flesh be justified in his sight: for by the law is the knowledge of sin' (Romans 3:19, 20).

Salvation by the works of the law is a foolish absurdity. The law demands perfection or punishment. It offers no alternatives. Behold the utter severity of God's holy law, and be warned!

Divine Forgiveness

Third, this passage of scripture teaches us much about divine forgiveness. It shows us that sin cannot be forgiven until God's broken law is silenced. God must do something for himself before he can do anything for a sinner. Let me show you what I mean by that.

Before this woman could be forgiven the law of God had to be dealt with. Her accusers had to be silenced. And before any of us can be forgiven, the accusations of God's law must be silenced. The law of God must be satisfied. Our Lord Jesus Christ came not to condemn, but to save. Yet, he came not to destroy the law, but to fulfil the law. Now, how could that be done? How could he fulfil the law and yet save this poor, guilty, adulterous woman? How could he fulfil the law and yet save us?

First, our Lord Jesus silenced this woman's accusers (vv. 6-9). At first, he ignored these religious hypocrites. He knew who they were, what they had done, and why they had done it. But they continued to press the issue, thinking that he was now trapped in the dilemma they had created. Then he drove away the woman's accusers.

He cast the light of judgment upon these men. Obviously, he wrote something on the ground that astonished these men, something that shocked them. He may have written some names, and times, and places involving these very men. He may have written the name of the man who was with this woman in the act of adultery. He may have written out the events exactly as they really happened. He may even have written something like this, 'Suppose a perfectly innocent one volunteer to take this woman's place? Let her go, and take me instead. I will give myself to be her Substitute.'

Whatever it was that he wrote, it seized these hypocrites with a legal conviction. They were pricked by their own guilty consciences. At last, they all left. There were no witnesses to accuse this woman, so the law had no claim upon her. The Lord Jesus silenced this poor woman's accusers and drove them away.

So, too, by his one, all-sufficient, sin-atoning sacrifice for us at Calvary, our Lord Jesus, our all-glorious Christ has forever silenced the claims of the law against us (Romans 8:1-4).

This is the only means by which the law of God can be satisfied and the mercy of God extended. Christ died as our Substitute, under the penalty of God's holy law for us. The substitutionary sacrifice of the Lord Jesus Christ at Calvary is the only basis of divine forgiveness; and justice satisfied demands that the sinner go free (Romans 8:31-34).

Our Lord Jesus Christ freely forgave this guilty woman. She was guilty, but not condemned! The law could not condemn her; and Christ would not condemn her, so she must be pardoned. She must go free. And that is what the Lord Jesus Christ has done for us. We were guilty. Indeed, we are guilty. But we shall never be condemned. Our sin is gone. Christ took it away. The law is silenced. It cannot charge us with sin. Justice is satisfied. The Lord Jesus Christ satisfied it.

> Christ Jesus my discharge procured,
> The whole of wrath divine endured:
> The law's tremendous curse He bore;
> Justice can never ask for more.

> Payment God cannot twice demand,
> First at my bleeding Surety's hand,
> And then demand the price from me,
> For whom Christ died at Calvary.

Be still, my soul, and find sweet rest –
The merits of my great High Priest,
His righteousness and precious blood,
Have satisfied the Holy God.

I'll trust Christ's efficacious blood,
And never fear the wrath of God,
Since Jesus Christ has died for me,
And lives for me to intercede.

There is no condemnation for any believer in Christ. There is no basis for condemnation. There is no condemnation now. There is no condemnation for the future. This pardon and forgiveness is absolutely free and unconditional. If our Lord had said, 'Go and sin no more, and I will not condemn thee', the poor woman would have been without hope. But he said, 'Neither do I condemn thee'. My pardon and forgiveness is free. 'Go and sin nor more.'

Who shall condemn to endless flames
The chosen people of our God,
Since in the Book of Life their names
Are written clear in Jesus' blood?

He, for the sins of His elect,
Has full, complete atonement made;
And justice never can expect
That the same debt should twice be paid!

Benjamin Beddome

As guilty sinners, worthy of eternal damnation, we worship and praise the Lord Jesus Christ, our Redeemer, for the free, full, everlasting pardon of sin through his blood. That precious blood is the only way God can or will forgive sin. And that shed blood is effectual, securing the forgiveness of every sinner for whom the Saviour died, every sinner who believes on the Son of God unto life everlasting.

Sovereign Grace
Fourth, we are here taught something about the mysterious ways of God's sovereign grace. Those scribes and Pharisees were doing exactly what they

wanted to do, without any force or compulsion except their own wicked wills. Yet, the Lord God was sovereignly controlling all the circumstances and events of the day. He was secretly working through these wicked men to bring this poor, guilty woman to her Saviour.

This poor, guilty, trembling woman was not seeking the Lord. But he was seeking her. He had chosen her. He loved her. He was about to redeem her. And now the appointed time of grace had come. She would be his. He used ungodly men to expose her shame. The very men who wanted her dead and sought her destruction were used by God to carry the chosen object of his sovereign love into the arms of her Saviour. He used her shame to humble her. He used even her loathsome sin to bring her to himself. He wisely, graciously, sovereignly, and tenderly made her willing to embrace the Saviour in the day of his power. At the time of grace, he wrought a mighty change in this woman's heart. Once she saw Christ, she hated her sin, and she fell in love with him.

True Repentance
One final thing that we are taught in this story is the nature of true repentance. The Apostle Paul tells us that there is a repentance that must be repented of, a repentance that 'worketh death' (2 Corinthians 7:10). True repentance is much more than a mere reformation of life. It is a change of heart and attitude toward the Lord Jesus Christ. In the presence of Christ this woman was convinced of her sin. She offered no plea in her own defence. She stood before the Lord silently in her guilt. The Pharisees were convinced of their guilt by their consciences. This woman was convinced of her guilt by the Saviour, by Christ Jesus making himself known to her. Theirs was a legal conviction of terror. Hers was a gospel conviction of brokenness and contrition before God.

This woman recognised Christ as her Lord. She did not ask for anything. She seems to have simply waited in submission before her sovereign Master, realising that he had the right to damn her and the power to save her. She refused to leave Christ. She was overwhelmed by his grace and conquered by his love. Her only hope was in the Saviour; and she knew it. She could not leave him. She had nowhere else to go. She submitted herself to the authority and dominion of Christ the Lord. From that day forth she took up her cross and followed him in the way.

We must place ourselves in this story. Are we the crowd who stood by? They witnessed forgiveness, but they did not enter into it. Are we the scribes and Pharisees? They were in the place where grace was bestowed, but they were too proud and self-righteous to seek it. Or, are we like this poor woman, crushed with guilt before God, broken with sin before the Son of God; guilty, dirty, exposed, naked? If we can take our place with this poor, adulterous woman before the Lord Jesus, he will forgive us too!

Chapter 59

'I am the light of the world'

'Then spake Jesus again unto them, saying, I am the light of the world: he that followeth me shall not walk in darkness, but shall have the light of life. The Pharisees therefore said unto him, Thou bearest record of thyself; thy record is not true. Jesus answered and said unto them, Though I bear record of myself, yet my record is true: for I know whence I came, and whither I go; but ye cannot tell whence I come, and whither I go. Ye judge after the flesh; I judge no man. And yet if I judge, my judgment is true: for I am not alone, but I and the Father that sent me. It is also written in your law, that the testimony of two men is true. I am one that bear witness of myself, and the Father that sent me beareth witness of me. Then said they unto him, Where is thy Father? Jesus answered, Ye neither know me, nor my Father: if ye had known me, ye should have known my Father also. These words spake Jesus in the treasury, as he taught in the temple: and no man laid hands on him; for his hour was not yet come' (John 8:12-20).

There is a very close affinity between light and life. Where there is no light there is no life. Light is vital to life. We see this in the very beginning of the book of God, in the very beginning of creation (Genesis 1:1-2:3). As it was in the creation of the world, so in the new creation of grace, when the Lord God moves upon the sin-darkened heart of his chosen, when he sends his Spirit to correct the chaos of the fall in his redeemed, he causes the Light to shine in our hearts to give the light of the knowledge of the glory of God; and that Light is our Lord Jesus Christ.

Throughout the Old Testament, our Lord Jesus was spoken of in type and in prophecy as the Light of Life. The Jews understood clearly that the Messiah would be the Light by which God would reveal himself to men (Isaiah 42:1-6; 49:6; 60:1-3). Christ was the pillar of fire that led and protected them. Christ was portrayed in the golden candlestick in the holy place. So, when the Lord Jesus announced in the temple treasury, 'I am the light of the world', those who heard him understood, or should have understood, that he announced himself as the Messiah, the Christ of God.[17]

Dark World
First, our Lord Jesus here reminds us that this world is a place of darkness, utter darkness. It is impossible to overstate the spiritual darkness of the world in which we live. I do not suggest for a moment that people are not enlightened academically, philosophically, and politically. Multitudes are. But still 'darkness covers the face of the earth, and gross darkness the people' (Job 5:14; 12:25; Isaiah 9:2).

What darkness, what thick, thick darkness engulfs this world! We live in a world morally degenerate and spiritually blind. What darkness people all around us live in day by day! Emotional anguish, mental torture, and domestic chaos are things with which multitudes constantly live in this world of darkness. What is the cause of the darkness? Why is it a constantly thickening blackness and darkness? Fallen men and women are devoted to their own hearts' lust (Ephesians 4:17-19).

Though learned in arts and sciences, the vast majority of men and women in this world know absolutely nothing about their own nature, the depravity of our race, the character of God, the person and work of the Lord Jesus Christ, sin, righteousness and judgment, the world to come, or God's salvation. I want to be as personal as I possibly can. If you are without Christ, you live in darkness. You have no moral compass. You have no spiritual understanding. You have no guide for life.

Christ The Light
Second, the Lord Jesus Christ is the Light, the only light that can dispel the darkness that engulfs your soul. Here, the Lord Jesus says of himself, 'I am the Light of the world'.

John's Gospel was specifically intended to demonstrate the eternal deity of our Lord Jesus Christ. John was inspired by God the Holy Spirit to demonstrate

---

[17] Our Lord had been interrupted by the Pharisees who brought the adulterous woman before him. Once he had bestowed on that poor sinner the mercy and grace of free forgiveness, he walked over to the treasury, the very prominent place where the priests put the temple offering boxes, and continued preaching.

the fact that our blessed Saviour is himself God. This is evident from the very first sentences of this gospel narrative (John 1:1-5).

As we have already seen, John tells us of seven distinct statements made by our Saviour in which he used the words 'I am' to display his Godhead, to declare himself the self-existent God who revealed himself to Moses in the burning bush. Every time we read where our Saviour said, 'I am', we should understand that he is declaring, 'I am Jehovah-Jesus, God your Saviour'!

'I am the bread of life' (John 6:48).
'I am the light of the world' (John 8:12).
'I am the door' (John 10:9).
'I am the good shepherd' (John 10:11).
'I am the resurrection and the life' (John 11:25).
'I am the way, the truth, and the life' (John 14:6).
'I am the vine' (John 15:5).

More than 50 times John quotes the Lord Jesus saying to men, 'I am he'! Here, in John 8:12 he calls himself 'The light of the world', telling us plainly that he alone is the Light, that there is no light except him, for he is God, Jehovah, the great 'I AM'! 'I am the light of the world' (John 9:5; 12:35-46). John picks up this same theme in his first Epistle (1 John 1:5).

The crucified Christ is risen like the sun, to diffuse light, and life, and peace, and salvation to sin darkened souls in the midst of a dark, dark world. What the sun is to the whole solar system; the centre of light, and heat, and life, and fertility, that and more the Sun of Righteousness is to all upon whom he shines the life-giving beams of his saving grace. The light of reason is unreasonable. The light of liberty is bondage. The light of education is ignorance. The light of conscience is unconscionable. The light of religion is blasphemy. He only is the true Light who came into the world to save sinners, who died as our Substitute on the cross, and sits at God's right hand to save to the uttermost all who come to God by him. 'For with thee is the fountain of life: in thy light shall we see light' (Psalms 36:9).

Immediately, the Pharisees jumped on our Lord with his own words (v. 13), quoting what he had said back in John 5:31. 'If I bear witness of myself, my witness is not true.' But, when they thought he was trapped by his own words, our Saviour seized the opportunity and asserted that he is the Son of God, One with the Father (vv. 16-18).

He was not separate from the Father when he walked through this world. He was in the Father's bosom in heaven, as the Son of God, though as the Son of man, our incarnate God, he was standing in front of them. And he was not alone in his testimony and judgment. Here, too, he and the Father were and are

One. As the Son reveals the Father, the Father verifies the Son. So, by the very law they hoped to use against him, the Saviour says to his detractors, 'the testimony of two men is true' (v. 17; Deuteronomy 19:15). He asserted again and again that he is the Christ, the Son of God; and the Father bore witness to his claims at his baptism, on the mount of transfiguration, by the rent veil, and by the outpouring of his Spirit.

Christ Jesus, our Lord, is the Light of the world. He alone reveals God to the world, man to himself, and salvation to sinners. By his substitutionary atonement at Calvary, he alone shows us how God can be just and yet justify guilty sinners.

Christ's Followers

Third, we see here that believers are people who follow Christ. 'Then spake Jesus again unto them, saying, I am the light of the world: he that followeth me shall not walk in darkness, but shall have the light of life' (v. 12).

To follow Christ is to commit yourself to him as your only Lord and Saviour. To follow Christ is to submit yourself to him, bowing to his will and his rule. 'Following' is just another word for 'believing'. It is the same act of soul, only seen from a different point of view. As Israel followed the pillar of cloud and fire in all their wilderness journey, moving whenever it moved, stopping whenever it stopped, asking no questions, marching on in faith, so we must follow Christ. Believers are people who 'follow the Lamb whithersoever he goeth' (Revelation 14:4). We follow his doctrine, his precepts, and his direction in our lives.

Those who follow Christ do 'not walk in darkness'. They are not left in ignorance, like the many around them. They do not grope in doubt and uncertainty, like the blind man our Saviour healed. They see clearly. They 'have the light of life'. They are all taught of God. Walking in the Light we see light. We see, and see clearly who God is; holy and sovereign, just and merciful, gracious and true. We see, and see clearly what we are. Sinners saved by grace! We see, and see clearly who Christ is, what he did, why he did it, where he is now, and what he is doing there. We see, and see clearly how God saves sinners, by divine resolve, by divine redemption, by divine regeneration, by divine resurrection and by divine righteousness.

Walking in the Light, we recognise that light has many different effects upon those upon whom it shines. Light is repulsive to creatures who love darkness. If you turn over a log in the woods, bugs will run everywhere, because they are creatures of darkness. Light is repulsive to them. In the same way, the light of the gospel is repulsive to men and women who live in darkness (John 3:14-19).

Light is revealing to those upon whom the light shines (2 Corinthians 4:3-6). Light revives the earth, and causes it to spring with life. Just as plants grow by the light of the sun, we grow in the grace and knowledge of our Lord Jesus Christ, as we walk in his light.

Light is restful. Like the light of the sun which warms us, creating a place of peace, Christ Jesus, the Light, brings us to a place of peace. We gain peace because the burden of sin is lifted and the path through life and to our eternal home is made clear and sure, all mapped out and arranged for us. We are secure in him; and that gives rest in our souls. It is like the joy and comfort of seeing the porch light at your home after being away from your family for a while.

And light is reflected. As the moon reflects the light of the sun, so when the Sun of Righteousness is risen upon the soul, the heaven-born soul reflects the Light in which he lives (Matthew 5:14-16).

Not In Darkness

Fourth, those who follow Christ the Light 'shall not walk in darkness'. We do not walk in the darkness of the unregenerate. Believers do not walk in the darkness of unbelief, the darkness of religious superstition, and the darkness of heresy. We walk in the Light of the gospel. That means that we know who we are, whose we are, and where we are going. Though we were blind, now we see. Though once we believed not, now we know in whom we have believed. Walking in the Light we know that we are in Christ and Christ is in us. We are in the covenant of grace and in the love of God, and are going to heaven and eternal happiness.

Christ is the Light that cannot be quenched. The lights with which many please themselves flicker in trial and go out in the valley of the shadow of death, and prove worse than useless. But the light that Christ is, and the Light he gives, shall never fail.

Know Not God

Fifth, those who do not know Christ, those who do not follow the Light do not know God. Our Saviour told the Pharisees standing before him that, with all their pretended light, they were utterly devoid of the knowledge of God (v. 19).

The Man Christ Jesus, our Mediator, the sinner's Substitute and Surety, is the only saving revelation of God. He is the Wisdom of God and the Word of God. To know him is to know God and have eternal life. To be ignorant of Christ is to be ignorant of God and dead in trespasses and in sins. May God give you grace to know him and to live by him. May God the Holy Spirit grant that we who know him and live by him may yet grow to know him better who loved us and gave himself for us (Philippians 3:10).

Do not I love Thee, O my Lord?
Behold my heart and see;
And turn the dearest idol out,
That dares to rival Thee.

Do not I love Thee, O my Lord?
Then let me nothing love;
Dead be my heart to every joy,
When Jesus cannot move.

Is not Thy Name melodious still
To mine attentive ear?
Doth not each pulse with pleasure bound
My Saviour's voice to hear?

Hast Thou a lamb in all Thy flock
I would disdain to feed?
Hast Thou a foe, before whose face
I fear Thy cause to plead?

Would not mine ardent spirit vie
With angels round the throne,
To execute Thy sacred will,
And make Thy glory known?

Would not my heart pour forth its blood
In honour of Thy Name?
And challenge the cold hand of death
To damp th' immortal flame?

Thou know'st I love Thee, dearest Lord,
But O, I long to soar
Far from the sphere of mortal joys,
And learn to love Thee more!

Philip Doddridge

Chapter 60

'If God were your Father ... '

' ... Jesus said unto them, If God were your Father, ye would love me: for I proceeded forth and came from God; neither came I of myself, but he sent me. Why do ye not understand my speech? even because ye cannot hear my word. Ye are of your father the devil, and the lusts of your father ye will do. He was a murderer from the beginning, and abode not in the truth, because there is no truth in him. When he speaketh a lie, he speaketh of his own: for he is a liar, and the father of it. And because I tell you the truth, ye believe me not. Which of you convinceth me of sin? And if I say the truth, why do ye not believe me? He that is of God heareth God's words: ye therefore hear them not, because ye are not of God ... ' (John 8:19-59).

Children almost always resemble their parents; and children of the same family almost always resemble one another. With some, the resemblance is stronger than it is with others; but it is a rare thing for children of the same family not to resemble one another, or not to resemble their parents.

In this eighth chapter of John's Gospel, as our Saviour taught in the Temple, the Pharisees, who were certain that they were distinctly the children of God, sought to discredit the Lord Jesus and tried to find a way to put him to death. These Pharisees, like the Jews as a whole, thought that they alone were the objects of God's love and they alone were the children of God. But the Lord Jesus stripped the mask off these hypocrites, saying to them, 'If God were your Father, ye would love me' (v. 42). In verses nineteen to fifty-nine the Lord Jesus Christ shows us seven things by which the children of God in this world are always identified.

429

There are some things by which God's elect are specifically identified, things explicitly named in holy scripture that always follow grace. Here are seven of those things.

God's People Know Christ

If God were your Father, you would know the Lord Jesus Christ. Everyone who is born of God knows Christ (v. 19).

'Then said they unto him, Where is thy Father? Jesus answered, Ye neither know me, nor my Father: If ye had known me, ye should have known my Father also.' These men boasted about their spiritual perception, the depth of their learning, knowledge, and understanding. They boasted about their knowledge of God. They knew just about everything there was to know; and they knew it. They knew the facts of Bible history, the tribes of Israel and their land grants, their creeds and customs, laws and punishments, rituals and ceremonies, the right animals for sacrifice, the sacrifices themselves, their sabbath days and holy days. They knew all about feasting, fasting, and tithing. They knew all about religion except the 'one thing needful'. They did not know God.

They did not know God at all. Here, our Saviour tells us plainly that they did not know God, because they did not know him. Can you imagine how offended they must have been? This was to them a public scorn. The Lord Jesus publicly denounced them, their religion, and their pretence of spiritual superiority. Learn this, there is no knowledge of God apart from Christ (John 1:18; 14:6; 17:3).

If you do not know the Lord Jesus Christ by God-given faith in him, you do not know God. Christ is the brightness of his Father's glory and the express image of his person. He that has seen the Son knows the Father; and, indeed, no one can know the Father, but he to whom the Son reveals him.

Having said that, I hasten to add that it means nothing to say, 'I believe in Jesus', if we do not know him as he is revealed in the scriptures (1 John 4:2, 3; 5:1; 2 John 7). Acknowledging Christ in name is meaningless, if we do not know him as the Prophets and Apostles have revealed him. If you do not know the Lord Jesus Christ as the incarnate God, the covenant Head of his Church, the Surety of his elect, the Law-fulfiller for his brethren, the mighty Sin-atoner of his chosen, and the effectual Saviour of his people, you do not know God, and you do not know his Son. If you do not know Christ as your Saviour, as your only wisdom, righteousness, sanctification and redemption, you do not know God and you do not know his Son.

Until you trust Christ alone for the whole of your acceptance before God, you are like these Pharisees, utterly ignorant of God and all things spiritual. Your trust in yourself; your knowledge, your experience, your feelings, your creedal ceremonies and religious rituals, your own righteousness, your prayers and fastings, your repentance and faith, your sorrow and tears, is proof that you neither know Christ nor the Father. All your imaginary righteousness is of no benefit to your soul, but shall be its everlasting ruin. All your imaginary good works are but works of iniquity, for which you must ever suffer the wrath of God. We must trust Christ and Christ alone, or we must forever die!

God's People Persevere To The End

If God were your Father, you would persevere in grace. All who are born of God persevere in grace (vv. 30, 31).

'As he spake these words, many believed on him. Then said Jesus to those Jews which believed on him, If ye continue in my word, then are ye my disciples indeed'. As our Lord Jesus told his hearers about his crucifixion and the knowledge the Jews should have of him after his sacrifice at Calvary, as he set before them the excellency and divinity of his doctrine, of his mission from the Father, and of the Father's presence with him, 'many believed on him'. Many who heard him preach trusted him. As the gospel was preached, it came to some in power, and faith came by hearing.

As it was then, so it is today and in every day. Some believed and some believed not (Acts 28:24). 'As many as were ordained to eternal life believed' (Acts 13:48).

To these new born babes in grace, the Lord Jesus declares, 'If ye continue in my word, then are ye my disciples indeed'. There are two kinds of disciples: professed disciples and true disciples. True disciples continue in the doctrine of Christ. False disciples go out from among us, because they were not of us (1 John 2:19). Those who do not continue in faith, who do not persevere in the faith of the gospel never were born of God, never were true believers. 'He that endureth to the end shall be saved' (Matthew 10:22; 1 Corinthians 15:1-3; Hebrews 3:6; 4:14; 10:23). All who are born of God, all who truly trust the Lord Jesus Christ shall persevere unto the end (Job 17:9; Psalms 1:3; 125:1; 138:8; Ecclesiastes 3:14; Isaiah 46:4; Jeremiah 32:40; Philippians 1:6).

God's People Are Free

If God were your Father, you would be free. All who are in Christ are the free-born children of God (v. 36).

'He that is called in the Lord, being a servant, is the Lord's freeman' (1 Corinthians 7:22). The Master said, 'Ye shall know the truth, and the truth shall set you free' (v. 32). Then, he declares in verse 36, 'If the Son therefore shall make you free, ye shall be free indeed'. All who are born of God are free indeed. Christ sets the captive free, free from sin, free from Satan, free from guilt, free from the law, free from the curse, free from religious bondage, free from superstition, free from the fear of death. In Christ we are free!

> Free from the law's great curse,
> In Jesus we are free:
> For Christ became a curse for us
> And died upon the tree.
> The rituals of the law
> And all the law's commands
> Have been fulfilled in Christ the Lord,
> Established by His hands.
>
> No cov'nant with the law
> Can now with us exist:
> Complete in Christ we stand by grace,
> Both free and ever blessed.
> No more the dread of wrath,
> No more constrained by fear,
> We worship and we serve our God
> With gratitude and cheer.
>
> In Jesus we are free,
> In Jesus we are free,
> Free from all sin and from all guilt,
> We live in liberty!
> We'll join the happy song,
> With all the blood-bought throng,
> And sing the praises of the Lamb,
> Whose grace makes us His own.

God's People Do The Works Of Abraham
If God were your Father, you would do the works of Abraham. All the children of Abraham do the works of Abraham (v. 39).

'They answered and said unto him, Abraham is our father. Jesus saith unto them, If ye were Abraham's children, ye would do the works of Abraham'. The word of God tells us plainly that all who trust Christ, be they Jews or Gentiles, and only those who trust Christ, Jew or Gentile, are the children of Abraham. These Pharisees were Abraham's physical seed. They were Jews. But the Lord Jesus declares plainly that they were not the children of Abraham. The children of Abraham are those who are the children of promise, the children of God, his spiritual children, the Church and Israel of God (Romans 2:28, 29; Galatians 3:29; Philippians 3:3).

What does our Saviour refer to when he speaks of his people doing the works of Abraham? What are the works of Abraham? What are these works that are characteristic of all who trust Christ? The works of Abraham were works of faith and love. Those are the things that characterize all believers. These proud Pharisees, who boasted of being Abraham's children, were trying to murder the Lord Jesus (v. 40, 41); but Abraham was a man who hazarded his own life to save the lives of others. Is that not what he did when he went to war to rescue Lot?

What are the works of Abraham which are performed by all who are born of God, the works of Abraham that characterize all the children of Abraham? Abraham forsook all for Christ (Genesis 12:1-4). Abraham cherished Christ, the Sacrifice of the covenant (Genesis 15). Abraham was a magnanimous, forgiving man. We see this throughout his life and most distinctly in his treatment of Lot. Abraham was a hospitable, generous man (Genesis 18). Abraham was a man who saw the Lord Jesus, and seeing him sacrificed everything to him (Genesis 22).

God's People Love The Lord Jesus Christ

If God were your Father, you would love the Lord Jesus Christ. All who have God for their Father truly love the Saviour (v. 42).

'Jesus said unto them, If God were your Father, ye would love me: for I proceeded forth and came from God; neither came I of myself, but he sent me'. 'We love him, because he first loved us' (1 John 4:19). We may differ on many points. But in this one thing every true child of God is like every other child of God: 'We love him'. We do not love him as we desire. We do not love him as we know we should. We do not love him as we soon shall. But we really do love our blessed Saviour. It is not possible for a man to experience the grace of God in salvation and not love the God of all grace. It is not possible for a person to know the efficacy of Christ's blood in his own soul and not love his gracious Redeemer. It is not possible to have a heart renewed by the power of the Holy Spirit and not love the Spirit of life. In spite of our many weaknesses, sins, and failures, we do honestly and sincerely confess, 'Lord, thou knowest all things, thou knowest that I love thee.'

We know also that we would never have loved him if he had not loved us first. The love of God for us precedes our love for him. 'He first loved us'. He loved us before we had any desire to be loved by him. He loved us before we sought his grace. He loved us before we had any repentance or faith. He loved us before we had any being. He loved us eternally. Does he not say, 'I have loved thee with an everlasting love, therefore with lovingkindness have I called thee'? He chose us, redeemed us, and called us, because he loved us.

Not only does God's love for us precede our love for God; but God's love for us is the cause of our love for him. 'We love him, because he first loved us'. This heart of mine was so hard, this will so stubborn, that I would never have loved the Lord Jesus, if he had not intervened to conquer me with his love. In the midst of my sin and corruption, he passed by and, behold, it was 'the time of love'! The triune Jehovah, the Lord God, the God of all grace revealed his great love for me in Christ. Beholding the crucified Christ dying in the place of sinners, the love of God conquered this rebel's heart. Trusting Christ as my only Saviour, I am compelled to love him, because he first loved me. And now I know that I am what I am by the grace of God, because he loved me. Tell me, my brother, tell me my sister, is it not so with you?

God's People Hear His Word
If God were your Father, you would hear his word. All who have God for their Father, all true believers, all true Christians hear God's word (v. 47).

'He that is of God heareth God's words: ye therefore hear them not, because ye are not of God.' All saved sinners believe the gospel. They all receive, embrace, believe, and rejoice in the doctrine of God. Regenerate men and women have eyes to see the glory of God in the face of Christ. This is not true of all religionists. Many religious people, very religious people, are will-worshipping Arminians. But believers 'know the truth' (v. 32; 1 John 2:21). Tell a believer about divine sovereignty, and he will fall down and worship. Tell him about covenant grace, and he will find comfort. Tell him about electing love, and he will sing with joy. Tell him about total depravity, and he will weep as he confesses it. Tell him about effectual blood redemption, limited atonement, and he will dance like David before the Ark of God. Tell him about irresistible grace, and he will shout, 'Amen'! Tell him about the security of the saints, the final perseverance of God's elect, and he will pray for grace to honour the God of all grace!

God's People Shall Never Taste Death
If God is your Father, you shall never taste death (v. 51).

'Verily, verily, I say unto you, If a man keep my saying, he shall never see death'. It is true, we shall drop these bodies of flesh; but that is not death. That is just laying aside a garment that is worn out and no longer needed or wanted. Like Enoch, we shall be translated, and never see death (John 11:26). Like Elijah, we shall be carried to heaven on a chariot of fire, and never taste death. Because the Lord Jesus tasted death for us (Hebrews 2:9), we never shall. We have everlasting life (Revelation 20:6; 2 Corinthians 5:1-9).

Chapter 61

God's Works Made Manifest

'And as Jesus passed by, he saw a man which was blind from his birth. And his disciples asked him, saying, Master, who did sin, this man, or his parents, that he was born blind? Jesus answered, Neither hath this man sinned, nor his parents: but that the works of God should be made manifest in him ... ' (John 9:1-41).

The Lord Jesus performed many miracles of mercy during the three years of his earthly ministry. He turned water into wine, calmed the stormy sea, and multiplied the loaves and fishes. He healed the sick, made the deaf to hear, caused the dumb to speak, made withered arms straight, caused the lame to walk, made the blind to see, and raised the dead to life. By all these things he made manifest the fact that he is God and he is the Messiah, the Christ, the Saviour of the world (Isaiah 29:18; 35:4-10; 42:6, 7; Matthew 11:4, 5).

Two of the Lord's miracles stand out as being of such great importance, so spiritually instructive that they each occupy an entire chapter in the volume of holy scripture. In the eleventh chapter of John's Gospel, the Holy Spirit gives us the very instructive story of Lazarus being raised from the dead. At the outset of that chapter, we are told that Lazarus' sickness and death was 'for the glory of God, that the Son of God might be glorified thereby' (John 11:4).

Here, in the ninth chapter of John's Gospel, the Holy Spirit holds before us a man who was born blind, whom the Lord Jesus healed. Here, too, the entire chapter is devoted to telling us about this great miracle. Like the resurrection of Lazarus, this man's healing is full of instruction for our souls. And, as we are told that Lazarus' sickness and death was 'for the glory of God', we read

435

in John 9:3 that this man's blindness was designed and intended 'that the works of God should be made manifest in him'. This great miracle is intended to illustrate and make manifest the works of God our Saviour in saving his people from their sins.

'Jesus passed by'

The story of this blind man's healing begins with the Lord Jesus. How appropriate! The fact is everything begins with God our Saviour. Before we read about this man, his blindness, or his healing, the Spirit of God tells us, 'And as Jesus passed by, he saw a man'. It was the Lord Jesus passing by and seeing him that led to the mercy he obtained. So it is in grace. There are no advances made by sinners to the Lord, until the Lord passes by and bids the sinner live. Salvation begins with God coming to man, not with man coming to God (Ezekiel 16:1-14). If we love him, it is because he first loved us (1 John 4:19).

The Son of God hid himself from those Pharisees in the Temple who despised him (John 8:59). He passed by them in judgment, leaving them to themselves steeped in religion and sealed to everlasting destruction in reprobation. Grace is always distinguishing and particular. 'And as Jesus passed by' those men in judgment, he passed by this man in mercy. He passed by our souls in eternal election and chose us unto salvation. He passed by our souls in predestination and arranged all things for our everlasting salvation. He passed by our souls at the appointed time of love and called us by his grace. There's hope for sinners when the Lord Jesus passes by. Bartimaeus understood that. 'And when he heard that it was Jesus of Nazareth, he began to cry out, and say, Jesus, thou Son of David, have mercy on me' (Mark 10:47).

'He saw a man'

Next, we read, 'He saw a man which was blind from his birth.' The word translated 'saw' carries the idea of staring, gazing upon, and watching. It also carries the idea of discerning, understanding, and knowing. Blessed are those people who are under the watchful eye of the Son of God! The Saviour 'saw a man'. He saw who he was. He saw where he was. He saw what he was. He saw all that he had done. He saw all that he had been. He saw that he was blind. And he saw all that he would do for this man! We see a similar passage in Luke 15:11-20, where the Spirit of God gives us our Saviour's parable of the prodigal son.

The sovereignty of God in the exercise of his grace is exemplified in this ninth chapter of John's Gospel. The Saviour saw the man; the man did not see him. The man did not call upon the Lord to have mercy upon him; the Lord was the one to take the initiative. That is the way it always is. 'Salvation is of the LORD'!

'Blind from birth'

This man, we are expressly told by God the Holy Spirit, 'was blind from his birth'. There is much to be learned from what is here stated about this man's blindness.

'And as Jesus passed by, he saw a man which was blind from his birth. And his disciples asked him, saying, Master, who did sin, this man, or his parents, that he was born blind? Jesus answered, Neither hath this man sinned, nor his parents: but that the works of God should be made manifest in him' (vv. 1-3).

The disciples thought, like most people, that bodily afflictions come upon people because of sinful behaviour, that sickness is an indication of divine displeasure and disapproval. Such thinking is wrong and betrays an underlying sense of superiority and self-righteousness.

The Lord's words in verse 3 do not suggest that the man and his parents were not sinners; for both were guilty of original sin, and both had committed actual transgressions (Romans 3:23; 5:12). The Master was simply declaring that it was not his parents' particular sin nor his own that was the cause of his blindness. We know, of course, that all sickness and death are the result of sin. Were there no sin, there would be no sickness and no death. But the assumption that sickness is an indication of God's judgment is a display of proud ignorance. That was the error of Job's three friends. Charismatic, Pentecostal, fake-healers teach the same foolishness.

The fact is this man's blindness, we are specifically told, was for the purpose of God's works being made manifest in him. His blindness was designed for his mercy. His blindness was an act of God's prevenient grace, by which God paved the way for the saving operations of his grace. His blindness was by the special arrangement of divine providence (Romans 8:28). The fact is, for God's elect, all our afflictions are designed and brought to pass for our everlasting benefit (2 Corinthians 4:17-5:1; 1 Peter 1:2-7).

Let us never imagine that anything comes to pass by accident, or without divine design. Many seem terribly confused by the fact of the fall and of sin's entrance into the world. They seem to think that Adam's fall took God by surprise, and that the Creator lost control of his creation when sin entered. But that is not the case at all. When Lucifer fell, it was by divine purpose; and when Adam fell, it was by divine purpose (Isaiah 14:12-14, 24, 26, 27; Psalms 76:10; Romans 11:33-36).

Just as this man's blindness made a way for God to display his works in him, the sin and fall of our father Adam, and the ruin of the human race in Adam's fall were designed by our God to make a way for the manifestation of his works of grace in Christ, of whom Adam was a type (Romans 5:14), to the praise of the glory of his grace (Romans 5:12-21).

Moreover, this man's blindness represents the spiritual blindness of all men by nature. This man's blindness of body gave occasion for the works of God to be made manifest in him. So, also, the blindness of soul affords opportunity for God in Christ to be magnified in the works of grace. We are all born in a state of spiritual blindness, a blindness from which we can never be delivered except by the Son of God. All are by nature blind to the knowledge of God the Father, blind to his everlasting love, blind to the Person, work, grace, mercy, favour, and all the ten thousand beauties and excellences which are in God the Son in his mediatorial character, as Head and Husband of his Church and people. All are blind to everything relating to the eternal power and Godhead of the blessed Spirit, both in his own essence and glory and in his grace and mercy to chosen sinners, blind to our own utterly lost, ruined and undone condition, blind to our need of a Saviour, and even blind to our blindness!

'Must work'
'I must work the works of him that sent me, while it is day: the night cometh, when no man can work. As long as I am in the world, I am the light of the world' (vv. 4, 5). How I like what I read here! The Lord Jesus Christ, the God-man, our Mediator, our covenant Surety, the sinners' Substitute, speaks of the work he did upon this earth as a work that had to be done, a work that he 'must work', a work that he must finish before he could leave this world and return to his Father and our Father who sent him. Jehovah's Servant must finish his work (John 10:14-18). And finish it he did! Righteousness is finished! Satisfaction is finished! Redemption is finished! Justification, forgiveness, sanctification is finished! Salvation is finished!

Our message is 'the gospel', good news, not good advice! The Lord Jesus said, 'I have glorified thee on the earth: I have finished the work which thou gavest me to do' (John 17:4). What could be more blessed? Redemption-work is finished. The Church of Christ is saved. Jehovah is glorified. 'How beautiful upon the mountains are the feet of him that bringeth good tidings, that publisheth peace; that bringeth good tidings of good, that publisheth salvation; that saith unto Zion, Thy God reigneth'! (Isaiah 52:7)

'Go wash'
In verses 6 and 7, the Lord Jesus used very unlikely means to perform his miracle of mercy on this poor, blind man. 'When he had thus spoken, he spat on the ground, and made clay of the spittle, and he anointed the eyes of the blind man with the clay, And said unto him, Go, wash in the pool of Siloam,

(which is by interpretation, Sent.) He went his way therefore, and washed, and came seeing.'

Our Saviour used means that had no virtue or healing power in themselves; and the means used were both foolish and distasteful to the natural mind. So it is that by the preaching of the gospel, by the foolishness of preaching, spiritually blind and dead sinners are made to see and live. Gospel preaching is foolishness to the world; but it is the power of God unto salvation to those who are saved (1 Corinthians 1:18-24).

Let us understand that the means used are useless, without the blessing of God upon them. The clay and the pool of Siloam, like gospel preaching, were merely instruments in the hand of Christ. But without him the clay would only have been a greater obstruction to sight, not a means of giving sight. Just so, what we call the means of grace, without his blessing, tend more to increase spiritual blindness than remove it (2 Corinthians 2:15, 16; Revelation 3:18).

'Dost thou believe?'

This man experienced an extraordinary miracle, a miracle that could not be denied. It was such an extraordinary thing that it brought him into conflict with the Pharisees. The Pharisees reviled him and finally excommunicated him. But he stood by his experience. He said, 'Nothing like this has ever happened to anyone in the history of the world. I know that I was born blind. I know that I now see. And I know that the man who did this great work for me and in me is of God.' But that is not salvation. It takes more than a miracle, even a notable miracle, to produce faith in the heart of a man. Saving faith is the gift of God. It comes only by divine revelation. Faith comes only by Christ revealing himself to us, and in us, by his omnipotent mercy and irresistible grace.

'Jesus heard that they had cast him out; and when he had found him, he said unto him, Dost thou believe on the Son of God? He answered and said, Who is he, Lord, that I might believe on him? And Jesus said unto him, Thou hast both seen him, and it is he that talketh with thee. And he said, Lord, I believe. And he worshipped him' (vv. 35-38).

This man had received sight; but he must have Christ revealed to him in order to believe on him as Prophet, Priest, and King; and Christ is revealed by the hearing of the word (Romans 10:9-17). God saves sinners by the means he has ordained; and that means is the preaching of the gospel (1 Peter 1:23-25).

'Made blind'

Now, look at verses 39-41, and learn that the very gospel that God uses to cause the blind to see, he uses to make those blind who think they see.

'And Jesus said, For judgment I am come into this world, that they which see not might see; and that they which see might be made blind. And some of the Pharisees which were with him heard these words, and said unto him, Are we blind also? Jesus said unto them, If ye were blind, ye should have no sin: but now ye say, We see; therefore your sin remaineth.'

Our Lord's judgment upon these Pharisees and his mercy upon the man born blind reminds me of the cloud in the camp of Israel that gave light to Israel, while engulfing Egypt in darkness (Exodus 14:19, 20). Christ is both the Rock of ages; the sure Foundation Jehovah has laid in Zion. 'He that believeth shall never be ashamed, nor confounded, world without end' (Isaiah 45:17). And he is a 'stone of stumbling, and a rock of offence'. On whomsoever he shall fall, 'it will grind him to powder' (Deuteronomy 32:4; Isaiah 28:16; 1 Peter 1:6-8; Matthew 21:44).

'Who is this that cometh from Edom, with dyed garments from Bozrah? this that is glorious in his apparel, travelling in the greatness of his strength? I that speak in righteousness, mighty to save. Wherefore art thou red in thine apparel, and thy garments like him that treadeth in the winefat? I have trodden the winepress alone; and of the people there was none with me: for I will tread them in mine anger, and trample them in my fury; and their blood shall be sprinkled upon my garments, and I will stain all my raiment. For the day of vengeance is in mine heart, and the year of my redeemed is come' (Isaiah 63:1-4).

'Dost thou believe on the Son of God?' God help you to believe. As this blind man was healed on the sabbath day (v. 14), on the day you believe on the Lord Jesus Christ, your everlasting sabbath rest begins (Matthew 11:28-30).

Chapter 62

The True Shepherd And The False

'Verily, verily, I say unto you, he that entereth not by the door into the sheepfold, but climbeth up some other way, the same is a thief and a robber. But he that entereth in by the door is the shepherd of the sheep. To him the porter openeth; and the sheep hear his voice: and he calleth his own sheep by name, and leadeth them out. And when he putteth forth his own sheep, he goeth before them, and the sheep follow him: for they know his voice. And a stranger will they not follow, but will flee from him: for they know not the voice of strangers. This parable spake Jesus unto them: but they understood not what things they were which he spake unto them' (John 10:1-6).

The Lord God made a promise to his church in Jeremiah 3:15. It is a promise made to those people to whom the God of heaven declares, 'I am married unto you ... I will bring you to Zion'. This is God's promise to his people for all time. 'I will give you pastors according to mine heart, which shall feed you with knowledge and understanding.'

Those pastors are the ascension gifts of Christ to his church, they are pastors after God's own heart, who feed the sheep with knowledge; gospel knowledge, Bible knowledge, the knowledge of God, of Christ, of grace, and knowledge of man in his fallen state and in his redeemed state. They constantly proclaim the word of the Lord. They constantly call eternity bound sinners to Christ, and urge God's people to 'walk in the old paths, where is the good way' that you may 'find rest for your souls'. They feed God's people with

441

understanding, too, understanding yourself, understanding the things of God, and understanding the times.

When the Lord God gives his church pastors after his own heart, who feed his sheep with knowledge and understanding, his sheep shall 'fear no more, are no longer dismayed, neither shall they be lacking' (Jeremiah 23:4). Blessed are those people, blessed is that church to whom God gives such a pastor!

What kind of pastor is he who is the gift of God to his people? These first six verses of John 10 show us. The word 'pastor' simply means 'shepherd'. Christ himself is the Good Shepherd, the Chief Shepherd, and the Great Shepherd of the sheep. All faithful pastors are under-shepherds, men to whom the Lord Jesus entrusts the care of his sheep, men responsible to feed his sheep with knowledge and understanding, men responsible to guide his sheep and protect his sheep. In this tenth chapter of John's Gospel, our Lord Jesus uses himself as the example, the pattern, the standard, by which all true shepherds are identified and known.

Context

It is impossible to understand the message of our Lord in this parable, if we fail to see the context in which it is given. In this parable our Master is distinctly addressing the Pharisees, religious leaders who use their office for their own gain, who come only to rob, and steal, and kill, those false shepherds who use and abuse his sheep.

In the ninth chapter, our Lord having healed the blind man, the Pharisees, now put him out of the synagogue, fearing they might lose power, position, and influence (John 9:39-41). Then the Master said, 'Verily, verily, I say unto you, he that entereth not by the door into the sheepfold, but climbeth up some other way, the same is a thief and a robber'. How those words must have stung those thieves and robbers, those destroyers of men's souls, those false shepherds!

Here is the false shepherd. 'Verily, verily, I say unto you, he that entereth not by the door into the sheepfold, but climbeth up some other way, the same is a thief and a robber'. With those words, our Master describes every false shepherd. Here is the true shepherd. 'But he that entereth in by the door is the shepherd of the sheep'. With those words, the Lord Jesus describes himself and every true shepherd of the sheep.

The False Shepherd

First, our Saviour describes every false shepherd, every false prophet, every false preacher. The most dangerous thing in this world is a false prophet, a false shepherd. The Pharisees of our Lord's day were all false shepherds. But we are plainly and repeatedly warned in the word of God that throughout the ages of time, until the very last day, false prophets and false shepherds, like those Pharisees, will only increase. And, like those Pharisees, the false shepherds will always be recognised, applauded, and promoted by a lost religious world; and the true shepherd will always be despised (Matthew 24:24; Acts 20:30; 1 Timothy 4:1; 2 Peter 2:1; 1 John 2:18; 4:1; 2 John 7).

Who is the false shepherd? The false shepherd is described in many ways in the scriptures; but in the passage before us the Lord Jesus lays the axe to the root of the tree and tells us that all false shepherds that will ever be in the world are those who enter not by the door, but climb up some other way into the sheepfold. The false shepherd is one who refuses to enter the kingdom of God by Christ the Door. He is a lost, self-righteous man, one who going about to establish his own righteousness, refuses to submit to and trust the righteousness of God.

There can be no question about this. Our Lord tells us plainly that he is the Door. 'I am the Door; by me, if any man enter in, he shall be saved, and shall go in and out, and find pasture' (v 9). So the one great mark by which false shepherds are identified is that they enter not by the Door: 'Verily, verily, I say unto you, he that entereth not by the door into the sheepfold, but climbeth up some other way, the same is a thief and a robber' (v. 1). This is the identifying mark of every false shepherd. He is not saved himself. He is a lost, unbelieving rebel.

He enters not in by the Door. He makes another way into the sheepfold. He offers another hope, another mediator. Truly, these are perilous times! Christ says, 'I am the Way'. The false shepherd says, 'There are other ways'. Christ declares, 'It is not of him that willeth, nor of him that runneth, but of God that showeth mercy.' The false shepherd says, 'God has done everything he can. Now, it's all up to you.' Christ says, 'I lay down my life for the sheep.' The false shepherd says, 'Christ died for everyone'. Christ says, 'By my own blood, I have purchased forgiveness, put away sin, obtained eternal redemption, made an end of transgression, and brought in everlasting righteousness.' The false shepherd says, 'Forgiveness, righteousness and redemption are possible since Christ died, if you will only accept it.' Christ says, 'It is the Spirit that quickeneth: the flesh profiteth nothing.' The false shepherd says, 'The Spirit wants to quicken; but it is really the will of your own flesh that profits you with salvation and eternal life.'

Antichrist

The false shepherd is antichrist. Antichrist is not a single figure in a red suit with horns, a tail, a pitch fork, and the number 666 tattooed on his forehead. Antichrist is often represented as one man; but really he is many. Antichrist is all freewill, works religion, and any who promote it.

Our Lord here speaks of one false shepherd, rather than of many, because all false shepherds are really one. All false shepherds are antichrist. All false shepherds are the man of sin. They all come into the sheepfold, the churches of Christ, by climbing over the wall, refusing to enter by Christ, the Door. Paul, Peter, and Jude describe them as those who sneak into the church under false pretence as the servants of God, those who come into the church 'privily' as promoters of righteousness.

The false shepherd is that man who would turn you away from the gospel of Christ unto another gospel, which is not another (Galatians 1:6-9). The false shepherd is one who tries to corrupt your mind from the simplicity that is in Christ, preaching another Jesus, another spirit, and another gospel (2 Corinthians 11:3, 4).

The apostle Paul spoke of a day when the man of sin must be revealed, and clearly identified him in 2 Thessalonians chapter 2. Here he is. You have seen him and heard him many times. You can find him in almost every place where men and women gather for worship. He is that one 'Who opposeth and exalteth himself above all that is called God, or that is worshipped; so that he as God sitteth in the temple of God, showing himself that he is God' (2 Thessalonians 2:7-12; Revelation 13:1, 2).

There is no question but that the great enemy of the sheep, the false shepherd, who comes like a lamb, but who has the paw of a bear, is Antichrist. He is empowered and directed by Satan himself. The false shepherd is antichrist. He is the preacher of freewill-works religion, the religion of man. Paul tells us in Romans 1 that that religion that changes the glory of the incorruptible God into the image of corruptible man, that religion that turns the truth of God into a lie, that religion that worships and serves the creature more than the Creator is the judgment of God upon a generation that refused to receive the love of the truth. The fruit of such religion is a constantly increasing moral degeneracy that is ultimately manifest in homosexuality and every imaginable deviant behaviour.

Really, sodomy is but a reflection of freewill-works religion. It is a pretence of love that involves no commitment. It is a union of men that can never produce life. It is the result of man's high opinion of himself, the fruit and exercise of his own will. It constantly seeks to recruit others. And it is condemned by God.

If we are saved from this curse, the curse of antichrist's religion, the only reason you and I are not engulfed in it is this: 'God hath from the beginning chosen you to salvation through sanctification of the Spirit and belief of the truth: Whereunto he called you by our gospel, to the obtaining of the glory of our Lord Jesus Christ' (2 Thessalonians 2:13, 14).

What is the false shepherd's object? What does he come to do? I often hear and read what others say when warning us of false prophets. They couch their warnings in such phrases that you would almost think they are saying, 'These men really are not so bad. Really, they are fine, fine brethren, whose brains are just a little muddled.' Our Lord does not speak like that at all. Does he?

The Master says, of every false shepherd, 'the same is a thief and a robber' (v. 1). In verse 10 he says, 'The thief cometh not but for to steal, and to kill, and to destroy'.

Satan's great object in this world is to steal, and to kill, and to destroy. That is the object of antichrist. That is the object of all false shepherds. They are God's enemies, Christ's enemies; and you ought to count them as your enemies. David did, and so did Paul (Psalms 139:21, 22; Galatians 5:12). They come for the express purpose of robbery and destruction, to rob God of his throne, to rob Christ of his glory, to rob the Son of God of his seed, his satisfaction for his soul's travail, to rob you and your children of the Way of life, to rob you of the only Door unto the Father, to rob you of redemption, salvation, forgiveness, peace, and eternal life, and to destroy your soul (Matthew 23:13).

Be warned. Flee, flee from antichrist! Flee from all freewill-works religion. Flee from every false shepherd. Twice, the wise man warns us to flee from that way which seems right to a man, because the end of that way are the ways of death (Proverbs 14:12; 16:25).

Be Warned
Beware of false shepherds. They always come in sheep's clothing; but inwardly they are ravening wolves. Their object is to devour and destroy by mixing works with grace, mingling law with the gospel, calling bondage liberty and liberty licentiousness, making salvation in some way, in some part, to some degree, to be dependent upon and determined by you, your will, your work, your worth, your experience and learning.

The True Shepherd
Second, the Lord Jesus describes himself and every true shepherd.

'But he that entereth in by the door is the shepherd of the sheep. To him the porter openeth; and the sheep hear his voice: and he calleth his own sheep by name, and leadeth them out. And when he putteth forth his own sheep, he goeth before them, and the sheep follow him: for they know his voice. And a stranger will they not follow, but will flee from him: for they know not the voice of strangers' (vv. 2-5).

The shepherd of the sheep is Christ himself. He says in verse 11, 'I am the Good Shepherd: the Good Shepherd giveth his life for the sheep'.' In verse 14

445

he says, 'I am the Good Shepherd, and know my sheep, and am known of mine.' He is the Good Shepherd because he died for his sheep. The sheep were condemned to die; but he died in our room and stead that we might live forever. He is the Good Shepherd because he seeks his sheep until he finds it. We were lost; but he sought us and found us. He is the Good Shepherd because, when he finds his sheep that was lost, he lays it upon his omnipotent shoulders, holds it in the grip of almighty grace, and carries it all the way home.

Christ is the true Shepherd. But, remember, his purpose in this parable is to show us a clear distinction between true shepherds and the false, between true pastors and the false. He uses himself as the example all true under shepherds follow. What does our Saviour tell us about the true shepherd, the true pastor?

The true shepherd is one who enters into the sheepfold by the Door (v. 2). 'He that entereth in by the Door is the shepherd of the sheep.' The door spoken of in verse 2 is commonly thought to be the word of God. And it is certainly correct to say that Christ came by the word of God, fulfilling all the scriptures. But our Lord tells us plainly in verse 9 'I am the Door'. How are we to understand this? Is he the Door? Yes. Did he enter by the Door? Indeed, he did. That is exactly what he did.

'Christ being come an high priest of good things to come, by a greater and more perfect tabernacle, not made with hands, that is to say, not of this building; Neither by the blood of goats and calves, but by his own blood he entered in once into the holy place, having obtained eternal redemption for us' (Hebrews 9:11, 12).

Our Saviour showed himself the Good Shepherd by entering in by the Door, the same Door through which we must enter the kingdom of God; that is, 'by his own blood, he entered in once into the holy place, having obtained eternal redemption for us'. True, if he had remained without his taking our sins upon him and making them his own, he would not need to have entered in, but he was made sin for us. He could not enter in any other way. But, blessed be his name forever, 'by his own blood, he entered in once into the holy place, having obtained eternal redemption for us.'

This is the first mark of every true shepherd Christ sends to tend his sheep. He comes in by the Door, by the blood of Christ. He speaks of sin, because he has seen its greatness. He speaks of pardon, because he has been forgiven. He proclaims free justification by the blood, because he is justified. He proclaims perfect righteousness, because Christ has been made righteousness to him. He preaches free grace, because he has been saved by free grace. He preaches the precious blood, because he has felt its power. He tells sinners of a new creation, because he experiences it. He preaches eternal security, because he is secure on the Shepherd's shoulders, in the Shepherd's grip.

'He that entereth in by the door is the Shepherd of the sheep.' Without this, no other qualification will do. All the learning a man can attain in college, or seminary, or by his own diligent study can never make him a pastor. All the eloquence in the world will never make a preacher. He who serves as Christ's shepherd must enter by the Door of the sheep.

The true shepherd is one who cares for the sheep. 'To him the porter openeth' (vv. 3, 4). The Holy Spirit opens the way for Christ. He also opens the way for his servants, his true shepherds. 'And the sheep hear his voice'. The sheep hear the Shepherd's voice, his gospel. They hear his voice through the lips of his true shepherds, faithful pastors (1 John 4:5, 6).

'And he calleth his own sheep by name'. Without question, this speaks of our Saviour's personal, particular, effectual call of his elect to life and faith in him by the power of his Holy Spirit. It also shows the complete knowledge Christ has of his sheep. He says, 'I know them' (v. 27). When Zacchaeus was a straying sheep, Christ said to him when he was up the tree, 'Zacchaeus, Come down; for today I must abide at thine house' (Luke 19:5). When Nathanael was a straying sheep under the fig-tree, Christ 'saw him' (John 1:48). After his resurrection, he saw Mary and said to her, 'Mary', and she turned herself and said unto him, 'Rabboni: which is to say, Master' (John 20:16). So it is still. Christ knows his sheep; and he calls his own sheep by name; and they follow him.

This also implies the love of Christ for his sheep. When you love someone, you love their name. Christ not only knows you, but he calls you by name. The Lord Jesus Christ loves the names of those for whom he died. Your name is graven on his heart, and on the palms of his hands.

But there is more here. Our Saviour gives his sheep a new name. He said to Abram, 'Thy name shall no more be called Abram, but Abraham shall thy name be' (Genesis 17:5). He said to Jacob, 'Thy name shall be called no more Jacob, but Israel: for as a prince hast thou power with God and with men, and hast prevailed' (Genesis 33:28). He said to Cephas, 'Thy name shall be called Peter' (John 1:42), which means a stone, a living stone in the house of God. When the Lord Jesus calls his sheep, they get a new name. Indeed, 'old things are passed away; and, behold, all things are become new' (2 Corinthians 5:17).

And, when we come to the temple above, he says, 'him that overcometh will I make a pillar in the temple of my God, and he shall go no more out; and I will write upon him the name of my God, and the name of the city of my God, which is new Jerusalem, which cometh down out of heaven from my God; and I will write upon him my new name' (Revelation 3:12). If you hear his voice and follow him, you have a new name, a name given to you by God himself. It is the name he gives his own darling Son, 'The Lord our Righteousness' (Jeremiah 23:6 and 33:16).

Those who are Christ's true shepherds, like Christ the Good Shepherd, love, care for, and are sympathetic with his sheep. Faithful pastors understand and know that Christ's sheep are just sheep; sinful, weak, defiled, and helpless, because they, too, are his sheep. But, like Christ, they call his sheep by his new name. They are his saints. Indeed, they are one with him, so thoroughly one with him that anything done for them is done for him; and anything done to them is done to him (2 Corinthians 6:11, 12).

This is the lesson exemplified by our Saviour in this parable, the lesson the Pharisees could not grasp, the lesson the religious leaders of our age cannot grasp, the lesson all who serve as his under shepherds must grasp. If we would influence men and women for good, if we would lead people, if we are to have any power with them, we must lead them by their hearts, with the power of love, and care, and sympathy. They must be convinced that we care for them.

The power to lead men lies in sympathizing with them, as one who walks in the same path with them. The man of influence is the man of sympathy. The man of power is the man of service. He that loves is he that leads. He that serves is he that rules. The hearts of men cannot be moved by mere external force or power. The heart cannot be influenced by mere logic, reason, and dogma. Hearts are moved by hearts!

You may chain the limbs of a man; you may coerce his actions or even his words by religious creeds, religious rules, intimidation or fear. But how can soul be in communion with soul, move and influence the will and win the affections? There is only one way. If we would influence men intimately, profoundly, really, we must enter into sympathy with them. No man is or can be a true shepherd of the sheep who has not entered the same Door, who does not walk in the same path, who is not himself one with the sheep.

This is the lesson our Master taught and confirmed by his own example. The Good Shepherd proved himself to be the Good Shepherd, and illustrated what a true shepherd is by his care, tenderness, sympathy, and love toward his sheep. He lived for them, walked with them, toiled, and hungered, and suffered with them.

Our blessed good Shepherd was and is one with his sheep. He entered into mortal life through a mother's womb, just as we do. He passed through life by the same path of toil and daily care as we do. He made his exit from this world through the same portal of suffering and death as we must. In life and death he walked with the sheep. Therefore, he could say, 'I am the Good Shepherd, not merely because I am commissioned and sent of my Father, not merely because I wield the power of omnipotence', but 'I am the Good Shepherd because I know my sheep and am known of mine.'

Here is another character of the true shepherd. 'He goeth before them' (v. 4). The shepherd always goes before the sheep; and they follow him. When he says, 'Let us go to the well', they follow him. When he says, 'Let us go down into that dark valley', they go after him. So it is with Christ. Christ never called a sheep to go where he never went himself. He has borne all that he calls his sheep to bear. Our Saviour went into the depths of sorrow, heart sorrow, soul sorrow, the very sorrow of hell for his sheep. Let us not be surprised when he calls us to suffer. We will not be called to go where he has not gone. Do not be afraid to put down your tender feet where he put down his. It is still true that he goes before you. Do not be afraid. Christ is always with you and is always before you (Isaiah 43:2).

So it is with all Christ's true shepherds. They are men who go before and lead the sheep. They do not whip the sheep, beat the sheep, bind the sheep, frighten the sheep, and drive the sheep. They go before the sheep, leading them (1 Corinthians 11:1; Philippians 3:17; 1 Thessalonians 1:6; Hebrews 13:7, 17).

Here is one more great distinction between the true shepherd and the false. 'The good shepherd giveth his life for the sheep' (vv. 10-15). Hirelings are just hirelings. They do not care for the sheep. Because they do not care for the sheep, they will abandon them whenever they can serve their own interests better by doing so. Not the good Shepherd. Our Lord Jesus came into this world, lived for, and gave his life for the sheep that they might have life. And all his true shepherds follow his example. The true shepherd's life is wrapped up in the sheep, in serving their eternal interests. The true shepherd is worthy of his hire; but he is no hireling. The true shepherd gives and lays down his life for the sheep.

Are you following Christ? Do you hear his voice in the word? Do you hear his voice in the preaching of the gospel? Do you follow him? Follow on to know the Lord fully. Soon we shall be where no tempting devil, no deceiving world, and no false shepherds are found. There we shall hunger no more, neither thirst anymore; neither shall the sun light on us, nor any heat. For the Lamb, which is in the midst of the throne, shall feed us, and shall lead us unto living fountains of water; and God shall wipe away all tears from our eyes (Revelation 7:16, 17). In that great eternal day there will be no more need of under shepherds; in that great eternal day there shall be one fold and one shepherd!

Chapter 63

The Sheep

'Verily, verily, I say unto you, he that entereth not by the door into the sheepfold, but climbeth up some other way, the same is a thief and a robber. But he that entereth in by the door is the shepherd of the sheep. To him the porter openeth; and the sheep hear his voice: and he calleth his own sheep by name, and leadeth them out. And when he putteth forth his own sheep, he goeth before them, and the sheep follow him: for they know his voice. And a stranger will they not follow, but will flee from him: for they know not the voice of strangers. This parable spake Jesus unto them: but they understood not what things they were which he spake unto them' (John 10:1-6).

There are some people among the fallen sons of Adam whom God Almighty has purposed to save. They are called 'his own sheep'. These sheep are sinners loved of God with an everlasting love, chosen by him unto salvation, and redeemed by Christ the Good Shepherd. They shall, each of them, be called to life and faith in Christ by the power of God's irresistible grace at his appointed time and preserved in him unto everlasting glory.

Sheep And Goats

According to the word of God, the whole human race is divided into two categories: sheep and goats. Sheep never become goats; and goats never become sheep. Our Lord plainly tells us that some men and women are his sheep; and some are not his sheep. Some are goats (Matthew 25:31-33; John 10:16, 26). This division of the human race was made in eternity in God's sovereign purpose of grace in eternal election. He chose some to salvation and passed by others.

This division is made manifest in time, at the time of love, when the sheep are called by the Holy Spirit through the preaching of the gospel to life and faith in Christ. The call of the Spirit and our resulting faith in Christ do not make the division or make us sheep; but the call of God and the gift of faith in Christ make the division manifest, and make it manifest that we are Christ's sheep, chosen, redeemed, and called by grace.

This division of the human race is a permanent, immutable division. Sheep never become goats; goats never become sheep.

Lost And Found
As the human race is divided into two categories, so, too, the Lord's sheep are divided into two categories: straying sheep and returned sheep, lost sheep and found sheep, wandering sheep and folded sheep. This is what Peter tells us in 1 Peter 2:25. 'For ye were as sheep going astray; but are now returned unto the Shepherd and Bishop of your souls.'

Whenever I preach the gospel, my mind is upon the sheep. My heart is fixed upon the sheep. I am not much interested in goats. I am on the trail of Christ's sheep. I have nothing for goats. And I am not disturbed by goats. My business is with sheep. I am seeking the Lord's sheep who are lost. I am sent of God to feed those sheep who are in the fold. Having my mind and heart fixed upon the sheep, I know that I have a good and noble object, and that I am in harmony with the will of the Shepherd, because the Shepherd's mind is ever upon his sheep. The Shepherd's heart is always upon his sheep. The Good Shepherd's glory is wrapped up in and is one with the salvation of his sheep.

Four Ways
The Lord Jesus often speaks of 'my sheep'. He calls his people 'his own sheep'. But how did he get his sheep? How did those who are his sheep come to be his sheep? I can find only four ways by which a shepherd can obtain the possession of sheep. Here are four ways in which God's elect belong to Christ as sheep belonging to a shepherd.

A man can come into the possession of sheep by a gift; and we were given to Christ as his sheep from eternity in the covenant of grace, and in time by the effectual call of the Holy Spirit (John 6:37-40). Those the Father gave to the Son from eternity, and those he is now giving to the Son in effectual calling, and those who come to believe on the Son by the gift of his grace, and those whom it is the Father's will that Christ raise up to eternal life at the last day are all the same people. They are 'his own sheep'!

A man may also obtain the possession of sheep by lawful purchase; and the Lord Jesus Christ, as the Good Shepherd, purchased his sheep out of the hands of divine justice by the lawfully demanded price of his own precious blood (John 10:11, 15).

Third, if a man owns a flock of sheep and those sheep give birth to other sheep, then the new born lambs belong to the original owner by birth. So it is that we belong to Christ instrumentally by birth, too (Isaiah 66:8).

And, fourth, a man may become the owner of sheep by inheritance. If the original owner gives his sheep to another person as his inheritance, then the sheep become his property by inheritance. We are the inheritance of our dear Shepherd, the Lord Jesus Christ. Therefore we are called 'God's heritage' (1 Peter 5:3; Ephesians 1:18; Psalms 2:8).

Ten Bible Descriptions

I have searched the scriptures and found ten things plainly revealed in the word of God about those people who are called by the Son of God 'his own sheep'.

1. All who belong to Christ as his sheep are chosen sheep (John 15:16; Ephesians 1:3-6; 2 Thessalonians 2:13). Sheep love the doctrine of election. We know that had there been no election of grace there would have been no salvation by grace. Election is the sheep's friend. And all sheep are the friends of election. They confess with Josiah Conder,

> 'Tis not that I did choose Thee,
> For, Lord, that could not be.
> This heart would still refuse Thee,
> Hadst Thou not chosen me.

2. All the Lord's sheep are, by nature, straying sheep (Isaiah 53:6). 'Sheep', a more suitable word could not be found to describe us. It is ever the nature of sheep to stray. We went astray in our father Adam. We went astray from the womb, speaking lies. We went astray all the days of our lives, by wilful, deliberate choice, each one to his own way, until God the Holy Spirit arrested us by his almighty grace (Ephesians 2:1-5).

We all know what it is to stray. None of us know how to return. Even after experiencing the grace of God in salvation, it is still the nature of our evil hearts to stray from our God. And, even now, when we stray, we would never return to him if he did not fetch us back to himself. Even now, we are compelled to cry, 'Turn us, O God of our salvation and we shall be turned. Draw me, and we will run after thee.'

None of the Lord's saved sheep have any problem with the doctrine of total depravity. It is the bitter reality of our daily experience!

> Prone to wander, Lord, I feel it,
> Prone to leave the God I love.
> Here's my heart. Oh, take and seal it,
> Seal it for Thy courts above!

Robert Robinson

3. I rejoice to read in the word of God that all the Lord's sheep are redeemed sheep (John 10:11, 15).

We have been eternally redeemed (Revelation 13:8), justly redeemed (Romans 3:24-26), particularly redeemed (John 10:25), vicariously redeemed (Galatians 3:13), and effectually redeemed (Hebrews 9:12). Talk to sheep about limited atonement, and they will rejoice. Tell them about effectual blood, and they will sing. Proclaim to sheep how that they have been particularly redeemed, and they will shout, 'Hallelujah'! And they will honour the man who preaches that message as God's messenger to their souls. Sheep honour the Shepherd's precious blood.

> Redeemed! How I love to proclaim it!
> Redeemed by the blood of the Lamb.
> Redeemed by His special atonement!
> His child and forever I am!

Frances J. Crosby

4. At God's appointed time, in the time of love, each and every one of those chosen, redeemed, straying sheep are called sheep. The Good Shepherd always seeks his sheep 'until he find it'. And when he finds it, he always fetches it home by his almighty, effectual, irresistible call. This irresistible call is what David described as fetching grace, when he commanded Ziba, his servant, to go bring Mephibosheth to his palace, saying, 'Fetch him'! So it is, in the time of love, that the Lord Jesus sends his Spirit to his chosen, redeemed, straying sheep, saying 'Fetch him'.

Notice how the Good Shepherd describes this call here in John 10:2-4. Our Good Shepherd calls 'his own sheep'. He never calls goats, but only 'his own sheep', his personally chosen, redeemed, predestinated sheep. When he calls his sheep, 'they hear his voice'. He never calls in vain. 'He calleth his own sheep by name'. That is a particular, personal, effectual call. And when the Son of God calls his sheep, he always 'leadeth them out'. His call is an almighty, effectual, irresistible call.

454

God's sheep rejoice in the knowledge of his almighty, irresistible grace. What sane man would quarrel with irresistible love? What sane man would be angered by infallible grace? What man in his right mind would ever get upset with a friend who snatched him from the jaws of death, when he was both unaware of his condition and unwilling and unable to do anything about it?

5. Every one of the Lord's sheep are specially known sheep (John 10:27). The Lord Jesus says, 'I know them'. The world does not know them (1 John 3:1). Before they are called, the church does not know them, the preacher does not know them, and they do not know themselves. Sometimes even after they are called, churches and preachers do not know them. But Christ says, 'I know them'. And that is enough! He knows them eternally. He knows them distinctively (Matthew 7:23; Romans 8:29). He knows them universally. He knows them wherever they are and knows everything about them. And he knows them savingly. All who are known by him are saved by him.

The Lord's sheep rest in his love. We rest in his distinguishing knowledge of us. It is his knowledge of us, not our knowledge of him, that is the source and cause of our salvation, justification, eternal life, and assurance. The experience of eternal life is found in our knowing him; but the cause is in his knowledge of us (Isaiah 53:10, 11).

6. Our Lord Jesus declares that all his sheep are knowing sheep (John 10:14). Not only does the Good Shepherd know his sheep, he says, 'I am known of mine'. They know him and 'they know his voice' (John 10:4). The Apostle John explains this for us in 1 John 2:20-27. Goats are driven to and fro with every wind of doctrine, because they do not know the Shepherd's voice. Sheep, all of them, know the Shepherd's voice and follow it (John 10:4, 5).

7. The word of God tells us that all of the Lord's sheep, as soon as they are called, are folded sheep (Ezekiel 34:11-15). When the Lord calls his sheep, he brings them into his fold. It seems to me that he is telling us here that he brings his sheep into his church. I realise that all true believers, when they are born of God are born into the church and kingdom of God. But Ezekiel's prophecy refers not to the church in its universal aspect, but to the local church. So that the promise is this: I will bring my sheep into the fold of a local church. Here he feeds them in a good pasture, refreshes them with living water, and causes them to lie down in peace and safety in this good fold.

I realise that many make light of believer's baptism and church membership. I recognise that neither baptism nor church membership has anything to do with our salvation. But we must never be seduced into thinking that the ordinances of Christ and the church of Christ are non-essentials. I cannot find in the word of God any evidence that the Lord's sheep are found outside his fold once they have been called (Ezekiel 20:37, 38). All Christ's sheep follow him into the watery grave of believer's baptism. And all Christ's sheep dwell with him and his sheep in the fold. Sheep need each other. They are never found alone unless they are either lost or sick.

8. All the Lord's sheep are following sheep (John 10:4, 27). None of the sheep follow the Shepherd by nature. Yet, our Lord says, 'They follow me'. How can both things be true? The answer is simple. The Shepherd causes the sheep to follow. Yet, he causes them to do so in such a way as to make them perfectly willing to follow him. He entices the sheep to follow him by his goodness. He lovingly forces his sheep to follow him with his rod. But the sheep, all the sheep, do follow the Shepherd. They follow the doctrine and counsel of his word, the direction of his Spirit and the revelation of his will. They all 'follow the Lamb whithersoever he goeth' (Revelation 14:3, 4).

9. Our Lord Jesus assures us that all his sheep are secure sheep (John 10:28-30). In this world the sheep must face many dangers. Many wolves seek to devour them. Their own flesh is ever opposed to them. The devil seeks by every means to destroy them. And the world, both the religious world and the material world, are instruments by which our adversary the devil seeks our ruin. But in the midst of all our enemies and all our dangers, all the sheep are perfectly safe. We are in the hands of our dear, Almighty Shepherd. And he and his Father are one. That is a simple declaration that our security is to be found in the Persons of the triune Godhead. The Father's purpose cannot be defeated. The Son's blood cannot be wasted. The Spirit's seal cannot be broken. Immutable grace cannot be altered. Omnipotent power cannot be subdued. The will of God cannot be resisted.

10. The word of God speaks of some sheep in a very singular way. They are called 'other sheep' (John 10:16). Our Saviour says, 'Other sheep I have, which are not of this fold: them also I must bring, and they shall hear my voice; and there shall be one fold, and one shepherd.' These other sheep belong to Christ as surely as the rest. The other sheep have been redeemed by Christ. The other sheep are safe and secure in the hands of Christ. The other sheep shall be effectually called by Christ. If you are one of these 'other sheep', the Good Shepherd says concerning you, 'Them also I must bring'. If you are one of these 'other sheep', the Good Shepherd will get you. He will return you to himself.

Chapter 64

'I am the door'

'Verily, verily, I say unto you, he that entereth not by the door into the sheepfold, but climbeth up some other way, the same is a thief and a robber. But he that entereth in by the door is the shepherd of the sheep. To him the porter openeth; and the sheep hear his voice: and he calleth his own sheep by name, and leadeth them out. And when he putteth forth his own sheep, he goeth before them, and the sheep follow him: for they know his voice. And a stranger will they not follow, but will flee from him: for they know not the voice of strangers. This parable spake Jesus unto them: but they understood not what things they were which he spake unto them. Then said Jesus unto them again, Verily, verily, I say unto you, I am the door of the sheep. All that ever came before me are thieves and robbers: but the sheep did not hear them. I am the door: by me if any man enter in, he shall be saved, and shall go in and out, and find pasture. The thief cometh not, but for to steal, and to kill, and to destroy: I am come that they might have life, and that they might have it more abundantly' (John 10:1-10).

Our Lord Jesus Christ is the great 'I AM', the one true and living God who spoke to Moses out of the burning bush, and revealed himself by that name, saying, 'I AM THAT I AM'. He is the eternal, self-existent God. In the New Testament he reveals himself with profound simplicity as the 'I AM' (John 6:35; 8:12; 9:5; 10:11; 11:25; 14:6; 15:1).

In all those places our Master showed himself to be the Master of simplicity. That means he was also the Master Preacher. He seldom used words with more than two or three syllables. He never once appeared scholastic. He

457

never attempted to impress his hearers with what he knew. His intent was to be heard and understood. So he always spoke with great plainness and simplicity. He had no use for rhetoric or eloquence. He did not attempt to prove or enforce his doctrine with complex arguments. He simply declared it. And he declared it with utter simplicity. Our Saviour took the most profound truths and put them in pictures that any child could see. None is more profoundly simple than the picture he gives us of himself as the way, the only way of salvation in John 10:1-10. In these verses our Saviour declares that the only way we can enter into heaven is by the door. Then, he says twice, 'I am the door'.

Christ is the Door, the only door, by which we can and must enter the kingdom of God. Of all the comparisons made use of by our Lord Jesus to illustrate and set forth what he is appointed of God to be to his people, none is more simple, and yet none more profound, than this, 'I am the Door'.

How merciful, how gracious, how kind he is! Our Saviour compares himself to a door, so that every time we enter or leave any building or room we may be reminded of him. Everyone knows what a door is and how it is used. A door lets people in who want in, and shuts people out you want to keep out. And a door lets people out who want out, and shuts people in you want to keep in. Our Saviour says, in verse 9, 'I am the door: by me if any man enter in, he shall be saved, and shall go in and out, and find pasture.'

'In' And 'Out'
It is easy enough to understand what he means by the words, 'I am the door: by me if any man enter in, he shall be saved, and shall go in'. But what does he mean by the last part of that sentence? 'I am the door: by me if any man enter in, he shall be saved, and shall go in and out, and find pasture.' If we enter into the kingdom of God, if we enter into salvation by Christ the Door, we must and shall go out of something else, and going out of that into the sheepfold of grace, we find pasture for our souls.

The Door Out
Christ Jesus is the only door out of death and into life. He is the Door, the only door out of our house of bondage. There are many houses of bondage in this world from which the there is no way out but Christ. We are all by nature condemned prisoners, shut up under the lock and key of God's holy law (Galatians 3:22). We are guilty, without excuse, debtors, criminals, under the wrath of God, condemned by conscience, condemned by the words of our own mouths, and condemned by God's holy law. There is a worse prison to come, but this is the way to it, the beginning of sorrows. Is there no door out of this prison, no way to pay the debt, no way to make satisfaction to divine justice,

that we may be discharged from this prison? Bless God, there is, and Christ is that Door; whosoever believes in him, shall not come into condemnation (Romans 8:1; Isaiah 61:1).

The Lord Jesus has set many captives free (Psalms 116:16; 1 Timothy 1:13-15). As he sent his angel to set Peter and John free from prison, he sends his servants preaching the gospel, to proclaim the opening of the prison, to proclaim liberty to all who believe, to all who will go out by him. This is righteously earned liberty, blood bought liberty, liberty by the cancellation of debt, liberty by the power of his Spirit.

As Israel came out of Egypt by the hand of Moses, by the blood of the lamb and by the power of God, passing through the Red Sea, so Christ is the Door out of our house of slavery, darkness, and bondage.

As we are all condemned prisoners by nature, we are all by nature bondmen to the law. Condemnation we fear and despise; but this bondage we love. It is the bondage of legalism and self-righteous, works religion. Oh, how men love the shackles of duty, the leg irons of ceremony, the stocks of piety, and the prison of legality! Serving the law, we were the servants of sin; and we loved that slavery.

The Lord Jesus is the Door, the only Door out of legal bondage (Matthew 11:28, 29). He is the Door out of Babylon. 'If the Son therefore shall make you free, ye shall be free indeed' (John 8:36). Yet there are many who not only will not be free themselves, but are enraged at those who are. As Ishmael the son of the bond-woman hated and persecuted Isaac the son of the free-woman, religious legalists hate and constantly oppose those who walk at liberty. Still, Christ is the Door of liberty and freedom from cruel, legal religion.

Who among the saints in the household of faith has never been in the bondage of affliction? Some endure great afflictions. I know many who seem to spend much of their lives in trouble and sorrow, in days of woe and nights of weeping, ever struggling with sickness and pain, domestic trouble and financial crises one after another. God's saints, as long as we live in this world, are engaged in warfare in themselves, warfare between the flesh and the spirit.

Spiritual trouble will not cease until we cease to live in this body of sin and death. 'Unto you it is given in the behalf of Christ, not only to believe on him, but also to suffer for his sake' (Philippians 1:29). Christ is the Door, the only Door out of our trouble. There is no other (1 Peter 5:6, 7; Psalms 27:8-10; 73:21-28). 'Humble yourselves therefore under the mighty hand of God, that he may exalt you in due time: Casting all your care upon him; for he careth for you.'

Soon you and I must take our place in the grave, where our bodies will rest, and rest in hope, because Christ is the Door, the only door, by which we shall escape that prison (John 11:25; Revelation 20:6; 1 Thessalonians 4:13-18).

Christ is the Door out of condemnation, bondage, legalism, trouble and the grave!

The Door In

As Christ is the Door out of bondage, so our Lord Jesus Christ is the Door, the only door into the sheepfold. When our Saviour says, 'I am the door: by me if any man enter in, he shall be saved, and shall go in and out, and find pasture', he is talking about entering into the kingdom of God, the sheepfold of grace.

There are many who enter into the kingdom outwardly, by climbing up some other way into the church of God, refusing to trust Christ. But those who enter in by Christ the Door, believing on him, shall be saved. Being saved, they go out of the house of bondage, and walk at liberty. Christ is the way in. He says, 'I am the door: by me if any man enter in, he shall be saved, and shall go in and out, and find pasture.' He is the Door; and the Door is open. All who enter in by the Door are welcome.

Christ is the Door, the only door by which sinners may come in unto God himself (Ephesians 2:13, 18; 3:12; Hebrews 10:19-22). Our Saviour died that he might bring us to God (1 Peter 3:18). He alone is the Door of atonement and reconciliation (Romans 4:25-5:11; 2 Corinthians 5:18-21). The Lord Jesus Christ is both the Ark of salvation and the Door into the Ark. The Son of God is both the Treasury of all good things and the Door into the Treasury. All the fulness of God is in Christ. All the fulness of grace is in Christ. All the fulness of glory is in Christ. All the promises of God are in Christ. All things are his and he is ours! All fulness is in Christ!

Twofold Promise

In John 10:10 the Lord Jesus makes a twofold promise to all who enter in by the door. He said, 'I am come that they might have life, and that they might have it more abundantly'. In John 10:9 he says, 'I am the door: by me if any man enter in, he shall be saved, and shall go in and out, and find pasture'.

Here is the first part of the promise: 'They shall be saved'. Christ pledges his word for it that those who enter in shall be saved. Those who do not enter in shall be damned. If you are not in Christ, you are without; and 'without are dogs, and sorcerers, and whoremongers, and murderers, and idolaters, and whosoever loveth and maketh a lie' (Revelation 22:15). But those who enter in 'shall be saved'. Immediately saved! Fully pardoned! Completely justified! Saved from all the evil consequences of sin! Eternally saved!

Here is the second part of the promise: 'and find pasture'. Come to Christ and find in him pasture for your soul. What luscious pasture there is for his sheep in his gospel! What great pasture we find for our souls in the ordinances of divine worship!

'I am the door'

Any Man

'I am the door; by me if any man enter in, he shall be saved'. The word of God makes many sweet promises of grace to sinners. But none is sweeter than this: 'I am the door; by me if any man enter in, he shall be saved'. Our Lord called the thirsty in Isaiah. 'Ho, every one that thirsteth, come ye to the waters' (Isaiah 55:1). In John 7:37 he said, on the last day, that great day of the feast, 'If any man thirst, let him come unto me and drink' (John 7:37). Near the end of the Book of Revelation he says, 'I will give to him that is athirst of the fountain of the water of life freely' (Revelation 21:6). In Matthew's gospel he addresses those who labour and are heavy laden. 'Come unto me all ye that labour and are heavy laden, and I will give you rest' (Matthew 11:28). In Zechariah he calls prisoners of hope. 'Turn you to the stronghold, ye prisoners of hope' (Zechariah 9:12). But here he says, 'If any man'. That is peculiarly precious. It is not said if any thirsty man, if any weary man, if any labouring man, if any heavy laden man, but 'if any man enter in he shall be saved'. That means any man: rich or poor, old or young, male or female, high or low, you or me. 'I am the door; by me if any man enter in, he shall be saved'.

Shuts In

Christ is the Door that shuts us in. When Noah entered into the ark, the Lord shut him in; and once we have entered into the Ark of God, Christ is the Door that shuts us in (John 10:28; Philippians 1:6; 1 Peter 1:5).

> A sovereign protector I have,
> Unseen, yet forever at hand,
> Unchangeably faithful to save,
> Almighty to rule and command.
> He smiles, and my comforts abound;
> His grace as the dew shall descend;
> And walls of salvation surround
> The soul He delights to defend.
>
> Inspirer and hearer of prayer,
> Thou shepherd and guardian of Thine,
> My all to Thy covenant care
> I sleeping and waking resign.
> If Thou art my shield and my sun,
> The night is no darkness to me;
> And fast as my moments roll on,
> They bring me but nearer to Thee.

461

Kind author, and ground of my hope,
Thee, Thee, for my God I avow;
My glad Ebenezer set up,
And own Thou hast helped me till now.
I muse on the years that are past,
Wherein my defence Thou hast proved;
Nor wilt Thou relinquish at last
A sinner so signally loved!

Augustus Montague Toplady

Chapter 65

Christ, Our Shepherd

'I am the good shepherd: the good shepherd giveth his life for the sheep. But he that is an hireling, and not the shepherd, whose own the sheep are not, seeth the wolf coming, and leaveth the sheep, and fleeth: and the wolf catcheth them, and scattereth the sheep. The hireling fleeth, because he is an hireling, and careth not for the sheep. I am the good shepherd, and know my sheep, and am known of mine. As the Father knoweth me, even so know I the Father: and I lay down my life for the sheep. And other sheep I have, which are not of this fold: them also I must bring, and they shall hear my voice; and there shall be one fold, and one shepherd' (John 10:11-16).

What a blessed, delightful, instructive subject we have before us! May God the Holy Spirit now take the things of Christ as our Shepherd and show them to us. The Lord Jesus Christ, the Son of God, is the Shepherd of his sheep. The Apostle Peter describes our experience of grace in these words, 'For ye were as sheep going astray; but are now returned unto the Shepherd and Bishop of your souls' (1 Peter 2:25).

Old Testament
Throughout the Old Testament scriptures, it was prophesied that Messiah, the Christ, the Son of God, our Redeemer would come into the world as a Man, and that one chief characteristic of his work of redemption and grace would be that of a shepherd buying, seeking, and gathering his sheep. The prophet Isaiah wrote, 'He shall feed his flock like a shepherd: he shall gather the lambs with his arm, and carry them in his bosom, and shall gently lead those that are with

young' (Isaiah 40:11). 'They shall not hunger nor thirst; neither shall the heat nor sun smite them: for he that hath mercy on them shall lead them, even by the springs of water shall he guide them' (Isaiah 49:10).

The Lord himself says in the Book of Ezekiel, 'For thus saith the Lord GOD; Behold, I, even I, will both search my sheep, and seek them out' (Ezekiel 34:11). 'Therefore will I save my flock, and they shall no more be a prey; and I will judge between cattle and cattle. And I will set up one shepherd over them, and he shall feed them, even my servant David; he shall feed them, and he shall be their shepherd' (Ezekiel 34:22, 23). 'And David my servant shall be king over them; and they all shall have one shepherd: they shall also walk in my judgments, and observe my statutes, and do them' (Ezekiel 37:24).

When David meditated upon these things, his heart bubbled over with joy, confidence, faith, and hope. He sang, 'The LORD is my shepherd; I shall not want' (Psalms 23:1).

New Testament

In the New Testament three distinct adjectives are used to describe the characteristics of Christ as our Shepherd. In his great work of redemption our Saviour is called 'The Good Shepherd'. He says, 'I am the good shepherd: the good shepherd giveth his life for the sheep' (John 10:11). In his resurrection glory he is called 'The Great Shepherd'. The apostle closes the Book of Hebrews describing our Redeemer as, 'that great shepherd of the sheep' (Hebrews 13:20). In reference to his glorious return Peter declares him to be 'the chief Shepherd' (1 Peter 5:4).

Our Lord Jesus Christ is the good Shepherd with reference to his work of redemption, the great Shepherd with reference to his resurrection, and the chief Shepherd with reference to his glorious return. These three adjectives are always distinct. They are never mingled together or interchanged. Each is used in its proper place and setting with reference to the Son of God, and the accomplishment of his mediatorial work for the salvation of his sheep.

The Good Shepherd

Our Lord Jesus Christ calls himself 'The Good Shepherd'. 'I am the good shepherd: the good shepherd giveth his life for the sheep.' 'I am the good shepherd, and know my sheep, and am known of mine' (John 10:11, 14). In the redemption and salvation of our souls the Lord Jesus Christ is 'The Good Shepherd'. The Apostle Peter takes up this theme of redemption in 1 Peter 2:21-25, and shows us five things about Christ as 'The Good Shepherd'. Remember, it is with reference to the redemption and salvation of our souls that Christ is called 'The Good Shepherd'.

The Good Shepherd Is The Suffering Shepherd
'For even hereunto were ye called: because Christ also suffered for us, leaving us an example, that ye should follow his steps' (1 Peter 2:21). Here is our calling, 'For even hereunto were ye called'. All true believers have been effectually and irresistibly called to Christ by the grace and power of God the Holy Spirit. We have been called to salvation, eternal life, and faith in him. And all who are called by grace are called to a life that involves suffering in this world (Philippians 1:29).

In this world we are called to suffer many things for Christ's sake, even as he suffered many things for our sakes. As he took up his cross and suffered for us, so we must willingly take up our cross daily and follow him. It is written, 'If we suffer with him, we shall also reign with him'. It is not possible to follow Christ without suffering with him and for him.

'Yet if any man suffer as a Christian, let him not be ashamed; but let him glorify God on this behalf' (1 Peter 4:16). Let us ever remember that those things we suffer as Christians, as believers, we suffer from Christ, with Christ, and for Christ. This is a great honour indeed. So let us glorify God in all that we may be called to suffer in this world as the children of God.

Here is our rule of life. 'Christ also suffered for us, leaving us an example, that ye should follow his steps'. Rebels must be ruled by law. Mercenaries are ruled by rewards. Believers are ruled by Christ. We do not live by the rule of religious custom and tradition, the rule of our own consciences, or even the rule of Mosaic law. We follow Christ. We live by the rule of his word, his example, and his Spirit.

But the primary thing to be seen in this verse is the fact that the Lord Jesus Christ, our good Shepherd, is the suffering Shepherd. 'Because Christ also suffered for us'. Apart from the sufferings of Christ for us, apart from him having fully suffered the wrath of God to the full satisfaction of divine justice, there could be no salvation for anyone. Be sure you understand this. The necessity for Christ's death was the holiness and justice of Almighty God (Romans 3:24-26). Had Christ not died in our stead, we could never have been made alive (John 12:24). Had Christ not suffered the curse of the law for us, we could never have been freed from that curse (Galatians 3:13). Had the Son of God not poured out his life's blood unto death upon the cursed tree, he could never have obtained eternal redemption for us. It was with 'his own blood (that) he entered in once into the holy place, having obtained eternal redemption for us' (Hebrews 9:12). Had not the good Shepherd suffered for us, he could never have saved us (1 Peter 3:18). But, since he has suffered the wrath of God in our stead to the full satisfaction of infinite justice, all for whom he suffered and died must and shall be saved. Else his suffering and death are vain; and the blood of Christ is of no effect!

The Good Shepherd Is The Sinless Shepherd

'He knew no sin'. He is 'holy, harmless, undefiled, and separate from sinners'. He 'did no sin, neither was guile found in his mouth' (1 Peter 2:22). Had the Lord Jesus Christ not been the sinless Shepherd, he could not have been the good Shepherd. Had he not been altogether without sin, he could not have atoned for our sins; he could not have been our Substitute. But since he is without sin, the Lord Jesus Christ is a suitable substitute for sinners, one who is able to save to the uttermost all who come to God by him.

Though he was made in the likeness of sinful flesh, 'he did no sin'. Though he lived among sinful men, there was never any 'guile found in his mouth'. Our Saviour had no sin: no original sin, no personal sin, no actual sin. Yet, this immaculately holy, sinless One was made sin for us; and now we are made to be the righteousness of God in him. He took our place in time that we might take his place for eternity (Romans 5:19; 2 Corinthians 5:21).

The Good Shepherd Is The Submissive Shepherd

'Who, when he was reviled, reviled not again; when he suffered, he threatened not; but committed himself to him that judgeth righteously' (1 Peter 2:23). There is, of course, no subordination within the Godhead. The three persons of the holy trinity are eternally and immutably equal in all things. But, in order to redeem and save his sheep, the Son of God agreed to become one of us. He willingly, voluntarily assumed all responsibility for his sheep. And in his office capacity as our Mediator, he submitted himself to the will of the triune God as our Shepherd. That is what is revealed in John 10:16-18.

He submitted himself to the will of God in the covenant of grace before the foundation of the world, and voluntarily became Jehovah's Servant (Exodus 21:5, 6; Psalms 40:6-8; Isaiah 50:5-7). The Lord Jesus voluntarily submitted himself to the will of God at the time of his incarnation (Hebrews 10:5-10). Our great Saviour, as our Representative in this world, voluntarily submitted himself to the will of God as a Man throughout the days of his life upon this earth. Both his first words and his last words in this world demonstrate his submission to the Father's will (Luke 2:49; John 12:27, 28; 19:30). His life might well be summarized in his own words as he knelt in dark Gethsemane, 'Not my will, thy will be done'. Our Lord Jesus Christ was a willing Victim, a voluntary Substitute, an unconstrained, unforced Sacrifice for sinners.

Now look at 1 Peter 2:24. Peter tells us that the Good Shepherd is the substitutionary Shepherd. 'Who his own self bare our sins in his own body on the tree, that we, being dead to sins, should live unto righteousness: by whose stripes ye were healed' (John 10:11, 14, 15). Substitution is the very heart of the gospel. That person who does not understand the doctrine of substitution has not yet even learned the ABC of Christianity. This is basic, fundamental, and essential (Isaiah 53:4-6, 9-11). The Lord Jesus Christ is an able Substitute, a willing Substitute, a legal Substitute, a satisfactory Substitute, and an effectual Substitute, because he is our real Substitute. He did not pretend to take our place, and take our sins, and take our guilt, and take our punishment. He really, actually, took all because he is a real Substitute.

Yes, the word of God does, most distinctly, teach the great and glorious doctrine of limited atonement. You simply cannot believe in substitutionary atonement without believing in limited atonement. The Son of God did not die for nothing. Christ did not shed his blood in vain! The scope, the object, the purpose, the goal, the benefits of Christ's atonement are limited to, specifically designed for, and shall be enjoyed by God's elect. His precious blood made definite satisfaction and complete atonement for the sins of his people. Christ died for those who are saved by his blood. The Good Shepherd did not lay down his life for the goats. Where does the word of God suggest such an absurdity? Nonsense! The Good Shepherd laid down his life for the sheep. That is not Baptist language, or Calvinistic language. It is Bible language! Is it not? Read John 10:11 and 15, and John 10:26 and 27.

There can be no compromise here. This is the place where the glory of God and the souls of men are at stake. Those who preach a universal atonement preach a false gospel, for they preach that the will of man is the effectual cause of salvation and redemption. Whereas the word of God declares, 'As many as received him, to them gave he power to become the sons of God, even to them that believe on his name: Which were born, not of blood, nor of the will of the flesh, nor of the will of man, but of God' (John 1:12, 13). 'So then it is not of him that willeth, nor of him that runneth, but of God that showeth mercy' (Romans 9:16).

Those who preach a universal atonement preach a false Christ; for they make the Son of God a failure in that which is declared to be his most glorious work, declaring that his blood was shed in vain for the multitudes in hell. Whereas the word of God asserts that 'He shall not fail' (Isaiah 42:4). All who preach a universal atonement preach a false god, for they declare that the love of God is mutable, the justice of God perverted, the purpose of God frustrated, and the word of God is a lie, when they assert that the sin debt fully paid by Christ may yet be demanded from those for whom it has already been paid! Whereas God declares himself to be 'A just God and a Saviour'! (Isaiah 45:21). And as God is just and cannot be unjust, we are assured, with A. M. Toplady,

> Payment God cannot twice demand,
> First at my bleeding Surety's hand,
> And then again at mine!

Those who preach a universal atonement preach a false spirit, for they declare that the Spirit of God convinces men of a lie when he convinces them of sin removed, righteousness established, and judgment finished. Whereas the Son of God asserts that these things are indeed done (John 16:8-13).

We cannot and must not tolerate such blasphemous perversions. I dare not hold my tongue, or guard my pen, while wolves in sheep's clothing seek to destroy the souls of men, and rob Christ of his glory as the Good Shepherd! Look once more at Peter's description of the Good Shepherd. He is the suffering Shepherd, the sinless Shepherd, the submissive Shepherd, and the substitutionary Shepherd. Then, in verse twenty-five the apostle tells us,

The Good Shepherd Is The Successful Shepherd
'For ye were as sheep going astray; but are now returned unto the Shepherd and Bishop of your souls' (1 Peter 2:25). It is our nature to stray. We are all depraved, sinful, straying creatures. We went astray in our father Adam. We went astray as soon as we were born, speaking lies. And we went astray by deliberate choice all the days of our lives. Poor, ignorant, lost sheep can never find their way home. Dogs can. Cats can. Horses can. Even goats and hogs can. But sheep simply do not have the ability to come home. Straying sheep can only stray. They are the dumbest, most helpless, most pitiful animals on earth.

You will notice that the Spirit of God does not say, 'You have returned', as if to imply that we decided by our own freewill to return to Christ. Oh, no! That would never happen! Dumb as we are, sheep know better than that! The text says, you 'are now returned unto the Shepherd and Bishop of your souls'. We 'are returned', because the good Shepherd sought us out and returned us! We went astray. He sought us out. We were lost. He found us. We were sliding into hell. He laid us on his shoulders. We would not and could not return to him. He returned us to himself. He who is the good Shepherd is the successful Shepherd. 'He shall save his people from their sins.' With reference to his great work of redeeming and saving his people, Christ is 'The Good Shepherd'.

The Great Shepherd
Now, let us look at Hebrews 13:20. Here the Holy Spirit shows us that with reference to his resurrection glory, our Lord Jesus Christ is the Great Shepherd.

'Now the God of peace, that brought again from the dead our Lord Jesus, that great shepherd of the sheep, through the blood of the everlasting covenant, Make you perfect in every good work to do his will, working in you that which is wellpleasing in his sight, through Jesus Christ; to whom be glory for ever and ever. Amen' (Hebrews 13:20, 21).

Notice how the Holy Spirit describes the God of glory. Though he is glorious in holiness, inflexible in justice, majestic in power, and terrible in wrath, the great and glorious Lord God is called 'the God of peace'! He is called 'the God of peace', because he is the Author of peace. He found the way of peace and devised the covenant of peace. He made peace. By the blood atonement of his dear Son, the Lord God is reconciled, propitiated, and satisfied. And he is the Giver of peace.

The resurrected, ascended, exalted Christ is called 'the great shepherd of the sheep'. He was the Good Shepherd in his humiliation, while he worked out and accomplished redemption for us. And he may yet be called 'The Good Shepherd', as he seeks and saves his lost sheep by his almighty grace. But we are no longer dealing with him in his humiliation. Here is the Shepherd who sits upon the throne of the universe. He is 'the great shepherd of the sheep'. He is great in his person. The God-man! He is great in his position. The Right Hand of the Majesty on High! He is great in his power; total sovereignty, absolute omnipotence! He is great in his possessions; all fulness! And he is great in his provisions; all grace, all glory, all things!

Our Lord Jesus obtained his greatness as our Shepherd in his resurrection glory 'through the blood of the everlasting covenant'. We read about that covenant in Jeremiah 31:31-34. The blood of the covenant is the precious, sin-atoning blood of the Son of God, the blood of the Lord Jesus Christ, our Saviour. But why is the resurrection of Christ connected with the blood of the everlasting covenant? The whole purpose of God in the everlasting covenant was contingent upon one thing. It all depended upon one ultimate, final, climactic thing. It all depended upon the sufficiency, efficacy, and satisfaction of the blood of Christ (Hebrews 9:12-17). When our Lord Jesus Christ cried from the cross, 'It is finished', and died, he had at last fulfilled all the terms and conditions of the covenant. He rendered unto God the Father complete satisfaction for the sins of his people. And the efficacy of his atonement demanded both his resurrection from the dead, and ours. It demanded both his release from all the consequences of sin, and ours. This was the Father's promise to the Son as our Surety in the covenant before the world began (Isaiah 53:10-12).

Our sins were made to be his, and were thus imputed to our blessed Christ. His death satisfied the justice of God for all the sins of his people, which he bore in his own body on the tree. Now death has no more dominion over him. And, because he is our Substitute, death has no more dominion over us (1 Peter 4:1, 2).

It is through this Great Shepherd of the sheep that God perfects his work of grace in his sheep. In Hebrews 13:21, Paul's prayer is that the God of peace may 'Make you perfect in every good work to do his will, working in you that which is wellpleasing in his sight, through Jesus Christ; to whom be glory forever and ever. Amen.' It is Christ the Great Shepherd who causes his sheep to do his will. It is Christ the Great Shepherd who works in us that which is well-pleasing in his sight. And it is Christ the Great Shepherd who shall have the glory and praise for all his works of grace for us and in us.

Our Lord Jesus Christ is 'the Good Shepherd' in his work of redemption and salvation. He is 'the Great Shepherd' in his resurrection glory.

The Chief Shepherd
The Apostle Peter declares our Lord Jesus Christ to be the Chief Shepherd in his glorious second advent. 'And when the chief Shepherd shall appear, ye shall receive a crown of glory that fadeth not away' (1 Peter 5:4). Christ is the Chief Shepherd. In the kingdom of God there is only one Chief. That Chief is the Lord Jesus Christ himself. All pastors, teachers, elders, evangelists, missionaries, apostles, and prophets are servants of the Shepherd, not lords over the flock. God's servants are examples to the flock, not tyrants over the flock. We are under-shepherds. Christ alone is the Chief Shepherd. And it is as the Chief Shepherd that our Lord Jesus Christ shall complete his work of grace in our ultimate and final glorification. Soon, Christ the Chief Shepherd shall appear. When Christ comes, he will raise our bodies up from the dead. And the Chief Shepherd shall give to all his sheep 'a crown of glory that fadeth not away'. We shall at last be perfectly conformed to Christ, even to the likeness of his glory as the God-man Mediator. Then, the purpose of our God shall be finished (Romans 8:28, 29; 1 John 3:1-3).

Try to remember these three pictures of Christ our Shepherd. Meditate upon them, draw comfort from them, and glorify Christ in your heart as the Good Shepherd who redeemed us, the Great Shepherd who rules from heaven for us, and the Chief Shepherd who is coming again to take us up unto himself in glory. It is Christ the Shepherd who is our Saviour. Salvation is altogether his work. He agreed to it in the covenant. He accomplished it on the cross. He applies it from his throne. He planned it. He purchased it. He performs it. He preserves it. He perfects it. And he alone shall have the praise for it.

Chapter 66

The Free Obedience Of Christ

'And other sheep I have, which are not of this fold: them also I must bring, and they shall hear my voice; and there shall be one fold, and one shepherd. Therefore doth my Father love me, because I lay down my life, that I might take it again. No man taketh it from me, but I lay it down of myself. I have power to lay it down, and I have power to take it again. This commandment have I received of my Father' (John 10:16-18).

Isaiah 53:10-12 describes the death of our Lord Jesus Christ as that which God the Father did to his Son when he made him to be sin for us.

'Yet it pleased the LORD to bruise him; he hath put him to grief: when thou shalt make his soul an offering for sin, he shall see his seed, he shall prolong his days, and the pleasure of the LORD shall prosper in his hand. He shall see of the travail of his soul, and shall be satisfied: by his knowledge shall my righteous servant justify many; for he shall bear their iniquities. Therefore will I divide him a portion with the great, and he shall divide the spoil with the strong; because he hath poured out his soul unto death: and he was numbered with the transgressors; and he bare the sin of many, and made intercession for the transgressors.'

Isaiah 50:5-7 describes our Lord's sacrificial obedience unto death, even the death of the cross as our voluntary Surety and Substitute. Like all the law of God given to Israel, the law regarding the bond slave in Exodus 21:1-6 was a messianic, prophetic law. It portrayed the work of our Lord Jesus Christ as Jehovah's righteous Servant. In the covenant of grace, before the worlds were

471

made, the Son of God, our Saviour, became Jehovah's voluntary Servant that he might redeem and save his people by his free obedience to God as our Substitute. This is what Isaiah describes in Isaiah 50:5-7.

'The Lord GOD hath opened mine ear, and I was not rebellious, neither turned away back. I gave my back to the smiters, and my cheeks to them that plucked off the hair: I hid not my face from shame and spitting. For the Lord GOD will help me; therefore shall I not be confounded: therefore have I set my face like a flint, and I know that I shall not be ashamed.'

Here in the tenth chapter of John's Gospel our Lord Jesus Christ speaks of himself as the Good Shepherd, who gave his life for his sheep. Let me never tire of reading, hearing, and meditating upon those blessed words of his: 'I am the good shepherd: the good shepherd giveth his life for the sheep' (v. 11). 'I lay down my life for the sheep' (v. 15). Then, in verse 16, our Saviour declares, 'And other sheep I have, which are not of this fold: them also I must bring, and they shall hear my voice; and there shall be one fold, and one shepherd.'

In verses 17 and 18, he tells us that he must bring all his sheep into his fold by laying down his life for the sheep in his own obedience to the Father as 'the shepherd of the sheep'. Oh, what a shepherd he is, who dies that the sheep may live! In these two magnificent verses of holy scripture, our Lord Jesus Christ describes his own death, the death he must accomplish at Jerusalem, as an act of voluntary, free obedience to his Father.

'Therefore doth my Father love me, because I lay down my life, that I might take it again. No man taketh it from me, but I lay it down of myself. I have power to lay it down, and I have power to take it again. This commandment have I received of my Father.'

In these verses we have a description of our Lord's sacrificial obedience unto death, even the death of the cross, as our voluntary Surety and Substitute.

A Question

The death of our Lord Jesus Christ is the most wonderful, astounding, magnificent event in the history of the universe. Nothing that is, has been, or shall hereafter be, can be compared to it. Yet, as he was suffering the wrath of God, bearing the sins of his people, dying as the voluntary Substitute for guilty, hell-deserving, hell-bent sinners, that we are, we hear the Son of God expressing the most woeful, unexplainable lamentation imaginable. 'Is it nothing to you, all ye that pass by? behold, and see if there be any sorrow like unto my sorrow, which is done unto me, wherewith the LORD hath afflicted me in the day of his fierce anger' (Lamentations 1:12).

When I hear those words falling from the lips of the Son of God as he hangs upon the cursed tree, I simply cannot avoid asking, 'Of whom does the bleeding Lamb of God speak these words? To whom is the death of Christ meaningless and insignificant?'

Nothing in all the universe is more wonderful and magnificent in the eyes of God than the death of his dear Son. The Saviour himself declares, 'Therefore doth my Father love me, because I lay down my life'! The angels of heaven, like the cherubim facing the mercy-seat, ever look into the mystery and wonder of redemption, by the blood of Christ, with astonishment. God's servants, faithful gospel preachers, are so overwhelmed with the wonders of redemption and the glory of the Redeemer that they never cease to study, glory in, and preach the cross of our Lord Jesus Christ (Isaiah 6:1-6; Galatians 6:14; 1 Corinthians 2:2). Redeemed sinners on the earth cherish nothing, delight in nothing, marvel at nothing as we do the death of our Lord Jesus Christ for us (Galatians 2:20; 1 John 3:16; 4:10). The ransomed in glory appear to think of nothing and speak of nothing except the dying love of the Lamb in the midst of the throne (Revelation 5:9-12). Hell itself looks upon the death of Christ as a wonderful, unexplainable, mysterious thing. I am certain that this is one thing that Satan himself did not understand, that Christ would triumph over him, and crush his head by his death upon the cross, else he would never have put it into the heart of Judas to betray the Master.

Yet, astonishing as it is to imagine, there are some to whom our darling Saviour speaks, as it were with astonishment, to whom his death is meaningless, insignificant, nothing. Who are these people to whom the death of Christ is nothing? Who is it that thinks little of the sin-atoning death of the Lord Jesus Christ? Our Lord is here addressing himself to everyone who passes by him, passes by his sacrifice, passes by his death as the sinners' Substitute. O unbelieving, Christless soul, it is you! Cold, calculating, heartless preacher, you who pass by the crucified Christ, and take to your lips meaningless, insignificant things (politics, social issues, denominational squabbles, religious history, traditions, etc.), it is you! Christ crucified is mundane, meaningless, and insignificant only to unregenerate, unbelieving souls.

It is my heart's prayer that the death of our Lord Jesus Christ will be made the most important thing in all the world to you who read these lines. I pray that you and I may become totally consumed with the crucified Christ, that our hearts, our lives, every fibre of our souls may be constantly dominated by the death of Christ as our sin-atoning Saviour.

Our Lord Jesus Christ, of whom it is written, 'grace is poured into thy lips', declares plainly that his death at Calvary was the free, voluntary act of his own obedience to his Father's will, by which he won his Father's love as a man, as our Mediator and Surety. 'Therefore doth my Father love me, because I lay down my life, that I might take it again. No man taketh it from me, but I lay it down of myself. I have power to lay it down, and I have power to take it again. This commandment have I received of my Father' (John 10:17, 18).

The Father's Commandment
In John 10, the Lord Jesus Christ speaks of himself not as God the eternal Son, but as the Good Shepherd, the Mediator, the Surety of his people. He says, 'This commandment have I received of my Father'. With those words, he declares that his death as our Substitute was arranged by God before the world began (Psalms 40:7; Hebrews 10:7-10). The death of Christ was not accomplished by the arrangement of men or by the arrangement of hell, but by the arrangement of the triune God (Acts 2:23; 1 Peter 1:18-20). The death of Christ at Calvary was accomplished by the arrangement of infinite love, through an eternal covenant, by the work of divine providence (John 3:16; Romans 5:6-8; Hebrews 10:5-14).

The Son's Obedience
The Lord Jesus Christ laid down his life voluntarily, as an act of free obedience to his Father. No man forced him to die. God the Father did not compel him to die, or take his life from him. Oh, no! Our Saviour died voluntarily, by his own will. His death was accomplished by his own will. 'He poured out his soul unto death'. It is true, as we have seen, 'it pleased the Father to bruise him'. The Father cried, 'Awake, O sword, against my shepherd, and against the man that is my fellow, saith the LORD of hosts' (Zechariah 13:7). But our blessed Lord Jesus, our precious Christ, took the cup of wrath in his own hands. The Son of God fell willingly upon the sword of justice. Our Saviour died by his own will. The Lord Jesus laid down his life for the satisfaction of justice. Our Saviour laid down his life as the Substitute for chosen sinners. The Son of God laid down his life for the glory of his Father. Our blessed Redeemer laid down his life, because of his love for us. The Lord Jesus Christ laid down his life that he might take it again (Romans 14:9; Philippians 2:5-11).

The Father's Love For The Son
Our Saviour says, 'Therefore doth my Father love me, because I lay down my life'. I know of nothing in heaven or earth so sweet to meditate upon and so impossible to explain as the Father's love for his darling, dying Son. The Father loved him for the loveliness of his Godhead. The Father loved him for the beauty of his holy humanity. The Father loved him, because he laid down his life for us. The Father loved him as the glorious, saving, effectual Mediator of his people.

God himself never saw anything in all the world so lovely, so infinitely worthy of his love, admiration, and honour as the death of his dear Son upon the cursed tree for his people. 'Herein is love'! Because of this great act of love, because of this great act of Christ's free obedience to the Father as our Surety, the Father has given his Son everything (Isaiah 53:4-12; John 3:35; 17:2).

Four Lessons
Let us learn from the words and example of our Lord and Saviour, that though God's child may suffer greatly in this world, may often have to carry a heavy cross, and may often have the Father's face hidden from him, yet he remains, he is still, the darling object of his Father's love. Never did the Father more fully love his Son than when he was heaping upon him the fury of his wrath.

Let us learn that God honours those who honour his Son. The only way a sinner can honour the Son of God is to trust him. The only way of access to God is Christ. Our only worthiness of the Father's love and approval is Christ (John 17:22-26). Yet, learn too, that in Christ, because of Christ, for Christ's sake, God loves us. God the Father gave his Son to die for us. God the Son laid down his life for us. God the Spirit now sprinkles us with the blood of Christ, and declares us, 'redeemed'. Child of God, learn this, you are not your own. 'For ye are bought with a price: therefore glorify God in your body, and in your spirit, which are God's' (1 Corinthians 6:20).

End of Volume 1

Index Of Bible Verses

17:3	33, 94, 127, 154, 182, 184, 223, 411, 430	2:24	120	2:16	291
17:4	304, 438	2:36	286	2:28, 29	433
17:5	19, 32	2:38	74	2:29	344
17:5, 20	293	2:39	42, 92	3:3, 4	42, 152, 160
17:6	354	2:40	38	3:10-23	198
17:9	354	3:19	235	3:12	166
17:9, 10	33	4:12	76, 164, 192, 339	3:19, 20	419
17:9, 20	347	5:36, 37	326	3:20	48
17:11	354	6	321	3:23	437
17:12	354	6:2	416	3:24-26	58, 80, 124, 192, 454, 465
17:13	127	7:51	178		
17:17	216	8:20	183	3:25	88
17:20-22	29	9:1-9	195	3:25, 26	134
17:22	19, 29	10:43	170, 342	3:31	338
17:22-26	475	13:27	41	4:5	76
17:23	371	13:36	252	4:8	107, 292, 293
17:24	49, 110, 354	13:48	42, 49, 92, 260, 375, 431	4:16	136, 206, 339
18:1	273			4:25	119, 224
18:1, 2	416	15:18	22	4:25-5:5	120
18:6	119	16	259	4:25-5:11	336, 405, 460
18:36	326	16:19	361		
18:37, 49	366	16:31	338	5:1	335
19:7	283	17:2, 3	302	5:1-11	171
19:10	314	17:31	285, 291	5:5-11	113
19:17-19	78	20:21	38	5:6-8	84, 247, 392, 474
19:19-22	366	20:28	385		
19:28-30	78	20:30	443	5:8	135
19:30	192, 466	21:30	361	5:8-10	83
19:38, 39	413	22:16	74	5:12	125, 296, 437
20:16	447	26:13-18	249		
20:21	252	28:24	431	5:12, 19	139
20:21-23	249			5:12-21	438
20:30, 31	337	Romans		5:14	438
21:1-18	100	1:1-3	93	5:18	135
21:15-17	120	1:4	120	5:19	223, 466
21:17	334	1:14-17	254	5:20, 21	55, 84, 322
21:25	20	1:15-17	91	6:1-6	236
		1:16	43, 91	6:1-7	74
		1:16, 17	185	6:3, 4	146
Acts		1:18-20	40, 291	6:3-6	159
1:7	289	1:18-21	35	6:4-6	29
1:8	118, 249, 252	1:18-32	198	6:11	279
		1:25	42	6:23	154, 183, 190
1:9-11	289	1:25-31	221		
2	342	1:28	311	7:9	141
2:22, 23	341	2:1-16	198	7:18	65
2:23	120, 379, 383, 402, 474	2:4, 5	291	7:24	262
		2:12	291	8:1	136, 293, 298, 459
		2:15	35, 291		

8:1-4	58, 338, 420	11:29	160, 293, 377	9:16	79, 83, 96
8:3	48	11:33-36	160, 284, 437	9:20-22	241
8:5	124			10:4	367
8:7	360	11:36	94, 343	10:11	272
8:14-17	213	12:1, 2	279	10:31	250, 252
8:17	293	14:7	241	11:1	449
8:27, 34	397	14:9	397, 474	11:20-26	86
8:28	94, 437	14:10	288	12:11, 18	148
8:28, 29	470	14:17	124	12:12	132
8:28-30	161, 282, 343	15:4	90, 329	14:8	54
8:28-31	65			14:33	320
8:28-32	27			15:1-3	431
8:28-39	348	**1 Corinthians**		15:9	401
8:29	370, 455	1:17	73	15:10	148
8:29, 30	132	1:17-31	85	15:24-28	397
8:30	377	1:18-24	439	15:47-49	224
8:31-34	420	1:18-25	96	15:51-58	290
8:32	66	1:18-31	114	15:58	91
8:32-34	293	1:21	91, 384	16:22	192
8:32-39	298	1:23	359		
8:33	76	1:26-29	260, 320		
8:33, 34	135	1:26-31	253	**2 Corinthians**	
8:34	23	1:30	155, 185	1:21, 22	149
8:37-39	349	1:30, 31	66, 191, 206, 221, 339	2:14-16	382
9:6	107			2:14-17	38
9:11-13	174	2	71	2:15, 16	439
9:11-28	311	2:1-5	96, 412	3:14-18	33
9:13-16	285	2:2	83, 473	4:3, 4	311
9:16	44, 102, 227, 467	2:2-5	94	4:3-6	164, 427
		2:8	182	4:4-6	196, 229
9:30-10:4	274, 359	2:9	14	4:5	401
10:1-13	65	2:9, 10	131	4:5, 6	94
10:4	20	2:9-14	154	4:6	29, 33, 50, 124
10:4-9	132	2:12-16	411		
10:8, 9	154	2:14	124, 131, 166, 346	4:6, 7	44, 114
10:9, 10	219, 236, 261			4:7	320
		2:14-16	71	4:17-5:1	437
10:9-13	215, 368	3:16	98, 276	5:1-9	434
10:9-17	439	3:16, 17	118	5:9	396
10:11-15	336	3:21-23	61	5:10	288
10:13, 14	337	4:3-5	288	5:10, 11	252, 287, 291
10:13-15	370	4:7	148, 359		
10:13-17	39, 183, 355	4:19	383	5:10-15	238
10:15	88	5:7	77, 116	5:14, 15	253, 293
10:17	39, 91, 96, 114, 156, 259, 267, 337, 355	6:9-11	242	5:16	23, 83, 91, 92, 185
		6:9-20	118		
		6:19	118	5:16, 17	94
		6:19, 20	279	5:17	108, 125, 223, 321, 447
11:1	160	6:20	475		
11:25	160	7:22	431	5:17-21	164, 267, 293
11:26	160	9:15	367		

www.ingramcontent.com/pod-product-compliance
Lightning Source LLC
Chambersburg PA
CBHW020456100426
42812CB00024B/2682